The Palgrave Handbook of Childhood Studies

The Palgrave Handbook of Childhood Studies

Edited By

Jens Qvortrup
Norwegian University of Science and Technology, Norway

William A. Corsaro
Indiana University, USA

Michael-Sebastian Honig
University of Luxembourg

First published in hardback 2009 and in paperback 2011 by
PALGRAVE MACMILLAN

Palgrave Macmillan in the UK is an imprint of Macmillan Publishers Limited,
registered in England, company number 785998, of Houndmills, Basingstoke,
Hampshire RG21 6XS.

Palgrave Macmillan in the US is a division of St Martin's Press LLC,
175 Fifth Avenue, New York, NY 10010.

Palgrave Macmillan is the global academic imprint of the above companies
and has companies and representatives throughout the world.

Palgrave® and Macmillan® are registered trademarks in the United States,
the United Kingdom, Europe and other countries.

ISBN: 978–0–230–53260–1 hardback
ISBN: 978–0–230–53261–8 paperback

This book is printed on paper suitable for recycling and made from fully
managed and sustained forest sources. Logging, pulping and manufacturing
processes are expected to conform to the environmental regulations of the
country of origin.

A catalogue record for this book is available from the British Library.

A catalog record for this book is available from the Library of Congress.

10 9 8 7 6 5 4 3 2 1
20 19 18 17 16 15 14 13 12 11

Printed and bound in Great Britain by
CPI Antony Rowe, Chippenham and Eastbourne

Contents

Figures, Tables and Boxes

Figures

Tables

Boxes

Notes on Contributors

Leena Alanen is a sociologist and Professor in Early Childhood Education and Docent in the Sociology of Childhood at the University of Jyväskylä, Finland. She has been active in developing Childhood Studies since the 1980s, through her own research and international research projects, and in the International Sociological Association. She is currently the book review editor for *Childhood* (Sage). Her research interests include children and childhood in social theory, generational relations and the intersection of gender and generation.

Adrian Bailey is Professor of Migration Studies in the School of Geography, University of Leeds, UK, and Adjunct Professor, Department of Geography, University of Illinois Urbana-Champaign, USA. He studies processes of transnationalization and how these circulate inequality, and convenes the Transnational Society Project.

David Buckingham directs the Centre for the Study of Children, Youth and Media at the Institute of Education, London University, UK. He is also a Visiting Professor at the Norwegian Centre for Child Research, NTNU, Trondheim. His research focuses on children's and young people's interactions with electronic media, and on media education. His most recent book is *Beyond Technology: Children's Learning in the Age of Digital Culture* (Polity, 2007).

Doris Bühler-Niederberger is Professor of Sociology of Family, Youth and Education at the University of Wuppertal, Germany. Her research interests include growing up in twentieth- and twenty-first-century Germany; social institutions, experts and political processes defining and structuring childhood and youth; growing up and social inequality. She is currently president of RC 53 'Sociology of Childhood' of the International Sociological Association.

Daniel Thomas Cook is Associate Professor of Childhood Studies and Sociology at Rutgers University, Camden, New Jersey, USA. He is editor of *Symbolic Childhood* (2002) and author of *The Commodification of Childhood* (2004) as well as a number of articles and book chapters on consumer society, childhood, leisure and urban culture. Cook also serves as an editor of *Childhood: A Journal of Global Child Research* (Sage).

William A. Corsaro is the Robert H. Shaffer Endowed Chair in the Department of Sociology at Indiana University, Bloomington, USA. Corsaro is the author of several books in the area of childhood studies and early education, including *Friendship and Peer Culture in the Early Years* (1985), *We're Friends, Right? Inside Kids' Culture* (2003), *The Sociology of Childhood*, 2nd edition (2005), and with Luisa Molinari, *I Compagni: Understanding Children's Transition from Preschool to Elementary School* (2005).

Gunilla Dahlberg is a professor at Stockholm University, Sweden. She has been a project and scientific director for several research projects dealing mainly with early childhood education, and she has served in several government commissions related to curriculum development for early childhood education. She has also been a deputy member CERI: the OECD's innovation and research organization in Paris. Her most recent publications are (with Moss and Pence) *Beyond Quality in Early Childhood Education and Care*, 2nd edition (2006), and (with Moss) *Ethics and Politics in Early Childhood* (2005).

Kirsten Drotner is a professor in the Department of Literature, Culture and Media Studies at the University of Southern Denmark and founding director of DREAM: Danish Research Centre on Education and Advanced Media Materials. Author or editor of 15 books, her research interests include media history, qualitative methodologies and young people's media uses. Her most recent work focuses on media globalisation as developed in out-of-school contexts and on digital forms of learning.

Ann-Carita Evaldsson is a professor in the Department of Education, Uppsala University, Sweden. Her work has mainly focused on preadolescent children's peer talk and peer culture, addressing topics such as the social organization of games, the accomplishment of identities (gender, class and ethnicity) in peer talk (accounts, disputes, gossip, insults, language alternation, bullying) and moral ordering in multiethnic school settings. Methodologically her research combines ethnography with conversation analysis and membership categorization analysis.

Laura Fingerson is an independent researcher in Minneapolis, Minnesota, USA. She is the author of *Girls in Power: Gender, Body, and Menstruation in Adolescence* (SUNY Press, 2006) and other articles and book chapters on adolescence, body, gender and media. Her next project is on how adolescents make their everyday food and physical activity decisions.

Michael Freeman is Professor of English Law at University College London, and a Fellow of University College London, UK. He is the founding editor of the *International Journal of Children's Rights*. He is the author of many books, including *The Rights and Wrongs of Children* (Frances Pinter, 1983), *The Moral Status of Children* (Martinus Nijhoff, 1997), *Children, Their Families and the Law* (Macmillan, 1992), *Understanding Family Law* (Sweet and Maxwell, 2007) and *The Best Interests of the Child* (Martinus Nijhoff, 2007). He is the editor of the *International Journal of Law in Context* and was the editor of *Current Legal Problems* and of the *Annual Survey of Family Law*. He is a non-practising barrister, and a Fellow of Gray's Inn.

Ivar Frønes is Professor of Sociology, University of Oslo, Norway. His scientific works cover a variety of fields, with emphasis on life course analysis, childhood, youth and studies of cultural and social trends. His publications include *Among Peers*, 1995; *Digitale Skiller* (Digital Divides), 2002; and *Moderne Barndom* (Modern Childhood), 2006. He is currently working on projects on the life course, childhood, and marginalization, and the development of social indicators for children's well-being and development ('Theorizing Indicators,' *Social Indicators Research*, 2007).

John Gillis is Professor of History Emeritus, Rutgers University, New Jersey, USA, now resident in Berkeley, California. He is the author or editor of ten books in European social and cultural history, touching on themes of age relations, family cultures and commemoration. Of late, he has turned his attention to global history, publishing *Islands of the Mind* in 2004. He is now at work on a cultural historical geography of coasts.

Harry Hendrick teaches history in the English Centre at the University of Southern Denmark, Odense. His main research interests are the history and sociology of childhood and youth. His forthcoming essay publications focus on young people and the emergence of the disciplinary state in late modernity. His book publications are *Images of Youth: The Making of the Male Youth Problem, 1880–1920* (Clarendon Press, 1990); *Child Welfare: England 1872–1989* (Routledge, 1994); *Children and Childhood in English Society, 1880–1990* (CUP, 1997); *Child Welfare: Historical Dimensions, Contemporary Debate* (Policy Press, 2003); and *Child Welfare and Social Policy: Essential Readings* (Policy Press, 2005).

Heinz Hengst was Professor of Social and Cultural Sciences, Hochschule Bremen, Department of Sozialwesen, Germany. His main research interests are in children's culture and changing generational relations. Major publications are *Kritische Stichwörter zur Kinderkultur* (co-edited with K. W. Bauer) (1978), *Kindheit als Fiktion* (co-authored with M. Köhler, B. Riedmüller, and M. M. Wambach) (1981), *Die Arbeit der Kinder* (co-edited with H. Zeiher) (2000), *Kinder, Körper, Identitäten* (co-edited with H. Kelle) (2003), and *Kindheit soziologisch* (co-edited with H. Zeiher) (2005).

Michael-Sebastian Honig has been head of the research department Children and Child Care in the German Youth Institute in Munich, and Professor of Pedagogy at the University of Trier, and is currently Professor of Social Work at the University of Luxembourg. His many publications include *Entwurf einer Theorie der Kindheit* (Towards a Theory of Childhood) (1999). He is co-editor of the journal *Zeitschrift für Soziologie der Erziehung und Sozialisation* (Journal of the Sociology of Education and Socialization), is a member of the editorial board for *Childhood* and edits the series published by Juventa *Kindheiten – Neue Folge* (Childhoods – New Series).

Allison James is Professor of Sociology at the University of Sheffield and Professor II at NOSEB, Trondheim. As one of the pioneers of childhood studies she has carried out a wide range of empirical and theoretical research, most recently exploring children's perceptions of hospital space and children's perspectives on food. Author of numerous books and articles, her latest book is *European Childhoods* (co-edited with A. L. James, Palgrave, 2008).

An-Magritt Jensen, PhD, is Professor of Sociology, Norwegian University of Science and Technology (NTNU). Selected publications are *Gender and Family Change in Industrialized Countries*, co-edited with K. O. Mason (Clarendon Press,

Oxford, 1995), and *Children and the Changing Family: Between Transformation and Negotiation*, co-edited with L. McKee (London, RoutledgeFalmer, 2003). She is Chair of COST A19 Children's Welfare (2001–2006) and principal editor of COST-country reports: *Children's Welfare in Ageing Europe*, Vols. I and II (Norwegian Centre for Child Research, 2004).

Natalie Hevener Kaufman is Professor Emerita, University of South Carolina, and author or co-author of *Globalization and Children: The Impact of Global Political and Economic Change on the Everyday Lives of Children, Measuring and Monitoring Children's Well-Being, Implementing the UN Convention on the Rights of the Child, The Participation Rights of the Child, Human Rights Treaties and the Senate: A History of Opposition, International Law and the Status of Women.*

Andreas Lange is a researcher in the Department of Family and Family Policies at the German Youth Institute in Munich and he teaches sociology at the University of Konstanz. He works and publishes on the ambivalent modernization of childhood and the family, including aspects of media and work life. Recently he has written an expert statement on children's perspectives on their parents' family and working times for the Seventh Family Report of the Federal Ministry of Family Affairs, Senior Citizens, Women and Youth.

John McKendrick is Senior Lecturer in Human Geography and Director of the Scottish Poverty Information Unit at the School of Law and Social Sciences, Glasgow Caledonian University. His research interests span the studies of the provision of environments for children, children's use of space, children's play and children and poverty. He is a committed applied researcher (see recent reports: *Life in Low Income Households with Children* and *School Grounds in Scotland, A National Survey*). He edited 'Children's Playgrounds in the Built Environment', a Special Issue of the *Built Environment* (Alexandrine Press, 1999) and *First Steps*, a collection of 21 'retrospective' autobiographical short notes written by geographers on one of their favourite readings from the geographies of children and youths (2004).

Berry Mayall is Professor of Childhood Studies at the Institute of Education, University of London. She has carried out many studies with parents and children, with a focus on their use of services. In recent years she has worked on the sociology of childhood, and her most recent work includes several contributions to European handbooks on the topic and a book exploring the social status of childhood – *Towards a Sociology for Childhood* (Open University Press, 2002).

Johanna Mierendorff is a sociologist and educationalist. From 1996 to 2007 she worked at the University of Halle, Germany, as research assistant and lecturer; since 2008 she has been Visiting Professor of Social Pedagogy at the University of Trier, Germany. Her work has mainly been theoretically and empirically focused on the interrelationship between childhood and the welfare state (child, youth and family politics). Furthermore, she is interested in questions of child poverty (child-centred qualitative approach and discourse analysis). Since 2003 she has been a member of the steering board of the section 'Sociology of Childhood' in the German Sociological Association.

Olga Nieuwenhuys holds degrees in sociology from the University of Paris (Sorbonne), the Free University Amsterdam and the University of Amsterdam. Her teaching and research interests include childhood in international development, children's geographies and the anthropology of childhood. She is co-editor of *Childhood* (Sage Publishers) and on the advisory board of *Children's Geographies* (Routledge). She is the author of *Children's Lifeworlds, Labour, Gender and Welfare in the Developing World* (London: Routledge, 1994, and New Delhi: Social Science Press, 1999) and of a number of scholarly articles and book contributions.

Thomas Olk is Professor of Social Work and Social Policy Research at the Martin-Luther University of Halle, Germany. His research focuses on the generational order in modern societies, children's citizenship and the relationship between children/childhood and the welfare state. He was a member of the EU COST-Network 'Children's Welfare' (2003–2006, Vice-Chair) and co-edited the book *Childhood, Generational Order and the Welfare State: Exploring Children's Social and Economic Welfare* (University of Southern Denmark Press, 2007).

Jens Qvortrup is a Professor of Sociology at the Norwegian University of Science and Technology, and former Director of the Norwegian Centre for Child Research, Trondheim. He directed the large international study Childhood as a Social Phenomenon (1987–1992), and was founding president of the International Sociological Association's section on sociology of childhood (1988–1998) and a co-editor of the Sage journal *Childhood* (1999–2008). He has published extensively in the field of childhood: *Childhood Matters,* 1994 (with Bardy, Sgritta and Wintersberger), *Childhood and Children's Culture,* 2002 (with Mouritsen) and *Studies in Modern Childhood,* 2005.

Irene Rizzini is a professor and a researcher at the Pontifical Catholic University of Rio de Janeiro, Brazil, and Director of the International Center for Research on Childhood (CIESPI). She serves as President of Childwatch International Research Network. She is the author of several books, among which are *Globalization and Children* (co-edited with Natalie Kaufman); *The Art of Governing Children: The History of Social Policies, Legislation and Child Welfare in Brazil; Desinherited from Society: Street Children in Latin America; The Lost Century: The Historical Roots of Public Policies on Children in Brazil; Images of the Child in Brazil: 19th and 20th Centuries; Children and the Law in Brazil – Revisiting the History (1822–2000); Niños, adolescentes, marginalidad y violencia en América Latina y el Caribe: relaciones indisociables?*

Katherine Brown Rosier is Professor of Sociology at Central Michigan University, USA. In addition to the series Sociological Studies of Children and Youth, which she co-edits, recent publications include *Mothering Inner-City Children: The Early School Years* (Rutgers, 2000), and several articles on the topic of covenant marriage. Her current interests are focused on children's identity issues, and the decline of children's freedom in post-9/11 America.

Heinz Sünker is Professor of Social Pedagogy and Social Policy in the Department of Educational and Social Sciences, Wuppertal University, Germany. He has studied German literature, philosophy, Protestant theology and pedagogy at the universities of Münster and Heidelberg. He received his PhD and his Habilitation at the University of Bielefeld. His main research interests and fields of publication are critical social theory, theory and history of social work and social policy, sociology and politics of education, German fascism, childhood studies, and child and youth welfare.

Martin Woodhead is Professor of Childhood Studies at the Open University, UK, where he has engaged in interdisciplinary and applied research, teaching and publishing for more than thirty years. His main interests relate to early childhood development, education and care, as well as child labour and children's rights, including policy studies and extensive international research. He is co-editor of the journal *Children & Society*, and a member of the editorial board for *Childhood* and of the advisory board for *Journal of Early Childhood Research*.

Helga Zeiher, sociologist, is a retired researcher from the Max Planck Institute for Human Development in Berlin, Germany. Until 1999 she was a founding chair of the Sociology of Childhood section in the German Association of Sociology, and now engages in work within the German Society for Time Policy. Her main book publications include *Orte und Zeiten der Kinder*, 1994 (with H. J. Zeiher); *Die Arbeit der Kinder*, 2000 (co-edited with H. Hengst); *Childhood in Generational Perspective*, 2003 (co-edited with B. Mayall); *Kindheit soziologisch* 2005 (co-edited with H. Hengst); *Flexible Childhood? Exploring Children's Welfare in Time and Space*, 2007 (co-edited with D. Devine, A. T. Kjørholt, H. Strandell); *Schulzeiten, Lernzeiten, Lebenszeiten*, 2008 (with S. Schroeder).

Why Social Studies of Childhood?
An Introduction to the Handbook

Jens Qvortrup, William A. Corsaro and Michael-Sebastian Honig

The Palgrave Handbook of Childhood Studies signals recognition of a significant area of study which began to assert itself a quarter of a century ago. Its publication is a sign that childhood studies have both matured and experienced remarkable diversification; it is an indication that these studies, like childhood, have being and legitimacy in their own right. But even if these perspectives and approaches have gained ground, a handbook will be helpful in making them better known both in academia and among the broader public.

So far childhood and children as studied in sociology, anthropology and geography, for instance, have not had their own handbooks in the English language,[1] and in general they have been poorly represented among *oeuvres* intended to provide the public or a more focused readership with an overview, such as dictionaries, encyclopaedias and the like. The nature of this representation, or perhaps underrepresentation, is interesting in itself as a sociology-of-knowledge issue. Even if one might argue that during the twentieth century we achieved an improved and friendlier understanding of children, Ellen Key's prophecy in exactly 1900 about the emergent *century of the child* (Key, 1900) is hardly reflected or realized in the way childhood and children are represented in these kinds of reference work.[2]

In standard works like the three international encyclopaedias of the social sciences published during the twentieth century (see Seligman, 1930–1935; Sills, 1968–1979; Smelser and Baltes, 2001), childhood is represented very differently. In the 1968–1979 work by Sills, we dare say, childhood as a social phenomenon is not represented at all. On page 390 in volume two of this monumental work (18 volumes) one reads the following:

> CHILD DEVELOPMENT, *see* developmental psychology; educational psychology; intellectual development; moral development; sensory and motor development; *and the biographies of* Gesell; Hall; Montessori.
>
> CHILD PSYCHIATRY, *see under* psychiatry.

As these cross-references make perfectly clear, children are seen purely in psychological and pedagogical terms, and nothing at the time pointed to a change in that, let alone to speculations about the failure to think of childhood in a broader social scientific context.

In a notable sense this was different in 1930–1935, when a 15-encyclopaedia volume was published. We find in this, under the entry 'Child', as many as 57 double-column pages. The entry is divided into 12 sections, which in addition to one about child psychology (written by Gesell) deal with what we might call social policy issues: child welfare, child hygiene, child mortality, child guidance, child marriage, dependent children, neglected children, delinquent children, institutions for the care of children, child labour, and child welfare legislation.

As to the most recent edition of the Encyclopaedia from 2001, technology has provided us with a search engine, which swiftly helps us with hits for 'childhood' or 'children'. Most of them, however, are about developmental or behavioural issues, or welfare issues; there is very little about what we in this volume present as social studies of childhood.[3]

These three different ways of presenting or representing children or childhood may to some degree reflect the time in which they were written. Even if in 1930 attitude changes towards sentimentalization (Zelizer, 1985) were in full swing, the problems facing children in the rich world between the two World Wars were still massive, and it is hardly a surprise that the Encyclopaedia at the time mirrored this reality.

In the late 1960s these countries were in the midst of welfare state development, where the social problems of children were less conspicuous, and thus it is perhaps less striking they were dealt with in merely psychological terms.

Though doubtless a coincidence, it is noteworthy that each of the three editions was published just a few years after the adoption of one of the three global children's rights documents. In 1924 the first international legal regulations were adopted by the League of Nations as the Geneva Declaration of the Rights of the Child; in 1959 a new Declaration of the Rights of the Child was issued by the General Assembly of the United Nations, and then in 1989 the much more encompassing United Nations Convention on the Rights of the Child (UNCRC) was adopted by the General Assembly. While the two Declarations were rather brief assertions of intent with the purpose of underlining children's need for protection, the Convention added most importantly a section on children's rights to participate (see in this volume Freeman; Kaufman and Rizzini). The somehow parallel sequence might suggest the impact of changing attitudes to children in the agenda-setting western world.

Preludes

This handbook is called *The Palgrave Handbook of Childhood Studies*. The formulation is not intended to monopolize the concept of childhood, as some might object – in particular since not all disciplines preoccupied with children are equally well represented. We are well aware of this fact and we do not seek to disguise that the volume is primarily about children and childhood in a broader social scientific context. We are well aware also of the merits of not least child psychology and the huge body of knowledge accrued from more than a century's study of the child. At the same time it was felt that a lack of potential new insights meant that sociology and anthropology – the two most obvious forerunners in the now interdisciplinary social studies of childhood – came to see difficulties in exploring children and childhood using their own disciplinary concepts and perspectives. It remains a predicament or at least a challenge (see Woodhead in this volume) to define the borders between sciences allegedly more focused on the individual, like psychology, and, for instance, sociology, anthropology, geography and law, which claim a much broader context as their remit.

It would be unacceptably arrogant to make it appear as if it was a complete novelty to talk about children or childhood as social phenomena. Numerous scholars within, for instance, philosophy and pedagogy have been fully aware of the impact of community and society on children's life worlds; individual gifted authors have persuasively demonstrated remarkable insight into childhood and society (Ariès, 1962; Mead, 1978; de Lone, 1979; Preuss-Lausitz et al., 1983; Zelizer, 1985; to mention just a few). In a Marxist and socialist tradition we find activists and thinkers like Key (1900), Kanitz (1925) and Bernfeld (1967), whom we would not perhaps count as traditional scholars, but who nevertheless contributed to our understanding of children's life and welfare. The same could be said about quite a few of the so-called child savers (like Jane Addams) who also produced significant thinking. At the same time it is in our view reasonable to argue that most of these people either were characterized by an enthusiasm and engagement on behalf of mostly poor and destitute children (like child savers, whether well understood or not; see Platt 1977, 'Introduction to Second Edition') or were lone riders who did not create a fashion, as it were.

We argue that it takes both ideas and organization to allow a take-off in setting new academic fashions or creating viable new paradigms. New ideas cropped up forcefully during the 1980s among individual scholars in different countries in the rich world, apparently independently of each other (for instance Jenks, 1982a; Corsaro, 1985; Qvortrup, 1985; and Thorne, 1987). Some of them were of course inspired by previous thinking, as mentioned above, but remarkably they also, without knowing each other, converged around some core ideas – in particular a criticism of socialization. Here it has to be said that they shared company with a few psychologists (see the collection by Dreitzel, 1973; see also Richards, 1974; Burman, 1994).

It is evident that social studies of childhood have become institutionalized in terms of professionalization, organization, public research programmes, teaching programmes and curricula at numerous universities and high schools, and in journals, book series and so on – in other words, they have caught the interest of more than a few farsighted scholars with alien ideas. Important has been the early establishment of a section on childhood under the International Sociological Association (Research Committee 53), which has given the field significant status among other research committees. Subsequently social studies of childhood under various names have found a place in several national disciplinary organizations – strongest perhaps in the United States of America and Germany.

While we argue that conditions in this sense were right for a take-off,[4] it is not easy, if possible at all, to make any definitive judgements about why social studies of childhood took off at that particular time in the early 1980s. Things were, however, on the move, as demonstrated by the UNCRC, the negotiations about which began in 1979. Social movements (Prout and James, 1990), and perhaps the women's movement in particular (Therborn, 1993), have also been mentioned as conducive to positive changes to the advantage of children, just as the continuous fertility decrease in Europe can be interpreted in terms of increased emotionality (family level) or as a sign of negative attitudes towards childhood in modern societies (society level). In general terms some sociologists of science, like Merton (1973), hold the view that no new directions in research are sustainable unless they reflect certain realities in the world (see also Adorno, 1973).

Social studies of childhood and their *raison d'être*

If one looks back it is possible to discern at least five characteristics of the 'new childhood paradigm', as it was called at the time: it aimed at studying childhood in its normality; it was critical of the conventional socialization perspective; it purported to give voice to or acknowledge agency in children; it tried to expose structural opportunities for and/or constraints on children; and it intended to use as far as possible ordinary sociological or anthropological methods in the study of children and childhood.

1. *The study of 'normal' childhood*: The impetus to set in motion social studies of childhood was not in the first place a social policy concern, even though there was resentment over adult society's offences towards children, anger over the way many children led their lives, or – as with all research – a hope that it would in the end be useful and serve humankind. We maintain that the new paradigm of childhood was one which did not primarily aim at responding to particular pressing social issues. The 'new childhood paradigm' was more than anything else directed at basic research with a primary interest in acquiring knowledge and insight about childhood and children as these notions and phenomena were understood in their normality and in seeing children as actors or agents on a number of stages and within many contexts.

In the *Encyclopaedia of Social Sciences* from 1930 the focus was, as noted above, almost invariably on children who in one way or another deviated from normality or from what was seen as a desired condition in social, economic, behavioural or whichever other ways children encountered problems. The situation in the 1920s and 1930s clearly invited, indeed demanded, that political efforts and resources be devoted to coming to terms with such issues.

Currently, just as in the 1960s or 1970s, when new encyclopaedias were published, nobody can claim that social, economic or other problems have been overcome or are close to being solved – not in the rich world and particularly not in the large poor world, where problems abound. However, it is precisely in this large, problem-ridden world that one has the right to suggest that an improvement of the daily lives of hundreds of millions of children presupposes as a minimum an understanding of problems of a larger order and children's place in them. Without denying the dire need to help individual children to overcome their subsistence or even their psychological problems, the new childhood paradigm would formulate its research questions in terms of socio-economic development of prosperous and healthy surroundings for children rather than child development.

2. *A critique of the conventional socialization perspective*: It is in retrospect clear that one significant feature of the new childhood paradigm was, negatively formulated, a reluctance to accept the socialization model understood as a functionalist understanding of child development. In positive terms the demand was to enhance the visibility of children here and now, while they are children, and to understand, accept and recognize children and their life worlds *in their own right*. Children are not here merely or first of all to become adults, though, of course, we all expect and hope that they will become adults. However, this expectation and hope had, in lore and science, gained so much attention and conveyed so much significance that it was more or less forgotten that children also have a life while they are children. To insist that this life has a worth in its own right amounts to saying that it should not necessarily be formed according to criteria for a successful later adult life. This important perspective has been very influential, whether one is studying children's agency or childhood in structural terms.

3. *Agency and voice for children*: Among those who embarked on the study of children within the framework of the new paradigm of childhood it was a common observation that children were largely appreciated as people who were on the receiving end in terms of provision and knowledge. Children were reduced to vulnerable people to be protected without being seen also as participants – in any case, not participants in the larger social fabric, which was an adult privilege and prerogative. Therefore it became imperative for social studies of childhood to look into these charges or prejudices. Was it 'naturally' or necessarily the case that children lacked qualities and capacities for participation? If this proved not to be so, were these qualities and capacities merely useful or applicable in a childhood context – because nobody would deny, of course, that children did possess resources, creativity and inventiveness.

Against this background it is interesting that the UNCRC was formulate during the same period as the breakthrough in childhood studies, because this momentous document also granted children participatory potential and endowed them with participatory rights, even though they were restricted compared to those held by adults.

Social studies of childhood have made available numerous studies about children's agency in circumstances and surroundings far beyond the more narrow vicinities in which children have so far been seen as victims conceptually and empirically.

4. *Structural constraints on childhood*: It followed from the new understanding of children and childhood as being part of not merely the particularistic world of family and locality, but also of the larger society, that they encountered new opportunities and constraints. The limited space so far allotted to them in research had not found much reason to explore these opportunities and constraints. Social studies of childhood found that parameters in terms of economics, technology, urbanization and even globalization are on many occasions highly relevant to the study of childhood – and these new perspectives and horizons are a great revelation. In fact, even within these large-scale frameworks children have been found to be not only victims but also actors and participants, for better or worse (see Bailey in this volume).

This commonality implies an opportunity to compare childhoods in various contexts, historically and interculturally. The historical perspective has been and remains an inspiration and an interest in itself, and it is of clear significance also in accounting for what childhood is like in other parts of the world, outside the most developed and rich nations. One the one hand, studies of childhood under various circumstances occasion variegated views of what children's life worlds are like. On the other hand, they also invite us to speculate about what these many life worlds have in common. To this end, our Handbook gives significance to a generational perspective in the sense that a relationship to adults is a reality for each and every child, just as there has always been a relationship between childhood and other generational segments, notably adulthood.

5. *The use of ordinary social scientific methods to study children and childhood:* Our suggestion above that childhood and children as research objects do not in principle deviate from other sociological or anthropological research objects implies that children are in fact humans and therefore also can and should be studied as such. They do not belong to another species requiring particular methods. Social studies of childhood do not deny, of course, that children are 'small' people, but this fact does not make them less human. Sometimes one gets the impression that the fact of their smallness is conducive to including them or conceptually incarcerating them in a micro world or a world of particularism; children are seldom studied as people who are part of a universal, cosmopolitan or global orbit. However, children are present in all societies and in most contexts and must therefore be accounted for in all these times and places. Indeed, childhood and children must be accounted for also in terms of influence from distant factors: even if children are not present at most adult work places, for instance, they are obviously impacted by parents' employment; even if children are far away from places where political and economic decisions are made, we still need to study the influence such decisions have on children's life worlds; children are obviously impacted heavily by environmental and climatic changes; what we do not know is whether, how and to what extent they are differently impacted than adults.

The structure and contents of the Handbook

A handbook is, as we understand it, a book whose chapters as far as possible give a state-of-the-art overview of their respective subjects. Its aim is to collect and present significant knowledge and to provide an overview on which the reader can rely. At the same time it must not lose the personal style and perspective of each chapter's author. It has been the intention of this Handbook to faithfully represent new insight and perspectives without necessarily concealing our own position. As a field develops, it will inevitably experience a proliferation of both subject areas and ways of seeing the subject at issue and its context. To remain an up-to-date and living document a handbook cannot and should not hide productive disagreements, and it is hardly a surprise that the epistemological debates found elsewhere are also represented among scholars of social studies of childhood.

A handbook is a book which can be used by scholars, students and the interested public. Each chapter should make the reader wiser and inspired; it must be a rounded piece in itself as well as one which generates interest in and references to further study. Such an ambitious aim is of course variously approached by the book's many authors, and we as editors have made no efforts to streamline the chapters theoretically or methodologically.

The Palgrave Handbook of Childhood Studies contains 28 chapters distributed over six sections: I: Concepts of childhood studies; II: Historical and socio-economic contexts of childhood; III: Generational relations; IV: Children's everyday lives/the local framework; V: Children's practice – children as participants; and VI: Children's rights and place in the world.

Section I of the Handbook is devoted to the conceptual and theoretical foundations of childhood studies. The first two chapters deal with two concepts which have simultaneously become signature themes in childhood studies. Through an understanding of childhood as a structural form, the field of childhood studies distinguishes itself from socialization research. Jens Qvortrup develops this idea in the context of the conceptual dualism of structure vs. agency (Chapter 1), which plays a significant role in the theoretical history of the social sciences. Conceiving childhood as a unit in the social structure makes it possible to distinguish the individual development of children from the historical and cultural history of childhood. Childhood as a structural form functions as a framework within which children lead their lives. This approach opens up childhood studies as a new and fruitful field of research.

Just as significant as the concept of childhood as a structural form is the idea of children's agency. Allison James (Chapter 2) anchors the idea of children's agency in the general shifts in social theory which took place in the 1970s and 1980s, which have both an epistemological and a political significance. James examines the concept of the social actor and its relationship to the concept of agency. Agency constitutes an individual competence of children, not a sign of their subordinate status in relation to adults. As agents, children make their own contribution to social and cultural reproduction. This thesis is supported with the research results of a variety of studies.

Agency as competence – this raises the question of how childhood studies approach the psychology of individual developmental processes. Martin Woodhead provides, in Chapter 3, a detailed and differentiated overview of the origins and extension of the development paradigm of childhood since the late nineteenth century. It will surprise some readers that many of the critiques of developmentalism were raised in the many controversial debates in developmental psychology itself. For example, William Kessen put forward the thesis of 'the child as a cultural invention' in the American Psychological Association's house journal as early as 1979. Woodhead shows that a strong research agenda on change and transition in children's growth, learning and well-being is essential for childhood studies.

This warning against too hasty a rejection of the developmental paradigm carries over correspondingly to the problem of socialization. Michael-Sebastian Honig puts forward, in Chapter 4, the proposition that childhood studies are to be based not on a demarcation from developmental psychology and socialization research, but on the ways and means by which they gain access to the reality of children's lives. He reminds us that one of the roots of childhood studies is the critique of the adult ideological viewpoint. Childhood studies can only move beyond this viewpoint when they make a distinction between children and childhood and ask: how is the child possible? This question can be answered not with an alternative image of the child, but through the analysis of the social conditions for making children observable.

This is followed by a brief critical evaluation of the empirical research practice of childhood studies. Andreas Lange and Johanna Mierendorff provide in their contribution (Chapter 5) an overview of the methodology and methods of childhood research. It revolves around the question of how the new epistemological agenda of childhood studies can be realized with the standards of social scientific research. The authors show that this question cannot ultimately be answered in a technical way; rather, we need to resolve the substantial problems of 'object adequacy'. They begin by identifying four methodological shifts which are characteristic of childhood studies, and link these to a discussion of tools for childhood research. In this way the methodological discussion turns into an overview of exemplary qualitative and quantitative projects in international childhood research.

Section II of the Handbook is devoted to the historical and social transformation of childhood. The first two chapters identify two historical focuses: Harry Hendrick examines the evolution of childhood in Western Europe; John Gillis concentrates on the nineteenth and twentieth centuries and the emergence of 'modern childhood'. In the two following chapters, Helga Zeiher and An-Magritt Jensen engage with the institutional and demographic aspects of the transformation.

Setting out from Ariès' famous thesis, Harry Hendrick first provides in Chapter 6 a clearly structured account of the various theoretical approaches in family historiography and the controversies surrounding the parent–child relationship. In the late middle ages, children and childhood were embedded in the familial house-hold and the family economy. Hendrick examines the cultural and economic changes which took place in European modernity as a process of 'dis-embedding'. He places this in five contexts: the rise of science, the transformation of religi-osity, poverty and its consequences, children's work and children's education. Fundamental changes took place in the meaning of 'childhood'. The evolution of childhood, according to Hendrick, is the evolution of an idea of childhood. Childhood had achieved at the beginning of the nineteenth century the status of a representation of the self in which a person's essence is expressed.

Like Harry Hendrick, John Gillis warns against the fiction of continuity (Chapter 7). Gillis sees the nineteenth century as constituting a historical break. Modernity means a comprehensive mobilization in time and space; it transforms children from 'beings' into 'becomings'. Development becomes the metaphor for childhood; age-group membership becomes the principle underpinning the social organization of the improvement and disciplining of the rising generation. On the one hand, children's space and time is placed under supervision; on the other, space and time become the most meaningful representation of childhood. Gillis examines as a key example the meaning of the child's birthday, which was almost non-existent before the nineteenth century; he discusses the ubiquity of children's photographs and draws attention to the stylization of past childhood as the most meaningful phase of life, the 'paradise lost' of adulthood. The costs of this sacralization (Zelizer) are high: children pay with their autonomy; for adults, having children gains a significance which is difficult to live up to – certainly an important reason for the epochal decline in fertility in Western Europe.

What Hendrick and Gillis describe as a historical phenomenon is represented by Helga Zeiher as a social process. The theme of Chapter 8 is the origin and transformation of childhood as an institution. Processes of institutionalization are many-sided and contradictory. Modern childhood is constituted by 'schol-arization' and 'familialization', which bring about a differential organization of children's space and time. The 'chronologization' of the life course revolutionizes childhood in modernity: it makes it possible to subject childhood to an ultimate goal, and to direct children over a period of time towards this goal through peda-gogy. The process of institutionalization liberates children structurally from their parents' personal power over resources, but subjects them to the rules and goals of both state and market organizations. In this respect all children are equal, but there are also new opportunities for the development of children's agency: individualization and institutionalization are complementary. Zeiher observes a trend towards de-standardization of contemporary childhood. She thus warns against also seeing that as a form of 'de-institutionalization' and misunderstand-ing it as 'liberation of the child'.

Since the nineteenth century industrialization has disrupted children's pos-ition within the family. Individual wage labour replaces the familial household as the basis for securing existence. Marriage correspondingly loses its signifi-cance for the legitimation of one's offspring. The lost monopoly of marriage at the birth of a child leads to a pluralization of family forms. An-Magritt Jensen

describes in Chapter 9 this secular tendency of modern societies in the industrialized West from children's perspective. Children who grow up with their
biological, married dual-earner parents are the winners in this change; children who grow up in consensual unions are the losers. They run a greater risk
that their parents will separate, that they will experience poverty and that they
will lose their relationship to their father. Jensen also draws attention to the
frequently overlooked consequences of familial 'pluralization' for children's
everyday life. She draws her discussion together in the thesis that adults, not
children, stand at the centre of the freedom of choice manifested in the transformation of the family – which provokes the question: Why should people
have children?

Section III contains contributions on generational relations and perspectives,
which for many childhood scholars are pivotal to the whole area and include in
principle a family and a societal level as well as a cross-sectional and a life course
perspective.

Although a generational perspective on childhood is not completely new,
Leena Alanen assumes in Chapter 10 the task of theoretically consolidating it
while including useful comparisons to class and in particular gender studies.
It is thus plausibly argued that just as studies of women are impossible without considering men, one cannot imagine a study of childhood without also
having adulthood in mind as an *internal* (necessary) relation. This is to say that
we must expect that there exists a generational order in society that pertains
to children, adults and other generational segments, just as one finds class
and gender orders which exist beyond face-to-face relations. This implies that
generational relations must include not only parent–child relationships, as in
families, but also, in a macro perspective, adult–minor relations that are pervasive and valid in many contexts. Alanen introduces and draws on Mannheim's
classic article on generation from 1928 (see also Hengst in this volume) and
thus suggests that childhood studies have a bearing on studies of social structure in general.

Berry Mayall in Chapter 11 suggests generational perspectives at a family level.
Her main focuses are socialization, changing families and interdependencies.
First, socialization has always been with us but has changed towards having
the nuclear family as our main child socialization agency. At the same time the
state has realized that children are too precious a good to be left to parents' discretion and thus intervenes – although with highly different energy and intensity from country to country. Schooling has become the undisputed arena for
public intervention, whereas preschool day care remains a contested terrain, the
more so the younger children are. Second, Mayall points to the significance of
family changes, not least due to an increasing incidence of family breakdown.
Furthermore and due to low fertility rates, even smaller families alter children's
daily lives in terms of decreasing opportunities for sibling relations, although
children might wish exactly this because their parents are working more and
more outside the home. Third, intergenerational interdependencies come more
frequently to include three generational relations, due to increased longevity.

These relationships have different meanings when they are seen from children's perspective or from a parental or grandparental perspective, and quite often children's activities and agency are not, in this development, taken into account.

Like Alanen and Mayall, Thomas Olk (in Chapter 12) also suggests a generational perspective, but first of all from a macrosociological perspective, the relations between generational groups in terms of, for instance, access to scarce resources, and how changes in relative positions between generations develop historically and possibly also in the future. While largely affirming Alanen's presentation, Olk presents the reader with various interpretations of the idea and concept of generational justice and shows how claims and duties of children are constructed accordingly. Even if children in general terms tend to share parents' welfare it does not follow that their claims on resources are the same as those of other generations. It is suggested that children have become marginalized: it is far from a matter of course that they are represented in philosophical and political discourses, and despite the UNCRC they are typically an at-risk group in terms of distributive justice. Whether children's position is a result of 'a conspiracy of the elderly', a consequence of a demographic logic and/or a reflection of changing ideological views is debatable, but in any case we are now confronted with historically new questions as to who carries responsibility and the financial burdens of the young and the old.

Heinz Hengst (in Chapter 13) like Alanen draws on Mannheim in an effort to come to terms with generation, but first of all with the notion of and what constitutes collective identities. The idea from Mannheim's 1928 essay about understanding generation in cultural terms is brought together with Margaret Mead's observation from the 1970s about a possible reversal of competencies between generations due to rapid modernization conditions which were internalized faster by the young than adults, not to mention the elderly, thus depriving the latter of advisory competencies. Hengst uses in particular Mannheim's notion from later writings of 'conjunctive experiential space' to denote similar experiences and thus similar basic awareness, which is not necessarily acquired consciously but rather as a result of 'structurally identical experiences'. Hengst uses as examples well-known media and consumption experiences which put youth and children ahead of their elders. It is suggested also that experience at an early stage (childhood, youth), and furthermore its deliberate and authentic nature, is stronger compared both to what is internalized later and to school experiences that are imposed on children.

Section IV considers the nature of children's everyday lives, including the activities and settings within which children live and construct their life worlds. The section also examines how children's everyday lives are perceived by peers and adults and how children's lives are enabled and constrained by specific aspects of the wider adult culture. The various chapters consider issues of children's bodies in their everyday lives, their experiences in early institutions like child care and preschool programs, constraints and opportunities in the localities in which they live, the nature and range of their use of time in leisure activities, and how their lives are affected by adult perceptions and actions that define the proper ways children are to participate in and are affected by the adult world.

In Chapter 14, Laura Fingerson discusses children's bodies. She argues that bodies are not static, but continually change through processes of aging, puberty and illness. Children's bodies change more dramatically and quickly than adults, and bodily change such as increased height (literally getting bigger) is an important marker of age and status for children and youth. Fingerson adds important insights to a growing interest in the body in the social sciences from the perspective of children and youth. She argues that the body is drawn on as a source of agency and power by children and concludes that to truly understand children's social lives we must understand their embodied lives.

Gunilla Dahlberg in Chapter 15 examines how the early institutionalization of children's lives has occurred through the rise in early childhood education and care brought about by increases in women's labour market participation and recognition of the learning potential and agency of preschool children. Dahlberg examines progressive social policies regarding early education and care primarily in Europe and the positive aspects of children's experiences and participation as they create and participate in the local school and peer cultures in these institutions. At the same time, Dahlberg also reflects on the merits and limitations of these policies from a critical poststructuralist and feminist perspective. Here she reviews the work of scholars of early education who eschew the view of children as unified, coherent and relatively static selves and instead propose and explore the perspective of young children as complex, changing and contradictory creatures.

In Chapter 16 John McKendrick considers the localities or sociocultural spaces in which children live their lives. He focuses on the neighbourhood and argues it is the primary realm within which most children undertake activity independent of adults. He considers the debates about problem neighbourhoods and neighbourhood problems which are symptomatic of dual conceptions of children as social problems and the social problems of children – the topic of Chapter 17 by Rosier, discussed below. For McKendrick well-designed neighbourhoods can facilitate children's independence with, for example, safe traffic-free pathways between significant sites in the neighbourhood (home, school, play space, shops, etc.). However, he argues further that design is only one component of successful neighbourhoods, maintaining that neighbourhoods must exude a culture of participation for children in which their presence, opinions and needs are equal to those of adults.

In Chapter 17 Katherine Brown Rosier argues that in the United States and many Western societies children and social problems have come to be seen in two interrelated ways. First, children are often seen *as problems* – as a nuisance and disruptive to respectable adult life, as a source of extreme worry and anxiety for adults, or as irresponsible by engaging in uncivil behaviours like using drugs, getting pregnant, dropping out of school, or committing property or violent crimes. This first perception, which Rosier argues is often exaggerated and unfair to children, draws attention away from the second perception, that children *have problems* and are very vulnerable to structural inequalities in Western societies (see Olk in this volume) and to the power of adults to mistreat and abuse them. Rosier addresses these two sides of the problematization of children and childhood, and considers the implications of the various ways that adults see children as problematic.

Ivar Frønes addresses children's leisure time and cultural activities in Chapter 18. He argues that leisure can be seen both within the framework of a child's life in the present and within the child's life course development or socialization. According to Frønes the perception and functions of children's leisure and cultural activities vary with children's cultural backgrounds and within and over historical periods. Frønes maintains that the amount of leisure, and the categorization of leisure activities, do not emerge from the activities as such, but from cultural framing. He argues that the culture of leisure activities is reflected in social structures, social change and cultural variations, but it also provides a sphere of autonomy, positioning the leisure activities of young people as indicators of social change and arenas of social tension.

Section V focuses on children's practices and their active participation in their societies and cultures. All of the chapters in this section see children as active agents and contributors to adult society, as discussed by James in Chapter 2. The various chapters address children's work, children's creation of and participation in their own peer cultures, children's participation in and transformation of play and games, children as active consumers of a wide range of societal goods and resources, children's active use and interpretation of visual media (especially television and films), and children's use and creative production of electronic or digital media.

Children's work from a historical and global perspective is explored by Olga Nieuwenhuys in Chapter 19. Nieuwenhuys reviews the changing nature of adults' perceptions of and the actual types of children's labour in both the developed North and the developing South. She points out how the importance of children's school work is often overlooked in the developed world and how concern for the protection of children by adults in the developed world often blunts our understanding of the complexity of and need for children's labour in developing countries. In the South many children combine schooling and work, and their labour (directly for their families and for others) is an economic necessity. She argues that those who wish to protect children from exploitation must recognize working children's movements as organizing for the right to work in dignity and to fight for their rights.

In Chapter 20 William A. Corsaro argues that children create their own peer cultures from very early in childhood. He maintains that these peer cultures are not separate from the adult world, but rather children's and adults' cultures are intricately interwoven in different ways across space and over time. Corsaro discusses two basic themes in children's peer cultures: communal sharing (as seen in children's sharing, participation and friendships) and resistance of adult authority (as seen in children's autonomy, control, conflict and differentiation). Corsaro explores a wide range of routines in peer culture in line with these two themes across historical time and in different parts of the world. He makes a strong argument for the diversity and universality of features of children's peer cultures.

Children's play and games are the topic of Chapter 21 by Ann-Carita Evaldsson. She considers play and games as social action with a focus on children's play and game participation in situated activities across various settings. Evaldsson's examination of children's play activities *in situ* provides a conceptualization for rethinking a whole set of binaries that consistently reappear in childhood studies, such as children's play as separate from the adult world; play and games as different activities; gender differentiation in play; the distinction of play and seriousness; and play and work. Evaldsson presents a review of approaches to children's play from developmental psychology and folklore, and more recent multidisciplinary approaches represented in anthropology, sociology and sociolinguistics. Overall, Evaldsson's analysis of play and games captures the importance of understanding children as active contributors to the complex process of cultural continuity and change within the peer group and in society at large.

In Chapter 22 Daniel Thomas Cook presents a comparative-historical analysis of children as consumers. Cook argues that for the better part of a century, merchants, marketers and advertisers have recognized, attended to and engaged with children as active consumers. Children's consumption, according to Cook, goes beyond singular purchases and into meaningful engagement with the world and, as such, needs to be understood not simply as individual acts but in reference to an encompassing consumer culture of childhood. Cook illustrates key themes in the consumer culture of childhood over time and across culture, class and gender. He concludes that the issue of children's place in consumer culture must be confronted in ways that take note of the hand of corporate power in the hyper-commercialization of childhoods while also granting that children's stake in commercial life is something other than exploitation

David Buckingham in Chapter 23 presents a detailed review of themes in research on children and television. He argues that children are singled out as a special audience for television even though they do not watch television any more than many adults. Further, he notes that as with many aspects of conceptions of childhood there is a dual concern regarding children and television: how television may have positive (e.g., educational) and negative (e.g., exposure to harmful material) effects on children. Buckingham reviews psychological and cultural studies research on children and television, noting how the two approaches differ in regard to their focus on the nature of television as a cultural medium of communication and their perspectives of children as individual and relatively passive rather than collective and active viewers or consumers. In discussions of the cultural studies approach Buckingham points to some of his own research which stresses how children define and construct their social identities through talk about television and other media. However, while favouring a 'child-centred' approach to television, Buckingham cautions against the view that if children are active they are somehow not influenced by what they watch. Here he argues that activity should not be equated with agency or social power and calls for a position in which children and television are best understood in the context of a wider analysis in which both are constructed and defined.

In Chapter 24, Kirsten Drotner considers the discourses of concern and discourses of celebration surrounding children's digital media practices (including computer gaming, the internet, mobile phones, and other features of the digital age). She notes that both optimists and pessimists take a normative stance in their descriptions and evaluations, but give more attention to emotionally charged issues like sex, violence and bodily harm associated with the digital world than to more insidious aspects of the power and control of large media conglomerates. Drotner goes beyond the discourses of concern and celebration to examine the intricate and complex nature of children's digital media practices in terms of semiotic codes, time, place and social relations. These media practices are in a state of continual development and flux. Drotner concludes that technology developers, content producers and avid young users will lead the way in the future of digital media practices, but is optimistic that 'level-headed' researchers will follow closely on their heels.

Section VI contains chapters about rights, interests and responsibilities, which are universal and enduring issues that assume various manifestations depending on time and place. The relations between them are not straightforward, and it remains a problem to establish connections between individualism and collectivism. This is not least pertinent as far as children are concerned: even if the UNCRC underlines *the child* as a rights subject, most parents, politicians and professionals would hesitate not to give substantial weight to the family and the public.

Chapter 25 by Michael Freeman is concerned with children, their rights and the background for the development of children's rights and the current situation since the UNCRC was adopted in 1989. The chapter is a defence of the principal importance of rights, despite attacks on this view; at the same time it is demonstrated that we still have a long way to go until it is taken for granted that children are rights subjects – for various reasons many different groups remain strongly against the view that children should be rights holders. The question is, though, whether there are – compared to other groups – good reasons for depriving children of rights – and that holds for welfare rights as well as for agency rights. Freeman guides us through what might be called a children's rights movement in an international context – from declarations in 1924 and 1959 to the pathbreaking Convention in 1989. Obviously, its nature as an international document immediately raises questions about its claim to be a universal document. The chapter, in terms of examples from the Convention's coming into existence and discussions about the ways in which articles were formulated, makes it clear that many compromises had to be made. At the end, however, an agreement was reached, but discussions are likely to continue about this important document and significant problems, such as the contents of rights versus the interests of children.

Doris Bühler-Niederberger and Heinz Sünker explore in Chapter 26 how interests in children and responsibilities for children have changed over time. They provide the reader with examples from European history, in particular France and Germany. The overall conclusion is that it is difficult to discern a clear interest in children that is not at the same time an interest in the family, in the society or in general terms an interest in the social order. This interest is thus paralleled by fitting responsibilities in terms of appropriate preventive measures and interventions and can be followed through to the present time under different names – from disciplining to building of human capital. As such, interest in children was largely dictated by the perceived benefits that were to be expected in adulthood from investing in them – economically, pedagogically, morally and/or ideologically. The chapter nevertheless ends with an optimistic note after considering the UNCRC and what it has signified. Even if this document also extends the protective mood from previous historical eras, it is likely to be less instrumental in its protective measures and in any case more emphatic about children's legitimate rights as participants.

In Chapter 27 Adrian Bailey addresses an important issue about children's mobility. Conventionally we think of children as living and staying more or less in the same place, but at any time some children have been moving in the sense of migrating with their parents. This has been accentuated over recent decades, with repercussions that need attention, theoretical and empirical. Migrating children have experiences and face problems that differ from those complying with 'sedentarist' ideals, and norms around mobility and sedentarism may collide. The various forms of staying together or being separated make networking difficult and complicated. Children may stay back while mothers live abroad, or alone or most often with parents they may meet a new community in a foreign country or continent with all that this implies in terms of coping with new life situations. The analysis of migrant children encounters a further problem: are they first of all children or migrants? The response to this question partly determines whether parents or the state assume the main responsibility for them or the extent to which tensions between parents and children are addressed. This again differs according to cultural background.

The last chapter, by Natalie Hevener Kaufman and Irene Rizzini (Chapter 28), presents and discusses on a global scale the children's rights situation and the indispensability of such rights in a world in which large numbers of children are troubled. Despite reluctance in some countries and cultures to regard children fully as humans, the authors demonstrate that much movement has taken place over recent decades to place children firmly on the legal map. We are in this respect not talking merely about the UNCRC as perhaps the most prominent document, but about a number of other documents containing articles in support of children's rights and well-being, among them the African Charter of the Rights and Welfare of the Child. As Freeman also makes clear, Kaufman and Rizzini underline the significance of having rights documents, if for no other reason than that it makes it difficult to move back from a given signature. Even if progress has been made, an appalling number of children live under unacceptable conditions and it cannot be denied that many hurdles remain before the written rights are brought to bear on all children. One hurdle is the extent to which the countries of the world are willing to endorse statutes which may be seen as reflecting the values of Western societies, even if practically all countries have in fact ratified the UNCRC. Another and much more difficult hurdle to overcome is the fact that the economic, social, and political realities are still too often counter the legal promises given in these texts.

Notes

1. In the German language, see Markefka and Nauck, 1993; Krüger and Grunert, 2002; in English, for an encyclopaedia from a historical perspective, see Fass, 2003; recently a handbook about children and the media was published in English; see Drotner and Livingstone, 2008.
2. No notice is taken here of the numerous handbooks of psychological child development and of pedagogy, which are beyond the scope of this handbook.
3. For instance, the entries on disorder, anti-social behaviour, therapy, cognitive development and many other entries dealing with psychological and social order problems; there are admittedly entries closer to this handbook's area, but they are few and far between, such as entries on anthropology of childhood and infant mortality.
4. It is something of a reckless act to mention particular influential works in these formative years, but if we nevertheless were to do so we believe that Jenks (1982b) deserves to be mentioned as the first collection with the title *Sociology of Childhood* and a symptomatic introduction by the author (Jenks, 1982a); we would also cite James and Prout's collection of chapters (1990) that (although not unequivocally) set the agenda for a *social constructionist approach*, and finally the volume *Childhood Matters* (Qvortrup et al., 1994), which (again not consistently) pursued the idea of perceiving childhood in a *structural perspective*.

References

Adorno, Th.W. (1973) 'Zum Verhältnis von Soziologie und Psychologie', in Th.W. Adorno (ed.) *Aufsätze zur Gesellschaftstheorie und Methodologie*. Frankfurt: Suhrkamp, pp. 7–62.

Ariès, Ph. (1962) *Centuries of Childhood. A Social History of Family Life*. New York: Vintage.

Bernfeld, S. (1967) *Sisyphos oder die Grenzen der Erziehung*. Frankfurt a.M.: Suhrkamp.

Burman, E. (1994) *Deconstructing Developmental Psychology*. London: Routledge.

Corsaro, W.A. (1985) *Friendship and Peer Culture in the Early Years*. Norwood, NJ: Ablex.

Dreitzel, H.P. (ed.) (1973) *Childhood and Sozialization. How Children Interact with Adults in the Family, the Commune, and the School*. Recent Sociology No.5. London: Macmillan Press.

Drotner, K. and S. Livingstone (eds) (2008) *The International Handbook of Children, Media and Culture*. London: Sage.

Fass, P. (ed.) (2003) *Encyclopedia of Children and Childhood: In History and Society*. New York: Macmillan Reference USA, 3 vol.

James, A. and A. Prout (eds) (1990) *Constructing and Reconstructing Childhood: Contemporary Issues in the Sociological Study of Childhood*. London and Washington DC: Falmer Press.

Jenks, C. (1982a) 'Introduction: Constituting the Child', in Jenks, 1982b, pp. 9–24.

Jenks, C. (ed.) (1982b) *Sociology of Childhood. Essential Readings*. London: Batsford Academic and Educational Ltd.

Kanitz, O.F. (1925) *Das proletarische Kind in der bürgerlichen Gesellschaft*. Urania-Verlags-Gesellschaft: Jena.

Key, E. (1900) *Barnets århundrade: studie*. (The Century of the Child: A Study). Stockholm: Bonniers förlag.

Krüger, H.-H. and C. Grunert (eds) (2002) *Handbuch Kindheits- und Jugendforschung*. Opladen: Leske and Budrich.

Lone, R. de (1979) *Small Futures: Children, Inequality, and the Limits of Liberal Reform*. New York and London: Harcourt Brace Jovanovich.

Markefka, M. and B. Nauck (eds) (1993) *Handbuch der Kindheitsforschung*. Neuwied, Kriftel, Berlin: Luchterhand.

Mead, M. (1978) *Culture and Commitment: the New Relationships between the Generations in the 1970s*. New York: Columbia University Press.

Merton, R.K. (1973) *The Sociology of Science*. Chicago and London: The University of Chicago Press.

Platt, A.M. (1977) *The Child Savers. The Invention of Delinquency*. 2nd edn. Chicago: The University of Chicago Press.

Preuss-Lausitz, U.a.o. (1983) *Kriegskinder, Konsumkinder, Krisenkinder. Zur Sozialisationsgeschichte seit dem Zweiten Weltkrieg*. Beltz: Weinheim.

Prout, A. and A. James (1990) 'A New Paradigm for the Sociology of Childhood? Provenance, Promise and Problems', in A. James and A. Prout (eds) *Constructing and Reconstructing Childhood*. London: The Falmer Press, pp. 7–43.

Qvortrup, J. (1985) 'Placing Children in the Division of Labour', in P. Close and R. Collins (ed.) *Family and Economy in Modern Society*. London: Macmillan.

Qvortrup, J., M. Bardy, G.B. Sgritta and H. Wintersberger (eds) (1994) *Childhood Matters: Social Theory, Practice and Politics*. Aldershot: Averbury.

Richards, M.P.M. (ed.) (1974) *The Integration of a Child into a Social World*. Cambridge: Cambridge University Press.

Seligman, E.R.A. (ed. with A. Johnson) (1930–1935) *Encyclopaedia of the Social Sciences*. New York: Macmillan.

Sills, D.L. (ed.) (1968–1979) *International Encyclopedia of the Social Sciences*. New York: Free Press.

Smelser, N.L. and P. Baltes (eds) (2001) *International Encyclopedia of the Social & Behavioural Sciences*. Amsterdam: Elsevier.

Therborn, G. (1993) 'The Politics of Childhood: the Rights of Children in Modern Times', in F.G. Castles (ed.) *Families of Nations*. Brookfield, USA: Dartmouth Publishing Company, pp. 241–291.

Thorne, B. (1987) 'Re-Visioning Women and Social Change: Where Are the Children?' *Gender and Society*, 1(1): 85–109.

Zelizer, V.A. (1985) *Pricing the Priceless Child. The Changing Social Value of Children*. Princeton, New Jersey: Princeton University Press (with a new preface 1994).

Section I
Concepts of Childhood Studies

1
Childhood as a Structural Form

Jens Qvortrup

The background

The twin concepts 'structure' and 'agency' have served philosophy and social science since time immemorial – occasionally under other names, perhaps. It is a commonplace to suggest, for instance, that social change is the result of the interplay between structural conditions, on one hand, and conscious and deliberate human interventions, on the other. The strength relation between the two largely determines the direction and rapidity of social change and it is thus of continuous interest to look for the relationship between structural forces and human agency, with the purpose of striking a balance. At the same time, it is a contested issue that almost unavoidably produces rigid fronts behind which either 'determinists' or 'voluntarists' barricade themselves – that is, at least, often the perception and mutual accusations of the adversaries.

Voices have often been raised against this and other binaries, and many doubt their usefulness. Nonetheless, the introduction and widespread application of structure and agency and their interrelatedness was new and seen as significant for childhood studies in the late twentieth century, and it justifies that the first two chapters in this Handbook deal with them specifically (see James in this volume).This is not to say that children have not been seen as active people before, or addressed as belonging to the same kind as adults. It does suggest, however, that with social studies of childhood, sociological and anthropological research for the first time begins – almost programmatically – to be serious about structure and agency as far as childhood and children are concerned.

This was, in fact, a novelty according to Canadian sociologist Anne-Marie Ambert, who two decades ago documented what she called 'the near absence' of studies on children in mainstream sociology. She included classical sociologists such as Comte, Marx, Pareto, Weber, Durkheim, Simmel, Mead, Parsons, and Merton, who circumvented childhood as an issue, on purpose or not, and she found that the situation was not much better in modern sociology textbooks and journals in the field (Ambert, 1986). The question could be and was raised as to whether this marginalization was symptomatic of the position of children in society.

It was a near absence, as Ambert writes; we can find publications from that time dealing with children – even publications that carry the title of 'sociology of childhood' or the like. And yet, by and large the contents of these works did not represent a new path, but remained faithful to socialization as the 'core issue of sociology of childhood', as one author contended (Fürstenau, 1973: 11). This was true also for some of the more well-known twentieth-century sociologists, such as Talcott Parsons and Kingsley Davis – renowned representatives of a structural-functionalist orientation. For someone interested in childhood and social structure, the title of an article by Davis from 1940 caused some expectation: 'The Child in the Social Structure'. However, no new directions were invoked in terms of recognizing childhood as a unit in the social structure; on the contrary, Davis made perhaps the most definitive strike against such an aspiration when he stated that:

> an individual's most important functions for society are performed when he is fully adult, not when he is immature. Hence society's treatment of the child is chiefly preparatory and the evaluation of him mainly anticipatory (like a savings account). Any doctrine which views the child's needs as paramount and those of organized society as secondary is a sociological anomaly. (Davis, 1940, 217)

Even if some sociologists actually did theorise around children, one might still suggest that Ambert's observation is confirmed by the way they approached the issue; namely, from a forward-looking, anticipatory, or, in Davis' words, 'preparatory' perspective. Despite eminent sociologists' impeccable record for appreciating the significance of social structure, they all, when it comes to children, fail to think in terms of *structure*, let alone of children as a *social group* or a *collective* – apart perhaps from the fact that they are *all* heading towards adulthood. Children have accordingly one significant thing in common, namely their 'getaway' from 'childhood'. The anticipation of and voyage towards adulthood not only characterise adults' attitudes to children, but also loom large for children; the features significantly determine adults' expectations of children and their behaviour towards them, as well as children's expectations of their own performance and achievement. The 'barbarian invasion of the stream of newborn infants', as formulated by Parsons, is, 'of course, a critical feature of the situation in any society' (Parsons, 1964, 208),[1] because it is a challenge for any society to socialise children to its norms, with the purpose of their full and final integration into society – that is, adult society. Parsons' formulations suggest that this did not always take place without tension and resistance.[2] He failed, however, to provide a satisfying sociological approach, because, in his and most other sociologists' view, children did not have agency, and the notion of childhood as a segment in the social structure was not in their minds.

The question is whether it is relevant and plausible to see children as constructive actors in society and to perceive childhood in structural terms. The latter is the theme of this chapter (see James on agency in the next chapter).

For scholars well versed in social studies of childhood this discussion may appear outdated. Yet, it does have a historical significance. The question to be answered, a quarter of a century ago, was how one might possibly deal with children in a more positive way, rather than simply tolerating them because of what they were to become.[3] How could we possibly do justice to childhood and children while they were still children and members of current childhood? This was not part of a revolutionary programme, but scarcely more than a modest analytical claim for providing children and childhood with 'conceptual autonomy', as formulated by Barrie Thorne in an important article (1987, 103). This claim entailed nothing but a demand for granting visibility to childhood and giving voice to children; or to use another typical phrase, dealing with childhood and children in its/their own right, that is, without necessarily making reference to children's futurity as adults.

Childhood as a segment in a social structure

In common parlance and scientific discourse childhood is routinely characterized as a *period*. The period one has in mind pertains to the individual and may be of various lengths; in any case it must be the time span demarcating the beginning and the end of an individual person's childhood. It is difficult to get away from thinking in these terms; each of us is used to – and eager to foresee – what happens to us during our own and our children's life phase. It is also in line with dominant discussions of individual mobility, which in turn concur with our society's individualistic ethos. To think in structural terms breaks with personal life plans; it asks you to think in terms not of child development, but rather of *development of childhood*.

In structural terms childhood has no temporal beginning and end and cannot, therefore, be understood periodically. Rather, it is understood as a *permanent form* of any generational structure. The two notions of childhood – as a period and as a permanent form – do not contradict each other. They can, and do, coexist side by side, but the meanings of the two are quite different, as illustrated in Figure 1.1.

This chapter does not detail various anticipatory approaches. It might be pedagogically helpful, though, to briefly put them side by side with a sociological approach in order to highlight the more important features of childhood as a structural form.

Figure 1.1 is thought to demonstrate both *childhood as a period* and *childhood as a permanent structural form*. Its first column illustrates a historical chronology in terms of generational distances between each cell – here set to 20 years. Its first row represents three generational units or age groups.[4]

Childhood as a period – the development of the child

In Figure 1.1 there are two arrows dealing with childhood as a period; we shall concentrate on the upward directed one,[5] which represents an *individual* and an *anticipatory* orientation. In this example the rising arrow has its beginning in the 1980s and ends in our current decade. It is a period of around 20 years, corresponding to the period of an individual's childhood. The child is born in, say, 1982 and thus – if she or he survives – reaches adulthood in 2000.[6] The

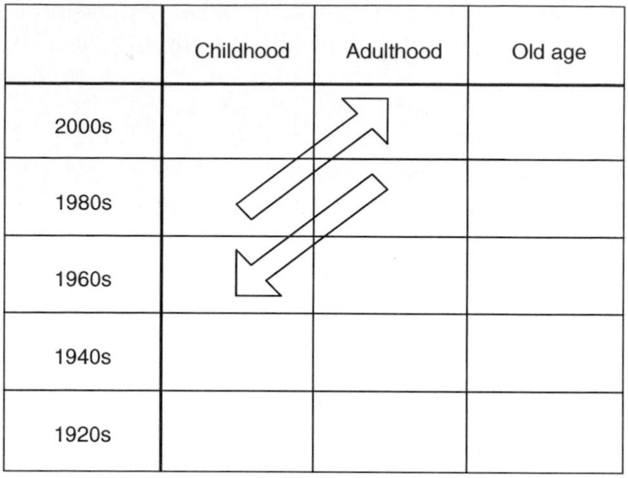

	Childhood	Adulthood	Old age
2000s			
1980s			
1960s			
1940s			
1920s			

Figure 1.1   Model of generational relations
Source: Author's own.

period or the child's individual life phase thus represents the transition towards adulthood.

We are, interestingly, using a characteristic terminology to describe this personal transition. The dynamics of *child development* lies in major changes in an individual's dispositions, as we know them from several models of child development (see Woodhead in this volume): from (e.g., sexual) immaturity to maturity, from (e.g., cognitive) incompetence to competence, from (e.g., motor functional) incapacity to capacity, and so on. Since these and most other changes described by developmental psychology are invariably depicted as movements from a less to a more desirable state, it seems to coincide with normatively stipulated anticipations of improvements as the child accomplishes the transition to her/his adult life phase.

Its anticipatory orientation is demonstrated by underlining socialization and upbringing methods with adulthood as a goal, or, to put it differently, with the purpose of overcoming one's individual childhood successfully. In some countries authorities explicitly talk of OBE – that is 'outcome-based education' – where outcome includes qualities such as being a good worker, spouse, parent, citizen, and so on.[7]

In this sense the wording is revealing when one encounters a typical phrase such as our objective to integrate the child successfully *into society*. The phrase suggests, perhaps unwittingly, that the child is not a member of society or, in other words, that society is identical with adult society. It is obviously true that a child is not an integrated adult in society, which does not seem, though, to be a necessary condition for being integrated as a person. Children are thus, by definition, excluded from society, since their integration into it marks the fact that their childhood has come to an end.[8]

Had it not been for this discourse's dominance, it might have gone without further notice. As used by dominant child sciences like psychology, paediatrics and pedagogy – but also in common parlance and by children themselves – the perspective illustrated by the rising arrow in Figure 1.1 is *anticipatory* at the *individual* level and describes a *transition* from one *period* to another in a person's life.

Childhood as a permanent segment – the development of childhood

Representatives of social studies of childhood seem to agree that the terminology of anticipation of the adult life phase is not helpful. A number of scholars have made statements, sometimes in the form of theses, about the nature of childhood in structural terms. Accordingly, childhood is 'a specific structural and cultural component of many societies' (Prout and James, 1990, 8), 'a component of the structures of society – not a preparatory stage' (Mayall, 1996, 58), 'placed in the context of societal development' (Zeiher, 1996, 37), 'a cultural pattern in historical change of generational relations' (Honig, Leu and Nissen, 1996, 21), and others could be mentioned (Alanen, 1992; Qvortrup, 1993; James, Jenks and Prout, 1998; Sgritta, 2002; and Corsaro, 2005). At the same time one often encounters use of the terminology which is far from consistent, oscillating between the individual and the structural understanding of childhood, and inattentively using child and childhood interchangeably.

To come to terms with a sociological understanding, Figure 1.1's vertical and horizontal dimensions are invoked. Each of the cells in the figure represents a structural form – at any given time – of childhood, adulthood or old age.[9] Each cell is defined by a set of societal or structural parameters. It is easy to name such parameters, but difficult to be exhaustive: we are talking about economic parameters, political, social, cultural and technological parameters, and we certainly have in mind also ideological and/or discursive parameters, that is, parameters representing understandings of and ideologies about children and childhood. It is the interplay between parameters[10] that produces all societal configurations, including sociological groups and relations between them. At any given time, thus, childhood is the result of strength relations between prevailing parameters, which must all be counted as structural forces.

Figure 1.1 gives us the opportunity to discuss – along the vertical dimension – the development of childhood, and – along the horizontal dimension – childhood as a generational unit.

The structural form of childhood (in France in the 1920s – to make a concrete allusion) was a result of the interplay of parameters which at this time and place assumed certain values. In the 1940s, 1960s, and so on, as the values of and relations between parameters in France changed, childhood as a structural form changed accordingly. In this sense childhood, as the social space within which children lead their life, changes constantly, just as adulthood and old age also change. These changes cannot hide, however, the *continuous existence and reality of childhood as a structural form*. In structural terms it is not transient and not a period; it has *permanence*. The *historical development of childhood* does not do away with its form, and contemporary *childhood's cultural variability* testifies to its universal presence.

Childhood is, in other words, *both* constantly changing *and* a permanent structural form within which all children spend their personal childhood period. Childhood is there as a social space to receive any child born and to include the child – for better or for worse – throughout his or her childhood period. When this child grows up and becomes an adult, his or her childhood comes to an end, but childhood as a form does not go away and will stay there to receive new generations of children. Hardman put it in this way in an early, but later reprinted, article from 1973: 'The children move in and out of this segment into another, but others take their place. The segment still remains' (2001, 504).

In Figure 1.1 this is seen in the double movement: from one historical time to another (1920s to 1940s to 1960s, etc.) childhood remains there, although it is subject to change; at the same time we also appreciate – if we follow the upward directed arrow – that all the individual childhood periods disappear completely.[11]

The vertical – historical – perspective thus illustrates, we might say, the development of childhood (rather than the development of the child). This notion, *the development of childhood*, suggests an understanding of childhood which is completely different from its individual counterpart. It is a notion whose dynamics lies in societal parameters, and not in individual dispositions.

Imagine that we are asked to envision childhood in France one hundred years ago. Since it is impossible to capture all French children's periodic childhoods we will most likely come to visualize quintessential French childhood, using our historical knowledge of the values and interactions of prevailing parameters which produced the structural form of French childhood at the beginning of twentieth century. It was a childhood which – compared to the situation today – was characterized by more siblings, higher child mortality, a dramatically lower level of technology (no cars, no IT, hardly any cinemas, few telephones), lower standards of education, poorer health, more children working, a lower divorce rate, and so on. Many of these parameters also impacted other age groups, so that we may argue in general terms that all generational units are in principle exposed to the same external parameters, even if they may be impacted with different intensity and strength.

Obviously, each French child's individual childhood within any historical time's childhood assumes unique manifestations, but it does not and cannot basically deviate from it. Even if we all agree that French childhood a century ago was not a unitary one, most of us would probably also agree that its parameters would assume quite different values than French childhood today – that it was very different from contemporary French childhood.

When we argue that childhood changes historically while remaining as a permanent form, we are claiming continuity and change. The parameters of childhood change their values constantly (but internally, with various paces and rates[12]), but childhood nevertheless keeps forms that are comparable over time, because it essentially keeps being impacted by the same set of parameters. Even over long historical or cultural distances childhood must be recognizable and identifiable as long as it makes sense to talk about childhood, that is, to use this concept. While childhood as a period is a transient phase for each child to become an adult, childhood as a structural form can never turn into anything else and least of all into adulthood as a structural form. Nevertheless, it is absolutely meaningful to talk about a transition from one historical childhood to another historical childhood.[13]

Childhood as a permanent segment – childhood as a generational unit

If we now look at the horizontal dimension of Figure 1.1, we are moving to think in terms of generational structuring (see the chapters in this volume by Alanen, Mayall, Olk, and Hengst). Compared with the arrow, where each individual child relates to his or her individual adulthood via a movement of 'becoming integrated into society', as we saw, childhood at the horizontal level *is* integrated in a generational structure at any time in history. We then perceive this structure cross-sectionally, as a coexistence of contemporaneous generational units. In this sense it would be meaningless to state that childhood is not an integrated part of society; on the contrary, it would not be imaginable to do without childhood, just as adulthood and old age necessarily must be there as generational segments.

It was suggested above that all generational units are in principle exposed to the same parameters – be they economic, technological, cultural, and so on. It is, though, reasonable to add that the generational units do not all experience or deal with the impact of these parameters in the same way. They are positioned differently in the social order. Means, resources, influence and power are differentially distributed between the units, whose abilities to cope with external challenges vary accordingly. Finally, the units may arguably have different interests, which raises the issue of how the interests are served, furthered and/or prevented, that is, the question of what in broad terms are called generational conflicts and how they are approached or solved.

Relations between generations do not necessarily take the form of conflicts or cleavages; they may simply be taken into account as differences or, in fact, as common interests. The important point is that a generational perspective is indispensable for coming to terms with the nature of the relationship.

It may be helpful to briefly compare this form with other structural forms such as a social class or a gender group. To the extent that these categories or structural forms are all social constructions in the sense of having been produced by a number of parameters, they are comparable to structural forms in generational terms. Their permanence implies that their existence does not depend on particular members, even if, of course, members may exert influence on them. A social class does not depend on one or another person leaving or entering it in terms of individual mobility. A gender group will likewise continue to exist as long as there are social differences between the life worlds of females and males; it does not disappear simply because someone dies and thus leaves the gender group. Social classes and gender groups have permanence, just as generational groups have permanence. At the same time they are all subject to change due to changing societal parameters and perhaps also changing size and composition.

The main particularity about structural forms in terms of generations – as compared with those in terms of class and gender – is the relatively quick turnover of their members: as far as childhood is concerned, one might say that it experiences a 100 per cent mobility towards adulthood – or, if you like, a total replacement every generation (however defined: currently every 18 years). In principle this is not different from other generational units (adulthood, old age) or indeed from gender groups. Replacements here also take place automatically, even if they take longer – again depending on historical and societal circumstances. Social class does not foresee a similar automatism in replacement of its members; nevertheless it extends its existence beyond its individual members.

Applications of a structural perspective[14]

One may, of course, ask why it is necessary or important to introduce a structural perspective on childhood – one that must be in generational terms. The immediate answer is that we pursue this task because we expect it to produce insights which will not be produced by other perspectives, including ingrained approaches to the study of the child and its life phase. It has to be borne in mind that as a structural form childhood is abstracted from individual children, and hence the method for acquiring insight into childhood, both historically and generationally, does not necessarily demand that children are directly observed or asked. What we are searching for is children's life worlds or the framework within which children lead their lives. At the end of the day it is obviously of greatest significance how both close and distant parameters have bearings on children, but we know equally well that many, perhaps most, powerful parameters influencing children's lives are set in motion without having children or childhood in mind at all.

Again it is useful to make a comparison with class and gender. As we know, important insight is gained about social class 'in itself', that is, about its putative objective circumstances, without necessarily knowing anything about individual workers and proletarians; likewise, we may obtain valuable knowledge about the relationship between men and women by studying historical developments in society – again without having known about one single woman or man.

Therefore, following our definition of childhood as a structural form above, we will – in order to come to terms with children's life circumstances – have to take into account and be deeply informed about the parameters which describe and explain these life circumstances.

In a historical context – what we called the development of childhood – one should in principle follow the ensemble of parameters as they change and interact with each other. This is – in perhaps a vague and sketchy way – what historian Philippe Ariès did as he followed the development of childhood from a time when it was not, putatively, a part of people's awareness, through 'a long process of segregation (...) which has continued into our own day, and which is called schooling [– this] isolation of children, and their delivery to rationality' (Ariès, 1982, 7). We may talk about an institutionalization of childhood and, more specifically, a scholarization of childhood as a result of demands from a changing economy and a changing polity. These developments changed children's life worlds dramatically. Even though there were actors who worked hard for the schooling of children, one wonders whether this would have been the case had it not been basically understood as an indispensable interest of the trades, burgeoning industry, society at large, and so on.

When anthropologist Ruth Benedict in a famous article suggested that 'From a comparative point of view our culture goes to great extremes in emphasizing contrasts between the child and the adult' and commented that 'these are all dogmas of our culture, dogmas which, in spite of the facts of nature, other cultures commonly do not share' (Benedict, 1938), her focus was interestingly not socialization or the child as such. It was rather observations about *the generational position of childhood*, which she summarized from various cultures during the first third of the twentieth century. The same was true for her colleague Margaret Mead, who – also drawing on experiences from coexisting cultures – observed *different relations between generations*. She distinguished between three different cultures – 'the *postfigurative*, in which children learn primarily from their elders, the *cofigurative*, in which both children and adults learn from their peers, and the *prefigurative*, where adults learn also from their children' (Mead, 1972, 31). What Benedict and Mead note as differences using contemporary evidence may also be appreciated as changes in historical comparisons of cultures and societies. The interesting questions are, however, why these differences exist, what their nature is, and why generational relations change historically.

Sociological answers to these questions cannot be found in changing individual dispositions or psychological readiness,[15] but rather in transformations of culture and society. People respond to new figurations of economic, social and technological conditions; and social groups enter into new mutual constellations at societal as well as local and familial levels.

This may be difficult to appreciate as far as children are concerned, because we are not used to understanding children in structural terms. In principle the situation is comparable to areas that are more familiar to us. There is no doubt, for instance, that relations have changed between women and men over time (and that contemporary cultures exhibit gender differences). These changes have scarcely come about because of some intrinsic changes in women and/or men, but rather because gender roles change as a result of societal alterations. Women came to receive education, and eventually they joined men in the labour market. Thus gender relations assumed new forms and contents in tandem with *structural transformations* – facilitated through the agency of women (and perhaps quite a few men as well, who in various positions found it to be in their interest).

It seems easy to appreciate changes in such familiar areas concerning adult collectives. Have there been similar changes between generations? As suggested by Benedict and Mead, children assume different positions vis-à-vis adults in different cultures or societies. Nothing is changed, of course, in the fact that each and every child is heading towards adulthood; it is the conditions or the circumstances under which they do this that differ. It is, in other words, *childhood in structural terms* which assumes different forms as a result of societal transformations.

The examples from Ariès, Benedict and Mead illustrate partly a historical development, and partly intercultural variations in the framework within which children lead their lives. These changes and variations have basically come about due to changes demanded by the economy and the polity. They are no less real for that, and it is up to researchers in childhood to unravel the new contexts of significance for children's life worlds.

An interesting and important example of changing intergenerational relations may be derived from demographic developments, that is, developments which children cannot be accused of having caused, but which will nevertheless impact them fundamentally. In the first place a population pyramid helps us visualize how childhood has been taking up ever less space over time; hence its structural form is minimized almost literally. The factors responsible for, or perhaps rather in accord with, these demographic changes are all ones that in other respects will come to influence childhood, such as economic growth, industrialization, urbanization, improved health, secularization, individualization, education, privatization of the family, and so on. As a result childhood has become smaller – both at the family and at the societal level. The attitude has become more sentimentalizing, more protective – at least at the family level. The sociologist James Coleman has used US statistics to show how children are affected in relative terms by the development: due to changing demographics the share of households without children currently living in them has increased from 27 per cent in 1870 to 64 per cent in 1983. Over the same time, per capita income of children relative to adults decreased from 71 to 51 per cent (Coleman, 1990, 590).

This example demonstrates how structural developments impact childhood differently whether we speak of a family or a societal level. One may argue that the relations between children and their own parents have become more close, caring and protective, while at the societal level they have come to be understood in terms of a structural heedlessness or indifference, to use a phrase from German sociologist Kaufmann (2005, 152ff).[16] When we look at Coleman's figures it is easy to appreciate that the decrease in children's income relative to *all* adults is a result of the fact that ever fewer adults, that is, fewer parents, are currently assuming responsibility for children. Even if it is (still) true that most adults have been or will be parents, it is at the same time true that nowadays children as a collective are at greater risk of low income or poverty than adults as a collective. The lower the birth rate the more likely is this scenario to be true. In previous eras, as Coleman's figures suggest, both resources and responsibilities were more equally spread over both life and community.

The examples of structural parameters' influence on childhood and children are legion. They are not invoked to suggest that they are superior to other methods used to achieve insight, but they must be invoked as an additional method for coming to encompassing understandings of how childhood develops and how children as a social group or collective fare compared with other generational units. It is not necessarily the case that the development falls out negatively for children or childhood. The point is not in the first place to ask this question at all. The point is to find out about the impact on childhood of these macro variables.

Recent years – in particular the past two decades – have seen a tremendous growth in computer technology. Margaret Mead did not know about this, even if it was in germ foreseen in her book mentioned above. If we follow her thinking, much indicates that children will have significant comparative advantages over their elders in society, and the oldest generation in particular may suffer drawbacks in mastering this new technology. At the same time the oldest generation is becoming more and more numerous and thus in principle gaining more and more political power. How this development will turn out – at the societal as well as at the family level – is difficult to say.

What is true, we suggest, is that studying the interrelations between generations as structural forms will be indispensable if we are to foresee and possibly improve *the future of childhood*. To come to terms with the future of childhood we need to think creatively of the future figuration of partly known parameters, and in particular the changing values of these parameters. This is again completely different from foreseeing the no less important future of the child.

Notes

1. Parsons may have borrowed the expression from Ortega y Gasset, who talked about children as an 'irruption verticale' of barbarians (see Meillassoux, 1994, p. 219) – that is, their (non-entitled?) intrusion or their (hostile?) invasion.
2. References to Parsons and Davis are made partly because they are sociologists and partly because their work – deliberately and consciously worked out and argued for – was indicative of our culture's perception of children's position, that is, in waiting. Numerous expressions in common parlance and in political documents (see James and James, 2008) speak of children merely in their futurity – such as 'children are our next generation', 'children are our future', and so on.
3. The now frequently encountered expression that children in traditional sociological thinking are perceived as 'not human beings but human becomings' was originally formulated during this period (see Qvortrup, 1985, p. 132).
4. Of course, the length of the childhood *period* has changed historically (see e.g., Gillis, 1974, pp. 2, 104 and 208) and is in any case debateable. One might also have added more generational units, such as youth. It is, however, the principle behind the relationships that is important to observe.
5. The downward directed arrow may aptly be called the psychiatric or the psychoanalytic arrow in the sense that an adult may be analysed by reverting to events and experiences in childhood to interpret an adult state and/or possibly cure calamities. The key to understanding, for instance, psychopathologies in adults thus is said to lie in past childhood, exactly as the key to understanding children's futurities as adults allegedly lies in current childhood.
6. Eighteen years of age is currently a typical end of the childhood period, corresponding also with the definition set by the UNCRC.
7. In principal OBE and other forward-looking orientations justify any method leading to the desired result, given that adulthood is paramount.
8. Whether all 'non-integrated' individuals for that matter are children is another question, which is not without interest; thus adults who due to, for instance, insanity, feeblemindedness or drug abuse are deprived of their majority in court consequently become legal minors; in a sense therefore they have been returned to childhood status.

9. Of course, other forms like youth or middle age might have been represented also, but the number is not important for the argument.
10. It goes without saying that, at the end of the day, these parameters are artificial in accordance with Marx's famous dictum from the *German Ideology*: 'Men make their own history, but not under conditions of their own choosing.' It is another matter whether children should be included in this notion of 'men'! See other chapters in this volume on children's agency, for instance those by James and Corsaro.
11. In this way it becomes possible to combine childhood and childhoods – that is, the singular and the plural forms. All the different individual-period childhoods disappear, but childhood as a structural form remains.
12. That is, values of the economic parameter do not change at exactly the same rate as values of, for example, the technological, cultural or social parameters, which in turn are likely to have different paces than, for instance, the discursive parameter, and so on.
13. The question is then whether we should here talk of childhood or childhoods?
14. In order to forestall criticism for one-sidedness, let alone determinism, I shall incidentally emphasize, that children as actors does have a significant place in this discussion. In the first place, in this Handbook's division of labour it is given space in several chapters (see, for instance, those by James, Corsaro, and Nieuwenhuys). Secondly, activities of children as they pertain to transforming social orders must always be a part of any description of structural forms, as they change accordingly (see Qvortrup, 1995, on change and continuity of children's obligatory activities; see also Corsaro, 2005, pp. 33ff). The extent to which children's agency is able to impact childhood as a form is another matter.
15. deMause comes close to such an interpretation with his psychogenetic theory of history (deMause, 1975, p. 3). His rejection of the role of technology and economics to the advantage of personality changes leaves his theory with limited credibility among social scientists.
16. The German language allows a useful distinction between these qualities of relations: at the family level *Beziehungen* and at the societal level *Verhältnisse* (cf. *Klassenverhältnisse*) (see Honig, 1999).

References

Alanen, L. (1992) *Modern Childhood? Exploring the 'Child Question' in Sociology.* Jyväskylä: University of Jyväskylä.

Ambert, A.-M. (1986) 'Sociology of Sociology: The Place of Children in North American Sociology', *Sociological Studies of Child Development*, Vol. 1, pp. 11–31.

Ariès, Ph. (1982) *Barndommens historie* (abbreviated Danish edition of L'Enfant et la vie familial sous l'ancien regime, 1960, including the author's preface to the new French edition from 1973). Copenhagen: NNF Arnold Busck.

Benedict, R. (1938) 'Continuities and Discontinuities in Cultural Conditioning', *Psychiatry*, 1(2): 161–167.

Coleman, J.S. (1990) *Foundations of Social Theory.* Cambridge, MA. and London: Belknap Press of Harvard University Press.

Corsaro, W.A. (2005) *The Sociology of Childhood.* Thousands Oaks, California: Pine Forge Press.

Davis, K. (1940) 'The Child and the Social Structure', *The Journal of Educational Sociology*, 14(4): 217–229.

deMause, L. (1975) 'The Evolution of Childhood', in Lloyd deMause (ed.) *The History of Childhood.* New York: The Psychohistory Press, pp. 1–73.

Fürstenau, P. (1973) *Soziologie der Kindheit.* Heidelberg: Quelle & Meyer.

Gillis, J.R. (1974) *Youth and History. Tradition and Change in European Age Relations 1770 – Present.* New York and London: Academic Press.

Hardman, Ch. ([1973] 2001) 'Can There Be an Anthropology of Children?', *Childhood*, 8(4): 501–517.

Honig, M.-S. (1999) *Entwurf einer Theorie der Kindheit*. Frankfurt am Main: Suhrkamp.

Honig, M.-S., H.R. Leu and U. Nissen (1996) 'Kindheit als Sozialisationsphase und als kulturelles Muster', in M.-S. Honig, H.R. Leu and U. Nissen (eds) *Kinder und Kindheit. Soziokulturelle Muster – sozialisationstheoretische Perspectiven*. Weinheim und München: Juventa, pp. 9–29.

James, A. and A. James (2008) 'Changing Childhood in the UK: Reconstructing Discourses of "Risk" and "Protection"', in A. James and A. James (eds) *European Childhoods: Cultures, Politics and Childhoods in Europe*. Palgrave Macmillan: Houndmills, Basingstoke, pp. 105–128.

James, A., C. Jenks and A. Prout (1998) *Theorizing Childhood*. Polity Press: Cambridge.

Kaufmann, F.-X. (2005) *Schrumpfende Gesellschaft: Vom Bevölkerungsrückgang und seine Folgen*. Frankfurt am Main: Suhrkamp.

Mayall, B. (1996) *Children, Health and the Social Order*. Buckingham: Open University Press.

Mead, M. (1972) *Culture and Commitment. A Study of the Generation Gap*. Herts: Panter Books.

Meillassoux, C. (1994) 'Kapitalistische Produktion von "Überbevölkerung" in Afrika', *Das Argument* 204, 36(2): 219–232.

Parsons, T. (1964) *The Social System*. London: Free Press.

Prout, A. and A. James (1990) 'A New Paradigm for the Sociology of Childhood? Provenance, Promise and Problems', in A. James and A. Prout (eds) *Constructing and Reconstructing Childhood*. London: Falmer Press, pp. 7–34.

Qvortrup, J. (1985) 'Placing Children in the Division of Labour', in P. Close and R. Collins (eds) *Family and Economy in Modern Society*. Basingstoke and London: Macmillan, pp. 129–145.

Qvortrup, J. (1993) Nine Theses about 'Childhood as a Social Phenomenon', in J. Qvortrup (ed.) *Childhood as a Social Phenomenon: Lessons from an International Project*. Eurosocial Report 47, Vienna: European Centre, pp. 11–18.

Qvortrup, J. (1995) 'From Useful to Useful: The Historical Continuity of Children's Constructive Participation', *Sociological Studies of Children*, Vol. 7, pp. 49–76.

Sgritta, G.B. (2002) 'Inconsistencies: Childhood on the Economic and Political Agenda', in F. Mouritsen and J. Qvortrup (eds) *Childhood and Children's Culture*. Odense: Odense University Press, pp. 209–260.

Thorne, B. (1987) 'Re-Visioning Women and Social Change: Where Are The Children?', *Gender and Society*, 1(1): 85–109.

Zeiher, H. (1996) 'Kinder in der Gesellschaft und Kindheit in der Soziologie', *Zeitschrift für Sozialisationsforschung und Erziehungssoziologie*, 16(1): 26–46.

2

Agency

Allison James

Introduction

In exploring the idea of children's agency this chapter introduces what has, in many ways, been one of the most important theoretical developments in the recent history of childhood studies – the shift to seeing children as social actors; a changed perception that dates from the 1970s. This entails, as we shall discover during the course of this chapter, a view of children as people worthy of study 'in their own right and not just as receptacles of adult teaching' (Hardman, 1973, 87), and is a change in perception that has, in turn, placed considerable emphasis on children's role as social agents. That is to say, as Mayall (2002) points out, children are now seen as people who, through their individual actions, can make a difference 'to a relationship, a decision, to the workings of a set of social assumptions or constraints' (2002, 21). As this chapter explores, what this focus on children's agency has achieved, therefore, is a reconceptualization not only of what 'childhood' is, but also of the ways in which children themselves can be understood as active participants in society. It is an important shift in thinking that has ramifications beyond childhood studies, however, since it reflects and refracts the everyday experiences of children in communities across the world. It is the aim of this chapter, therefore, to not only chart the historical development and significance of this changing epistemology within the social sciences, but also to underscore its wider social political significance for children's own experiences.

Being or becoming an individual?

Lee observed that 'a division is often drawn between adult "human beings" and child "human becomings"' (2001, 7). Such a distinction, he continues, shows that we have:

> grown used to making sense of childhood *through* adulthood, interpreting everything children do, or have done to them, in terms of how this will affect their journey toward adulthood, or in terms of what it tells us about how far a

34

given child has travelled. Children's lives and activities in the present are still envisaged in the main, as a preparation for the future. (2001, 8)

And, since, traditionally, adulthood is held to represent some kind of end point to children's journey, it is assumed that it is:

adults' stability and completeness... [that] allow them to act in society, to participate independently in serious activities like work and politics [while] children's instability and incompleteness mean that they are often understood only as dependent and passive recipients of adults' actions. (2001, 8)

And, indeed, prior to the 1970s it was precisely such a view of children that predominated within the social sciences. The study of children as individual social actors was simply not yet part of its agenda and children were studied predominantly as representatives of a category whose significance lay, primarily, in what they revealed about adult life.

The dominance of this view can be traced back to the growth and influence of developmental psychology, for the study of children had long been its special province and expertise. Since as far back as the late nineteenth century children had been intensively observed and studied. However, this was not for the intrinsic interest of understanding what it was like to be a child or to get a glimpse into their everyday lives. Rather, these early scientists viewed children primarily as people who were interesting for what they revealed about the sources and origins of humankind in general. Being as yet unsullied by much contact with the social world, young children were seen as ripe for investigation by those scientists interested in discovering the stages of development through which could be charted the physiological and psychological changes that occur between 'childhood' and 'adulthood'. Ascribing to the view that the growth of the infant child's body and mind was shaped by a 'normal core of development unfolding according to biological principles' these early child studies laid the foundations, therefore, for developmental psychology's later concern to uncover the many commonalities of physical and psychological development that help transform 'children' into 'adults' (Burman, 1994, 12). Within this approach, however, children as individuals were granted significance if they deviated from the 'standard' model of 'the (developing) child' which was gradually emerging. Thus, by the 1930s as Burman shows:

clear lines of demarcation were being drawn between the elabouration of developmental norms for diagnostic use (seen as the domain of general psychology and medicine) and psychoanalysis (seen as the arena of the particular personality traits and specific idiosyncratic processes). (1994, 13)

For developmental psychology, therefore, and within the work of one of its most prominent proponents Jean Piaget, the individual child, the child whom he studied in his laboratory, was ironically only of interest for what that child revealed about children's thinking *in general*. Piaget's concern was to understand how children develop the rationality characteristic of adult thought. Thus, he set out to map, systematically and through experimentation, the changes that occur in children's ways of thinking as they grow older and gradually learn to adapt to more complex environments. And in the construction of his hierarchical, universal path of human development, the actions and reactions of individual children were interesting 'insofar as they were instantiated and provided a forum for investigating, general epistemological questions about the origins and growth of thought' (Burman, 1994, 153). Thus, Burman concludes, 'Piaget depicted a subject who is irrevocably isolated and positioned outside history and society', and a subject largely without subjectivity and individuality (1994, 154).

However, it was not just within the discipline of developmental psychology that the present lives of children as individual actors played second fiddle to a focus on children as 'becomings'. Within the culture and personality school of anthropology that flourished in the United States from the late 1920s – and continues to the present, see for example, Levine 1994 – the future that children represent is also a key focus. As social anthropologists seeking to understand what lies behind cultural differences, the study of children is used to counter the universalizing tendencies of developmental theory through demonstrating the effects that culture can have upon child development. Thus, through her work with children and young people in Samoa, Mead (1928) sought to demonstrate the ways in which culture can act to temper the developmental path from childhood to adulthood, and was able to reveal the absence among Samoan youth of what, at that time, was regarded as the 'natural', universal rebelliousness of adolescence. Similarly, focusing on the child-rearing practices of the Zuni, Donu and Kwakiutl, Benedict (1935) also demonstrated the plasticity of children's development, finding marked differences in the responsibilities given to children in these different societies. Thus, although offering an important challenge to the idea of the universalism of children's trajectories towards adulthood that was implied by developmental theories, the culture and personality writers were also focused on children primarily as becomings, rather than beings. They studied children in order to get to know more about processes of cultural reproduction, rather than to understand their present lives.

And within sociology things were no better. The study of individual children's lives and experiences was subsumed by an overarching interest in socialization (see Prout and James, 1990). Regarded as the process whereby children were informed and transformed into society members, traditional socialization theory drew heavily on the concepts and models of developmental psychology and argued that:

> socialising agents [who] teach, serve as models and invite participation. Through their ability to offer gratification and deprivations they induce cooperation and learning and prevent disrupting deviance. (Elkin, 1960, 101)

Reaching its apogee in the work of Talcott Parsons (1951), as Lee observes, social-ization was seen as 'a process that rescues each child from the incompleteness of "nature", and thereby rescues society from the disorder and decay that would result if its population were incomplete' (2001, 40). Once more, therefore, the focus was on the category of children providing the vehicle for the reproduction of adult life, with the emphasis this time being placed on the facilitating role of social institutions such as the family and the school.

Across all three areas – developmental psychology, social anthropology, soci-ology – prior to the paradigm shift that took place in the 1970s and 1980s there were, therefore, many similarities in the ways in which 'the child' was conceptual-ized and the manner in which children were made the focus of scientific enquiry. Lee (2001, 42–43) has described this as a 'dominant framework' which can be summarized as follows: although children are regarded as inadequate, incomplete and dependent, society must invest in their care, training and upbringing since it is children who represent the future of the social world. Within this concep-tualization of 'the child', therefore, there was little room for any notion of the agentic child – the radically different model of 'the child' that was to become a key feature of the 'emergent paradigm' within the new sociology of childhood (Prout and James, 1990).

A break with tradition?

What then accounts for the paradigm shift that occurred in the 1970s and 1980s? In part this can explained by the shifts in social theorizing that were occurring at this time, described below, but it also reflects a changing awareness of children's place and position in society. The year 1979 saw the launch of the International Year of the Child and the emergence of the idea of the 'world's children', which through showing to western audiences the consequences that war, famine and poverty have on children across the world 'threw the very idea of childhood into stark relief' (Prout and James, 1990, 2). Child abuse also began to become a more public issue, raising a wider public consciousness that some children do not inhabit the idyllic world of 'Happy, Safe, Protected, Innocent Childhood' (Holt, 1975, 22–23). Children could no longer be seen as waiting, unproblematically, in the wings of adulthood. Childhood was no longer a known quantity, as images of radically different childhoods began to penetrate the television screens of west-ern homes and to populate the billboards and hoardings of western streets.

Within the academy there were also signs of an emerging critique and unease about traditional perspectives on children. Developmental psychologists such as Donaldson (1978) were beginning to challenge some of Piaget's work on child development through, for example, demonstrating that the social context of the laboratory experiment, which was unfamiliar to children, inhibited their responses. When this context was changed young children's thought and rea-soning could be shown to be much more sophisticated than Piaget had claimed (see also McGarrigle and Donaldson, 1974). Thus, 'what appears to be "faulty" reasoning actually indicates children's ingenious attempts to create sensible meanings for what are, to them, nonsensical situations and contexts' (Woodhead and Faulkner, 2000, 25). The work of the Soviet psychologist L.S. Vygotsky, a contemporary of Piaget, was also becoming recognized as important for what it revealed about children's active role in human development. He argued that through social interaction, children learned to internalize the skills and competencies they observed in others (see for example Vygotsky, 1978). Here 'the child' is not just engaging in activities as an individual that promote changes in cognition in the manner envisaged by Piaget; rather, the child becomes involved in social relations and activities of different kinds and is thus positioned, foremost, as a *social* actor.

Within the social sciences, the 1950s and 1960s saw the emergence of new interpretive and interactionist approaches to understanding everyday life that launched a critical attack on the structural functionalist agenda. Through its emphasis on the role of social structures and institutions in shaping society, structural functionalism had left little room for consideration of the role which individuals played in society. Wrong (1961) accused Parsons of having an over-socialized conception of humankind, while Rafky (1973) and Mackay (1973) later took socialization theory itself to task by claiming a more active role for children in the process of cultural assimilation. Elsewhere the rise of structuralism and semiology was generating interest in the ways in which social life is not only ordered, but also apprehended, through the use of language (see Ricoeur, 1978) and the non-verbal symbols and signs in everyday life (see for example Hebdige, 1979). Thus, it is not surprising that at a time when Berger and Luckmann (1967) were exploring the social construction of reality, a debate about the socially constructed character of childhood emerged, following Ariès' now famous claim that 'in medieval society the idea of childhood did not exist' (1962, 125; James and Prout, 1990). In such an intellectual climate, childhood could no longer be seen, simplistically, as just the early part of the life-course.

In addition, the counter-cultural movements of the 1960s, the rise of feminism and anti-colonial movements had challenged the hegemony of existing social and political relations, stimulating social science interest in the world-views being articulated by different sub-cultural groups (see Hall and Jefferson, 1976). This work revealed the existence of radically alternative perspectives on the social world that, finally, signalled the death knell to traditional socialization theory. Through their detailed ethnographic work, Willis (1977) and later Corrigan (1979) demonstrated the subtle ways in which young working-class lads learned to apprehend the social world, the often very different meanings they attributed to it and the accommodations and challenges they made to it. And it was within this tradition that Hardman (1973) became one of the first to suggest that children, too, might inhabit a 'self-regulating, autonomous world which does not necessarily reflect early development of adult culture' in which they could be seen as social actors (1973, 87).

But perhaps of greatest theoretical significance for the paradigm shift that occurred in conceptualization of children and childhood was the recognition, within social theory, of the significance of great divide – and the need to find some resolution to it. That is to say, the recognition of the importance for social science of both those theories that sought to explain the structure of social life and those which explored the actions and meanings of individuals, a first attempt at reconciliation which took place in Giddens' (1979) account of structuration theory. Here he suggested that social scientists had to take account of both agency and structure in their explanations of the social world for, as he argued:

> every act which contributes to the reproduction of a structure is also an act of production and as such may initiate change by altering the structure at the same time as it reproduces it. (69)

Given the ways in which children and childhood had traditionally been conceptualized, it is perhaps not surprising that this intellectual debate helped prompt the major paradigm shift that gave birth to childhood studies. What the structure–agency debate did was to raise important questions about the part that children themselves played in their own growing up and socialization – something which, as we have seen, had been underplayed within the traditional, dominant framework. If Giddens was correct about the interaction between structure and agency, then children, as much as adults, could be envisaged as active participants in society. They too could be seen as people who were as much contributors to its shape and form, as well as being 'socialized' by it and, indeed, there were already available accounts of children's lives that indicated the ways in which this process could be seen to be happening.

Published in 1979, Bluebond-Langner's account of the private worlds of dying children reveals 'structure' and 'action' both at play, and presents children – literally – as actors in the scripting of death on a cancer ward. Based on a nine-month ethnographic study in the Department of Pediatrics in a large Midwestern teaching hospital in the United States, Bluebond-Langner's aim had been to 'get as close as possible...to their thoughts, their interactional strategies, and their structuring of the situation' (1979, xi). Taking up Denzin's point that traditional structural-functionalist and psychological-functionalist theories of socialization fail to grasp the 'shifting, unfolding, creative aspects of all human behaviour', Bluebond-Langner reveals children's role in the everyday structuring of hospital life and parent–child relations on the ward (Denzin, 1973 cited in Bluebond-Langner, 1979, 5). In her words, she wanted to show 'the child's role in the initiation and maintenance of the social order' – and this she proceeds to do, quite clearly (1979, 5). Thus, for example, she reveals children acting as active interpreters of the social world of the cancer ward:

> A five-year-old boy interprets his mother's crying as indicating that he is very sick. 'See my mommy's red nose, that's from me. Everybody cries when they see me. I'm pretty sick'. He also notes that he is getting more presents than his sister. 'I get more presents than when I had my tonsils out. My sister gets the same.' Finally, he has been behaving in ways that are ordinarily cause for reprimand and finds that he is not reprimanded...He acts the sick role and claims his right

on the basis that he is truly ill. For example, Beth snatching a toy from her sister, said, 'Gimme that. I'm the sick one, not you'. (Bluebond-Langner, 1979, 9)

But, through their actions, these children also help construct the everyday world of the hospital and its structures. At a time when death from childhood leukaemia was more likely than it now is, Bluebond-Langner argued that the leukaemic children were 'an affront to the doctors' sense of mastery to their training, their profession and their self-concept' since they cannot easily offer cure or comfort (1979, 219). But, as Bluebond-Langner showed, by pretending that they did not know they were ill or that they were going to die, a knowledge which clearly they did have, the children engaged their doctors and their parents in a game of mutual pretence. It was a game, she said, that allowed 'participants to fulfil their role expectations and retain social membership in the face of a threat to such membership' (1979, 219). That is, it was a game played by children and by adults that enabled the status quo of the power and authority of the hospital setting, of ideas about parenting, and ideas about children, to remain unchallenged in the face of a progressive and fatal disease.

But what exactly does the concept of 'social actor' entail and how does it relate to that of 'agency'? While the historical account provided above details the *emergence* of this idea within childhood studies, in relation to the wider development of social theory, its nuances and ramifications have yet to be explored. This is the task of the next section.

Actors, agents and processes of reproduction

By now, the idea that children are social actors is a commonplace one. However, as noted above, this has its origins in the intellectual debates of the 1960s and 1970s that culminated in a new paradigm for the social study of childhood. Summing up these developments in 1990, James and Prout provide a definition of what this notion of children as social actors might embrace:

> children are and must be seen as active in the construction of their own lives, the lives of those around them and of the societies in which they live. Children are not just the passive subjects of social structures and processes. (1990, 8)

That said, they thought it equally important to acknowledge that:

> children's social relationships and cultures are worthy of study in their own right, independent of the perspective and concerns of adults. (1990, 8)

And indeed, both these statements remain important since they entangle the twin concepts of actor and agency, an entanglement that is core to contemporary childhood studies. As Mayall writes:

> it is clear enough, without carrying out formal research studies, that children are social actors: that is, they take part in family relationships from the word

go; they express their wishes, demonstrate strong attachments, jealousy and delight, seek justice (2000, 21)

But, as she goes on to say, what really 'put children into sociology' was the collective endeavour to say more than this – that is, to argue that they had agency (2000, 21). For Mayall (2002) the actor is someone who does something; the agent is someone who does something with other people, and, in so doing, makes things happen, thereby contributing to wider processes of social and cultural reproduction. Thus, to study children as social actors is to see them as 'active in the construction of their own lives' and as leading lives that are 'worthy of study in their own right' and not just for what they reveal about the future or about the development of humankind. But, following Mayall's argument, to see children as agents is to regard them as also having a part to play 'in the lives of those around them' in 'the societies in which they live' and as forming independent 'social relationships and cultures'. It is then a more developed and rounded conception of what it means to act that the concept of 'agency' provides, and it is this that forms the point of departure for many contemporary studies of children's everyday lives.

Corsaro (2005), for example, draws on this in his discussion of what he calls the process of interpretive reproduction (see also Corsaro, this volume). Drawing on his extensive fieldwork with young children in America and Italy that has explored their social lives *as children*, Corsaro developed this term to capture the '*innovative* and *creative* aspects of children's participation in society' (emphasis in original, 2005, 18). For him, the notion of reproduction is not a passive process that describes children 'simply internalizing society and culture' (2005, 19). Instead, reproduction refers to the twin processes of children, on the one hand, actively 'contributing to cultural production and change' and, on the other, their being constrained by the 'societies and cultures of which they are members' (2005, 19). Children, he says, participate in cultural routines, such as learning to talk and playing games like peekaboo with their parents, from a very early age – that is, children are *social* actors from the start. But, as they act, over time, children also:

strive to interpret or make sense of their culture and to participate in it. In attempting to make sense of the adult world, children come to collectively produce their own peer worlds and cultures. (2005, 24)

This process of reproduction is neither linear nor an exact copy, however, since there are any number of misunderstandings, ambiguities and difficulties that children need to resolve and interpret on the way. And, as actors who have agency, this they do. Thus, for example, Corsaro (1985) shows how nursery school children reinforce the school rule that forbids them to bring personal items from home into school, because these often become the focus for disputes, by actively reinterpreting it. Forbidden from having these items on view in the classroom, the children hid small cars, candy and toy animals in their pockets. These they revealed to their friends in secret and out of view of the teachers. And that they did (but also didn't!) obey the rule served, Corsaro argues, to both reinforce and reproduce it.

What this act of defiance also achieves, however, as Corsaro points out, is to help build a peer culture among the children themselves, and within childhood studies the collective agency of children has become a significant focus of study. In Connolly's (2004) work, for example, he shows the very different routes to displays of masculinity that Northern Irish middle-class and working-class boys take in their everyday engagement with school rules and in playtime activities. The middle-class boys act in ways which demonstrate their 'acceptance of being closely controlled and emphasis on knowledge and mental skills', a collective compliance that reproduced not only the school environments, but also their home environments. (2004, 150). The middle-class boys asserted their masculinity by disrupting the girls' skipping games and policing the behaviour of any boy who showed an interest in joining in. By contrast, the working-class boys acted in ways that emphasized 'practical and material concerns' focused on the 'here-and-now and on surviving', reflecting the dangerous, and often violent, neighbourhoods in which they lived (2004, 189). For these boys, the assertion of masculinity was far less cerebral, involving instead:

> external expressions of masculinity in terms of muscles and strength as well as physical skills such as fighting and wrestling... [and], through the discourses on girlfriends and boyfriends they also place an emphasis on being physically attractive and...on displays of (hetero)sexuality. (2004, 193)

It is not, however, just within the context of their peer cultures that children's agency – their ability to act creatively and to make things happen – can be seen taking place. Children live their lives in and between any numbers of social institutions; be it the school, the family, the legal system. It is these institutions which constitute the structure of society – that structured complexity which shapes the fabric of our everyday lives. What might an agency-centred account of children and childhood contribute to understanding the broader issues of social and cultural reproduction?

Children as agents

According to Mayall (2002), significant insight into understanding children's agency can be gained from the critical realist account of the relationship between structure and agency which places importance on the historical dimension of social life. Through its emphasis on the continuities embedded in social structure, continuities that precede and will outlive the individual, critical realism underscores the transformatory character of a social life that takes place in and through social relations of different kinds. And it is these social relations, which take place between people who occupy distinctive social positions, that can be, unintentionally (and sometimes intentionally), transformative of social structure. For Mayall (2002, 33) of particular importance for childhood studies, is the child–adult relation, a generational and hierarchical relationship that offers both opportunities and limitations for children's agency. Thus, rather than a concern to explore how children gradually learn to interpret the world, and achieve an understanding of it that they then reproduce, albeit perhaps in modified form (see Corsaro's interpretive reproduction above), here the focus is on the contribution that children's actions, over time, might make to structural change continuity (James and James, 2004). Here, then, it is not the life world of the child as individual agent who is the subject of study, but the child as a member of the generational category of children.

This research perspective on children as agents has been characterized as the minority-group approach in that it is concerned to explore the characteristics of children's agency in relation to their subordinate position, vis à vis adults within the social order (James, Jenks and Prout, 1998). This can be envisaged as a child in relation to a parent, a pupil in relation to a teacher or as a political minor in relation to the adult majority. These different social positions, which can be – indeed usually are – occupied by any child *simultaneously*, all offer different opportunities and constraints for children to act and, in doing so, exercise their agency. Thus, for example, in work that explores English children's experiences of family breakdown, Smart, Neale and Wade (2001) reveal the different kinds of agency that children in different families are able to exercise to ameliorate the changes that are occurring in family life following the divorce of their parents.

Similarly, in their research on children's experience of abusive families in Australia, Mason and Falloon (2001) reveal children exercising agency in the form of choice – that is choosing not to reveal their experiences to agencies. This 'choice' similarly reflected children's understanding of familial care, which serves to balance out the inequalities associated with the exercise of power and control. Unlike their experience of adult power in the context of schools, the children felt that 'their parents did "care" about them and that this provided some, even if limited, leverage for negotiation and agency on the child's part' (2001, 112).

Conclusion: agency and action

For many adults, that children might be regarded as having agency may raise questions about what kind of agency that might be and how much freedom children might be permitted to have in the exercise of it. It is, for example, a concern that is voiced most prominently in public debates about children's access to media. Here most children's apparent facility with technology (when compared to that of many adults!) and their ready access to new media of different kinds has raised old and new moral panics about the nature of childhood itself. A main feature of this anxiety, ironically, is whether children are to be regarded as passive receivers of media's messages or, instead, as savvy and competent, media-wise children who are active decision-makers, able to exercise control over it (Buckingham,

2001). However, as Buckingham argues, rather than simply celebrate or condemn children's potential empowerment as media consumers:

> we need to understand the extent – and the limitations – of children's competence as participants in the adult world. In relation to the media, we need to acknowledge children's ability to evaluate the representations of that world that are made available to them; and to identify what they might need to know in order to do so more productively and effectively. (2000, 193)

In that childhood is fragmented by social variables such as class, gender, ethnicity and health status; not all children may have the same opportunities to access media; nor, indeed, are all children equally competent in its use. Thus, despite the frequent tying of ideas of children's agency to a political agenda to expose children's minority status vis-à-vis adults, agency, in the end, is an attribute of individual children. It is something which they may or may not choose to exercise, rather than a symbol of their minority social status. This observation raises other questions, therefore, about children's rights *to* agency. Do all children have the same capacity for agency? What might inhibit or prevent particular children from exercising it, and under what kinds of circumstances?

References

Ariès, P. (1962) *Centuries of Childhood*. London: Jonathan Cape.
Benedict, R. (1935) *Patterns of Culture*. London: Routledge and Kegan Paul.
Bluebond-Langner, M. (1979) *The Private Worlds of Dying Children*. Princeton, NJ: Princeton University Press.
Buckingham, D. (2001) *After the Death of Childhood*. Cambridge: Polity Press.
Burman, E. (1994) *Deconstructing Developmental Psychology*. London: Routledge.
Connolly, P. (2004) *Boys and Schooling in the Early Years*. London: Routledge/Falmer.
Corrigan, P. (1979) *Schooling the Smash Street Kids*. London: Macmillan.
Corsaro, B. (1985) *Friendship and Peer Culture in the Early Years*. Norwood, NJ: Ablex.
Corsaro, B. (2005) *The Sociology of Childhood*, 2nd edn. Thousand Oaks, CA: Pine Forge Press.
Donaldson, M. (1978) *Children's Minds*. London: Fontana.
Elkin, F. (1960) *The Child and Society*. New York: Random House.
Giddens, A. (1979) *The Central Problems of Social Theory*. Cambridge: Polity Press.
Hall, S. and T. Jefferson (eds) (1976) *Resistance through Rituals*. London: Hutchinson.
Hardman, C. (1973) 'Can There Be an Anthropology of Children?', *Journal of the Anthropological Society of Oxford*, 4(2): 85–99. (Reprinted in *Childhood* (2001) 8(4): 501–517).
Hebdige, D. (1979) *Subculture: The Meaning of Style*. London: Methuen.
Holt, J. (1975) *Escape from Childhood*. Harmondsworth: Penguin.
James, A. and A. Prout (eds) (1990) *Constructing and Re-constructing Childhood*. Basingstoke: Falmer Press.
James, A. and A.L. James (2004) *Constructing Childhood: Theory, Policy and Social Practice*. Basingstoke: Palgrave Macmillan.
James, A., C. Jenks and A. Prout (1998) *Theorizing Childhood*. Cambridge: Polity Press.
Lee, N. (2001) *Childhood and Society*. Buckingham: Open University Press.
MacKay, R. (1973) 'Conceptions of Childhood and Models of Socialization', in H.P. Dreitzel (ed.) *Childhood and Socialization*. London: Collier-Macmillan.

Mason, J. and J. Falloon (2001) 'Some Sydney Children Define Abuse: Some Implications for Agency in Childhood', in L. Alanen and B. Mayall (eds) *Conceptualizing Child-Adult Relations*. London: Routledge/Falmer.

Mayall, B. (2002) *Towards a Sociology of Childhood*. Buckingham: Open University Press.

McGarrigle, J. and M. Donaldson (1974) 'Conservation Accidents', *Cognition*, 3(4): 341–350.

Mead, M. (1928 [1969]) *Coming of Age in Samoa*. Harmondsworth: Penguin.

Parsons, T. (1951) *The Social System*. London: Routledge and Kegan Paul.

Prout, A. and A. James (1990) 'A New Paradigm for the Sociology of Childhood? Provenance, Promise and Problems', in A. James and A. Prout (eds) *Constructing and Re-constructing Childhood*. Basingstoke: Falmer Press.

Rafky, D.M. (1973) 'Phenomenology and Socialization: Some Comments on the Assumptions Underlying Socialization', in H.P. Dreitzel (ed.) *Childhood and Socialization*. London: Collier-Macmillan.

Ricoeur, P. (1978) *The Rule of Metaphor*. London: Routledge and Kegan Paul.

Smart, C., Neale, B. and Wade, A. (2001) *The Changing Experience of Childhood*. London: Polity Press.

Vygotsky, L.S. (1978) *Mind in Society*. Cambridge, MA: Harvard University Press.

Willis, P. (1977) *Learning to Labour*. Aldershot: Avebury.

Woodhead, M. and Faulkner, D. (2000) 'Subjects, Objects or Participants? Dilemmas of Psychological Research with Children', in P. Christensen and A. James (eds) *Research with Children*. London: Falmer Press.

Wrong, D. (1961) 'The Oversocialized Conception of Man in Modern Sociology', *American Sociological Review*, 26(2): 183–193.

3
Child Development and the Development of Childhood

Martin Woodhead

Developing children

Development is a core construct within Western societies. Gardeners nurture the development of plants, managers construct a development plan for their company, rich nations offer aid to developing countries, and so on. In each case, 'development' is about change; with a strong sense that these changes follow an ordered, rule-governed plan and that the outcome will be a more advanced, complex or sophisticated level of organization. In the same way, development of children has been generally understood to be about physical and psychological growth in the young of the species, as they transform from foetus, to infant, to child, to adolescent, to adult. Belief in development as progress has been an important subtext – for example expressed through images of the immature, dependent infant maturing to a state of rational, moral autonomy. As one child development textbook put it:

> ...these changes usually result in new improved ways of reacting – that is in behaviour that is healthier, more organised, more complex, more competent or more efficient. (Mussen et al., 1984, 7)

Power relationships are also implicit within developmental discourses, whereby the course of a child's development is, to greater or lesser extent, nurtured, shaped and defined by people, institutions, policies and practices. The current Wikipedia entry encapsulates this view of the child:

> Child development is the study or examination of mechanisms that operate during the biological and psychological process of growth of a child to adolescence, from dependency to increasing autonomy...The optimal development of children is vital to society... (http://en.wikipedia.org/wiki/Child_development, accessed 28 November 2007)

Child development research became an established and highly influential field of enquiry during the twentieth century, especially via the comprehensive theories of intellectual, moral and personal development, constructed especially by Piaget, Kohlberg, Erikson and others (Piaget, 1929; Erikson, 1968; Elkind, 1969). Equally all-embracing sociological accounts were also being constructed, which emphasized the way the children's primitive natures were socialized within social institutions, notably family and school (e.g., Elkin, 1960; Denzin, 1977). In similar vein, students of anthropology explored the origins of culture in infant- and child-rearing practices (e.g., Mead and Wolfenstein, 1955; Montgomery, 2008).

Child development has until recently been the most influential child research paradigm within modern Western societies, whether measured in terms of scientific journals, professional associations, university courses, textbooks or in terms of impact in child policies and practices (especially in education, child care and social work). But in many ways it is misleading to suggest child development is a single paradigm, given the diverse, often competing theories and perspectives that characterize this field of scholarship. One short chapter cannot begin to do justice to the core features of the paradigm, nor to the diversity of scholarship summarized in numerous textbooks (e.g., Mussen et al., 1984; Berger, 1991; Shaffer, 1993; Durkin, 1995; Cole and Cole, 1996; Schaffer, 1996; Slater and Bremner, 2003; Smith et al., 2003; Smidt, 2006; Harris, 2008). The aim of this chapter is more modest: to ask about the influence of child development theorizing on the ways childhood has been understood and shaped in contemporary societies, and vice versa. I will briefly trace the origins of scientific child development research, and identify some of its major features as these have shaped constructions of childhood. I will then summarize influential critiques and offer some reflections on the position of developmental concepts within contemporary Childhood Studies.

A science of childhood

Scientific studies of children's development began to attract attention during the latter decades of the nineteenth century, because of their ability to offer solutions to the childhood issues confronting industrializing, urbanizing societies (Cunningham, 1991; Hendrick, 1997). For example, in England, poverty, high density housing, high infant mortality, migration, changing employment patterns and family care systems, variously set new challenges for nineteenth century social reformers. More than ever before, urban childhoods were about children *en masse*, in factories, in overcrowded slums, in the streets and in schools. Mass education contributed to children becoming a distinctive subgroup within society, their lives separated off and institutionalized, especially within education (compulsory in England from 1880).

Importantly for this chapter, childhood was being constructed – and children known – not only by their name, gender, religion, class and other social categories. They were also increasingly marked off and organized according to their age (made more precisely possible once universal birth registration was established, in England from 1837). For the first time, the great mass of children could be regulated using age as a metric, to identify the end as well as the beginning of their childhoods, along with all the subdivisions and transitions along the way (notably school starting age, criminal responsibility, full-time employment, marriage, right to vote, etc.). A new breed of childhood professionals was now charged with identifying children's distinctive needs for care, discipline and teaching (Kellmer-Pringle, 1975; Woodhead, 1997), protecting children's welfare, and promoting their learning. Since children were now organized – and thought about – in terms of age-linked school grades or classes, it became a priority to know the kinds of instruction that was appropriate for each grade. Tools were also needed that could enable professionals to sort and select children according to their abilities and potential (Rose, 1985; Burman, 1994; Woodhead, 2003a). In short, the implication of nineteenth-century 'education for all' policies in industrial societies was that for the first time the lives of all children were regulated in terms of normative expectations; a forerunner to the universal standards now being applied through global Educational for All (EFA) initiatives (Woodhead, 2003a).

There were also more scholarly reasons why children's development increasingly became a legitimate subject of scientific scrutiny. The industrial revolution that so powerfully shaped the lives of children also coincided with a revolution in the biological sciences which radically altered ideas about development, whether of species, of societies, or of human beings. Darwin's evolutionary theory (set out in 'Origin of Species', 1859) challenged beliefs about creation and about the relationship of humans to other species. It also focused attention on new questions about the significance of immaturity in young humans. Why does the human species – in many ways the most complex and sophisticated animals on earth – give birth to offspring that are so helpless and so dependent for care and nurturance over such a relatively long period? What is the extended period of childhood for? What are children's distinctive psychological as well as physical needs? Is it possible to discover a natural progression from infancy to maturity and beyond? In short, Darwin's theories fundamentally changed the lens through which scholars and experts observed children:

> Children's bodies were weighed and measured. The effects of fatigue were studied, as were children's interests, imaginings, religious ideas, fetishes, attitudes to weather, to adults, drawings, dolls, lies, ideas and, most importantly for us their stages of growth ... children as a category were being singled out for scientific study for the first time. (Walkerdine, 1984, 171)

Child development priorities

Some major priorities for the new field of child development research were: to describe the major developmental milestones; to explain the processes underlying development; and to identify the causes and significance of environmental factors in shaping deviations from the norm.

Arnold Gesell was among the earliest to tackle the first of these priorities, by founding the Yale Clinic of Child Development in 1911. A huge, glass-enclosed child observation room combined with the newly available movie camera technologies enabled Gesell to assemble a massive data bank of young children's behaviour at various ages and stages. He distilled his research into 'normative summaries', representing the milestones of normal development for each age group, which were in turn used to assess individual children's developmental progress (Gesell, 1925; Gesell and Ilg, 1946). Gesell's mission (and that of numerous others since) was to identify universal, rule-governed patterns of behaviour, thinking and reasoning, and especially how far these follow a predictable, stage-like sequence. Individual differences in developmental pathway were recognized, but the emphasis was on what children have in common – on identifying 'normal' patterns of development, and deviations from the norm in terms of developmental precocity and delay. For the most part, developmentalists have been much less interested in patterns of growth and change towards developmental goals that might be unique to specific individuals, contexts or cultures. The use of the singular noun 'child' in textbooks on 'Child Development' has been a highly informative 'calling card' for the paradigm!

A second priority for developmental research is to explain these patterns, to find out what drives processes of growth and change. Introductory textbooks typically identify a range of theoretical perspectives. Maturationist theories emphasize respects in which development involves natural processes of maturation, the unfolding of a genetically encoded development plan. These are sometimes also referred to as 'nativist' theories of development, by contrast with 'environmentalist' theories that emphasize the influence of learning and experience, notably behavioural approaches most strongly advocated by B.F. Skinner. Most theories lay between these two extremes, including Piaget's constructivist model (or 'Genetic Epistemology') in which development is seen as the product of the maturing child's activity in constructing an internal representation of their environment, and Vygotsky's sociocultural perspective, which recognizes the powerful role of social processes and cultural tools in mediating the direction and process of learning (summarized in Oates et al., 2005).

A third priority has been to measure the impact of environmental factors in shaping individual differences in growth and development, identifying risks to psychological adjustment and well-being, and especially the role that adversities play as causal factors in maladjustment, delinquency or other deviations from normality. Longitudinal studies, following a cohort of children from infancy to maturity have made a major contribution to these issues. The Oakland Growth Study of children born in 1920/21, and the Berkeley Guidance Study of a slightly younger cohort were among influential early studies (Elder, 1974), establishing birth cohort designs as a feature of the developmental toolkit. More recent studies have highlighted the complexity of causal processes, notably children's resilience to adversities in certain circumstances, as well as their vulnerabilities (Werner and Smith, 1982; Masten, 2001; Luthar, 2003).

By the 1970s, developmental theories and research methodologies appeared to encompass virtually every aspect of childhood study, especially when taken alongside insights from sociology and anthropology of childhood. On the other hand, study of childhood was not and never has been built around consensus, between or within disciplinary boundaries. Theoretical border crossings added to the eclecticism of scholarly offerings available to the inquisitive student at that time. For example, a dedicated handful of developmentalists were interested in cross-cultural studies (e.g., Bruner et al., 1966; Cole et al., 1971; Segall et al., 1990). Most significantly, The Six Cultures Project provided the first systematic and detailed recordings of children's behaviour in different cultures and provided a wealth of information on children's work, play and social interaction, as well as on caregiver beliefs about development (Whiting and Whiting, 1975).

The 1970s also saw the first major critiques of Piaget's account of developmental stages, which had dominated psychological and educational theory in Europe, and to a lesser extent North America (Walkerdine, 1984). A series of imaginative variations on Piaget's classic experiments convincingly demonstrated young children's capacities for reasoning embedded in 'human sense' and drew attention to the ways social context and social process shapes children's development (Donaldson, 1978). Reappraisal of Piaget's account of developmental stages coincided with the wider availability in English of sociocultural theories, notably Vygotsky (1978), whose core ideas have proved highly influential on recent generations of developmentalists (e.g., Cole, 1996; Rogoff, 2003).

The coexistence of competing accounts of the child's development also posed a problem to a research community dedicated to discovering universal laws. In 1979, the core issue was confronted head-on within the pages of the American Psychological Association's house journal. Developmental researchers were implored:

> to peer into the abyss of the positivistic nightmare – that the child is essentially and eternally a cultural invention and that the variety of the child's definition is not the removable error of an incomplete science. (Kessen, 1979, 815)

More radical critiques also began to appear about the ways childhoods were being represented in developmental accounts (Ingleby, 1974; Henriques et al., 1984) and about the role of child research in regulating children's lives (Rose, 1989). The foundation concept of 'child development' itself came under increasing scrutiny, coupled with the demand that children be respected as subjectivities, as meaning makers, as social actors, and more recently as rights bearing citizens (e.g., Bradley, 1989; Stainton-Rogers and Stainton-Rogers, 1992; Walkerdine, 1993; Burman, 1994, 1997; Morss, 1996; Woodhead, 1999b, 2005, 2006).

Developmentalism and childhood studies

The critique of developmental accounts has been closely linked to the emergence of Childhood Studies. Indeed, the new social studies of childhood have been premised on a proposal by one group of scholars to consign developmental psychology to the dustbin of history, along with psychoanalysis and common sense (James et al., 1998). This rhetorical challenge is unrealistic and in many ways inappropriate – especially bearing in mind that many of the strongest challenges to developmentalism have come from within the research discipline itself, as the following sections highlight.

Child or childhoods?

The first challenge has been that the singularity implied by the phrase 'child development' serves to naturalize, essentialize and universalize particular cultural forms of childhood. This critique draws attention to the cultural specificity of much that is presented as child development orthodoxy, in textbook knowledge, in policies and practice, notably in statements about children's fundamental needs (Woodhead, 1997). The challenge is especially salient at the start of the twenty-first century, when developmental research has become a vibrant, eclectic, global activity, and developmental concepts are pervasive, including within the interpretation of the UN Convention on the Rights of the Child (UNCRC, 1989) which affirms that children have a right to development (Article 6), and refers to protecting 'the child's physical, mental, spiritual, moral and social development' (e.g., Articles 27 and 32) (Hodgkin and Newell, 1998; Woodhead, 2005).

Building the UNCRC around concepts of development has been challenged as inviting overgeneralization of developmental theories and evidence, promoting globalized standards for judging other people's childhoods, (Burman, 1996; Boyden, 1997). According to some commentators, it is a case of 'thinking locally, acting globally' (Gergen et al., 1996). For example, at the time of writing (2007) the World Bank website proposed that the first eight years of life can be summarized in seven 'Developmental Stages'. In each case, children are described in terms of 'What they do' and 'What they need'. For example, 'children' at one to two years '...enjoy stories and experimenting with objects, walk steadily, climb stairs, run, assert independence...' and by two to three and a half years require opportunities 'to engage in dramatic play, increasingly complex books, sing favourite songs, work simple puzzles...' (www.worldbank.org). No cultural qualifiers are offered, nor even acknowledgement that millions of the world's children may never have even seen a staircase – far less had opportunity to climb one, nor have access to story books. Asserting independence is moreover far from universal as a developmental goal (Greenfield, 1994; Kagitcibasi, 1996; Woodhead, 1996).

The salience of developmentalism is greatly amplified in contexts where all births are registered, and birthdays are both celebrated as a symbolic marker of growing maturity and as a life course marker, linked to significant changes in capacities, role and status, as well as to key transition events, such as starting pre-school, transfer to primary school and so on (Dunlop and Fabian, 2007). 'How old are you?' is one of the first questions adults in the UK usually ask when they meet a child for the first time and children themselves soon come to recognize the salience of age as a constraining factor as they negotiate their activities and identities. Knowing a young person's age positions them in relation to expectations about their competencies, their proper treatment and their progress through childhood stages. It opens the way to questions about what class they are in at school, whether they have exams looming and so on.

What is frequently overlooked in developmental accounts is that giving primacy to children's age as a proxy for their developmental stage is not inevitable, nor 'natural'. In many regions of the world, a child's age has not traditionally been the most salient factor shaping their childhood – birth dates have not been recorded nor annual birthdays celebrated. A child's ethnicity, social class/caste and gender have frequently been much more powerful determinants of their daily activities, and the ways they have been valued and treated. Many exceptions to this cultural myopia could be listed, of course. For example, cultural psychologists have offered a much more balanced account of processes of child care, pathways to language and learning, and experiences of adolescence (e.g., Rogoff, 1990, 2003; Nsamenang, 1992; Cole, 1996). But, as a generalization, it is fair to say that knowledge of developmental experiences for the great majority of the world's children has been and still is in very short supply (Woodhead, 1999a).

Building the research networks that can help redress that global imbalance is a high priority for child research. This issue is not just about sensitivity to other people's childhoods 'out there' but also about acknowledging the complexity of childhoods within modern societies. Studying a classroom of 25 children can be an encounter with 25 cultural stories, many of which are multiple stories – as ethnographic accounts reveal (Connolly, 1998; Bray et al., 2008). These examples serve as a reminder that the childhoods described by developmental research are not static, but changing, not least under the pervasive influence of developmental constructions of childhood as these permeate parent advice, school curricula and welfare systems. In this respect, universalized discourses of development have become something of a self-fulfilling prophecy.

Object or participant?

A second challenge to developmentalism has been that scientific studies risk objectifying the young people in ways that take little account of their subjectivity and agency:

> Since for most of this century, mainstream child psychology conceptualized the child in much the same way as a chemist conceptualizes an interesting compound, it made absolute sense for the psychologist to take the child into a laboratory for closer inspection and testing. (Greene, 1998, 257–258)

It is important to emphasize that objectification does not as a rule extend into fieldwork itself, during which developmental researchers engage with children in ways that are at least as sensitive and respectful as for children's encounters with any number of adults during their lives at home and at school. Yet, when it comes to thinking about and writing about these same children, the scientific paradigm continues to expect developmental researchers to adopt an objective stance. Their subject – the child – is transformed into a de-personalized object of systematic enquiry, their individuality evaporated into a set of measurable independent and dependent variables, condensed into data sets that can address the hypothesis being tested, and abstracted into a general developmental pattern, (Woodhead and Faulkner, 2008). For example, according to a new grand theory of development reported in the journal Child Development:

> the infant is viewed as an integrated system consisting of multiple reciprocally coupled components...embedded within a specific context. (Spencer et al., 2006)

While children have been seen as scientifically interesting for more than a century, research into children's lives has been largely shaped by adult agendas for children, and reflected dominant power relationships between expert researchers and innocent, vulnerable, developing children. Recognizing that children are 'subjects with concerns' as well as 'subjects of study and concern' (Prout, 2000) has become one of the rallying calls for new interdisciplinary childhood studies. Yet, here we face one of the many paradoxes in child development research, in that the current emphasis within child research on recognizing the child as active, competent and socially engaged is in many respects consistent with long-standing insights from developmental theory. For example, developmental research has long emphasized that newborn babies are pre-adapted for social engagement, actively seeking out social relationships through which their security is assured, emotions regulated and cognitive and communicative competence fostered (reviewed by Schaffer, 1996). Piagetian constructivist theories took for granted that children actively engage with their physical and social environment, constructing cognitive models to make sense of the world and gradually acquiring increasing sophistication in their intellectual, social and moral understanding (Elkind, 1969). Studies of social development emphasized children's role as social actors and meaning makers (Bruner and Haste, 1987), partners in social interaction, reciprocal exchanges and transactional patterns of mutual influence (Sameroff, 1987). In short, for much of the past century, developmental researchers have described children's active role in their development, even while they objectified children within discourses of research. These complexities surrounding the relationships between the researcher and the children they study require to be articulated not assumed, far less dismissed (Woodhead and Faulkner, 2008).

It could be argued that the field of Childhood Studies should be reserved for research that engages directly with children's experiences and perspectives, for example through ethnography (James et al., 1998) and participatory research (Johnson et al., 1995; Woodhead, 1999c). But this would exclude much research that is more broadly about improving children's well-being, and which may to a greater or lesser degree involve consulting with them directly, as the principal stakeholder. In the same way, ensuring that children are recognized as participants in research is open to a variety of meanings. A weak interpretation would be about obtaining informed consent, avoiding deception, being transparent about purposes and uses, and so on. There are many intermediate stages towards a strong interpretation of participation where children are co-researchers, with much greater control at each stage of the research process: defining research questions, planning research, carrying out fieldwork, interpreting/analysing research and so on (West, 1995; Kellett et al., 2004). One of the benefits of a broad interdisciplinary Childhood Studies is to encourage a very high level of debate, critical analysis and methodological innovation regarding the status of children in research.

Project or person?

A third challenge has been that developmental research reinforces power relationships within which children's lives, learning and prospects are socially regulated, in families, schools and society. Underpinning this challenge is the claim that developmentalism privileges idealized constructions of adulthood, as the reference point for describing, explaining, controlling and intervening in the lives of children. As Verhellen (1997) put it, within the developmental paradigm, children are in a state of 'not yet being'. As immature learners of life, they are a set of 'potentials', a 'project in the making', researched within an evaluative frame that is mainly interested in their position on the stage-like journey to mature, rational, responsible, autonomous, adult competence (James et al., 1998). Qvortrup (1994) crystallized the dilemma, by drawing on the distinction between studies of children as 'human becomings' rather than 'human beings'. The risks are greatest where discourses devalue children's current interests and capacities and/or value them mainly for their future potential.

As one of the principle exponents of a developmental paradigm, Piaget would undoubtedly have rejected any accusation that he devalued children's ways of thinking and learning. On the contrary, he showed profound respect for children's ways of thinking and behaving – as different and logical in their own terms. This was signalled in the preface to one of his most influential early works, 'The Language and Thought of the Child' in which the new (in 1926) insights offered by Piaget's psychological approach was celebrated because it did *not* take adult modes of thinking as a standard, but sought to understand children's own ways of thinking (Piaget, 1926, x–xiii). Piaget, along with other developmental researchers, sought to enhance more child-centred practices in twentieth century Europe, not diminish them. Developmental insights informed child-centred education especially, based around respect for the integrity of children's interests, activities and ideas, rather than the imposition of an adult frame of reference upon them (Walkerdine, 1984). The details of these theories have been challenged, as noted earlier (e.g., Donaldson, 1978). But they were progressive at the time, in their attempt to make sense of and respect observed differences between children at different points in their journey from infancy to adulthood – differences that remain even if cruder forms of developmentalism are cast aside.

Encouragingly, the core issue of studying children as human 'beings' versus human 'becomings' has itself come under renewed scrutiny, not least because children's accounts of their own 'being' almost invariably includes a strong sense of 'becoming'. Children's current state includes anticipating what they will become:

> It was not merely psychologists and parents who were looking forward to adulthood on behalf of 'the child'; also children were anticipating adulthood in ways that contributed to forming their childhood in the here and now. (Qvortrup, 2004, 269)

From a theoretical perspective, looking beyond the dichotomy is more product-ive than perpetuating it (see Uprichard, 2008). But vigilance is still needed where public policies and professional practices continue to position children more as 'becomings' than as 'beings', especially when developmental concepts are translated into the language of economics (Penn, 2002; Woodhead, 2006). For example, evidence that early childhood is a period of rapid growth and change, and that early interventions are most likely to produce positive child outcomes underpins the World Bank's vision for early childhood education, as presented on their website:

> A healthy cognitive and emotional development in the early years translates into tangible economic returns. Early interventions yield higher returns as a preventive measure compared with remedial services later in life. Policies that seek to remedy deficits incurred in the early years are much more costly than initial investments in the early years. (Source: http://web.worldbank.org)

In similar vein, the *Lancet* published a series of high profile articles during 2007, estimating that over 200 million children under five years of age are failing to achieve their developmental potential, and advocating early intervention pro-grammes as a cost-effective solution (Engle et al., 2007; Grantham-McGregor et al., 2007).

Framing developmental research evidence in economic terms can be politic-ally persuasive. But it can also be challenged for appearing to construct children mainly as a potential social cost, but offering an attractive rate of return from well-timed and targeted investment. The same applies to the ways future-oriented developmental principles justify decisions made on behalf of children in more everyday contexts at home and school. In short, embedding respect for children's status as human beings from the beginning of life still has a long way to go (Knuttson, 1997; Santos-Pais, 1999).

Child development in childhood studies?

In this chapter, I have drawn attention to the pivotal but contested place of devel-opmental concepts in child research, in everyday discourses, as well as in policies and professional practices. In this final section I look ahead and ask about the place of child development in interdisciplinary Childhood Studies. The answer to that question depends on what is meant by interdisciplinary. Three possibilities spring to mind:

- A 'clearinghouse' model would encompass all studies of children and childhood, all research questions, methodologies and disciplinary approaches;
- A 'pick 'n' mix' model would be more selective but still incorporate a wide range of approaches. The selection criteria might be about the specific topics studied or orientation to the field;
- A 're-branding' model might appear to have interdisciplinary aspirations, but would mainly be about redefining a traditional field of enquiry while still adhering to conventional disciplinary boundaries.

I would argue all three models are to be found in current expressions of Childhood Studies (Woodhead, 2003b). For example, the journals *Childhood* and *Children & Society* accommodate papers on a wide range of topics and approaches, consistent with a clearinghouse model. Curricula for the growing numbers of University programmes in Childhood Studies are similarly broad in their coverage; a version of pick 'n' mix, perhaps? At the same time, the thrust of much theoretical work appears to be more focused; in some cases with the apparent goal of re-branding traditional academic identities, especially sociology (James et al., 1998). Of course, developmental research is not static either. Similar radical reversion of developmental themes has taken place, with the growth of critical psychology, social constructionist and discursive approaches, and sociocultural studies (Stainton-Rogers and Stainton-Rogers, 1992; Burman, 1997; Woodhead, 1999a).

While clearing house and pick 'n' mix models might be seen as risking being too inclusive in terms of forging a positive interdisciplinary identity for childhood studies, risks also attach to 're-branding' traditional disciplines, which inevitably exclude other traditions.

My conclusion – not surprisingly – is that we may agree with James et al. (1998) and consign cruder versions of developmentalism to the dustbin of history. But it would clearly be a mistake to discard a field as diverse as developmental psychology. The consequence could be for Childhood Studies to be seen as a minority interest rather than of mainstream concern and relevance. This is not just about acknowledging the continuing dominance of developmental approaches within academic research. The proverb about not throwing out the 'baby' with the 'bathwater' is relevant here. If 'developmentalism' is discarded (as bathwater), the core issues of change during infancy, childhood and youth remain of central concern, as it is understood in science, in policy and by teachers, parents and children. Childhood is transitional however it is culturally constructed (Hockey and James, 1993, 2003). This period of the human lifespan is marked by major changes in physical size and maturity, relationships and identities, interests, activities, skills and perspectives, including perspectives on development. These changes are, of course very differently expressed within specific cultural settings and socioeconomic contexts. Yet, immaturity remains one of the most distinctive features of the young of the human species (Bruner, 1972), whether constructed in terms of nurturance and vulnerability, teaching and learning, socialization and development or respect for their rights.

For example, respecting children's rights, especially their participatory rights, is a priority for education, social care, health care and legal systems, and an underpinning principle for Childhood Studies. One of the most debated areas of professional practice is about adapting practices to children's maturity and understanding, their 'evolving capacities' in the language of the UNCRC (Lansdown, 2005) including techniques for 'listening to children'. Acknowledging children's agency, competence and participatory rights is the beginning, not the end of the story. More rigid versions of developmental theory undoubtedly undervalued children's social awareness and capacities for understanding and empathy (Dunn, 1988) – and implicitly overestimated possession of these attributes among the adult community. Yet concepts and tools are still needed that acknowledge children are, for much of the time and in many contexts, relatively more vulnerable, dependent and inexperienced. They require (and often seek) guidance, support and teaching from more experienced members of society – through enabling structures and pedagogies for participation. Relevant concepts and tools are provided by more recent branches of developmental research: for example 'scaffolding', 'zone of proximal development', 'guided participation', 'cultural tools', 'communities of practice' (e.g., Wood, 1988; Rogoff, 1990; Lave and Wenger, 1991; see also Woodhead, 1999b and Smith, 2002). Of course, these learning relationships are much more fluid and varied than a crude developmental model might suggest, and they are not inevitably based on rigid age-based hierarchies. In some circumstances, children may be more competent, resourceful and resilient than those who formally care for and teach them; and the significance of peer relationships has generally been underestimated (Corsaro, 1992; Mercer and Littleton, 2007). In short, a strong research agenda on change and transitions in children's growth, learning and well-being (including children's perspectives on these themes) is essential for Childhood Studies, even if we choose no longer to describe this agenda as about 'child development'.

References

Berger, K. (1991) *The Developing Person through Childhood and Adolescence*, 3rd edn. Worth: New York.

Boyden, J. (1997) 'Childhood and the Policy-Makers: A Comparative Perspective on the Globalization of Childhood', in A. James and A. Prout (eds) *Constructing and Reconstructing Childhood*, 2nd edn. London: Falmer Press, pp. 190–229.

Bradley, B. (1989) *Visions of Infancy: A Critical Introduction to Child Psychology*. Cambridge: Polity Press.

Bray, R., I. Gooskens, L. Kahn, S. Moses and J. Seekings (2008) Growing up in South Africa: Childhood and Adolescence in Post-Apartheid Cape Town. Draft unpublished manuscript, Centre for Social Science Research: University of Cape Town (Unpublished manuscript).

Bruner, J.S. (1972) 'Nature and Uses of Immaturity', *American Psychologist*, 27(8): 687–708.

Bruner, J.S. and H. Haste (eds) (1987) *Making Sense: The Child's Construction of the World*. London: Methuen.

Bruner, J.S., R. Olver and P.M. Greenfield (1966) *Studies in Cognitive Growth.* New York: Wiley.

Burman, E. (1994) *Deconstructing Developmental Psychology.* London: Routledge.

Burman, E. (1996) 'Local, Global or Globalized? Child Development and International Child Rights Legislation', *Childhood*, 3(1): 45–67.

Burman, E. (1997) 'Developmental Psychology and Its Discontents', in D. Fox and I. Prilleltensky (eds) *Critical Psychology: An Introduction.* London: Sage, pp. 134–149.

Cole, M. (1996) *Cultural Psychology.* Cambridge, MA: Belknap Press of Harvard University Press.

Cole, M. and S. Cole (1996) *The Development of Children.* New York: W.H.Freeman.

Cole, M., J. Gay, J.A. Glick and D.W. Sharp (1971) *The Cultural Context of Learning and Thinking.* New York: Basic Books.

Connolly, P. (1998) *Racism, Gender Identities and Young Children: Social Relations in A Multi-Ethnic, Inner-City Primary School.* London: Routledge.

Corsaro, W.A. (1992) 'Interpretive Reproduction in Children's Peer Cultures', *Social Psychology Quarterly*, 55(2): 160–77.

Cunningham, H. (1991) *The Children of the Poor: Representations of Childhood since the Seventeenth Century.* Oxford: Blackwell.

Denzin, N. (1977) *Childhood Socialization.* San Francisco: Jossey Bass.

Donaldson, M. (1978) *Children's Minds.* London: Fontana.

Dunlop, A. and H. Fabian (eds) (2007) *Informing Transitions in the Early Years. Research, Policy and Practice.* London: Open University Press.

Dunn, J. (1988) *The Beginnings of Social Understanding.* Oxford: Blackwell.

Durkin, K. (1995) *Developmental Social Psychology.* Oxford: Blackwell.

Elder, G.H. (1974) *Children of the Great Depression: Social Change in Life Experience.* Chicago: University of Chicago Press.

Elkin, F. (1960) *The Child in Society: The Process of Socialization.* New York: Random House.

Elkind, D. (ed.) (1969) *Studies in Cognitive Development: Essays in Honor of Jean Piaget.* London: Oxford University Press.

Engle, P., M. Black, J. Behrman, M. Cabral de Mello, P. Gertler, L. Kapiriri, R. Martorell and M. Young (2007) 'Strategies to Avoid the Loss of Developmental Potential in More Than 200 Million Children in the Developing World', *The Lancet*, Vol. 369, pp. 229–242.

Erikson, E. (1968) *Identity: Youth and Crisis.* London: Faber & Faber.

Gergen, K.J., A. Gulerce, A. Lock and G. Misra (1996) 'Psychological Science in Cultural Context', *American Psychologist*, 51(5): 496–503.

Gesell, A. (1925) *The Mental Growth of the Pre-school Child.* New York: Macmillan.

Gesell, A. and F.L. Ilg (1946) *The Child from Five to Ten.* New York: Harper and Brothers.

Grantham-McGregor, S., Y.B. Cheung, S. Cueto, P. Glewwe, L. Richter, B. Strupp and International Child Development Steering Group (2007) 'Developmental Potential in the First 5 Years for Children in Developing Countries', *The Lancet*, 369(9555), pp. 60–70.

Greene, S. (1998) 'Child Development: Old Themes, New Directions', M. Woodhead, D. Faulkner and K. Littleton (eds) *Making Sense of Social Development.* London: Routledge, pp. 250–268.

Greenfield, P.M. (1994) 'Independence and Interdependence as Developmental Scripts', in P.M. Greenfield and R.R. Cocking (eds) *Cultural Roots of Minority Child Development.* Hillside, New Jersey: Erlbaum, pp. 1–39.

Harris, M. (2008) *Exploring Developmental Psychology.* London: Sage

Hendrick, H. (1997) *Children, Childhood and English Society 1880–1990.* Cambridge: Cambridge University Press.

Henriques, J. et al. (eds) (1984) *Changing the Subject: Psychology, Social Regulation and Subjectivity.* London: Methuen.

Hockey, J. and A. James (1993) *Growing-up and Growing Old.* London: Sage.

Hockey, J. and A. James (2003) *Social Identities Across the Life Course.* Basingstoke: Palgrave Macmillan.

Hodgkin, R. and P. Newell (1998) *Implementation Handbook for the Convention on the Rights of the Child.* New York: UNICEF.

Ingleby, D. (1974) 'The Psychology of Child Psychology', in M.P.M. Richards (ed.) *Integration of a Child into a Social World.* London: Cambridge University Press, pp. 295–308.

James, A. and A. Prout (eds) (1997) *Constructing and Reconstructing Childhood,* 2nd edn. London: Falmer Press.

James, A., C. Jenks and A. Prout (1998) *Theorizing Childhood.* Cambridge: Polity Press.

Johnson, V., J. Hill and E. Ivan-Smith (1995) *Listening to Smaller Voices: Children in an Environment of Change.* London: Actionaid.

Kagitcibasi, C. (1996) *Family and Human Development across Cultures: A View from the Other Side.* London: Erlbaum.

Kellett, M., R. Forrest, N. Dent and S. Ward (2004) 'Just Teach Us the Skills Please, We'll Do the Rest: Empowering Ten-Year-Olds as Active Researchers', *Children & Society,* 18(5): 329–343.

Kellmer-Pringle, M. (1975) *The Needs of Children.* London: Hutchinson.

Kessen, W. (1979) 'The American Child and Other Cultural Inventions', *American Psychologist,* 34(10): 815–820.

Knuttson, K.E. (1997) *Children: Noble Causes or Worthy Citizens.* Aldershot: Arena/Unicef.

Lansdown, G. (2005) *The Evolving Capacities of Children: Implications for the Exercise of Rights.* Florence: UNICEF Innocenti Research Centre.

Lave, J. and E. Wenger (1991) *Situated Learning: Legitimate Peripheral Participation.* New York: Cambridge Press.

Luthar, S.S. (2003) *Resilience and Vulnerability: Adaptation in the Context of Childhood Adversities.* Cambridge: Cambridge University Press.

Masten, A.S. (2001) 'Ordinary Magic: Resilience Processes in Development', *American Psychologist,* 56(3) 227–238.

Mead, M. and M. Wolfenstein (eds) (1955) *Childhood in Contemporary Cultures.* Chicago: University of Chicago Press.

Mercer, N. and K. Littleton (2007) *Dialogue and the Development of Children's Thinking.* London: Routledge.

Montgomery, H. (2008) *Small Strangers: A Cross Cultural Introduction to Childhood.* Oxford: Blackwell.

Morss, J.R. (1996) *Growing Critical: Alternatives to Developmental Psychology.* London: Routledge.

Mussen, P.H., J.J. Conger and J. Kagan (1984) *Child Development and Personality.* New York: Harper Collins.

Nsamenang, A.B. (1992) *Human Development in Cultural Context.* London: Sage.

Oates, J., K. Sheehy and C. Wood (2005) 'Theories of Development', in J. Oates, C. Wood and A. Grayson (eds) *Psychological Development and Early Childhood.* Oxford: Blackwell/Open University, pp. 47–88.

Penn, H. (2002) 'The World Bank's View of Early Childhood', *Childhood,* 9(1): 118–32.

Piaget, J. (1926) *The Language and Thought of the Child.* London: Routledge & Kegan Paul.

Piaget, J. (1929) *The Child's Conception of the World.* London: Routledge & Kegan Paul.

Prout, A. (2000) 'Children's Participation: Control and Self-Realisation in British Late Modernity', *Children & Society,* 14(4): 304–315.

Qvortrup, J. (1994) 'Childhood Matters: An Introduction', in Qvortrup et al., pp. 1–23.

Qvortrup, J. (2004) 'Editorial: the Waiting Child', *Childhood,* 11(3): 267–273.

Qvortrup, J., M. Bardy, G.B. Sgritta and H. Wintersberger (eds) (1994) *Childhood Matters. Social Theory, Practice and Politics.* Aldershot: Avebury.

Rogoff, B. (1990) *Apprenticeship in Thinking: Cognitive Development in Social Context.* New York: Oxford University Press.

Rogoff, B. (2003) *The Cultural Nature of Human Development.* Oxford, UK: Oxford University Press.

Rose, N. (1985) *The Psychological Complex.* London: Routledge.

Rose, N. (1989) *Governing the Soul: The Shaping of the Private Self.* London: Routledge.

Sameroff, A. (1987) 'The Social Context of Development', in N. Eisenberg (ed.) *Contemporary Topics in Developmental Psychology.* New York: Wiley.

Santos-Pais, M. (1999) *A Human Rights Conceptual Framework For Unicef.* Florence: ICDC.

Schaffer, H.R. (1996) *Social Development.* Oxford: Blackwell.

Segall, M.H., P.R. Dasen, J.W. Berry and Y.H. Poortinga (1990) *Human Behaviour in Global Perspective. an Introduction to Cross-Cultural Psychology.* New York: Pergamon.

Shaffer, D.R. (1993) *Developmental Psychology,* 3rd edn. Pacific Grove, CA: Brooks/Cole Publishing Company.

Slater, A and G. Bremner (2003) *An Introduction to Developmental Psychology.* Oxford: Blackwell.

Smidt, S. (2006) *The Developing Child in the 21st Century: A Global Perspective on Child Development.* London: Routledge.

Smith, A. (2002) 'Interpreting and Supporting Participation Rights: Contributions from Sociocultural Theory', *International Journal of Children's Rights,* 10(1): 73–88.

Smith, P., H. Cowie and M. Blades (2003) *Understanding Children's Development.* Oxford: Blackwell.

Spencer, J., M. Clearfield, D. Corbetta et al. (2006) 'Moving toward a Grand Theory of Development: in Memory of Esther Thelen', *Child Development,* 77(6): 1521–1538.

Stainton-Rogers, R. and W. Stainton-Rogers (1992) *Stories of Childhood: Shifting Agendas of Child Concern.* Hassocks: Harvester.

Uprichard, E. (2008) 'Children as "Being and Becomings": Children, Childhood and Temporality', *Children & Society,* 22(4): 303–313.

Verhellen, E. (1997) *Convention on the Rights of the Child.* Leuven: Garant Publishers.

Vygotsky, L.S. (1978) *Mind in Society: the Development of Higher Psychological Processes.* Cambridge, MA: Harvard University Press.

Walkerdine, V. (1984) 'Developmental Psychology and the Child-Centred Pedagogy: the Insertion of Piaget's Theory into Primary School Practice', in J. Henriques et al. (eds) *Changing the Subject; Psychology, Social Regulation and Subjectivity.* London: Methuen, 153–202.

Walkerdine, V. (1993) 'Beyond Developmentalism?' *Theory and Psychology,* 3(4): 451–470.

Werner, E. and R. Smith (1982) *Vulnerable but Invincible.* New York: McGraw-Hill.

West, A. (1995) *You're on Your Own: Young People's Research on Leaving Care.* London: Save the Children.

Whiting, B.B. and J.W.M. Whiting (1975) *Children of Six Cultures: A Psycho-Cultural Analysis.* Cambridge, MA: Harvard University Press.

Wood, D. (1988) *How Children Think and Learn.* Oxford: Blackwell.

Woodhead, M. (1996) *In Search of the Rainbow: Pathways to Quality in Large-Scale Programmes for Young Disadvantaged Children.* The Hague: Bernard van Leer Foundation.

Woodhead, M. (1997) 'Psychology and the Cultural Construction of Children's Needs', in A. James and A. Prout (eds) *Constructing and Reconstructing Childhood,* 2nd edn. London: Falmer Press, pp. 63–84.

Woodhead, M. (1999a) *Is There a Place for Work in Child Development?* Stockholm: Rädda Barnen.

Woodhead, M. (1999b) 'Reconstructing Development Psychology – Some First Steps', *Children & Society,* 13(1) 3–19.

Woodhead, M. (1999c) 'Combating Child Labour: Listen to What the Children Say', *Childhood,* 6(1) 27–49.

Woodhead, M. (2003a) 'The Child in Development', in M. Woodhead and H. Montgomery (eds) *Understanding Childhood: An Interdisciplinary Approach.* Chichester: Wiley/Open University, (Childhood Vol. 1), pp. 85–124.

Woodhead, M. (2003b) *Childhood Studies: past, Present and Future.* Paper presented to Childhood and Youth Studies Launch Conference. Milton Keynes: Open University.

Woodhead, M. (2005) 'Early Childhood Development: A Question of Rights', *International Journal of Early Childhood*, 37(3) 79–98.

Woodhead, M. (2006) 'Changing Perspectives on Early Childhood: Theory, Research and Policy', *International Journal of Equity and Innovation in Early Childhood*, 4(2) 5–48.

Woodhead M. and D. Faulkner (2008) 'Subjects, Objects or Participants? Dilemmas of Psychological Research with Children', in A. James and P. Christensen (eds) *Research with Children: Perspectives and Practices,* 2nd edn. London: Falmer Routledge, pp. 10–39.

4
How Is the Child Constituted in Childhood Studies?

Michael-Sebastian Honig

The social study of childhood has become, in a relatively short time, an international and interdisciplinary research field with a recognized place in the scientific community and an acknowledged voice in the public discourse about children (Qvortrup, 2005b). The adoption by the United Nations of the Convention on the Rights of the Child in 1989, and its associated international implementation process, was an important element in this success story. However, the tension between science and civil rights claims also creates some serious problems for the constitution of this field of study. It has been consistently pointed out that the social studies of childhood appear to be characterized by an orientation towards the perspective of the child and his or her under-appreciated capacities, towards highlighting, instead of their becoming and their development into fully functioning adults, children's present reality and their meaning-making activity (Prout and James, 1990). But what is a 'child' for childhood studies? Does the term refer to every human being from birth to the age of majority? Is it a matter of children, or childhood? Doesn't the international character of the research field already require speaking of *childhoods* in the plural? And what – going the other way – are we to make of 'the child' as encompassing what individual children have in common?

How, then, do childhood studies constitute their object? The central thesis of the following discussion is that the social studies of childhood distinguish themselves from those other sciences dealing with children, not with an alternative image of the child, but through a systematic differentiation between children and childhood. On the basis of this distinction, the question of the child is framed in terms of its observability. In the concept of the generational order, extending the core thesis, both aspects are linked together, and this is why it is of central significance for childhood studies.

The inspiration: the question of the child

In the United States of America, Great Britain and the Nordic countries, it is possible to identify authors who in the 1980s consciously took up a sociology of childhood perspective. Exemplary here are Chris Jenks for Great Britain (Jenks,

[1982] 1992b), Jens Qvortrup for the Nordic countries (Qvortrup, 1985, 1987) and Barry Thorne for the United States of America (Thorne, 1987). For Germany, too, Heinz Hengst was a pioneer of the new social studies of childhood (Hengst, 1981, 1985). Nonetheless, the project of 'rethinking childhood' (Skolnick, 1976) should be characterized as being less about individuals than about approaches and constructions of problems: this becomes especially striking when they are formulated by individuals who did not at the time see themselves as childhood researchers, but whose works have today acquired the status of classics.

One of these was the British anthropologist Charlotte Hardman. Her article 'Can There Be an Anthropology of Children?' (Hardman, [1973] 2001) was first published in 1973, but re-printed almost 30 years later in *Childhood* because of its significance. Hardman examined a collection of children's rites and rhymes, jokes and jeers, laws, games, and secret spells collected by Iona and Peter Opie after the Second World War, and first published in the late 1950s. Hardman asked whether these children's games and rhymes can be seen as an expression of an immature mode of being, comparable to primitive folklore. With this question, she alludes to the evolutionary mainstream of classical ethnology and cultural anthropology. Would it not, however, make sense, asks Hardman, to study children's games and rituals in their own right, as documents of an autonomous system of meaning? What beliefs, value orientations, interpretations and viewpoints do they develop on the basis of their daily experiences in the world in which they live?

> My proposed approach regards children as people to be studied in their own right, and not just as receptacles of adult teaching. My search is to discover whether there is in childhood a self-regulating, autonomous world which does not necessarily reflect early development of adult culture. (Hardman, [1973] 2001, 504)

In the dominant diachronic and universalistic perspective in anthropology, there was no basis for seeing children's collective forms of expression as anything more than expressions of the essence of 'being a child'. With her synchronic perspective Hardman brings into view oral traditions, interactions and iconic representations which are exclusive to children. It is a matter of an autonomous segment of socioculture which is distinct not just from other segments, but also from the individuals who populate this segment: 'The children will move in and out of this segment into another, but others take their place. The segment still remains. The segment may overlap with others, may reflect on others, but there is a basic order of beliefs, values and ideas of one group which bounds them off from any other group' (Hardman, [1973] 2001, 504).

Hardman's discovery of children's culture produced a distinction between children and childhood in the emerging field of childhood studies. This distinction functions as a heuristic for children's agency (James, this volume), but it also raises the resulting question of how the agency of children is related to childhood as a trans-individual sociocultural reality. In order to answer this question Hardman refers to the Russian cultural psychologist Vygotsky. Already, in the

1930s, Vygotsky had criticized Piaget's presumption of a genetic epistemology of cognition. For Piaget, children work through their law-governed cognitive development through active exploration of their material and social environment. Vygotsky, in contrast, outlines the playful self-organization of knowledge acquisition in the context of the child's social world. Children's play is a social form within which children organize their development. It makes it possible to distinguish the infant fusion of word and object as elements of a system of meaning which orders children's objects and behaviour according to particular rules (Hardman, [1973] 2001, 509, 514). As children express children's culture, a collective system of meaning, they become competent actors in their world and thus generate at the same time the framework which makes it possible for them to be competent in the adult world.

Another classic writer in childhood studies, the American sociologist and student of Goffman, Matthew Speier, shows that the world of children is a distinct world: 'Children's cultural activities have a viable organization of their own and it is this organized world that is not very visible to adults. The nature of the child's organized world is hardly understood as yet' (Speier, 1976, 172). But children's culture is not simply one section of reality; it is universe of meaning, and thus poses an epistemological problem. Speier's provocative thesis is that researchers solve this problem by mobilizing an 'adult ideological viewpoint' in the scholarly study of children. The term 'adultism' refers to the epistemologically relevant elements of the adult conception of children which unconsciously underpin the scientific consideration of children: 'The sociologist has incorporated his status as an-adult-in-society into his thinking about childhood' (Speier, 1976, 170). The question then raised for the social studies of childhood is how it is possible to gain insights into the world of children which transcend the 'adult ideological viewpoint'. Speier does not argue for research from children's perspective, but outlines the division between the world of children and that of adults. There are two cultures, engaged in a process of meaning negotiation (Speier, 1976, 174). The new social studies of childhood need to look behind the previous presumed familiarity with children. 'The first problem is to examine interactional events in children's cultural activities, such as talking, play and games. The second problem pertains to the distinction between children's and adult's cultures' (Speier, 1976, 174; cf. Waksler, 1991).

Hardman and Speier are important for the theoretical history of childhood studies not because they identified children as a sociological theme, but because they asked what turns children into children, instead of simply assuming that one knows how one should understand children. The British sociologist Chris Jenks identified, in a text which some see as the most important source for the new social studies of childhood, the *differentia specifica* of a sociology of childhood. It posed the question which tends to be forgotten by those who study children: 'It is as if the basic ontological questions, "What is a child?", "How is a child possible as such?" were … answered in advance of the theorizing and then dismissed' (Jenks, [1982] 1992a, 10). With these questions, the human sciences will recover childhood as a theoretical problem: 'The child is familiar to us and yet strange, he inhabits our world and yet seems to answer to another, he is essentially of ourselves and yet appears to display a different order of being' (Jenks, [1982] 1992a, 9).

The child as social construct?

In any case childhood studies did not begin at zero. The question of the child is a modern question. Jean-Jacques Rousseau (1712–1778) posed it on the eve of the French Revolution as a question of the child's *nature*, which in turn was understood as a question of *human* nature. 'Nature' does not mean biological nature. The 'discovery of the child' in the eighteenth century was the discovery of the indeterminacy of the future determination of humans, who had to develop themselves as historical and social beings (Benner, 1999). Thinkers such as Johann Gottfried Herder (1744–1803) thus developed the question of the child in a historical anthropology in which language was of key significance. In the nineteenth century, the question of the nature of the child was reformulated in terms of evolutionary theory. Childhood became an ontological recapitulation of phylogenesis, which had no independent significance other than as individual development attaining every stage of maturation and rationality which manifests itself in the typical adult. Children become human beings who are not yet adult. It is this answer to the question of the child, in terms of a deficit, that the emerging sociology of childhood decisively opposes. The pointed demarcation from a socialization paradigm is one of the identifying characteristics of childhood studies (exemplary authors include James, Jenks and Prout, 1998, 22ff.). The American developmental psychologist Arlene Skolnick had already formulated essentially similar arguments in the 1970s (Skolnick, 1975). Many of the contributions to her edited collection, bearing the programmatic title *Rethinking Childhood*, are among the classic texts of childhood studies (Skolnick, 1976).

In his essay 'Constituting the Child' – the introduction to a collection of the source texts of a future sociology of childhood – Chris Jenks formulated and explained the objection to the socialization paradigm (Jenks, [1982] 1992a, 1996b). Theorists of socialization and development, argued Jenks, focus on the distinction between children and adults. Instead of examining how children are different from adults, and how they might not be, they assume that children are 'other' (Christensen, 1994):

> The adult member [is] being considered naturally as mature, rational and competent, the child is viewed in juxtaposition as less than fully human, unfinished or incomplete. Such dichotomous discrimination in terms of socio-cognitive competence assumes its most explicit form in theories concerned with the learning process. (Jenks, [1982] 1992a, 19)

The observation that children and adults in modern Western societies are located in separate, indeed conflicting, worlds is one of the basic premises of the 'rethinking' of childhood (Benedict, 1976). 'These oppositions are familiar ones and they include: childhood vs adulthood; private vs public; nature vs culture; irrational vs rational; dependent vs independent; passive vs active; incompetent vs competent; play vs work' (Prout, 2005, 10). The response of socialization and development theorists to the hypothesized distinction between children and adults, according to Jenks, is to be concerned with the integration of children into the order of adult society. Socialization is the epitome of an adultistic concept (Speier, 1976, 173) which first constitutes 'childhood'.

As a classic example of this mode of thinking, Jenks criticizes Talcott Parsons' theory of socialization and Jean Piaget's theory of cognitive development. Jenks portrays Parsons' approach as driven by an obsession with norms: 'The social norms become both the means and the ends of all action within the system. ...they become the source of "identity" between the actor and the system, and the social order itself resides in this identity between the actor and the system' (Jenks, [1982] 1992a, 17). Jenks identifies the underlying concept of Parsons' theory as the transformation of living organisms into machines, from content to form. 'Through the central concept of socialization Parsons commits a theoretic violence, particularly upon the child, through seeking to convert their worlds from content to form' (Jenks, [1982] 1992a, 16). Parsons' conceptual operations constitute the transformation of life into death: 'In Parsons' world life passes into death at the hands of the theorist and socialization is the key to this mortification' (Jenks, [1982] 1992a, 17).

Behind this pathos, however, there lies a theoretical problem. Jenks' diagnosis of a conceptual violence inflicted on the child cannot deny that every question concerning the child depends on some theoretical framework if it is to provide any sort of answer. With Parsons it is the Hobbesian question of how social order is possible. Jenks should have framed his critique of Parsons' concept of childhood as an alternative answer to the conditions of possibility of social order, instead of criticizing Parsons' approach in the name of the child. Theories of socialization are theories of the constitution of sociality; they operate with particular conceptions of society. The question is: how is personality constituted in social terms? The pathos of the critique obscures the fact that Jenks is not at all interested in this question. Jenks shifts the theoretical framework and analyses 'socialization' as a form of thinking about the child, as a social form of knowledge, as a construct: 'The idea of childhood is not a natural but a social construct; as such its status is constituted in particular socially located forms of discourse. ...The child is constituted purposively within theory' (Jenks, [1982] 1992a, 23). The point of this position does not lie in a rejection, but in a de-naturalization of the socialization paradigm: socialization is understood as a discourse that constitutes 'the child'.

Approaching the child as a construct is one of the central premises of a sociology of childhood. Already, in 1977, Norman K. Denzin had written: 'There is nothing intrinsic to the object called "child" that makes that object more or less "childlike"' (Denzin, 1977, 2). The construct 'the child' is an abstraction with its own social reality: 'To be defined as a child is to be a child' (Denzin, 1977, 16). Jenks links up with this seamlessly: 'It makes reference to a social status delineated by boundaries incorporated within the social structure and manifest through certain typical forms of conduct, all of which are essentially related to a particular cultural setting' (Jenks, [1982] 1992a, 12). In any case, this formulation carries with it the danger of confusing the object-related and the epistemological levels of the construct concept. This danger becomes even clearer in Leena Alanen's critique of the socialization paradigm (Alanen, 1988a, 1988b, 1990). More strongly than Jenks, she draws in the interactionist critique of the structural-functionalist concept of socialization, as it had developed since Dennis Wrong's critique of the 'oversocialized conception of man' (Wrong, 1961). She criticizes the neglect of interaction within socialization in relation to its outcomes, and the selectivity of the attribution of outcomes to processes in the light of a functional perspective (see also Dreitzel, 1973). In any case, she goes beyond the classical interactionist critique when she sees the 'adult ideological viewpoint' as constituting the 'exclusive power of adults in defining children' (Alanen, 1988a, 58). The socialization framework makes it difficult 'even to imagine, and even harder to conceptualize children as veritable social actors' (Alanen, 1988a, 57). Making children conceptually invisible leads to a denial of their value as autonomous human beings.

Alanen's critique of the socialization paradigm is directed at a mode of thought which justifies the social marginalization of children as well as the measurement of normal childhood in terms of the infant's physical weakness and need for protection and the regularities of physical growth and psychic development. The proximity of this approach to the feminist critique of science is striking. The sociology of childhood is the antithesis. It regards children as social actors, not as objects of socialization; as sociology from the child's standpoint, it places children's life projects in the conceptual foreground (Alanen, 1992). The ambivalence of this position lies in the coupling of an epistemological critique with a normative position. It carries with it the danger of an ontologization of power and a naturalization of the concept of the actor. For when the power of adults over children is regarded as a condition for the possibility of knowledge about children, this has to underpin all knowledge; it can no longer be part of the question of the possibility of knowledge, or of its dichotomous structure. This makes it possible to understand why the social studies of childhood have no theory of age differentiation (institutionalized age-membership: Honig, 1999, 191ff.), and speak more of school-age children with essentially the same conceptual apparatus as they do of children still unable to talk – if they are given any attention at all. If childhood studies have nothing to say about children growing up, they will have been constituted with a disinterest in children's growing up. It is thus significant when the feminist sociologist Barry Thorne draws attention to the fact that children are also often overlooked in feminist analyses (Thorne, 1987). The dichotomous schema of the powerful and the powerless falls short. The underlying ideal of autonomy itself needs to be problematized, the relationship between autonomy, vulnerability and dependency needs to be examined – and certainly not only in relation to children (Thorne, 1987, 104ff.; Lee, 2005).

In an interactionist or social constructivist research tradition, socialization can be described as a process of interaction between adults and children (Musolf,

1996). In this process, children as actors play a constitutive role. 'The child, like the adult, is able to shape, define, and negotiate its relationship to the external world of objects, others and social situations. Such a self-conscious organism can define its own reality and its own relationship to that reality' (Denzin, 1977, 10). Socialization means 'how the object called "child" comes to enter into the very processes that produce and shape its own self-consciousness and awareness of others' (Denzin, 1977, 10; see Bluebond-Langner, 1978). In his studies of interactions between adults and children in public life (1986, 1987, 1990) Spencer E. Cahill shows how conceptions of childhood regulate the contact between adults and children in a self-evident way. They constitute the context in which the competent acquisition of capacities to participate in public life takes place. The process in which children develop this ritual competence links together the participation rights anchored in the conceptions of childhood with forms of the presentation of self. This linkage develops, according to the model, as the novice's internal conversation, which provides emotions with a vocabulary of motive and with forms of public self-representation (Cahill, 1987, 313). The process is completed when the child – even if specifically in relation to particular arenas – is acknowledged as a personality. A key element of this process is the infringement of moral conduct in public life:

> Children's ceremonial acts are essential elements of the process through which they are socialized to civility. ... The caretaker–child relationship absorbs children's ceremonial deviance, makes that deviance a proper concern in its own right, and acts on that deviance so as to reduce its reoccurrence in the future. (Cahill, 1987, 318)

Here the collectivity of children plays a key role. 'Children develop a sense of group identity and acquire knowledge of the codes of conduct which adults sustain by attempting to cooperatively circumvent the constituent rules of those codes of conduct' (Cahill, 1987, 320). Socialization takes place with the cooperation of child actors but in the meantime the concept of socialization has itself also quietly been transformed: cooperation is not subjection, and childhood socialization means socialization towards being a child, not a development towards adulthood (Handel, Cahill and Elkin, 2007). Socialization and development, since Durkheim and Parsons two sides of one coin, are uncoupled; this makes it possible to understand socialization in a non-teleological way.

With William Corsaro it becomes even clearer that an approach to the socialization paradigm from the perspective of the child places the collectivity of children at the centre of attention (Corsaro, this volume). In his comparative ethnographic studies, Corsaro described Italian and American nursery schools, with reference to Goffman, as 'underlife', and as a key element of the interpretive reproduction of adult culture (Corsaro, 1992). As one commentator sums it up, 'Corsaro emphasizes children's transformative power through their appropriation of adult culture, creatively interpreted and reproduced within peer culture' (Musolf, 1996, 314). Socialization is understood as a social and collective process which takes place among children. 'The biological child enters into a social nexus and through self-generated actions with others builds up a social understanding which becomes a developing core of social knowledge on which he/she build throughout the life course' (Cook-Gumperz and Corsaro, 1986, 9). Here Corsaro draws – like Charlotte Hardman – on Vygotsky's cultural psychology (Rogoff, 2003). Vygotsky conceived the development of competency not in linear but in reproductive terms, and reproduction as a reconstruction in the medium of language:

> Thus the interpretive model extends the notion of stages by viewing development as a productive-reproductive process of increasing density and reorganization of knowledge that changes with the children's developing cognitive and language abilities and with changes in their social worlds. (Corsaro, 1992, 162)

Corsaro gave this approach systematic form in a microsociology of childhood (Corsaro, 2005).

A transcendence of the socialization paradigm of childhood is ambivalent. It promises an autonomous field to childhood studies, but carries with it the danger of a self-misunderstanding. This danger consists of confusing the objective and methodological levels of the critique of the socialization paradigm of childhood, and simply reversing the dichotomies in the new framework of childhood, when they approach children as competent social actors, as beings vs becomings, and 'in their own right' (James, Jenks and Prout, 1998, chapter 10; Prout, 2005, 62ff.). Childhood socialization is a field of the social construction of childhood, and to that extent a key theme in the social studies of childhood.

From the new social studies of childhood to generational studies – and beyond

In the context of the social studies of childhood, the question of the child is the question of the observability of children; that is, the question of the child is a methodological question. The concept of childhood operates, correspondingly, as an epistemological construct mediating the distinction between childhood as a symbolic order of knowledge and children as social actors. This distinction makes it possible to make an empirical theme of the relationship between children and adults and the agency of children within a de-naturalizing perspective. Chris Jenks, for example, examines the symbolic forms of childhood (Jenks, 1996a); Jens Qvortrup analyses childhood as an element of a generational social structure (Qvortrup, 1985, 2005a; Qvortrup, this volume); Leena Alanen highlights the institutionalized practices and social struggles: 'Childhood was – and in its modern version is – the ever-constituted result of decisions and actions of particular historical social actors in their economical, political and cultural struggles that potentially concern the whole spectrum of their interests' (Alanen, 1988a, 64). But how are children to be empirically studied in this perspective? Empirically children are unthinkable in the absence of childhood – as they were, so to speak, pre-social neonates. Research into childhood which focuses on unmediated children would ontologize its object before even knowing what it is talking about. An answer to this difficulty is promised by the concept of generation, which is why it has become a key concept of a theory of childhood.

The concept of generation has two axes: along one axis things turn around the relationship between older and younger; along the second axis things revolve around the relationship of members of a generation with each other. In other words, it concerns generational relationships and generational membership. The two classical concepts of generation address both these axes. In the first third of the nineteenth century, Friedrich Schleiermacher (1768–1834) developed the concept of generation as a concept of the mediation of individual and society, of social integration and social reform, of the present and future of the child in modern society, into a foundational concept of a scientific pedagogy. In this approach the concept refers to a social form of cultural mediation between old and young, revolving around the question of the interest of the old in the social reproduction of society through their own offspring. The second classical concept of generation is more widespread in the history of sociological theory. Karl Mannheim formulated his approach to the problem of generations in the 1920s. He showed the internal connection between generations as experiential collectivities, and examined its contribution to the dynamics of modern societies; this approach has for some time been of great significance in youth research (Hengst, this volume).

With respect to children and childhood, both classical concepts of generation focus on the relationship between children and parents, or children and adults. The duality of children and adults refers to a social, developmental and future-oriented dimension, that of children and parents to an individual, genealogical and past-oriented dimension. This is why it is possible in the context of childhood studies to speak of generations in a familial sense, but also, for example, of generations in the welfare state.

The work of Leena Alanen was groundbreaking for the concept's reception in childhood studies (Alanen, 1992; Alanen, this volume). In her dissertation she developed the idea of a generational ordering of childhood as social and cognitive organization of biological distinctions along lines of power, analogous to the concept of gender as it had been developed in feminist social science (Alanen, 1994). Alanen refers in her discussion, alongside the feminist discussions, to the work of John Fitz und John Hood-Williams (Fitz and Hood-Williams, 1982; Hood-Williams, 1990) on age patriarchy as well as to the analyses of Jens Qvortrup on the transformation of the generational division of labour (Qvortrup, 1985, 1995), and to Viviana Zelizer's work on the historical shifts in the social value of children (Zelizer, 1985). The differing implications of familial and non-familial generational relationships are not relevant for Alanen (for discussions of generational order in the German literature, see Honig, 1999; Bühler-Niederberger, 2005; Andresen, 2006).

Alanen detaches the concept of generation from its genealogical or life-course framework and abstracts it to a relation of power. Children and adults are relationally asymmetrical categories which are embedded in generationally ordered spheres, such as 'public' vs 'private' or 'rational' vs 'irrational'. These are normatively structured, characterized by unequal opportunities for participation, and constitute settings for learning processes. Children become children, and adults become adults, through 'generationing', through institutionalized practices of distinction. Alanen later further developed her concept systematically in an engagement with Karl Mannheim's classical approach (Alanen, 2001; Alanen and Mayall, 2001) and uses it, inter alia, to demonstrate the active role of children in the process of generationing.

'Children' and 'adults' are, in this concept of generation, conceived relationally. This makes it possible to abandon a substantive concept of childhood and adulthood, since children and adults are mutually determined through relational difference. But this difference is also determined by power relations which precede it as much as the relational difference asserts and differentiates these power relations. 'Doing generation' couples questions of epistemological possibility to questions of social praxis; in other words, the mechanisms of the constitution of children legitimate themselves as 'fair to children'. As representations of power, distinctions become differences, categories become population groups. The emphasis on the differences between children and adults corresponds to a stress on the communality among children (see the tribal child, James, Jenks and Prout, 1998, 214ff.), as it is described in countless studies of the social world of children.

Leena Alanen has attempted to develop the concept of generation, analogously to the concept of gender, into a structural category of sociality. However, this is bound up with a loss of differentiation. This becomes clear when one distinguishes between an analytical and an empirical concept of generation. This distinction makes it possible not to see children and adults automatically as opposing groups. On the analytical level, generations constitute conceptual entities which mutually exclude and presuppose each other. Empirically, however, generations never exist in isolation, but always in relation to other generations. Generational orders are thus not dichotomous; it is more that generational membership and generational distinctions display 'polyphony' (Mannheim) of biographical and historical temporality (see also Matthes, 1985). Generations, in other words, despite their differences, are also bound together by their location in history. The concept of generational order can, however, obstruct our view of the *specific* social form of these modes of organizing social relationships. Rolf Nemitz refers to the *permanent distinction* which legitimates *ever-changing differences* as the 'pedagogic difference' (Nemitz, 1996, 2001). Childhood and adulthood are constituted through historically specific forms of 'the structuring of the life course, the establishment of the transition point [from childhood to adulthood – MSH], and the extent of the legitimacy of this two-fold division' (Nemitz, 1996, 149; transl. MSH). The 'pedagogic difference' is based not on cultural mediation, a power relation, but on 'origins' as an anthropological condition for the possibility of 'the new'. The concept does not regard the distinction between children and adults as objective, but as *constitutive* of its object – a distinction which *generates* varying forms of difference. It is a matter of an epistemological concept of generation, which needs to be developed within a theory of the generativity of the social (Liegle and

Lüscher, 2008, 141, 149ff.). It does not refer to a body of knowledge about what a child 'is', but asks, how is the child possible?

For the social studies of childhood, this means studying the relationship between children and childhood in the semantics and praxis of social relationships. This opens up access to the various generational orderings of childhood as a social phenomenon (Qvortrup et al., 1994):

- Social relations between children and adults as well as among children can be analysed as interacting moral orders in Erving Goffman's sense (Denzin, 1973).
- At the level of social structure, it is possible to identify a political economy of generational relations which works with a concept of order revolving around welfare politics and theories of policy (Wintersberger et al., 2007).
- At the level of semantics, it is possible to analyse symbolic forms of childhood in terms of Basil Bernstein's theory of codes and Foucault's theory of discursive orders (Jenks, 1995; Cook, 2002; Bühler-Niederberger, 2005).

The avoidance of a concept of generation organized around group-formation also has the great advantage of making it possible to pose the question of the *limits* of a generational approach in childhood studies. They are made evident by the following empirical points:

- There is *not just one* generational order; it is more the case that various binary codes of childhood and adulthood coexist. Jürgen Zinnecker distinguishes scripts of postmodern childhood, advanced modernized childhood, traditional modernized childhood and fundamentalist childhood (Zinnecker, 2001, 25ff.).
- In a rich overview of research in media and cultural studies, Andreas Lange shows numerous indications of a *mixture* of generational arrangements, also and precisely in the context of the 'normal' family (Lange, 2004).
- Childhood is also constituted *beyond* generational difference. The 'mediatization' of children's experience is not determined by its position in the generational order. Heinz Hengst speaks of children's 'temporal comradeship' (Holloway and Valentine, 2003; Hengst, 2005; Hengst, this volume). With her concept of pre-figurative culture, Margaret Mead had already in the 1970s observed that adults' knowledge advantage is systematically shrinking.
- The generational order only *partially* determines the social position of children. Social origin, sociocultural milieu, gender and ethnicity overlay the significance of the adult–child distinction (Betz, 2008). If one considers childhood as a social position, one can observe a diversity of unequal childhoods (Lareau, 2003).
- Last but not least: To speak of children is a de-differentiating abstraction. Does one mean infant, school children or legally restricted competent actors? The age diversity of childhoods plays hardly any conceptual role in childhood studies. Helga Kelle and Heinz Hengst have warned of a 'partially unreflective

"juvenilization" of the collective subject of research on children and child-hood' (Hengst and Kelle, 2003, 9; transl. MSH).

The empirical evidence suggests tensions between homogeneity, identity, diversity and divergence between children and childhood – not to be forgotten are tendencies towards a new universalization of childhood in the medium of consumer culture (Cook, this volume) and international children's rights (Kaufman and Rizzini, this volume). As a dichotomous concept, the concept of generation is at best meaningful in the context of family life. The constitution of the child, however, takes place to an increasing extent beyond the familial context; this requires a 'de-centring' of the category of generations (Hengst, this volume). It concerns in any case children *and* adults. The central question then remains, exactly what turns children into 'children'?

The future of childhood studies

What distinguishes the social studies of childhood from all the other forms of knowledge concerned with children is the perspective on the constitution of their object with which they approach children and childhood. Childhood studies ask: How is the child possible? The classical answer runs as follows: children are human beings in transition from nature to reason in the unity of possibility and reality (Rustemeyer, 2002). A concept of possibility and an ideal of perfection are thus linked together; childhood in modernity becomes the promise of the future, the promise of better possibilities in reality. This classical modern concept of childhood is paradigmatically bound to a concept of generation which links together cultural transmission and social change.

Childhood studies are faced with the demand to speak of childhood at the same time that its classical framework is dissolving. Childhood can only inadequately be described as a protection realm of learning and development, certainly not as some sort of promise. There is a de-pedagogization of the generational order taking place, which also dissolves the old power relations. This eliminates the ambition in the field conceptually to emancipate children as competent social actors from their tutelage under an age patriarchy. This has been entirely achieved since the competent child has been put forward as the leading image of a knowledge-based economy (Magalhaes and Stoer, 2003). In this development, there lies an opportunity. Childhood studies, which began with a critique of the adult ideological viewpoint, can become aware of the fact that the erosion of the classic European model of childhood determines the social conditions of the possibility of constituting childhood as an object of knowledge. Because the natural and cultural self-evidence to which childhood studies refer is disappearing, they have to conceive their object and their approach in a more abstract and complex way (examples in the German literature include Luhmann, 1991; Reyer, 2004). This insight can enable recourse to the theoretical history of childhood studies.

One often-overlooked danger of reification is carried within a national–cultural perspective. The international research community has so far barely begun to engage with the task of intercultural and international comparison. This is why children and childhood often appear implicitly as transcultural entities. But it has also failed to examine the diversity of childhood sociologies in different countries (Bühler-Niederberger and van Krieken, 2008). In the process, the specific conditions in particular countries have led to different theoretical preferences.

The future of childhood research lies in not simply separating children because it understands itself as a science from the child's perspective or takes children's rights as the reference point for childhood research, because it cannot presuppose a concept of the child. Previously the critique of the 'othering' of children (Christensen, 1994) has already sharpened the sensibility for the differences among children and the multiplicity of childhoods. When the natural and cultural references which allow us to speak of 'children' become inconclusive, the microsocial practices of children's production and self-expression as children, as well as the question of what children and adults have in common, must be placed more in the foreground (Audehm, 2007), perhaps along with vulnerability, dependency and non-reciprocal care – until now neglected dimensions of the relationality of generational orders. This is also certainly a reason why one can observe the discovery of the child's body (Fingerson, this volume), and with it a renaissance of historical anthropology (Prout, 2000; Hengst and Kelle, 2003). The early, pre-linguistic phase of life, even pre-birth childhood, has generally been factored out by childhood studies, even though it is precisely in this arena that the social studies of childhood need to clarify what they mean when they are speaking of 'children' (Denzin, 1977). Perhaps the most important desideratum for childhood research which is cognizant of the relationality of childhood and adulthood, and a product of the liberation of the social studies of childhood from the suggestive evidence of the empirical child, is, however, the analysis of adulthood.

It is not the child, and also not the generational order, but generativity as a mode of the constitution of sociality which is the leading theoretical concept of the future study of childhood.

References

Alanen, L. (1988a) 'Rethinking Childhood', *Acta Sociologica*, 31(1): 53–67.
Alanen, L. (1988b) 'The Social Construction of Childhood: Towards a History and Theory of Childhood Constructs' in H. P. Hepworth (ed.) *Canadian Seminar on Childhood. Implications for Child Care Policies.* Vienna: European Centre, pp. 93–101.
Alanen, L. (1990) 'Rethinking Socialization, the Family and Childhood', in P. Adler and P. Adler (eds) *Sociological Studies of Child Development, Vol. 3.* Greenwich, London: JAI Press, pp. 13–28.
Alanen, L. (1992) *Modern Childhood? Exploring the 'Child Question' in Sociology.* Jyväskylä: University of Jyväskylä.
Alanen, L. (1994) 'Gender and Generation. Feminism and the "Child Question"', in J. Qvortrup, M. Bardy, G. Sgritta and H. Wintersberger (eds) *Childhood Matters. Social Theory, Practice and Politics.* Aldershot a.o.: Avebury, pp. 27–42.

Alanen, L. (2001) 'Explorations in Generational Analysis', in L. Alanen and B. Mayall (eds) *Conceptualizing Child-Adult Relations*. London and New York: Routledge/Falmer, pp. 11–22.

Alanen, L. and B. Mayall (eds) (2001) *Conceptualizing Child-Adult Relations*. London and New York: Routledge/Falmer.

Andresen, S. (2006) *Sozialistische Kindheitskonzepte. Politische Einflüsse auf die Erziehung.* München: Reinhardt.

Audehm, K. (2007) *Erziehung bei Tisch. Zur sozialen Magie eines Familienrituals.* Bielefeld: transcript.

Benedict, R. (1976) 'Continuities and Discontinuities in Cultural Conditioning', in A. Skolnick (ed.) *Rethinking Childhood. Perspectives on Development and Society.* Boston/Toronto: Little, Brown and Company, pp. 19–28.

Benner, D. (1999) 'Der Begriff moderner Kindheit bei Rousseau, im Philanthropismus und in der deutschen Klassik', *Zeitschrift für Pädagogik*, 45(1): 1–18.

Betz, T. (2008) *Ungleiche Kindheiten. Theoretische und empirische Analysen zur Sozialberichterstattung über Kinder.* Weinheim und München: Juventa.

Bluebond-Langner, M. (1978) *The Private Worlds of Dying Children.* Princeton, NJ: Princeton University Press.

Bühler-Niederberger, D. (2005) *Kindheit und die Ordnung der Verhältnisse. Von der gesellschaftlichen Macht der Unschuld und dem kreativen Individuum.* Weinheim und München: Juventa.

Bühler-Niederberger, D. and R. van Krieken (2008) 'Persisting Inequalities: Childhood between Global Influences and Local Traditions', *Childhood*, 15(2): 147–155.

Cahill, S.E. (1986) 'Childhood Socialization as a Recruitment Process: Some Lessons from the Study of Gender Development', in P.A. Adler and P. Adler (eds) *Sociological Studies of Child Development, Vol. 1.* Greenwich: JAI Press, pp. 163–186.

Cahill, S.E. (1987) 'Children and Civility: Ceremonial Deviance and the Acquisition of Ritual Competence', *Social Psychology Quarterly*, 50(4): 312–321.

Cahill, S.E. (1990) 'Childhood and Public Life: Reaffirming Biographical Divisions', *Social Problems*, 37(3): 390–402.

Christensen, P.H. (1994) 'Children as the Cultural Other', *KEA: Zeitschrift für Kulturwissenschaften*, 6: 1–16.

Cook, D.T. (ed.) (2002) *Symbolic Childhoods.* New York: Peter Lang.

Cook-Gumperz, J. and W.A. Corsaro (1986) 'Introduction', in J. Cook-Gumperz, W.A. Corsaro and J. Streeck (eds) *Children's Worlds and Children's Language.* Berlin/New York/Amsterdam: Mouton de Gruyter, pp. 1–11.

Corsaro, W.A. (1992) 'Interpretive Reproduction in Children's Peer Cultures', *Social Psychology Quarterly*, 55(2): 160–177.

Corsaro, W.A. (2005) *The Sociology of Childhood*, 2nd edn. Thousand Oaks, London, New Delhi: Pine Forge Press.

Denzin, N.K. (1973) 'The Work of Little Children', in N.K. Denzin (ed.) *Children and Their Caretakers.* New Brunswick: Transaction Books, pp. 117–126.

Denzin, N.K. (1977) *Childhood Socialization.* San Francisco a.o.: Jossey-Bass.

Dreitzel, H.P. (ed.) (1973) *Childhood and Socialization.* New York: Macmillan.

Fitz, J. and J. Hood-Williams (1982) 'The Generation Game: Playing by the Rules', in D. Robbins (ed.) *Rethinking Social Inequality.* Aldershot: Gower, pp. 65–95.

Handel, G., S.E. Cahill and F. Elkin (2007) *Children and Society. The Sociology of Children and Childhood Socialization.* New York, Oxford: Oxford University Press.

Hardman, C. ([1973] 2001) 'Can there be an Anthropology of Children?', *Childhood*, 8(4): 501–517.

Hengst, H. (1981) 'Tendenzen der Liquidierung von Kindheit', in H. Hengst, M. Köhler, B. Riedmüller and M.M. Wambach (eds) *Kindheit als Fiktion.* Frankfurt am Main: Suhrkamp, pp. 11–72.

Hengst, H. (ed.) (1985) *Kindheit in Europa. Zwischen Spielplatz und Computer.* Frankfurt am Main: Suhrkamp.

Hengst, H. (2005) 'Kindheitsforschung, sozialer Wandel, Zeitgenossenschaft', in H. Hengst and H. Zeiher (eds) *Kindheit soziologisch.* Wiesbaden: VS Verlag für Sozialwissenschaften, pp. 245–265.

Hengst, H. and H. Kelle (2003) 'Kinder – Körper – Identitäten. Zur Einführung', in H. Hengst and H. Kelle (eds) *Kinder – Körper – Identitäten. Theoretische und empirische Annäherungen an kulturelle Praxis und sozialen Wandel.* Weinheim und München: Juventa.

Holloway, S.L. and G. Valentine (eds) (2003) *Cyberkids. Children in the Information Age.* London and New York: RoutledgeFalmer.

Honig, M.-S. (1999) *Entwurf einer Theorie der Kindheit.* Frankfurt am Main: Suhrkamp.

Hood-Williams, J. (1990) 'Patriarchy for Children: On the Stability of Power Relations in Children's Lives', in L. Chisholm, P. Büchner, H.-H. Krüger and P. Brown (eds) *Childhood, Youth and Social Change. A Comparative Perspective.* London, New York, Philadelphia: The Falmer Press, pp. 155–177.

James, A., C. Jenks and A. Prout (1998) *Theorizing Childhood.* Cambridge: Polity Press.

Jenks, C. ([1982] 1992a) 'Constituting the Child', in C. Jenks (ed.) *The Sociology of Childhood. Essential Readings.* Aldershot: Gregg Revivals, pp. 9–24.

Jenks, C. (ed.) ([1982] 1992b) *The Sociology of Childhood. Essential Readings.* Aldershot: Gregg Revivals.

Jenks, C. (1995) 'Decoding Childhood', in P. Atkinson, B. Davies and S. Delamont (eds) *Discourse and Reproduction: Essays in Honor of Basil Bernstein.* Cresskill: Hampton Press, pp. 173–190.

Jenks, C. (1996a) *Childhood.* London/New York: Routledge.

Jenks, C. (1996b) 'Constituting Childhood', in C. Jenks *Childhood.* London/New York: Routledge, pp. 1–31.

Lange, A. (2004) 'Kindheitsforschung und Generationenkonzept. Eine medien- und kulturwissenschaftliche Skizze', *Zeitschrift für Soziologie der Erziehung und Sozialisation,* 24(3): 303–318.

Lareau, A. (2003) *Unequal Childhoods. Class, Race, and Family Life.* Berkeley, Los Angeles, London: University of California Press.

Lee, N. (2005) *Childhood and Human Value. Development, Separation and Separability.* Maidenhead: Open University Press.

Liegle, L. and K. Lüscher (2008) 'Generative Sozialisation', in K. Hurrelmann, M. Grundmann and S. Walper (eds) *Handbuch der Sozialisationsforschung.* Weinheim und Basel: Beltz, pp. 141–156.

Luhmann, N. (1991) 'Das Kind als Medium der Erziehung', *Zeitschrift für Pädagogik,* 37(1): 19–40.

Magalhaes, A.M. and S.R. Stoer (2003) 'Performance, Citizenship and the Knowledge Society: A New Mandate for European Education Policy', *Globalisation, Societies and Education,* 1(1): 41–66.

Matthes, J. (1985) 'Karl Mannheims "Das Problem der Generationen", neu gelesen. Generations-"Gruppen" oder "gesellschaftliche Regelung von Zeitlichkeit"?', *Zeitschrift für Soziologie,* 14(5): 363–372.

Musolf, G.R. (1996) 'Interactionism and the Child: Cahill, Corsaro, and Denzin on Childhood Socialization', *Symbolic Interactionism,* 19(4): 303–321.

Nemitz, R. (1996) *Kinder und Erwachsene. Zur Kritik der pädagogischen Differenz.* Berlin, Hamburg: Argument-Verlag.

Nemitz, R. (2001) 'Frauen/Männer, Kinder/Erwachsene', in H. Lutz and N. Wenning (eds) *Unterschiedlich verschieden. Differenz in der Erziehungswissenschaft.* Opladen: Leske + Budrich, pp. 179–196.

Prout, A. (2000) 'Childhood Bodies: Construction, Agency and Hybridity', in A. Prout (ed.) *The Body, Childhood and Society.* Houndmills a.o.: Macmillan, pp. 1–18.

Prout, A. (2005) *The Future of Childhood*. London/New York: RoutledgeFalmer.

Prout, A. and A. James (1990) 'A New Paradigm for the Sociology of Childhood? Provenance, Promise and Problems', in A. James and A. Prout (eds) *Constructing and Reconstructing Childhood*. London/New York/Philadelphia: Falmer Press, pp. 7–34.

Qvortrup, J. (1985) 'Placing Children in the Division of Labour', in P. Close and R. Collins (eds) *Family and Economy in Modern Society*. London: Macmillan, pp. 129–145.

Qvortrup, J. (1987) 'Introduction: The Sociology of Childhood', *International Journal of Sociology*, 17(3): 3–37.

Qvortrup, J. (1995) 'From Useful to Useful: The Historical Continuity of Children's Constructive Participation', in A.-M. Ambert (ed.) *Sociological Studies of Children*. Greenwich/London: JAI Press, pp. 29–76.

Qvortrup, J. (2005a) 'Kinder und Kindheit in der Sozialstruktur', in H. Hengst and H. Zeiher (eds) *Kindheit soziologisch*. Wiesbaden: VS Verlag für Sozialwissenschaften, pp. 27–47.

Qvortrup, J. (ed.) (2005b) *Studies in Modern Childhood. Society, Agency, Culture*. Houndmills: Palgrave Macmillan.

Qvortrup, J., M. Bardy, G. Sgritta and H. Wintersberger (eds) (1994) *Childhood Matters. Social Theory, Practice and Politics*. Aldershot a.o.: Avebury.

Reyer, J. (2004) 'Integrative Perspektiven zwischen sozialwissenschaftlicher, entwicklungspsychologischer und biowissenschaftlicher Kindheitsforschung?', *Zeitschrift für Soziologie der Erziehung und Sozialisation*, 24(4): 339–361.

Rogoff, B. (2003) *The Cultural Nature of Human Development*. Oxford, New York: Oxford University Press.

Rustemeyer, D. (2002) *Wie ist Pädagogik möglich?* Manuscript, Universität Trier.

Skolnick, A. (1975) 'The Limits of Childhood: Conceptions of Child Development and Social Context', *Law and Contemporary Problems*, 39(3): 38–77.

Skolnick, A. (ed.) (1976) *Rethinking Childhood. Perspectives on Development and Society*. Boston/Toronto: Little, Brown and Company.

Speier, M. (1976) 'The Adult Ideological Viewpoint in Studies of Childhood', in A. Skolnick (ed.) *Rethinking Childhood. Perspectives on Development and Society*. Boston/Toronto: Little, Brown and Company, pp. 168–186.

Thorne, B. (1987) 'Re-Visioning Women and Social Change: Where are the Children?', *Gender and Society*, 1(1): 85–109.

Waksler, F.C. (ed.) (1991) *Studying the Social Worlds of Children. Sociological Readings*. London, New York, Philadelphia: The Falmer Press.

Wintersberger, H., L. Alanen, T. Olk and J. Qvortrup (eds) (2007) *Childhood, Generational Order and the Welfare State: Exploring Children's Social and Economic Welfare. Vol. I of COST A 19: Children's Welfare*. Odense: University Press of Southern Denmark.

Wrong, D.H. (1961) 'The Oversocialized Conception of Man in Modern Sociology', *American Sociological Review*, 26(2): 183–193.

Zelizer, V.A. (1985) *Pricing the Priceless Child. The Changing Social Value of Children*. New York: Basic Books.

Zinnecker, J. (2001) 'Children in Young and Aging Societies: The Order of Generations and Models of Childhood in Comparative Perspective', in S.L. Hofferth and T.J. Owens (eds) *Children at the Millenium: Where Have We Come from, Where Are We Going?* Amsterdam, London, New York a.o.: JAI, pp. 11–52.

5
Method and Methodology in Childhood Research

Andreas Lange and Johanna Mierendorff

Introduction: the object(s) of childhood studies and the standards of social scientific research

For more than two hundred years different scientific and political interests in children and childhood have existed and, due to this, there have been many changing ideas and methods for how to get a view inside children's thinking, children's actions and children's worlds (Waksler, 1991). Parallel to the rise of organized modernity, children and 'their worlds' were more and more seen as 'constructed' and constituted differently from adults, and, thus, a specific and more and more differentiated treatment of the 'strangeness' had to be developed to gain knowledge of the inner world of the 'other' (Honig, 1999). Educational research, developmental psychology and paediatrics have developed a wide range of very specific, partly 'artificial' methods to work with the 'otherness' of children and with their specific cognitive conditions (Hasselhorn and Schneider, 2007). The fundamental motivation for this research agenda was to get more and deeper knowledge about the learning mechanisms and the parameters of the 'normal development' (cf. Smith, 2007) of children's minds and bodies in respect of the idea that childhood and the development of children is controllable and that future citizenship can be 'created'. However, childhood is framed mainly as the 'educational project of modernity'. The effects of traditional methods on children were to some extent intrusive and alienating (Mey, 2003, 8).

What has changed in the meanwhile? What is the specific new sociological approach to children's worlds, to childhood as a social pattern and to childhood as an element of social structure? The traditional view, first, of children as natural, as dependent, and as in development, was criticized because of the uncertainty and instability of late modernity (Heaphy, 2007), due to general methodological doubts concerning the question of what we know if we look at the so-called rapidly changing 'realities' – which no longer seem to be realities – and due to the growing paradigm of individualism and pluralism. Second, the ideas about controlling children's development became more and more theoretically dubious. A new paradigm for children and childhood evolved from these doubts and uneasiness (see Honig, this volume; Qvortrup, this volume). Childhood was conceptualized as historically contingent and socially constructed and, more importantly, as a central element of social structure. Furthermore, children were seen as active in the permanent social reproduction of everyday life, of children's culture and of society. The main objects of sociological childhood research have changed fundamentally (for recent reviews see Kränzl-Nagl and Mierendorff, 2007; Matthews, 2007; Schweizer, 2007).

Thus, it becomes necessary to think about research strategies and methodology to realize and implement these 'new' research agendas. Childhood is no longer solely seen, first, as a natural stage in the life course, or, second, as a secure stage of development, but as an element of social structure and as a social context of children's lives. This context, and especially the sociality of this context, becomes one of the most striking features of, and a theoretical starting point for, research in the field of the 'new sociology of childhood' (James and James, 2004; Prout, 2005). This does not mean that 'old' methods and traditional knowledge about children have to be abandoned, but methodological access, the choice of methods and the interpretation of data have to be changed. In this context, it has to be mentioned that sociology as an academic discipline itself has not yet developed a very intense concern about the special aspects of researching children. In most textbooks about methods of social research, researching children is not even a topic (see, for example, Diekmann, 2007, for a quantitatively oriented textbook in the German context, and Flick, 2007, for a qualitatively oriented textbook).

One of the important theoretical implications of this sociality is that childhood as an element of social structure has to be understood in terms of its generational order (Honig, 1999; Alanen and Mayall, 2001; Mayall and Zeiher, 2003; Qvortrup in this volume). Seen in this light, childhood can no longer be understood theoretically as divided from adulthood. It is constructed in its relations to adulthood, which implies certain power relationships and the research question of the social positioning of children in society. By understanding the generational order as the normative and structural fundament of this social context, a new sociological object and a new epistemological agenda has been created. The permanent process of reproduction of this social context and the consequences for children as a group or as individuals steps into the floodlight of research (Corsaro, 1997; see also the next section of this chapter). Although this assumed generational order and its reproduction are not always the central object of research, the social fundament of the social phenomenon called 'childhood' is. Genuine sociological research and methodology, starting from this theoretical perspective, must be aware of its own role in the permanent reproductive process of generationing.

For heuristic purposes it seems useful to distinguish four central dimensions of these social contexts:

(a) the cultural, societal and political contexts in which the generational order structures the power relationship between children and adults;
(b) the ongoing interactions among children and adults or among peers in private, informal or institutional areas;

(c) the permanent reproduction of children's so-called culture within the culture of a society (or more and more of globalized 'world society');
(d) children's views on the social world in which they are permanently involved.

The methodological challenges are how is it possible to obtain knowledge about these social contexts and the corresponding processes of interpreting these structures and acting according to them? What are the appropriate methods needed to obtain empirical data about childhood as a cultural pattern and as an element of social structure? How can we, in a methodologically controlled way, delve into different patterns of childhood in diverse and varying cultural and societal contexts?

Unfortunately, these questions have often been reduced to purely technical matters. Thus, for example, in the case of managing interviews with children, researchers try to lessen the difficulties and limits of interviewing by using dolls, coloured pictures or anything else to foster the attention and capability of the child or to make their own language more understandable. Although such questions are important for the design of research, they are not the only and not the main ones in discussing methodological approaches to children. It is not only about technique – it is much more about shifts in the epistemological frame of conducting and interpreting research. In brief, our review tries to show how, on the one hand, childhood research has to rely on the general and rigorous standards of social scientific research and, on the other hand, how sociological childhood research has to reflect on the special chances and risks of applying these methods to the population of children – including the question of in what circumstances special techniques need to be developed.

Methodological linchpins and paradigms

Important methodological shifts have taken place which are very useful in transferring these big questions into researchable topics. The other way round: new research topics force scientists to adapt their methodological repertoire, as can be seen in the case of culture and media analyses. Some general methodological starting points have been emerging which are different from traditional empirical studies on children in developmental psychology, educational psychology and educational sciences. Indeed, these different scientific fields have developed and changed their methodologies during the last decades (see Mey, 2005) as well. However, the 'old' methods have not been submerged; now these old 'tools' are often used in a different way in sociological research.

First: the ethnographical shift

A direct 'import' from sociology which has been widely applied in research on children and children's cultures is ethnography in its widest sense. Ethnography is an umbrella term for a diverse set of research tools that emphasize the discovery of participants' understanding of their social and symbolic worlds. Ethnography does not 'test' hypotheses or try to find connections among a set of pre-defined variables. Rather, ethnographic researchers set out to be taught the ways, language and expectations of the social group or special population they seek to study. One aim is to get a glimpse of the knowledge and competences of the groups of actors to be studied (Corsaro, 1997, 2003). Another aim is to get inside the mechanisms of children's culture and into the processes of generationing (Alanen and Mayall, 2001; Kelle, 2001; Thorne, 1993). Anthropologists originally developed ethnography as a general research approach, as a means of understanding and describing other cultures. It was adapted and adopted by sociologists in their investigations of other cultures within western societies – for instance, in the early phases of the urban sociology of the so-called Chicago School. Looking from an ethnographic viewpoint at children and children's culture can be seen as a major advance in commonly held research ideas of 'testing children' – but this access in itself constructs children as 'others'.

Second: a shift away from households and families

A second important methodological step was the recognition that the re-definition of the 'statistical point of reference' in large data sets is important to harvest new ideas about the position of children as a social group in society (Saporiti, 1994). The group of children is ascribed the status of a unit of observation of their own; since the population of children and/or the individual child is statistically 'freed' from the household or the family, children are treated as a single statistical unit. The family is acknowledged to be an important part of the environment of the child – but not the main unit to be looked at. One of the most important examples that document the benefits of this perspective is the research on child poverty: it makes an important difference whether poor families or single children in their families are observed. The number of children shows immediately greater proportions when the research uses single children as the statistical unit, because very often more than one child is living in a family (Saporiti, 1994, 209). Since the 1990s, many macro-theoretical empirical studies about children's health, socio-economic status, education and so on have been reworked for a child-centred data set. These forms of secondary analysis, for instance, have been a very important starting point in Europe and the United States for the sociology of childhood. The path-breaking project Childhood Matters (Qvortrup et al., 1994) is an excellent example.

On a qualitative level, researching children in the context of families also concealed children as actors for a long time (Solberg, 1996). As Wyness (2006, 187) subtly comments:

> Thus, even when we are in a position to explore the interior of family life, mothers and fathers are perceived to be the key actors, with routines assumed to flow through the controlling forces of adults. We come up against the perennial problem of 'second-hand data' in child research. That is, researchers in the

past have tended to omit from their research proposals the voices of children as crucial mediators of parents' worlds. As with research in other fields such as education and social policy, we learn about how children view their worlds from the perspective of significant adult figures.

Third: the social recognition of children as reliable informants

According to the assumptions of the two first steps, children are increasingly seen as important participants in social life and as worthwhile informants for policy research, institutional evaluations, social accounting, social reporting and macrosociological comparative research (Ben-Arieh et al., 2001, 90). The insight that social planning, institutional change or specific politics cannot be implemented and realized if the individuals are against it or if they do not want to cooperate additionally forced the development of child-centred surveys or censuses. To gain access to children's opinions and meanings about the social world, living conditions, environment and so on, different and multiple verbal and non-verbal methods emerged. The main task is to understand and to interpret children's expressions – namely to get access to the so-called perspective of children (Heinzel, 2000). This access has its own academic value – but it is also a very important step in creating concrete and successful participatory projects.

Fourth: analysing the societal context of childhood from a constructionist and structuralist perspective

To get a broader and deeper picture of the social context of childhood, it is important to analyse not only children's expressions or the data about children's living conditions. The normative constructions, rulings and institutionalizations, which are the seedbeds in which childhood is permanently re-constructed, also have to be looked at. This includes the analysis of law, institutions, professions, and political and institutional discourses – not to forget their repercussions in the print and electronic media. Therefore, social-constructivist methodology, specifically discourse analysis, is one cornerstone of the new social studies on children and childhood. However, the other part of research, which has begun, concerns the structural effects of norms and regulations on children's lives (Hagen, 2007; see below).

Tools for sociological childhood research

In the last two decades, since the so-called shift in childhood research, many traditional psychological and sociological methods have been changed and modified and some new methods have evolved. In the following discussion we provide a very brief overview of the main and most prominent methods in childhood research and their methodological challenges and boundaries. This overview makes no claim to be exhaustive, as only the main approaches are presented. The chosen studies are exemplars intended to show specific approaches or peculiar features clearly.

Quantitative approaches: the group of children as a statistical unit

Official data sets and secondary analyses

The idea of painting a picture of children's social situation is realized by using official data sets to make secondary analyses. The target is to make children visible in these data sets (Saporiti, 1994). As mentioned above, in macro-analyses a lot of child-related data – about housing conditions, income situation, health situation, death rate, schooling, siblings, employment status of the parents and demographic aspects – are collected to get knowledge, first, about the social status of children in society compared to other age groups such as adults or elderly people and, second, about 'childhood as a status, that is, the social conditions shared by the child population' (Saporiti, 1994, 192). In this sense, large-scale official statistical data sets are important for capturing the diversity of childhood and also of children's daily life experience to get an idea of the broader social position of this age group in relation to the group of adults (Qvortrup, 1990, 2000).

These analyses, especially comparative ones, are often very difficult to realize because the database is still insufficient in many countries or the data are extremely heterogeneous and only partly comparable because of different traditions in statistical data sets, as the 13 Country Reports of COST A19 – Children's Welfare have shown (Jensen et al., 2004). Often data are extremely out of date (Bradshaw, 2007, 94).

Children's surveys

Following the mainstream of sociology, one important tool for uncovering the social situation or the well-being of children as a special population and the special situations of different groups of children (migrants, boys, girls, social strata), and for delineating relevant facets of their world, is the use of surveys, sometimes even representative ones (Ben-Arieh et al., 2001; Alt, 2004). The surveys sometimes use different methods: collecting objective data by standardized or semi-standardized questionnaires, interviews with children and parents, or data from official data sets. The research focus is, to some extent, the well-being or the quality of life of children or partly the conditions for 'good development'. Great efforts in this direction have been made by the International Society for Child Indicators, which tries to develop internationally accepted and theoretically legitimated indicators for children's well-being (ISCI, http://www.childindicators. org/; Ben-Arieh, 2005; Ben-Arieh and Frønes, 2007).

As in the case of qualitative interviews, there is a rich literature on the special needs of children concerning the details of wording, questioning and so on. Recently, indicating advances in this topic, even survey experiments about the quality of survey data obtained from children and youths compared to adults have been conducted. Fuchs (2004) concludes that children and juveniles process survey questions in a more segmented fashion and they are influenced to a greater degree than adults by the information provided in the text and by the response categories of each given question. That the response categories are very sensitive issues can be shown concretely in the case of self-reports of media use (Jordan et al., 2007). The answer 'often' with respect to TV viewing means 50 per cent more minutes than in the case of being online.

The concrete methodological challenges of the enterprise to conduct a survey with children can be grasped by looking at the German Childhood Panel (Alt, 2004). This is a longitudinal survey with three waves of data. It provides insight into the basic circumstances of children's situations and lives, as well as the perception of important domains of children's lifeworlds from their point of view, for example their family, schools, friends and so on. Due to the fact that mothers and fathers have also been interviewed, many possibilities for comparing the different perspectives are given, making this an important tool for assessing the dimensions and ambivalences of the generational ordering of childhood. If we look at the methodological aspects, it is quite complicated to develop appropriate questions for children and to include these questions in a standardized instrument. It was recognized in the pre-test that interviews longer than 20 to 30 minutes led to an increase in concentration problems and signs of exhaustion. These restrictions were overcome by allowing the children to take an active part in the interview after 20 to 25 minutes. Haunberger (2007), in a careful review of the methodological implications of the interview situations in the Panel, comes to the following conclusions:

- children have no inclination to answer in a socially desirable modus – but their mothers do!
- children do not stay attentive for long in surveys, but children from the age of eight years on can be interviewed for about 45 minutes;
- the only real distortion which can be shown is the presence of a third person in the interview situation.

An innovative approach to elicit children's responses in a quantitative design was implemented by van Deth et al. (2007). Their interest was in the political knowledge and attitudes of children in the first grade. Because most of these children were not able to read and write and the authors wanted to use the context of the school class to gather as many children as possible, they developed a questionnaire based purely on pictorial representations. The researchers projected the questions with an overhead projector and read them aloud to the children. The children could answer the questions about the complex topics of authority, political parties and so on by choosing various sorts of 'smiley' images. Another answering format was to write an X in a circle under the possible answer.

In summary, the survey approach involving children as informants has meanwhile reached a high level of sophistication and is a pillar of modern childhood research. The same can be said about the qualitative counterpart.

Qualitative interviews: pathways to children's perspectives

A window on children's perspectives and world views

The qualitative research interview has been one of the most used methods in the microsociological approaches of a new sociology of childhood (Westcott and

Littleton, 2005). Here, different from traditional approaches for interviewing children in developmental and forensic psychology, the child is construed not as passive but as active, and the character of the interview as a social and negotiated situation is intensively reflected. Westcott and Littleton (2005) underline that one has to see the potential of the interview and its limitations as depending on the implicit contract between researcher and child: is there an experimental contract or a didactic contract? Or, more desirable, following the new social studies of childhood approach, is there an explicit and reflexive contract which tries to acknowledge the co-construction of meaning between interviewer and child? This reflexivity is also needed because one has to be aware of the different frames that interviews can activate in the minds of children. One has to avoid such frames, which can distort the process, for example the frame of 'school'. Children then think they have to give 'adequate answers'. Another aspect of the interview relationship is the balance of power between the adult interviewer and the child. One approach to this problem is not to interview children alone, but in pairs or groups, so that the collective position of children empowers them in this situation.

As in ethnographic research (see below), qualitative interviews have to cope with the problem of child–adult roles in the interview setting (Mandell, 1988). As in the discussion of surveys, the framing of questions and the appreciation of children's competencies is hampered by the ambivalence of trying to empower the children and see them as competent interviewees, on the one hand, and the need to find some age-specific resources, on the other hand. This dilemma can be partially solved by mixing 'ordinary methods' which are also used with adults and special, child-centred methods (Hill, Laybourn and Borland, 1996).

Turning to the material fields of the application of interviews, the new objects of sociological childhood research and areas of interest are children's world views and perspectives, and there exists a rich array of topics from the perspective of children. The wide spectrum of issues can be seen in the following topics, which are only examples and are not exhaustive: *family, family relationships* (Rigg and Pryor, 2007); *divorce* (Zartler, Wilk and Kränzl-Nagl, 2004); *credentials/school report* (Beutel, 2005); *everyday life in day care* (Roux, 2002); *poverty* (Ridge, 2007); *quality of children's television* (Plenk, 2005); *methods used in research and consultation* (Hill, 2006); and *home ventilation* (Earle et al., 2006). It is obvious that the topics are becoming more and more specific and sophisticated. These studies should not be interpreted solely in terms of the differences between children, youths and adults concerning the issues mentioned. They are valuable in showing how children experience and interpret important segments of their lifeworld and their environment. As a result, it is the aim of several studies to evaluate political measures against the yardstick of children's preferences and understanding, and they can be used in the training of teachers and other professionals who care for children. One can see the emergence of the idea that children should have a voice in decision making at all levels. Research methods, then, are one important means of implementing this agenda (cf. the contributions in Hallett and Prout, 2003). In the domain of research on divorce and new family forms, this empowering use of new research methods helps to correct an old-fashioned view of children as 'victims' who are not able to cope with new situations and constellations.

Glimpses into the modernization of children's lives and into unequal childhoods

Qualitative interviews with children have been widely used in research into children's life conduct under conditions of modernity or postmodernity in Germany (Büchner et al., 1994; Zeiher and Zeiher, 1994). The intention behind these projects is to uncover the mechanisms by which individualization, pluralization and the blurring of boundaries between social systems (Jurczyk and Lange, 2007) unfold into the lifeworlds of children. Children in their middle childhood were asked about their everyday-life activities, their family lives, their aspirations and so on. By comparing children's answers and sorting them into different theoretically derived dimensions, various typologies of the 'modern child' were developed. Another variant of research, the setting and interpretation of interview data, was developed by Zeiher and Zeiher (1994), and Kirchhöfer (1998) applied these methods to document the effects of the German reunification on children's morning rituals. These researchers went into the details of the children's enacting agency in the microstructures of their everyday lives and developed elements for a theory of the children's decision making: in which situations are children self-determined; in which situations do they behave habitually; and in which situations are they influenced by the structures of institutions? An exciting new question for future research which has to be explored methodologically and sensitively concerns different forms of agency. Analytically, two variants of agency can be differentiated (Laurendeau and Shahara, 2008): forms of reproductive agency, on the one hand, and those of resistant agency, on the other hand, which have the power to partially transform the generational order. Both forms have to be analysed in the settings in which children and grownups are negotiating the status and the rights of being a child. Beside the general trends of modernization, interviews are useful tools to explore the facets of unequal childhoods – inequalities generated by ethnic background and social class (Lareau, 2003).

Reconstructing children's biographies

A new and exciting strand of qualitative interview concerns children's construction of their biographies. Whereas developmental psychologists are concerned with the deficiencies of children's accounts of their life history, sociologists, such as Behnken and Zinnecker (1998), credit modern children with the necessary competencies and reflexivity for constructing them. Differential perspectives and approaches, as suggested by Ecarius (1999), try to disentangle the factors that are responsible for the 'autobiographical competencies' of children. In this vein, it seems that reflexivity and modernity are the main generators of children's autobiographical narrations, whereas tradition and living in rural areas hamper the development of a modern form of presenting one's identity.

Focus groups

More and more attention is now given to interviews with more than one child as a promising tool – the so-called focus group methodology (Lamnek, 2005). There are reasons why focus groups are especially suitable for use with children. They create a safe peer environment and are similar to the types of setting that children are familiar with from their schools. Another factor is that the provision of peer support can soften the power imbalance between adult and child that exists in one-to-one interviews. Children may also be encouraged to give their opinions when they hear others and their memories may be triggered by the contributions of the other children (Kölbl and Billmann-Mahecha, 2005).

A very important feature of group discussions is their potential to give a detailed picture of the role of peers and social institutions in the production of the social world of the child and in this way to de-individualize childhood. One main modus of the process of peer self-socialization – the ritual – has been researched via focus groups by Wulf et al. (2004) and Tervooren (2006) to discover the mechanism of the transition from childhood to youth. As an example of this form of ritual, eight girls aged between 11 and 13 are depicted who manage their initiation into adolescence through initiation into a clique. The children are simultaneously those initiated and those initiating. Through admission into and advancement within the clique, the children are able to negotiate and practise an adolescent habitus.

Observations: from content to meaning, agency and performativity

A growing use in the sociology of childhood can be attested for observational methods. Some of the most innovative empirical insights into the lifeworlds of children have been produced in this way, especially by participant observations. It seems reasonable that in gathering detailed information about the physical environment, activities, social partners and roles that are available to children, combined with information about key adults and peers, processes of social construction, children's agency and children's perspective become visible (Kelle, 2001). An important advantage of observational methods is that researchers are examining experiences and actions as they are unfolding over time, and not, as in interviews, as retrospective accounts of what has happened. One main problem of this approach is the role that the adult researcher plays: the sheer physical presence of the adult researcher can be an obstacle to entering children's cultures. One 'solution' was found by Mandell (1991), by performing what she calls the 'least adult role'. She tried by various means to minimize the significant differences between herself and her research subjects. For instance, she refused to do 'teacherly' things, which also implied ignoring requests from children for help and social support.

These examples of observation studies also show one facet of a special research task when working with children – the handling of ethical dilemmas and responsibilities. Researchers constantly reflect on the appropriateness of their social construction of the children in the concrete research situation and they have to decide whether to give their information to teachers or parents in cases of emergency (Christensen and Prout, 2002). On this subject, it has to be mentioned that the current climate of concern about child abuse and paedophilia in western societies is very problematic while trying to construct confidential relationships among children and the childhood researchers (Pole, 2007).

Corsaro and Molinari (2000) took a different stance towards this and used their 'master statuses' as adults as a key to immerse themselves within the children's cultures. Molinari, as an Italian, was the key to gaining access to an Italian preschool for Corsaro to observe. Corsaro drew on his foreignness, his explicit distinctiveness from children, as a means of entering their social worlds. In this case, working with groups of Italian children, this meant Corsaro's nationality as an American as well as his adult status. The children would introduce him to their norms, routines and language games as an 'incompetent adult'. Children's familiarity with their preschool or school can accentuate the researcher's strangeness.

Mandell (1991) and other researchers who used participant observation methods (Thorne, 1993) report difficulties which are generated by the differences in the interpretation of the physical aspects of children's interactions and especially their play; there is always an ambivalence between the need to allow children to express themselves through their own actions and the demands of the 'social order'. Thus, children have, for instance, another view on bullying or harming someone, and adults tend to intervene in seemingly chaotic interaction chains in the best interest of the child, but perhaps not in the best interest of valid childhood research.

For the purpose of reconstructing the details of the microsociological unfolding of the interplay of structure and agency, the new technical devices of video-analysis and recording of observations should also be mentioned. The researcher is able to repeat intersecting sequences of action so that parallel interaction strands among children in the school or the playground, for example, can be analytically separated (see Evaldsson, this volume). Another important advantage is that these techniques of recording are able to document more than texts, including bodily movements, mimicry and so on. In this way they shed new light on children's sociality, especially in their peer worlds (Wagner-Willi, 2007). They also open up new theoretical vistas for the sociology of childhood.

Approaches to the performativity and iconicity of social life (Maar and Burda, 2004) have been especially productive in recent years. Informed by the sociology of Goffman and theatre sciences (Fischer-Lichte, 2004), the social life of children is seen and modelled as a theatrical performance, with a special emphasis on the body as the basis of identity and conduct and looking at the power of images in opposition to the reduced perspective of discourse.

The merits of these new perspectives are shown in the field of gender roles by Tervooren (2006). She has researched the complex process of sex role identification at the end of childhood and used observations of the interactions between boys and girls in schools. She refers to the conceptual tool of 'doing gender', and develops this further by looking at the resources and restrictions which can be utilized by the boys and girls in performing their sexual identities. From her carefully designed observations she is able to demonstrate that the accomplishment of gender roles is not reached by imitating rigid sex role scripts, but by a complex production of mimetic and bodily grounded actions and performances (see Fingerson, this volume). In middle childhood, children 'test out' the sex roles by transgressing them, probing the physical and emotional codes of being a man or woman. This is done not in individual isolation but within the peer group; it is not done solely in their minds by way of cognition. Gender becomes simply a knowledge structure, which, as a part of children's agency, can be performed and actualized, as a result of combining traditional and new ways of being a boy or a girl. But as Tervooren is also able to demonstrate, there is more scope for girls to experiment with gender roles; boys are more restricted in trying out feminine forms of conduct.

Documentary analysis

Texts and representations of and about children in differing social situations (political, professional and institutional) are researched with conventional content analyses and the new tools of social semiotics and discourse analyses. These analyses are able to demonstrate why the social representations of children in modern societies are often framed in terms of a rhetoric of decay and missing competencies (Best, 1994; Rosier, this volume). The main goal is to deconstruct the ideas, the models and knowledge about children and childhood as social constructions that are embedded in specific historical situations and interests (Davis and Bourhill, 1997; Bühler-Niederberger, 1998, 2005; Kjørholt, 2002).

A further field of content is provided by the reconstruction of the normative context of childhood in child law and political regulations of childhood. The analyses of Therborn (1993, 1996) and Hendrick (1997, 2003) should be mentioned as the most advanced approaches. Therborn analyses the European development in children's rights as a changing of the integration of children in modern civil society (see Ostner, 2007). Hendrick looks from a wider perspective at the political regulation of childhood and especially the regulation of children's welfare, spanning a longer historical time. Using and analysing laws, decrees, parliamentary debates and legitimating processes they reconstruct the social circumstances of changing childhood patterns. In this vein, they can, for instance, also deconstruct otherwise hidden trends towards a normalization of childhood by way of medicalizing it (Kelle, 2007).

These public discourses are linked to the world views of parents and children. As Davies and Machin (2000) have shown, children know about the public opinions concerning television programmes. The article addresses the persistent tendency of this discourse to express socially responsible and public service values in evaluating programmes. This finding is explained both in terms of children's ability to adapt to the requirements of the public consultation task they were taking part in and in terms of their obvious ability to access different kinds of adult discourse available in the culture at large, in particular various representations of childhood expressed in policy and regulatory documents and in literature. Hagen (2007) extends these arguments by showing how the public scripts circulating in the various discourses are utilized in constant negotiations between parents and children about the right approach to the media, the most important topic being the 'right use of time' (see Buckingham, this volume). In this way, discourse analysis is also a key contribution to answering important questions about the positioning of children in the generational order. 'In the negotiations between children and parents, the children positioned themselves as wannabe autonomous actors. Parents used rules and negotiations in the attempts to position themselves as good parents who teach their children values and sensible media use habits. In these negotiations both children and their parents drew upon public discourses or scripts' (Hagen, 2007, 388). Additionally, Aarsand (2007) demonstrates that children and parents can use media rhetorical devices from public discourses as interaction resources in successfully 'doing' family life.

Conclusions

Having reviewed methods and methodologies in childhood research, we want to go back again to the starting point. It was argued that a sociological view of childhood and children bears new objects of research – namely the social and cultural context of childhood, the generational order and the agency of children. Therefore, to gain insight into these social relations, circumstances and processes, traditional methods in child research were challenged from a reflexive methodological position.

Looking back at the methods presented, it is obvious that no completely new methods have come to the fore, with the one exception of the use of video as a new form of observation. Interviews, traditional observations, large-scale data collections and surveys, discourse analysis, content analysis and so on are all instruments which are quite well known, sometimes adapted and modified to children's assumed stage of development (understanding, capability of expression, cognitive competencies), although used also in adult-focused research. As in research which deals with adults, the high standards of the serious social sciences have to be enforced – namely reliability, objectivity, validity, transparency and inter-subjectivity in both quantitative and qualitative approaches.

Nevertheless, in reviewing the whole discussion we can discover some constitutive methodological changes in sociological research on children and childhood. The changed scientific access to the relationship between researcher and the research 'object' in all kinds of methods is remarkable: the data material is collected and interpreted from the perspective of a child or from the perspective of the group of children, and less from the viewpoint of an assumed and desirable outcome of socialization processes. These changes mean, first, that the reflection of our scientific knowledge about children and childhood becomes a starting point and part of the interpretation process – traditional 'near and dear' assumptions about how children and childhood have to be reflected. Second, if traditional knowledge about the object of research has become more uncertain,

then sensitive processes of understanding the 'strangeness' have to be methodologically promoted. Thus, an altogether 'ethnographic attitude' has emerged in
almost all research settings. Third, thinking from the children's perspective also
means children are positioned in the research focus as serious research units and
informants, as was mentioned before.

Due to an emerging 'basic ethnographic attitude', it is interesting to pay more
attention to the above-mentioned iconic and bodily change in childhood sociology. The discovery of the body, gesture and mimicry and, thus, the broader
emergence of (video) observations are shifts in the whole of sociology which challenge the dominance of the linguistic approach. For childhood sociology, this is
of special importance, because language as a symbol of power is one of the strong
conditions of an unequal relationship between children and adults. Thus, the
method of (video) observation can help to minimize the unequal power relationships between researcher and child that result from language differences. The
observation of mimicry and gesture may also open a forward-looking access not
only to children's cultures, but also to the interdependencies and power structures between adults and children.

If the wide range of applied methods in childhood research starts from the
assumption, first, that children are reliable 'clients' and active social persons and,
second, that childhood has a worth in itself as well as being a segment of social
structure, then possible consequences of this kind of research need to be explored.
Better still, assumable consequences such as more visibility of children, a greater
acknowledgement of children's permanent agency or a potentially higher status in society have to be asked for. At the same time, a paradox in childhood
research has to be accepted – on the one hand, the differences between children
and adults were posited as a dilemma for children in the sense of their weak position in society, in economy, in daily power relationships between the child and
the adult. Discovering this by research is seen as part of a crucial deliberating process. On the other hand, by seeing the child more and more as an unknown, as
well as a research unit which has to be addressed in a specific way, the difference
between childhood and adulthood, between children and adults, is permanently
reproduced through childhood research. How to cope with this paradox, with
the consequences of scientific constructions of 'strangeness' and 'otherness' in
research (see Hengst, 2005), is one of the most important questions for further
methodological reflection.

References

Aarsand, P.A. (2007) 'Computer and Video Games in Family Life. the Digital Divide as a
    Resource in Intergenerational Interactions', *Childhood*, 14(2): 235–256.
Alanen, L. and B. Mayall (eds) (2001) *Conceptualizing Child-Adult Relations*. London:
    Routledge.
Alt, Ch. (2004) 'The DJI Panel Study on Childhood: how do children grow up in Germany?',
    in S. Hübner-Funk (ed.) *Research in Progress. Selected Studies of the German Youth Institute*.
    München: Deutsche Jugend Institut, pp. 75–85.

Behnken, I. and J. Zinnecker (1998) 'Kindheit und Biographie', in R. Bohnsack and W. Marotzki (eds) *Biographieforschung und Kulturanalyse. Transdisziplinäre Zugänge qualitativer Forschung.* Opladen: Leske + Budrich, pp. 152–166.

Ben-Arieh, A. (2005) 'Measuring and Monitoring Children's Well-Being: The Role of Children', in Ch. Klöckner and U. Paetzel (ed.) *Kindheitsforschung und kommunale Praxis.* Wiesbaden: VS-Verlag, pp. 57–76.

Ben-Arieh, A. et al. (2001) *Measuring, and Monitoring Children's Well-Being.* Dordrecht: Springer Netherlands.

Ben-Arieh, A. and I. Frønes (2007) 'Indicators of Children's Well-Being: Theory, Types and Usage', *Social Indicators Research*, 83(1): 1–4.

Best, J. (ed.) (1994) *Troubling Children. Studies of Children and Social Problems.* New York: Aldine de Gruyter, pp. 3–19.

Beutel, S.-I. (2005) *Zeugnisse aus Kindersicht. Kommunikationskultur an der Schule und Professionalisierung der Leistungsbeurteilung.* Weinheim, München: Juventa.

Bradshaw, J. (2007) 'Some Problems in the International Comparisons of Child Income Poverty', in H. Wintersberger et al. (eds) *Childhood, Generational Order and the Welfare State: Exploring Children's Social and Economic Welfare.* Odense: University Press of Southern Denmark, pp. 93–107.

Büchner, P., M. du Bois-Reymond, J. Ecarius, B. Fuhs and H.-H. Krüger (1994) *Kinderleben. Modernisierung von Kindheit im interkulturellen Vergleich.* Opladen: Leske + Budrich.

Bühler-Niederberger, D. (1998) 'The Separative View. Is there any Scientific Approach to Children', in D.K. Behera (ed.) *Children and Childhood in our Contemporary Societies.* Delhi: Kamla-Raj Enterprises, pp. 51–66.

Bühler-Niederberger, D. (2005) *Kindheit und die Ordnung der Verhältnisse. Von der gesellschaftlichen Macht der Unschuld und dem kreativen Individuum.* Weinheim, München: Juventa.

Christensen, P. and A. Prout (2002) 'Working with Ethical Symmetry in Social Research with Children', *Childhood*, 9(4): 477–497.

Corsaro, W.A. (1997) *The Sociology of Childhood.* Thousand Oaks: Sage.

Corsaro, W.A. (2003). *We're Friends, Right?: Inside Kids' Culture.* Washington, DC: Joseph Henry Press.

Corsaro, W.A. and L. Molinari (2000) 'Entering and Observing Children's Worlds. A Reflection on a Longitudinal Ethnography of Early Education in Italy', in P. Christensen and A. James (eds) *Research with Children. Perspectives and Practices.* London: Falmer, pp. 179–200.

Davies, M.M. and D. Machin (2000) 'It Helps People Make Their Decisions. Dating Games, Public Service Broadcasting and the Negotiation of Identity in Middle-Childhood', *Childhood*, 7(2): 173–191.

Davis, H. and M. Bourhill (1997) '"Crisis": The Demonization of Children and Young People', in Ph. Scraton (ed.) *Childhood in 'Crisis'?* London: UCLR Press, pp. 28–57.

Deth, J.W. van, S. Abendschön, J. Rathke and M. Vollmar (2007) *Kinder und Politik. Politische Einstellungen von Kindern im ersten Grundschuljahr.* Wiesbaden: VS-Verlag.

Diekmann, A. (2007) *Empirische Sozialforschung. Grundlagen – Methoden – Anwendungen.* Reinbek: Rowohlt.

Earle, R.J., J.E. Rennick, F.A. Carnevale and M. Davis (2006) 'It's Okay, It Helps Me to Breathe: The Experience of Home Ventilation from a Child's Perspective', *Journal of Child Health Care*, 10(4): 270–282.

Ecarius, J. (1999) '"Kinder ernst nehmen". Methodologische Überlegungen zur Aussagekraft biographischer Reflexionen 12-jähriger', in M.-S. Honig, A. Lange and H.-R. Leu (eds) *Aus der Perspektive von Kindern? Zur Methodologie der Kindheitsforschung.* Weinheim, München: Juventa, pp. 133–152.

Fischer-Lichte, E. (2004) *Ästhetik des Performativen.* Frankfurt a.M.: Suhrkamp.

Flick, U. (2007) *Qualitative Sozialforschung.* Reinbek: Rowohlt.

Fuchs, M. (2004) 'Kinder und Jugendliche als Befragte. Feldexperimente zum Antwortverhalten Minderjähriger', *ZUMA-Nachrichten*, 28(54): 60–88.

Hagen, I. (2007) 'We Can't Just Sit the Whole Day Watching Tv. Negotiations Concerning Media Use among Youngsters and Their Parents', *Young*, 15(4): 369–393.

Hallett, Ch. and A. Prout (eds) (2003) *Hearing the Voices of Children. Social Policy for a New Century*. London: Routledge.

Hasselhorn, M. and W. Schneider (2007) 'Gedächtnisentwicklung', in M. Hasselhorn and W. Schneider (eds) *Handbuch der Entwicklungspsychologie*. Göttingen: Hogrefe, pp. 266–276.

Haunberger, S. (2007) 'Wenn Kinder antworten: Erfahrungen mit der standardisierten Befragung', in Ch. Alt (ed.) *Kinderleben – Start in die Grundschule*, Band 3: Ergebnisse aus der zweiten Welle. Wiesbaden: VS-Verlag, pp. 325–344.

Heaphy, B. (2007) *Late Modernity and Social Change. Reconstructing Social and Personal Life*. New York: Routledge.

Heinzel, F. (ed.) (2000) *Methoden der Kindheitsforschung. Ein Überblick über Forschungszugänge zur kindlichen Perspektive*. Weinheim, München: Juventa.

Hendrick, H. (1997) *Children, Childhood and English Society 1880–1990*. Cambridge: University Press.

Hendrick, H. (2003) *Child Welfare. Historical Dimensions, Contemporary Debate*. Bristol: Policy Press.

Hengst, H. (2005) 'Kindheitsforschung, sozialer Wandel, Zeitgenossenschaft', in H. Hengst and H. Zeiher (eds) *Kindheit soziologisch*. Wiesbaden: VS-Verlag, pp. 245–265.

Hill, M. (2006) 'Children's Voices on Ways of Having a Voice: Children's and Young People's Perspectives on Methods Used in Research and Consultation', *Childhood*, 13(1): 69–89.

Hill, M., A. Laybourn and M. Borland (1996) 'Engaging with Primary-Aged Children about Their Emotions and Well-Being: Methodological Considerations', *Children and Society*, 10(2): 129–144.

Honig, M.-S. (1999) *Entwurf einer Theorie der Kindheit*. Frankfurt a.M.: Suhrkamp.

James, A. and A.L. James (2004) *Constructing Childhood. Theory, Policy and Social Practice*. Basingstoke: Palgrave Macmillan.

Jensen, A.-M. et al. (2004) *Children's Welfare in Ageing Europe*. Vol. I and II. Trondheim: Norwegian Centre for Child Research.

Jordan, A.B., N. Trentacoste, V. Henderson, J. Manganello and M. Fishbein (2007) 'Measuring the Time Teens Spend with Media: Challenges and Opportunities', *Media Psychology*, 9(1): 19–41.

Jurczyk, K. and A. Lange (2007) 'Blurring Boundaries of Family and Work – Challenges for Children', in H. Zeiher, D. Devine, A.T. Kjørholt and H. Strandell (eds) *Flexible Childhood? Exploring Children's Welfare in Time and Space*. Odense: University Press of Southern Denmark, pp. 215–238.

Kelle, H. (2001) 'The Discourse of "Development". How 9 to 12-Year-Old School Children construct "Childish" and "Further Developed" Identities within their Peer Culture', *Childhood*, 8(1): 95–114.

Kelle, H. (2007) 'Ganz normal: Die Repräsentation von Kinderkorpernormen in Somatogrammen. Eine praxisanalytische Exploration kinderärztlicher Vorsorgeinstrumente', *Zeitschrift für Soziologie*, 36(3): 197–216.

Kirchhöfer, D. (1998) *Aufwachsen in Ostdeutschland. Langzeitstudie über Tagesläufe 10 bis 14-jähriger Kinder*. Weinheim, München: Juventa.

Kjørholt, A.T. (2002) 'Small Is Powerful. Discourses on "Children and Participation" in Norway', *Childhood*, 9(1): 63–82.

Kölbl, C. and E. Billmann-Mahecha (2005) 'Die Gruppendiskussion. Schattendasein einer Methode und Plädoyer für ihre Entdeckung in der Entwicklungspsychologie', in G. Mey (ed.) *Handbuch Qualitative Entwicklungspsychologie*. Köln: Kölner Studienverlag, pp. 321–350.

Kränzl-Nagl, R. and J. Mierendorff (2007) 'Kindheit im Wandel – Annäherung an ein komplexes Phänomen', *SWS-Rundschau*, 47(1): 5–28.

Lamnek, S. (2005) *Gruppendiskussion. Theorie und Praxis*. Stuttgart: UTB.

Lareau, A. (2003) *Unequal Childhoods: Class, Race, and Family Life*. Berkeley: University of California Press.

Laurendeau, J. and N. Shahara (2008) ' "Women Could Be Every Bit As Good As Guys". Reproductive and Resistant Agency in Two "Action" Sports', *Journal of Sport & Social Issues*, 32(1): 24–47.

Maar, Ch. and H. Burda (eds) (2004) *Iconic Turn. Die neue Macht der Bilder*. Köln: Dumont.

Mandell, N. (1988) 'The Least-Adult Role in Studying Children', *Journal of Contemporary Ethnography*, 16(4): 433–467.

Mandell, N. (1991) 'The Least-Adult Role in Studying Children', in F.C. Waksler (ed.) *Studying the Social Worlds of Children, Sociological Readings*. London: Falmer Press, pp. 38–59.

Matthews, S.H. (2007) 'A Window on the "New" Sociology of Childhood', *Sociology Compass*, vol. 1, online version.

Mayall, B. and H. Zeiher (eds) (2003) *Childhood in Generational Perspective*. London: Institute of Education.

Mey, G. (2003) *Zugänge zur kindlichen Perspektive. Methoden der Kindheitsforschung*. Forschungsbericht aus der Abteilung Psychologie im Institut für Sozialwissenschaften der Technischen Universität Berlin, Vol. 2003–1.

Mey, G. (ed.) (2005) *Handbuch Qualitative Entwicklungspsychologie*. Köln: Kölner Studien Verlag.

Ostner, I. (2007) 'Whose Children? Families and Children in "Activating" Welfare State', in H. Wintersberger et al. (eds) *Childhood, Generational Order and the Welfare State: Exploring Children's Social and Economic Welfare*. Odense: University Press of Southern Denmark, pp. 45–57.

Plenk, A. (2005) 'Die Perspektive der Kinder auf Qualität für Film und Fernsehen', *Televizion*, 18(2): 60–64.

Pole, Ch. (2007) 'Researching Children and Fashion: An Embodied Ethnography', *Childhood*, 14(1): 67–84.

Prout, A. (2005) *The Future of Childhood*. London: Falmer.

Qvortrup, J. (1990) 'A Voice for Children in Statistical and Social Accounting: A Plea for Children's Right to Be Heard', in A. James and A. Prout (eds) *Constructing and Reconstructing Childhood: Contemporary Issues in the Sociological Study of Childhood*. London: Falmer Press, pp. 78–98.

Qvortrup, J. (2000) 'Macroanalysis of Childhood', in P. Christensen and A. James (eds) *Research with Children: Perspectives and Practices*. London: Falmer Press, pp. 77–97.

Qvortrup, J., M. Bardy, G.B. Sgritta and H. Wintersberger (eds) (1994) *Childhood Matters. Social Theory, Practice and Politics*. Aldershot: Avebury.

Ridge, T. (2007) 'Negotiating Childhood Poverty: Children's Subjective Experiences of Life on a Low Income', in H. Wintersberger et al. (eds) *Childhood, Generational Order and the Welfare State. Exploring Children's Social and Economic Welfare*. Odense: University Press of South Denmark, pp. 161–187.

Rigg, A. and J. Pryor (2007) 'Children's Perceptions of Families: What Do They Really Think?' *Children and Society*, 21(1): 17–30.

Roux, S. (2002) *Wie sehen Kinder ihren Kindergarten. Theoretische und empirische Befunde zur Qualität von Kindertagesstätten*. Weinheim, München: Juventa.

Saporiti, A. (1994) 'A Methodology for Making Children Count', in J. Qvortrup, M. Bardy, G.B. Sgritta and H. Wintersberger (eds) *Childhood Matters. Social Theory, Practice and Politics*. Aldershot: Avebury, pp. 189–210.

Schweizer, H. (2007) *Soziologie der Kindheit. Verletzlicher Eigensinn*. Wiesbaden: VS- Verlag.

Smith, L. (2007) 'Norms in Human Development: Introduction', in L. Smith and J. Voneche (eds) *Norms in Human Development*. Cambridge: Cambridge University Press, pp. 1–30.

Solberg, A. (1996) 'The Challenge in Child Research: from "Being" to "Doing"', in J. Brannen and M. O'Brien (eds) *Children in Families. Research and Policy*. London: Falmer Press, pp. 53–65.

Tervooren, A. (2006) *Im Spielraum von Geschlecht und Begehren. Ethnographie der ausgehenden Kindheit.* Weinheim, München: Juventa.

Therborn, G. (1993) 'Children's Rights since the Constitution of Modern Childhood. A Comparative Study of Western Nations', in J. Qvortrup (ed.) *Childhood as a Social Phenomenon: Lessons from an International Project.* Eurosocial Report 47, Vienna: European Centre, pp. 105–138.

Therborn, G. (1996) 'Child Politics: Dimensions and Perspectives', in E. Verhellen (ed.) *Monitoring Children's Rights.* The Hague, Boston, London: Martinus Nijhoff, pp. 377–391.

Thorne, B. (1993) *Gender Play: Girls and Boys in School.* New Brunswick, NJ: Rutgers University Press.

Wagner-Willi, M. (2007) 'Videoanalysen des Schulalltags. Die dokumentarische Interpretation schulischer Übergangsrituale', in R. Bohnsack et al. (eds) *Die dokumentarische Methode und ihre Forschungspraxis. Grundlagen qualitativer Forschungspraxis.* Wiesbaden: VS-Verlag, pp. 125–145.

Waksler, F.C. (1991) 'Beyond Socialization', in F.C. Waksler (ed.) *Studying the Social Worlds of Children: Sociological Readings.* Bristol PA: Falmer Press, pp. 12–22.

Westcott, H.L. and K.S. Littleton (2005) 'Exploring Meaning in Interviews with Children', in S. Greene and D. Hogan (eds) *Researching Children's Experience. Approaches and Methods.* London: Sage, pp. 141–157.

Wulf, Ch. et al. (2004) *Penser les pratiques sociales comme rituels. Ethnographie et genèse de communautés.* Paris: L'Harmattan.

Wyness, M. (2006) *Childhood and Society. An introduction to the Sociology of Childhood.* Houndsmills: Palgrave.

Zartler, U., L. Wilk and R. Kränzl-Nagl (eds) (2004) *Wenn Eltern sich trennen. Wie Kinder, Frauen und Männer Scheidung erleben.* Frankfurt a.M.: Campus.

Zeiher, H. and H. Zeiher (1994) *Orte und Zeiten der Kinder. Soziales Leben im Alltag von Großstadtkindern.* Weinheim, München: Juventa.

Section II

Historical and Socio-Economic Contexts of Childhood

6

The Evolution of Childhood in Western Europe *c.*1400–*c.*1750

Harry Hendrick

Prologue

First, a word of caution. The history of childhood and children tends to be written from the adult perspective – this distinguishes it from other schools of historical writing and, therefore, from other interpretative paradigms. The disparity lies in the disassociation between historian and subject. The privileged status of adulthood is obvious if we consider the processes involved in selecting, assembling and assessing sources. Our cultural omnipotence – our powers, prejudices, ambitions, anxieties and memories – ensures that at almost every juncture there exists among us a commonality of outlook, which usually governs or at least influences our perception of childhood as an 'idea' and of children as individual persons. Many historians, who defer to class, ethnicity, gender, and gay and lesbian culture, seem to have rather less empathy with children. Indeed, throughout the myriad of discourses by which the history of social life is established, known and experienced, children are frequently excluded from being 'present' as persons with standpoints – their distance from us, established as it is through *difference*, turns them into 'liminal' figures, representations of the 'limit condition' of humanity (Kennedy, 2006, 7) – they are the 'absent referent', the archetypal 'Other'.

It is also important to appreciate the distinction between a *concept* of childhood, which can mean that all societies have an understanding of children as *different* from adults 'in respect of some unspecified set of attributes', and a *conception* of childhood, which is 'a specification of those attributes' (Archard, 1993, 21–22). Furthermore, since 'childhood' (and 'adulthood') – conceptually and experientially – has been subject to historical transfiguration through varying biological, legal, educational, religious, social and political ascriptions (Kennedy, 2006, 5–13), we have to be careful about using the term with respect to the vast contextual landscape that is late medieval and early modern Western Europe. This may seem to be only a matter of linguistic clarity and yet to speak of 'childhood' during the period is to risk describing a condition which, as is shown below, in its dissimilarity from modernity, loses explicatory value, providing no more than an illusion of continuity.

Controversial issues in the historiography of the family

Ariès and the medievalists

Since Philippe Ariès' *Centuries of Childhood* (1962), although heavily criticized, remains such a generative text, we should be clear as to his claims. His most controversial assertion portrayed the medieval period as being without a *sentiment* of childhood (the French word, usually translated as 'idea', is not quite the same): there was no 'awareness of the particular nature of childhood'; once children left infancy (5 to 7), they began to be integrated into the social relationships and tasks governing society (but without sharing the same status as adults). Ariès' underlying theme, which had been anticipated by Norbert Elias in *The History of Manners: The Civilising Process* (1939, 1978), was that between the fifteenth and early eighteenth century, 'childhood' became separated off from 'adulthood' (an identity that was itself being refined). For Elias (and Ariès), 'The distance in behaviour and whole psychological structure between children and adults increases in the course of the civilizing process' – a process that involved controlling the instincts, which had barely begun before the end of the Middle Ages (quotation in Cunningham, 2005, 4).

In a crucial development, which was his second claim, around the seventeenth century, moralists began promoting a view of children as having been hitherto neglected but whose 'innocence and weakness' (and potential for evil) were now in need of protection, education and discipline. These needs necessitated that schools be confined to children (rather than pupils of all ages, as in the past), who found themselves subject to physical and emotional oppression. Thus children were segregated from adults, and 'childhood' became fixed as a preparatory stage in the life course. Third, from the late seventeenth century, as the family became increasingly privatized through a decline in its sociability, and parents began to regard their children as sweet, simple, 'coddlesome' creatures, so attention was obsessively focused on their physical, moral, religious and sexual welfare, which also served to emphasize discipline and to further 'quarantine' them from the public world.

Much of the criticism of Ariès came from medievalists (and early modernists), who argued not only for a 'particular nature' of childhood, but also that children were often treated with greater sensitivity than in later centuries (Pollock, 1983; Hanawalt, 1986, 1993; Shahar, 1990; Orme, 2001). Nicholas Orme insists that 'Medieval people...had a concept of what childhood was, and when it began and ended. The arrival of children in the world was a notable event, and their upbringing and education was taken seriously' (Orme, 2001, 5). And he continues: 'it cannot be overemphasized that there is nothing to be said for Ariès' view of childhood in the Middle Ages, nor indeed of a major shift in its history during the sixteenth and seventeenth centuries, as opposed to changes of detail' (Orme, 2001, 9). As evidence of a medieval awareness of 'children', critics often cite the contemporary view of life as progressing through 'stages': 'the ages of man', which categorized young people as *infantia* (birth to 7), *pueritia* (7 to 12/14, depending on gender) and *adolescentia* (12/14 to 21) (Shahar, 1990,

21–3; 1Heywood, 2001, 14). This is said to be proof that childhood was conceptualized in the writings of scholars, poets, priests and lawyers (Orme, 2001, 7). It is true that in several spheres of rights and duties, children were often distinguished from adults (Orme, 2001, 7–9). But in the popular imagination (if not that of the intellectual elite), this could easily be referring to *social roles* rather than to a societal *concept*. The latter implies more than mere 'difference' for it looks to a 'general notion' or an 'abstract idea' (*OED*) – of the kind found during the early modern centuries onwards owing to the consciousness-changing influences of the Renaissance, the Scientific Revolution, religious reformations and the Enlightenment.

The 'dark legend' view: deMause, Shorter and Stone

The 1970s saw the publication of a trio of influential studies (deMause, 1976; Shorter, 1976; Stone, 1977) which, although critical of Ariès, shared his view that the period had witnessed significant conceptual and attitudinal changes regarding childhood, resulting in new forms of conduct. deMause, a psycho-historian, advocated a 'psychogenic' theory of historical change where the evolution of parental relationships is seen as a motor force of history, rather than, say, technology or economics. Over the centuries, parents are said to have become more liberal and sensitive as they progressed through a number of child-rearing modes: infanticidal, abandonment, ambivalence, intrusion, socialization and, currently, 'helping' – characterized by empathy. deMause famously (infamously) asserted: 'The further back in history one goes, the lower the level of child care, and the more likely children are to be killed, abandoned, beaten, terrorized, and sexually abused' (deMause, 1976, 1). This was a direct contradiction of Ariès' central claim that (in deMause's words) 'the traditional child was happy because he was free to mix with many classes and ages' but that once 'childhood' was invented, the result was 'a tyrannical concept of the family which...deprived children of freedom, inflicting upon them for the first time the birch rod and the prison cell' (deMause, 1976, 5).

While deMause addressed himself directly to the parent–child relationship, Shorter had comparatively little to say about children in the creation of the modern family, confining his remarks to a discussion of changes in how mothers (mainly French) treated their babies. In his provocative words, 'Good mothering is an invention of modernization.' In earlier times, mothers regarded infants with a certain indifference, whereas in 'modern society, they place the welfare of their children above all else' (Shorter, 1976, 168). There was, in what he identified as a seminal historical shift, 'a surge of sentiment' among the French middle class in the eighteenth century, which owed much to the displacement of a traditional 'moral economy' by market capitalism, accompanied by a growth in individualism and competition. This more developed sentiment, he says, can be seen in the rise of maternal breastfeeding (as opposed to wet-nursing) and the decline of swaddling, both of which led to greater intimacy between mother and child. In time, 'good mothering' filtered downwards through the social classes, and so the 'modern' family was born.

The third pioneering text was Stone's study of the English family. In contrast to Shorter, Stone agreed with Ariès that the significant filial changes occurred during the early modern period, which he divided into three overlapping stages of development: the 'open lineage family', 1450–1630; the 'restricted patriarchal family', 1550–1700; and the 'closed domesticated nuclear family', 1640–1800. Stone made the parent–child relationship pivotal to the evolution of consanguinity, arguing that *c.* 1500–1800 relations between upper-class parents and their children progressed from being 'usually fairly remote' (1450–1630), through the authoritarian and physically punitive second stage (1550–1700), to the 'child-oriented family type' (1640–1800). Emphasizing ideas and culture rather than economic modes of production, Stone saw the gradual shift in family affinities as being caused by changes in political, religious and philosophical thought, together with the 'rise of affective individualism' as a new self-confident middle class began to usurp the position of the aristocracy. But he was emphatic that no clear, linear pathway could be discerned in either family form or parent–child relations, instead there was a continuing series of competing and conflicting ideas and vested interests.

The 'white legend' critique

Each of these authors (including Ariès), collectively known as the *sentiments* school for their focus on emotions and attachments, provoked a furious response as all aspects of their interpretations were subjected to withering criticism from the 'revisionists'. Michael Anderson, a historical sociologist, raised the crucial matter of the role of ideas as 'prime movers of social change', and asked how their actual *impact* on family behaviour was to be established. He warned against overestimating the importance of 'culture' and called for more attention to be given to the 'household economics approach', which emphasizes familial economic conduct (Anderson, 1995).

The best known critic is Linda Pollock, whose *Forgotten Children* (1983) was enthusiastically welcomed by reviewers, the majority of whom were beguiled by its central thesis, namely that parental care is unchanging and is always practised in the best interests of children (see also Macfarlane, 1970; Wrightson, 1982; Houlbrooke, 1984). Drawing upon a sociobiological framework that sees children as being in need of protection, affection and socializing for normal development, which all parents are said to provide, Pollock made extensive use of hundreds of diaries and autobiographies to elucidate what she claimed to be 'the actuality' of children's lives, rather than the *idea* of childhood. When looked at in this way, she argued, *continuity* was the principal characteristic of the parent–child relationship – there was no reason to assume that parental care must vary according to societal change as a whole. She concluded: 'Instead of trying to explain the supposed changes in the parent–child relationship, historians would do well to ponder just why parental care is a variable so curiously resistant to change' (Pollock, 1983, 271). This is precisely the view that is contested not only by the sentiments school but also by numerous other historians of social life.

Although warmly received, there have been several criticisms of Pollock's study: over-extending insights from diaries (Anderson, 1995); reducing the history of childhood to a timeless universality (Graff, 1995); being uncritical with regard to the evolution of the diary as a genre (Dekker, 2000); and assuming that absence of reference to abuse is evidence of non-abuse (Fleck, 1987). Nor was much thought given to children's perspectives. In ignoring their experiences of love, loss, pain and grief, Pollock presented an *adult-centric* interpretation of human emotions. And in claiming that parents usually try to do what is best for their children 'within the context of their culture', she eschewed the historian's obligation to examine the workings of power and authority in a particular historical context and, just as important, the extent to which children were prisoners of their culture (Archard, 2003, 45–47; Hendrick, 2005, 61–63). In effect, she more or less simply 'read off' from adult records protestations of 'love' without endeavouring to discern how they disclosed themselves in domestic intimacies. Put another way, she disregarded 'the connections between language use and the unequal relations of power' (Fairclough, 1989, 1).

The parameters of childhood

Definitions

According to Peter Burke, the cultural historian, between '1500 and 1800, the major economic, social and political changes...had their consequences for culture...', which he defines as 'a system of shared meanings, attitudes and values, and the symbolic forms...in which they are expressed or embodied' (Burke, 1978, 244). There are two reasons why this is a good place to begin our consideration of the parameters of childhood (meaning those features that define the concept and determine its performance). First 'childhood' as an *idea* is embedded in 'culture', and children are participants (with varying degrees of agency) in many if not all of those relationships that are governed through cultural practice. Second, Burke's reference to social change being consequential for culture underlies the approach adopted here, which is that if we are to identify the principal overarching environments of childhood, it is important to be sensitive to the significant political, economic, religious and social developments that occurred during our period, particularly the Reformation and Counter-Reformation, the Renaissance and the rise of Humanism, the Scientific Revolution, the transition from feudalism to capitalism, the emergence of centralized government, the Enlightenment and the early years of Romanticism, evangelical revivalism and industrialization. Through the interplay of these transformations, a capitalistic and gradually urbanizing Europe developed in which nation states slowly became committed to the values of humanism, science, secularism, reason, individualism, and the rule of law. As a result, people's lives changed immeasurably. That there were certain biological continuities: the need for food, shelter, companionship, sex and care of children, is unquestionable, but neither should there be any doubt that these needs and practices were shaped in response to the demands of evolving public and private circumstances.

However, to be more precise about the nature of the 'parameters', we need to distinguish between *cause* and *effect*. Ascribing such status in the realm of social phenomena is notoriously difficult and carries with it the risk of descending into arid semantics. Nevertheless, in identifying the influences governing the multiple meanings and experiences of childhood, it will be helpful to attempt a distinction between 'prime movers' of social change (Anderson, 1995), and 'outcomes' or 'consequences'. Examples of the former include the great historical reconfigurations mentioned above, notably those of religion, politics and economics as well as accompanying changes in attitudes and values. Among the more influential 'outcomes' were wet-nursing, abandonment, physical and emotional well-being, and parental and scholastic approaches to discipline and punishment. Assigning child labour and education, ubiquitous conditions of so many children is, as we shall see, more problematic.

The Enlightenment, science and individualism

Broadly speaking, the decisive shifts in early modern European history can be seen as contributory 'prime movers' in the evolution of childhood as new patterns of thought and behaviour were established, which collectively identified (created) childhood's distinctive characteristics. For instance, the Age of Reason, the Enlightenment and the Scientific Revolution, affected a range of human relationships with animals and nature, and between husbands and wives, masters and servants, clerics and parishioners, monarchs and subjects, and children and adults (Thomas, 1984). The scientific revolution, in posing fundamentally alternative ways of viewing the cosmos, incorporated the concept of childhood into a 'scientific' (rather than a religious) perspective on the meaning of the universe, in part through the philosopher John Locke's secular emphasis in privileging nurture over nature – 'man is made not given' (Porter, 1997, 9; Heywood, 2001, 35–36). Locke (1632–1704) was the seminal voice in arguing against innate original sin in children, in portraying 'child development' as a mental and physical, rather than religious, process, and he impressed upon his readers the necessity of providing children with a rational education which, although allowing for repression of will and deferred gratification, implicitly recognized their particular natures (Ezell, 1983–1984; Cunningham, 2005, 59–62).

But child-centredness as an end in itself never assumed the final objective of Enlightenment (and Humanist) pedagogy; it was always subordinate to the production of the responsible adult: a new kind of 'self', suitable for the later stages of proto-industrialization, the developing nation state and the onset of industrial capitalism. Nonetheless, as Lawrence Stone argues, between 1640 and 1810 there occurred the growth of 'affective individualism', in accord with the emergence of individualism in society, which was expressed as a demand for personal autonomy (Stone, 1975, 150–151). The manifestation of affective relations within what Stone terms 'the closed domesticated nuclear family' (among the upper elite), made marriage more companionable, liberalized relations between husbands and wives, and gave rise to the 'Child-oriented, Affectionate and Permissive Mode' of child-rearing among the professional classes, the gentry and later the nobility (Stone, 1975, 149–180, 254–299).

Religion (early education and child rearing)

Desiderius Erasmus, the theologian, expressed the common view of Renaissance Humanism that children be regarded as investments in maintaining the cohesion of the state (and the family) and, therefore, were in need of academic and moral tutoring (from fathers) to mould their natures, especially in their early years, the neglect of which he regarded as more important than infanticide. In emphasizing and linking both the futurity of childhood and the social and political significance of early education, Erasmus influentially prefigured two of the defining features of childhood which, with the coming of the Reformation, were shared by Protestant (and Roman Catholic) moralists and educationalists, and became pivotal to the idea of the Christian family (Gavitt, 1991; Cunningham, 2005, 42–58).

One particularly important impact of radical religious change was the spread of formal learning so as to extend literacy for Bible reading, to train the clergy and as a means through which moral and legal codes could be promulgated (Stone, 1964). But the sixteenth-century Lutheran Reformation did more than popularize academic knowledge; it sought to intensify the intimate relationship between family and state and, 'through the spiritualization of the household' (Hill, 1964), to integrate itself into the domestic psyche. During the 500 years when the Catholic Church was dominant, baptism freed the child from the burden of original sin. With the Protestant Reformation came a new and sterner faith, one that took childhood seriously as it promoted a spiritual education, advising that 'children learn to die' (Quoted in Houlbrooke, 1984, 149), be made aware of their sins, and be instructed in a life dedicated to the pursuit of redemption (Fletcher, 1994; Ozment, 1983). We can only speculate as to the manner whereby the obsession with death as a hallmark of religious instruction affected children's psychological universe (Avery and Reynolds, 2000).

The reformation also influenced the nature of the demand for obedience and submissiveness, which were fundamental features of parental and educational relationships. Relieving children of their sinful souls and compelling them to attend to their school work were convenient excuses for the use of 'the rod' as the implement of correction (which undoubtedly concealed sadistic and sexually abusive impulses). The child's will was to be bent in the direction of Godliness, even if it were to be broken in the process. The ideal child, a contemporary wrote, is 'pious, disciplined, obedient and teachable' (Cunningham, 2005, 47; see also 45–58; Houlbrooke, 1984; Morgan, 1986; Fletcher, 1994). But it would be wrong to think that a single form of parental discipline was universal. In his study of child-rearing in early America, Philip Greven identified three modes: 'evangelical', 'moderate' and 'genteel', and it is probable that similar distinctions, often related to social position, were to be found in Europe (Greven, 1977).

Several historians present physically oppressive discipline in a manner sympathetic to parents. Caning, apparently, was 'a last resort' and it seems that many parents found corporal punishment 'a distasteful task' (Pollock, 1983, 143–202; Houlbrooke, 1984, 141). The complaints of moralists that parents were too lenient and ignored the strict prescriptive advice on beating are also summoned as evidence of parental love and affection (Fletcher, 1994; Cunningham, 2005). In similar vein, punitive child-rearing in sixteenth-century Germany has been described as *rational* in seeking to produce 'social beings' to build a socially cohesive society (Ozment, 1983, 132–177). And violence does indeed often have its own political logic. Clearly, in a period marked by religious and political turbulence, child upbringing had several different objectives from those of later centuries (Collinson, 1988; Fletcher, 1994). In reaching this conclusion, however, we should remember that these discussions utterly ignore the feelings of the children concerned.

Poverty and its consequences: abandonment, infanticide and wet nursing

The risk of death, as an outcome of poverty, by accident, neglect, malnutrition or, indirectly for babies through maternal ill-health, has always been a determinant of childhood. Infant mortality reached record levels during the period with perhaps as many as a quarter of infants dying within their first year (Cunningham, 2005, 91). Accidental deaths from drowning and fire were frequent occurrences (Hanawalt, 1986, 1993). Death also figured prominently in respect of the outcomes of abandonment, infanticide and wet-nursing. Understanding these practices, however, not only means seeing poverty as pervasive, especially in rural areas, but also appreciating that in one way or another this exacerbated circumstances whereby large numbers of children were deserted and, in a minority of cases, either 'murdered' by their parents or simply 'allowed' to die.

Abandonment, infanticide and wet-nursing were undoubtedly striking features of the continuity of childhood across the centuries, although parental motives are not always easily discerned and have been subject to considerable debate. We know that abandonment continued well into the nineteenth century with perhaps over 100,000 babies given up every year in Europe, mainly in Catholic countries owing to the large number of foundling hospitals for the protection of illegitimates – to prevent infanticide. In eighteenth-century Paris, 70 to 80 per cent of abandoned infants were illegitimate. Often the custom, which has been described as 'wet-nursing at public expense', was a temporary measure used to alleviate economic hardship and other forms of family distress with parents reclaiming their children after a year or so. But there were also a substantial number of babies who, primarily for reasons of poverty, were permanently deserted. Seen as threats to the social order, these children represented a constant source of anxiety for governments and religious and philanthropic organizations (Boswell, 1988; Shahar, 1990; Kertzer, 1993; Heywood, 2001; Jackson, 2002).

Since the term 'infanticide' covers a broad category of child murder, distinguishing between it and abandonment is a complex matter. Infants may be killed for economic reasons, to preserve a balance between livelihood and demographic growth, to rid the family of a sick or handicapped member or, as in Mediterranean areas, to satisfy an unwed mother's honour. Infanticide had been accepted in the ancient world until after the fourth century when, under influence of Christianity, it come to be seen as both a sin and a crime, so that by the late Middle Ages false accusation was regarded a slander. From the sixteenth century onwards, the practice was increasingly associated with rural illegitimacy, the principal causes being either poverty or popular prejudice against unwed mothers, particularly servants (Hanawalt, 1986, 1993; Shahar, 1990; Kertzer, 1993; Heywood, 2001, 74–77).

In addition to abandonment and infanticide, babies were also at extreme risk from being wet-nursed, usually by country women. In eighteenth-century Hamburg there were between 4000 and 5000 wet nurses in a population of 90,000; and in Paris, of the 21,000 babies born annually, 19,000 were given over to wet nurses (Shahar, 1990, 55). Aside from the probable emotional upset experienced by babies at being separated from their mothers, travelling to and fro, and having to adapt to changes of nurse (Shahar, 1990, 67), the infants were exposed to appallingly high infant mortality rates. At the same time, in urban France the infant morality rate was between 180 and 200 per thousand live births for those maternally fed whereas the figure was from 250 to 400 for those wet-nursed in the countryside. Foundling hospitals, however, had even higher rates (Sussman, 1982, 67; Fildes, 1998; Heywood, 2001, 65). Although wet-nursing was frequently condemned by Enlightenment moralists and physicians who urged mothers to exhibit 'maternal solicitude', in many parts of Europe it remained common among all social classes until well into the nineteenth century.

Several reasons have been advanced for its popularity. Upper-class mothers were said to wish 'to remain smooth and beautiful and sleep the night through'. But these mothers were also probably responding to a cultural perception of 'inferior humans' ('Negroes', the Irish, the poor, the mad, children and adolescents), which portrayed pregnancy as 'breeding' (with non-human animal connotations) and saw 'suckling' as a 'debasing activity' (Thomas, 1984, 43). Fathers were equally enthusiastic since it was believed that sexual intercourse during lactation would spoil the milk and, therefore, wives might be reluctant to satisfy their husband's sexual requests. Among the lower classes and the poor, in freeing mothers for wage labour or in allowing them to provide vital assistance in family run businesses, the wet nurse was a key figure in sustaining a viable household economy. Mothers who for medical reasons were unable to suckle their own children had little or no alternative but to put them out, for until the 'Pasteurian' revolution in the late nineteenth-century wet-nursing offered the safest alternative to maternal milk (Sussman, 1982; Fildes, 1998; Heywood, 2001).

There is some debate as to whether the high infant morality rates blunted parental grief and reduced emotional investment in infants. The 'white legend' account, in stressing parental benevolence across cultures in the face of material and psychic impoverishment (Pollock, 1983; Houlbrooke, 1984; Gavitt, 1990; Kertzer, 1993), tends to oversimplify the inherent ambivalences and ambiguities in child care, especially in poverty stricken environments. An account of motherhood in late Victorian-Edwardian London, drawing on anthropological research, identifies 'selective neglect' of sickly children, and suggests that 'material deprivation may structure mothering and calls into question notions of nurturance, attachment, and bonding as universal or biological' (Ross, 1993, 185; also Dekker, 2000, 127–138).

Child labour

Large numbers of working children were a continuous presence throughout our period, subject to little or no contemporary comment as regards the morality of their employment. Not until the late eighteenth century did child labour begin to receive the attention of reformers who implied the specificity of childhood in writing of the young workers: 'They are CHILDREN', which suggests a conceptual awareness not found in earlier centuries (Quotation in Cunningham, 1991, 64). In important respects, the involvement of children in community toil was a 'consequence' of a timeless unspoken understanding, which viewed their participation as 'natural'. And yet it would also be true to say that the identification of child labour as a feature of the 'natural order' defines it as *causal* in shaping both the perception and experience of childhood. Thus, where 'prime movers' of social change are concerned, it is tempting to see the employment of children as an example of 'circular causation' (leaving aside the theory's tautological shadow). The direct 'consequences', which are much easier to determine, were the mainly detrimental effects of the labour: ill health (and disablement), physical and sexual abuse, lack of schooling and perhaps also an *emotional* disregard by parents for children who had minimal economic value. There is no clear evidence on 'interest and emotion', although nineteenth-century studies suggest that family ties were economically instrumental rather than purely affective (Cunningham, 2005, 103). The extent to which children working within their communities may have derived positive feelings of self-fulfilment from their experience is hard to assess (and, with respect to contemporary child labour, remains controversial).

There was rarely an appointed day at which children formally joined the labour force, rather the entry process was gradual according to their age (which was often difficult to determine), gender, parental circumstances, and the nature of local economies. Except for upper-class children (usually boys) who normally left home from age seven and upwards to become servants in other prosperous families, the majority of young workers were in agriculture, industry (especially clothing) and services, which exerted the principal demands on female and child labour until well into the nineteenth century. Nor should we see the period of employment as being for fixed days and weeks; more likely it was casual and seasonal as children moved almost imperceptibly between domestic tasks, the organized public labour market, a little schooling and playing. In the absence of reliable population censuses, it is impossible to know what percentage of children were *gainfully* employed at what ages; however, the general view is that below the age of 10, the figure was 8 or 9 per cent, and that between 10 and 14 years of age the percentages varied according to industry or occupation (Hanawalt, 1986, 107–123, 156–168; Cunningham, 1991, 50–97; Kirby, 2003; Rahikainen, 2004). But we have to remember that definitions of 'wage labour' and of 'labour' itself are culturally and historically variable. In practice, the reality was probably more fluid than we can account for here, particularly within agricultural and domestic industrial environments, which underwent considerable evolution during the period with the emergence of new technologies and a greater emphasis on capitalistic and international production (Rahikainen, 2004).

There are a number of conclusions to be drawn about working children. First, since the early modern era child labour has been a demand-led rather than a supply-led phenomenon, which increased during the pre-industrial period and accelerated rapidly with industrialization. But the 'demand' was not confined to private employers (and parents in home industries) since, abiding by the belief that the devil finds work for idle hands, throughout Europe orphan and pauper children were put to work in orphanages and Poor Law institutions. Second, while child labour has been more or less compulsory for children, it has been connected to the freedom adults have in choosing their work. Children, it seems got the jobs nobody else wanted. Third, child labour has always stood in relation to the lives of non-working middle- and upper-class children: employed children were 'exploited for the benefit of the social ambitions of masters' children'. Fourth, since child labour was used extensively in the leading industries, which pioneered industrial growth, it appears to have been indispensable for European economic development (Rahikainen, 2004).

Education

Whilst it was not a 'prime mover' in the manner of, say, the Reformation, the long process from the sixteenth century onwards to expand educational provision and, very importantly, to confine schooling to children (overwhelmingly middle and upper-class boys), rather than to pupils of all ages, undoubtedly yielded a new understanding of, and interest in, 'childhood' as a stage in the life course and, therefore, the *original* status of education is better defined as causal rather than consequential (see above re child labour to 'circular causation'). The school formalized a number of adult attitudes (prejudices) to the so-called subculture of children: 'a casual attitude to private property, an addiction to mischief, and a predilection for...noise and dirt' (Thomas, 1989, 57–63). And to counter this 'subculture' obedience, discipline and corporal punishment were the order of the day – the emblem of the schoolmaster was the birch rod, as pupils lived under 'a repressive regime' (Thomas, 1976; Hanawalt, 1983, 84; Orme, 2001).

Prior to the late nineteenth century, 'education', however it is defined in relation to academic learning, tended to be the privilege of those who are economically and socially secure. Locke's treatise, for example, prescribed an essentially moral education for the sons of the gentry and nobility to produce 'vertuous, useful, and able Men in their distinct Callings' (Quoted in Ezell, 1983–1984, 142). Since the 'natural' condition of childhood prioritized 'work', formal education only gradually came to be seen as an essential prerequisite for the journey to adulthood. In rural areas, with their high seasonal demand for child labour, educational opportunities were more restricted than in urban centres and were generally dependent on local and family economies. However, some form of schooling was fairly widespread, although average attendance was usually irregular and rarely lasted for more than three years (Houston, 1988).

Schools (religious and secular), open to all-comers, first began to develop in England in the twelfth century in response to the need for a literate clergy, and although they proliferated during the Reformation, perhaps no more that 12 per cent of the population had ever been pupils (drawn mainly from the urban middle and upper class). At the time, however, the ability to read and write was becoming increasingly necessary for apprentices to the London gilds (Morgan, 1986; Hanawalt, 1993, 82–85; Orme, 2001, 11–42). By the late seventeenth century, aside from the requirements of religion to read the Bible and learn the catechism, schools of all types were under pressure from the demands of nation states for administrative personnel and from a developing commercial capitalism for clerks and bookkeepers. This period, then, marks a shift from a religious dominance to that of industry, commerce and local and national administration. Schooling, as it became more firmly established, not only linked ideas of childhood and the treatment of children to economic and political change, but was also reinforcing the view of childhood as a 'becoming' stage in preparation for adult roles (a condition that was increasingly universalized through compulsory mass education in the later nineteenth century).

Childhood and an emerging sense of 'self'

The subtle and gradual evolution of ideas about childhood that had been in progress from the late Middle Ages continued to the point where there was a 'new world of children in eighteenth-century England' (Plumb, 1975). So it was that *c.* 1750 fresh social, philosophical and psychological speculations abounded, partly under the continuing influences of science and the Enlightenment, but also in three innovative directions: first, Rousseau's revolutionary advocacy in *Emile* (1762) of the child in the man, rather than the man in the child (as it was usually presented), along with the natural goodness of children; second, the omnipotence of Romanticism which, in its protest against the 'Experience of Society', privileged 'childhood' as the *source* of the imagination; and, third, and of shorter duration but with considerable effect at the time, the Evangelical Revival with its pessimistic emphasis on original sin and the need for redemption. One hitherto neglected way of grasping these shifts in perceptions and understandings, which marked a seminal stage in adult–child relations is, in an exploratory manner here, to think of them in terms of a developing psychology of subjectivity – a more intricate sense of the adult 'self' (closely related to the 'new world' of children) – that became so characteristic of nineteenth-century industrial 'modernity'.

In pre-Lockean society the concept of childhood excluded virtually any awareness of individual psychological progression (Shahar, 1990, 21–32). Children were 'silent witnesses' to the breakdown of domestic and social order for although parents were concerned about their physical and spiritual well-being, they were less inclined to pay attention to their mental welfare either in terms of protecting them from an abusive environment or by recognizing that they could become emotionally disturbed (Foyster, 1999, 57–73). However, in thinking 'psychoanalytically' (without being anachronistic), it is useful to remember that 'subjectivity' had been evolving since the Renaissance gave rise to new expressions of the self in biography, autobiography, portraiture and self-portraiture, and that Descartes promoted the individual mind in its association with knowledge as well as the importance of self-criticism as an individual rather than a social act (Burke, 1997; Sawday, 1997; Smith, 1997). Locke's achievement in separating personal identity from theological imperatives and linking it to consciousness was a crucial step towards symbiotically attaching 'the child' to 'the man'. These intellectual and cultural spurts undoubtedly were affecting definitions of the self vis-à-vis individualism as it connected to behaviour between husbands and wives, parents and children, brothers and sisters and other kin. Exactly how this worked in practice is difficult to ascertain, but clearly the mindset of society was very different between *c*.1400 and *c*.1750 from what it was by the end of the eighteenth century (Fletcher, 1999, 7).

In trying to identify the evolutionary process regarding 'childhood', we may ask how, under the influence of a growing recognition of a person's 'essence', adults began to assemble their own childhood (Kennedy, 2006, 5–8). That the trajectory between 'becoming' (as child) and 'being' (as adult) was known is clear from Rousseau writing in his *Confesssions* (1783), 'Who wants to know me as an adult, has to know me as a child.' This sense of child/self, impregnated with the great geographical and cultural disruption caused by the industrial revolution, produced 'the genre of adult autobiography called "Childhood"', which altered the nature of 'homeland', relocating it psychologically within the individual (Kennedy, 2006: 4). In other words, autobiographers began to realize that 'as children they had experienced another reality' (Dekker, 2000: 114). Thus, 'memory' was structured to advance the status of childhood – but in pursuit of the adult life: 'the child we once were' (Rose, 1997, 239–240; Tomaselli, 1997, 90–91; Woolff, 1998; Dekker, 2000, 109–126). This explains why, as our period closes, and industrial society became increasingly complex not only in terms of gendered and class relations but also of governmentality, the 'child figure' assumed literary popularity for authors (and their readers) as a malleable mediator in attempting to reconcile the perplexed 'self' with the ever expanding 'social' (Berry, 1999). We should not be surprised if this reminds us of how the evolution of childhood may be deployed in a variety of circumstances and how children, often at great risk to their own welfare, throughout the centuries have unknowingly helped us to augment our freedom of choice in a variety of circumstances.

References

Anderson, M. (1995) *Approaches to the History of the Western Family, 1500–1914*. Cambridge: Cambridge University Press.

Archard, D. (1993) *Children, Rights and Childhood*. London: Routledge.

Archard, D. (2003) *Children, Family and the State*. Aldershot: Ashgate.

Ariès, Ph. (1962) *Centuries of Childhood*. Harmondsworth: Penguin. Originally published as *L'Enfant et la vie familiale sous l'ancien regime* (1960).

Avery, G. and Reynolds, K. (eds) (2000) *Representations of Childhood Death*. Basingstoke: Macmillan.

Berry, L.C. (1999) *The Child, the State and the Victorian Novel*. Charlottesville and London: University Press of Virginia.

Boswell, J. (1988) *The Kindness of Strangers: The Abandonment of Children in Western Europe from Late Antiquity to the Renaissance*. London: Allen Lane.

Burke, P. (1978) *Popular Culture in Early Modern Europe*. New York: Harper Torchbooks.

Burke, P. (1997) 'Representations of the Self from Petrarch to Descartes', in R. Porter, (ed.) *Rewriting the Self. Histories from the Renaissance to the present*. London: Routledge, pp. 17–28.

Collison, Patrick (1988) *The Birthpangs of Protestant England*. London: Palgrave Macmillan.

Cunningham, H. (1991) *The Children of the Poor: Representations of Childhood since the Seventeenth Century*. Oxford: Blackwell.

Cunningham, H. (2005) *Children and Children in Western Society since 1500*. Harlow: Pearson Longman.

Dekker, R. (2000) *Children, Memory and Autobiography in Holland: From the Golden Age to Romanticism*. London: Macmillan.

deMause, Ll. (ed.) (1976) *The History of Childhood*. London: Souvenir Press.

Elias, N. (1939; 1979) *The History of Manners: The Civilising Process*, Vol. 1. New York: Pantheon.

Ezell, M.J.M. (1983) 'John Locke's Images of Childhood: Early Eighteenth Century Response to Some Thoughts Concerning Education', *Eighteenth-Century Studies*, 17: 139–155.

Fairclough, N. (1989) *Language and Power*. London: Longman.

Fildes, V. (1988) *Wet Nursing: A History from Antiquity to the Present*. Oxford: Blackwell.

Fleck, E. (1987) *Domestic Tyranny*. New York: Oxford University Press.

Fletcher, A. (1994) 'Prescription and Practice: Protestantism and the Upbringing of Children, 1560–1700', in D. Wood (ed.) *The Church and Childhood*. Oxford: Blackwell, pp. 325–346.

Fletcher, A. and Hussey, S. (eds) (1999) 'Introduction', in their *Childhood in Question: Children, Parents and the State*. Manchester: Manchester University Press, pp. 1–14.

Foyster, E. (1999) 'Silent Witnesses? Children and the Breakdown of Domestic and Social Order in Early Modern England', in A. Fletcher and S. Hussey (eds) *Childhood in Question*. Manchester: Manchester University Press, pp. 57–73.

Gavitt, Ph. (1990) *Charity and Children in Renaissance Florence: The Ospedale degli Innocenti, 1410–1536*. Ann Arbor: University of Michigan Press.

Graff, H. (1995) *Conflicting Paths: Growing Up in America*. Cambridge MA: Harvard University Press.

Greven, Ph. (1977) *The Protestant Temperament: Patterns of Child-Rearing, Religious Experience, and the Self in Early America*. New York: Alfred A. Knopf.

Hanawalt, B. (1986) *The Ties that Bound: Peasant Families in Medieval England*. New York: Oxford University Press.

Hanawalt, B. (1993) *Growing Up in Medieval London: The Experience of Childhood in History*. New York: Oxford University Press.

Hendrick, H. (ed.) (2005) *Child Welfare and Social Policy. an Essential Reader*. Bristol: Policy Press.

Heywood, C. (2001) *A History of Childhood: Children and Childhood in the West from Medieval to Modern Times*. Cambridge: Polity.

Hill, Ch. (1997) 'The Spiritualisation of the Household' in his *Society and Puritanism in Pre-Revolutionary England*. London: PalgraveMacmillan, pp. 382–416.

Houlbrooke, R. (1984) *The English Family, 1450–1700*. London: Longman.

Houston, R.A. (1988) *Literacy in Early Modern Europe: Culture and Education, 1500–1800*. London: Longman.

Jackson, M. (ed.) (2002) *Infanticide: Historical Perspectives on Child Murder and Concealment, 1550–2000*. Aldershot: Ashgate.

Kennedy, D. (2006) *The Well of Being. Child, Subjectivity, and Education*. Albany: State University of New York Press.

Kertzer, D. (1993) *Sacrificed for Honour: Italian Infant Abandonment and the Politics of Reproductive Control*. Boston: Beacon Press.

Kirby, P. (2003) *Child Labour in Britain, 1750–1870*. Basingstoke: Palgrave Macmillan.

Macfarlane, A. (1970) *The Family Life of Ralph Josselin, A Seventeenth Century Clergyman*. Cambridge: Cambridge University Press.

Morgan, J. (1986) *Godly Learning: Puritan Attitudes towards Reason, Learning, and Education, 1560–1640*. Cambridge: Cambridge University Press.

Orme, N. (2001) *Medieval Children*. New Haven & London: Yale University Press.

Ozment, S. (1983) *When Fathers Ruled: Family Life in Reformation Europe*. Cambridge MA: Harvard University Press.

Plumb, J.H. (1975) 'The New World of Children in Eighteenth-Century England', *Past and Present*, 67: 64–93.

Pollock, L. (1983). *Forgotten Children: Parent-Child Relations from 1500 to 1900*, Cambridge: Cambridge University Press.

Rahikainen, M. *Centuries of Child Labour*. Aldershot: Ashgate.

Rose, N. (1997) 'Assembling the Modern Self' in R. Porter (ed.) *Rewriting the Self. Histories from the Renaissance to the present*, London: Routledge, pp. 224–248.

Ross, E. (1993) *Love & Toil. Motherhood in Outcast London, 1870–1918*. New York: Oxford University Press.

Sawday, J. (1997) 'Self and Selfhood in the Seventeenth Century' in R. Porter (ed.) *Rewriting the Self. Histories from the Renaissance to the Present*. London: Routledge, pp. 29–48.

Shahar, S. (1990) *Childhood in the Middle Ages*. London: Routledge.

Shorter, E. (1976) *The Making of the Modern Family*. London: Fontana.

Smith, R. (1997) 'Self-Reflection and the Self' in R. Porter (ed.) *Rewriting the Self. Histories from the Renaissance to the present*. London: Routledge, pp. 49–60.

Stone, L. (1964) 'The Educational Revolution in England, 1560–1640', *Past and Present*, 28: 41–80.

Stone, L. (1977) *The Family, Sex and Marriage in England, 1500–1800*. London: Weidenfeld and Nicolson.

Sussman, G. (1982) *Selling Mother's Milk: The Wet-Nursing Business in France, 1715–1914*. Urbana: University of Illinois Press.

Thomas, K. (1976) *Rule and Misrule in the Schools in Early Modern England*. Reading: Reading University Press.

Thomas, K. (1984) *Man and the Natural World*. Harmondsworth: Penguin.

Thomas, K. (1989) 'Children in Early Modern England', in G. Avery and J. Briggs (eds), *Children and Their Books*. Oxford: Oxford University Press, pp. 45–77.

Tomaselli, S. (1997) 'The Death and Rebirth of Character in the Eighteenth Century' in R. Porter (ed.) *Rewriting the Self. Histories from the Renaissance to the Present*. London: Routledge, pp. 84–96.

Woolff, L. (1998) 'Then I Imagine a Child: The Idea of Childhood and the Philosophy of Memory in the Enlightenment', *Eighteenth-Century Studies*, 31(4): 377–401.

Wrightson, K. (1982) *English Society. 1580–1680*. London: Longman.

7
Transitions to Modernity

John Gillis

Modernity is notoriously difficult to pin down. What we can say is that it is not so much a thing but an orientation to things. The beginnings of modernity have been assigned to various periods and places, but it is generally agreed that it became a central force on a global scale only in the nineteenth century. Today it is imperative that we speak of modernities, for it is now clear that it has taken many different forms, not only across the world, but also within western societies themselves, always inflected by class, gender, race and ethnicity (Qvortrup et al., 1994; Stearns, 2006). Everywhere, however, modernity is associated with radically new orientations towards time and space.

Modern time is linear, unstoppable and unrepeatable, what Edward Casey has called 'self-emptying time' (Casey, 1993, 7). Modern space is also perceived as empty, 'increasingly placeless, a matter of mere sites instead of lived places, of sudden displacements rather than perduring implacements' (ibid., xv). In modernity, everything is in motion, everything is perceived to be in a state of becoming rather than being. This revolutionary shift in perception has altered every dimension of human existence, but none so radically as childhood, which of all the modern stages of life is seen as the most evanescent, the most subject to loss and displacement.

While there are those who claim to find similarities between the treatment of children in the pre-industrial period and children today, the case for historical continuity is not convincing. One can argue that children as such were not that different than they are now, but this is not the same as arguing that the concept of childhood itself is unchanged. It is generally agreed that the idea of childhood as a special time deserving of its own special space is itself an artifact of modernity.[1] The idea that every child should be afforded such a childhood is a very recent thing, an aspiration of the privileged few that was democratized in western countries only in the twentieth century and has yet to gain full acceptance in many parts of the world.

In earlier periods, adults were no less concerned with the well-being of children, recognizing that their own existence depended on youngsters' contributions to the household economy, but the idea that they deserved a time and a space all their own was as unthinkable as it was impracticable. Prior to the nineteenth

114

century, the lives of children and adults were inseparable, embedded in highly localized place-worlds of the pre-industrial society's basic social and economic unit, the patriarchal household. Childhood was not so much a specific age, but a social role that could be occupied by a wide range of age groups. It was not a precise chronological category, but a social status associated with dependency. Parenthood was also sociologically rather than biologically defined, such that the 'children' of the patriarchal household included not only kin but also servants, slaves and apprentices, everyone subject to the immense authority conferred on those who headed households.

Pre-modern society could imagine no times or spaces for children outside the household. Schooling was still for the privileged few. Child's work and play were inseparable from that of other members of the household; and it was accepted that children should eat, drink and sleep with adults. The household was 'family', superseding the biological parent–child bond in law and customary practice. In the pre-industrial regime of high mortality and high fertility many biological families had insufficient resources to provide for all their own children. In England, prior to the middle of the nineteenth century, 17 per cent of children were fatherless by the age of ten and 27 per cent by the age of fifteen. It has been estimated that between half and two-thirds of all young women had lost their father by the time they married in their twenties (Gillis, 1996, 9).

But orphans were not the only ones found in the households of strangers. Due to conditions of poverty, children routinely moved out of their natal homes in their teenage years to work as servants or apprentices, thus unburdening their biological parents while supplying the labour needs of better-off households. We know that in late medieval and early modern Europe two-thirds to three-quarters of all young people spent some part of their childhood or youth away from their birth families. In England, one-fifth of all rural people before the nineteenth century were living in households other than their own (ibid., 9). For many, the dependency associated with childhood was perpetual. They, like the slave populations of the same period, were considered boys and girls regardless of age.

In pre-industrial societies it was the houses of the rich rather than the poor that contained the largest number of children. In the household economy, the 'big houses' benefited from the surplus labour of their poorer neighbours, while at the same time relieving them of the feeding and housing costs of their high rates of fecundity. The big houses also provided services that the church and state were yet unable or unwilling to supply. They were the primary educational institution of pre-industrial society, the local equivalent of the police and welfare services, offering a measure of security to those who, orphaned, abandoned or simply poor, had no place to turn. Households provided training, shelter and authority. They, not the nuclear family, were the basic unit of society, without which neither the economy nor the social order could have functioned.

The household was also the psychological equivalent of today's single family house, the place where people felt 'at home'. Households were focuses around which life revolved in an era when time was still perceived as cyclical rather than linear and when space was still felt centripetal. Before the nineteenth century time did not stretch backwards and forwards much beyond the present. In the seventeenth century, Sir Thomas Browne could declare: 'Think not thy time short in this world, since the world itself is not long. The created world is but a small parenthesis in eternity; and a short imposition, for a time, between such a state of duration as was before, and may be after it' (quoted in Gifford, 71–72). The past was seen as being within easy reach, the future not very far off and the present, the *now*, very full rather than as perpetually emptying out. In an era when the perceived edge of space was only as far away as the forest or the next village, the household was still the navel of the world. This very condensed sense of the *here* as well as the *now* contributed to a powerful sense of place that satisfied contemporaries' need for existential as well as material sustenance. Home was the place that nurtured and sheltered you at the moment, not, as we have come to understand it, as one special place associated with the biological family of origin (Gillis, op. cit., 9–10, 32–33). The household seemed to provide sufficient time and space for all age groups.

Before the nineteenth century it was the household that gave people their primary identity and legal status. In colonial New England people were prohibited from living on their own; and the single family house was an exceptional living arrangement. This did not mean, however, that the population was immobile. Children circulated in much greater numbers and with much greater velocity than in modern low fertility/low mortality stay-at-home society, where growing up with one's biological family has become the norm. But, given the closed notion of time and the centred understanding of space that prevailed then, neither ageing nor movement was experienced as displacement or loss. The experience of homesickness, while reported among Swiss mercenaries in the early modern period, was not associated so much with the absence of particular homesteads or families as with the loss of familiar landscapes.[2]

The sense of loss that is precipitated by the passage of linear time and movement through vacant space was not experienced by those still living in a 'small parenthesis'. In a world envisioned as static and concentric, the life course was represented in the classical image of the 'Ages of Man', a great arc that encompassed everyone from cradle to grave, all pictorially represented within a single spatial frame, suggesting that different age groups were variations on a single theme (Sears, 1986). In this conception of life, children were lesser versions of adults rather than a different species of being. Under these conditions it is understandable why prior to the nineteenth century numerical age was largely irrelevant and few marked their birthdays until the very last years of their lives when the approach of death made them more time conscious. As long as childhood was embedded in place, still a state of being rather than becoming, the time of the child was rarely marked, much less celebrated.

The notion of childhood

All this was to change, however, when new concepts of time and space, institutionalized in the course of the nineteenth century with the onset of industrialization and the formation of the modern nation state, swept away the spatial and temporal order of the old household economy. This did not happen simultaneously in all places; nor did it happen overnight. It began in north-western Europe and in parts of North America; first, among the Protestant middle classes, who had embraced the idea of linear time and infinitely expanding space as part of their vision of a new world order based on industrial capitalism. The industrial revolution would ultimately remove production from the household to the office and the factory, thus creating for the first time a separate domestic sphere (Gillis, op. cit., chapter iv).

Other regions of the world were much slower to abandon the household economy; indeed, there are many parts of Africa and Asia where it still remains intact. Nor did change happen quickly or uniformly across European and American societies, where the working people were less likely to separate home and work than were the middle classes. Not until the middle of the twentieth century did female servants disappear completely from middle-class domiciles in Europe and America, a sign that the ancient institution of the household had finally given way to the ideal of the single family home. It was only then that modern childhood can be said to have become universal in western societies.

The Protestant middle classes were the first to embrace the idea of development through time, privileging becoming over being (Lowe, 1982). This meant that both individuals and societies were seen as moving through a sequence of unrepeatable stages. The life course was initially organized around childhood, youth, adulthood and old age, but was later fine-tuned to include further categories like infancy, adolescence and middle age. Organized as a normativized narrative, the developmental sequence was both a voyage through time, complete with beginnings, middles and end points, and movement though space, starting with a fixed point associated with the natal home, always moving upward and outward in the world (Cole, 1991).

The concept of development was from the moment of its inception strongly inflected by notions of class and gender, however. It was adult, middle-class males who were supposed to venture forth both into the future and the world at large. Bourgeois females were assumed to be inherently sessile homebodies waiting to welcome home their returning husbands and sons. Assumed to be more attached to the past, females were perceived to be less capable of the displacements in time and space demanded of bourgeois men. Peasants and workers were initially believed less fit for development, but ultimately autonomy became the norm for all males, highlighting the gendered nature of the notions of time and space associated with modernity.

The masculinized norm of development meant not only turning one's back on the past but on place as well. With so many new fields of conquer, leaving things behind became an imperative, even a virtue, for new self-made man. In turn, this confirmed the connection between femininity and domesticity, and reinforced the association of childhood with the woman's world of home and family. Young children, regardless of sex, were understood to be feminized, the reason why it was deemed necessary for boys to leave behind domestic things in order to claim the fullness of masculine adulthood. By the end of the nineteenth century, series of rites of passage, ranging from breeching to going away to school, had been created exclusively for young males to assist their distancing from the times and spaces of childhood.

The life course of females involved no such displacement, as their place remained within the natal home, but among middle-class males the profound sense of lost times and abandoned places produced a nostalgia for childhood and for home that became a central feature of modern western culture. 'God has given to each of us our own Paradise, our own old childhood, over which old glories linger – to which our hearts cling, as all we have ever known of Heaven upon earth,' wrote Anthony Froude (quoted in Gillis, op. cit., 103–104). Men like Lewis Carroll were particularly obsessed with young girls, who represented for them a connection with an earlier feminized self they were desperate to recover (Robson, 2001). The late nineteenth century was the moment when the longing for childhood and home-sweet-home surfaced in western bourgeois societies, ultimately becoming the driving force behind the modern obsession with creating special times and spaces for childhood, even in the absence of actual children to populate them. In the twentieth century this would become common across all classes and ethnic groups.

Age segregation

The erosion of the household as the central social as well as economic institution of western society precipitated a great debate about the place of children. The initial response to its demise was a universal panic about the children of families too poor to meet the imperatives of the new middle-class norms of domesticated, feminized childhood. The crisis was particularly acute in the nineteenth-century cities, where 'nomadic', 'savage', 'street' children seemed to be out of control, contributing to fears about juvenile delinquency, moral degeneration, even civilizational collapse. When traditional charities and volunteerism proved ineffective, public authority was forced to step in with coercive measures. The first phases of compulsory schooling, beginning in the second half of the nineteenth century, were designed not so much to educate as to discipline (Cunningham, 1991; Mintz, 2004, chapters vii–viii). The youngest age groups were first to be subject to what amounted to an internal civilizing mission, but in the early twentieth century older ages, now increasingly defined by the term 'adolescence', were subjected to tighter control.[3] By 1900, children were segregated from adults in the spheres of both production and consumption. There had evolved a whole new set of times and spaces of childhood, initiated and policed by self-proclaimed 'child savers', who were quick to transform themselves into professionals acting in the name of children and adolescents (Platt, 1969; Gillis, 1974, chapter iv).

Anxiety about children out of place by no means disappeared in the twentieth century, but, in the course of time, child protection institutions – schools, juvenile courts, borstals, orphanages, playgrounds – were established in all western societies and exported as part of imperial projects to other parts of the world. Today we have a further set of age-calibrated institutions – daycare centres, halfway houses and summer camps – that service everything from infancy to young adulthood (Naban, 1994). Every age now has its own medical, psychological and therapeutic special-izations, constituting a body of special interests that compete with one another for attention and funding. But, despite these multiple focuses, all child savers share the basic modern assumptions about the essential innocence and vulnerability of children which justifies the prescription of special times and places for childhood.

Age segregation has often moved apace with class, gender and racial separation. Until well into the twentieth century it was assumed that boys and girls of differ-ent class strata should be educated separately. And, as long as it was assumed that mature masculinity required separation from the world of women, sex segrega-tion would also remain a central feature of modern childhood. First institutional-ized in elite male boarding schools and military academies, it became a feature of public secondary and university education in the twentieth century. In South Africa and the American South, the establishment of sex-segregated schooling went hand in hand with racial apartheid.

Subject to increased adult supervision in school and in public spaces in general, children came in the course of the late nineteenth and early twentieth centuries to have less access to the times and places of adults in general (Zeiher and Zeiher, 1994, chapter i). Excluded by protective labour laws from most workplaces, chil-dren and juveniles were less likely to be in the company of their elders except within the increasingly narrow precincts of domestic space. The street, the city equivalent of the rural common, became off-limits to them; and the establish-ment of age limits on drinking further segregated them. In the early twenti-eth century, a multitude of products designed specifically for young age groups reached the market. Highly specialized children's food, furniture, clothing and toys were on offer. At first affordable only by affluent parents, these ultimately constituted a mass market of huge proportions. Stores added children's depart-ments as advertising increasingly targeted younger age groups. In the wake of the Second World War, teenagers became consumers in their own right, prompting the development of other age-graded niche markets that colonized every dimen-sion of the age scale. Today, children are encouraged to enter into consumption at ever-earlier ages, enticed by marketing strategies aimed at building product and brand loyalty even among preschoolers (Cross, 1997).

The emergence of mass media also reinforced modern notions of childhood. Children's books and magazines proliferated in the nineteenth century, as part of an effort to protect children from the supposedly corrupting influences of adult literature (Drotner, 1988). The advent of movies was initially perceived as a threat to the ideal of childhood innocence, but, in time, the film industry learned how to profit from the new genre of cartoons and features for children. Radio and, later, television programming moved quickly to segregate child from adult audi-ences. Children's hours were established and content carefully regulated, though preventing access to adult media became increasingly difficult in the 1980s and 1990s when children came into possession of their own televisions and video equipment.

Now, with the advent of the internet, the boundaries between age groups are again challenged, but the current panic seems only to reinforce the spatial and temporal norms of childhood as parents and legislators work furiously to shore up what they believe to be the inviolable age boundaries, never questioning the idea of childhood innocence itself (Drotner, 2004, 584–589).

The modern idea of childhood has shown itself capable not just of surviving, but of adapting to the changing conditions of modern life. Children have recently gained access to previously segregated domains of adulthood, while adults have been invading places reserved for younger age groups. As early as the 1980s, Joshua Meyrowitz was warning that 'each stage of socialization has been associated with its own physical location', but now 'the idea of special places for special stages of life is fading' (1988, vii, 157). Over recent decades the physical landscapes that had earlier sustained not just age but also gender, race and ethnic distinctions have been radically eroded, creating deep anxieties, expressed in an extensive literature proclaiming the 'disappearance of childhood', 'children without childhoods', and the 'adult-like child' (Meyrowitz, 1984). But the category itself has not been seriously challenged and seems to be gaining strength in the current panic over child molestation. Despite evidence that children are quite resilient, the spaces and times of childhood are under greater surveillance than ever before (Kincaid, 1992).

Virtual children

As Viviana Zelizer pointed out some time ago, children became more precious at the moment when they lost their economic value as wage earners and became a cost rather than a benefit to their parents (Zelizer, 1985). Developed societies have become extraordinarily child-centred even as children have become an ever smaller part of the population. Never have children been so valued, but never have so many adults lived apart from children. In 1870, the proportion of American households without children was 17 per cent; today it has reached 64 per cent. It is far more common for households to have pets (80 per cent) than offspring, in part because of falling birth rates and increased voluntary childlessness, but also because of the greater longevity of adults, who are far more likely to live apart from their children in old age. Yet never has the image of the child been so pervasive in our politics, commerce and culture. Childhood has become more luminous even in the absence of real children (Gillis, 2002).

This paradox is explained by the changing nature of family life itself. No longer held together by the shared functions of a household, modern family life has become vicarious. Family members no longer share common here and now, but are brought together at specially designed family times, calendrical celebrations and reunions, events that were wholly absent in pre-industrial society. These provide the sense of family past and future that contemporary families live *by* even when they do not live *with* other family members. In the same way, the designation of a family homeplace, even if it is no longer lived in or rarely visited, sustains at a symbolic level families' sense of continuity and connection (Gillis,

1996, 234–235). Family time is no longer something that, as in the days of the household, simply happens, but is now a special occasion that must be organized, planned for, and, if it meets the high expectations we have come to expect of these moments, recorded and commemorated (Gillis, 2001). The amount of time invested today in anticipation and commemoration of family often exceeds that actually spent in the actual presence of family members.

If the amount of real time and space shared with children has greatly diminished, the number of special occasions devoted to them has increased enormously. Children have become the symbols of modern family life. A wedding does not make a family; the birth of a child does, even in absence of marriage as such. It becomes the point of origin, the first act from which everything else follows. Children's birthdays, ignored before the nineteenth century, have become central to families' celebration of themselves. What is now commonly referred to as 'family time' – homecomings, mealtimes, bedtimes – all involve children. A host of major child-centred holidays, notably Christmas but also summer vacations, have emerged to become the events around which family history is narrated and recorded. Some of these take place in commercial venues, but the preferable location of special family times is the place of home; if not the actual place of residence than some other location, a country cottage or summer place that has become, though the amount of time spent together there is limited, the Mecca for scattered family members. In Europe and North America second homes and weekend retreats have become the places where precious images of childhood are captured on film or tape and preserved for posterity (Gillis, 2004).

As time has accelerated and physical distance increases, the demand for special times and places multiplies. Providing them is generally considered women's work, and so, as women have returned to the workforce, the production of family time and space has come under increasing strain. The family meal has lost ground, and homecomings and bedtimes have also come under pressure. In this era of 'time famine', what were once domestic occasions have been outsourced. In Nordic countries, McDonalds has become a favourite location for the celebration of children's birthdays (Brembeck, 2008).

Much of what is designated as family life today is spent either in anticipation of these moments or in remembering them. What has come to be called 'quality time' with children is now associated with a set of specially designed spaces, sep arate from everyday existence. Commercialized playrooms, children's museums and theme parks lure families through the promise of experiences no longer available closer to home. But in the United States outsourcing has not discouraged the building of ever bigger houses, with larger kitchens and family rooms. Even though they often remain unused, such houses continue to be in demand, for they have become 'the place we stage the life we wished we had time to live' (Garber, 2001, 207).

In the modern era, we are surrounded by virtual children. Their photographs cover our walls; their toys and school books fill our attics and basements. Children are the most photographed and now most videoed members of the human species. It is estimated that half of all film stock is devoted to them

(Spence and Holland, 1991; Higonnet, 1998, 87–96). This virtual landscape of childhood is created and sustained by a unique set of rituals and narratives which have developed in the modern era. Photographs of children, especially young children, taken almost exclusively on festive occasions, have become the favoured means of sustaining idealized, highly stereotyped images of childhood that never seem to change from generation to generation. 'Children – and especially girl children – must learn to present them as an image', writes Patricia Holland (1992, 17).

In these special times and spaces, childhood is a kind of performance, when children are expected to act like children. Even as the time spent with children erodes, and children cease to do childish things at ever-earlier ages, the ideal is thereby sustained and reinforced. On family occasions children act out the prevailing notions of childhood before an appreciative audience of adults, eager not only to confirm their idea of what childhood should be but also to revisit their own 'lost' childhoods vicariously. To achieve the best results, the contemporary performance of childhood is enacted in a time and space apart, which, like a theatrical stage, is removed from everyday existence. A visit to a theme park or playroom is one way of achieving this, but, for those who can afford it, private venues are preferable. The home has traditionally served as the site of most child-centred rites, but in recent decades, as the residence has ceased to be a shelter from the outside world, the weekend or seasonal house has become the favoured location for the theatre of childhood.

The memorial child

Childhood is modernity's most memorable stage of life. It is impossible to write autobiography without dwelling extensively on the earliest years. We suppose, contrary to abundant evidence, that what happens then is determinative. People said to have been deprived of their childhoods are to be pitied no matter what their subsequent achievements may be. We are convinced that childhood innocence lost can never be recovered. We do not worry ourselves about the evanescence of middle or old age, but we regard childhood as paradise lost; the object of a perpetual recovery project that helps explain our desperate efforts to sustain an idealized notion of childhood, often even at the expense of real children.

Childhood has become modern society's myth of both origin and destiny, our explanation of who we are and what we will become. As Maria Warner points out, 'children have never been so visible as points of identification, as warrants of virtue, as markers of humanity' (Warner, 1995, 57, 60). Childhood is a screen on which adults project their greatest hopes and deepest fears, making it difficult to see children for what they really are. Children are often seen either as little angels or little monsters, but rarely as complex human beings; and this condition is compounded by the fact that so few adults now live with children and thus experience them in a variety of different situations where all their human dimensions are visible.

In the modern era, childhood has had to bear an enormous symbolic burden. As Elizabeth Goodenough has put it:

> childhood is both a chronological stage and a mental construct, an existential fact and a locus of desire, a mythical country continuously mapped by grown-ups in search of their subjectivity in another time and place. (Goodenough, 2000, 180)

Childhood remains a prime source of selfhood, the thing that adults use to explain themselves to themselves, and to others. In a secular age, which has ceased to believe in eternity, childhood has become a guarantee of immortality, the one solid thing when all else seems to melt into thin air. It is through photography that 'we find off death's terrors, snapshot by snapshot', observes Anne Higonnet, 'pretending to save the moment, half time, preserve childhood intact' (Higonnet, 1998, 95). And in the latest phase of western culture's obsessions with origins, attention is increasingly focused on the image of the unborn child, the foetus becoming the ultimate representation of the original, uncorrupted self.

Children to live by

Children have always been subject to the authority of adults, serving their needs in all kinds of capacities. What is different about the modern era are the ways that adult needs have changed, especially in the developed world. No longer are European and American children necessary as workers, however much the global economy itself may still be dependent on child labour. To be sure, as Jens Qvortrup has pointed out, never have so many children been employed at another kind of work – school work – which now absorbs ever increasing numbers of years (Qvortrup, 1995). Children may no longer serve the immediate material needs of adults, but never before have they been so necessary to their existential well-being. As Karen Fog Olwig and Eva Gulløv have argued, 'childhood bears this heavy burden of providing a source of identification and rootedness for adults' (Olwig and Gulløv, 2003, 2).

It is at the interface between adult needs for an idealized childhood and the interests of real children that the contradictions of the transitions to modernity are most evident. It is abundantly clear that the *time of childhood* as constructed by adults and *time for children* as actually lived by children are not the same (James et al., 1998, 61). This is equally true of the spaces that children create for themselves, apart from those adults create for them. Since the first days of compulsory schooling, children have resisted the time imposed by their elders, playing the truant at every opportunity. In the same way they trespass the spaces modernity has assigned them, creating their own territories just as they create their own temporalities.

Such transgressions have led to ever-greater surveillance and efforts at control, always in the name of the protection of a pure childhood that has never really existed except in the minds of adults. Under conditions where adult identities are so tied up with idealized notions of childhood, it is inevitable that all deviations are perceived as threatening, producing anger and sometimes violence against the very children who are supposed to be protected (Demos, 1986). Never before in history have moral panics been so focused on children.

The idea of childhood over-determines relations between adults and children in ways that have costs for all those involved. For children, the price is the loss of autonomy. There is no historical evidence that children behave better or worse today than they did in the past, but it is clear that today's offspring lead increasingly scripted lives. The costs to adults are no less considerable, not only in funds expended on schools and correctional institutions, but also on the new therapeutic and medical approaches that are now marketed throughout the western world. But perhaps the greatest burden of all is psychological, for, an effort to live *by* the standards of modern childhood makes it increasingly difficult to live *with* real children.

Falling birth rates and the unprecedented decision to remain childless by young couples have a multitude of causes, but one is most certainly the modern concept of childhood itself, which not only raises the material standards and costs of raising children, but, at a time when the nuclear family is ever more on its own when it comes to childrearing, makes enormous demands on parents' time and psychological resources. The idea that children need their separate spaces within the home has led to the building of ever bigger but also more isolated houses. Suburbanization, a trend driven by the notion that cities are unfit for children, has further eroded the time that families can actually spend together because so much effort is now put into transporting children from home to school and extracurricular activities that were once within walking distance are now often miles apart. Modern space, like modern time, has become less and less child-friendly even as it has embraced the concept of childhood.

Were it not for the almost religious belief in the value of children, western rates of reproduction would be even lower. As long as the notion of 'our children, our future' remains an article of faith, the replacement rate will probably continue to hover just below the replacement level. But, as David Lowenthal recently suggested, faith in the future has been faltering in recent decades, and, should our sense of posterity become detached from a desire for progeny, it is questionable whether some hidden natural instinct to reproduce would come to the rescue (2006, 42–43). Western Europe is already becoming reliant on the surplus populations from Africa and the Middle East as a source of young labour. In North America, the robust reproductivity of Latin America is already changing the age as well as the ethnic composition of the United States (Qvortrup, 1994).

Alison Gopnik has suggested that it might be better if we stopped thinking of children in terms of potentiality and treated them as beings in their own right, what she calls the 'intrinsic view – the view that childhood and caring for children are valuable of and for themselves' (Gopnik, 2000). This is easier said than done, however, for the modern notions of time and space do not allow for concentrating on the here and now, on children as they really are as opposed to what they might become. As long as we live *by* modernity's iconic childhood, we will not easily find a way of living comfortably *with* children, providing a place for them in our adult worlds. Perhaps a condition which some have described as 'postmodernity', which rejects both linear time and ever-expanding space, will relieve this condition, but there is not much evidence, despite its many prophets, that its day has arrived. In the meantime, the best we can do is be sensitive to the contradictions that the transitions to modernity have brought us, constantly reminding ourselves that childhood and children are two very different things.

Notes

1. Linda Pollock and others have found the beginnings of something like modern parent–child relationships in early modern Europe. But, as Peter Stearns asserts, they do not show that the concepts and institutions of childhood as we know them were present before the nineteenth century (Pollock, 1983, 1987; Stearns, 2006, chapter vi).
2. On homesickness, see Lowenthal, 1985, p. 10.
3. The word adolescence had existed in earlier periods, but became normative and institutionalized only in the later nineteenth century.

References

Brembeck, H. (2008) 'Inscribing Nordic Childhoods in MacDonalds', in M. Gutman and N. de Coninck-Smith (eds) *Designing Modern Childhoods: History, Space, and the Material Culture of Children: An International Reader.* New Brunswick, New Jersey: Rutgers University Press, pp. 269–281.

Casey, E.S. (1993) *Getting Back into Place: Toward a Renewed Understanding of the Place-World.* Bloomington IN: Indiana University Press.

Cole, T.R. (1991) *The Journey of Life: A Cultural History of Aging in America.* Cambridge: Cambridge University Press.

Cross, G. (1997) *Kid's Stuff: Toys and the Changing World of American Childhood.* Cambridge MA: Harvard University.

Cunningham, H. (1991) *Children of the Poor: Representation of Childhood since the Seventeenth Century.* Oxford: Blackwell.

Demos, J. (1986) *Past, Present, and Personal: The Family and the Life Course in America.* New York: Oxford University Press.

Drotner, K. (1988) *English Children and Their Magazines, 1751–1945,* 2nd edn. New Haven: Yale University Press.

Drotner, K. (2004) 'Childhood and the Media', in P.S. Fass (ed.) *Encyclopedia of Children and Childhood in History and Society.* New York: Macmillan, vol. 2, pp. 584–589.

Garber, M. (2001) *Sex and Real Estate: Why We Love Houses.* New York: Pantheon.

Gifford, D. (1991) *The Farthest Shore: A Natural History of Perception.* New York: Harper Collins.

Gillis, J.R. (1974) *Youth and History: Tradition and Change in European Age Relations, 1770 to the Present.* New York: Academic Press.

Gillis, J.R. (1996) *A World of Their Own Making: Myth, Ritual, and the Quest for Family Values.* New York: Basic Books.

Gillis, J.R. (2001) 'Never Enough Time: Some Paradoxes of American Family Time(s)', in K.J. Daly (ed.) *Minding the Time in Family Experience: Emerging Perceptions and Issues.* Amsterdam: Elsevier.

Gillis, J.R. (2002) 'Birth of the Virtual Child: Origins of our Contradictory Images of Children', in J. Dunn and J. Kelly (eds) *Childhood and its Discontents.* Dublin: Iffey Press, pp. 31–50.

Gillis, J.R. (2004) *Islands of the Mind: How the Human Imagination Created the Atlantic World.* New York: Palgrave/Macmillan.

Goodenough, E. (2000) 'Introduction to Special Issue on the Secret Spaces of Childhood', in *Michigan Quarterly Review*, xxiv (Spring), pp. 179–193.

Gopnik, A. (2000) 'Children Need Childhood, Not Vocational Training', *The New York Times*, 24 December.

Higonnet, A. (1998) *Pictures of Innocence: The History and Crisis of Ideal Childhood.* London: Thames and Hudson.

Holland, P. (1992) *What is a Child? Popular Images of Childhood.* London: Virago.

James, A., C. Jenks and A. Prout (1998) *Theorizing Childhood.* New York: Teachers College Press.

Kincaid, J. (1992) *Child-loving: The Erotic Child and Victorian Culture.* New York: Routledge.

Lowe, D. (1982) *The History of Bourgeois Perception.* Chicago University Press.

Lowenthal, D. (1985) *The Past is a Foreign Country.* Cambridge: Cambridge University Press.

Lowenthal, D. (2006) 'The Past of the Future: From the Foreign to the Undiscovered Country', *History Today*, 56(6): 42–49.

Meyrowitz, J. (1984) 'The Adultlike Child and the Childlike Adult: Socialization in an Electronic Age', *Daedalus* 113(3): 19–48.

Meyrowitz, J. (1988) *No Sense of Place: The Impact of Electronic Media on Social Behavior.* New York: Oxford University Press.

Mintz, S. (2004) *Huck's Raft: A History of American Childhood.* Cambridge MA: Harvard University Press.

Naban, G. P. (1994) *Geography of Childhood: Why Children Need Wild Places.* Boston: Beacon Press.

Olwig, K.F. and E. Gulløv (2003) 'Towards An Anthropology of Children and Place', in K.F. Olwig and E. Gulløv (eds) *Children's Places: Cross-Cultural Perspectives.* London: Routledge.

Platt, A.E. (1969) *The Child Savers: The Invention of Delinquency.* Chicago: University of Chicago Press.

Pollock, L. (1983) *Forgotten Children: Parent-Child Relations from 1500–1900.* Cambridge: Cambridge University Press.

Pollock, L. (1987) *A Lasting Relationship: Parents and their Children over Three Centuries.* London: Fourth Estate.

Qvortrup, J. (1994), 'A New Solidarity Contract? The Significance of a Demographic Balance for both Children and the Elderly', in J. Qvortrup et al. (1994), pp. 319–334.

Qvortrup, J. (1995) 'From Useful to Useful: The Historical Continuity of Children's Constructive Participation', *Sociological Studies of Children*, 7: 49–76.

Qvortrup, J., M. Bardy, G.B. Sgritta and H. Wintersberger (1994) *Childhood Matters: Social Theory, Practice, and Politics.* Aldershot: Avebury.

Robson, C. (2001) *Men in Wonderland: The Lost Childhood of the Victorian Gentleman.* Princeton: Princeton University Press.

Sears, E. (1986) *The Ages of Man: Medieval Interpretations of the Life Cycle.* Princeton: Princeton University Press.

Spence, J. and P. Holland (1991) *Family Snaps: The Messages of Domestic Photography.* London: Virago.

Stearns, P.N. (2006) *Children in World History.* New York: Routledge.

Warner, M. (1995) *Six Myths of Our Times: Little Angels, Little Monsters, Beautiful Beasts and More.* New York: Vintage.

Zeiher, H. and H. Zeiher (1994) *Orte and Zeiten der Kinder: Soziales Leben im Alltag von Großstadtkindern.* Weinheim/Munich: Juventa.

Zelizer, V. (1985) *Pricing the Priceless Child: The Changing Social Value of Children.* New York: Basic Books.

8
Institutionalization as a Secular Trend

Helga Zeiher

Looked upon from a societal viewpoint, childhood shows up as a configuration of social processes, discourses and structures which relate to ways of living as a child at a particular time in a particular society, and which gain a certain permanency by being reproduced in social life.[1] Focusing on the configuration as a whole, childhood may be regarded as a *societal institution,* and the term institutionalization then means the totality of processes of establishing and further developing childhood as a societal institution. The secular process of the emergence of childhood as a social institution may be seen as part of the trend of institutionalization of the life course, which was conceptualized by sociologists in the 1980s in order to analyse the historical emergence and transformations of age-related societal regimes in people's lives in modernity (Kohli, 1985; Mayer and Müller, 1985; Hareven, 1986).

In order to describe and analyse social childhood, the terms institution and institutionalization are used in a narrower sense and relate to concrete entities within social childhood, each of which is meant to normalize particular needs, activities or life arenas and to provide opportunity structures; these may be called *childhood institutions.* In this sense the family is a childhood institution, and so is the educational and childcare system of a country as well as its components, including schools, daycare and leisure institutions.

Moreover, in colloquial language even a single school or care facility is called *an institution* or *an organization.* The terms are not clearly separable, yet the term organization may be seen as pointing more to the fulfilment of the purpose through organizational structures and processes, while the term institution highlights the permanence of a structure. A single organization or institution in that sense provides a particular life space, which consists of purposefully created and maintained opportunity structures as well as informal opportunity structures that the users develop within their daily life inside a facility.

This chapter is about institutionalization as a *secular trend* in social childhood, hence the dynamics of change in childhood. It focuses on recent changes that are part of the transition from industrial to late modern society. First, the chapter provides a short overview of the two main processes of the societal formation of childhood in modernity, *scholarization* and *familization,* thereby enquiring into the social dynamics that have progressed and changed the character of these processes in the course of recent decades. The next focal topic is the organization of children's activities, activity sequences and patterns within schools, daycare and leisure institutions. This section particularly emphasizes the *organization of time and space,* and looks into social dynamics within the institutionalization processes arising in the context of the recent social changes in the use of time and space in late modern society. The third issue is the dynamics in the institutionalization processes due to interdependent developments of *institutionalization and individualization.* Finally, the chapter looks at processes of de-institutionalization on the level of institutional structures as well as on the level of the individual's agency and perception.

Secular trends: scholarization and familization

The historical transition towards modern industrialized societies beginning in the late eighteenth century included a new organization of the generational order (Hendrick, Gillis, this volume). For all children, learning became separated from paid labour and placed in schools, thereby separating children's school work from adults' gainful work and hence childhood from the adult world of work. Furthermore, paid labour became spatially and temporally separated from the family household, a process that resulted in the privatization of the core family, including the familization of childhood. Both changes positioned children in a new way in society, namely confined within two societal institutions, each specialized to perform a particular part of societal reproduction: the care-specialized family and the learning-specialized educational system.

These two main childhood institutions differ fundamentally in that the school is a place of formally organized affiliation, and the family is the place where the particular child is in focus. The related secular processes, familization and scholarization, have since been developing in parallel and antagonistically, in competition and conflict, with mutual support, influence and interpenetration.

Increasing scholarization

In the period of early industrialization, the implementation of compulsory schooling was driven forward by social dynamics arising from industrialization and the interests of the state. Economic developments created demand for higher qualification ('human capital'), and the shift in poor children's work from help within the family domain towards industrial work gave rise to policy measures, since these children's health was endangered and children's low wages threatened the adult workers' income. Compulsory schooling also functioned as a state measure for socializing children in addition to family socialization. In the course of the twentieth century, attempts at implementing new political values in the population, be they totalitarian or democratic, were used as efforts by the state towards forming and controlling school education, in order to transmit the respective politically highlighted values to the young population.

The process of institutionalization of childhood through scholarization has expanded until the present along with developments in society and the economy. These processes differ between nations; however, some general trends may be identified. One trend is towards more schooling for more children. This trend was strongly pushed in the 1960s, when economic production began to shift from industrial labour towards knowledge and service-related work, and then again in the beginning of the twenty-first century, in the context of the recent radical economic and social changes. In both periods, a growing demand for more qualification was met by campaigns in favour of diminishing social class and gender disadvantages in educational opportunities, which were to be satisfied by prolongations of the duration of compulsory schooling as well as by efforts to enhance pupils' academic achievement through more detailed curricula and tests. As to the institutionalization of childhood, these purposes led to a growing number of schools and teachers, to young people spending more life time in schools on average, and to more formalized learning organization and achievement control.

In the countries of the North, scholarization has spread into the lives of young children under school age and into older children's out-of-school time since the 1960s. Daycare institutions have expanded in number, and many more facilities for structured leisure activities, including sports and cultural activities which supplement school activities, are now offered to and engaged in by children (see Dahlberg, this volume). The increasing scholarization outside of school was brought about by the coincidence of three social developments: First, the expanding participation of mothers in the workforce created a need for care and leisure institutions. Secondly, the economic demand for young people to gain better qualifications has become much debated in the public arena. Child development, socialization processes and the need for changes in the perception of the child have become pertinent issues in child-related sciences, in teachers' education, and in public discourse. Since that time, middle-class parents have become much concerned about their children's future chances on the labour market, and encourage them to attend frequent out-of-school learning institutions. Thirdly, processes of urban development have reduced opportunities for younger children to meet and play outdoors on their own in many regions in the same period. Regarding their children as endangered by high levels of traffic and the anonymous nature of urban shopping areas, parents prefer to keep them in safe places, leading to increased demand for structured facilities.

Familization and state interventions

The family must be regarded as a childhood institution insofar as the children's position within the family as well as the parents' tasks, duties and rights in relation to children are formally and informally regulated on the societal level. The family model in modernity – the male-breadwinner model – placed childhood within the nuclear family, which thereby became specialized in bringing up children. The model is characterized by a particular configuration of gender and generational relationships: it is based on a gendered division of labour, the financial provision being the father's duty and household and care work being the mother's duty. This family model was strengthened by the state (and still is by some states) through family-focused legislation. With regard to civil rights and financial matters, parents became obliged by law to care for their children's physical needs and health. Means to that end include men's income being high enough for the family, the social-health system being family- and not individual-based, and schools and daycare institutions opening only in the morning and not offering meals, thereby forcing mothers to stay at home or work only part-time (Qvortrup et al., 1994). This family model was predominant in the ideology and legislation of the welfare states in most Western countries until the mid-twentieth century, even though there were great national variations in the type and extent of its realization (Jensen et al., 2004; Dahlberg, this volume).

Early in the history of modernity, states began to take a subsidiary role to the family in order to prevent children from serious risks; children's homes being one example. In the twentieth century, care and provision for children of poor families in need became a welfare state task to be performed by professionals including family supervisors, care givers and therapists. Over the course of time, related concepts, social professions and personnel as well as specialized institutions grew in number. The kind of risks that demanded and allowed for state intervention in the family became legally defined and hence institutionalized, as did the intervention measures.

Besides interventions in cases of particular need, states also increasingly influenced and controlled all parents' child-directed behaviour, thereby removing care duties from the family (Näsman, 1994). States created laws and measures in order to protect all children from daily risks, thereby institutionalizing functions previously held informally by the family. Most of such interventions are age-graded laws, including the age children are allowed to cycle on roads, to watch certain movies or to buy alcohol or tobacco. A pertinent field of state control over all parents' care behaviour is health control (Mayall, this volume; Mayall, 1996). Historical studies reveal the growth of paediatric advice directed at mothers since the late eighteenth century (Turmel, 1997). While this advice at first informed mothers about childcare and child diseases, today standardized control of physical and mental health and also language competence aims at controlling child development and school entrance maturity, whereby a 'functional symbiosis' of paediatric and pedagogic purposes takes place (Kelle, 2007). In many countries, regular age-graded children's health control is compulsory for all young children. The World Health Organization provides an international classification of child health norms and thus an attempt towards a worldwide normalization of childhood. Yet this development has been criticized. In her analysis of the spread of dyslexia in Switzerland in the 1980s, Bühler-Niederberger (1991) investigated processes of creating definitions of deviation and showed that the number of children labelled as affected had grown when the amount of knowledge and therapy measures and the number of specialized therapy personnel had been augmented.

The most important field of child-related tasks taken over by the welfare state from the family is doubtlessly childcare. Here, institutionalization became enforced by the growing weight on institutionalized learning, on the one hand, and by changes in the gendered division of labour on the other. Since the 1960s, economic demands for women's labour power as well as women's demands for emancipation from the traditional gender hierarchy (the male-breadwinner-family model) led to increasing participation of mothers in the labour market in all countries of the North – to a varying extent. As a result, most families outsource childcare for some proportion of the day (see Dahlberg, this volume; Mayall, this volume).

The secular process of childhood familization is contradictory. On the one hand, childhood becomes increasingly institutionalized outside the family by structured care and leisure as well as by children's rights – also rights that restrict parents' decision-making on behalf of the child – and thereby less subjugated to the family as an institution (see below), a tendency that is accomplished by lessened hierarchical relations between child and parent (see below). On the other hand, the family is still a strong childhood institution. Parents' responsibilities for their children's socialization and learning achievement as well as for their mental development are enlarged and enforced, and children are increasingly confined within the family space as opposed to the local environment. In spite of more children's rights and less hierarchical adult–child relations, children are still dependent to a high degree on their parents' economic resources and decisions, including place of residence, mobility, and participation in daycare and school (Jensen, 2007).

Organizational means: time and space

Institutions exert social power over children not least through temporal and spatial organizational means.

Time

In many respects, age serves as a suitable category for differentiating and rationalizing norms, rules and organizational structures, because it is defined within modernity's concept of time, namely in objective, linear progressing, fragmental and measurable time (Gillis, this volume). Childhood can be said to be that part of the 'institutionalized life course' (Kohli, 1985) that is age-structured in the most detailed way, hence chronologized. Concerning childhood, age-grading seems particularly self-evident because it relates to the life period of physical growth. Psychological conceptualizations of step-by-step child development underline and justify the complex age-graded childhood regime.

Chronologization impacts directly on individuals' lives in that set temporal structures must be respected. The institutionalized time regime furthermore supports the individual's continuous awareness of the respective next age step, in that temporal structures are mirrored by individual representations of age-defined periods. Children usually perceive themselves and are perceived by adults as being on a step-by-step path towards adulthood – most children even long for such upgrading. Age representations serve as criteria for perceiving and valuing one's own present and future life as well as that of others (James, 2005) and thereby enforce the acceptance of what is socially 'normal'. Hence, there is general support for the chronologization trend.

The historical process of chronologization of childhood began through scholarization. School entrance and leaving, learning curricula and access to educational achievement degrees are organized by age. In the course of the twentieth century, a multitude of further age-steps related to care, health, civil rights, voting, use of transportation, alcohol and drug consumption, and access to public places and events were also institutionalized. Welfare state monetary transfers for families and maternal and paternal leave from work are also regulated by children's age. Age levels are an issue of political debates and are changed according to social changes of different kinds, including economic demand for young people's learning outcome, children's rights and urban development.

Time structuring is also a pertinent issue in childhood institutionalization processes as a *means of organizing* the daily practice within schools and school-like structured leisure facilities. The clock is an indispensable means for coordinating, fragmenting and sequencing activities performed in groups of pupils and teachers. Doubtless, how time structures are shaped must be oriented to efficient synchronization. Furthermore, one might presume that efficiency related to the purpose of the institution, namely learning, would have priority. However, a look at the historical development of the time organization of school learning reveals the strong impact of another criterion, namely the aim of adapting the structures of school time organization to those in the adults' working world; from the beginning, the school time regime has been isomorphic to the organization of work in industrial modernity. As Meyer and Rowan (1977) argued, the most important purpose of school organization is to legitimate itself towards society at large rather than to affect positively teaching and learning processes. This purpose becomes most obvious in the similarity of the organizational structures of schools and institutions in the economic arena.

The argument is underlined by the hesitance and slow pace of the recent changes from the traditional Taylorist school learning time regime towards a more individualized time organization, advocated by reform-oriented pedagogues. Of course, the mere persistence of fixed structures tends to inhibit changes, and usually rather strong pressure is needed in order to change fixed organizational structures. However, pedagogical efforts did not bring about the beginning of fundamental changes; rather these changes came about only when they were urged by economic demands for adapting young people to the less standardized and more individualized time use in the working world. Hence, these recent changes have been encouraged and performed through pedagogical efforts, but not caused by them.

Space

Many formally organized opportunities for children's activities, including school learning, institutional care or sport, are fixed to particular places, which are specialized for the respective institutional purpose. Thus, institutionalization binds children to sheltered places. The historian Ariès (1962) pointed out the increasing confinement of children that came about with scholarization and Zinnecker (1990) described that trend as *'domestication* of childhood' in the dual sense of the word of being confined in fenced areas and houses and being tamed.

Children come to an institution's place in order to do the particular activity, and they go to other institutions' places when they intend to do another – institutionalization is related to functional specialization and differentiation of space. All places that a child uses in the course of the day and week are located in archipelagos of more or less distant islands. A child's activities are thereby spatially segregated, and often his or her social relationships along with them. Such *insularisation* (Zeiher, 2001) impacts on children's ways of shaping daily life, in that it enforces an individual way of managing one's time, hence individualization (see below).

Since social space is no longer only physical space but also enlarged by the internet to include virtual space, media development also has to be examined for its impact on the institutionalization trend in childhood (see below).

Children's position within childhood institutions

Embedded and hidden in the family

In the generational order of modernity, the family became a particular childhood institution in that parents' division of labour, tasks and rights in relation to the child were informally and formally regulated by social values, norms, rules and laws. The family, represented by the parents, was related to the society at large, while children were positioned within the family and dependent on parents. Hence, children were treated as members of the family but not of society.

However, as a characteristic of modernity, children's family dependency became increasingly restricted. First, by separation and institutionalization of tasks; as a secular process, generational reproduction tasks have been transferred increasingly from the family towards state institutions. This began with the scholarization of children's learning and went on by institutionalizing care and leisure activities. Secondly, while welfare state interventions into the family in order to control the quality of care for children's health and to provide material resources were until recently directed towards the family and not the child, they are now subject to critical debate in order to address children in their own right (e.g., Olk and Wintersberger, 2007). Thirdly, in the course of establishing children's rights since the 1980s (see Freeman, this volume), state legislation has transferred more and more rights from the parents to the children themselves, including, for instance, laws which restrict the parents' rights of decision-making on the child in cases of parents separating or serious disease.

Individuation through institutionalization

In principle, institutions treat individuals by no other features than by belonging to a certain category, as holders of roles. Institutions are indifferent to other particularities of the person. As a client of schools, care and leisure organizations, the child is the basic unit of formal membership, rights, obligations, supports and control, and not the family. Hence, the secular transfer of tasks from the family to formal organizations is setting children partly free from being subjugated to the personal regime of the family, and placing them directly vis-à-vis structures defined on the level of society at large. In this sense, institutionalization goes along with individualization of the position in society or 'individuation' – a term preferred by some authors (Frønes, 1994; Näsman, 1994; Turner, 1986).

Ordering people into rational administrative categories without regard to their particular personality and personal life context means treating everybody in a similar way. Thus, individuation implies an emphasis on equality of individual rights and obligations as well as inclusion in mass society. In this sense, increasing institutionalization may be seen as an important moment on the historical path towards children's position in society as a population group in their own right, and children's participation in democratic rights.

Because individuation means, in principle, a disregard of family background and equality in respect to the purposes of the institution, social class differences are ignored in principle. Thus, compulsory schooling can serve as a policy measure in order to provide equal educational chances for children without regard to social class, gender or ethnicity. Since the 1960s, politicians have made efforts to increase institutionalized learning for all children from an early age. In this process, they have been highly aware of the fact that today's knowledge and service-oriented economies demand better qualification for all children, and that equal opportunities can be enhanced by more institutionalization – thus combining economic and democratic aims.

Individualized agency

Western modernity means not only increasing institutionalization and individuation but also the promise of individual autonomy. Since the eighteenth century, individualization in the sense of individual freedom and autonomy has been conceptualized in philosophical and educational theories, human rights and democracy have become political goals, and the self-reflexive and self-determined personality has become a key issue in social sciences and the arts. In sociological and public discourses on modernity, the aim of individualization was regarded as jeopardized by the standardization and structural control which became increasingly exerted on people's lives by the organizational means used in industrialized modernity. Contradictions between the trends of institutionalization and individualization were critically highlighted, one well-known example being Max Weber's ([1922] 1972) pessimistic view on increasing bureaucratic power.

Concerning children, such contradictions have been debated by educationalists since the beginning of the twentieth century and have led to reform efforts towards supporting individualized learning. Yet it is only in recent decades that the idea of the child as a subject has become the prevailing concept in child-related sciences, including pedagogy, child development psychology, socialization theory and new childhood sociology. This conceptual development changed the pedagogical practice in that parents and teachers are no longer supposed to behave in authoritarian ways but rather to treat children as responsible individuals, and negotiate rather than command (Honig, 1999). These developments are now gaining influence in that individualized learning has become most emphasized and is being increasingly implemented in schools. However, as mentioned above, while respective recent changes in the organization of schools and other child-related institutions were explicitly motivated by pedagogical concepts, the changes must basically be understood as part of and pushed by overwhelming societal processes.

It is not least the dynamics in the secular institutionalization process itself that have caused changes in children's agency. Two aspects can be identified: First, the expansion of learning, care and leisure institutions in the 1960s and 1970s described above led at the same time to an increase in differentiation of educational types and levels within schools, as well as outside school, where a variety of structured leisure, care and learning opportunities emerged. Institutions thereby evolved in a way that offered a wider range of options. Especially in the arena of leisure activities, children are required to make choices between structured opportunities, and to coordinate the temporal and spatial placement of activities and meetings in the course of their day and week. This development has fundamentally changed the relationship between the child and such institutionalized facilities. On the one hand, children's everyday lives have become related to more structured options and thereby more institutionalized; on the other hand, children are now required to carry out an additional new activity, namely individualized rational time-space management (Zeiher, 2001). In short, institutionalization supports individualization in that institutional structures are becoming more optional. However, as long as individualized agency is restricted to choices between packages of pre-organized activities, the child still has to adapt to each package. This reveals a new contradiction between institutionalization and individualization. While increasing institutionalization, on the one hand, augments the perceived options to shape life individually, on the other hand more institutionalization means more subjection to constraints concerning the performance of the chosen options (e.g., Beck, 1992). Concerns for 'the over-regulated child', which became an issue of public debate in the 1980s, may be seen as a reaction to the restricting impact of optionalization.

Secondly, in today's 'late', 'fluid' or 'reflexive' modernity, the organization of activities within institutional structures is also changing in character. Social structures tend to become de-standardized in that the organization of time and space is left more to individuals. Time is dealt with more flexibly and is less future-oriented, activities are less fixed to places and many distances can be bridged immediately by virtual means (e.g., Bauman, 2000). These changes first emerged in the world of work. Organizational forms of children's school learning are now becoming isomorphic to those of paid labour, in order to provide the young generation with time-organization-related qualifications needed in their future working life (Zeiher et al., 2007). This development is welcomed and realized by educationalists, who have long advocated such changes. However, some authors now question the limits of children's new individual autonomy by pointing out an even stricter dependency in that children are urged to internalize the societal control. The debate was started in Nordic countries, where such pedagogic changes had been implemented rather early (Warming Nielsen and Kampmann, 2007). The aforementioned contradiction between institutionalization and individualization, both permanent tendencies of modernity, seems not to be reduced in late modernity but rather sharpened due to progress in both tendencies.

Recent developments in the family as a childhood institution have also emerged as contributing to the individualization of children's agency. Changes in the gendered division of labour lead to young children spending more care time outside the family as well as to older children spending more time at home on their own (Solberg, 1990). 'Autonomous mothers need autonomous children' was a saying in the 1980s. The trend towards more parents separating may be pointed out as well. When a child no longer relies only on one family but rather on two single parents or these parents' new families, social spaces are constituted where the child temporally is positioned in spatial distance to the respective other parent. This may create reflexive distance and demand for individual agency (Jensen, 2007; Jensen, this volume).

Children meet social demands for individualized agency differently depending on their social background. Some authors (e.g., Warming Nielsen and Kampmann, 2007) indicate social class and ethnic differences in children's ability to cope with such demands, thus identifying a new source of social inequality.

De-Institutionalization?

Is there a trend towards de-institutionalization in today's childhood? Regarding the ongoing scholarization trend as well as the increasing welfare state activity in institutionalizing former family tasks, a general tendency towards de-institutionalization in social childhood cannot be established at all. Powerful economic interests in the labour power of the next generation and of women are pushing both scholarization and state interventions in the family in order to control and take over tasks.

But are there dynamics within that development that might counterbalance the institutionalization trend and change its impact on children? When we consider two general contradictions in the dynamics of modernity, a de-institutionalization trend may be expected. First, the structural influence over individuals' lives exerted by institutions contradicts modern society's basic promise to realize individualism and autonomy. If today's children experience institutional control less directly because of the aforementioned individualizing tendencies within the educational system and the family, it does not equate to a loss of control. Rather, a shift from external towards internalized control is taking place.

Secondly, organizational structures as such tend to resist changes. Inertia of structures contradicts the basic tendency of modernity to get everything static moving (Rosa, 2005, 156). Until now the development of modern society has been characterized by accelerated progress, thus creating increasing pressure for change. Does such pressure tend to inhibit further institutionalization or even destroy existing institutions? To what degree do institutions resist? Indeed, recent debates in sociology on changes from industrial towards late modernity often identify a recent shift from fixed towards more fluent social conditions, namely to a de-standardization of social structures, to tendencies towards flexibility and individualization in people's social and working life, and to erosions of border-lines within modernity's social order of gender, generation and social class (e.g., Bauman, 2000). The question of how childhood is included in such trends may be applied to the borderlines of childhood institutions.

Looked upon from the children's life situation as a whole, de-institutionalizing dynamics can be revealed as coming about in line with children's changing ways of living. Today's children use the tremendous amount of information offered by electronic media and thereby do an important part of learning on their own, and when older children increasingly participate in gainful work alongside school, they blur the institutional boundaries of modern childhood, according to which the learning child was confined within schools and separated from the world of work.

Pluralization of institutionalized options (see above) is accompanied by a choice in identity scripts transmitted by the media and the market. Not only does the mere optionalization seem to create the individuals' distance from an institution, but also the growing cultural emphasis on individual agency related to shaping one's own life and establishing a personal identity (Hengst, 2007). In the arena of young people's leisure time preferences, a de-institutionalizing activity exerted by the children themselves is also emerging rather clearly. Research into young people's sport preferences reveals a trend away from for-mally structured athletic training arrangements and towards a preference for individual performance of sporting skills practised in streets and other pub-lic areas using skates or special bikes. These young people are obviously with-drawing from adult-made-structured settings and strict time-space regimes, and creating their own common habits, which may be seen as a rather informal self-made institutionalization of social forms for individualized sport performance (Alkemeyer, 2003).

To sum up: On the level of daily life as well as on the mental level, children's position in relation to school and the family may be said to be becoming more 'individualized', and the relations between the childhood institutions and the children's perception of these are becoming more relaxed. However, while a multitude of small freedoms and blurring borderlines occur on the front stage of institutional frameworks, strong societal forces, not least economic ones, in the end restrict children's autonomy in relation to childhood institutions. On the social structure level, institutionalization is still increasing; scholarization is still progressing due to developments in knowledge and the economy, and the 'social investment state' is augmenting investments in children and thereby the institu-tionalization of childhood.

Note

1. The reasons for and mechanisms of the genesis, reproduction and impact of institutions have been an issue of various sociological approaches the range of which covers ques-tioning for the internalization of external systems of norms and rules as well as more recent 'neo-institutionalist' concepts (e.g., Dobbin, 1994) which highlight the impact of cultural perceptions and meanings.

References

Alkemeyer, T. (2003) 'Zwischen Verein und Straßenspiel', in H. Hengst and H. Kelle (eds) *Kinder, Körper, Identitäten*. Weinheim & München: Juventa, pp. 293–318.

Ariès, Ph. (1962) *Centuries of Childhood: A Social History of Family Life*. London: Jonathan Cape.

Bauman, Z. (2000) *Liquid Modernity*. Cambridge: Polity Press.

Beck, U. (1992) *Risk Society. Towards a New Modernity*. (First published in German 1986). London: Sage.

Bühler-Niederberger, D. (1991) *Legasthenie – Geschichte und Folgen einer Pathologisierung*. Opladen: Leske & Budrich.

Dobbin, F. R. (1994) 'Cultural Models of Organization: The Social Construction of Rational Organizing Principles', in D. Crane (ed.) *The Sociology of Culture: Emerging Theoretical Perspectives*. Cambridge: Blackwell, pp. 117–141.

Frønes, I. (1994) 'Dimensions of Childhood', in J. Qvortrup, M. Bardy, G. Sgritta and H. Wintersberger (eds) *Childhood Matters. Social Theory, Practice and Politics*. Aldershot: Avebury, pp. 145–164.

Hareven, T. (1986) 'Historical Changes in the Social Construction of the Life Course', *Human Development*, 29(3): 171–180.

Hengst, H. (2007) 'Not Quite Here and Not Quite There. Metamorphoses of the World within Reach', in H. Zeiher, D. Devine, A.T. Kjørholt and H. Strandell (eds) *Flexible Childhood? Exploring Children's Welfare in Time and Space*. Odense: University Press of Southern Denmark, pp. 95–119.

Honig, M.-S. (1999) *Entwurf einer Theorie der Kindheit*. Frankfurt am Main: Suhrkamp.

James, A. (2005) 'Life Times: Children's Perspectives on Age, Agency and Memory across the Life Course', in J. Qvortrup (ed.) *Studies in Modern Childhood*. Basingstoke: Palgrave Macmillan, pp. 248–266.

Jensen, A.-M. (2007) 'Mobile and Uprooted? Children and the Changing Family', in H. Zeiher, D. Devine, A.T. Kjørholt and H. Strandell (eds) *Flexible Childhood? Exploring Children's Welfare in Time and Space*. Odense: University Press of Southern Denmark, pp. 121–141.

Jensen, A.-M., A. Ben-Arieh, C. Conti, D. Kutsar, M. Nic Ghiolla Phadraig and H. Warming Nielsen (eds) (2004) *Children's Welfare in Ageing Europe*. Vol. 1 and 2. Trondheim: Norwegian Centre for Child Research.

Kelle, H. (2007) '"Ganz normal": Die Repräsentation von Kinderkörpernormen in Somatogrammen', *Zeitschrift für Soziologie*, 36(3): 199–218.

Kohli, M. (1985) 'Die Institutionalisierung des Lebenslaufs. Historische Befunde und theoretische Argumente', *Kölner Zeitschrift für Soziologie und Sozialpsychologie*, 37(1): 1–29.

Mayall, B. (1996) *Children, Health, and the Social Order*. Buckingham: Open University Press.

Mayer, K.U. and W. Müller (1985) 'The State and the Structure of the Life Course', in A.B. Sørensen, F.E. Weinert and L.R. Sherrod (eds) *Human Development and the Life Course. Multidisciplinary Perspectives*. Hillsdale NJ.: Erlbaum, pp. 217–245.

Meyer, J. and B. Rowan (1977) 'Institutionalized Organisations: Formal Structure as Myth and and Ceremony', *American Journal of Sociology*, 83(2): 340–363.

Näsman, E. (1994) 'Individualization and Institutionalization of Childhood in Today's Europe', in J. Qvortrup, M. Bardy, G. Sgritta and H. Wintersberger (eds) *Childhood Matters. Social Theory, Practice and Politics*. Aldershot: Avebury, pp. 165–187.

Olk, T. and H. Wintersberger (2007) 'Welfare States and Generational Order', in H. Wintersberger, L. Alanen, T. Olk and J. Qvortrup (eds) *Childhood, Generational Order and the Welfare State. Exploring Children's Social and Economic Welfare*. Vol. 1 of COST A19. Odense: University Press of Southern Denmark, pp. 59–90.

Qvortrup, J., M. Bardy, G. Sgritta and H. Wintersberger (eds) (1994) *Childhood Matters. Social Theory, Practice and Politics*. Aldershot: Avebury.

Rosa, H. (2005) *Beschleunigung. Die Veränderung der Zeitstrukturen in der Moderne.* Frankfurt am Main: Suhrkamp.

Solberg, A. (1990) 'Negotiating Childhood: Changing Constructions of Age for Norwegian Children', in A. James and A. Prout (eds) *Constructing and Reconstructing Childhood.* Brighton: Falmer Press, pp. 118–137.

Turmel, A. (1997) 'Childhood and Normalcy: Classification, Numerical Regularities, and Tabulations', *International Journal of Educational Research*, 27(8): 661–672.

Turner, B.S. (1986) *Citizenship and Capitalism. The Debate over Reformism.* London: Allan & Unwin.

Warming Nielsen, H. and J. Kampmann (2007) 'Children in Command of Time and Space?', in H. Zeiher, D. Devine, A.T. Kjørholt and H. Strandell (eds) *Flexible Childhood? Exploring Children's Welfare in Time and Space.* Odense: University Press of Southern Denmark, pp. 191–214.

Weber, M. (1972) *Wirtschaft und Gesellschaft.* (First published 1922). Tübingen: J.C.B. Mohr.

Zeiher, H. (2001) 'Children's Islands in Space and Time: The Impact of Spatial Differentiation on Children's Ways of Shaping Social Life', in M. Du Bois-Reymond, H. Sünker and H.H. Krüger (eds) *Childhood in Europe. Approaches – Trends – Findings.* New York: Peter Lang, pp. 139–159.

Zeiher, H., D. Devine, A.T. Kjørholt and H. Strandell (eds) (2007) *Flexible Childhood? Exploring Children's Welfare in Space and Time.* Vol. 2 of COST A19: Children's Welfare. Odense: University Press of Southern Denmark.

Zinnecker, J. (1990) 'Vom Straßenkind zum verhäuslichten Kind', in I. Behnken (ed.) *Stadtgesellschaft und Kindheit im Prozess der Zivilisation.* Opladen: Leske + Budrich, pp. 142–162.

9
Pluralization of Family Forms
An-Magritt Jensen

Why should people have children? Why should they marry and stay together? Questions that are seldom posed in poor societies now haunt the rich. Having children, forming families and staying in them were a matter of survival. This is no longer the case. The 'child issue' is part of an ever more difficult decision among young people who discuss, postpone and eventually reduce the intrusion of the ever more demanding presence of children in their personal lives. I shall venture the hypothesis that pluralization of family forms is about the increasing economic and social costs of children in the family. As children no longer represent a positive material gain to parents, the social institution for having them, marriage, transforms. The primary implications can be traced in the changing role of marriage followed by a host of new family forms, among which extramarital births, consensual unions and stepfamilies are the most widespread. The fading centrality of marriage represents a key point through which the marginalization of children in adults' lives is reflected.

It was through marriage, Foucault (1992) argues, that 'descendants' (children) could be legitimated and obtain citizenship in society. The Family Father of Roman law had three basic powers: *the right* over children, wife and property. As expressed by Therborn (2004, 13): 'The rule of the father and the rule of the husband, in that order.' Children were the centre of rotation and marriage was the social institution constructed to overcome the biological insecurity of fatherhood. Through marriage '...the rights of husbands to the exclusive sexual use of women's bodies and the right to the title of father of a particular woman's children' were ensured (O'Brien, 1981, 55). Formalizing families was a method of gaining control over the resource represented by children. Gillis (2000) describes pre-modern Europe as a society where the family father was a basis upon which property, power and prestige rested, while bachelors had no social position.

With industrialization the centrality of children to people's (men's) lives was lost. The immediate consequences were decimation in the number of children around the turn of the twentieth century (named the First Demographic Transition). This historic change transformed western societies. As children no longer were an economic benefit to the family, the need to produce a large quantity of them was substituted by the need to invest in fewer but 'quality' children. Educated children would ensure social mobility for the family. For the first decades marriage remained strong and the mid-century is regarded as the golden era of the house-wife. Divorce rates were low but the breadwinner/home-carer family was short-lived. As women entered the labour market on a mass scale the next transition was set in motion. The Second Demographic Transition 'marked the end of Ariès' era of the "child-king". It inaugurated a period of adult-centred preoccupations with self-fulfilment', Lesthaeghe maintains (1995, 19). As mothers left their household work to take up paid work the last justification for marriage evaporated. The change was first noted in the more secularized countries of northern Europe but gradually the changes were traced all over the western world. New family forms were more com-plex, less strictly patterned and, first and foremost, less stable.

The pluralization of family forms is the story of how changes at the macro level impact on childhood and children's lives. The character, scope and consequences of these changes are part and parcel of structural changes outside the family realm. As children no longer are vital for family survival, social prestige and accu-mulation of power, maintaining patriarchal rule over children and women was no longer necessary. Social ends are not achieved in the family but located in the labour market. In 'liquid modernity' long term attachment is counter-productive and the fast movers are the winners, Bauman (2000) argues. Children and mar-riage are postponed, avoided and shifted to short-lived and plural family forms. Family forms are subjected to 'flexibilization' along with the demands of the labour market. Children's family forms are in the midst of deep cutting changes of childhood, rightly described as a revolution by Hernandez (2001). Until the mid-century the majority of children in western countries were born after their parents' marriage, with bread-winning fathers and home-caring mothers. Since then the two-parent/one-time-married family is losing ground.

Children's lost monopoly on marriage

The rise of births outside marriage is the centre of gravity in this revolution. It works in concert with decreasing stability and shorter duration of all family forms, an outflow of fathers and an influx of new men in children's lives. Although the scope of change differs between countries, the process is general and has been accelerating over the last few decades.

Historically only the legitimate children counted. One destiny can illustrate the depth of shame and misfortune of children who happened to be illegitimate. The Norwegian writer Henrik Ibsen had his first child, Hans Jakob, in 1846. Ibsen was 17 and not married to the mother, a maid who was ten years older. Hans Jakob was doomed to a life of utmost poverty and so were his six children, grandchildren of Ibsen. None of them survived their thirtieth birthday. Ibsen reluctantly accepted the fatherhood of Hans Jakob, but there was no contact between this son and the father. The destiny of the first son stands in sharp contrast to Henrik Ibsen's second son, Sigurd, born in marriage 13 years later. Sigurd was awarded a doctoral degree in law at the age of 22. In 1895 he failed to be appointed as the first professor of soci-ology in Norway,[1] but became prime minister during the transition to independence from Sweden in 1905. Ibsen's legal descendants have formed a powerful line in the Norwegian intellectual and art elites for generations. What this destiny illustrates is that it was not any child who counted. Unmarried motherhood (and to some degree fatherhood) was a disgrace. For children, being born and raised in a marriage was the key to access to the highest rungs of the social ladder. Many European countries have similar stories to tell about the children who failed to be born into marriage. In Norway the resentment was strong and non-marital partnerships were even forbidden by law from 1842 until 1972. Children of unmarried mothers met a harsh destiny. Many did not survive childhood, struggled in utter poverty, and were stigmatized by disgraceful nicknames, like bastard, illegitimate or 'spurious'. Premarital pregnancy was widespread (about every second pregnancy), but only the unfortunate children did not succeed in being born in marriage. In Scandinavia, as was also the case for England, marriage was more about legitimizing children than controlling sexuality (Prinz, 1991; McRae, 1997).

By the turn of the twenty-first century children were more likely to be born into populations where more and more people did not have children. Children were also likely to be born outside marriage, to experience family shifts, to have few siblings, and to live either in a dual-earner or a one-parent family. The direction of change has been remarkable and uniform although the pace of change varies. It has gained its momentum during just one generation and is evolving across countries and continents in the rich world: in Europe, the United States of America, Canada and Australia. Despite cultural and religious resistance, marriage control over children is weakening everywhere.

Figure 9.1 (starting in 1970) demonstrates that the likelihood of a child being born to unmarried mothers in Europe was well below a 10 per cent line (with Iceland and Sweden as exceptions). Some 30 years later all countries display growth in the proportion of children born to unmarried mothers. In the Nordic countries this has exceeded or is about every second child and in most countries it accounts for more than 30 per cent. Some countries, like France, have a strong but even development throughout the period (7 per cent in 1970 to 46 per cent in 2004). In other countries the trend has accelerated since 1990, such as in Bulgaria. Until 1990 (the transition to the market economy) only slow changes took place (8.5 per cent in 1970 to 12 per cent in 1990). Since then, the increase is remarkable (49 per cent in 2004). The development is described as being in radical contradiction to the Eastern Orthodox tradition of the country.[2] Also in Ireland the acceleration took place after 1990 (3 per cent in 1970, 8.5 per cent in 1985 and 32 per cent in 2004). In some cases, like Germany, specific situations prevail. Before the unification the two parts of Germany had very different paths, with a strong increase and high levels of births among unmarried mothers in East Germany and a modest level in West Germany (55 per cent versus 21 per cent in 2002). After 2002, information is no longer given separately, and the proportion (29 per cent in 2004) is a mean of the two extremes. The overwhelming picture is one of general increases in children's likelihood of being born outside marriage, with a gradient from North to South, and (a less clear one) from West to East. The development runs across religions, as manifested by Catholic Ireland and the Eastern Orthodox tradition of

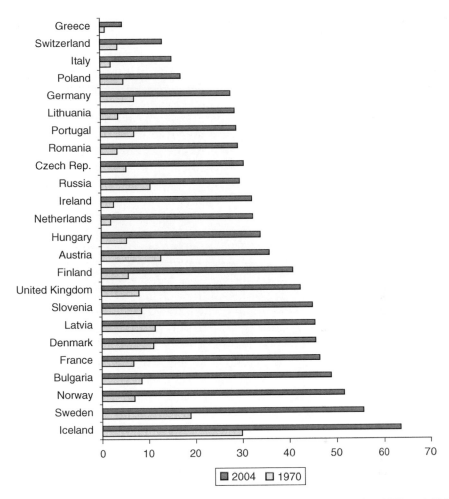

Figure 9.1   Extramarital births (per 100 births) among European countries, 1970 and 2004

Source: Sardon, Jean-Paul (2006) 'Recent Demographic Trends in the Developed Countries'. *Population* (English Edition), 61(3), 197–266.

Bulgaria, and political systems, as manifested by socialist East Germany and capit-alist West Germany. Country-specific manifestations can explain the change, but they all sum up to a rise in births outside marriage.

An unmarried mother used to be synonymous with a single mother. This is no longer the case. Many children are born to unmarried but not single mothers. In most Scandinavian countries (Norway, Sweden and Denmark) births outside marriage are absorbed in consensual unions (Statistics Sweden, 1992; Jensen and Clausen, 1997; Christoffersen, 1998). Around 5 to 6 per cent of all children were estimated to be born to mothers living alone and no changes have been noted in the proportion of children born to a two-parent family. Similarly in France, where the proportion of 'illegitimate' children grew five-fold (from 6 per cent to

30 per cent) between 1965 and 1990, only 4 per cent of these children did not have parents living together at the birth and were conceived in their parents' already existing union (Toulemon, 1995). On the other hand, in England extra-marital births are associated with an increase both in single motherhood and in consensual unions (Clarke and Jensen, 2004). Outside Europe, in the United States of America almost 40 per cent of all children born to unmarried mothers were born in a consensual union in the mid-1990s, up from 30 per cent in a decade, while the increase in children born to single mothers was much more modest (from 15 per cent to 17 per cent) (Bumpass and Lu, 2000). The countries may differ but increasing shares of children start their life in other family forms than to married parents.

Despite the historical resentment of unmarried mothers and their children, social scientists did not take much interest during the first decades of upsurge. In everyday life the transformation from a formal marriage to a 'paperless' union was invisible and largely unnoticed. The children did not carry any visual signs of distinctiveness or disgrace. No one would call them names. Neighbours would not know. As cohabitation diffused the issue, marriage seemed irrelevant. The lack of a marriage certificate was seen as insignificant as long as the children continued to be born into two-parent families. It was a widespread understanding that marriage and consensual unions were of the same kind. Statistics and research focused on the number of parents in families, single parent or two parents, ignoring the distinction between marriage and consensual union. Gradually, and with reluctance, awareness surfaced about the fundamental shift children's families had undergone. The lost monopoly of marriage at the birth of a child was the first step on the road to pluralization of children's family forms during childhood. Most important is the likelihood of these children not sharing their everyday life with the father, experiencing increased instability and precarious economic conditions in mother-only families. Being born to married parents is still the gateway to children's welfare.

Diversity, fragility and instability

The new family forms are not only plural. They are also fragile. Children are more likely to spend parts of their childhood in different family arrangements. In general, studies have confirmed that children born in consensual unions have greater risk of parental dissolution compared to children born to married parents (Jensen, 1992; Toulemon, 1995, 1997; Jensen and Clausen, 1997; Ottosen, 2000; Oláh, 2001; see Kiernan, 1999 for Europe in general). This picture accords with findings in the United States of America, where the trends for children born outside marriage are similar (Bumpass and Lu, 2000; Manning, 2004). Due to increasing fragility Bumpass and Lu estimated that two-fifths of all American children will spend some parts of their childhood in a consensual union, and about a third of the time with unmarried mothers is spent in cohabitation: 'we simply cannot address the changing family experiences of children while ignoring cohabitation', they conclude (39).

Children are increasingly planned but a pregnancy no longer leads to marriage, as it traditionally did. Furthermore, fewer cohabiting parents marry later. Consensual unions are 'here to stay' Toulemon (1997) stated a decade ago. Unmarried cohabitation had become a permanent mode of life and the motives to marry have shifted away from children to parents' relationships. The traditional 'protective' impact of children on family stability is weakening. Toulemon (1995) confirms for France that marriages are more stable than consensual unions. In addition the impact of children on family stability has declined and on the whole, Toulemon concludes, 'It is marriage, rather than the birth of a child, which appears to be a better guarantee of the stability of the couple' (1995, 183). There is ample research on family instability both in marriages and in consensual unions, but the likelihood of disruption is much higher where parents are not married, as we shall see later (Manning, 2004). The spread of consensual unions is a major factor leading to an increase in children not living with both parents, and it is working in concert with the escalation in divorce. The de-formalization of family types has hampered the possibilities of following children's families through statistics, while surveys have become the main method of mapping. Among these the WHO-based Health Behaviour in School-Aged Children (HBSC) is unique.[3] Figure 9.2 shows the average percentage of children aged 11 to 15 years living with one parent for a group of European countries.

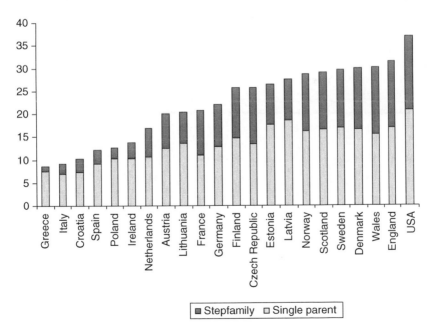

Figure 9.2   Percentage of children in European countries not living with both parents, 2000/2001

Source: Currie et al., 2004, fig. 2.7.

The majority of children in all countries live with both parents but Figure 9.2 also shows that substantial numbers of children in some countries do not. American children more often report other family forms (37 per cent). Among European countries about 30 per cent of the children in the northern countries have other family forms while for children in central and southern Europe other family forms, are rare. In Greece, 91 per cent of the children report living with both the mother and the father, while in Germany this is the case for 77 per cent. Children's families are pluralized by two mechanisms: at birth or through changing families during childhood. Hence, there is some, although not complete, correspondence between the proportion of children born to unmarried mothers and children living in other family forms. The children are not asked about the marital status of the parents and hence there is no distinction between marriage and cohabitation. But they are asked about step-parents and we can see that where the large majority of children (about 80 per cent) live with both parents, the rest are likely to live in single-parent families. By contrast, increased levels of destabilization also mean that more children are living with step-parents. Many aspects are not covered in this figure. Manning and Brown (2006) divide American children into six categories of prevailing family forms: married two biological parents (61 per cent), cohabiting two biological parents (3 per cent), married with one step-parent (8 per cent), cohabiting with one step-parent (3 per cent), single mother (21 per cent) and single father (3 per cent). The picture accords with the trends in many European countries as well. In the research network COST A19 Children's Welfare, all countries reported a destabilization of children's families. Despite this, there was very little effect on the gendered division of parenthood. The proportion of children living with their fathers, and not with their mothers, is typically reported to be about 2 to 3 per cent (Jensen et al., 2004). Children's families are diversified, but it is fathers (not mothers) who are less likely to share the everyday life with a child, and new men increasingly enter the family as a step-parent. Men are no less a part of children's families but their biological fathers are increasingly likely to live with other children. Figure 9.3 illustrates how children's families change while the two-adult family remains strong.

Figure 9.3 refers to Norway as an example of a general development. In 1989, 78 per cent of children under 18 lived with married parents. By 2006 this percentage was 59. Counting the number of parents, irrespective of marriage or consensual unions, we find that more children lived with both parents and the change is smaller. Furthermore, counting the number of adults, irrespective of biological bonds, we can see that 85 per cent of all children lived with two adults and there has been almost no change over the period. The cross-sectional picture of children's families displays the family forms but not the dynamics. About 40 per cent of the children born in the beginning of the 1990s are estimated not to live with their father throughout childhood (Jensen and Clausen, 1997). Among children with a parental break-up, divorce now accounts for only half, while the other half are children whose parents have broken up from consensual unions, or from a stepfamily – which is the most fragile family form (Statistics Norway, 2001). Similarly, for American children it is estimated that despite only 3 per cent

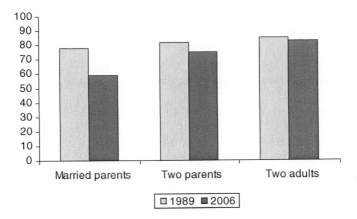

Figure 9.3 Children 0 to 17 years by their parents' status, Norway
Source: Statistics Norway – annual family statistics. Author's calculations.

of the children having cohabiting parents at any point in time, 40 per cent will spend a part of their childhood in this family form (Bumpass and Lu, 2000). It is the instability and the weakening position of fathers through the decline of marriages rather than single-parent families which are the important elements in children's families. The decline of the married-two-parent family is remarkable.

The fragility of consensual unions is a crucial factor in the pluralization of children's families. However, this is not the whole story. Comparing England & Wales to Norway highlights the importance of socio-economic forces in family formation and break-up (Clarke and Jensen, 2004). In Norway more children are born into a consensual union than in England & Wales. Still, more children experience a parental break-up in the latter countries. In both cases the relationship between cohabitation and fragile families is confirmed. But the overall risk of dissolution, in terms of both divorce and cohabitation, was much higher in England & Wales. The study also found that cohabiting mothers and fathers have lower education and income than married parents in both countries. But parents were more disadvantaged in England & Wales. Consensual unions were associated with less resources and higher risks among the least resourceful. Furthermore, the latter have a less generous welfare system for families with children. Hence, even if the mechanisms were the same, the effect on children's families was graver in England & Wales. The study concluded that there is an interaction between family forms, socio-economic resources and a risk of break-up: 'It is the well-known story where children of the "haves" are better off than children of the "have-nots". It may be masked as family changes, but behind this is the old pattern of social stratification' (Clarke and Jensen, 2004, 65). The study disclosed that the socio-economic disadvantages of cohabiting parents compared to married ones were a likely explanation for the differences. The issue is further explored below.

The concern about how a pluralization of family types may impact children's welfare has focused on two factors. The first is the economic consequences for the children. The second is the children's relationship with their father, and men in general. A third aspect, the impact on the children's everyday life, is seldom the focus of the debate. Here these three aspects are discussed one by one.

Economic responsibility for children

The pluralization of family forms has gone hand in hand with the upsurge in mothers taking employed work. In Scandinavia, with the highest rates, 70 to 80 per cent of mothers have an income of their own. In Norway, a survey on children's families revealed that the majority of children had parents who shared the child-related expenses[4] (Jensen and Clausen, 2000). However, focusing on those children where one of the parents covered most expenses alone (about one third) showed some interesting variations. In the modern family forms, such as consensual unions and stepfamilies, the mother was more likely than the father to cover the child-related expenses. By contrast, it was only in the families with traditional marriages that the father was more likely to cover such expenses. The mother's income seems to expand her economic responsibility for children and this responsibility accelerates along with new family patterns. Children having mothers with high earnings and living in consensual unions or stepfamilies were significantly more likely to have their expenses covered by her alone than children with low-earning mothers who were living with married parents. Mothers take over more economic responsibility for children in modern families. Furthermore, children in modern family structures more often live in conflict-ridden families. Money is at the heart of such conflicts.

Children born in consensual unions have in general parents with fewer educational and monetary resources compared to those born in marriage, as discussed above. Even if the cohabiting parent pioneers were found among higher educated people in the student population, in a short time this family type was followed up among the less well off. In fact, the cost of the wedding itself is an obstacle to marriage and young people with less resources give priority to other expenses (McRae, 1999). As seen, the case of England & Wales and Norway demonstrates the negative association between education, income and cohabitation which is traced in several countries (Manning and Lichter, 1996). Other studies in the United States of America have shown that college-educated women are more likely to marry and less likely to divorce than less educated women (McLanahan, 2004). As a result, children with parents breaking up from a consensual union are likely to suffer a stronger loss in resources than children experiencing divorce. The former group of children are more likely to be found among the less resourceful families from the beginning, and within this group the even less resourceful parents are more likely to separate.

The combined effect of parental resources, fragility and mothers' continued responsibility for children has resulted in a polarization of children's material welfare. The economic impact of family changes is essential as children's access to family resources declines sharply, McLanahan argues (2004). Children's access to family resources is most critical where the income was already low.

All over the western world children increasingly depend on two incomes for their economic welfare and working mothers are seen as a safety net for child poverty. Through working more parents can offer their children more. However, the number of children living in a one-parent family is increasing and all over Europe children in a single-earner family are at risk of poverty (Jensen et al., 2004). Actually, children in one-income families have high levels of poverty even if their parents live together (UNICEF, 2005). Italy and the United Kingdom are among the countries with the highest rates of child poverty in Europe for two different reasons. In Italy traditional family types of bread-winning fathers and home-caring mothers prevail. In the United Kingdom modern family types with high rates of single-mother families are significant. In both cases there is only one earner, while two incomes are needed. The provision of children is left to family systems with shrinking economic capacity. Italy and the United Kingdom are here used only to exemplify a condition with growing relevance to modern childhood. UNICEF finds that in most countries in Europe child poverty increased during the 1990s.[5] With more earning power among mothers in general, the economic resources in the family are expanded provided the parents stay together. Children with stable, two-earner families are the economic winners. Children without such families are the losers. But in this process of polarization the children who happen to be born to stable and dual-earning parents are getting fewer. Pluralization of family types increases the economic inequality among children and parental break-up is the single most important factor pushing children down the economic ladder.

An important mechanism through which inequality expands is the stability in the gendered division of parenthood. With more children remaining with the mother, a long-term shift from male to female economic responsibility over children is taking place. The more powerful (men) are substituted by the weaker (women) as the economic agent of the family. In Scandinavia, where much emphasis is given to promoting female employment, the gender segregation of the labour market is among the strongest in Europe. The welfare state allows only a small proportion of children to fall into poverty (about 3 per cent), but is at the same time an employer to many mothers who are paid low earnings in the care sectors. Paradoxically, children's well-being is jeopardized in a double sense since children are a main reason why women earn less than men do.

Fathers and men in children's life

Much attention is given to fathers as carers. When little Leo was expected, a public debate in Britain questioned whether or not the father, prime minister Tony Blair, ought to take paternity leave. The fact that this was debated at all reflects a change in the cultural expectations of fatherhood. In several countries public policy has supported fathers' possibilities of taking a more active role in the care of small children. In Sweden and Norway[6] the introduction of a 'daddy quota' in parental leave has been welcomed. Fathers have used their rights and across countries a positive association is found between the proportion of children born outside marriage and the father's use of time in child care (Thomson, 2003). In Sweden, often regarded as one of the countries where genders are the most equal, cohabiting fathers are more likely to use their 'daddy quota' than married fathers (Oláh, 2001). Hence, in the new family types fathers are more active in child care and cohabiting fathers seem to be at least as, if not more, involved with their children than married fathers. Finally, consensual fathers do not seem to have less frequent visiting patterns with their child after dissolution (Jensen and Clausen, 1997; Skevik, 2006).

Despite the 'new role of fathers' children are no less the responsibility of their mother (Jensen at al., 2004). In general, children live with their mother, but the likelihood of living with the father depends on the family type and is lower if parents were not married. Since the legal rights of parental responsibility[7] traditionally have followed marriage, many unmarried fathers did not share this responsibility with the mother at the time of the break. Much political attention is given to strengthening the linkages between children and their fathers after break-up. The weaker parental rights of cohabiting fathers have been an important issue in policy. The expected result of strengthening such rights is more equality in parenting after break-up. In Sweden, where equalization of parental rights was implemented in the early 1990s, a further escalation in break-ups took place in the following years (Oláh, 2001). As an explanation it is suggested that fathers who previously would maintain a less favourable relationship are freer to leave such a union as these rights are secured. Hence, making the rights of fathers independent of their marital status has increased children's likelihood of not living with him.

The combination of modern family patterns with ideologies of gender equality is important to children and father involvement. While cohabiting fathers are more oriented towards child care than married fathers, they are also less likely to remain living with their children. The fatherless society is featured as *the crisis* of our day (as described by Blankenhorn, 1995, among others). Keeping in contact with the father is seen as the solution to the problems that family dissolutions may cause. However, commuting does not solve all problems for children with parents living apart; it may even create some new ones.

Children as family nomads

The movement of children between parental homes is primarily a result of parents' decisions and wishes about where to live, and whether to live together or not. The often referred to notion of Beck and Beck-Gernsheim (2002, 91) that 'Family life no longer happens in one place but is scattered between several different locations' captures a condition of childhood about which little is known. With more parents living apart, children maintain family ties by commuting. Children's relations to the non-resident parent are part of a bureaucratization of parenthood, often by a written contract between the parents. Children keep in contact with their fathers in this situation, but we may ask whether they have a right to an agenda of their own. Children's own leisure and activities with friends are likely to be subordinated to the visiting schedules their parents have agreed upon, often in a heated and conflict-ridden situation after a break-up.

Children's mobility between parental homes may remove them spatially from their friends, leisure activities, home and community, while attaching them emotionally to the parents. The everyday lives of children living within walking distance between parental homes (and within a short distance in general) may benefit from a shared neighbourhood. It may be easier to maintain friends and leisure activities. Distance impacts children's influence on the visiting schedules, as well as their satisfaction with the arrangement. Children in walking distance have more control and are more satisfied with their visiting frequencies than the long-distance travellers. But not all children have walking distance between their parents.

In Norway the majority of children have longer distances. Furthermore, age is important for children's visiting frequencies. In general older children have fewer visits than younger children, but they also have more influence. Over time, children's mobility between parental homes has been increasing, as has the incidence of children living in two households on a shared basis (Jensen, 2007). About 10 per cent in Norway and 18 per cent in Sweden are in this situation. In England, Wade and Smart (2003) have shown that while there is a growing presumption that 'equal' parenting is fair, children over time start questioning why they must carry the burden of commuting. Time has become the yardstick for a 'fair' sharing of children, while children may feel that they are shared as if they are parental property. Another study (Robinson et al., 2003) found that children often lamented the practical issues involved in changing homes, lack of space in their (often temporary) new home, difficulties with their parents' new partners, and lack of time alone with the non-resident parent. But they also had a growing capacity to manage their 'time-maps'. The contact with the other parent represented emotional 'highs' but also 'lows'. The situation is complicated to resolve. Children had a desire for 'normality' when visiting the other parent, as they longed for 'the rest of their lives'. While enjoying being together with one parent, they often missed the other. Their life was divided into whom to be with, and what to do, depending on whom they visited.

Potential problems associated with commuting have been under-explored in research. Most children will be able to master travelling alone. But there are clearly also those who will not. The very lack of attention to the issue raises the question of whether potential conflicts between children's welfare and father contact have been covered up by interests stronger than children themselves. Children are exposed to the 'world of travellers' when their parents separate. Their mobility is justified by the general assumption that the most important problem of family dissolutions is too little contact with the absent parent. However, while losing contact can be detrimental to children's welfare, challenges and uncertainties in moving between homes may undermine their interests in ways gaining less attention. Children's spaces are expanded as their homes are divided. The social and geographically located space of a home is gradually exchanged for maintaining emotional relationships. But children's time is subjected to new demands out of their own control.

Structural changes and children's agency

The relationship between structure and agency is at the core of sociological controversies: where does agency start, and how does it interact with structure? From Marx and Durkheim onwards, the sociological legacy tells us that individuals do not choose their life in a vacuum but act within a system of social relationships. More recent sociologists, such as Beck and Beck-Gernsheim (2002), argue that the process of individualization undermines the traditional social institutions to the advantage of the individual as a basic unit of social actions. While we may discuss the degree to which the parental generation, man and woman alike, are free to choose their family form at any stage of a historical process, it is clear that the pluralization of family forms is driven by adults, not children. For example, pregnancy used to be an important reason to marry and children were a major reason to stay in marriage. In this sense children influenced their parents' behaviour first to marry and next to keep on in the marriage 'for the children's sake'. This 'symbolic power' that children possessed over their parents' entrance into and exit out of marriage is now largely lost (Jensen, 2003). It was not openly recognized as a kind of 'child power', but was working through the collective consciousness of marriage as the only place for having and rearing children. This power vanished during the 1970s and after. We may argue over whether children's power to influence marriage patterns was to the benefit of children or not. Many accounts are given about children growing up in families full of misery, where their best interest would have been a split-up. On the other hand, are we sure that the substitute for children's power over marriage (pluralization of family forms) is in accordance with their best interests?

Are children actors in changing families? Many will argue that the negotiating position of children within the family has been augmented. Children are listened to and have a say in contrast to the more remote relations between the generations in previous times (Hendrick, 1997; du Bois-Reymond, 2001). In the mass media the negotiating power of children is often portrayed as a problem. Discipline is on the decline and exhausted parents do their best in trying to satisfy their children's demands. But where should we draw the limits of children's negotiating powers? Robinson et al. (2003) analysed the agency of English children in their parents' divorce. They found that most children had little information about why their parents divorced or what this would mean for them. Furthermore many children found that their parents 'moved on' with their lives and were reluctant to dwell on the divorce, as were their own siblings as well. Children had to turn to other places for comfort and support. Grandparents often provided a 'safe' and 'neutral' territory. Likewise, friends could comfort, but often in privacy and only the trusted ones. Most children told that they kept the divorce secret to reduce the risks of being different. Their parents' new relationships represented a major challenge, and many children expressed ambivalence about this. In particular, getting to know about the new partner seemed critical as several parents initially kept the relationship secret and children got to learn about it in unexpected ways.

Only a minority of the children were consulted about important issues such as where to live and how to stay in contact with the other parent, but those children who were involved also reported more satisfaction. Despite stumbling blocks in the process, over time children demonstrated a growing capacity to balance a number of competing demands. Robinson et al. (2003, 88) conclude that 'children do not experience their parent's divorce passively: they are involved, creative and resourceful participants'. Children have some agency but seemingly this is kept in a rather limited space, and a major space of this agency is traced in their capacity to adjust.

Pluralization of family forms can be understood both on a structural level and on the level of actors. Children, as a rule, have modest influence in both cases. On the macro level the drivers of the pluralization are traced in the structural forces of society, in the new demands on adults' lives. While the large majority of children half a century ago were born into a nuclear family, with married parents of largely homogeneous backgrounds, they are now born into a host of different family types, including those not discussed above (same-sex partnerships, self-chosen single parenthood and a multitude of mixtures of ethnic, cultural and religious attributes). In this sense, pluralization is outside the scope of children as actors. Pluralization can also be understood on an individual level and concerns the stability of whatever family type children are born into. The question is whether children are more likely to experience several family forms due to changes during their childhood. Once again, the children are in most cases left without much influence. Their parents are the decision makers. Still, if children have no say in the broad processes of pluralization, formation and dissolution of families, they do play important roles in adjustments to the family type within which they live their lives.

Pluralization of family forms provides a particularly interesting case of changes in the relationship between structure and agency because the agency in question belongs to the adults. Adults, not children, are at the centre of the broad transformations of families. This raises the question: is choice and freedom for adults enhanced at the expense of safety and security for children? Outside the scope of agency the pluralization of children's family types should be understood in the context of a market society where families are a barrier to the full utilization of the labour supply in society. As noted by the Australian demographer John Caldwell (1982, 237) capitalism needs individuals, not families.

Notes

1. After this, a professorship in sociology was not established until 1949.
2. Communicated by Prof. Mihael Mirchev, University of National and World Economy, Sofia, Bulgaria, March 2007.
3. It was established in 1982 with five countries, and has grown to cover more than 30 countries and regions. In every country about 1500 children aged 11, 13 and 15 years are filling out a questionnaire about, among other aspects, their family situation (Currie et al., 2004).
4. Child care, clothes, leisure and transport.

5. In the United Kingdom a decline has taken place. However, the level is still among the highest.
6. Recently also introduced in Germany.
7. This is the right to be involved in important decisions such as education, religion and health matters for the child. It must not be confused with the child's residential home.

References

Bauman, Z. (2000) *Liquid Modernity*. Cambridge: Polity Press.
Beck, U. and E. Beck-Gernsheim (2002) *Individualization*. London: Sage Publications.
Blankenhorn, D. (1995) *Fatherless America. Confronting Our Most Urgent Social Problem*. New York: Basic Books.
Bumpass, L. and H.-H. Lu (2000) 'Trends in Cohabitation and Implications for Children's Family Context in the United States', *Population Studies*, 54(1): 29–41.
Caldwell, J.C. (1982) *Theory of Fertility Decline*. London: Academic Press.
Christoffersen, M.N. (1998) 'Growing up with Dad – a Comparison of Children Aged Three to Five Years Old Living with Their Mothers or Their Fathers', *Childhood*, 5(1): 41–54.
Clarke, L. and A.-M. Jensen (2004) 'Children's Risk of Parental Break-Up: Norway and England/Wales Compared', *Acta Sociologica*, 47(1): 51–70.
Currie C., C. Roberts, A. Morgan, R. Smith, W. Settertobulte, O. Samdal and V.B. Rasmussen (2004) *Young People's Health in Context. Health Behaviour in School-Aged Children (HBSC) Study: International Report from the 2001/2002 Survey*. Health Policy for Children and Adolescents, no. 4, Geneva: WHO.
du Bois-Reymond, M. (2001) 'Negotiation Families', in M. du Bois-Reymond, H. Sünker and H.-H. Krüger (eds) *Childhood in Europe. Approaches – Trends – Findings*. New York: Peter Lang, pp. 63–90.
Foucault, M. (1992 [1984]) *The Use of Pleasure. The History of Sexuality: 2*. London: Penguin Books.
Gillis, J.R. (2000) 'Marginalization of Fatherhood in Western Countries', *Childhood* 7(2): 225–238.
Hendrick, H. (1997) *Children, Childhood and English Society 1880–1990*. Cambridge: Cambridge University Press.
Hernandez, D. (2001) ' "Revolutions in Children's Lives." With David E. Myers', in A.S. Skolnick and J.H. Skolnick (eds) *Family in Transition*. 11th edn. Boston: Allyn & Bacon, pp. 288–297.
Jensen, A.-M. (1992) *Det vaklende faderskapet? Barns familier etter samlivsbrudd*. [The Fragile Fatherhood? Children's Families after Family-Dissolution.] Report no. 9, Oslo: Norwegian Institute for Urban and Regional Research.
Jensen, A.-M. (2003) 'For the Children's Sake: Symbolic Power Lost?', in A.-M. Jensen and L. McKee (eds) *Children and the Changing Family. between Transformation and Negotiation*. London: RoutledgeFalmer, pp. 134–148.
Jensen, A.-M. (2007) 'Mobile and Uprooted? Children and the Changing Family', in H. Zeiher, D. Devine, A.T. Kjørholt and H. Strandell (eds) *Flexible Childhood? Exploring Children's Welfare in Time and Space*. Odense: University Press of Southern Denmark, pp. 121–141.
Jensen, A.-M. and S.-E. Clausen (1997) *Barns familier. Samboerskap og foreldrebrudd etter 1970*. [Children's Families. Consensual Unions and Parental Break-Up since 1970] Report no. 21, Oslo: Norwegian Institute for Urban and Regional Research.
Jensen, A.-M. and S.-E. Clausen (2000) *Barndom – forvandling uten forhandling? Samboerskap, foreldreskap og søskenskap*. [Childhood – Transformation without Negotiation? Consensual Unions, Parenthood and Siblings]. Report no. 6, Oslo: Norwegian Institute for Urban and Regional Research.
Jensen, A.-M., A. Ben-Arieh, C. Conti, D. Kutsar, M. Nic Ghiolla Phádraig and H. Warming Nielsen (eds) (2004) *Children's Welfare in Ageing Europe*. Vol. 1 and 2, Trondheim: Norwegian Centre for Child Research (NOSEB).

Kiernan, K. (1999) 'Cohabitation in Western Europe', in *Population Trends* 96. London: The Stationery Office.

Lesthaeghe, R. (1995) 'The Second Demographic Transition in Western Countries: An Interpretation', in K.O. Mason and A.-M. Jensen (eds) *Gender and Family Change in Industrialized Countries*. Oxford: Clarendon Press, pp. 17–62.

Manning, W.D. (2004) 'Children and the Stability of Cohabiting Couples', *Journal of Marriage and Family*, 66(3): 674–689.

Manning, W.D. and D.T. Lichter (1996) 'Parental Cohabitation and Children's Economic Well-Being', *Journal of Marriage and Family*, 58(4): 998–1010.

Manning, W.D. and S. Brown (2006) 'Children's Economic Well-Being in Married and Cohabiting Parent Families', *Journal of Marriage and Family*, 68(2): 345–362.

McLanahan, S. (2004) 'Diverging Destinies: How Children are Faring Under the Second Demographic Transition', *Demography*, 41(4): 607–627.

McRae, S. (1997) 'Cohabitation: a Trial Run for Marriage?' *Sexual and Marital Theraphy*, 12(3): 259–273.

McRae, S. (1999) 'Cohabitation or Marriage? – Cohabitation', in G. Allan (ed.) *The Sociology of the Family. a Reader*. Oxford: Blackwell Publishers, pp. 172–190.

O'Brien, M. (1981) *The Politics of Reproduction*. London: Routledge & Kegan Paul.

Oláh, L. Sz. (2001) 'Policy Changes and Family Stability: The Swedish Case', *International Journal of Law, Policy and the Family*, 15(1): 118–134.

Ottosen, M.H. (2000) *Samboskab, Ægteskap og Forældrebrud. En analyse af børns familieforhold gennem de første leveår*. København: Socialforskningsinstituttet 00:9.

Prinz, C. (1991) Marriage and Cohabitation in Sweden. Paper prepared for the European Population Conference, 21–25 October, Paris.

Robinson, M., I. Butler, L. Scanlan, G. Douglas and M. Murch (2003) 'Children's Experience of Their Parents' Divorce', in A.-M. Jensen and L. McKee (eds) *Children and the Changing Family. between Transformation and Negotiation*. London: RoutledgeFalmer, pp. 76–89.

Skevik, A. (2006) 'Absent Fathers or "Reorganized Families"? Variations in Father-Child Contact after Parental Break-up in Norway', *The Sociological Review*, 54(1): 115–132.

Statistics Norway (2001) *Å gjete kongens harer*. (To herd the king's hares – Norwegian saying). http://www.ssb.no/magasinet/analyse/art-2001-12-11-01.html (date accessed 17 February 2003).

Statistics Sweden (1992) *Barnens familjeförhållanden år 1985* (Children's families 1985). Örebro: Statistiska meddelanden (juli).

Therborn, G. (2004) *Between Sex and Power. Family in the World, 1900–2000*. London: Routledge.

Thomson, E. (2003) *Partnerships and Parenthood: A Comparative View of Cohabitation, Marriage and Childbearing*, CDE-Working Paper No. 18, University of Wisconsin-Madison: Center for Demography and Ecology.

Toulemon, L. (1995) 'The Place of Children in the History of Couples', *Population: an English Selection*, 7: 163–186.

Toulemon, L. (1997) 'Cohabitation Is Here to Stay', *Population: An English Selection*, 9: 11–46.

UNICEF (2005) *Child Poverty in Rich Countries 2005*. Report Card No. 6, Florence: Innocenti Research Centre.

Wade A., and C. Smart (2003) 'As Fair as It Can Be?', in A.-M. Jensen and L. McKee (eds) *Children and the Changing Family. Between Transformation and Negotiation*, London: RoutledgeFalmer, pp. 105–119.

Section III
Generational Relations

10
Generational Order

Leena Alanen

Introduction

As distinctively sociological approaches to the study of childhood were debated and the novel field of childhood studies began to emerge in the 1980s and 1990s, *generation* was identified early on as a key concept for establishing this new manner of thinking in the social sciences. Jens Qvortrup (1985, 1987) was one of the first to argue the case; he wrote that in industrial society the concept of generation has acquired a broader meaning than in earlier societal formations as 'children' and 'adults' have now assumed structural attributes relative to each other. It was therefore useful, he wrote, to treat 'childhood' and 'adulthood' as structural elements in an interactive relation and childhood as a particular social status (Qvortrup, 1987, 19).

Generation, of course, is not a new term in sociology. It has been conceptualized in a number of ways and several analytical frames exist for studying generational issues. The best known of them is probably the cultural study of historical generations, introduced into sociology by Karl Mannheim in the late 1920s and enjoying something of a revival since the beginning of the 1990s (e.g., Pilcher, 1994, 1995; Becker, 1997; Corsten, 1999; Edmunds and Turner, 2002). The term also appears in studies of age categorization, where it tends to be used synonymously with 'age group' or 'cohort'. There is also a broad range of studies that focus on changes in intergenerational relationships; these were particularly promoted in the 1950s, often with functionalist overtones with a focus on problematical relations between the 'young generation' and their parent generations (e.g., Eisenstadt, 1956). More recently the focus has been extended to cover a broader range of intergenerational relationships, including multigenerational relationships (e.g., Liebau and Wulf, 1996; Arber, 2000).

Qvortrup's proposal for a *structural* use of the terms 'childhood' and 'adulthood' however points in a different direction. It particularly marks a difference from the everyday common-sense meanings of the terms as well as from the meanings that are attached to them in mainstream social science.[1] In both everyday discourse and social science contexts, the terms childhood and adulthood are mostly taken to refer to two 'stages' in the biography of human individuals: childhood comes first and is followed – through the transitional stage of youth – by adulthood and, later, by 'old age'. Generational relations then denote the relationships between individuals located in different life stages (intergenerational relations) or between individuals sharing the life stage (intragenerational relations). 'Children', for example, in this understanding simply denotes those individuals that are currently living their lives within the childhood stage.

In modern Western societies this division (or 'structuring'; Hockey and James, 1993) of the course of individual life into stages has been standardized, normalized and institutionalized in multiple ways by legislation and welfare state institutions (e.g., Kohli, 1986). People are routinely and across most, if not all, social domains defined in terms of their (chronological) age and assigned to the appropriate life stage, and their behaviour and management is prevalently judged against standard models of their life stage (e.g., Blatterer, 2007a). In social science, conceptual and methodological tools have been developed to study the phenomenon of life course, its divisions and internal transitions, and the changes at, and current reality of, each stage (e.g., Hockey and James, 1993; Giele and Elder, 1998; Hareven, 1999).[2]

In contrast, the newly proposed idea of childhood as an element of social structure calls for differently composed sociological tools. These acknowledge as their basis and starting point for (re)conceptualization, research methodology and empirical exploration, the fundamentally *relational* nature of the social categories of childhood and adulthood. Fitz and Hood-Williams were ahead of their time (1982, 65) when they pointed out that:

> If we wish to understand 'youth' and childhood we have to proceed not by studies of discrete phenomena but by studies of *relationships*, since youth [or childhood/LA] is not a function of age but a *social category constituted in relation to*, and indeed in opposition to, the category adult (as is feminine to masculine). (Emphasis added by LA)[3]

Fitz and Hood-Williams (1982, 66) also observe that the family is the key institutional setting for the child–adult relationship, but children and adults of course also meet in several other settings. They therefore suggest that it would be more appropriate to speak of the adult–minor relation and its constitution.[4] To denote the structured system of child–adult relations, Fitz and Hood-Williams adopt the concept of 'patriarchy' from the historical and anthropological study of kinship relations and Max Weber's analysis of patriarchal relations of authority (see also Hood-Williams, 1990). Similarly Qvortrup's designation of childhood as a particular social *status* (Qvortrup, 1987, 19) underlines the economic and political nature of child–adult relations.[5]

In this chapter 'generation', and not 'patriarchy' or other terms deriving from patriarchal discourse, is adopted as a key term in developing a structural, generational approach for the sociological study of childhood.

Generational order

A generational perspective was adopted in the research of the international Childhood as a Social Phenomenon project (1987–1992), which was established to study the characteristic social features of childhood across a number of Western societies. The core idea in the project's approach was the idea of dynamic social relations between generations, which now were understood as the elements (or units) of a generational structure. In the final product of the project (Qvortrup et al., 1994) a number of analyses were presented on the relations between childhood and adulthood at the social macro level, and also a number of new concepts were suggested to develop further the new sociological thinking (Qvortrup, 1994). The idea of a *generational order* was one of them; it was presented as a useful analytic tool to work on and to refine, and to develop into a comprehensive framework for the social study of childhood (Alanen, 1994; also Alanen, 1992, 64–71).

The core idea in the notion of a generational order is that there exists in modern societies a system of social ordering that specifically pertains to children as a social category, and circumscribes for them particular social locations from which they act and thereby participate in ongoing social life. Children are thus involved in the daily 'construction' of their own and other people's everyday relationships and life trajectories.

Among social scientists, Philippe Ariès (1962) was the first to promote the view that childhood had been only fairly recently created as a distinct (relational) location for the younger members of modern society. While there has been a fair amount of debate on the argument of childhood as a historical invention and on the adequacy of the historical evidence that Ariès presented, his work has to be credited for preparing ground for discussing the emergence of a specific structural position of childhood and of children as a separate social category that is interrelated to other social categories.

This idea of an internal (necessary) relationality (Sayer, 1992, 88–92) between generational categories is a grounding assumption for the new manner of thinking. Their interdependence means that they stand in a relation of mutual constitution – they reciprocally presume each other. For social practice the implication is that childhood and adulthood are produced and reproduced in the interactions taking place between members of existing generational categories – in other words, in intergenerational practices. Through such practices a particular social structure also recurrently emerges. And as this structure is a particular organization of social relations, in this case relations between generational categories, it is fitting to call it a *generational* order.

Childhood, not to mention adulthood, will hardly be a homogeneous entity, for within each broad generational category subcategories will probably emerge. What these subcategories are in each case, and how they emerge and are recognized, both socially and practically, will always be an empirical question to study. A preliminary summary definition for a generational order at any point of time and place is: a generational order is a structured network of relations between generational categories that are positioned in and act within necessary interrelations with each other.

The importance of generation: intersectionality

The importance of recognizing generational ordering as a distinct organizing principle of social relations is that it proposes one further socially determining structuration for social scientists to consider in addition to the more recognized social class, gender, 'race', ethnicity, dis/ability and sexuality/sexual orientation (see also Prout, 2002). Each of these categories was long understood as a pre-given condition within the natural order of things, and each of them has now been submitted to critical social analysis and deconstruction. Their 'socially constructed' nature has been revealed and their long-lived 'misrecognition' (Bourdieu) as natural facts (albeit always marked by time and place) has been undermined. New questions on their construction, operation and effects have been raised for study, driving forward their reconceptualization to the point that now each of these structural categories has a place within social theory and research, even if they have remained contested concepts. And as they all operate in the same social space – 'society' – their interconnections (which is the issue of intersectionality) has also emerged as a theoretical topic for social science research (e.g., McCall, 2005; Walby, 2007).

One significant implication of the idea of a generational order is that the social world is not only simultaneously gendered, classed, 'raced', and so on; it is also organized in terms of generational ordering – it is also 'generationed' – and it is this insight that calls for structural and relational rethinking in the sociology of childhood.

Such an argument reveals a certain discrepancy between the terminological practice that prevails in the 'new' social study of childhood and the newly suggested understanding (concept) of generational ordering. To begin with, to take generational ordering seriously is to assume that children's lives and experiences are in addition to being gendered, classed, raced, and so on, also – and first of all – generationed. This calls us to accept that not everything observable and knowable about the lives and the experiences of the human individuals that we in everyday speech call children can be attributed to their 'childness' (cf. Cook-Gumperz, 1991), that is the generational 'segment' of their lives and experiences.[6] Quite obviously these human individuals are also, and simultaneously, girls and boys, so the very same lives and experiences also need to be seen as gender-ordered, and through an appropriate analytical gender 'lens' we would be led to discern determinate processing of gendering that has impacted the lives and experiences of these (young) individuals. The same logic also applies to social class, race/ethnicity, dis/ability and the other recognized powerful structurations: each of them also has determinate effects on the everyday lives, experiences and understandings of those human individuals whom we in our everyday terms continue to speak of and identify (terminologically) as 'children'. As if we could subsume them totally under just one form of organizing social relations which – paradoxically – would be a *generational* order of relations still waiting to be recognized, investigated and conceptualized.

Is it therefore not rather interesting that in our scientific discourse we seem to practice *terminological* generationing when focusing research interest on 'children' while at the same time we lag in *theoretical* generationing? Sociology lacks conceptual tools that will help to produce knowledge on the generational 'segment' of individuals' lives, in this case the material, social and cultural processes through which individuals acquire the social quality of 'childness' and the status of 'child'. Presumably there are still some hidden generational discourses in action in much sociological thinking which would need to be challenged and deconstructed in order to open up new ways to develop generational analysis. To begin to do so, 'conceptual autonomy' (cf. Thorne, 1987) needs now to be granted to the generational segment of the social world. Developing 'generation' as a parallel to other powerful social structures (gender, race, etc.) will also help to integrate the study of childhood issues into intersectional analyses that will be able to account for the complex social phenomena that make lived childhoods.

This chapter, then, proposes that 'generational order' provides a conceptual starting point and an analytical tool for framing the study of childhood in ways that will capture both the structured nature of childhood and children's active presence in generational structures. The following sections introduce some conceptual resources for advancing in this direction.

First, the concept of generation is revisited: the theoretical and methodological use into which Karl Mannheim put the notion when developing his cultural theory of generations is briefly reviewed and some insights are drawn from his thinking. These then are discussed in the context of class theory and structural concepts of social class. Feminist work on gender and the gender order provides the third pool of analytical resources for further elaborating the concept: by cautiously paralleling 'generation' with 'gender' (as with class), we hope the contours of a conceptual frame for generational analysis will emerge. Moreover some of the first attempts to study generational order(ing) will be presented in the sections to follow.

Mannheim's concept of generation

Important lessons may be learned, first, by studying Karl Mannheim's idea of (cultural) generations and the analogy he makes between generation and (social) class.

In his famous essay from the end of the 1920s, Mannheim's interest was focused on generations as cultural phenomena and their historical emergence. Mannheim's special interest was in the role that culturally formed generations could take in social change (Matthes, 1985; Corsten, 1999); in his own formulation he proposed a 'theory of intellectual evolution' (Mannheim, 1952 [1928], 281).

Generations are formed, he wrote, when members of a particular age group (or a cohort) during their youthful years live through the same social and historical events and experience them as significant to themselves. Through such shared

experience, members of the age group come to develop a common consciousness, which is observable even to outsiders and is expressed in a shared world
view and shared social and political attitudes. Mannheim assumed that youth
would be the key period for 'making fresh contact with social life' and forming
generational experiences. Shared world views and attitudes would however tend
to persist over the life course of the cohort members, making membership in
the (cultural) generation identifiable even in later life to members themselves as
well as to outsiders. Generations, thus, are groups formed within specific social
and historical contexts, and according to Mannheim such groups may also act as
collective agents and as (cultural) bearers of social transformation – this was the
aspect of generation formation that was Mannheim's specific interest. To summarize, a generation is a historically positioned age group whose members undergo a
similar socialization process which brings about a shared frame of experience and
action and makes them into an 'actual', active generation.[7]

According to Mannheim's way of thinking there is a particular point of interest which can lead us from his specifically *cultural* concept of generation to an
approach that will more readily help include children in generational analysis.
This is one of Mannheim's basic ideas that the 'generational location' in his theory
of cultural generations is the logical – and not merely metaphorical – equivalent
of 'class location' as presented in theories of social class:

> Location can be defined (in relation to both classes and generations/LA) only
> by specifying the structure within which and through which location groups
> emerge in historical-social reality. Class-position was based upon the existence
> of a changing economic and power structure in society.

> While [g]eneration location is based on the existence of biological rhythm in
> human existence – the factors of life and death, a limited span of life, and age-
> ing. Individuals who belong to the same generation, who share the same year
> of birth, are endowed, to that extent, with a common location in the historical
> dimension of the social process. (Mannheim, 1952 [1928], 289–290)

What the concepts of class and generation share is a formally similar relation to a
social structure, albeit to a different social structure in each case: a class-position
is a constitutive element of the class structure (in Mannheim's terms: 'economic
and power structure') and a 'generation location' a constitutive element of a generational structure that Mannheim describes in terms of the existential basis of
human life and society, 'governed by both biological and extra-biological factors'
(Mannheim, 1952 [1928], 310).

The sense of class that Mannheim refers to seems to be of the Weberian kind:
class is defined by the situation of people – 'the probability of their enjoying the
benefits of material goods, gaining a position in life and "inner satisfactions" as
a result of a relative control over goods and skills' (Weber, 1968 [1922], 302). A
class then refers to all those people who share the same class situation, that is: the
same set of life-chances and of opportunities in property and employment markets (Crompton, 1998, 57; Turner, 1999, 225). A slightly different, and alternative,

concept of class is available in class theories that take their inspiration from Marx and his theory of capitalism and his understanding of internally related classes. This concept of class is discussed next.

Generation categorically and relationally

The idea to begin with is 'class' defined by the economic relations of production in which the members of one economic class stand towards the members of another class. What is important to note is that both of these notions – the Weberian and the Marxist 'class' – are relational, but there is a significant difference between the kinds of interrelations that can exist between members of different social classes. In the Weberian case the relations between members of different classes tend to be *external*, or contingent, in the sense that class is defined in terms of a number of shared attributes (age, income, education, attitudes, life-chances, etc.). In contrast, class theories based on Marxian dialectics assume that relations between classes are *internal*, or necessary, in the sense that what one class is dependent on its relation to the other, and the existence of one necessarily presupposes the other (Sayer, 1992, 89–90; Ollman, 2003).

The idea of a modern 'nuclear family' exemplifies the case of a generational structure in which the relations are also internal: it is a system of relations, linking to each other the husband/father, the wife/mother and their children, all of which can be conceived as positions within the structured network of relations (cf. Porpora, 1998, 343). Internality implies that the relations of any holder of one position (such as that of a parent) cannot exist without the other (child) position. What parenting is or becomes – that is, action in the position of a parent in its defining relations – is dependent on the reciprocal action taken by the holder of the position of child. Similarly, a change of action in one position will probably effect change in the other position. The interdependency – of positional performance as well as identity – does not work only one way, unidirectionally, from parental position to child position. Interestingly, the term that in the family example corresponds to the positional performance of the holder of the child position is missing from both everyday and sociological discourse, presumably because the culturally normative basis for understanding the child–parent relationship tends to be one way only. Logically, 'childing' (Mayall, 1996, 49) would be the needed counter term to 'parenting'.

A parallel example is easily given by the structured system of teacher–student positions. The case can be expanded by bringing in the complexities in which the holder of a teacher position also defines a position only within a broader schooling system. The structure of schooling (including the family system) will probably be found to exist in an equally internal relation to a particular welfare state structure, or a labour market structure, and these in turn will be internally related to wider economic and cultural structures that potentially extend to global structures.[8] Thus the generational structures that we may find to exist as truly relational structures can be expected to be embedded in chains of further relational structures, be they generational or otherwise (e.g., class or gender structures); thus, the determinations of generational structures and positions are always dynamic and complex.

The distinguishing feature by which we may find relational social structures in existence and the way to 'determine' the possibilities of actual performance of the holders of its structured positions is *interdependency*. However, as Sayer (1992, 89–91) notes, the relationship need not be, and often is not, symmetrical in both directions. The familial generational structure, for instance, is (usually) one of asymmetry, as is the generational structure of teacher–student, and many other structures of relations embedded in the organization of the welfare state.

Additionally the Marxist concept of economic class is one that clearly hinges upon internal relations: capital necessarily presupposes wage labour, and outside this relationship, it is no longer capital (Sayer, 1992, 88–92). In non-Marxist analyses as well as in popular discourse, classes (or, more often, strata) are defined differently, mostly in terms of the attributes that members of the category share, such as income, education and status. Accordingly the class structure (or stratification system) is a construction by researchers, who classify individuals according to their correspondence to the chosen criteria of class (stratum). The relations between classes (that is, relationships between groups of holders of class positions) are in this mode of analysis most likely external and contingent rather than internal and necessary, because the constructed class positions do not reciprocally define and imply each other, as they do within internal (necessary) relations.

Here it is instructive to think of gender (gender structures) as being composed of internal relations and then relate this idea to a concept of gender based on external relations. Connell (1987) does this, although his terminology is somewhat different from the above. He examined some of the most current frameworks of gender theory, among them theories that he called *categorical* (Connell, 1987, 54–61). In an analysis based on categorical theorizing, the gender categories as they exist for us – mostly men and women, or some subcategories of each – are taken as the starting point and the study aims to find out how the categories relate to each other in terms of a chosen aspect – for example, life-chances or resources. The problematic point in categorical theorizing, Connell concludes, is that an analysis that begins by setting a simple line of demarcation between gender positions is not able to pay attention to the process of how the gender categories and the relations between the categories are constituted in the first place and are subsequently reproduced or, as it may be, transformed. The consequence is that categorical theories of gender are forced to treat both genders in terms of internally undifferentiated, homogeneous and general categories, thereby inviting criticism of false universalism and sometimes even of falling back on biological thinking. To resolve this 'categoricalism' Connell advocates what he calls 'practice-based' theorizing that focuses on 'what people do by way of constituting the relations they live in' (Connell, 1987, 61–64).

The risk of undifferentiated treatment of category members is also evident in the structural approaches to childhood that start from the social category of children as their unit and demarcate this unit (mostly) on the basis of chronological age (see Qvortrup, 1994, 2000). Children, as well as their counterparts in the analysis (e.g., adults), are in fact brought into the analysis as demographic age categories or sets of birth cohorts. The translation of the 'generational' into the social construct of age moves the analysis close to cohorts-based (statistical) generational analysis. In Qvortrup's structural approach the (contingent) relations between the categories of children and adults are given an economic interpretation, and (macro)economic processes are brought into the analysis to 'explain' the economic situation of the age-defined category of children. Thereby Qvortrup's approach could be seen as a modification of Mannheim's generational analysis, only children are now shown to form not a cultural, but an economic generation in that they are shown to share a set of economic risks and opportunities. In this view, the definition of their generational nature – 'childness' – seems to be based on an observable similarity or shared attribute, or sets of them, among individual children, and therefore more external than internal.

There is also another interesting feature in category-based analyses in which the focus is on the economic aspects of generational relations. An example is David Oldman's thought-provoking framing of children's activities (Oldman, 1994); his aim is to show how in capitalist societies the relations between the (generational) classes of children and adults have become organized as *economic* relations. The suggestion is that adults and children are social categories which exist principally by their economic opposition to each other, and in the ability of the dominant class (adults) to exploit economically the activities of the subordinate class (children). Children, through their various everyday activities, in fact produce value to adults who perform 'childwork', that is work in which children are the objects of the adults' labour (Oldman, 1994, 43–47). As family is only one of many sites where this class opposition and exploitation takes place (school being another), Oldman concludes that there exists a distinctive *generational mode of production* that articulates with two other existing modes of production: the capitalist mode that dominates in the industrial sphere, and the patriarchal mode that dominates in the domestic sphere (ibid., 55–58).

In his bold interpretation of child–adult relations Oldman clearly confines the generational ordering of social relations under the logic of production. Many of the analyses that have focused on structural relations between childhood and adulthood have followed the same idea when outlining the evolving structures of *economic* relations between the two generational categories of children and adults (e.g., Qvortrup, 1995; Wintersberger, 1998, 2005; Hengst, 2000; Olk and Wintersberger, 2007). In contrast, the notion of a generational order promoted in this chapter intends to provide a frame for analysis, by leaving it to empirical study to find out what actually is the constitutive principle in the social ordering, and organizing, of child–adult relations in each (e.g., national) case and in different social fields. In some cases it may be primarily economic; in the case of other structures the cultural may dominate. In any case this approach enables a more dynamic conceptualization of generational structures than seems possible if the starting point is based on generational categories. The analysis would aim to identify the *internal* relations that link children to the social world, the (relational) *positions* that define childness in each historical time-space, and the social (relational) *practices* (cf. Connell, 1987) in which the positions constitutive of childness are concurrently produced and maintained, and occasionally transformed. Gender research provides some examples and tools for developing a dynamic, relational frame for generational analysis.

From gender to generation

The crafting of new analytical tools that since the 1970s has taken place in women's/feminist studies provides a rich source for proposing and also elaborating generational concepts (Alanen, 1992, 26–52). The invention of *gender* in particular, with its many derivations in feminist theory and research, is in addition a powerful resource for conceptually developing the study of generation.

Children, too, are gendered, but the usefulness of the notion of gender lies beyond this. Gender is essentially a relational concept, but so also is generation. As 'men' and 'women' do, so also 'children' and 'adults' name two social categories that are positioned within a relation to each other, the first in a gender relation, the latter in a generational relation. By elaborating on the relational logic of gender, a clearer relational understanding of generation can also be expected to develop.

The notion of gender permitted feminist scholars to move from a parallel view in sociology of women in relation to male society and to reclaim such questions. Explanations for the existence of the social category of women were sought by studying the historicity and social constructedness of 'women'. This scholarship led to a view of gender as a *structural* formation of power relations that exists beyond the face-to-face situated interactions of individual men and women (e.g., Connell, 1987; Marshall, 1994; Ferree et al., 2000). The assumption of such a system of power implies in turn *structuring processes*, that is gendering – the social processes that effect the regulating, organizing and positioning of people into different social locations within the gender structure or gender order (Connell, 1987). Differential positioning in turn implies, and helps to explain, the differential access of women and men to participation in social life, which over time has resulted in social divisions and patterned inequalities between men and women, and particular gendered identities, experiences and knowledges (Marshall, 1994). Social relations moreover have been shown to be gendered at every 'level', and similarly the existing systems of symbols, meanings or significations that constitute the cultural and discursive dimension inherent in gendering.[9]

The immense theoretical productivity of the sex/gender distinction for elaborating the sociality of gender suggests that also generation, as a social and relational phenomenon, can be profitably theorized by taking into use parallel terms. By conceptually privileging the asymmetry between children and adults, childhood and adulthood, space is opened for empirically exploring

1. the *generational structures* that are composed of generational categories (positions) of childhood (or childness) and adulthood (or adultness: Blatterer,

2007a), and linking them into a reciprocal interdependency, as well as relationships of power;
2. the material, social and cultural processes in which children and adults, as both individual and collective actors, are involved, and in which also their everyday activities are embedded so that *generational (re)structuring* is recurrently effected; and finally
3. the cultural systems of *meanings, symbols and semantics* through which existing generational categories and their interrelationships are produced and rendered culturally meaningful.

One instance of generational ordering can already be detected in the institutionalized and culturally normative division of social spheres into 'public' and 'private'. The locations of 'childhood' can be seen to order children particularly into the 'private' world of home, family and care, and out of the world of economy and politics. Thereby a child's place is ordered to be within the family, in relation to and in difference from its adult members.

The working of an established generational order usually becomes first apparent when its rules are violated, when, for example, children work for wages instead of going to school or when they disregard their 'obligations' to their parents as a dependent being by taking to autonomous living (e.g., in the streets). Such instances begin to reveal a social order composed of, but also constraining and coordinating, children's relations in the social world, in a pervasive and systematic way. Children also become designated as social actors with valuable social contributions within the various social practices intersecting their daily lives. The social positions that such structures order children to take not only allow but in fact constrain children to actively participate in ongoing social life. The nature of their participation can be expected to differ from that of other social categories, and the practices through which children's participation is organized will probably limit the range of their agency more extensively than is the case with most adults. The freedoms and limitations, options and constraints that are inherent in modern forms of childhood are, however, social and sociological issues to explore, and not simply to assume.

The notion of a generational order and childhood as a position in a network of relations also suggests that children need to be respected as 'knowers' who gain practical knowledge of what it is to be in the world, as a 'child' in the kind of society in which they are positioned as 'children'. Children, too, reflect on their experiences, build on them and arrive at a body of understanding which they commonly revise. They will have, in other words, an understanding – their own, based on their social location – of the very same world that sociology has mainly described and explained from conventional adult (and adultist) viewpoints (Blatterer, 2007a). Children's positional knowledge is also a valuable data source for researchers, and the feminist standpoint methodology as developed for a sociology for women (Smith, 1988, 2005, Alanen, 1992, 1994; Mayall, 2000) is also useful in the case of children: taking a child's structural standpoint as a guideline will help researchers to open up the social world from children's positions in a generationally ordered social world, and to explain the world from children's positions – a case of sociology for children (cf. Mayall, 2002). Moreover, the business of doing research itself is a case of generational ordering, and also has implications for the methodology and ethics of (adult) researchers studying children and childhood (Mayall, 2000, 2002).

The analytical frame supported by the notion of generational order is a structural one, and a specific concern in structural theorizing is to secure *agency* for children; this needs to be built into both its theory and methodology. In relational thinking this is confirmed through attention to interdependencies of structural positions and to the reciprocal constitution of these positions in relational practices. Agency is conceptualized in terms of the 'powers' (or lack of them) of those positioned as children to influence, organize, coordinate and control events taking place in their social worlds. Such positional 'powers' can be revealed by studying the possibilities and limitations of children's action as 'determined' by the specific structures within which persons are positioned as expressly children. Therefore, in order to detect the range and nature of the agency of concrete, living children, the exploration needs to be oriented towards identifying the generational structures from which children's powers (or lack of them) derive: the source of their agency in their capacity as children is to be found in the social organization of generational relations.

Thus in a generationing frame as has been outlined here the primary focus of childhood research will be on revealing (1) those *structures* that can be identified as specifically generational, (2) the interdependent *positions* that these generational structures define for generational groups to take and to act from, and (3) the social and cultural *practices* of positioning – both self- and other-positioning – through which the current generational structures, and the generational order as their composite structure, are generated, maintained and (occasionally) transformed.

Generationing practices include 'childing' practices through which people are constructed as children as well as 'adulting' practices through which a distinct adult position is produced. Few attempts yet exist at studying the generational order empirically. The relational frame and particularly the concept of generationing have been met with some approval in the childhood research literature (e.g., Mannion and L'Anson, 2004; Punch, 2005; Brownlie and Anderson, 2006; Vanobbergen, 2007). Samantha Punch (2005) has explored generationing practices as they take place within families and among siblings by interviewing siblings individually and in focus groups where some sibling interaction could also be observed. She notes that, for instance, the ways in which children talk about the differences between their relationships with their parents and their siblings indicate that there are a range of generationing practices in families. These are distinguishable in the particular behaviours that were acceptable to engage in with other children, in parents' positional power as well as in the power that inheres in the interaction between children and parents, and between siblings.[10]

Conclusion

The basic principles of the social order – that is, the ways in which members of a society relate to each other and to the whole of their society – also include the arrangement of relations between generational groups. In this sense the social order is also always a generational order (e.g., Bühler-Niederberger, 2005, 9; cf. Honig, 1996, 1999, 190).

It would then seem inevitable that if the sociology of childhood is to advance theoretically the notion of generational order(ing) is worth developing and being empirically tested and refined. This would seem critical even for the sociology of childhood as it struggles to become recognized as a field of study that is also indispensable for the broad sociological endeavour of accounting for the organization of social life, its (changing) divisions, their intersections and the resulting complexity in individual lives and social relationships. Moreover, if the body of knowledge in general sociology remains ignorant of generational ordering as a distinct organizing principle of social relations, the social study of childhood is at risk of remaining isolated from the main areas of social research.

Notes

1. Mannheim's conceptualization comes closest to the new meaning of generation, as will be discussed later in this chapter.
2. In the life course approach, childhood is the primary stage of individual growth, development and socialization, and childhood is the time and place when the individual is being prepared to replace the adult members of present society. In this the life course approach aligns with much developmental psychology.
3. Interestingly, sociological theory has in fact contained a relational view on childhood from its beginning. As Jenks (1982, p. 10) writes, it has been 'impossible [for theory] to produce a well defined sense of the adult and his society without first positing the child'. This insight on relationality, however, has been a twisted one: the child–adult relation has been understood asymmetrically in that the child was taken to instance difference and particularity in relation to the adult, and therefore could be conceptualized only from the point of view of how childhood's difference could and needed to be integrated into the social order of adult society. To accomplish this, sociologists relied on notions of individual development and socialization, and thus the basic (ontological) question of ' "What is a child?" [...was] so to speak, answered in advance of the theorizing and then dismissed' (ibid.).
4. It is significant to note the extent to which the shadow of family life, captured for example in the doctrines of *parens patriae* and *in loco parentis*, falls upon these meetings (Fitz and Hood-Williams, 1982, p. 65).
5. Hood-Williams (1990) makes the further distinction between 'age patriarchy' (child–parent relations) and 'marital patriarchy' within family patriarchy.
6. A similar argument also applies to the social category of adulthood and 'adultness' as the embodiment of adulthood (see Blatterer, 2007a, 2007b). Blatterer (2007a, pp. 772–776) calls attention to the lack of sociological analyses of adulthood, which has helped to retain it as an uncontested, taken-for-granted construct while being the always present point of reference for sociologists when their concern has been with childhood, youth or old age. The very same claim – phrased as adultism, adult-centredness, adult ideological viewpoint and so on – had been made earlier in the context of childhood study (see e.g., Joffe, 1973; Goode, 1986; Waksler, 1986; Blitzer, 1991; Alanen, 1992). One implication of Blatterer's claim of an adultist bias in studies of old age is that the idea of generationing is also applicable to the social and sociological construction of old age.
7. For interpretations of Mannheim's theory of generations see for example Pilcher (1994, 1995), Corsten (1999) and Edmunds and Turner (2002).

8. It is commonly assumed that social structures include only 'big' objects such as the international division of labour, whereas they include also small ones at the interpersonal and intrapersonal levels, for example conceptual structures (Sayer, 1992, p. 92).
9. For a more detailed exposition of what useful lessons may be learned from gender research and theory see Alanen (1992, 1994).
10. Alanen (2000) and (2001) presents an empirical study on children's lives in Central Finland, as an early attempt to put a relational methodology to use in researching childhood.

References

Alanen, L. (1992) *Modern Childhood? Exploring the 'Child Question' in Sociology.* Jyväskylä: University of Jyväskylä.
Alanen, L. (1994) 'Gender and Generation: Feminism and the "Child Question"', in Qvortrup et al. (1994), pp. 27–42.
Alanen, L. (2000) 'Childhood as Generational Condition: Towards a Relational Theory of Childhood', in *Research in Childhood: Sociology, Culture & History.* Odense: University of Southern Denmark, pp. 11–29.
Alanen, L. (2001) 'Childhood as a Generational Condition: Children's Daily lives in a Central Finland Town', in L. Alanen, and B. Mayall (eds) *Conceptualizing Child-adult Relations.* London: Falmer Press, pp. 129–143.
Arber, S. (ed.) (2000) *The Myth of Generational Conflict: The Family and State in Ageing Societies.* London: Routledge.
Ariès, P. (1962) *Centuries of Childhood. A Social History of Family Life.* London: Jonathan Cape.
Becker, R. (ed.) (1997) *Generationen und sozialer Wandel. Generationsdynamik, Generationenbeziehungen und Differenzierung von Generationen.* Opladen: Leske & Budrich.
Blatterer, H. (2007a) 'Contemporary Adulthood. Reconceptualizing an Uncontested Category', *Current Sociology,* 55(6): 771–792.
Blatterer, H. (2007b) 'Adulthood: The Contemporary Redefinition of a Social Category', *Sociological Research Online,* 12(4) http://www.socresonline.org.uk/12/4/3.html.
Blitzer, S. (1991) '"They Are Only Children, What Do They Know?" a Look at Current Ideologies of Childhood', in S.E. Cahill (ed.) *Sociological Studies of Child Development, 4.* Greenwich, London: JAI Press, pp. 11–25.
Brownlie, J. and S. Anderson, (2006) '"Beyond Anti-smacking". Rethinking Parent-Child Relations', *Childhood,* 13(4): 479–498.
Bühler-Niederberger, D. (2005) *Kindheit und die Ordnung der Verhältnisse.* Weinheim, Basel: Juventa.
Connell, R.E. (1987) *Gender & Power. Society, the Person and Sexual Politics.* Cambridge: Polity Press.
Cook-Gumperz, J. (1991) 'Children's Construction of "Childness"', in B. Scales, M.C. Almy, A. Nicolopoulou, and S. Ervin-Tripp (eds) *Play and the Social Context of Development in Early Care and Education.* New York: Teachers College Press, pp. 207–218.
Corsten, M. (1999) 'The Time of Generations', *Time & Society,* 8(2): 249–272.
Crompton, R. (1998) *Class and Stratification.* Cambridge: Polity Press.
Edmunds, J. and Turner, B. (2002) *Generations, Culture and Society.* Buckingham: Open University Press.
Eisenstadt, S.N. (1956) *From Generation to Generation. Age Groups and Social Structure.* New York: Free Press.
Ferree, M.M., J. Lorber, and B.B. Hess (eds) (2000) *Revisioning Gender.* Lanham: Rowman & Littlefield.
Fitz, J. and J. Hood-Williams (1982) 'The Generation Game: Playing by the Rules', in D. Robbins (ed.), *Rethinking Social Inequality.* Aldershot: Gower, pp. 65–95.

Giele, J.Z. and G.H. Elder (1998) *Methods of Life Course Research: Qualitative and Quantitative Approaches*. Thousand Oaks: Sage.

Goode, D.A. (1986) 'Kids, Culture and Innocents', *Human Studies*, 9(1): 83–106.

Hareven, T. (1999) *Families, History and Social Change: Life Course and Cross-cultural Perspectives*. Boulder: Westview Press.

Hengst, H. (2000) 'Die Arbeit der Kinder und der Umbau der Arbeitsgesellschaft', in H. Hengst and H. Zeiher (eds), *Die Arbeit der Kinder. Kindsheitskonzept und Arbeitsteilung zwischen den Generationen*. Weinheim, Basel: Juventa, pp. 71–97.

Hockey, J. and A. James (1993) *Growing Up and Growing Old. Ageing and Dependency in the Life Course*. London: Sage.

Hood-Williams, J. (1990) 'Patriarchy for Children: On the Stability of Power Relations in Children's Lives', in L. Chisholm, P. Büchner, H. -H. Krüger, and P. Brown (eds), *Childhood, Youth and Social Change*. London: Falmer, 155–171.

Honig, M.-S. (1996) 'Wem gehört das Kind? Kindheit als generationale Ordnung.', in E. Liebau and C. Wulf (eds), *Generation. Versuche über eine pädagogisch-anthropologische Grundbedingung*. Weinheim: Deutscher Studien Verlag, pp. 201–221,

Honig, M.-S. (1999) *Entwurf einer Theorie der Kindhe*it. Frankfurt am Main: Suhrkamp.

Jenks, C. (1982) 'Introduction', in C. Jenks (ed.) *The Sociology of Childhood. Essential Readings*. London: Batsford Academic and Educational Ltd., pp. 9–24.

Joffe, C. (1973) 'Taking Young Children Seriously', in N.K. Denzin (ed.) *Children and Their Caretakers*. New Brunswick: Transaction Books, pp. 101–116.

Kohli, M. (1986) 'Social Organization and Subjective Construction of the Life Course', in A. Sorensen, F.E. Weinert and L.R. Sherrod (eds) *Human Development and the Life Course: Multidisciplinary Perspectives*. Hillsdale, NJ: Lawrence Erlbaum, pp. 271–291.

Liebau, E. and C. Wulf (eds) (1996) *Generation. Versuche über eine pädagogisch-anthropologische Grundbedingung*. Weinheim: Deutscher Studien Verlag.

Mannheim, K. (1952 [1928]) *The problem of generations. Essays in the Sociology of Knowledge*. London: Routledge and Kegan Paul.

Mannion, G. and J. L'Anson (2004) 'Beyond the Disneyesque. Children's Participation, Spatiality and Adult-child Relations', *Childhood*, 11(3): 303–318.

Marshall, B.L. (1994) *Engendering Modernity. Feminism, Social Theory and Social Change*. Cambridge: Polity Press.

Matthes, J. (1985) 'Karl Mannheims "Das Problem der Generationen", neu gelesen.' *Zeitschrift fü Soziologie*, 14(5): 363–372.

Mayall, B. (1996) *Children, Health and the Social Order*. Buckingham: Open University Press.

Mayall, B. (2000) 'Conversations with Children. Working with Generational Issues', in P. Christensen and A. James (eds), *Research with Children: Perspectives and Practices*. London: Falmer Press, pp. 120–135,

Mayall, B. (2002) *Towards a Sociology for Childhood*. Buckingham: Open University Press.

McCall, L. (2005) 'The Complexity of Intersectionality', *Signs: Journal of Women in Culture and Society*, 30(3): 1771–1800.

Oldman, D. (1994) 'Adult-Child Relations as Class Relations', in Qvortrup et al., pp. 43–58.

Olk, T. and H. Wintersberger (2007) 'Welfare States and the Generational Order', in H. Wintersberger, L. Alanen, T. Olk and J. Qvortrup, J. (eds), *Childhood, Generational Order and the Welfare State: Exploring Children's Social and Economic Welfare*. Odense: University Press of Southern Denmark, pp. 59–90.

Ollman, B. (2003) *Dance of the Dialectic. Steps in Marx's Methods*. Urbana: University of Illinois Press.

Pilcher, J. (1994) 'Mannheim's Sociology of Generations: an Undervalued Legacy', *British Journal of Sociology*, 45(3): 481–495.

Pilcher, J. (1995) *Age and Generation in Modern Britain*. Oxford: Oxford University Press.

Porpora, D.V. (1998) 'Four Concepts of Social Structure', in M. Archer, R. Bashkar, A. Collier, T. Lawson and A. Norrie (eds) *Critical Realism*. London: Routledge, pp. 339–355.

Prout, A. (2002) 'Researching Children as Social Actors: An Introduction to the Children 5–16 Programme', *Children & Society*, 16(2): 67–76.

Punch, S. (2005) 'The Generation of Power: A Comparison of Child-parent and Sibling Relations in Scotland', in *Sociological Studies of Children and Youth, 10*. Amsterdam: Elsevier, pp. 169–188.

Qvortrup, J. (1985) 'Placing Children in the Division of Labour', in P. Close and R. Collins (eds) *Family and Economy in Modern Society*. London: Macmillan, pp. 129–145.

Qvortrup, J. (1987) 'The Sociology of Childhood. Introduction', *International Journal of Sociology*, 17(3): 3–37.

Qvortrup, J. (1994) 'Childhood Matters: An Introduction', in Qvortrup et al., 1994, pp. 1–23.

Qvortrup, J. (1995) 'From Useful to Useful: The Historical Continuity in Children's Constructive Participation', in *Sociological Studies of Children 7*. Amsterdam: Elsevier, pp. 49–76.

Qvortrup, J. (2000) 'Macro-Analysis of Childhood', in P. Christensen and A. James (eds) *Research with Children: Perspectives and Practices*. London: Falmer Press, 77–97.

Qvortrup, J., M. Bardy, G.B. Sgritta and H. Wintersberger (eds) (1994) *Childhood Matters. Social Theory, Practice and Politics*. Aldershot: Avebury

Sayer, A. (1992) *Method in Social Science*. London: Routledge.

Smith, D.E. (1988) *The Everyday World as Problematic. A Feminist Sociology*. Milton Keynes: Open University Press.

Smith, D.E. (2005) *Institutional Ethnography. a Sociology for People*. Lanham: Altamira Press.

Thorne, B. (1987) 'Re-Visioning Women and Social Change: Where are the Children?' *Gender & Society*, 1(1): 85–109.

Turner, B.S. (1999) *Classical Sociology*. London: Sage.

Vanobbergen B. (2007) ' "Soon He Will Boil over like a Kettle": Visualizing the Invisible – the Representation of *Hyperactivity* in Women's Magazines and Professional Journals for Teachers in Flanders (1965–2005)', *History of Education*, 36(2): 173–189.

Waksler, F.C. (1986) 'Studying Children: Phenomenological Insights.' *Human Studies*, 9(1): 71–82.

Walby, S. (2007) 'Complexity Theory, Systems Theory, and Multiple Intersecting Social Inequalities', *Philosophy of the Social Sciences*, 37(4): 449–470.

Weber, M. (1968 [1922]) *Economy and Society*. Berkeley: University of California Press.

Wintersberger, H. (1998) 'Ökonomische Verhältnisse zwischen Generationen – Ein Beitrag zur Ökonomie der Kindheit.' *Zeitschrift für Soziologie der Erziehung und Sozialisation*, 18(1): 8–24.

Wintersberger, H. (2005) 'Work, Welfare and the Generational Order: Towards a Political Economy of Childhood', in J. Qvortrup (ed.) *Studies in Modern Childhood*. Basingstoke, New York: Palgrave Macmillan, pp. 201–220.

11
Generational Relations at Family Level

Berry Mayall

This chapter aims to consider intergenerational relations in families in the light of the social structures that shape them. It is thus designed to act as a complement to the consideration of theoretical approaches to these relations (see Olk, this volume; Alanen, this volume). I set out here, briefly, the standpoint that informs this chapter, and go on to consider intergenerational relations under three headings: socialization; the changing family; and interdependencies.

Starting points

In this chapter, first, I take the view that childhood is a subsection of society, which, like adulthood, is subject to political, socio-economic forces, but in specific ways. These forces impact on the character of childhoods in relation to social institutions (outside families), in relation to how social institutions shape families, and also in relation to how childhood is worked through within families. Key to understanding childhood as understood and operationalized within families is the relation between the state (or society more generally) and families. In many societies, care and socialization of children is a shared responsibility in extended families and local networks (e.g., Le Vine, 2003; Gottlieb, 2004); in modern Western societies, nuclear families (two-generational) are regarded as the principal site of child socialization, with parents responsible for the moral training, as well as for the health and welfare, of their children. States vary in how much they help with the costs of child-rearing, and how far they intervene to modify childhood and parental practices. These interventions will be a principal theme in this chapter.

Second, I rely on the view that 'child' is relational with 'adult', in the sense that 'the child' is defined in its difference from 'adult'; similarly childhood differs from adulthood. Generally these differences include denigration of 'the child' by comparison with 'the adult'. Thus common ideas about 'the child' are that relatively s/he is incompetent, irrational and morally immature. Childhood is relational with adulthood, too, in the sense that relational processes between the two may lead to changes, both within families and within society more generally. Changes in perceptions of one social group may emerge, and change in one social group will, in the end, lead to changes in the other. Thus if children are increasingly understood as competent, knowledgeable and morally reliable, their parents will be less required to, and will see less reason to, control their children's every move.

The common association of age with 'child' carries problems, since everyone less than 18 years of age may get bracketed together in terms of societal assumptions and legal provisions. Very young people are physically weak, lacking in knowledge and experience. But these biological vulnerabilities are often the basis for more socially constructed vulnerabilities, whereby negative characteristics may be assigned to people in the later stages of their development (Lansdown, 1994). This problem points to an important theme in this chapter, which is that those people who inhabit childhood as socially defined may in practice behave in ways not associated with those definitions. For instance, whilst learning at school is commonly thought to be children's main activity in Western societies, children themselves may regard contributions to their family's economic welfare as also appropriate, as is usual across the world (Mackinnon, 2003). Children may demonstrate moral competence through their care for and about other family members (Ridge, 2006). They may surprise their elders by their agency in providing continuity in family relations when parents split up.

Socialization?

A key change over the centuries in Western societies in the structural function of families is described by Ariès (1960): towards families as child socialization agencies. This constituted a break with traditions common across the world – of families as joint enterprises assuring their economic welfare down the generations. In the last hundred years, additionally, Western psychology has propounded the view that mother–child relations are of paramount significance for child development and thus has emphasized the societal importance of two-generational families.

Whilst the aim of educating a child so that s/he can function well in a given society seems fundamental, psychology and sociology became interested in examining the concept towards the end of the nineteenth century (Clausen, 1968). 'Socialization' suggested a passive recipient and a future-oriented set of procedures, but during the twentieth century, these disciplines have discovered the child as active participant in learning and this child has become well established in psychological theory (Elkin and Handel, 1978; Wood, 1986; Greene, 1999) and in more general social science work (Denzin, 1977). Since psychology has been a dominant influence in shaping our understanding of children's capabilities and relation activity, one might expect psychology's discovery of the child as active participant in learning to have infiltrated Western socialization agendas. But children are too valuable a national resource to be left to the vagaries of individual actors. A large-scale structural aim reinforces the construction of children as relatively passive socialization objects – the perceived need to weld societies together and to assure the state of a useful future citizenry. Thus, for example, in France at the turn of the twentieth century, the threat of revolution was an important backdrop to Durkheim's formulation of sociology of education. He wanted moral unity and solidarity for French society; mothers and then teachers were to teach conformity (Wilson, 1962). In the United States at that time, concern about threats to the 'American way of life' from waves of immigrants from southern and eastern Europe can be seen as powerful influences: children were defined as key objects for the transmission of social values and as raw material for the building of citizenship (Denzin, 1977, 6); and in this project, the school was a key institution. In Britain, similar concerns, this time about the lower classes then corralled in publicly funded schools, led to highly instrumental curricula, designed to teach children their place in the class structure. These concerns to turn out citizens appropriately moulded for social needs continue to operate, and the specific sets of ideas moulding state education in the early days continue to be influential (Alexander, 2000). State interventions have also included measures to modify mothers' childcare behaviour, through the training and work of health visitors and social workers.

As regards children nowadays, socialization agents vary according to differing societal trends and pressures. Women's changing status intersects with developments in welfare states. Most of northern Europe, through comprehensive welfare provisions, has promoted dual-career parents, extensive parental leave and daycare. However, the model of the mother as housewife retains currency in, for instance, the Netherlands and Germany, and these states have not (yet) provided daycare for the youngest children. In the UK policy encourages mothers to do paid work (partly to reduce child poverty), but although it has a well-established welfare state, the political will (in a socially divided society) to provide adequate daycare has so far been lacking. In most Mediterranean countries, where welfare states have been slower to gain ground and where until very recently the mother at home was the norm, a new generation of young women are expecting to engage in paid work; hence the grandmother is currently the main source of care. More general economic pressures are seen in Russia, where inadequate supply of housing forces three-generational families to live together, and where the supply of daycare has been in decline since the demise of the USSR; in complement to these pressures, the idea and presence of the matriarchal *babushka* persists (Attias-Donfut and Segalen, 1998: chapter 6).

However, across Europe, daycare is a common experience for children by the age of three, and children must respond to its ideologies and related practices. Children enter the relational practices of daycare not as dependent members of a family but as persons, and the state must consider what kind of care and environment is appropriate. In entering into direct relations with the state, children's agendas intersect with the state's socialization aims. One society's daycare may promote the notion of children as collaborating citizens of a socialist society (USSR); another's (France) fosters children as heirs to national culture (Alexander,

2000); in the United States of America emphasis will be on citizenship but also on competition between individuals (Whiting, 1963; Penn, 2005).

Parents whose children attend daycare are exposing them to these forces and to possible conflicts between the moral character of home and daycare. Daycare puts children in the hands of staff trained in accordance with societal views on socialization. Children face a new kind of adult; the professionalization of staff may act as a barrier to constructing a *gemenskap* – a community based on mutual trust and solidarity with which children identify (Liljeström, 1983). In some countries, Western ideas about childhood and child–adult relations are imposed on the local culture (Penn, 2002). Dencik (1995), reflecting on the wholehearted Nordic development of daycare centres, alleges that children will engage in 'dual socialization': at home in the context of long-term commitment by parents for whom the child is special and unique, and in the institution, where staff may come and go and may inhibit deep emotional involvement with the children. So children will learn a new set of social competences: to be emotionally independent and flexible, to be self-reliant and self-disciplined. Recognition that in some institutions the social ethos may be harmful and may neglect children's participation rights is one context for developmental work towards the institution as a little democracy where adults and children collaborate (Malaguzzi, 1998; Clark, Kjørholt and Moss, 2005).

If next we look at school-age children, it is clear that characteristics of the education/care system will affect relations within families, including socialization. In some societies (e.g., France and Finland), the remits of the home and of the education system are broadly discrete: the home provides the school with children morally trained and fit to be educated and the state delivers the education it deems appropriate. At another extreme is the English education system, which enlists parents in the educational enterprise, to help with homework, and to collaborate with school agendas. So the extent to which the home is haven from the instrumental public world depends partly on what assumptions underpin the education system. More socially equal societies may rely without question on parental behaviour; more socially divided societies may question and seek to modify it and children will have to cope with resulting triangular tensions between themselves, parents and teachers. Further, school and home penetrate each other: the child sent to school unfed and undisciplined will be a problem for the teacher; the child who does well at school casts reflected glory on the home.

Beyond the school day, Western societies are now developing out-of-school services to meet the 'demands' of the adult working day. This extended institutionalization of children is an example of structural disregard: how policies may develop with due regard for only some of the groups (adults here) affected. Whilst children may enjoy institutional life, they have no choice but to be there. Further, whilst attendance there increases children's direct relation to the state, institutionalization can also be seen as reinforcing their separation from their family as an ongoing economic enterprise and more generally from the socio-economic business of adult life.

Changing family structures

Families in Western societies have become interesting to commentators recently, first because they are changing in character and structure and are therefore up for political debate (what is a family, what is its function, is it in decline?); second perhaps because sociological work, in its consideration of the reflexive self (Giddens, 1992) and of individualization (Beck, 1992), has turned to consideration of adult sexual partnerships (Smart and Neale, 1999: chapter 1).

Whilst studies of families within developmental psychology have traditionally focused on parents and children, more open-ended enquiries reveal that family in the minds of its members includes extended relations – horizontally and vertically (see Jensen in this volume). Children themselves may include a wide range of resident and non-resident relatives, both as comprising their family and as important to them (Morrow, 1998; Brannen et al., 2000; Ross et al., 2005). Family members as resources (care, finance) also come into focus when adult partnerships fall apart. Kinship relations are perhaps distinctive from other relationships simply because, by inhabiting the status of child, parent and grandparent, people must consider, to some extent, the relational character of that status with the other two. As noted above, older people may inhabit two or all three statuses, and this will give cause for thinking about relations with the others.

Observers have identified key ways in which families are changing in Western societies: that people are living longer; that marriage and cohabitation are less stable; and that people have fewer children. This section considers these three points, with particular reference to implications for children.

As *people are living longer*, the large-scale problem perceived is that states are faced with providing financial help to people in retirement from paid work, over longer periods. Since there are fewer children growing up to engage in paid work and since pensions are paid out of current payroll or social security taxes, solutions need to be sought (Thomson, 1995). Complementary suggestions are that states should oblige people to save and to save more during their paid work years, and that women should be persuaded to have more children. Both of these suggestions have implications for state intervention in family life and for children's lives in families. Measures to even out incomes and overcome relative poverty are clearly important. Measures to enable women to bear and raise children and to engage in paid work are also essential; these include parental leave arrangements and enough good quality care services for children up to an age where they are deemed able to care for themselves. As noted above, societies vary in their commitment to these measures.

Children's lives are influenced in other ways by adult longevity. For if adults live longer they will be asked to do paid work longer. In order to match job availability to those who then need jobs, children will be excluded from the labour force for longer. This complements the current view that children need longer years of education and training to compete in complex global employment markets. So children are assigned to childhood dependency for longer – at school and at home. Questions arise here: How do teenagers, who are schoolchildren,

consumers and accomplished moral agents, relate to adults? What are the implications of children's longer status as schoolchildren/students for societal recognition of their other kinds of work – unpaid work in households and, in family
businesses, paid work?

'Family breakdown' – divorce and separation – is increasingly common in Western
societies. Much psychological research has stressed trauma for children and adverse
financial, social and educational consequences. A benefit of research studying children's own experience and views has been to modify or complement these points.
The many studies (see Jensen and McKee, 2003) indicate that children wish to be
kept informed; many wish to participate in decision-making but they then make
the best of the outcome, and work their way through to an acceptable life.

Feminist work has pointed to advantages for women and their children in leaving
patriarchal abusive relationships and in taking control of their lives. Women and
children may collaborate towards a better life (Alanen, 1992; Mullender et al., 2003);
space at home may be more equally shared; and morally they may become more
equal partners. However mothers still hold and control the economic resources and
their work patterns structure children's use of time. Changes in the social power of
women (more in paid employment, more divorces initiated by women) lead to the
'feminization' of children's lives: after separation most children live with mothers;
daycare and education in the early stages is run by women; some fathers will be less
involved (Jensen, 1994). The extent to which the state supports these changed and
changing family structures will affect children's welfare. A substantial threat to
children when parents split up is poverty (Clarke and Joshi, 2003). Support based on
children's needs rather than on a two-parent family is an important development.

If *parents have fewer children*, children's opportunities for sibling relations
decrease. And if their lives are increasingly compartmentalised, within their generation and social contacts restricted mainly to those with other children, then
perhaps relations with children assume particular salience. Sibship provides a
source of identity and of relations across time, and is shaped by negotiated power
relations (Edwards et al., 2006: chapter 4); in this, sibling relations differ from
child–parent relations, where adult power is less negotiable (Punch, 2005). But
for children lines between 'peers' and 'sibs' may also become blurred as children
build new relations with step-parents and their children. Sibship can be seen
as not only a biological relation but a social construction (Edwards et al., 2006:
chapter 2), and children themselves (for instance, in Asian families) may blur
boundaries further, as their use of the term 'my cousin brother' suggests. Perhaps
the most important point here is that children think other children are important social contacts. Research indicates three kinds of benefit from child–child
interaction: intellectual learning; moral development; friendship. Friendship is
especially important for children, as fun, defence and support.

Intergenerational interdependencies[1]

Given that people live longer nowadays in welfare states, children, parents
and grandparents have longer to inhabit kinship statuses with living relatives

(Attias-Donfut and Segalen, 1998, 2002; Vollenwyder et al., 2002). So, one may be a child to one's parents for 60 years, a parent for 70 years and a grandparent for 30 years. And one may occupy more than one of these positions simultaneously. Furthermore, nowadays childhood lasts longer, since longer scholarization lengthens children's dependency on parents and/or the state. These points mean, first, that children are more likely to have one or more living grandparents and to know them over several years, even into their own adulthood; and, second, people have a long time to reflect on what it means to be a child, parent, grandparent, on what changes have taken place in the character of child, parent and grandparent, and on how relations across the generations change over time, generally, and in individual cases in response to structural and individual changes. These continuous processes of 'socialization' therefore extend across life: people continually learn, negotiate and renegotiate the social order: at work, in families and in the community (Brim, 1968; Denzin, 1977, p. 111).

Family structure in traditional societies has been described as a closely knit extended group, across three generations, living under one roof or nearby and characterized by close emotional reciprocity and sharing of economic resources; Kagitcibasi (1996: chapter 5) finds no evidence that this structure has to give way to modernizing, industrializing forces. However, some argue that the welfare state has weakened family ties (Dench, Gavron and Young, 2006). And according to the individualization thesis, people in advanced societies are less firmly tied to family traditions, but make their own choices of career and lifestyle, no longer tied by duty to their elders (Beck, 1992; Lüscher, 2000).

Whether or not there was once a clearly accepted contract of duty across, and especially up, the generations in families, it is argued that nowadays we have normative guidelines and varying notions of responsibility negotiated within families over time (Finch and Mason, 1993: chapter 6). Intergenerational transmissions will change over time as circumstances vary, as people get older and as people work through their ideas about responsibility and expectation, building on past experience.

The above studies are about adults, with children as socialization projects. If we start from children's standpoints and activities, we may have to modify our account of intergenerational relations. First I look at affective relations, and then more specifically at children's contributions to the division of labour.

At the level of affective child–parent relations, some things remain unchanged. Whilst welfare state provisions work towards fairer distribution of income across social classes and generations through intervention in the world of paid work, they have left untouched the domain of unpaid work, and therefore have not dealt with gender issues: the unpaid work of women across the generations (Schunter-Kleeman, 2000; Wintersberger, 2000). Patriarchy can be considered as firmly in place (Hood-Williams, 1990). Some aspects of child–parent relations remain constant: the pivotal role of women in caring work; the authority and responsibility of parents; the parental teaching role; children's dependency; continuity of care and concern over time. In these circumstances, children unsurprisingly continue to stress the centrality of emotional ties in the family, with mother as the central figure.

Yet general changes towards democratization are perceived in Western child–parent relations over time: a diminution of the social space between parents and children (Zeiher, 2003; Wade and Smart, 2005). 'In the old days' children obeyed without question; were not asked for or allowed to express their views; had poor knowledge; could count less on continuity of care by mother; had a much narrower lifestyle, but greater physical freedom. Nowadays children can discuss with parents, they are better informed; generally they can count on mothers' continued presence; they have less physical but more intellectual freedom.

As to relations with non-resident relatives, such as fathers and grandparents, power to promote and maintain these rests more with adults than with children. And if in Western societies the concept of duty and respect up the generations has slid from central significance in family relations, then children's relations with grandparents may be individualized and contingent on factors such as geographical proximity and grandparents' and mothers' work in encouraging and facilitating the development and maintenance of solid relations. So in children's relations with non-resident fathers and grandparents we find least certainty and most variation (van Ranst et al., 1995; Brannen et al., 2000; Dench and Ogg, 2002; Ross et al., 2005). Some fathers relinquish their children. Children's grandparents are not archetypal (retired, kindly, old-fashioned) but a varied and individual set of people, healthier than previous cohorts; they may live near or far away, may be busily employed, and may adopt involved, distant or companionate stances with children and grandchildren (Wilk, 2000). An important consideration is children's in/ability to take independent action. Children may visit a relative living nearby on their own initiative, but travelling further distances is outside their assigned competence. It has been noted that 'opportunity structures' for contact are at least as important as personal motivation (Oppelaar and Dykstra, 2004).

However, from children's viewpoints, family provides a uniquely valuable forum for support, advice and concrete help, in contrast to the more formal 'helping' agencies. It is in their family that children have the best chance of being taken seriously as persons, and listened to. When children need help, most commonly their main confidant is their mother. But they turn also to other family members, young and old. Grandparents are particularly important as non-judgmental listeners (Ross et al., 2005), whilst parents may intervene (sometimes against the child's wishes) to solve the problem. Children confide little in professionals (such as teachers, social workers); this reflects the same point (Williamson and Butler, 1995; Hallett, Murray and Punch, 2003; Mullender et al., 2003).

We consider next children as agents in a range of family contexts, engaged in work and affective relations (as feminists point out, these are conceptually indivisible). Children's work in Western societies has been slow to gain recognition, but it is comparable – though less time-consuming – to the work children do in the Majority World to contribute to their families' economic welfare (see Nieuwenhuys, this volume). A first social context is the family as a going concern, where children engage in a range of kinds of work, including housework and caring for and about family members (or 'people work'); they are participating in the enterprises of keeping the family going, as a healthy productive organism.

Children's visibility in such work owes something, by extrapolation, to feminist thinking which pointed to women's activities at home as work. Many children engage in paid work (Mizen et al., 2001), and this too, from children's perspectives, is undertaken partly as a contribution to the family's economic welfare; children may work to finance school meals, games equipment, presents for the family.

A second social context is children's membership of families which are overtly understood by their members – children and adults alike – to be economic projects, assuring family welfare across the generations. Commitment to the family's interests, reciprocity, ideas about duty and respect towards older generations are general across the world, and continue, as we learn from newer members of Western societies – for instance, children and adults with roots in Asian countries (Afshar, 1994; Mayall, 2002: chapter 6; Ross et al., 2005). As new arrivals, and especially if families settle in areas already colonized by people from their country of origin, people will rely heavily on family and be suspicious of welfare state provisions and interventions (Sachs, 1983: chapter 4; Attias-Donfut and Segalen, 1998, 185). Some grandparents born abroad take responsibility for transmitting the culture, skills and language of their country of origin, whilst the children may reciprocally help their parents and grandparents make sense of the new society – teaching them its language and interpreting for them (Jessel et al., 2004; Zelizer, 2005). Children may participate in the work of family businesses, such as 'takeaways' (Song, 2001) and corner shops (Chandra, 2000), and through their household work and care of siblings release their parents for work in these enterprises.

A third social context is where children step out of local understandings of childhood and contribute to solving specific problems in the family. Thus in the United Kingdom, some thousands of children reverse the normal direction of care-giving and care for their ill or disabled parents; this work gives rise to debate whether these are proper activities for children (Aldridge and Becker, 2002). Children's caring work has been described for Zimbabwe, where the young carers saw it as an activity 'separate from the ordinary' (Robson and Ansell, 2000), but not as a conceptual problem. The widespread vision of 'AIDS orphans' in parts of southern Africa simply as uncared-for victims has been challenged by work demonstrating how children are 'embedded in and commandeer their way' through extended social relations with both adults and children (Henderson, 2006, 304; see also Barnett and Whiteside, 2002).[2]

Final points

Families across at least three generations have attracted renewed academic and policy-related attention because of increased longevity, perceived breakdown of marital relations, mothers' paid employment, parental illness and death from drugs and AIDS, and state funding crises. Much of this work (in the United States of America and Francophone countries) has focused on adults, with children as socialization projects (e.g., Attias-Donfut and Segalen, 1998; Bawin-Legros, 2002). Work on intergenerational duty and responsibility in families has also been largely adult-focused (e.g., Finch and Mason, 1993). Children's own contributions to intergenerational relations have been studied empirically in some European work, and in work on Africa and Asia (Le Vine, 2003).

Macro-analyses of how intergenerational relations are developing (see Olk in this volume) can be complemented by empirical studies of people's understandings and activities. In particular we can learn from children's standpoint on their social status, their agency, the constraints and opportunities they face. Research remains to be done linking empirical data from children with sociological concepts of childhood. Thus, at the family level, we may ask, for instance, how far children, as dependants within adult-ordered contexts, can act as agents in forming and maintaining the intergenerational links at issue here. Children's understandings of intergenerational relations may be structured by family cultural and religious traditions as much as by personal inclination. Further, children's own understandings of their childhoods (acquired from parents, sibs and friends) within families may serve to structure their intergenerational relations.

More broadly, children's own contributions to social relations will be shaped by societal expectations about what childhood does and should consist of. Children in Western societies are largely excluded conceptually from engagement with economic activity, though studies of what they actually do are beginning to challenge this concept, and widening understandings of what economic activity consists of – to include domestic and caring work – point towards the rightful inclusion of children as economic actors (Zelizer, 2005). But we have to note too that, within Western societies, the project of forming one's own individual life may constitute a powerful structuring context for how children perceive intergenerational relations. The scholarization of childhood complements this individualization, suggesting to children and adults that children's lives are to be shaped by educational agendas. Within these, children's activities tend to be organised within fixed timetables, thus constraining their use of time. Of interest too would be tensions between people's understanding of education as defined by the state, and education as concerned with understanding of one's own relational position within kinship networks – and how these relate to wider social forces.

Notes

1. Within the word limit of this chapter it is relations across three generations that are the main focus.
2. To the extent that this section draws on some empirical studies, I note difficulties encountered by researchers in accessing three-generational families: volunteers may be biased towards enthusiasm for intergenerational links. More general samples of children (classes at school, large-scale surveys) show some variation in how much contact there is and how important it is (Dench and Ogg, 2002).

References

Afshar, H. (1994) 'Muslim Women in West Yorkshire', in H. Afshar and M. Maynard (eds) *The Dynamics of Race and Gender: Some Feminist Interventions*. London: Taylor and Francis, pp. 127–150.

Alanen, L. (1992) *Modern Childhood? Exploring the 'Child Question' in Sociology*. Research Report no. 50. Finland: University of Jyväskylä.

Aldridge, J. and S. Becker (2002) 'Children Who Care: Rights and Wrongs in Debate and Policy on Young Carers', in B. Franklin (ed.) *The New Handbook of Children's Rights*. London: Routledge, pp. 208–222.

Alexander, R. (2000) *Culture and Pedagogy: International Comparisons in Primary Education*. Oxford: Blackwell.

Ariès, P. (1960) *Centuries of Childhood*. Harmondsworth: Penguin.

Attias-Donfut, C. and M. Segalen (1998) *Grandparents: La famille à travers les Generations*. Paris: Editions Odile Jacob.

Attias-Donfur, C. and M. Segalen (2002) 'The Construction of Grandparenthood', *Current Sociology*, 50(2): 281–294.

Barnett, T. and A. Whiteside (2002) *AIDS in the Twenty-first Century*. London: Palgrave Macmillan.

Bawin-Legros, B. (2002) 'Introduction – Filiation and Identity: Towards a Sociology of Intergenerational Relations', *Current Sociology*, 50(2): 175–183.

Beck, U. (1992) *Risk Society*. London: Sage.

Brannen, J., E. Heptinstall and K. Bhopal (2000) *Connecting Children: Care and FamilyLife in Later Childhood*. London: Routledge Falmer.

Brim, O.G. (1968) 'Adult Socialization', in J. Clausen (ed.) *Socialization and Society*. Boston: Little, Brown and Co, pp. 182–226.

Chandra, V. (2000) Children's Work in the Family. Unpublished PhD thesis, University of Warwick.

Clark, A., A.M. Kjørholt and P. Moss (2005) *Beyond Listening: Children's Perspectives on Early Childhood Services*. Bristol: Policy Press.

Clarke, L. and H. Joshi (2003) 'Children's Changing Families and Family Resources', in A.-M. Jensen and L. McKee (eds) *Children and the Changing Family*. London: Routledge Falmer, pp. 15–26.

Clausen, J. (ed.) (1968) *Socialization and Society*. Boston MA: Little Brown and Company.

Dench, G. and J. Ogg (2002) *Grandparenting in Britain*. London: Institute of Community Studies.

Dench, G., K. Gavron and M. Young (2006) *The New East End: Kinship, Race and Conflict*. London: Profile Books.

Dencik, L. (1995) 'Modern Childhood in the Nordic Countries: "Dual Socialisation" and Its Implications', in L. Chisholm, P. Buchner, H.-H. Kruger and M. Du Bois Reymond (eds) *Growing up in Europe: Contemporary Horizons in Childhood and Youth Studies*. Berlin and New York: Walter de Gruyter, pp. 105–120.

Denzin, N.K. (1977) *Childhood Socialization*. San Francisco: Jossey-Bass Publishers.

Edwards, R., L. Hadfield, H. Lucey and M. Mauthner (2006) *Sibling Identity and Relationships*. London: Routledge.

Elkin, F. and G. Handel (1978) *The Child and Society: The Process of Socialization*. 3rd edn. New York: Random House.

Finch, J. and J. Mason (1993) *Negotiating Family Responsibilities*. London: Routledge.

Giddens, A. (1992) *The Transformation of Intimacy*. Cambridge: Polity Press.

Gottlieb, A. (2004) *The After-Life Is Where We Come From: The Culture of Infancy in West Africa*. Chicago: Chicago University Press.

Greene, S. (1999) 'Child Development: Old Themes, New Directions', in M. Woodhead, D. Faulkner and K. Littleton (eds) *Making Sense of Social Development*. London: Routledge, pp. 250–268.

Hallett, C., C. Murray and S. Punch (2003) 'Young People and Welfare: Negotiating Pathways', in C. Hallett and A. Prout (eds) *Hearing the Voices of Children: Social Policy for a New Century*. London: Routledge Falmer, pp. 123–138.

Henderson, P.C. (2006) 'South African AIDS Orphans: Examining Assumptions Around Vulnerability, from the Perspective of Rural Children and Youth', *Childhood*, 13(3): 303–328.

Hood-Williams, J. (1990) 'Patriarchy for Children: On the Stability of Power Relations in Children's Lives', in L. Chisholm, P. Buchner, H.-H. Kruger and P. Brown (eds) *Childhood Youth and Social Change: A Comparative Perspective*. London: Falmer, pp. 155–171.

Jensen, A.-M. (1994) 'The Feminisation of Childhood', in J. Qvortrup, M. Bardy, G. Sgritta and H. Wintersberger (eds) *Childhood Matters*, Aldershot: Avebury Press, pp. 59–76.

Jensen, A.-M. and L. McKee (eds) (2003) *Children and the Changing Family: Between Transformation and Negotiation*. London: Routledge Falmer.

Jessel, J., E. Gregory, T. Arju, C. Kenner and M. Ruby (2004) 'Children and Their Grandparents at Home: A Mutually Supportive Context for Learning and Linguistic Development', *English Quarterly*, 36: 16–23.

Kagitcibasi, C. (1996) *Family and Human Development: A View from the Other Side*. Hove: Lawrence Erlbaum.

Lansdown, G. (1994) 'Children's Rights', in B. Mayall (ed.) *Children's Childhoods: Observed and Experienced*. London: Falmer, pp. 33–44.

Le Vine, R.A. (2003) *Childhood Socialization: Comparative Studies of Parenting, Learning and Educational Change*. Hong Kong: University of Hong Kong.

Liljeström, R. (1983) 'The Public Child, the Commercial Child and Our Child', in F.S. Kessel and A.W. Siegel (eds) *The Child and Other Cultural Inventions*. New York: Praeger, pp. 124–151.

Lüscher, K. (2000) 'Ambivalence: A Key Concept for the Study of Intergenerational Relations', in S. Trnka (ed.) (2000) *Family Issues between Gender and Generation*. Luxembourg: Office for Official Publications of the European Communities. pp. 11–25.

Mackinnon, D. (2003) 'Children and Work', in J. Maybin and M. Woodhead (eds) *Childhoods in Context*. Chichester: John Wiley and Sons, pp. 129–172.

Malaguzzi, L. (1998) 'History, Ideas and Basic Philosophy: An Interview with Lella Gandini', in C. Edwards, L. Gandini and G. Forman (eds) *The Hundred Languages of Children: The Reggio Emilia Approach*. Greenwich CT: Ablex, pp. 41–90.

Mayall, B. (2002) *Towards a Sociology for Childhood: Thinking from Children's Lives*. Buckingham: Open University Press.

Mizen, P., C. Pole and A. Bolton (eds) (2001) *Hidden Hands: International Perspectives on Children's Work and Labour*. London: Routledge Falmer.

Morrow, V. (1998) *Understanding Families: Children's Perspectives*. London: National Children's Bureau.

Mullender. A., G. Hague, U.M. Imam, L. Kelly, E. Malos and L. Regan (2003) 'Could Have Helped But They Didn't': The Formal and Informal Support Systems Experienced by Children Living with Domestic Violence', in C. Hallett and A. Prout (eds) *Hearing the Voices of Children: Social Policy for a New Century*. London: Routledge Falmer, pp. 139–157.

Oppelaar, J. and P.A. Dykstra (2004) 'Contacts between Grandparents and Grandchildren', *Netherlands Journal of Social Sciences*, 40: 91–113.

Penn, H. (2002) 'The World Bank's View of Early Childhood', *Childhood*, 9 (1): 119–132.

Penn, H. (2005) *Unequal Childhoods*. London: Routledge.

Punch, S. (2005). 'The Generationing of Power: Comparison of Child-Parent and Sibling Relations in Scotland', *Sociological Studies of Children and Youth*, 10, 169–188.

Ridge, T. (2006) 'Childhood Poverty: A Barrier to Social Participation', in K. Tisdall, J.M. Davis, M. Hill and A. Prout (eds) *Children, Young People and Social Inclusion*. Bristol: Policy Press, pp. 23–38.

Robson, E. and N. Ansell (2000) 'Young Carers in Southern Africa: Exploring Stories from Zimbabwean Secondary School Students', in S. Holloway and G. Valentine (eds) *Children's Geographies: Playing, Living, Learning*. London: Routledge, pp. 174–193.

Ross, N., M. Hill, H. Sweeting and S. Cunningham-Burley (2005) *Grandparents and Teen Grandchildren: Exploring Intergenerational Relationships*. End-of-Project Report to ESRC. London: ESRC.

Sachs, L. (1983) *Evil Eye or Bacteria: Turkish Migrant Women and Swedish Health Care.* Stockholm: Department of Social Anthropology.

Shunter, Kleeman S. (2000) 'Gender Mainstreaming as a Strategy for Modernising Gender Relations?' in S. Trnka (ed.) *Family Issues between Gender and Generation.* Luxembourg: Office for Official Publications of the European Communities, pp. 79–85.

Smart, C. and B. Neale (1999) *Family Fragments?* Cambridge: Polity Press.

Song, M. (2001) 'Chinese Children's Work Roles in Immigrant Adaptation', in Mizen, P., C. Pole and A. Bolton (eds) *Hidden Hands: International Perspectives on Children's Work and Labour.* London: Routledge Falmer, pp. 55–69.

Thomson, P. (1996) 'Justice between Generations and the Plight of Children' in H. Wintersberger (ed.) *Children on the Way from Marginality Towards Citizenship. Childhood Policies: Conceptual and Practical Issues.* Eurosocial Report 61. Vienna: European Centre, pp. 43–66.

Van Ranst, N., K. Verschueren and A. Marcoen (1995) 'The Meaning of Grandparents As Viewed by Adolescent Grandchildren: An Empirical Study in Belgium', *International Journal of Aging and Human Development*, 41(4): 311–324.

Vollenwyder, N., J.-F. Bickel, C.L. d'Epinay and C. Maystre (2002) 'The Elderly and Their Families, 1979–94: Changing Networks and Relationships', *Current Sociology*, 50(2): 263–280.

Wade, A. and C. Smart (2005) *Continuity and Change in Parent-Child Relationships over Three Generations.* End-of-project report to ESRC. London: ESRC.

Whiting, B. (1963) *Six Cultures: Studies of Child Rearing.* London: Wiley.

Wilk, L. (2000) 'Intergenerational Relationships: Grandparents and Grandchildren', in S. Trnka (ed.) *Family Issues between Gender and Generation.* Luxembourg: Office for Official Publications of the European Communities, pp. 26–29.

Williamson, H. and I. Butler (1995) 'Children Speak: Perspectives on Their Social Worlds', in J. Brannen and M. O'Brien (eds) *Childhood and Parenthood.* London: Institute of Education, pp. 294–308.

Wilson, E.K. (1962) 'Introduction' to *Moral Education* by E. Durkheim. New York: Free Press of Glencoe, pp. ix–xxviii.

Wintersberger, H. (2000) 'Family Issues between Gender and Generation', in S. Trnka (ed.) *Family Issues between Gender and Generation.* Luxembourg: Office for Official Publications of the European Communities, pp. 5–8.

Wood, D. (1986) 'Aspects of Learning and Teaching', in M. Richards and P. Light (eds) *Children of Social Worlds.* Cambridge: Polity Press, pp. 191–212.

Zeiher, H. (2003) 'Intergenerational Relations and Social Change in Childhood: Examples from West Germany', in B. Mayall and H. Zeiher (eds) *Childhood in Generational perspective.* London: Institute of Education, pp. 157–178.

Zelizer, V. (2005) 'The Priceless Child Revisited', in J. Qvortrup (ed.) *Studies in Modern Childhood: Society, Agency, Culture.* London: Palgrave Macmillan, pp. 184–200.

12
Children, Generational Relations and Intergenerational Justice
Thomas Olk

Introduction

Usually research on social inequality uses social characteristics like class, gender and ethnicity to characterize similar social positions within a hierarchical distribution system of societal resources. For example, categorizing children as dependent members of family households has enjoyed widespread consensus. In contrast, it is less common to take age or generation as a constituting characteristic of social inequality. This means that social-characteristic-based research conceives of children as part of a collective unit which comprises adults (parents) and children, and not as autonomous claims makers themselves with respect to societal resources (e.g., income). Consequently, research which analyses the position of children in the system of unequal distribution of resources from a generational perspective is still quite rare. Over the past few decades, under the label of 'new social studies of childhood' (Qvortrup et al., 1994), a macrosociological approach has been developed in the field of childhood research. According to this approach all children in a given society are part of the generational unit of childhood, and thus related to other generational units, like adulthood and old age, from which they can be systematically differentiated. As members of the generational unit of childhood they have something in common with all other children besides the fact that different groups of children – for example, boys and girls, children from rural and urban regions, children with different social backgrounds, and so on – may be exposed to different living conditions. Children as children share a certain degree of commonality in terms of rights, power, law, access to welfare and to space, and so on which differentiates them from the members of other generational units already mentioned.

With respect to generational relations between children and other generations, two levels of analysis can be identified: a microsociological and a macrosociological level (Kaufmann, 1993). From a microsociological perspective children are rendered as individual social actors who interact with other persons and groups. If it is the case that their interaction partners are adults, then they are involved in 'intergenerational relationships' (*Generationenbeziehungen*). From a macrosociological perspective, however, childhood can be described as a collectivity, which can be compared to collectives, for example adulthood and old age (cf. Qvortrup, 2000, and this volume). Insofar as children (understood as a collective) are related to other collectives as mentioned before the focus is on intergenerational relations' (*Generationenverhältnisse*).

The following analysis is interested in exploring both to what extent children have access to scarce resources compared to other generational groups like adults and the elderly and (historically speaking) how the relative position of different generations changes under the impact of economic, social and demographic parameters. As such, the arguments presented in this chapter are restricted to the macrosociological level of intergenerational relations, and thus do not address intergenerational relationships.

A theoretical approach which is interested in analysing the position of children in a generational order is focused on social processes which help to produce, reproduce and change generational relations – including childhood. When conceptualizing the historical dynamic of the relations between different generational units, it is not enough, however, to analyse the social structural position of childhood or children and adulthood or adults as isolated social categories. Rather, a relational understanding of generations is needed which is interested in exploring the relations between all generational units and the shifts in these relations over time.

As Alanen (2001, and this volume) has pointed out, two different approaches in the implementation of such relational generational analyses can be identified: Whereas one approach treats generations, that is generational units, as dependent variables, the other treats them as independent variables. At present, it is common for researchers to conceptualize generations as dependent variables. The members of a generational unit are defined as a demographic group – for example children, adults or the elderly – which is differentiated from other demographic groups by chronological age. The category 'birth cohort' is often employed when distinguishing between various generations in a historical sense. The crucial question of such research is what influence do independent societal forces, such as market, state, laws, demographic trends, and so on, have on different generational units or groups. This means that children are defined on the basis of an external and contingent characteristic – in most cases by their chronological age. Following Alanen, the other type of generational analysis is interested in the *internal* relations of children to the social world. In such analyses the term generational structure or order refers to the totality of social (relational) processes by which some persons are considered 'children' and others 'adults'. These are interactive processes of social construction that are ultimately responsible for determining whether one belongs to the category of children or to the category of adults. Such 'social practices' are named 'generationing' (Alanen, 2001). Generationing takes place both at the level of everyday interactions – for example between children and adults in families, between pupils and teachers in schools, and so on – and at the level of collective social practice in society.

The robustness of this approach, which focuses on the 'internal' relations of generations in the process of generationing, can be identified from the fact that it avoids any reference to given contingent categories – like chronological age or belonging to a birth cohort – in defining the contours of generational units. Instead, the processes of production, reproduction and change of the contours of generational units are themselves at the centre of this kind of research. This approach makes it possible to reconstruct how, that is via which social practices, some members of society are *made* 'children' and others are *made* 'adults', as well as what this means for their agency and their opportunity structures.

Until recently, generational analyses based on such an approach did not exist. In the following I refer to research which treats generational units or groups as 'dependent variables'.

Different concepts of generational justice

In the following I ask how children and childhood are localized in the system of claims and duties between the generations. Which concepts of generational justice dominate and what is the position of children and childhood within the existing system of generational resource distribution? To this end it is necessary to understand what is meant by the concept of generation. In the public debate as well as in philosophy and social theory four concepts of generation are relevant, which correspond to different, partly conflicting understandings of re-distributive justice (Laslett/Fishkin, 1992; Cohen, 1993; Arber/Attias-Donfut, 2000; Nullmeier, 2004). Depending upon the underlying concept of generational justice, the legitimate claims and duties of children are constructed in different ways:

(1) One possible definition of the concept of generations focuses on children, adults and the elderly as personal units coexisting at a specific historical point in time. Usually, talk of the relationship between 'the young' and 'the old' refers to younger and older people living in the present. Insofar as age groups are classified by their chronological age the term age *classes* is used; in contrast the term age *groups* refers to the social dimensions (historical events, group consciousness, etc.) as discriminating factors (Marshall, 1983).

(2) Another understanding of the concept of generation focuses on the succession of different generations (age groups) over the course of time. These are clusters of birth cohorts affected by specific historical events, the results of which are qualitative differences between one generation and another (Marshall, 1983). Factors leading to the formation of different generations can be economic changes (e.g., 'the children of the Great Depression'; see Elder, Jr., 1999), political (e.g., the post-war generation) and social developments (e.g., the post-materialistic generation). With regard to the position of different generations in the system of re-distributive justice it is of particular interest to see to what extent the combination of economic, demographic and political factors contributes to the formation of distinguishable generations which differ in their life chances and opportunity structures.

(3) In this context an understanding of the concept of generation that has been gaining influence compares complete life courses, and in doing so

compares the balance sheets of age cohorts (generational accounting) (Kotlikoff, 1992). Following this approach the economic situation of the elderly living in the present is compared to the economic situation of the elderly in the future. This can be done by drawing up for each successive cohort, both in the present and in the future, a financial balance sheet of contributions paid to the state against allowances and benefits received throughout the life course. From these calculations, estimates are made concerning the contributions which future generations will have to pay whilst taking into account fluctuations in economic growth. The results demonstrate that the social rights currently being acquired by present generations will theoretically weigh heavily upon future generations. Following this concept of generational justice a just treatment of successive cohorts would mean ensuring that the rights of future generations, for example to some minimum level of pension, have to be equivalent to those of today's older generation.

(4) Another version of the concept of generation focuses on 'future generations'. These are distant generations which do not overlap with living generations (Tremmel, 2006). This concept highlights the burdens which living generations produce, and in doing so limit the life chances of future generations. Early on, ecological destruction was the central issue in this debate. Today, however, the issue of public debt is becoming more and more important.

The position of children in the system of intergenerational distribution of resources – a marginalized group?

The social movements and conflicts of the last 200 years have contributed to the expansion of political and social citizenship rights to different groups of adults beyond merely occupation, gender, ethnicity, and so on. However, the same cannot be said for children, who are rendered as dependent member of their parents' households. Denying political and social citizenship rights to children is in perfect harmony with classical concepts of citizenship in philosophy and social theory. For example, in agreement with liberal theory, T.H. Marshall (1964 [1949]) assigned full citizenship rights exclusively to adults. According to liberal theory the central criterion which transforms individuals into citizens is maturity and capability. The moral status of an autonomous rights holder is the idea of self-government and the competency to follow one's own free will. Children are not assigned full-fledged citizenship because they do not have the competency to organize their individual preferences into a stable hierarchy and to follow their own free will by taking responsibility for their own fate. Thus, being dependent on other persons (normally parents) makes it impossible to assign full political and social citizenship rights to them (Mortier, 2002). Although the United Nations Convention on the Rights of the Child (UNCRC) from 1989 has made a strong contribution towards strengthening children's rights, especially children's social citizenship rights, their status is still somewhat vague. Even though Art. 27 UNCRC safeguards a child's right to a decent standard of living, in paragraph 2 parents or the child's legal guardians are made responsible (within their means and financial capacities) for securing the conditions of living necessary for the child's development. Paragraph 2 is not intended to release governments from any responsibility to the children. State parties are only obligated to take the appropriate measures in assisting parents concerning the implementation of this right. In cases of acute need, this also means providing material assistance and support programmes, particularly with regard to nutrition, clothing and housing. This means that the primary responsibility for the material well-being of the child lies not with the government but rather with the parents. As a result, we must also accept that a child's standard of living may vary in accordance with that of its parents.

From a life course perspective the marginalized position of children compared to other age groups is considered not only unproblematic but even legitimate. In contrast to other ascribed characteristics like gender or ethnicity, which normally cannot be changed, individuals move from one age group to another simply by getting older. Due to the fact that people normally are members of different age groups during their life course, Daniels (1988) concludes that treating people unequally during different periods of their life is legitimated and fits the criteria of justice. Making access to rights and resources dependent on an individual's age appears unproblematic as long as this mechanism remains stable over time, that is provided each respective age group will be treated equally regardless of the point in time. Therefore, treating childhood as a status without legitimate rights and claims remains unproblematic. Due to the chronological ageing over the course of a person's life, every child will be treated as an adult and will have access to full-fledged citizenship rights in the future. However, as Sgritta (1994) has pointed out, this line of argumentation is not convincing. The assumption that every generation will be treated like the generations before and after is totally unrealistic because it is based on the idea of an ahistorical and stable society (Sgritta, 1994, 357–358). In fact, social change is universal; economic, political, demographic and social factors make sure that every generation starts off under different conditions and is confronted with opportunity structures during their life course which differ from those of other generations in the past and in the future.

It follows from Daniels' argument that it is important to clarify the underlying understanding of generation and to keep in mind possible interactions with other concepts of generation. Daniels' position only applies to age, and not to historical generations. He only considers age in the sense of a natural process of ageing which is undergone by every individual during the life course. He neglects the process of historical and social change which ensures that the process of ageing takes place under different societal conditions. Furthermore, his approach is individualistic insofar as children are only considered as individuals who will (hopefully) become adults during their life course. In contrast structural relations between generational units like childhood and adulthood are systematically neglected. From this follows that the generational order, that is the system of dominance and subordination, of ruling and being ruled, among the age groups living at the same point in time remains unobserved.

Children and childhood in an ageing society – exploitation of the young by the old?

The argument above should have made it clear that an analysis of children's rights compared to those of other age groups cannot be restricted to identifying the rights and life chances of children in a specific historic situation. Rather, the access of children to societal resources compared to other generations can (and does) vary during the process of historical development. Differences in the life chances of birth cohorts can be influenced by economic developments such as severe recessions, for example the Great Depression of the 1930s (cf. Elder, Jr., 1999), and periods of continuing economic growth, for example as experienced during the 1960s and 1970s. Furthermore, demographic trends, such as increasing or decreasing fertility rates – for example, the baby boomers – or the increasing number of old people compared to young people as a consequence of the ageing of population, can play an important role (Easterlin, 1980). After the Second World War it was the welfare state which increasingly conditioned the future prospects and life chances of different birth cohorts or generations. In this context the term 'welfare state generations' (Leisering, 1992) has become more and more common. It was the American demographer and sociologist Preston (1984) who for the first time stressed divergent paths in the development of living conditions among children and the elderly in the United States after the Second World War. According to his analysis the living conditions of the elderly in the United States have undergone a continuous process of improvement, whereas, over the same period of time, the living conditions of children and families became more and more harsh. He ascribed the reduction of poverty among the elderly and the increase of poverty among younger age groups to the fact that welfare programmes for children and families have been cut back in the United States, whereas those for the elderly have continuously expanded.

Extending a point Thomson (1989, 1996) makes in his comparison of New Zealand to other OECD countries, the development of the welfare state can be considered a process of increasing usurpation by one specific generation – in this case today's elderly. Following Thomson's line of thought the birth cohorts between 1915 and 1935 benefited from the expansion of welfare state provisions and were able to transfer their privileges into the period of their own old age (at the expense of the successive generations), because welfare state priorities have been shifted from the younger to older people. The most disadvantaged birth cohort consists of the children of the baby boom generation. Due to its relatively high numbers, this generation has been confronted with hard competition for scarce resources like places in schools and jobs. Moreover, during their period of employment they have to carry the financial burden of the pensions of the even larger baby boom generation, whereas at the same time – because of the small number of successive birth cohorts – they have to accept reduced social benefits when they retire.

The advantage of Thomson's line of argumentation is the fact that he goes beyond a solely cross-sectional analysis and realizes a balance sheet over the whole life course. This makes it possible to analyse the distributional effects of welfare state benefits irrespective of short-term economic fluctuations. Preston's and Thomson's arguments can be understood as an example of the shift in the discourse on generational justice. Preston emphasizes the conflict between age groups with regard to welfare state benefits: A growing number of well-secured older people are faced with a decreasing number of disadvantaged younger people. Welfare state re-distribution is understood as a zero-sum game between the old and the young in the sense that giving to one group means taking away from another group. This assumption is debatable. The degree and composition of welfare state transfers is heavily dependent on political decisions. The state may support the productivity of the economy or it may increase taxes and social contributions to gain an extended scope for re-distribution.

In contrast, Thomson stresses conflicts between birth cohorts: Instead of asking for distributional justice for age groups living at the same period in time, he focuses on generational equity between birth cohorts. He criticizes the exploitation of one historical cohort by another; the criterion of justice is related to the equal treatment of the collective balance sheets of different generations over the historical course of time. The shift in the prevailing concepts of generational justice is combined with the increased relevance of a precisely calculated account of generational relations. The traditional concept of the generational contract is not so much focused on the economic equity or inequity of generations but rather on the contributions of successive generations in securing the living of the young and the old as dependent generations at a given point in time. With increasing frequency the question is raised as to what quantitative extent one generation finances the other without getting something back in the future. Which generation carries which financial burdens and to what extent are these burdens distributed equally?

It is not the economic relations between individuals – that is the old and the young – or generational units which are at stake but the economic relations between succeeding historical generations. Thus, two different concepts of generational justice, which partially conflict, are combined (Nullmeier, 2004). One concept is focused on generational justice between successive generations, and as a consequence following generations may not be disadvantaged economically compared to previous generations. Here, equity is understood as securing the economic status between different birth cohorts. Another concept of generational justice replaces the concept of generational solidarity with the concept of generational self-responsibility. According to this concept a given generation may not hand over financial burdens to the next generation but has to make sure that its own financial savings suffice to secure its own living costs in the period of time when productive contributions are no longer possible. Each generation shall – calculated over the whole life course – safeguard its own living. Processes of exchange between the generations are possible and occasionally might even be necessary. But when it comes to intergenerational exchange processes – as is usual in cases of social security systems – it has to be guaranteed that one generation's contributions are balanced by equivalent contributions of another generation.

In any case, the two concepts are not compatible. The first concept focuses on economic equity over the whole life course between the generations. This means that succeeding generations shall enjoy the same economic living conditions as previous generations. The second concept, however, highlights each generation's self-responsibility. The result may be a balanced exchange relationship between two generations which may live under completely different material living conditions. This is the case because in this concept of generational self-responsibility economic equity is only called for with respect to exchange processes between generations and not with respect to living standards.

In the current discourse on intergenerational justice both concepts are linked by the assumption that a balanced exchange relationship between the generations would make it possible for the younger generations to achieve the living standard of the elder generation. This is based on the assumption that the deterioration of life chances of successive generations is a result of the exploitation of the younger by the elder generations due to unbalanced exchange relationships. This is what Thomson (1989, 1996) is driving at when he argues that the deprivation of younger generations is a consequence of a 'conspiracy' of the elderly against the young. There are two counter-arguments that can be raised: First, there is no empirical evidence to support the claim that the actions of the elderly are intentional in the sense of a 'selfish generation' enriching themselves at the expense of the young. Second, this argumentation does not consider that even in a situation of a balanced exchange relationship between generations the successive generation may be confronted with a deterioration of life chances compared to the life chances of former generations.

As a recent comparative study by Lynch (2006) demonstrates, privileges and disadvantages among generations in modern welfare states cannot be explained solely in terms of factors like the egoism of the elderly or their organizational power. Based on a calculation of the proportion of direct social spending for elderly and non-elderly, Lynch determined that among OECD countries there are significant differences with respect to their age-orientation on social policies. Whereas the social programmes of some countries can be characterized by a clear elderly orientation (e.g., the United States and Japan) others are relatively youth-oriented (e.g., Denmark, Sweden and Ireland). Other countries like Germany, France and Belgium, for example, hold a position somewhere in between. Contrary to Thomson's thesis concerning a 'conspiracy' of the old against the young there is empirical evidence that in some countries the elderly are in fact privileged regarding social programmes but there are other countries in which children and families profit substantially from welfare benefits. A given age-orientation corresponds neither to conventional welfare state typologies (e.g., de-commodification-typology by Esping-Andersen) nor to other variables like the extent of social expenditure, the proportion of elderly in the total population or the power of interest organizations for the elderly.

Following Lynch (2006: 55–69) the prevailing age-orientation of a country can be explained by the path-dependent development of the national political and social institutional system. She identifies the late nineteenth and early twentieth centuries as the first juncture. During this historical period two different types of welfare state with radically different institutional logics were established: a universal citizenship-based system, on the one hand, and an occupational- and insurance-based welfare state, on the other. Citizenship-based programmes become more youth-oriented with the passage of time, while occupationalist programmes developed along the line of an elderly orientation. The Second World War marks a second juncture. The different welfare state systems had to adapt to changing economic, social and political conditions. During this period the occupational-based countries split into two further groups. While one group reduced its elderly orientation by adding universal programs to its base of occupational programmes, the other group remained purely occupational-systems-oriented and continued to develop highly elderly-oriented spending patterns. Lynch explains this process of deviation from the previous path of occupation-orientation via the dominant mode of political competition in these countries. The period including the Great Depression and the Second World War was a time of great institutional fluidity, where many developed countries had the chance to rebuild their welfare state institutions after the crises of the twenties and thirties. Furthermore, the threat of war reinforced national unity, and consequently led to new social programmes being chosen. Lynch points out that the countries which managed to organize a shift from an occupational-based to a citizenship-based welfare state were able to establish a mode of programmatic political competition. As such, this shift encouraged universal-oriented and inclusive political programmes that benefited society at large over more focused programmes designed to benefit selective groups, for example the working class. Hence, the age-orientation of welfare in a specific country is not the result of a conspiracy against the young on the part of the elderly but the, more or less, unintended consequence of the structure of social programmes and the mode of political competition.

Is there any social justice for children?

As discussed above, an extension of Thomson's conclusions indicates that all OECD countries are confronted with an erosion of welfare state support for children. According to Lynch this does not hold for all countries. In the meantime each developed country has institutionalized, more or less, generous child benefit packages, including child benefits, tax allowances and benefits for families, childcare institutions, and so on. Furthermore, it cannot be denied that the material welfare and well-being of children has increased in these countries compared to previous times. However, the living conditions of children remain precarious and insecure. Not being accepted as claims makers and full-fledged citizens with social rights, they benefit more or less by chance from welfare programmes, and the extent of welfare support is heavily dependent upon political constellations and discretion. Whereas after the institutionalization of public pension systems the state is responsible for the living conditions of the elderly, the responsibility for securing the maintenance costs for children remains a private matter for the parents. Due to the ban on child labour and the introduction of compulsory school attendance, children cannot contribute to the family income, and instead represent a financial burden for their parents. As a result, their living conditions depend on the market capacity of their parents, which in turn ultimately means on the labour market. Lacking the right to make claims vis-à-vis the state, children have at best the right to share the living conditions of their parents. Due to the fact that they are excluded from participation in the (labour) market and that they are treated as dependent members of the family household, children are dependent on other actors – foremost on their parents but also on the welfare state if the parents fail to secure their living.

Empirical indicators demonstrate that this precarious status results in a relative deprivation of children and childhood compared to other generations. For example, the relative equivalent income of children decreased in the period from 1985 to 1995 compared to other age groups. In all countries their per capita income is lower than the income of the active population. The income situation of the elderly has improved in most of the countries, but is still beneath the level of the active population (Förster/Pearson, 2002). Furthermore, the relative poverty rate of the under-18 age group in ten out of fifteen researched countries is above the level of the total population and the poverty rate of the elderly (Jesuit/ Smeeding, 2002).

How can such a distribution of societal resources be assessed under the criterion of re-distributive justice? In this respect Bojer (2000, 2005) has made an ambitious attempt to explore the issue of social justice for children as children based on John Rawls' theory of justice (1973). Bojer comes to the conclusion that most of the theories of distributive justice do not say much about children. Although John Rawls also did not focus explicitly on the issue of social justice for children, Bojer points out that Rawls' theory of social justice is the only theory which is principally able to treat children as fully acknowledged human beings and as independent subjects of social justice (Bojer, 2000, 30). However, she formulates her argument concerning the inclusion of children in a theory of social justice from the perspective of the life course. Childhood – so her argument goes – can be seen as a necessary stage of life for all human beings on their way to becoming adult decision makers. The conditions under which they are living their childhood will have a great impact on their future perspectives as adults. Under conditions of social inequality there is a high probability that children will live their childhood in a harsh economic environment. From this it follows that these children will have fewer opportunities to make their own decisions and to improve their welfare position when they become adults. This cannot be justified, because children are not able to choose their parents – and this means they are not in a position to choose the quality of their childhood. Therefore, it may be justifiable to enhance life chances during the period of childhood by providing them with primary goods.

Lastly, Bojer justifies the societal right to a re-distributive intervention in the social conditions of childhood by pointing to the relevance of childhood for their later lives as adults. From this it follows that her argumentation is principally future oriented and fails to justify a good childhood as intrinsically valuable.

For example, it remains questionable whether this argumentation would justify investing in those children who might have no chance of becoming an adult.

However, this argumentation can provide a tentative basis for justifying investments in a good childhood. This is where Esping-Andersen (2002; Esping-Andersen and Sarasa, 2002) starts from when he argues that the welfare and well-being of tomorrow's elderly primarily depends on the welfare and well-being of the present child generation, because that is the generation of tomorrow's workers. In addition, Esping-Andersen points out that the possible distributional conflict between the old and the young in the here-and-now can be mitigated by transforming it into the temporal dimension. By doing this it would be possible to transform the zero-sum game into a positive-sum game. The argument goes at follows: The economic welfare of future generations of old people depends on the productivity of future generations of workers – this means the current generation of children. By investing in the life chances of children in the present the productivity of future workers will be improved – from which it follows that the future generation of workers will be better able to finance the pensions of the then old generation.

In contrast to Bojer's argument, in which the intervention in the conditions of childhood is legitimized by the future advantages for the children themselves, Esping-Andersen extends the future profit of the investments in children to the totality of the successive generations of the elderly. The connection between an investment in children and the effects upon the living conditions of the elderly is reformulated as an interrelationship between cohorts. Thus, Esping-Andersen identifies the following consequence: If the welfare of tomorrow's elderly should be improved, it is necessary to invest in present children. In this manner welfare programmes for children acquire an instrumental character. The only legitimation to invest in children, then, is to raise the productivity of the demographically caused shrinking number of children who will be the workers of the future and will be responsible for financing the pensions of future generations of the elderly. The paradigm of 'distributive justice' is replaced by the paradigm of 'productive justice'. Accordingly, it is justified to invest a larger proportion of resources in children at the cost of other age groups because doing so would result in a collective benefit for all future generations. Seen in this light, Esping-Andersen's line of argumentation is far from being a convincing contribution to a theory of justice for children as children.

Esping-Andersen's utilitarian approach fails because it legitimizes the investment in children by referring exclusively to their productive activities in the future. A convincing argument must rely on the usefulness of the activities of children as children. Just such an argument was proposed by Qvortrup (1995). It goes without saying that children in pre-industrial societies were useful in the sense that they participated to a great extent in the important productive activities connected to the household and local community, thereby contributing to the lives of their family members (see Nieuwenhuys in this volume). At first glance, this usefulness seems to have been lost by the ban on child labour and the integration of children into the educational system. Qvortrup (1995) pointed out that this transition to modernity is not characterized by a movement of children from 'usefulness' to 'uselessness', as, for example, Zelizer (1985) formulated, but rather might be better understood as a movement from one kind of 'usefulness' to another kind of 'usefulness'. Although the form and content of obligatory activities children performed underwent a dramatic change, there was still continuity in the sense that children moved from one productive activity (work in the labour market) to another (school work). In fact, participating in manual work has become dispensable due to technological progress and innovations in the labour world. However, under the conditions of an advanced service economy it is more important that children are involved in processes of self-qualification via school work in order to prepare themselves for the highly qualified jobs demanded by the future labour market. To this extent, school work is seen as an integral part of a complex system of a diachronic division of labour: The integration of children in schools is part of a system in which the end product – for example goods and services – is the result of a multi-level system of successive steps of production. The fact that the continuous usefulness of children is neglected at the societal level has far-reaching consequences for children, their parents and the entire society. This is because the ban on child labour and the integration of children into the educational system make it impossible for parents to exploit the manpower of their children without providing them with financial compensation. From this it follows that while the cost of living for children has to be covered exclusively by the parents, all societal institutions and the entire generation of adults profit from the children's productive activities. This has caused a decrease in fertility and a shrinking number of children and has modified the distribution of welfare between the generations with the consequence that living conditions of younger generations have deteriorated compared to the living conditions of older generations. A pre-condition for reversing this trend could be found in acknowledging the productive activities of children. This means that we would need to regard children as a collective good (Folbre, 1994); to remunerate parents for their contributions in raising their children as well as children for their productive activities of 'self-qualification'. Social provision would no longer be considered 'undeserved benefits', but rather a 'deserved compensation' for socially valued activities. At the same time, this would be a convincing strategy for designing social justice vis-à-vis children not only as an expression of intergenerational equity but most of all as justice vis-à-vis children as children.

References

Alanen, L. (2001) 'Explorations in Generational Analysis', in B. Mayall and L. Alanen (eds) *Conceptualizing Child-Adult-Relations*. London/New York: RoutledgeFalmer, pp. 11–22.

Arber, S. and C. Attias-Donfut (eds) (2000) *The Myth of Generational Conflict. The Family and State in Ageing Societies*. London/New York: Routledge.

Bojer, H. (2000) 'Children and Theories of Social Justice', *Feminist Economics*, 6(2): 23–39.

Bojer, H. (2005) 'Social Justice and the Rights of Children', in J. Qvortrup (ed.) *Studies in Modern Childhood. Society, Agency and Culture*. Basingstoke/New York: Macmillan Palgrave, pp. 221–230.

Cohen, L.M. (ed.) (1993) *Justice across Generations. What Does It Mean?* A Publication of the Public Policy Institute, American Association of Retired Persons, Washington DC.

Daniels, N. (1988) *Am I My Parents' Keeper? An Essay on Justice Between the Young and the Old.* New York/Oxford: Oxford University Press.

Easterlin, R.A. (1980) *Birth and Fortune. The Impact of Numbers on Personal Welfare.* New York: Basic Books.

Elder, Jr., G.H. (1999) *Children of the Great Depression: Social Change in Life Experience.* 25th Anniversary Edition. Boulder, Colorado: Westview Press.

Esping-Andersen, G. (2002) 'A Child-Centred Social Investment Strategy', in G. Esping-Andersen, G. Duncan, A. Hemerijck and J. Myes (eds) *Why We Need a New Welfare State.* Oxford/New York: Oxford University Press, pp. 26–67.

Esping-Andersen, G. and S. Sarasa (2002) 'The Generational Conflict Reconsidered', *Journal of European Social Policy*, 12(1): 5–21.

Folbre, N. (1994) 'Children as Public Goods', *The American Economic Review*, 84(2): 86–90.

Förster, M. and M. Pearson (2002) *Income Distribution and Poverty in the OECD Area: Trends and Driving Forces.* OECD economic studies. Paris.

Jesuit, D. and T. Smeeding (2002) *Poverty and Income Distribution.* LIS Working Paper 293. Luxembourg.

Kaufmann, F.-X. (1993) 'Generationenbeziehungen und Generationenverhältnisse im Wohlfahrtsstaat', in K. Lüscher and F. Schultheis (eds) *Generationenbeziehungen in 'postmodernen' Gesellschaften. Analysen zum Verhältnis von Individuum, Familie, Staat und Gesellschaft.* Konstanz: Universitäts-Verlag Konstanz, pp. 95–108.

Kotlikoff, L.J. (1992) *Generational Accounting: Knowing Who Pays, and When, for What We Spend.* New York: Free Press.

Laslett, P. and J.S. Fishkin (eds) (1992) *Justice between Age Groups and Generations.* New Haven/London: Yale University.

Leisering, L. (1992) *Sozialstaat und demographischer Wandel. Wechselwirkungen, Generationenverhältnisse, politisch-institutionelle Steuerung.* Frankfurt/New York: Campus Verlag.

Lynch, J. (2006) *Age in the Welfare State. The Origins of Social Spending on Pensioners, Workers, and Children.* Cambridge: Cambridge University Press.

Marshall, V.W. (1983) 'Generations, Age Groups and Cohorts: Conceptual Distinctions', *Canadian Journal of Aging*, 2(2): 51–62.

Marshall, T.H. (1964) 'Citizenship and Social Class', in T.H. Marshall (ed.) *Class, Citizenship and Social Development.* New York: Doubleday, pp. 65–122 (first published 1950, first held 1949 as Marshall Lecture at Cambridge University).

Mortier, F. (2002) 'The Meaning of Individualization for Children's Citizenship', in F. Mouritsen and J. Qvortrup (eds) *Childhood and Children's Culture.* Odense: University Press of Southern Denmark, pp. 79–99.

Nullmeier, F. (2004) 'Generationengerechtigkeit – aus politikwissenschaftlicher Sicht', in Verband Deutscher Rentenversicherungsträger (ed.) *Generationengerechtigkeit – Inhalt, Bedeutung und Konsequenzen für die Alterssicherung. Jahrestagung 2003 des Forschungsnetzwerkes Alterssicherung (FNA) am 4. und 5. Dezember 2003 in Erfurt.* DRV-Schriften, Band 51.

Preston, S.H. (1984) 'Children and the Elderly: Divergent Paths for America's Dependents', *Demography*, 2(4): 435–457.

Qvortrup, J. (1995) 'From Useful to Useful: The Historical Continuity in Children's Constructive Participation', *Sociological Studies of Children*, Vol. 7, pp. 49–76.

Qvortrup, J. (2000) Generation – an important concept for the study of childhood. Paper presented to American Sociological Association's meeting, Washington D.C.

Qvortrup, J., M. Bardy, G.B. Sgritta and H. Wintersberger (eds) (1994) *Childhood Matters. Social Theory, Practice and Politics.* Aldershot: Avebury.

Rawls, J. (1973) *A Theory of Justice.* Oxford: Oxford University Press.

Sgritta, G.B. (1994) 'The Generational Division of Welfare. Equity and Conflict', Qvortrup et al., 1994, pp. 335–362.

Thomson, D. (1996) 'Justice between Generations and the Plight of Children', in H. Wintersberger (ed.) *Children on the Way from Marginality Towards Citizenship. Childhood Policies: Conceptual and Practical Issues.* Eurosocial Report 61, pp. 43–66.

Thomson, D. (1989) 'The Welfare State and Generational Conflict: Winners and Losers', in P. Johnson, C. Conrad and D. Thomson (eds) *Workers Versus Pensioners: Intergenerational Justice in an Ageing World.* Manchester/New York: Manchester University Press, pp. 33–56.

Tremmel, J.C. (ed.) (2006) *Handbook of Intergenerational Justice.* Cheltenham/Northampton: Edward Elgar.

Zelizer, V. (1985) *Pricing the Priceless Child: The Changing Social Value of Children.* New York: Basic Books.

13
Collective Identities

Heinz Hengst

This chapter addresses the question of collective experiences and categorizations of children living today in western societies. The question is translated by cultural analysis into the search for commonalities that children express in their thoughts, emotions and actions. The thoughts that follow are linked together by reference to the works of Karl Mannheim. The starting point is Mannheim's concept of generation. It differs from the sociostructural concept of generation, which examines how the generational order of society – the oppositional positioning of children and adults – is (re)produced. Mannheim's sociocultural approach considers, embedded in a wider concern to explain social and cultural change, generations as consisting of cohorts born at approximately the same time in a specific area of the world. It stresses that shared experience, values and attitudes are formed through the perception and processing of that world. It assumes that the members of generations retain these patterns their whole lives long. Since the key notion in this chapter is collective identities, not generation, reference is also made for interpretational purposes to those works that were posthumously published. They provide insights into Mannheim's understanding of collective phenomena and demonstrate his conceptualization of a fundamental sociality, the medium within which individuals are able to constitute themselves. The key focus here is on Mannheim's concept of 'conjunctive experiential space' and on the significance he attached to pre-reflexive, 'atheoretical' knowledge. In the following – to ensure present-day relevance – these elements are placed in the context of mediated experience. Collective identity – like identity in general – is understood to be a *process*. We need to distinguish between two kinds of discourse about collective identity: a way of talking in speech, and a way of social action.

Negotiating identities

Issues relating to collective identity need to be discussed in the context of identity in the very general sense. Associated with the concept of identity is the question as to how people understand who they are, and how they distinguish themselves from others. Identity thus provides the key linkage between the individual and societal levels. In present-day societies – such is our everyday

experience – connecting the individual and social level has become more difficult and increasingly fraught with risks. The range of adoptable, traditionally
prescribed identity patterns has shrunk in size in a pluralized, individualized and
de-standardized world. Many collective identities, including class, gender, generation, and race, appear to be less clear than before. Identities have to be actively
negotiated, without recourse to any clearly defined scripts. In other words, people
are expected to do the bulk of the work involved in defining their place in society.
In the de-essentialized versions that have come to the fore in cultural studies and
social sciences, identity is conceived of as a never-ending constructional process.
Proponents of a reflexive social psychology emphasize besides the lifelong development of identity the heterogeneity of identity states and their openness (Keupp
et al., 1999). Their aim with the former point is mainly to indicate that what used
to be a typical problem confronting young people is increasingly a problem for
adults as well. One need only refer to the heterogeneity of lifeworlds in which
everyday identity work is performed to illustrate that children are in no different
situation than the members of other age and population groups. Children act in
the family, kindergarten or school, and in peer groups inside and outside institutions, and gain experience with a multifarious, omnipresent and mediatized
consumer world. They are active and addressed as children, as girls and boys of
different ages, as schoolchildren, friends, as members of a particular nationality
or ethnicity and as consumers.

Growing up in a consumer-media culture

Any adequate analysis of present-day conditions and the emergent tendencies
towards mediatization in developed consumer societies is not possible if the
media are (only or primarily) viewed as new vehicles of socialization. Media
penetrate every aspect of life. Media are 'the symbolic fabric of our lives', and supply the 'raw material out of which our brain works'. 'The media are an expression
of our culture, and our culture works primarily with the materials provided by
the media' (Castells, 1998, 365). And commodities are not just objects for barter,
but also goods with which people think and speak. Media and commercial culture can no longer be viewed as something separable from society, social change,
cultural work and the conduct of lives. They affect relationships, the framing
of events and the construction of individual and collective identities. Although
there are many factors that currently influence children's collective identities,
those that stand out are consumer culture and media culture. Children of today
can obtain access to virtually all cultural domains independently of parents and
teachers. Media and commercialized culture have revolutionized the pathways
for knowledge acquisition, and the manner in which children create images of
themselves, of others and of the world in general. Parents and other adult references can no longer influence the acquisition of knowledge in a traditional
way, with recourse to clearly defined age-related norms and concepts, from the
ubiquitous flood of information. The consumer careers of almost all children –
also as experience with places where goods are sold – begin when they are still

babies. In the new super-script centred on market interests, the teleological component, the notion of further development as higher development and of adulthood as being qualitatively different, no longer has any meaning. It distinguishes between consumers with much or little purchasing power, with longer and shorter life expectancy, with greater or lesser influence on buying decisions. It knows children as a target group with quite specific needs and interests that are essentially equal in value to those of adults. It is on criteria such as these that attempts to define children as a market, and to segment them accordingly, are based.

Collectivity and generation

In his 1928 essay on 'The Problem of Generations', Karl Mannheim distinguishes between three generational phenomena: *Generationslagerung* (social location), *Generationszusammenhang* (actual generation) and *Generationseinheit* (generational unit) (Mannheim, 1965 [1928]). Social location encompasses all those people who live under the same historical and hence social conditions, have approximately the same life data, and are exposed to the same societal events and states. An actual generation is when people process and interpret identical experiences in a similar way, are aware of this commonality and develop world views, lifestyles, attitudes and patterns of behaviour on that basis. When the social location is approximately the same and the actual generation is essentially identical, and these result in a similar interpretation of societal reality in order to develop specific world views or political perspectives, then the people concerned form a generational unit. In more recent contributions to research, these three manifestations of generation are read explicitly and implicitly as a continuum. Generational units are then the entities in Mannheim's model that are the most strongly 'psyched' for 'unitary response' (Schäffer, 2003, 66).

One fundamental principle is that, if war and other disasters are left aside, social change would be impossible and inconceivable unless younger people continually acceded to the existing culture. For Mannheim, successor generations are new 'bearers of culture' that 'have "new access" to accumulated culture'. By 'new access' he means both novel forms of distancing and innovative forms of 'appropriating, processing and developing what exists' (Mannheim, 1965, 37). Mannheim emphasizes yet another point: He sees the 'practical' importance of the generation concept, as soon as the aim is a 'more precise understanding of the accelerated transformations in the immediate presence' (ibid., 31–32). Rapid and all-embracing modernization conditions a growing distance between the past and the future. This is paralleled by shrinkage of the knowledge gap between young and old, and of the latter's advisory competence. The future is a matter for the younger generations, for those who can train themselves in and through the structures and elements of social change that are relevant for the future, without being weighed down by the ballast of tradition. This version brings his concept of generation close to what Margaret Mead (1970) termed 'pre-figurative culture'. Mead noted: 'In the past there were always some elders who knew more than any children in terms of their experience of having grown up within a cultural system. Today there are none. …There are no elders who know what those who have been reared within the last 20 years know about the world into which they were born' (ibid., 61).

Both ideas imply a special form of being culturally set free in societies undergoing rapid and extensive sociocultural change. Whereas Margaret Mead essentially leaves it at conceptually fixing an understanding of generation that was newly emergent in the late 1960s, Karl Mannheim developed a concept in the 1920s – in response to accelerated modernization (in the lagging nations of Germany, Austria, Italy and Hungary) – that enables the interrelationships between macrosocial frameworks, subjective access and coping patterns to be analysed in the context of collectivity formation. The fact that generational concepts are currently in vogue in cultural studies and the social sciences is crucially related to renewed and – to use Mannheim's terminology – 'accelerated transformations in the immediate present'.

The terms with which Mannheim reflects on the relationships between macrosocial frameworks and subjective access are – analogous to Marx's concept of class – 'social location' for characterizing the object side and the notion – adapted from Dilthey – of the 'layering of experience' (*Erlebnisschichtung*) for the subject side. Mannheim defines the interrelationship between the two as the 'non-contemporaneity of the contemporaneous'. He proceeds from the assumption that each individual lives 'with people of the same age and a diversity of others in a wealth of contemporaneous possibilities', sharing a common contemporaneity, whereas on the other hand 'the same time is a different time' for everyone 'that he shares only with people of the same age'. From this he derives the demand to organize the diagnosis of the contemporary age (*Zeitdenken*) polyphonically, namely in such a way that one can hear 'in every "moment of time"…the separate voices of the different generations' (Mannheim, 1965, 28–29).

If diagnosing *our* times is organized polyphonically, one cannot readily assume the formation of distinct identities – in the sense of identities that are primarily generational in character. In recent years, some significant examples have been provided for the relativized importance of generational membership in Mannheim's sense (cf. among others Bohnsack and Schäffer, 2002; Wimmer, 1998). In place of *stable* generations, one must assume (heuristically) the existence of collectives which do not form any distinct generational identities, whose lived, qualitative contemporaneity or synchronicity is also characterized – at least temporarily – by other memberships (having changing meanings), the habitus and actions of which always make contemporaries identifiable. This change of perspective can not only render problematic the significance of the generational collective for shared experience, mentalities and structures of feeling, but can also mean the rethinking of other collectives. One conceptual consequence of this would be to structure generational analyses research concerning collective identities as studies into 'differential contemporariness' (Hengst, 2004).

The problem of 'first impressions'

The key notion for Mannheim's concept of generation and for his cultural sociology, the 'layering of experience' (*Erlebnisschichtung*) already mentioned, relates to a specific layering and processing of experiences. Mannheim distinguishes between consecutive layers in time that relate reflexively to each other. Of crucial importance here is the contention that incisive experiences occur during the youth phase. 'First impressions have a tendency to establish themselves as a natural world view.' Mannheim speaks of a 'predominance of first impressions'. Although these do not determine further layering, they do influence reactions to new experience (Mannheim, 1965, 40–41). One now refers to the 'revisability' of first impressions (cf. Corsten, 2003). In Bourdieu's sociology of culture, habitus – a concept which has obvious parallels with the 'layering of experience' – is already 'incorporated' in early childhood (cf. *inter alia* Bourdieu, 1982). The question as to whether generational impacts can occur as early as childhood, contrary to Mannheim's assumptions, has never really been researched. The same is true of the events and conditions that can initiate such impacts. Whereas the depth and sustainability of first impressions gained by those who experienced war as children can be convincingly documented (Corsten, 2003, 59), it is much more difficult to identify consumer children or media children as generations.

To define the sociogenesis and characteristics of collective experience more precisely the concept of knowledge needs clarifying. That holds not only for Karl Mannheim, but also for Margaret Mead's use of the term in her aforementioned reference to 'pre-figurative culture'. She is well aware of the issue and notes in one passage that 'feeling' captures the essence better than 'knowledge' (Mead, 1970, 63). There is some agreement here with Mannheim (1980) to the extent that he, too, conceives of generation-specific experiential knowledge as implicit or 'atheoretical' knowledge, as a form of knowledge that structures the actions of a generation, but which is barely accessible to reflection by the same actors. Different from Margaret Mead, Mannheim provides a conceptual framework that enables the genesis of generation-specific orientations to be analysed. In his 1928 essay on generations, he identifies 'milieu' as the 'middle layer' that acquires key importance in the shaping of generation-specific orientations. Referring to milieu, Mannheim solves the problem of macro–micro relations by introducing a 'meso-level' (cf. Bohnsack and Schäffer, 2002), a collective plane located below the societal framework, but where more happens than in the family and at school.

There is no point at this juncture in stopping still at the generational approach. Rather, we should, as already indicated, integrate into the present analysis Mannheim's work on the sociology of knowledge that was posthumously published in *Strukturen des Denkens* (Mannheim, 1980). It is now possible to read and better understand Mannheim's notion of milieu by linking it to the concept of 'conjunctive experiential space' developed in these works. A conjunctive experiential space is distinguished by the fact that those participating in it have a similar basic stock of awareness (Mannheim speaks of 'that store which distinguishes our world view' [ibid., 207]). What he is referring to here is a form of primordial understanding within a collective, for which Mannheim coined the term 'contagion'. The phenomenon of contagion is a pre-reflexive one, and preceded any explication using concepts. However, it does require language before it can provide people with release from captivity in the momentary. Language and conceptual fixation alone can enable what Mannheim calls 'we-circles' and the 'extension of experiential space' (ibid., 216). Here especially are similarities to Bourdieu's habitus concept, which likewise refers to a broad range of non-linguistic, pre-reflective practices. Schäffer brings Mannheim and Bourdieu closer together by proposing that the cultural sociology of the latter be read as the 'sociogenesis of conjunctive experiential spaces' (Schäffer, 2003, 79).

Of decisive importance for an understanding of generational shaping, the 'layering of experience', is its connection to practice. The praxeological basis for Mannheim's sociology of knowledge states that only knowledge that has genu inely been acquired by oneself is engrained and (collectively) binds. This basis is not provided in the (merely communicative) transfer of knowledge from older to younger people, or through schooled learning, which is why neither can be constitutive of a generation. (On the other hand, of course, making school compulsory for everyone has created an essential foundation on which children and youths can experience themselves as collectives – beyond class and gender boundaries.) One important aspect is that Mannheim's conjunctive experiential space is not about 'membership' in the sense of 'community', but 'structurally identical experience…, experience that is also shared by those who do not even know each other' (Bohnsack and Schäffer, 2002, 254). In other words, even 'imagined communities' (Anderson, 1983) can be conjunctive experiential spaces (on the enlargement of specific conjunctive communities based on shared experience, see *inter alia* Mannheim, 1980, 226). The formation of generations is not confined to communication among persons present (Mannheim, 1965, 33–34). It is located within a continuum, within which there are implicitly not only processes within specific groups (e.g., peer groups or families), but also experiences with and within communicational contexts of which technology-based media are an integral element (Schäffer, 2003, 88).

Children's conjunctive experiential spaces

For some years now, studies on computer and Internet use and so on have been a primary focus of research on new generation-forming experience. Interest in the cultural practices developed through daily use of these technologies is to be seen in the following context. It is assumed that the shared (structurally identical) experience of discontinuities (and breaches with tradition) exerts an influence on the generation-specific layering of experience when this is rooted in everyday practice, in the modifications and refractions of such practice. This is especially the case where everyday cultural practices are fundamentally changed, for example by technical innovations (Bohnsack and Schäffer, 2002; Schäffer, 2003).

German researchers who have conducted empirical studies (being orthodox Mannheimians on this point) assume that the characterizing force of experience – natural and practical everyday interaction with personal computers, for example – is strongest in the youth phase. Where comparative research is being conducted, the computer activities of youths are compared to those of adults, not to those of children. However, it has repeatedly been found that the – mostly male – youths who are deemed to have a new, generationally specific, access to the world of computers can look back to relevant cultural practices in which they were already engaged in their primary school years. The interpretation then ascribes an 'initiation function' to these early activities (Bohnsack and Schäffer, 2002, 266). This initiation function is rarely subjected to differentiated analysis. Although the differences between cultural practices of children and youths cannot simply be levelled, any rigid dichotomization into children's media culture and youth media culture is a form of conventionalism that has no justification in fact. Moreover, it obscures the fact that the activities of both age groups occur increasingly under a common umbrella.

Just how taken for granted conjunctive experiential spaces communicated by media have become for children can be demonstrated with a study by Dominique Pasquier (1996), which focused on cultural practices relating to television. The study relates to teenager series that have become increasingly important in French television since the early 1990s. These series, directed at teenagers by the producers responsible, not only achieved huge resonance among their target group, but above all were an absolute hit among much younger children. The series advanced to become the preferred topic of discussion in classrooms, above all among primary-school children. Especially the girls in the latter age group participated actively, using the intertextual material, in the cult surrounding the series. The study shows (based on a survey, on observation, on interviews and on the analysis of fan letters) that the series were used by children 'to explore alternative identities concerning gendered roles and to discuss, within the peer group, the ethic of relationships' (ibid., 354). One can see here how something that was traditionally viewed as a typical developmental task on the part of youths extends back far into childhood. What also becomes clear is that the intersubjectivity with which such handling is achieved is synchronized through media. We need to notice here a transformation of the world within children's reach (Hengst, 2007), including a virtualization of 'contagion' (enlargement of the significant others, para-social interactions, interpenetration of real and virtual spaces, etc.).

These interpretations are in line with the findings of Claudia Mitchell and Jacqueline Reid-Walsh (2002) on the websites of primary-school girls. According to Mitchell and Reid-Walsh, they are a typical phenomenon of present-day youth culture. Internet activities are comparable to other forms of popular-culture activities, such as listening to music, skating or dressing in the latest fashions. Age limits are overcome when performing any of these activities. What is also clearly evident is that whenever children use the Internet, they are involved in different forms of community formation. The authors of the study refer in this context to Paul Willis' (1990) concept of 'proto-community', meaning new groups that emerge spontaneously because a number of individuals are interested in a popular text.

At this juncture it is necessary to address the fact that the people involved in new kinds of 'conjunctive experiential space' are not always peer groups as traditionally conceived of by childhood and youth research. Peers are first and foremost people of like mind, but not necessarily people of the same age. Being a peer is defined more strongly by shared interests than by a common age in years. Because hybrid media and pop-culture environments are often independent of age and are accessible, they open up a range of new opportunities – intergenerational peer groups are now arising with increasing frequency, but do not feature at all in childhood research.

Reversal of expertise?

In the interpretations of new, generationally specific access to media, and inter-active technologies especially, (institutionalized) formal learning is very often used as the contrast medium. In other words, new accession to (admittedly new) cultural elements has the effect of devaluing the variant of learning considered in modernity to be the best available alternative. 'Autodidactic' is an attribute repeatedly encountered in such interpretations. The concept of *Basteln* (fiddling around [with the computer]) is offered as a generic term for self-managed collect-ive processes of learning and appropriation. Reference is made to the tentative aspect of such active practices and to the 'playful' and independent mode in which such fiddling around is performed. It is invariably noted that the know-ledge acquired in a 'fundamentally collective' process can be transferred 'quite casually into work contacts' (Bohnsack and Schäffer, 2002, 266). A 'partial, novel and asymmetrical relationship' is diagnosed in educational contexts (i.e., adults, including teachers, learn from youths). A 'reversal of expertise' is noted, some-what less cautiously (cf. Schäffer, 2003, 225–226).

The new information and communications technologies play a special role in current discourses about the tendency towards informalization of learning. Digital technologies, in contrast to the bulk of products from the leisure and entertainment arsenal of the culture industries, are increasingly being sold to parents (and schools) for the cognitive and motivational potential they are pur-ported to have. If one looks at where and how children (and youths) make use of the relevant products, and at the activities they devise, it is clearly evident that they operate more on their own terrain of children's and youth culture than on that of formalized school learning. It would appear that the 'educationally valu-able' label also functions (here) as a ticket to a digital game world. Internet use, and especially online chatting, can be seen as a way of maintaining the enjoy-ment of play once one has (long since) grown out of the role-play age.

As already indicated, there is an understandable tendency to study the reversal of expertise, and so on, above all in connection with technological innovations, and especially with new communications technologies. These are often declared to be the media and technologies of young people. However, it is essential to focus not only on the entire media landscape, but also on the entire consumer culture – and on the global scale – if one is to grasp the extent to which the collective experience of present-day children and youths has undergone change. Youths are the key market for the entire range of global goods, from PlayStations to mobile phones to designer sports clothes, and they spend their everyday lives at local level within the context of global capitalism.

It comes as little surprise that learning processes within conjunctive experiential spaces are defined as identity work by the youths involved – in complete contrast to the experiential spaces they encounter in school (Schäffer, 2003). This correlates to the findings of a study in which English and German children defined themselves, in response to the question 'What are you?', in terms of their favourite leisure activities and hobbies, but never in terms of their school performance (Hengst, 1997, 51). The Finnish educational sociologists Ari Antikainen and Juha Kauppila (2005) have reported results from a generational study showing that the members of the youngest generation of teachers participating in the study remembered their hobby-related experiences as being identity-forming (in which media and consumer industry products played an integral role), but ascribed a mere commodity function to schooled learning, which they describe as something they took purely for granted. A comparison with members of the older generations of teachers shows clearly that a significant change has occurred here (cf. Antikainen and Kauppila, 2005, 224–233), and one that is not confined to Finland. This illustrates how difficult it is to distinguish between different age-, generation- and period-related effects – but it probably makes sense to assume the existence of a new generational 'type' whose social origins date as far back as the 1960s.

Terms and concepts of self-categorization

Technical communication media unleash their effects in a historical, social and cultural world. The latter consists of collective regimens and orientations that frame action even where some of them have become fragile or questionable. The starting point and basis for interacting with new cultural elements is the everyday world, organized as it always has been by routines and recipes of various descriptions. The stock of social knowledge that we share with our fellow human beings makes it easier for us to engage in activities in our daily lives. This resource provides the typification for every potential trajectory and also for the (groups of) people involved. The notions which people use to perform (collective) self-categorizations act as conveyors of this trace of everyday life.

In his thoughts on 'the role of notions and language in conjunctive recognition', Karl Mannheim makes a distinction between general abstract terms (meaning terms that extract what is designated from the specific experiential context) and terms that may be abstract 'compared to the fullness of each experience', but despite this abstractness are not free of perspectivity, of being closely linked to the 'special experiential space'. He refers to the latter as 'conjunctive terms' (Mannheim, 1980, 223–224).

If the aim is to understand the current collective terms and concepts of children, especially those they spontaneously express, then it is essential to take into due consideration their conjunctive dimension, in the sense of the constitutive interpretation of the everyday. In the given context, for example, this means that terms such as children, adults, girls, boys, or playing, learning and working are all conjunctive terms. How they are actually used and what they actually stand for is not always in line with contemporary experience. Where these terms are constantly being used and accompany our actions, they transport regimes, sequences of activity and positionings in a stereotypical manner. How children see themselves as children is ultimately reflected – in any case when they express themselves spontaneously – in the language with which they are labelled in everyday life. It is therefore no wonder when they see a fundamental difference between children and adults, when they see children primarily as an age group, have a traditional view of young and old, or view themselves as not-yet-adults or as adults in the making. Such social self-categorizations demonstrate the existential importance of generational order in many areas of their everyday life. On the other hand, they show that what is associated with collective terms – not only by children – is often lagging behind the experiences they have on a pre-reflexive level. This is also the case, as already intimated, for the terms used to typify activities such as playing, learning and working.

New elements in collective notions and self-categorizations are not reached unless one takes seriously the fact that collective identity can only really be understood in processual terms, and grasps this process as a doubly discursive construct. When attempting to analyse this process, it is essential to bring out the pre-reflexive dimension. This does not mean playing it off against the habitualized connotations of collective notions. The process of identity work involves both aspects. Research on younger children and gender has shown that essentialist collective notions can also function to provide a (secure) basis from which excursions can be made into less familiar terrain (Harris, 1998; James, 1993).

Berry Mayall (2003) interviewed children in London about their thoughts and reflections regarding childhood and adulthood. She refers to what she uncovered as an interesting mixture of generally widespread views (common-sense notions) and sociological reflection. Among the ideas expressed by the children she interviewed, there are some in which childhood is conceived of as a transitional phase, and others in which childhood is seen as a social position that is always present in society and which is determined by its differences and relationships to adulthood. Mayall identifies the children she interviewed as members of a generation, to the extent that they are not only socially and historically localized in a very specific way, but also recognize that they share a particular social situation with other children, and correspondingly see the strategies with which they respond not only as individuals but as shared answers to the social processes that affect them. They grow up with major changes in the living and working arrangements with the family. For them, it is commonplace that parents have difficult working hours, and that they separate and start new relationships. Mayall, who works with Mannheim's concept of generation, sees a (historical) 'generational context' insofar as children actually do 'participate' in the 'common fate' of their generation (ibid., 331).

The results of an empirical study on children's constructions of collective identity, conducted in the mid-1990s in Bremen and Manchester (Hengst, 1997), show that children are basically of the view that intergenerational relations are all about age. The 'Children's International' that they are constructing is above all an expression of their awareness of a fundamental difference between children and adults. Yet when they attempt to define this difference, they very often ascribe to their own group attributes that reflect elements taken from the scripts of the media and culture industries. In some contexts it is particularly evident that the (collective) age-specific self has acquired historically specific aspects in their own minds, in this case in the form of a fixation on western lifestyles and ways of livings, on consumerism as a way of life.

A comparison with the first two post-war decades lends supports to the assumption that the criteria for similarity applied by children are being increasingly culturalized. Whereas, in the large-scale (UNESCO) study by Lambert and Klineberg (1967), the Japanese were characterized by children from western nations as being different, western lifestyle as an orientation criterion has led to present-day children discovering similarities even with the Japanese. This is understandable when one considers the Japanese presence on the world markets for media and commercial (children's) culture. On the basis of technological and leisure criteria, the West also includes Japan. Through entertainment products such as computers, computer games and martial arts, the Japanese have made a name for themselves. That a major role must be attributed to the media and/or to mediatized consumer culture – also and precisely in the context being addressed here – is shown also by a study carried out by Sarah L. Holloway and Gill Valentine (2000). They analysed the 'images' that British and New Zealand children have of the people and life-worlds in the respective other nation. They found that children from high-status, rich societies tend to define each other as similar, as 'us' rather than as 'them', playing down or overlooking other features in the process. The study corroborates the influence of television, entertainment media and global consumption circles on the manner in which children form a picture of everyday life in other societies.

When the children in the study on their constructions of collective identity were asked to define 'we', in answer to the question 'Who do you think of when you say "we"?' it became quite evident – large collectives play an at least very insubordinate role. 'We' are the people in the relevant microworlds for activities and relationships in everyday life: family, friends, the clique, the school class, sometimes relatives. And the more reflective or eloquent children know that belonging to the group we call 'we' is ultimately dependent on the specific context (cf. Hengst, 1997, 60).

Final remark

Whatever these thoughts on children's collective identities leave open, they perhaps can sensitize us to the fact that sociocultural change is directly experienced in many cases – that is without having to pass the 'generationing' filter – into the experience and constructions of meaning on the part of present-day children. There is much to suggest that children's 'imagined communities' are being constructed anew under conditions of globalization. It is doubtless the case that the constructions of such communities are encroached upon not only by markets and media, but also by many other factors – one being the fact that very many of these children are growing up in migration societies, just as many others among them acquire experience as tourists. It must be assumed that the processes involved are complex and interdependent. However, in view of the omnipresence of the media in the everyday life of children, and the fact that media offerings constantly present 'others' (members of different nations and ethnic groups, men and women, children, youths, adults and old people) in distinct and significant environments, one can assume that this information and these images penetrate the collective self-images and images of others that today's children hold   tendentiously from infancy onwards.

References

Anderson, B. (1983) *Imagined Communities: Reflections on the Origins and Spread of Nationalism*. London: Verso.

Antikainen, A. and J. Kauppila (2005) 'Educational Generations and the Futures of Adult Education: A Nordic experience', in A. Antikainen (ed.) *Transforming a Learning Society. The Case of Finland*. Bern: Peter Lang. pp. 217–233.

Bohnsack, R. and B. Schäffer (2002) 'Generation als konjunktiver Erfahrungsraum. Eine empirische Analyse generationsspezifischer Medienpraxiskulturen', in G. Burkart and J. Wolf (eds) *Lebenszeiten. Erkundungen zur Soziologie der Generationen*. Opladen: Leske + Budrich, pp. 249–273.

Bourdieu, P. (1982) *Die feinen Unterschiede. Kritik der gesellschaftlichen Urteilskraft*. Frankfurt: Suhrkamp.

Castells, M. (1998) *The Rise of the Network Society*. Oxford: Blackwell.

Corsten, M. (2003) 'Biographical Revisions and the Coherence of a Generation', in B. Mayall and H. Zeiher (eds) *Childhood in Generational Perspective*. London: Institute of Education. pp. 46–67.

Harris, J.R. (1998) *The Nurture Assumption: Why Children Turn Out the Way They Do*. New York: The Free Press.

Hengst, H. (1997) 'Negotiating "Us" and "Them". Children's Constructions of Collective Identity', *Childhood*, 4(1): 43–62.

Hengst, H. (2004) 'Differenzielle Zeitgenossenschaft', in D. Geulen and H. Veith (eds) *Sozialisationstheorie interdisziplinär. Aktuelle Perspektiven*. Stuttgart: Lucius & Lucius. pp. 273–291.

Hengst, H. (2007) 'Metamorphoses of the World within Reach', in H. Zeiher, D. Devine, A.T. Kjørholt and H. Strandell (eds) *Flexible Childhood? Exploring Children's Welfare in Time and Space*. Odense: University Press of Southern Denmark, pp. 95–119.

Holloway, S.L. and G. Valentine (2000) 'Corked Hats and Coronation Street: British and New Zealand Children's Imaginative Geographies of the Other', *Childhood*, 7(3): 335–358.

James, A. (1993) *Childhood Identities. Self and Social Relationships in the Experience of the Child*. Edinburgh: Edinburgh University Press.

Keupp, H., T. Ahbe and W. Gmür (1999) *Identitätskonstruktionen. Das Patchwork der Identitäten in der Spätmoderne*. Reinbek: Rowohlt.

Lambert, W.E. and O. Klineberg (1967) *Children's Views of Foreign Peoples. a Cross-National Study*. New York: Appleton-Century-Crofts.

Mannheim, K. (1965) 'Das Problem der Generationen', in L.v. Friedeburg (ed.) *Jugend in der modernen Gesellschaft*. Köln und Berlin: Kiepenheuer & Witsch, pp. 23–48.

Mannheim, K. (1980) *Strukturen des Denkens*. Frankfurt: Suhrkamp.
Mayall, B. (2003) 'Kindheiten verstehen. Kommentare aus London', in H. Hengst and H. Kelle (eds) *Kinder – Körper – Identitäten. Theoretische und empirische Annäherungen an kulturelle Praxis und sozialen Wandel*. Weinheim und München: Juventa. pp. 319–332.
Mead, M. (1970) *Culture and Commitment. A Study of the Generation-Gap*. Garden City and New York: Doubleday and Company Inc.
Mitchell, C. and J. Reid-Walsh (2002) *Researching Children's Popular Culture. The Cultural Spaces of Childhood*. London: Routledge.
Pasquier, D. (1996) 'Teen Series' Reception. Television, Adolescence and Culture of Feelings', *Childhood*, 3(3): 351–373.
Schäffer, B. (2003) *Generationen–Medien–Bildung. Medienpraxiskulturen im Generationenvergleich*. Opladen: Leske + Budrich.
Willis, P. (1990) *Common Culture. Symbolic Work at Play in the Everyday Cultures of the Young*. London: Open University Press, Milton Keynes.
Wimmer, M. (1998) 'Fremdheit zwischen den Generationen. Generative Differenz, Generationsdifferenz, Kulturdifferenz', in J. Ecarius (ed.) *Was will die jüngere mit der älteren Generation? Generationsbeziehungen in der Erziehungswissenschaft*. Opladen: Leske + Budrich. pp. 81–113.

Section IV

Children's Everyday Lives/
The Local Framework

14
Children's Bodies

Laura Fingerson

As humans, we experience every moment of our lives as embodied. We are immersed in a world where our lived meanings and experiences have a bodily dimension, yet are not biologically determined. This approach to understanding social action, called embodiment, recognizes the body's corporeality and materiality as well as the social interactions and interpretations with which it is shaped and given meaning (Nettleton and Watson, 1998). The body is a variable in social interaction. For example, having a cold can make us irritable and grumpy, being in shape can compel us to start up a neighbourhood pickup basketball game and having frozen toes at an outdoor football game can force us to retreat to a heated home before the game is over. Socially, we interact differently with children's bodies or pregnant bodies or bodies belonging to those of a different race, ethnicity, dis/ability or gender.

Bodies are not static, but constantly change and shift through processes such as ageing, puberty or illness. This is particularly true for children whose bodies change even more dramatically and quickly than those of adults. When something changes about our physical bodies, it changes the way we interact with others. We are all 'embodied social agents' (Nettleton and Watson, 1998).

Individuals are constrained by the conditions in which they live and it is through their bodies, through embodied practices, that they can become subjects, participate in the construction of their conditions, transcend these conditions and act upon their worlds. Consequently, the body is implicated in processes involving power and agency (Foucault, 1977). Power, fluid and constantly shifting, is a fundamental aspect of all social interaction. Power is both the ability to influence behaviour and the capacity to use resources to achieve desired ends. For example, children and adolescents use power to influence others' views, to control conversation and to increase their social status. They use resources such as social status, their bodies and their knowledge to achieve their interactional goals.

When trying to explain individual action, there is a tension between attributing action to an individual's own power and desires versus the constraints of society, or structure, on that individual's actions. Keeping in mind this tension (or continuum as Fuchs [2001] advocates), agency involves individual and/or collective assertion of power over and choice in the larger circumstances (or structure) in which people find themselves. Power and agency both are negotiated and discursively produced through relationships, social interaction and language rather than being an essential element that an individual or group does or does not possess.

Bodies themselves can be used in an agentic manner as they help to shape the course of social interactions (Connell, 1995; Fingerson, 2006). Connell's (1995) term 'body-reflexive practices' refers to theorizing the body as both an object and an agent in social processes; as such, the body is a location for the negotiation of power. This sort of embodied agency is flexible and is not used in the same fashion by all individuals. Children and adolescents draw on their bodies in creative ways in social interaction, as discussed below, providing evidence for agency (also see James, this volume).

These notions of embodiment, agency and power are consistent with recent thinking in the sociology of childhood. Corsaro's (2005) theory of interpretive reproduction holds that children do not simply mimic adult (dominant) culture, but rather appropriate aspects of adult worlds into their own unique peer cultures. At the same time, children actively contribute to cultural production and social change. The dominant model of socialization relegates children and their bodies to a passive role, emphasizing societal moulding rather than children's actions (Prout, 2000). Corsaro instead finds that children are agents in their lives as they appropriate, reinvent and reproduce constructs from the larger social world.

By understanding how children and adolescents socially experience their bodies, we can learn about broader aspects of their everyday lives. We can learn about the shifting power in their social interactions, the resources from which they draw power, the ways in which they construct their social worlds and the ways in which they define each other as gendered, raced and aged beings. Surprisingly, although the literature on children, and adolescents' social lives has grown significantly in these past twenty years, there have been few empirical or theoretical contributions to research done on children's and adolescents' embodied lives. This chapter outlines some of these developments.

Salience of the body in childhood

Prout (2000) observed that the sociology of the body and the sociology of childhood have developed substantially in recent years, often along parallel lines. However, there has been surprisingly little contact between these two fields. This is due to how sociologists have traditionally addressed the body and to a lack of recognition of children's agency and distinct childhood cultures (James, 2000, this volume). However, children and adolescents are particularly defined by their bodies as their body marks status and their bodies change rapidly (Eder, Evans, and Parker, 1995; Fingerson, 1999; James, 2000; Fingerson, 2006).

For example, children are labelled based on their age and the abilities of their bodies, such as the terms 'baby', 'toddler', or 'adolescent', and each of these age markers signify a different structural placement in childhood. Height is a significant marker of age and status for children (James, 2000). Children use height to mark their social rank within the larger group and their progress towards being an adult, a position of power and maturity. James (2000) finds that children are involved in 'body work', as they constantly negotiate the presentation of their body, their body's actions and their body's appearance. For example, children work to make themselves appear taller or to stay within cultural prescriptions of thinness.

Adolescence is classified not only by growth but also by pubertal changes in the body, including secondary sex characteristics such as facial and public hair and primary sex characteristics such as menstruation. Fingerson's (2006) research focused on menstruation, which is a physical process that is intimately tied to social life, constrained by cultural and social interactional expectations and integrated into social discourse and power relations. Importantly, for a brief time, menstruation is new and has a great impact on girls' and boys' lives. For a brief time, menstruation is salient. By adulthood, women's and men's management of menstruation has become routine. Adolescent bodies are changing and growing as they make the transition between pre- and post-pubertal forms. The body and the body's experiences significantly shape human experience and human experience in turn shapes the body.

Christensen (2000) finds that children experience their bodies in terms of the social consequences the body has on their lives. In describing their bodily functions, children emphasize their own actions and their interactions with others, rather than simply talking about their bodies as isolated entities. Children think of illness, such as catching a cold, not as simply a bodily phenomenon, but rather as a disruption to their everyday social activities and routines. Recovery and feeling better are also expressed in terms of the social. For example, one of Christensen's participants, a seven year old, said that recovering meant a resumption of her daily activities: 'to do as I usually do'. She frames her recovery in terms of social interaction, not how her body is feeling.

Also demonstrating the salience of the body to childhood, Fingerson (1999) explored how nine to eleven-year-old girls interpreted family television programs and finds that these girls focused on humour relating to the body. During the group interviews, the girls appeared happier and more comfortable when collaboratively talking and laughing about body-related humorous sequences, than when answering other questions about the programs. These sequences included references to body image and body control through the topics of wearing revealing bikinis, being clumsy and using portable toilets. The laugh track of each program designates humorous sequences in the show and there were many such designated sequences the girls did not discuss. The content of media interpretations depends not only on the group dynamics and program content, but also on the particular issues raised in the program and how salient those issues are to the individual viewers. The girls focused their attentions on humour related to the body, as the body is indeed salient for pre-teen girls whose bodies are maturing into women's bodies rapidly.

Body and agency

Prout (2000) finds that although empirical work on children's agency is strong, few researchers take this work beyond the level of description (also see James, this volume). Fingerson (2006) attempts to fill this gap by proposing a theory of agency and the body, where the body both exerts agency and is a source of agency. These analytic tools can be used to understand how bodies can be used in negotiating power relations in daily interaction among all ages and groups.

Using the example of menstruation in adolescence, Fingerson first finds that the body itself exerts agency in girls' everyday lives. Some of the girls at times feel out of control when they are menstruating and wish they could plan exactly when their bleeding would start. Secondly, Fingerson shows that many girls, rather than being simply discouraged by their lack of control over their bodies, respond by drawing on their bodies as a source of power and agency in their interactions with other girls and with boys. Boys might have the power in the interactions when they teased or embarrassed girls about menstruation. But girls also had significant sources of power as they used boys' and men's embarrassment about menstruation to achieve desired ends (such as getting out of gym class or compelling boys to leave the conversation); developed an engaging social discourse with other girls and women about their shared bodily experiences; and developed a discourse of competence, where girls felt they could handle the pain and management of menstruation because they were girls, whereas they thought boys would not be able to handle it. Thus, the body is directly engaged in agency, both as it exerts agency and as it is a source of agency in the actor's social interactions.

As with many things in childhood, adults have a hard time imagining how the body can be so salient to children and adolescents. Beyond the importance of growth and puberty, adults wonder if adolescents, in particular, really talk about their bodies and other bodies in social interaction. But, as Fingerson (2006) demonstrates, teens talk openly in mixed-gender settings about menstruation and the body, something most adults never would have done in their own adolescence. Children and adolescents are living in a world that is generally comfortable with discussing the body and sex. There is openness in our culture today that was not there even in the late 1970s or the 1980s, only 20 to 30 years ago.

First, the prevalence of mass media exposes teens to a much larger cultural world than they used to be. No longer are children's social interactions limited to people they can talk to in person in their communities. Children and adolescents can follow along with the lives and conversations of characters in numerous television shows, movies and real-life celebrities. Further, there is a sensationalism and intense competition in the mass media where every show has to be more daring and more explicit than the last show. Issues of sex, violence and the body that were once taboo are now talked about routinely, all day and on network television, not just in the evening hours or on cable. This casualness of media talk filters into children's, and adolescents' lives and influences their peer cultures.

Secondly, as Jane Brody (2003) in a *New York Times* article explains, the AIDS epidemic has changed the way body and sexuality are talked about in the media and in everyday life. In order to talk about AIDS transmission and prevention, doctors, journalists and health writers learned to discuss explicit sexual activities without being embarrassed or prudish. The Monica Lewinsky–former-President Bill Clinton affair with the blue dress and detailed sexual information was plastered over the daily news. Similarly, with the bulk of US population, the baby boomers, moving into old age, there is an increasing attention to disease and illness such as breast cancer, impotence and menopause. Infertility is also increasingly common and discussed on the national scene. Brody recalls that when she started reporting on health issues in 1966, editorial policy severely limited her ability to describe any sex-related issue in a meaningful, forthright manner. This has changed significantly.

Thirdly, connecting both increased media prevalence and more open talk about body and sexuality, is the effect of third-wave feminism on children's and adolescents' cultures. Third-wave feminism is the current feminist movement primarily driven by younger women. Among the priorities of third-wavers are women's rights to sexual pleasure and women's rights to use and display their bodies as they choose. For example, girls and women feel that they have control and power over their own bodies and body expression, so they dress as sexily as they please for their own pleasure. They argue that this is not for the pleasure or objectification of boys and men. By dressing sexily, these third-wavers claim power over their surroundings and over their appearance. Thus, they gain control over the effects of their appearance on boys and men. We can see such control by media icons such as Madonna and Brittany Spears. Also, any walk through a local school reveals that girls, even in elementary schools, wear outfits baring their midriffs, or shorts with words on the rear. Such forms of attire can lead to school dress codes, which are often strongly resisted by both children and parents. Third-wavers' constructions of the body and sexuality have benefited from the second-wave feminist movement, such as the publication of *Our Bodies, Ourselves* (Boston Women's Health Collective, original publication date 1976), which is credited with launching the women's health movement.

These issues have changed what is acceptable to talk about, discuss and debate in public space. Children and adolescents today, in 2007, were born after 1990. They do not remember Reagan's presidency. Girls have always been welcome and involved in school sports. Former US Senator Bob Dole is best known for talking about impotency, not running for president. Most of them know someone who was born with the help of infertility science. The technologies for genetic testing, DNA analysis and Magnetic Resonance Imaging (MRIs) have always been available (for more, see the annual Beloit College 'Mindset List'). In Fingerson's (2006) research, some of the teens had even been to a local production of 'The Vagina Monologues'.

The body, agency and social interaction

Although the connection between sociology of childhood and sociology of the body is a new and underdeveloped area, several contributions have been made (see also Corsaro and Fingerson, 2003). This research demonstrates how children can draw on the body as a source of agency in everyday life.

In terms of gender, Martin (1996) finds that adolescents use their bodies and their sexuality as sources of agency. Yet, girls may feel that they have little control over their bodies because of the lack of both cognitive and subjective knowledge about their bodies. Tolman (2002) adds that adolescent girls are limited by their language in expressing sexual desire. They are not given language or space to express sexual pleasure or to explore positively their sexuality. This lack of sexual subjectivity limits girls' sexual agency, which makes girls susceptible to sexual and domestic abuse and unfulfilling sexual relationships throughout the life course. In sexual relationships, girls often have less power precisely because they are unfamiliar and uncomfortable with their own genitalia, and they do not have access to comfortable language to express either discomfort or pleasure. Girls are thus more vulnerable in sexual situations and being pressured to do things they do not want to do. Boys, on the other hand, are culturally supported in their sexual explorations and sexual knowledge. Boys learn through puberty that their bodies are a source of power and control (Martin, 1996). They use their knowledge and language in sexual interactions with girls to gain and hold the upper hand (Eder, Evans and Parker, 1995). Martin (1996) finds that girls use sports and school participation to express control in their lives.

Thorne (1993) finds that children use differences between their bodies as ways to tease the other sex and highlight the differences between the sexes. She contends that power differences between US fourth and fifth grade boys and girls are communicated and learned through social interaction, which focuses on the body. She talks about 'gender play', which is where children use the frame of 'play' as a cover for serious, gender-based messages that their play conveys about sexuality and aggression. Examples of gender play include bra-snapping and 'cooties' rituals. In cross-gender interactions, girls are more 'polluting' than boys are. Girls give cooties more often to boys than boys give them to girls. Also, Thorne found that the name 'cooties' was frequently changed to 'girl stain' or 'girl touch'. The most unpopular girls were sometimes called 'cootie queens' or 'cootie girls' and no such similar terms were used for unpopular boys. This shows that boys are more powerful; they are masculine and not stained by femininity.

Boys define themselves and their masculinity in opposition to femininity. For example, male athletes and coaches often use terms such as 'girl' and 'pussy' to insult those players who lack toughness (Eder, Evans and Parker, 1995). It is important for boys to be tough and aggressive, and at the same time to belittle and separate themselves from anything that is weaker or feminine (Fine, 1987). The girls' treatment as a source of contamination highlights the social power differences between superior boys and inferior girls. Boys and girls learn this difference through embodiment and body-based social interaction.

In another, striking example of using the body as a source of agency, Parr (2005) discusses how in 2002, approximately 29 child and adolescent asylum seekers in Australia attempted self-harm, such as hunger strikes and slashing their arms, to resist and to draw public attention to their placement in detention centres as they waited for the government to handle their cases. The children used their bodies as a direct source of agency in defiance of the structure that placed their bodies in detention.

Children also use their bodies, bodily functions and bodily waste products to resist authority. For example, children tell dirty jokes, disobey the dress code and use taboo bodily waste to shock teachers and other adults. Simpson (2000) relates one incident where a boy deliberately stabbed himself with a pencil to draw blood so he could leave the classroom lesson and visit the nurse. Resistance to the 'boredoms' of school lessons is well documented (Best, 1983; Everhart, 1983), but in this case it is the body that is directly used as the object of resistance.

At play, the physicality of the games shows how children can use their bodies as sources of power in their interactions. Several researchers have found that girls use their bodies in more restricted and inhibited ways in play and on the playground (Young, 1990; Thorne, 1993; Karsten, 2003). Thorne (1993), for example, finds in her US research that girls generally use less space and a smaller range of space on the playground than boys. Both boys and girls used their bodies to designate and patrol the borders of their space. In Karsten's (2003) research among children in Amsterdam, she finds that boys have claim to a higher, more valuable status on the playgrounds because of their bodily positions and visibility. Boys outnumber the girls, they are on the playground for more hours than girls are, they control more territory and space with their physical play than girls and their social networks were larger and more developed. At the same time, some girls challenged this gender divide by physically joining in games with boys. Boys were far less likely to join in girls' games.

However, in Evaldsson's (2003, this volume) research with girls and boys of immigrant backgrounds playing foursquare during recess in Sweden, she finds that power and agency in the social interactions of the game are attained by physical skills in throwing, not by gender status. Evaldsson finds that girls use their physical skills and power stances to demonstrate social power and competency in their play, rather than following dominant norms of feminine docile bodies. This is similar to Goodwin's (1998) research where she shows that Latina and African American girls in the United States use their bodies in hopscotch to display and assert power, challenge other players and resolve conflict. The girls are not simply playing passively and cooperatively, but call out fouls, dispute about rules and physically position themselves within the game to assert power. In another example, Messner (2000) observed four- and five-year-old girls in the United States and saw the girls using their bodies and voices to celebrate their soccer team, called the 'Barbie Girls.' An opposing boys' team was chanting in opposition to the girls' celebration of Barbie. Yet, the girls were not silenced and instead, they chased the boys off. The girls used their bodies to both proclaim their allegiance and to drive off the opposition.

In schooling, children's bodies are ordered and controlled. In preschools, Martin (1998) uncovers a hidden school curriculum designed to control children's bodily practices. Teachers require that children walk properly and quietly down the hall, sit up straight and try not to fidget. It is only on the playground that children are free to move about across different spaces, move their bodies as much as they please and play with whomever they choose (Evaldsson, 2003). Simpson (2000) finds that children's bodies are perceived as dangerous and troublesome and thus many school rules are designed to control students' bodies and their attentions. Further, when kids misbehave in school, their bodies are used in the punishment. For example, a child who was talking while the students were lining up for the dining room was punished by being made to stand in the main passage with his back to the rest of the school. He was bodily put on display. In this way, Simpson contends that the body is central to power relations among children and between children and adults in the schools. For children in school, being invisible, unnoticed and just a part of the group means they have managed to stay out of trouble. One effective punishment for kids who misbehave in school is to physically segregate and mark them.

Similarly, children, more so than adults, work particularly hard to fit in with others, as James (2000) learns in her classroom ethnography. Children do not want to stand out as different from their peers. To do this, they must make their bodies appear a certain way, such as changing the appearance of their bodies to conform to what other children in the group are doing, or in the classroom, blending in by sitting straight and still so the teacher will not notice them. In fact, children are not generally so orderly and well behaved, but children work to promote this view of themselves.

Health and the body

Health and health behaviours have direct implications for how children and adolescents experience their bodies and live embodied lives. For example, children who experience chronic illness may have many restrictions on their social lives. Clark (2003) explores US children's experiences of severe asthma and diabetes and finds that children have creative and powerful ways of coping in their social interactions with others, such as the use of imagination and play. The health decisions that children and adolescents have the most control over and that contribute significantly to youth physical well-being are eating and physical activity. The so-called obesity epidemic in the United States is getting a lot of press, particularly as it relates to children. Unhealthy diets and low physical activity can result in a myriad of physical and mental health problems (CDC, 2003), which are not only distressing in themselves, but also influence children's ability to participate in everyday activities and their social interactions.

According to the most recent Center for Disease Control (CDC) data (2003), approximately 15 per cent of youth in the United States ages six to nineteen are now overweight. This is triple the proportion from 1980. Among adolescents aged twelve to nineteen, African Americans are 24 per cent more likely and Mexican-Americans are 13 per cent more likely to be overweight than their non-Hispanic white counterparts (NCHS and CDC, 2002). The CDC (2003) reports that more than 60 per cent of youth eat too much fat and over 80 per cent do not eat enough fruits and vegetables. More than one-third of high school students do not regularly engage in vigorous physical activity. Daily Physical Education (PE) exists nationwide at only 8 per cent of elementary schools, 6.4 per cent of middle schools and 5.8 per cent of high schools (Weir, 2004). Illinois is the only state that mandates PE every day for every student, but about 25 per cent of Illinois school districts have been given waivers that relax the PE requirement (Weir, 2004).

The structure and institutions in adolescent social lives limit their power and agency in making their eating and physical health decisions. Social class groupings affect children and adolescents' physical health. For example, in terms of physical activity, middle-class youth are much more likely than working-class youth to be involved in extra-curricular organized sports, often several sports at one time (Lareau, 2003). Middle-class parents feel pressured to give their children the most opportunities possible and to have their children's time structured and supervised by adults. Working-class youth have more limited access to organized sports due to the financial and parental-time cost of participation (Lareau, 2003). Working-class adolescents may also not have enough financial resources to belong to health clubs and often live in unsafe neighbourhoods where they would not feel comfortable going out for a run (Duncan and Robinson, 2004). Space to play pickup games of basketball or soccer is often defined by social class through city and local politics (Bettis and Adams, 2005). Weight is particularly tied to class as the achievement of a slim, toned and muscular body ideal is a privilege afforded by the middle- and upper-classes who have the time and funds to spend on body projects (Lupton, 1996). As with many other areas, much of the research on class interactions with food and physical activity has been done on the adult world.

In terms of children's own power and agency to make their physical health decisions, age has the biggest influence. Jacobson and Maxwell (1994) found that children as young as kindergarten are making more of their own food choices than ever before. However, in Lupton's (1996) research, younger children felt a marked lack of power over food and relished young adulthood where they had new-found autonomy over the food they could choose, prepare and eat. Generally, adolescents have much more autonomy in their health decisions than younger children.

Adolescents' age and social location influence their mobility and financial resources. Adolescents are more limited in their movements and choices than adults because they are subject (at least somewhat) to their parents' or guardians' rules and household activities. Adolescents can be limited by family mealtimes or food selections available at home or at school. However, adolescents have more choices than younger children do to choose their own food and activities through increased access to money and to private and public travel to friends' homes, the park, the mall, restaurants or other social events. Adolescents often have larger allowances or work for wages in part-time jobs (Fine, Mortimer and Roberts, 1990). They also eat fewer meals with their parents and play and exercise less with their parents than younger children (Galinsky, 1999). Junk food is particularly attractive to adolescents because it is associated with parties, being with friends and being away from home (Lupton, 1996). Additionally, adolescents' eating and physical activity decisions and interpretations are more visible than those of adults because teens' social networks are more concentrated and physically proximate. Their bodily behaviours are on display for their peers and families and these behaviours are often scrutinized and commented on (Lupton, 1996).

More research on children's and adolescents' eating and physical activity behaviours is needed, particularly as they relate to peer groups. The 'obesity epidemic' in Western societies, particularly in the United States, continues to receive a great deal of press and children's food choices and opportunities for physical activity significantly affect their embodied lives.

Conclusion

As the research reviewed in this chapter shows, the body is experienced, managed and understood socially. The body is both a direct source of agency and can be drawn on as a source of agency and power in social interaction. For children and adolescents, in particular, the body is salient in their lives and affects their social interactions. In order to truly understand children's social lives, we must understand their embodied lives.

References

Beloit College (2006) 'Beloit College Mindset List'. http://www.beloit.edu/~pubaff/mindset/. (accessed 18 December 2006). Beloit, Wisconsin.

Best, R. (1983) *We've All Got Scars: What Boys and Girls Learn In Elementary School*. Bloomington IN: Indiana University Press.

Bettis, P.J. and N.G. Adams (2005) 'Landscapes of Girlhood', in P.J. Bettis and N.G. Adams (eds) *Geographies of Girlhood*. Mahway NJ: Lawrence Erlbaum, pp. 1–16.

Boston Women's Health Collective (1998) *Our Bodies, Ourselves for the New Century: A Book By and For Women*. New York: Touchstone Books.

Brody, J. (2003) 'Trans Fats to Safe Sex: How Health Advice Has Changed', *New York Times*. New York.

Center for Disease Control (CDC) (2003) 'Preventing Obesity and Chronic Diseases Through Good Nutrition and Physical Activity'. *CDC.gov Fact Sheet*. Atlanta. http://www.cdc.gov/nccdphp/publications/factsheets/Prevention/obesity.htm (accessed 12 December 2006).

Christensen, P.H. (2000) 'Childhood and the Cultural Constitution of Vulnerable Bodies', in A. Prout (ed.) *The Body, Childhood and Society*. Houndmills, Great Britain: MacMillan Press, pp. 38–59.

Clark, C.D. (2003) *In Sickness and in Play: Children Coping with Chronic Illness*. New Brunswick NJ: Rutgers University Press.

Connell, R.W. (1995) *Masculinities*. Berkeley: University of California Press.

Corsaro, W.A. (2005) *The Sociology of Childhood*, 2nd edn. Thousand Oaks CA: Pine Forge Press.

Corsaro, W.A. and L. Fingerson (2003) 'Socialization in Childhood', in J. DeLamater (ed.) *Handbook of Social Psychology*. New York: Kluwer-Plenum.

Duncan, M.C. and T.T. Robinson (2004) 'Obesity and Body Ideals in the Media: Health and Fitness Practices of Young African-American Women', *Quest*, 56: 77–104.

Eder, D., C.C. Evans and S. Parker (1995) *School Talk: Gender and Adolescent Culture*. New Brunswick NJ: Rutgers University Press.

Evaldsson, A.-C. (2003) 'Throwing Like a Girl? Situating Gender Differences in Physicality across Game Contexts', *Childhood*, 10(4): 475–497.

Everhart, R.B. (1983) 'Student "Power"', in R.B. Everhart (ed.) *Reading, Writing and Resistance: Adolescence and Labor in a Junior High School, Critical Social Thought.* Boston: Routledge and Kegan Paul.

Fine, G.A. (1987) *With the Boys: Little League Baseball and Preadolescent Culture.* Chicago: University of Chicago Press.

Fine, G.A., J.T. Mortimer and D.F. Roberts (1990) 'Leisure, Work, and the Mass Media', in S.S. Feldman and G.R. Elliott (eds.) *At the Threshold: The Developing Adolescent.* Cambridge: Harvard University Press, pp. 225–253.

Fingerson, L. (1999) 'Active Viewing: Girls' Interpretations of Family Television Programs', *Journal of Contemporary Ethnography,* 28: 389–418.

Fingerson, L. (2006) *Girls in Power: Gender, Body, and Menstruation in Adolescence.* Albany: SUNY Press.

Foucault, M. (1977) *Discipline and Punish: The Birth of the Prison.* New York: Vintage Books.

Fuchs, S. (2001) 'Beyond Agency', *Sociological Theory,* 19(1): 24–40.

Galinsky, E. (1999) *Ask the Children: What America's Children Really Think about Working Parents.* New York: William Morrow and Company, Inc.

Goodwin, M. (1998) 'Games of Stance: Conflict and Footing in Hopscotch', in S.M. Hoyle and C.T. Adger (eds.) *Kids Talk: Strategic Language Use in Later Childhood.* New York: Oxford University Press, pp. 23–46.

Jacobson, M.F. and B. Maxwell (1994) *What Are We Feeding our Kids?* New York: Workman Publishing Company.

James, A. (2000) 'Embodied Being(s): Understanding the Self and the Body in Childhood', in A. Prout (ed.) *The Body, Childhood and Society.* Houndmills, Great Britain: MacMillan Press, pp. 19–37.

Karsten, L. (2003) 'Children's Use of Public Space: The Gendered World of the Playground', *Childhood,* 10 (4): 457–473.

Lareau, A. (2003) *Unequal Childhoods: Class, Race, and Family Life.* Berkeley: University of California Press.

Lupton, D. (1996) *Food, the Body and the Self.* London: Sage Publications.

Martin, K.A. (1996) *Puberty, Sexuality, and the Self: Girls and Boys at Adolescence.* New York: Routledge.

Martin, K.A. (1998) 'Becoming a Gendered Body: Practices of Preschools', *American Sociological Review,* 63(4): 494–511.

Messner, M.A. (2000) 'Barbie Girls Versus Sea Monsters: Children Constructing Gender', *Gender & Society,* 14(6): 765–784.

National Center for Health Statistics (NCHS) and Center for Disease Control (CDC) (2002) 'Obesity Still on the Rise, New Data Show'. Press Release. Hyattsville, MD. October 8, 2002.

Nettleton, S. and J. Watson (1998) 'The Body in Everyday Life: An Introduction', in S. Nettleton and J. Watson (eds.) *The Body in Everyday Life.* London: Routledge, pp. 1–24.

Parr, A. (2005) 'The Deterritorializing Language of Child Detainees: Self-Harm or Embodied Graffiti?' *Childhood,* 12(3): 281–299.

Prout, A. (2000) 'Childhood Bodies: Construction, Agency and Hybridity', in A. Prout (ed.) *The Body, Childhood and Society.* Houndmills, Great Britain: MacMillan Press, pp. 1–18.

Simpson, B. (2000) 'Regulation and Resistance: Children's Embodiment During the Primary-Secondary School Transition', in A. Prout (ed.) *The Body, Childhood and Society,* Houndmills, Great Britain: MacMillan Press, pp. 60–78.

Thorne, B. (1993) *Gender Play: Girls and Boys in School.* New Brunswick NJ: Rutgers University Press.

Tolman, D. (2002) *Dilemmas of Desire: Teenage Girls Talk about Sexuality.* Cambridge, MA: Harvard University Press.

Weir, T. (2004) '"New PE" Objective: Get Kids In Shape', in *USA Today,* pp. 1A, 4A.

Young, I.M. (1990) *Throwing Like a Girl and Other Essays in Feminist Philosophy and Social Theory.* Bloomington IN: Indiana University Press.

15
Policies in Early Childhood Education and Care: Potentialities for Agency, Play and Learning

Gunilla Dahlberg

In recent years the institutionalization of childhood has accelerated dramatically, resulting in the rapid expansion of Early Childhood Education and Care (ECEC). Consequently, as lifelong learning increasingly begins with the very young, ECEC is moving with comparable speed up the policy agenda of nation states, as well as within different international organizations, including the European Commission, the OECD, the World Bank and UNESCO.

With some exceptions, interest and investment in ECEC on the part of both nation states and international organizations have historically been driven by different factors such as the desire to increase women's labour market participation by enabling reconciliation of work and family and the perceived long-term cost-effectiveness of such participation for a competitive economy (Dahlberg, Moss and Pence, 2007). However, today there is growing awareness of the structural shortcomings of neo-liberal economies and advanced liberal welfare states in terms of the construction of a sound ECEC. Recently, in the context of a knowledge society characterized by lifelong learning, the OECD (2006) has recognized the importance of understanding ECEC as *a human right for all children* and as a *public good* to be funded by the state and not as private commodities and businesses competing in the marketplace. On the basis of results from recent peer reviews of 20 member states, 'Starting Strong I and II: Early Childhood Education and Care' OECD (2001; 2006) maintains that a sound ECEC policy cannot be a quick fix from the outside, but rather the fruit of democratic consensus generated by careful consultation with major stakeholders. The OECD (2006, 126) equally argues that the 'belief that quality improvement can be left to market competition is naïve'.

This is a very powerful statement and similar statements have also been made of late by others in the field of ECEC (e.g., Corsaro, 2005; Dahlberg and Moss, 2005; Polakow, 2007). American sociologist William Corsaro (2003) argued for renewed civic engagement and greater public investment in the United States. Today, many American families must rely on private, for-profit early education and care for their children that is both costly and often of poor or barely adequate quality, provided by teachers lacking training and experience. Corsaro states that such programmes offer little to kids beyond custodial care. The idea of private profit which characterizes the American system creates a school of very low quality. A similar critique of US policy was recently put forth by Valerie Polakow (2007) in her book *Who Cares for Our Children?* Drawing on international comparisons, Polakow calls for urgent action in relation to, what she calls, the shameful record of the United States in caring for all its children. In the same spirit as the OECD, she urges us to view child care as a human right for all children and as a vital component of social citizenship rights for women. Prominence is placed on the Nordic countries and on some communities in northern Italy where, for several decades, the state and/or local authorities have focused on ECEC as a serious and long-term public project that, to a great extent, needs to be publicly funded.

Different curricular discourses and children's agency

In recent reviews, ever sensitive to context, the OECD has also explored the contrasts and complexities of different policies and approaches to ECEC. In so doing, it has identified two broad categories of pedagogical practices and traditions across Europe in particular: the *pre-primary tradition* and the *social pedagogic tradition* (Bennett, 2005). In the pre-primary approach, found in Belgium, France, Ireland, the Netherlands and the United Kingdom, but also in the United States, the focus on cognitive goals and readiness for school is an important aim. Accordingly, it is teacher-directed and children's performance is often benchmarked and assessed via prescribed targets generally pertaining to cognitive development. In the social pedagogic approach, found largely in the Nordic countries and Central Europe, the focus is more on children's play and social development with an accent on children's agency. This approach defines broader developmental goals that enable staff to tailor the programme to local conditions and base evaluation and assessment on more diverse targets rather than prescribed outcomes.

Conscious that different pedagogical approaches and definitions of quality are inextricably linked to different perceptions of childhood, the OECD, as concerns the pre-primary approach, expresses concern associated with the risk of placing too much emphasis on formal teaching and seeing school as a benchmark, which results in a form of 'schoolification'. By citing the 1989 United Nations Convention on the Rights of the Child and contesting a dominant notion of education as transmission and reproduction of content knowledge, the OECD advocates a view of curriculum in which young children should have a high degree of initiative and agency. It concomitantly stresses the importance of identifying and reinforcing 'those aspects of curriculum that contribute to the well-being and involvement of the child' (Bennett, 2005, 7). Instead of assessing a child's progress by grading or ranking, the OECD challenges member states to provide a positive, non-judgmental learning environment for the young. The OECD also ascribes much value to short national frameworks used to orient rather than define in detail content or methodology, and, in lieu of predetermined targets and outcomes, recommend a more supportive and participatory approach through observation and documentation of children's activities (Bennett, 2005). To this end, they propose principles that may counter the tendency to see school as a benchmark and to impose external targets and skills on young children (OECD, 2006, 207): (1) a focus on the agency of the child, including respect for the child's natural learning strategies (Sweden and Norway); (2) listening, project work and documentation as a primary means of working with young children (Reggio Emilia, Italy).

These two principles are viewed as contributing to children's well-being and desire and curiosity for learning, as well as building confidence in their own learning process. The focus has also been driven by the desire to introduce young children to participatory and democratic relations by teaching them to live together in a respectful fashion, to dialogue, and to open up for experimentation, research and reflection. The choice of Sweden and Norway is largely in light of the strong sense of collective responsibility that prevails in these countries, combined with individual freedom – values long upheld by the Nordic countries (Esping-Andersen, 1995). The idea of the competent child and children's agency has also been a fundamental part of the modernity project in most Nordic countries, which relates to modern institutions such as the negotiating family at home and a dialogical pedagogy in preschools, daycare institutions and schools (Brembeck, Johansson and Kampman, 2004). The curriculum for the Swedish preschool, which is a short national framework, proposes that local authorities and preschools focus on pedagogical practice over assessing children's progress by way of predetermined targets and outcomes. Likewise, the early childhood experience in the Italian city of Reggio Emilia and much of northern Italy (see Corsaro and Molinari, 2005) has been substantially shaped by its social and historical context in the aftermath of fascism, and is chiefly concerned with maintaining a construction and vision of a rich and competent child who can act and think independently and building a democratic culture of participation through the notion of learning as a relational space (New, 1993; Project Zero and Reggio Children, 2001; Rinaldi, 2006; Dahlberg, Moss and Pence, 2007).

Ethnographic studies on children's agency and play

Along the same lines as the OECD proposals cited above, recent ethnographic research related to the field of sociology of childhood challenges the idea of viewing children as passive recipients of pre-constituted and unquestionable knowledge transmitted by teachers with a privileged voice of authority and a privileged relation to the meaning of knowledge (James et al., 1998; James, this volume). In several influential ethnographic studies on early childhood settings in Italy and the United States, William Corsaro (2003, 2005, this volume) found that children, in their play, had a more agentic relationship with the world than previously ascribed to them. He states that in peer cultures, children develop a sense of collective community and a desire to share and participate in routines, activities and artefacts, with a potential for exceeding and transgressing the limits of knowledge transmitted to them by adults (Corsaro, 2005). Two other studies report similar results; the Swedish study 'Preschool Children's Play – an Arena for Cultural and Social Construction of Meaning' carried out by Annica Löfdahl (2002), and the Finnish study 'Social Places of Encounter for Children: Levels of Activity and Cultures of Negotiation in Day-Care Centers' carried out by Harriet Strandell (1994, 1997). In her study Löfdahl found that children were experimenting with new patterns and cultural themes while at the same time taking responsibility for themselves and others. Like Corsaro and Löfdahl, Strandell provides interpretations of children's play that reveal how children, in a very intelligent, creative and complex fashion, relate to their environment, and how play and playfulness are communicative resources that children employ to create and experiment with new cultural themes. Accordingly, Strandell argues that children's recognition of the transformative power of play becomes an important element of peer culture – a power that challenges the power position of children vis-à-vis adults. In this respect, the daycare setting can be understood as a structure and culture of negotiation.

Strandell (1994) also found that an overly controlled pedagogical approach translated into children becoming less engaged in activities, while participation, negotiation and taking responsibility for the learning process, together with adults and other children, did the contrary. Other researchers in the field express a similar concern in studies demonstrating that the prescription of detailed learning goals linked to formal teaching can place children in a position where they experience prolonged feelings of inadequacy which can impact negatively on their self-esteem and motivation to learn (Sylva and Wiltshire, 1993; Schweinhart and Weikart, 1997). The longitudinal IEA Pre-primary project (Weikart, 2000) has also shown that unstructured activities driven by children's interest produce better results than programmes geared towards pre-academic activities such as literacy and numeracy.

From the norm of the natural child towards the norm of the autonomous child?

Both the pre-primary and the social pedagogic tradition outlined by the OECD as well as ideas regarding children's agency need to be handled with caution and further scrutinized in terms of governing in the broadest sense. Researchers, particularly those who subscribe to the thinking of Michel Foucault and post-structuralism, have, over the last decades, challenged the forms of benevolent governing that is seen as placing great trust in the child and have asked us to become more reflective about the truths of children and how we are creating governable children of the present (e.g., Bloch, 1992; Burman, 1994; Lubeck, 1994; Cannella, 1997; Lenz Taguchi, 2000; Dahlberg, Moss and Pence, 2007).

Recent critically oriented research has issued warnings about the rhetoric regarding the active, autonomous, competent and flexible child, the child who is independent and capable of problem-solving and furthermore responsible for her/his own learning process through self-reflection and flexibility. Nicolas Rose (1999) has demonstrated how the trend towards autonomist and flexible behaviour is spreading to every reach of our society as we move towards a post-industrial knowledge and network society. We currently find ourselves in a situation where the state no longer figures as the central governor, and the individual is expected to assume responsibility for his/her own life through informed choices and activity (e.g., designing his/her own life via a continuous process of lifelong learning (see Deleuze, 1992; Rose, 1999; Fendler, 2001; Popkewitz, 2003; Dahlberg and Moss, 2005). These researchers argue that the child is supposed to play an active role in governing the self, by taking responsibility for his/her own actions and risks and exercising the choice and freedom of the flexible and informed consumer, ever ready to adapt to the needs of a rapidly changing marketplace. In this individualizing regime children are urged to practice continuous self-explication, self-evaluation and self-reflection, not only to acquire particular skills and competencies, but to become active, autonomous and self-governing children who are 'fit for purpose' in a neo-liberal world characterized by risk and unpredictability. In this neo-liberal discourse, freedom, or the 'duty to be free', implies an immense responsibility for each child and it may result in new forms of normalization and marginalization.

Rethinking narratives of children's agency, play and learning and early childhood education

In accord with the above, researchers, over the course of the last decades, have undertaken critical examination of how poststructuralist, feminist and postcolonial thought can be used to rethink children's agency, play and learning beyond normalization. In lieu of viewing the subject as a unified, coherent and relatively static self, these researchers explore the subject as a complex, changing, and contradictory creature. This generation of alternative constructions and practices of the child, hopefully more equitable ones, may pave the way for change (Davies, 1989).

In the poststructuralist spirit, Bronwyn Davies, alongside early childhood educators, has troubled narratives of children's play and interactions and encouraged readers to reconstruct new understandings about the nature of children's identities and relationships in preschools. In her groundbreaking study *Frogs and Snails and Feminist Tales: Preschool Children and Gender* Davies (1989) examines how gender myths (e.g., 'truths' about small children) influence teachers' thinking and action and, hence, regulate children's behaviour subjectivities and possibilities for being. For two years, in different cities in Australia, she observed children's play and their conversations. She also read feminist stories such as 'The Paper Bag Princess' together with the children and followed their understandings of the stories. Her data showed how children are constrained by the dualistic nature of the male–female categories, and this prompted her to ask how we, in educational practices, might move beyond said dualism. She states that the 'knowledge of oneself as male or female, encoded in one's body, makes possible, or precludes, certain forms of relationship with others and with the landscape. How one understands what one's body can or cannot do immediately affects the way one's body relates to the environment. That is, the idea of femaleness and the adoption of practices relevant to that idea have a material effect on the child's body'. She continues by saying: 'Each child must get its gender right, not only for itself to be seen as normal and acceptable within the terms of the culture. But it must get it right for others who will be interpreting themselves in relation to it as other' (1989, 20).

In a recent book, *Doing Foucault in Early Childhood Studies,* Glenda MacNaughton (2005) has described how she, together with educators, has attempted to become what they have called poststructurally reflective in relation to truths about children. Taking an activist stance, and using Gilles Deleuze and Felix Guattari's (1987) rhizoanalysis as a means of deconstructing a text to explore how it organizes meaning and power through offshoots, overlap, conquest and expansion and how it connects with things beyond it, these thinkers have tried to open the door for reconstructions of the everyday work of observing, documenting and analysing children's learning and their relationships. In another thought-provoking study entitled 'Queering Home Corner', Affrica Taylor and Carmel Richardson (2005) recorded children's sociocultural interactions during free play in an early childhood centre in the Australian Capital Territory. By queering home corner, they sought to expose the ways in which the premises of childhood innocence, domestic natural order and developmental appropriateness are embedded in the architecture of home corner, and hence become naturalized as part of the everyday landscape of 'normal' childhood. While playing in the home corner, they state, children are both symbolically and physically guided by the imagery, layout and artefacts of the home corner to undertake particular forms of domestic play, as the semiotic function of the home corner, with its decidedly straight, white and middle-class aesthetic, reproduces a universalized ideal of utopian domestic space and normative family relations. In their study they juxtaposed a range of role-plays enacted in home corner by drawing attention to the ways in which some children manage to subvert the intended design by transforming the space and performing counter-normative practices and identities. They then showed how children's desires exceeded the conventional wisdom of prevailing normal development paradigms and, hence, blurred the boundaries of identity categories by disrupting the assumed-to-be coherent gender categories of discrete, uncomplicated and unambiguous boyness on the one hand, and discrete, uncomplicated and unambiguous girlness on the other. Drawing on the work of Gilles Deleuze, Taylor and Richardson argue that for these children the home corner helps vacillate children's desires to become other in a series of fluid movements – as pleasure-based 'lines of flight.' Based on these results they call attention to how the semiology of the domestic architecture of home corner represents a culturally specific and highly nostalgic adult projection of a normative, idealized and segregated childhood innocence instead of the broad scope, complexity and diversity of contemporary children's lives. These norms function as disciplinary mechanisms that simultaneously limit the ways in which adults make sense of childhood and regulate the repertoire of identities that children have available to them.

The Swedish researcher Ulla Lind (2005) has also examined children's play at preschool from a poststructuralist perspective. Drawing on, among others, Elizabeth Grosz's Deleuzean-inspired thinking, she asks what kind of body regimes children produce in their play. Her findings show how the body, rather than being seen as an organic totality capable of wholesale expression of subjectivity, can be seen more as an assemblage of processes, pleasures, passions, activities and behaviours, linked by fine lines and unpredictable networks to other elements, segments and assemblages; for example, as conjunctions of events and as becomings – as lines of flight.

In another poststructuralist study 'Pedagogical Environments and Children's Construction of Subjectivity' Elisabeth Nordin-Hultman (2004) has explored the relationship between processes of normalization and the preschool environment. Her study is a call to action for a pedagogy that takes notice of and pays attention to the unique events of the here and now. By understanding the environment, not as a static and 'timeless' object but as a temporal flow of process, she pays close attention to the unique events of the here and now and she demonstrates that it is in the events, in unpredictable encounters with the environment, that children become engaged in what is interesting and meaningful for them, and she states that it is then that 'good' practice takes place.

In a forthcoming study, Liselott Olsson (2009) ventures further in the investigation of the potential contribution of Deleuze and Guattari to the field of early childhood education. Proceeding on the basis that most education entails taming children's desires, she boldly proposes a pedagogical relationship that constitutes 'events of encounters of desires', events in which the desires of the children meet those of the teachers. Using Deleuze and Guattarri's concept of 'assemblage of desire' (*agencement de désir*), together with events from pedagogical practice, she introduces an approach to learning with a focus on unconscious desire as the production of the real instead of the psychoanalytical definition of desire as fantasized lack. This incites preschools to rethink the logic of desire and no longer ask what children 'need', but rather what kinds of desires they are experimenting with, thereby enabling children and teachers to take part in producing new realities in the preschool classroom. In keeping with Deleuze and Guattari, Olsson states that learning may be seen from the perspective of the 'assemblage of desire' that takes place through logic of affect more than through rational, conscious thinking.

Subjectivity and learning as a relational space

The poststructuralist and Deleuzean-inspired studies cited above can help us produce greater intelligibility in children's play, interactions and the preschool world. They may also serve as a basis for framing alternative theories for policy analysis and action. By troubling theories of identity, one could argue that these researchers have succeeded in constructing an image of subjectivity and learning as a relational process of becoming. In so doing, they have considered the question of subjectivity less in terms of what the child IS; what kind of child is produced, as a self, an individual, an agent with his/her identity, and instead directed attention towards the AND – towards encounter, connections, transformations and becomings.

No doubt the thinking of Gilles Deleuze has been instrumental in this process. Following children's play and interactions from a Deleuzean perspective means viewing the early childhood milieu as something into which children are already plunged, and in which they are moving about and exploring by means of dynamic trajectories (Deleuze, 1997). For Deleuze, that milieu is made up of substances, powers and events, and, in a milieu like a preschool, materials such as drawings, documentation, play tools, furniture and noises in the shape of children's talking, singing, walking and drama are all pathways that merge not only with the subjectivity of the child, but with that of the milieu itself, insofar as it is reflected in those who travel through it. In this respect, other children and pedagogues are a milieu through which children travel; they pass through its qualities and powers and make a map out of them. In any milieu, persons and objects open or close doors, are guardians of thresholds, or are connectors or disconnectors of zones.

Hence, with a focus that is both experimental and pragmatic, Deleuze (1997) invites us to be attentive to processes, trajectories and becomings; to be alert to the way in which different learning processes are produced and function and the social consequences and effect they have. These trajectories and becomings should not, in his mind, be judged by their end products, their results, their precalculated outcomes, but by the way they proceed and by their power to continue. He asserts that we have to start to believe in the world again by multiplying the potential for precipitating events, life-giving confrontations and provocations, while undermining techniques of normalization and totalizing systems of classification and representation. He also states that an entire doctrine of judgment has been elaborated and developed, from Greek tragedy to modern philosophy, judgments that presuppose pre-existing criteria (higher values), criteria that pre-exist for all time (to the infinity of time), so that one can neither apprehend what is new in an existing being nor even sense the creation of a mode of existence. This prevents the emergence of any new mode of existence, as such a mode is created vitally through life-giving confrontations and provocations (Deleuze, 1997).

As evidenced at the outset of this chapter, OECD reviewers and researchers are clearly pursuing a valuable line of inquiry by signalling Sweden, Norway and Reggio Emilia as noteworthy examples of curricular development with an accent on children's agency and play. So are those researchers in the field of the sociology of childhood, while showing how children in a creative way are competent to handle and exert influence on the processes of control that they are subjected to in the course of their everyday life in the preschool. However, as pointed out above, the construction of the active and agentic child needs to be further scrutinized. In a postmodern society characterized by decentralization and uncertainty, new forms of control are developing, a control between the child and the adult that is no longer built on strong hierarchical rules, but more via children's and teachers' inner self-control (Rose, 1999). Similarly a growing body of technologies and strategies, which are supposed to support the active and self-managing child, are now invented; for example, portfolios, documentation, self-narratives and story-lines, and so on (Dahlberg, Moss and Pence, 2007). Making children's play and learning more visible through these strategies can imply that children's meaning-making and learning are taken more seriously and with more respect. But if we are not careful this visibility can prove to be more of an infringement on both children's and pedagogues' lives (Rose, 1999; Fendler, 2001). Whether Deleuzean-inspired research that is paying attention to more complex, ambivalent and nomad processes of the childhood landscape is able to address the reality of a postmodern knowledge society characterized by lifelong learning and uncertainty is an open question for further research.

References

Bloch, M.N. (1992) 'Critical Perspectives on the Historical Relationship between Child Development and Early Childhood Education Research', in S. Kessler and B.B. Swadener (eds) *Reconceptualizing the Early Childhood Curriculum: Beginning the Dialogue*. New York: Teachers College Press, pp. 3–20.

Bennett, John (2005) 'Curriculum Issues in National Policy-Making', *European Early Childhood Education Research Journal*, 13(2) 5–23

Brembeck, H.B., B. Johansson and J. Kampmann. (2004) *Beyond the Competent Child. Exploring Contemporary Childhoods in the Nordic Welfare States*. Roskilde: Roskilde University Press.

Burman, E. (1994) *Deconstructing Developmental Psychology*. New York: Routledge.

Cannella, G. (1997) *Deconstructing Early Childhood Education. Social Justice and Revolution*. New York: Peter Lang.

Corsaro, W.A. (2003) *We're Friends, Right? Inside Kids Culture*. Washington DC: Joseph Henry Press.

Corsaro, W.A. (2005) *The Sociology of Childhood*, 2nd edn. Thousand Oaks, CA: Pine Forge Press.

Corsaro, W.A. and L. Molinari. (2005) *I Compagni: Understanding Children's Transition from Preschool to Elementary School*. New York: Teachers College Press.

Dahlberg, G., P. Moss and A. Pence. (2007) *Beyond Quality in Early Childhood Education. Languages of Evaluation*, 2nd edn. London: Routledge.

Dahlberg, G. and P. Moss. (2005) *Ethics and Politics in Early Childhood Education*. London: Routledge.

Davies, B. (1989) *Frogs and Snails and Feminist Tales: Preschool Children and Gender*. Sydney: Allen & Unwin PTY Ltd.

Deleuze, G. (1992) 'Postscript on the Societies of Control', *October*, 59, 3–7.

Deleuze, G. (1997) *Essays Critical and Clinical*. Minneapolis: University of Minnesota Press.

Deleuze, G. and F. Guattari. (1987) *A Thousand Plateaus: Capitalism and Schizophrenia*. London: The Athlone Press.

Esping-Andersen, G. (1995) *The Three Worlds of Welfare Capitalism*. Cambridge: Polity Press.

Fendler, L. (2001) 'Educating Flexible Souls: The Construction of Subjectivity through Developmentality and Interaction', in K. Hultqvist and G. Dahlberg (eds) *Governing the Child in the New Millennium*, New York: Routledge, pp. 119–143.

James, A., C. Jenks and A. Prout. (1998) *Theorizing Childhood*. Cambridge: Polity Press.

Lenz Taguchi, H. (2000) Emancipation och motstånd. Dokumentation och kooperativa läroprocesser i förskolan. (Emancipation and Resistance. Documentation and cooperative learning-processes in preschool). Doctorial dissertation. Stockholm: HLS-Förlag.

Lind, U. (2005) 'Identity and Power, "Meaning, Gender and Age". Children's Creative Work as a Signifying Practice', *Contemporary Issues in Early Childhood*, 6(3): 256–268.

Löfdahl, A. (2002) Förskolebarns lek – en arena för kulturellt och socialt meningsskapande. (Preschool Children's Play – an Arena for Cultural and Social Construction of Meaning). Karlstad University Studies, 2002: 28.

Lubeck, S. (1994) 'Is Developmentally Appropriate Practice for Everyone?' *Early Education and Development*, 2(2): 168–174.

Mac Naughton, G. (2005) *Doing Foucault in Early Childhood Studies. Applying Poststructural Ideas.* London: Routledge

New, R. (1993) 'Italy', in M. Cochran (ed.) *International Handbook of Child Care Policies and Programs*. Westport: The Greenwood Press.

Nordin-Hultman, E. (2004) Pedagogiska miljöer och barns subjektskapande. (Pedagogical Environments and Children´s Construction of Subjectivity). Stockholm: Liber.

OECD (2001) *Starting Strong I.* Early Childhood Education and Care. Paris: OECD.

OECD (2006) *Starting Strong II.* Early Childhood Education and Care. Paris: OECD.

Olsson, L. (2009) *Movement and Experimentation in Young Childrens' Learning: Deleuze and Guattari in Early Childhood Education.* London: Routledge.

Polakow, V. (2007) *Who Cares for Our Children? the Child Care Crisis in the Other America.* New York: Teacher College Press.

Popkewitz, T.S. (2003) 'Governing the Child and Pedagogicalization of the Parent. A Historical Excursus into the Present', in M.N. Bloch, K. Holmlund, I. Moqvist and T. S. Popkewitz (eds) *Governing Children, Families and Education. Restructuring Welfare.* New York: Palgrave Macmillan.

Project Zero and Reggio Children (2001) *Making Learning Visible. Children as Individual and Group Learners.* Reggio Emilia: Reggio Children.

Rinaldi, C. (2006) *In Dialogue with Reggio Emilia. Listening, Researching and Learning.* London: Routledge.

Rose, N. (1999) *Powers of Freedom. Reframing Political Thought.* Cambridge: Cambridge University Press.

Schweinhart, L.J. and D.P. Weikart. (1997) *Lasting Differences: The High/Scope Preschool Curriculum Comparison Study through Age 23.* Ypsilanti, MI: High/Scope Press.

Strandell, H. (1994) *Sociala mötesplatser för barn. Aktivitetsnivåer och förhandlingskulturer på daghem.* (Social Places of Encounter for Children. Levels of Activity and Cultures of Negotiation in Day-Care-Centers). Helsinki: Gaudeamus.

Strandell, H. (1997) 'Doing Reality with Play: Play as a Children's Resource in Organizing Everyday Life in Daycare Centers', *Childhood*, 4(4): 445–464.

Sylva, K. and J. Wiltshire. (1993) 'The Impact of Early Learning on Children's Later Development', *European Early Childhood Education Research Journal*, 1(1) 17–40.

Taylor, A. and C. Richardsson. (2005) 'Queering Home Corner', *Contemporary Issues in Early Childhood*, 6(2) 164–173.

Weikart, D. (2000) *Early Childhood Education: Need and Opportunity.* UNESCO: Paris.

16

Localities: A Holistic Frame of Reference for Appraising Social Justice in Children's Lives*

John McKendrick

In this chapter, it is argued that localities are an integral and central part of the experience of childhood. Much of the chapter focuses on neighbourhood, as this is the dominant locality in children's lives. Supporting arguments in favour of these premises can be found throughout the *children's everyday lives* section of this book as neighbourhood settings feature prominently in discussions of children's bodies, family life, time use, daycare settings, problems and environments. Here, the focus shifts directly to the nature of localities, to complement those insights gleaned from essays in which locality is a canvas on which key elements of children's everyday lives are portrayed.

First, some general points on how locality is understood in the spatial sciences (what is locality) precede an introductory overview of the importance of locality in childhood studies. It is shown that locality is often implicit in childhood studies, although the contribution of localities to children's lives has been articulated (why we need to be here). The opening section concludes by amplifying what a localities perspective might contribute to the broader endeavour of childhood studies (where we need to go). Next, the chapter re-evaluates neighbourhood problems and problem neighbourhoods, two issues which are at the heart of public debate on children's everyday lives. Having considered the issues that are of most concern to the wider public, the discussion moves on to consider issues that are pertinent to understanding childhood, that is control and presence, and opportunity and constraint. Once more, it is argued that there is a need to move beyond prevailing thought if we are to fully appreciate children's everyday experiences. Finally, we consider locality as a political project, that is the formal attempts by local government and international organizations to promote Child Friendly Cities (CFC) and neighbourhoods. The chapter concludes by arguing that we need to move towards a multi-scale approach to locality if we are to better understand children's life experiences and to use this knowledge to improve the quality of children's lives.

Locality and childhood

What is locality?

Locality means many things in the spatial sciences (Painter, 2000). At its most straightforward, it is a descriptive concept delimiting places or regions at the sub-national scale; for example, the administrative area served by a municipal government. A second interpretation also considers locality to be a descriptive concept, but with the caveat that the area described must be one that is meaningful in terms of socio-spatial relations or processes that occur within, that is a locality is an area in which people share experiences; this area may not coincide with the boundaries drawn externally for administrative purposes. Thirdly, locality is understood dynamically, as part of a dialectical process. Not only are localities created by the playing out of socio spatial relations and processes in place, but in turn localities shape socio-spatial relations and processes; for example, where we are from (place identity) can influence people's reactions to us. The final two examples give less prominence to space. Fourthly, some interpretations of locality focus exclusively on the social dimensions, understanding localities to be the sum of energy and agency of people sharing a particular place, that is what matters is the outcome of people's interactions, rather than the character of the area. Finally, localities are also understood to be provisional networks of social relations, with no pre-given identity, permanence or pre-determined geographical form.

Elements from all traditions of locality studies will be evident throughout this chapter. However, the main approach adopted in this chapter is closest to the second tradition described above. Thus, for the purpose of this essay, localities are understood to be realms of meaningful everyday experience to children, within which *it might be expected* that key services are provided and children are accorded the right to encounter the world beyond the home independently of adults. As shall become clear, expectations are not always realized.

Localities in childhood studies

Why we need to be here

Academics, practitioners, service providers and service users each acknowledge the importance of localities in children's lives. At times, this recognition is implicit and inadvertent; at other times it is explicit and deliberate. The importance of locality can be evidenced through our concern with children and neighbourhood provision, design and access.[1]

Policy makers also extol the importance of localities in children's lives. The announcement by the UK Government during December 2007 to invest £1 billion in England from 2008/09–2010/11 through their *Children's Plan* provides an illustrative example of the acknowledged importance of neighbourhoods in children's lives in that the investment is to be targeted at specific localities ('deprived communities') in England (DCSF, 2007). *Provision* is to the fore in that £225m will be allocated over three years to build or upgrade more than 3500 playgrounds and establish 30 new supervised adventure playgrounds designed for the 8–13 age group. Furthermore, it is intended that schools become more central to their communities as child health services, social care, advice, welfare services and police will where possible be located on the same sites, aiming to make services more integrated and more convenient for children and their families. *Design* is also important in that £160m will be allocated to improve the quality and range of places for young people to go and things for them to do. According to the government, this could mean either 50 new state-of-the-art youth centres or 500 refurbished, or alternatively 2000 smaller-scale centres or mobile units. The concern to improve children's *access* to the neighbourhood is evidenced through the assertion by the Minister that, 'we want to move away from the "no ball games" culture of the past so that public spaces in residential areas are more child friendly. Local authority planning guidance will help to "prioritize a world designed for the needs of young people"'.

Thus, the acknowledged importance of localities in the lives of children manifests itself as a concern to improve what neighbourhoods have to offer children. The benefits are both material (improving provision, design and access) and symbolic (affirming that children are an integral part of neighbourhood life). In planning and policy, neighbourhoods tend to be viewed as discrete bounded spaces and the objective is to improve what they offer to the point where they can be described, for example, as 'child friendly', 'home zones', or constituted of 'safe routes'.

Where we need to go

When it is acknowledged that neighbourhood is important, there is a tendency to focus exclusively on neighbourhood space to the exclusion of the wider worlds of childhood within which the neighbourhood is located (e.g., Chin, 1993). Thankfully, Holloway and Valentine (2000) have progressed our understanding of children's spaces beyond being mere containers of children's services by illustrating the porosity of place. That is, they caution against a tendency to conceive of specific sites as discrete realms within which rules, behaviours, activities and norms prevail. Instead, they acknowledge that the boundaries of sites are porous and that while site-specific cultures may prevail within, these cultures are shaped by external forces (influences which are transmitted, for example, through mass media or the direct experiences which people encounter in other realms). In turn, site-specific cultures become external forces when children and other agents carry their experiences from within these sites to other domains. They use the examples of schools and homes, although the same principle applies equally to the neighbourhood and other localities; neighbourhood character is moulded within, although shaped directly and indirectly by the world beyond its boundary.

A localities focus should do more than describe what neighbourhoods have to offer children. A localities focus should also do more than consider the permeability of the neighbourhood to the influences of the world beyond its boundaries. A localities focus should ultimately serve as a holistic frame of reference for appraising social justice in children's lives. The neighbourhood is an important and meaningful realm within which children spend a significant proportion of their time at rest, play, education and work (Bernard, 1939; van Vliet, 1983; Gaster, 1991). Any failing of a neighbourhood to offer children what they need should be conceived of as a social injustice to be contested by those concerned with the quality of children's everyday lives. This is not to argue for a utopian blueprint for neighbourhoods comprising an extended list of provisions, design standards and rights of access. Following Holloway and Valentine (2000), there is a need to acknowledge the domestic circumstances of the family household (micro-scale) and the world beyond the neighbourhood (macro-scale) when appraising what individual neighbourhoods might be expected to offer their children (see Sibley, 1995, for insights at the domestic scale).

Neighbourhood problems, problem neighbourhoods

Children and neighbourhoods have increasingly been juxtaposed as problems in recent times. Thus, before turning to consider what neighbourhoods should offer children, there is a need to appraise neighbourhood problems and problem neighbourhoods.

Neighbourhood problems

Far from being the idyllic realm of childhood, children's presence in the neighbourhood and the lack of neighbourhood provision for children are increasingly viewed to be neighbourhood problems (Valentine, 1996). For example, Tables 16.1 and 16.2 summarize what the people of Scotland particularly dislike (Table 16.1) and like (Table 16.2) about their neighbourhood. A representative sample of adults in Scotland was asked to identify all of the traits they disliked or liked in their neighbourhood from a list of 22 possible dislikes and 17 possible likes.

'Young people hanging around and having nothing to do' is perceived by adults to be the biggest neighbourhood problem in Scotland at the current time; one in six people consider this to be problem (16 per cent). Furthermore, where neighbourhoods are rated less favourably, there is a greater likelihood of people expressing concern at 'young people hanging around and having nothing to do'; more than half of the people living in neighbourhoods which are considered to be 'very poor' also perceive young people to be a problem (52 per cent). Young people in the neighbourhood are considered to be more of a problem than traffic, litter, vandalism, crime and transport. Concerns are also raised at children having nowhere to play, although this is not as common a problem (4 per cent on the whole, and 18 per cent in the poorest neighbourhoods). Even the more positive finding that 'poor local schools' is one of the least problematic aspects of neighbourhood life must be qualified (only 1 per cent cite this as a neighbourhood problem) because fewer than one in ten people consider 'good local schools' to be among the aspects of the neighbourhood they particularly like. Ambivalence towards local schools is the most accurate way to describe their status among

Table 16.1   Aspects of neighbourhood particularly disliked by rating of neighbourhood as a place to live in Scotland, 2005/2006

		Percentage of adults				
		Rating of neighbourhood				
	Problems in the neighbourhood	Very good	Fairly good	Fairly poor	Very poor	All
1	Young people hanging about/ nothing for young people to do	8	20	46	52	16
2	Vandalism and graffiti	3	10	30	44	16
3	Fast/speeding traffic	6	8	8	10	7
4	Parking problems	6	8	7	6	7
5	Litter and rubbish	3	8	20	29	7
6	Drug abuse and dealing	1	7	29	44	6
7	Too much traffic	5	6	4	5	5
8	Poor public transport	6	4	5	6	5
9	Problems with neighbours	2	5	19	27	4
10	Alcohol abuse	1	5	20	28	4
11	Nowhere for children to play	2	6	13	18	4
12	Poor local shops	3	4	7	8	4
13	Problems with dogs	2	5	6	10	4
14	Poor local leisure facilities	3	4	8	9	4
15	Environmental noise	2	4	10	12	3
16	Area poorly maintained/run down	1	3	17	25	3
17	Unsafe area/crime	1	3	17	30	3
18	Problems with road/pavements/ drainage	2	1	0	*	1
19	Lack of amenities (doctor, bank, post office, etc.)	1	1	1	1	1
20	Poor outlook/view	0	1	3	7	1
21	Other	1	1	1	2	1
22	Poor local schools	0	1	1	2	1
23	Pollutions/smells/problem with industry	1	1	0	0	1
	Base	*14,862*	*11,182*	*1,396*	*706*	*28,261*

Notes: The columns add up to more than 100 per cent, as respondents were asked to identify all of the dislikes in the neighbourhood. The All Scotland rows totals also account for the opinion of the 115 respondents who had 'no opinion' on the overall quality of their neighbourhood; these data are omitted from this table.

Source: (Corbett et al., 2007, table 4. 28)

residents. Perhaps the most damning finding is that only 3 per cent of people in Scotland were of the opinion that 'good facilities for children and young people' were among the features of the neighbourhood they particularly liked.

Although lack of provision is a problem, young people are also considered to be a problem per se. Most concern is directed at teenagers and older children. Elsewhere in this volume, Katherine Rosier has considered this issue at greater length. For now, it is important to recognize that the perception of children and

Table 16.2   Aspects of neighbourhood particularly liked by rating of neighbourhood as a place to live in Scotland, 2005/2006

Likes in the neighbourhood	Percentage of adults				
	Rating of neighbourhood				
	Very good	Fairly good	Fairly poor	Very poor	All
1 Quiet/peaceful	70	49	14	6	57
2 Good neighbours	43	32	23	15	37
3 Convenient shop/other amenities	33	36	29	18	34
4 Friendly people	37	26	13	6	30
5 Good outlook/view	28	16	10	6	22
6 Good public transport	17	22	17	8	19
7 Safe area/low crime	25	12	4	1	18
8 Good local shops	13	15	10	7	13
9 Area well maintained	15	8	3	1	11
10 Community spirit	14	8	5	3	11
11 Good local schools	**10**	**9**	**7**	**5**	**9**
12 Clean/tidy place to live	9	6	2	1	7
13 Good local leisure facilities	7	7	5	2	7
14 Other	7	7	7	5	7
15 No/little traffic	6	4	3	1	5
16 Accessible/good location/handy	3	3	2	1	3
17 Good facilities for children and young people	**3**	**2**	**1**	**1**	**3**
18 Always lived here/been here a long time	1	1	2	1	1
Base	*14,862*	*11,182*	*1,396*	*706*	*28,261*

Notes: The columns add up to more than 100 per cent, as respondents were asked to identify all of the aspects of their neighbourhood that they particularly liked. The All Scotland rows totals also account for the opinion of the 115 respondents who had 'no opinion' on the overall quality of their neighbourhood; these data are omitted from this table.

Source: (Corbett et al., 2007, table 4. 25)

young people in the neighbourhood must be changed, if neighbourhoods are to be transformed into more rewarding environments for children.

Problem neighbourhoods

For a variety of reasons, neighbourhoods with a greater proportion of people experiencing poverty are more likely to be run-down and even dangerous environments (Andrews, 1985; Garbarino and Sherman, 1980). The urban landscape both reflects the poverty of its people and exacerbates their problems. Children are affected by living in such environments. 'Sick' buildings increase illness among children, vandalism (often instigated by youths) and neglect deprive them of community facilities and transportation planning has prioritized the motor-user over the pedestrian, inhibiting street play and cycle exploration.

A common response to the problems of deprived neighbourhoods is to implement a programme of area regeneration. This may involve whole-area slum clearance, refurbishment of housing or encouraging mixed tenure (encouraging owner-occupiers to move into areas formerly given over to social housing). Regeneration schemes transform the built environment, improving the quality of buildings and tidying up the appearance of the area. 'Redundant' spaces are transformed once more into useful spaces.

Or are they? Spaces temporarily abandoned by adults – where housing once stood and will stand again – are often colonized by children and will remain so until the latter stages of redevelopment (Ward, [1978] 1990); rubble and building sites may be eyesores for adults, but they are resources and environments for exploration in the eyes of children. Forbidding children to use these spaces can serve to heighten their attraction.

The loss of these environments as redevelopment progresses is simply urban change and it would be unreasonable to expect that children could have any more than a limited time-life use of these opportunities for play. More worrying is that redevelopment often removes play space. In one neighbourhood in northern England, redevelopment led to the removal of an all-weather sports pitch (one of only two playing fields on the estate), upon which new private houses were built, the Valley that surrounded the estate (affording opportunities for 'mountain' biking and winter sledging) was earmarked for a new municipal golf course, and design defects in the built environment which were exploited by children were erased (such as the hollow in the roadside beside which boys would congregate on rainy days to be splashed by passing cars). By themselves, these losses may be inconsequential, but collectively they cannot be ignored. The great irony is that it is these marginal environments that are currently more likely to present a richer array of opportunities for children. What adults abandon, children colonize. 'Regeneration' merely threatens those spaces that, in no small way, help compensate for the material deprivation that accompanies poverty.

There is a need to problematize 'problem neighbourhoods' when thinking of children. This is not to argue against regeneration (or to argue for deprivation); rather, it is to recognize children's perspectives on these issues. Improving the built environment and transforming the public realm should not, and need not, lead to a deterioration of children's neighbourhood opportunities.

Children's issues in the neighbourhood

If children are to capitalize upon neighbourhood opportunities, it follows that children must have a presence in the neighbourhood. Several factors mitigate against children's unfettered use of neighbourhood space and overly restrictive control over children's use of space is a problem that should be addressed. However, the response must be proportionate; enabling children to capitalize upon neighbourhood opportunities necessitates a measured degree of adult intervention and control.

Presence and control

Presence

Rules forbidding children to venture far from home is a consistent finding from the many studies that have examined children's access to their neighbourhood (Valentine and McKendrick, 1997). In one of the classical studies of children's play in urban England, Hole (1966) presented findings that, at the time, were taken as indicative of how children's home range – the distance they are permitted to venture unaccompanied from the home – has shrunk through time. Yet, from the vantage point of the twenty-first century, these children had a freedom to roam which would be unrecognizable to many of today's children. One-sixth of children (3–14 years) were allowed to travel alone to places which were at least two miles away from the family home: one-third of 7–8 year olds were allowed to travel up to half a mile away; and two-thirds of 9–10 year olds were allowed to leave their estate alone.

Age is the key factor shaping children's access to their neighbourhood (Hillman et al., 1990), but other factors are important too. Within urban areas, those from the most built-up areas are, on the whole, accorded less freedom to visit places of interest to them, girls are not permitted to venture as far away as boys (Matthews 1987; Cunningham and Jones, 1991) and, in a study of access to playgrounds and ethnicity in Amsterdam, Lia Karsten (1998) found that Dutch-Amsterdam children are more likely to experience both free-play within their home area and chaperoned access to clubs and sporting activity beyond their neighbourhood, relative to children of Turkish/Moroccan or Surinam/Antillean origin (also Woolley and Amin, 1995). This is an important finding that challenges the widely held beliefs that parents compensate children for the lack of independent neighbourhood play by taking them to formal leisure and sports activity. Even so, almost one-third of Dutch-Amsterdam children were only permitted to play around the home. The neighbourhood cannot (now) be assumed to be a realm for all children.

Controlling children's presence in the neighbourhood

This contraction of children's neighbourhood space can be accounted for in various ways. Children are themselves electing to spend less of their time in the wider neighbourhood and to spend more of their time in those parts of the neighbourhood close to home. This may reflect alternative opportunities (as the home emerges as a play space, comprising an array of electronic and other toys which are the personal possessions of children). This trend may also reflect self-imposed constraint, as some children do not venture into the neighbourhood for fear of danger posed by other children, unknown adults or environmental dangers such as traffic.

However, children's use of neighbourhood space is also constrained by the interventions of adults. First and foremost, 'informal' control is exerted by parents' rules governing children's neighbourhood transactions. Underlying parental concerns is a sense that the neighbourhoods have become more dangerous places for their children as a result of increased traffic, unruly children and the threat posed by dangerous adults (Valentine and McKendrick, 1997). Ironically, media attention tends to fuel parental fears, reinforcing restrictive parenting, rather than challenging misplaced perceptions and encouraging alternative solutions to restricting children's use of space.

Secondly, 'formal institutional' control is exerted through legally enforceable means such as child curfews (sometimes presented as 'child safety' orders) and antisocial behaviour orders (Matthews et al., 1999; Collins and Kearns, 2001). Local child curfews – schemes through which adults in positions of authority legally impose time-space restrictions on young people's use of space – are inherently geographical. Child curfews first became popular in the late nineteenth century in North America and remain so today: over three-quarters of cities of at least 100,000 people in United States of America have curfew laws. Most curfews apply to the night-time hours and have a crime prevention focus. The focus of attention of curfews is often on residential neighbourhoods, although the regulations apply throughout the city. Critics have described and expressed concern over attempts to impose local curfews on children, examining experiences in North America (United States of America and Canada), New Zealand and the United Kingdom, although it should be noted that some children welcome curfews (primarily, as a means for protecting them from other children).

Finally, subtle 'informal institutional' control over children's use of space is also exerted inadvertently. For example, the requirement of children to complete homework and to prepare themselves for examination outside school hours (having already spent a significant proportion of their day completing educational work in school), restrict the opportunities open to young people to partake of neighbourhood opportunities. Similarly, underinvestment in neighbourhood facilities by municipal government also makes the neighbourhood a less attractive realm for children and young people.

Presence and control

Some commentators lament the amount of control and some of the modes that are used to exert control over children's use of neighbourhood space (Matthews et al., 1999; Collins and Kearns, 2001). However, it is important to emphasize that control per se is not problematic. Table 16.3 can be used to illustrate this point. Rows in the table are used to summarize children's neighbourhood presence, which may be either omnipresent ('full', top row), limited ('site-specific', middle row) or absent ('no', bottom row). The amount of adult control exerted over children's use of space (either through parental control, direct institutional control or indirect institutional influence) in represented in columns, ranging from total control over children ('full', first column), limited control ('time' or 'domain' specific, middle column) or an absence of control ('no' far right column).

Three conclusions can be drawn. First, an absence of children in the neighbourhood should always be viewed negatively (bottom row), regardless of whether this results from full adult control, limited adult control or from children's own decision making. If children are not using the neighbourhood, then there is a problem with that neighbourhood or with the conditions that govern children's access to it. Secondly, and on the other hand, the omnipresence of children in the

Table 16.3 Evaluating neighbourhoods in terms of children's presence and adults' exertion of control over children

Children's presence in the neighbourhood		Full	Limited (time or domain specific)	No
	Full	+ & –	+	+ & –
	Limited (site specific)	– > +	+ & –	+ > –
	No	–	–	–
		Adult control over children in the neighbourhood		

neighbourhood is not necessarily positive. For example, although we may welcome children's presence in the neighbourhood, where this presence results from adults forcing children out of the home space and into the neighbourhood, or from children not heeding adults, then concerns should also be raised at children's neighbourhood presence. Thirdly, what is to be sought is the neighbourhood that facilitates children's presence with proportionate constraint from adults. Calls for a greater neighbourhood presence for children should not be misinterpreted as a call for adults to withdraw from controlling children. Rather, what are required are measured interventions that support, enable and inspire children to capitalize upon the opportunities afforded by their neighbourhood.

Opportunities and constraints

Neighbourhoods provide all manner of opportunities and possibilities to enhance the quality of children's lives. However, it must also be acknowledged that with some opportunities come constraint and with some constraints come opportunity.

Opportunities

Neighbourhoods can provide an array of opportunities for children. These opportunities tend to be understood in terms of services and facilities, such as schools, libraries and other community learning facilities, community centres, informal play space, formal grounds for play, youth organizations, leisure clubs and sport groups. However, the value of these services and facilities rests not only with the activities associated with them (education in schools, for example); neighbourhood facilities and services offer the opportunity for children to broaden their horizons, develop a sense of self, acknowledge their relation to and importance of other people, and to develop competencies (Hart, 1979; Moore, 1986). Indeed, the neighbourhood is the primary realm within which most children undertake activity independent of adults. A well-designed neighbourhood can facilitate such independence with, for example, traffic-free pathways between significant sites in the neighbourhood (home, school, play space, shops, etc.) (Department of Environment, 1973; Berg and Medrich, 1980). However, design is only one component of the successful neighbourhood. Neighbourhoods must exude a culture of participation for children in which their presence, opinion and needs are an integral part of neighbourhood life.

Opportunity as constraint

Inadvertently, four constraints can emerge as a result of attempts to improve what neighbourhoods have to offer children. First, any attempt to provide for children carries the potential risk of setting apart children from the wider life of the neighbourhood (McKendrick, 1999). For example, the provision of education through schools tends to corral children into a designated space, set within but existing apart from the wider neighbourhood. However, provision for children need not imply setting them apart. For example, schools can seek to integrate children fully within their community by providing opportunities for field-based learning and class-based local interest studies, by encouraging the wider community to contribute to the life of the school and by embedding the school more directly in the life of the neighbourhood.

Second, provision of specific sites for leisure can imply that leisure should only take place within these designated areas. For example, providing football parks implies no ball games outside these sports fields, providing shelters for teenagers implies no young people 'hanging around' other public spaces such as bus stops, and providing playgrounds implies that all children's play needs have been met. There is a need to challenge the conception that provision of sites for leisure is part of a compact that implies the withdrawal of children from other spaces, and rather to conceive of provision as means to enhance the quality of opportunity and to provide additional quality opportunities for play and leisure.

Third, adult-led provision of an array of organized leisure is often supported on the grounds that it provides 'gainful activity' which may steer children away from unproductive antisocial behaviour. In a similar vein to the designation of sites for leisure, there is a need to acknowledge that children also have a right to use, and a need to use, neighbourhood space in informal ways.

Finally, regeneration of neighbourhoods is sometimes accompanied by a transition from informal space to formal space. For example, many schools in Scotland have replaced grass playing fields with a more limited number of all-weather sports pitches that are open to the community to use out of school hours. Although the quality of facility is enhanced, there emerges the possibility that some children will have less opportunity to partake of leisure where access to leisure is dependent on the ability to pay. Indeed, some regeneration projects will restrict rather than facilitate participation and may further exclude children experiencing poverty from neighbourhood life (Box 16.1).

Constraint as opportunity

Just as opportunities can imply constraint, so constraints can imply opportunities for children in the neighbourhood. Again, attention can be drawn to four

Box 16.1   Sholver, a 'problem neighbourhood' from Oldham Metropolitan Borough in North West England

Perched 800 feet high on the north-eastern extremity of Oldham town on the upper slopes of Besom Hill, lies the public housing estate of Sholver. Its environmental and geographical marginality compounds the social exclusion that is characteristic of life at the margins of poverty. Once *the* problem estate of the town, its identity is now fractured into Low Sholver (where two small pockets of public housing which survived the bulldozer are now hemmed in by private housing developments) and Top Sholver (where public housing persists into decay as other, now larger, public housing estates in the town are redeveloped and renovated).

However, the quality of an environment for children should not be measured by bricks and mortar, or by its location relative to the commercial centre of the town. Indeed, the topography and position of the land known as Sholver affords a wealth of opportunities for children's leisure. The slopes of varying lengths and steepness are used by children of all ages for snow slides in winter and off-road bike runs in summer; the open woodland and heathland that borders the estate is an environment which can be used for group games and personal exploration, the countryside beyond this offers similar opportunities and others such as fishing and water-based exploration. Spaces temporarily abandoned by adults – where housing once stood and will stand again – are colonized by children and will remain so until the latter stages of redevelopment; rubble and building sites may be eyesores for adults, but they are resources and environments for exploration in the eyes of children. And children are both seen and heard in Sholver – they are an integral part of the peopled landscape.

It is ironic that redevelopment is the major threat to children in Sholver. Already, an all-weather sports pitch (one of only two playing fields on the estate) has been lost to private housing developers, the Beal Valley that lies at the bottom of the hill has been earmarked for a municipal golf course, the rubble wastelands are being reclaimed for housing development, and the design defects which were exploited by children are being erased (such as the hollow in the roadside beside which boys would congregate on rainy days to be splashed by passing cars). By themselves, these losses may be inconsequential, but collectively they cannot be ignored. Redevelopment, we may ask, for whom?

Source: Author's own

ways in which curtailing children's neighbourhood presence creates its own opportunities.

First, paternalistic control over children's use of space and time will serve the best interests of some of the children, some of the time. For example, schooling not only dictates what children must do for much of the year, it also educates, develops competencies and broadens minds. Parental rules can protect children from the physical dangers that exist in the neighbourhood, for example by forbidding children from flying kites beneath overhead electricity lines and by not collecting stray balls that have entered electricity substations. Adult interventions in children's neighbourhood lives can enhance the quality of life as lived and can enable children to achieve their potential in the future.

Second, where constraint curtails children's use of the wider neighbourhood, the result is often an enrichment of play opportunities in the domestic realm. Back gardens are more likely to be given over to children's play, more opportunities for play in the home are facilitated and streets immediately outside the home are often populated by children at play (albeit under the watchful eye of their parents). This is not to suggest that the withdrawal of children from wider neighbourhood space is unproblematic; however, it should be recognized that other opportunities are afforded with some constraints.

Third, it is important not to universalize children. Curtailing the movements of some young people may be to the advantage of others. For example, older children often 'take over' playgrounds when younger children are forbidden from playing outside later in the evening. On a different tack, the removal of more unruly children from the neighbourhood (for example, through antisocial behaviour orders or incarceration) may afford more opportunities for victimized children to partake more freely of neighbourhood opportunities.

Finally, although children's opportunities for independence are curtailed as a result of the insistence of some organizations that adults bring them to, and collect them from, neighbourhood activities, such restrictions do provide opportunities for children to spend more time with parents. For example, many schools are insistent on children being collected from school by an adult in the first year; some youth organizations also require parents to bring their children to and from activities.

Localities as a political project: child friendly initiatives

The United Nations Child Friendly Cities Initiative (CFCI) was launched in 1996 as an outcome of the World Conference on Human Settlements (Habitat II) resolution to make cities liveable places for all. The sense that insufficient attention was being given to the specific needs of children for safe, secure and healthy living conditions provided the stimulus for this work. An International Secretariat for CFC was established in September 2000 with the aim of providing information and support to interested municipalities. Its key objective is to share experiences and to encourage networking among cities committed to improving the quality of life for their children and fulfilling their rights.

The core idea is that a child friendly city is one in which children participate (Box 16.2). The UN Rights on the Convention of the Child provides a reference point against which standards are set in the realms of family support, home and the surrounding area, and the neighbourhood. The blueprint (Hart, 1996) identifies obstacles and solutions with regards to values (relating to children), provision of information, resources and services, and structures for service delivery.

A different approach to child friendliness has been taken by Chris Cunningham and Margaret Jones (1991, 1994) based on work undertaken in Australia. Although keen to stress that their vision of a child friendly neighbourhood is not a literal design template and that it requires a shift in thinking towards designing *for* children, they provide a model of the key elements that might be found in a child friendly neighbourhood (Figure 16.1).

There are five key elements in this 'design'. First, bushland and manipulable environments should be provided within 200 metres of every house. As was noted

Box 16.2   UNICEF's nine building blocks of a child friendly city

1. Children's participation: promoting children's active involvement in issues that affect them; listening to their views and taking them into consideration in decision-making processes
2. A child friendly legal framework: ensuring legislation, regulatory frameworks and procedures which consistently promote and protect the rights of all children
3. A city-wide Children's Rights Strategy: developing a detailed, comprehensive strategy or agenda for building a Child Friendly City, based on the Convention
4. A Children's Rights Unit or coordinating mechanism: developing permanent structures in local government to ensure priority consideration of children's perspective
5. Child impact assessment and evaluation: ensuring that there is a systematic process to assess the impact of law, policy and practice on children – in advance, during and after implementation
6. A children's budget: ensuring adequate resource commitment and budget analysis for children
7. A regular State of the City's Children Report: ensuring sufficient monitoring and data collection on the state of children and their rights
8. Making children's rights known: ensuring awareness of children's rights among adults and children
9. Independent advocacy for children: supporting non-governmental organisations and developing independent human rights institutions – children's ombudspeople or commissioners for children – to promote children's rights.

Source: UNICEF Innocenti Research Centre (2008)

above, this is particularly important to ensure that girls – with their more limited home range – have access to quality spaces for play. Secondly, streets should be conceived as social spaces in which traffic must adjust to the pace of the pedestrian. Limits of 30 kilometres per hour are recommended for ring roads, with cars being required to slow down to walking pace in residential feeder roads. Thirdly, paths and cycleways should link the focal points of the neighbourhood (key community and retail services) to afford children safe and interesting ways of moving about their neighbourhood. Fourthly, neighbourhood parks should accommodate still and running water, and habitats for aquatic and land-based wildlife as a means of fostering stronger relations between people and the environment. Finally, the question of supervision – by parents and other figures of authority in the community – should be facilitated in neighbourhood design.

Theirs is an interesting proposal. It is one that is child-focused, while attending to the concerns of adults. It is a proposal that is as concerned with quality, as it is with safety. It is also a proposal that addresses issues of deeper significance in society (such as people–environment relations). It is a proposal that is worthy of some serious consideration.

The provision of playgrounds and blueprints for child friendly neighbourhoods/cities are merely indicative of the wide range of ways in which localities are being (re-)designed to account for the particular needs of children (Chawla, 1998; Lynch, 1977). In the United Kingdom, *Safe Routes to Schools* is a project led

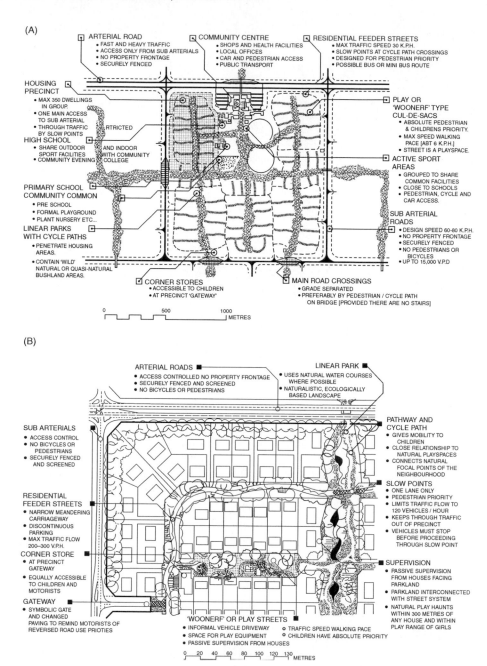

Figure 16.1 Model of a child friendly neighbourhood (A, Layout; B, Detail)

Source: Cunningham and Jones (1994). All attempts to trace copyright holders have been made; the editors and publishers would be happy to correct any errors or omissions if the copyright holders contact us directly.

by Sustrans which aims to transform routes to primary and secondary schools in the hope that it will encourage more widespread use of environmentally friendly modes of transport; *Home Zones* is a project managed by the Children's Play Council which aims to make streets more liveable by according greater priority to the pedestrian and cyclist (as opposed to drivers of motorized vehicles) and Grounds for Learning/Learning Through Landscapes are independent charities in Scotland and England/Wales respectively, which aim to support schools to provide richer school grounds which, in turn, could be utilized more often by children in their schooling.

Each, however, must not be misunderstood to be an exercise in design determinism, that is where the fabric of the environment determines its use (Berg and Medrich, 1980). Rather, each is grounded on the principle that children should participate more in their local environments. Best practice not only provides for children, but also should design with children.

Conclusion: scale, politics and the future of 'localities'

It has been argued that localities matter to children and that the neighbourhood is the locality that matters most of all. There are complications and nuances that must be acknowledged and addressed; steps must be taken to challenge the perception that young people are, per se, a neighbourhood problem; the notion that regeneration will lead to more child friendly environments must be challenged; adult control must be proportionate and must not overly restrict children's use of neighbourhood space; and it must be acknowledged that with new opportunities come constraint – hence the need to appraise in the round, whether each intervention improves the quality of children's everyday lives.

Contemporary concerns to improve neighbourhoods – to make them child friendly, safe home zones, or constituted by safe routes – are to be welcomed. However, it should not always be assumed that these schemes promote the best interests of children. Children have a right to an everyday environment that allows them to enjoy life and to realize their potential. Childhood studies must focus on the neighbourhood as a whole and must maintain this holistic focus to appraise this realm and to ensure that it serves children well. However, there is also a need to develop a multi-scale localities framework to explore the interactions between different sites in children's lives; in the terminology of Holloway and Valentine (2000), the porosity between home space, neighbourhood space and wider settlement space must be explored to fully appreciate the nature of the multiple overlapping localities within which children spend their everyday lives.

Thus, locality is a political project, but it is one that must not be conceived in isolation to children's wider worlds. It is also important that campaigning or implementing action to ensure that neighbourhoods better meet the needs of all children is grounded in children's rights. There are basic neighbourhood entitlements – such as the right to play, the right to space for play, the right to move freely and safely through the neighbourhood, and so on – that must be met for children. However, locality as a political project must extend beyond children's rights. What is required is a framework that negotiates children's rights with those of the wider neighbourhood. There is a need to work towards neighbourhoods that work better for all. Social justice is a holistic approach that moves beyond the particular concerns of any single group. If children's neighbourhoods are to be improved, then it requires a shift in attitudes and an openness to acknowledge not just to what children are entitled, but also to what is an equitable neighbourhood solution for children given the competing and often contradictory demands that are placed on neighbourhood space.

Notes

* Unless referring specifically to a particular sub-group of children – for example teenagers, girls, disabled children – the chapter refers to all young people aged less than 18 years.

1. To demonstrate the array of locality issues that pertain to particular neighbourhoods, this paper concentrates on providing evidence from the United Kingdom. The examples are indicative of neighbourhood conditions in developed countries, although the emphasis given to particular issues outside the United Kingdom may vary by degree. The principles and core argument – the plea to consider children's needs, but to do so within the wider frameworks of children's wider worlds and the needs of others in the neighbourhood – apply equally to the very different material conditions of children's neighbourhood experiences in the Majority World (e.g., Chawla, 1998).

References

Andrews, H.F. (1985) 'The Ecology of Risk and the Geography of Intervention: From Research to Practice for the Health and Well-Being of Urban Children', *Annals of the Association of American Geographers*, 75(3): 370–382.

Berg, M. and E.A. Medrich (1980) 'Children in Four Neighborhoods: The Physical Environment and its Effect on Play and Play Patterns', *Environment and Behavior*, 12(3): 320–348.

Bernard, J. (1939) 'The Neighborhood Behavior of School Children in Relation to Age and Socio-Economic Status', *American Sociological Review*, 4: 652–662.

Chawla, L. (1998) 'Growing Up in Cities: A Project to Involve Young People in Evaluating and Improving Their Urban Environments', *Environment and Urbanization*, 9(2): 247–251.

Chin, E. (1993) 'Not of Whole Cloth Made: The Consumer Environment of Children', *Children's Environments*, 10(1): 72–84.

Collins, D.C.A. and R. Kearns (2001) 'Under Curfew and under Siege? Legal Geographies of Young People', *Geoforum*, 32(3): 389–403.

Corbett, J., P. MacLeod and S. Hope (2007) *Scotland's People: Results from the 2005/06 Scottish Household Survey*. Edinburgh: Scottish Executive.

Cunningham, C.J. and M. Jones (1991) 'Girls and Boys Come Out to Play: Play, Gender and Urban Planning', *Landscape Australia*, 4: 305–311.

Cunningham, C.J. and M. Jones (1994) 'The Child Friendly Neighbourhoods: Some Questions and Tentative Answers From Australian Research', *International Play Journal*, 2: 79–95.

Department for Children, Schools and Families (2007) *The Children's Plan: Building Brighter Futures*. London: DCSF.

Department of Environment (1973) *Children at Play*. Design Bulletin 27. London: HMSO.

Garbarino, J. and D. Sherman (1980) 'High-Risk Neighborhoods and High-Risk Families: The Human Ecology of Child Maltreatment', *Child Development*, 51(1): 188–198.

Gaster, S. (1991) 'Urban Children's Access to Their Neighborhood: Changes Over Three Generations', *Environment and Behavior*, 23(1): 70–85.

Hart, R. (1979) *Children's Experience of Place*. New York: Irvington.

Hart, R. (1996) *Children's Rights and Habitat* (The UNICEF preparatory document for Habitat II: The UN Conference on Human Settlements). New York: UNICEF.

Hillman, M., J. Adams. and J. Whitelegg (1990) *One False Move: A Study of Children's Independent Mobility*. London: Policy Studies Institute.

Hole, V. (1966) *Children's Play on Housing Estates*. National Building Studies Research Paper 39. London: HMSO.

Holloway, S.L. and G. Valentine (2000) 'Spatiality and the New Social Studies of Childhood', *Sociology: The Journal of the British Sociological Association*, 34(4): 763–783.

Karsten, L. (1998) 'Growing up in Amsterdam: Differentiation and Segregation in Children's Daily Lives', *Urban Studies*, 35(3): 565–581.

Lynch, K. (1977) *Growing Up in Cities*. Cambridge MA: MIT Press.

Matthews, M.H. (1987) 'Gender, Home Range and Environmental Cognition', *Transactions of the Institute of British Geographers*, 12(1): 43–56.

Matthews, H., M. Limb and M. Taylor (1999) 'Reclaiming the Street: The Discourse of Curfew', *Environment and Planning A*, 31(10): 1713–1730.

McKendrick, J.H. (1999) 'Not Just a Playground: Rethinking Children's Place in the Built Environment', *Built Environment*, 25(1): 75–78.

Moore, R.C. (1986) *Childhood's Domain: Play and Place in Childhood Development*. London: Croom Helm.

Painter, J. (2000) 'Locality', in R.J. Johnston, D. Gregory, G. Pratt and M. Watts (eds) *The Dictionary of Human Geography*. 4th edn. Oxford: Blackwell, pp. 456–458.

Sibley, D. (1995) 'Families and Domestic Routines: Constructing the Boundaries of Childhood', in S. Pile and N.J. Thrift (eds) *Mapping the Subject: Geographies of Cultural Transformation*. London: Routledge, pp. 123–137.

UNICEF Innocenti Research Centre (2008) *The Child Friendly Cities Initiative*. http://www.childfriendlycities.org/about/index.html (accessed 5 June 2008).

Valentine, G. (1996) 'Children Should Be Seen and Not Heard: The Production and Transgression of Adults' Public Space', *Urban Geography*, 17(3): 205–220.

Valentine, G. and J.H. McKendrick (1997) 'Children's Outdoor Play: Exploring Parental Concerns About Children's Safety and the Changing Nature of Childhood', *Geoforum*, 28(2): 219–235.

Van Vliet, W. (1983) 'Exploring the Fourth Environment: An Examination of the Home Range of City and Suburban Teenagers', *Environment and Behavior*, 15(5): 567–588.

Ward, C. ([1978] 1990) *The Child in the City*. London: Architectural Press.

Woolley, H. and N. Amin (1995) 'Pakistani Children in Sheffield and Their Perception and Use of Public Open Spaces', *Children's Environments*, 12(4): 479–488.

17
Children as Problems, Problems of Children

Katherine Brown Rosier

In the United States and many other societies, children are viewed in two interrelated ways. First, children are seen *as* problems for adults – disrupting, disquieting and disturbing the everyday activities of adult life. And second, children *have* problems that can only be addressed and/or lessened by dedicated adult action and resources. This chapter addresses these two sides of the problematization of children and childhood, and considers the implications of the various ways that adults see children as problematic.[1]

Children as problems

When we consider children *as* problems for adults, three basic constructions are apparent. First, children are often seen as a nuisance and disruptive to respectable adult life, an inferior out-group that nevertheless has considerable power to inconvenience and embarrass adults. Secondly, adults' extreme worry and anxiety about vulnerable children's safety makes the protection of children a near-constant problem and concern. Thirdly, some children are seen as problems of their own doing, and adults resent and disdain those irresponsible children and youth who use drugs, are truant, get pregnant, run away, or who commit property or violent crimes.

Children as nuisance

Children are (and probably always have been) problematic for adults who are attempting to go about their everyday business of presentation of self, face-work, and routine public interaction (Goffman, [1955] 1982). As novice members of society, children present unique challenges to the taken-for-granted-ness of polite adult society.

Cahill (1987) impressively dissects children's initiation into the contemporary public life of adults, and its 'religion of civility.' Here, individual human personality is sacred, and a code of ceremonial conduct supports the goal of respecting and upholding other adherents' personalities as presented in their ritual performances.

As members of secular civil society, we have multiple, small interactional rituals that we perform – like the common practice of 'civil inattention' (Goffman,

1963) – that effectively communicate to others that we present no threat, have no desire to challenge their presentation of self and respect their individual personhood. These rituals are often referred to as simply 'etiquette' – how we should, and for the most part do, act in our impersonal encounters with strangers and casual acquaintances.

Children threaten these routines. All parents can produce stories of their children's public behaviours and pronouncements that violate the code Cahill describes, and mortify their caregivers. (A favourite of mine involved my then four-year-old daughter's conversational observation in a clinic waiting room: 'That lady looks just like a witch – look at her nose!') As novice, incomplete converts to the religion of civility, children upset adults' routine performances with some regularity, and they maintain at all times the potential to do great damage to adults' public 'face' (Goffman, [1955] 1982; Cahill, 1987). In *quid pro quo* response to the disrespectful treatment children often receive from adults, Cahill observes that at times they also engage in some deliberate 'playful terrorism,' purposefully sabotaging adults' performances.

Such threats to the polite conduct of adult routines demonstrate one basic way that children are problems to both their caregiving guardians and other adult bystanders. That is, children are often seen as an out-group, inferior to adults, and as such are seen as a disruptive nuisance to be avoided if not controlled (see Leach, 1994; Corsaro, 2005). Such a view contributes to discrimination against children as a group, and restrictions and prohibitions on their access to businesses, facilities, housing and even whole communities.

It is common to see postings in businesses – for example, a sign in an Antique Shop warning that 'Unattended Children will be Eaten'; a convenience store posting of 'No more than two children allowed at a time' – that communicate children's subordinate status and their nuisance character. Many facilities and businesses prohibit *unaccompanied* children, arguably long past an age when supervision is necessary for children's safety, or for their successful participation. For example, many gymnasiums require children under age 12 or 14 to be accompanied by a parent or other responsible adult, as do other public and private recreational facilities such as golf courses and swimming pools. Many of these facilities also provide child-free periods – for example, a community pool sets aside time for adult lap swims during which children can be neither in the pool nor pool-side. Corsaro cites an advertisement for a 'kid-free' cruise upon which adults are free from the nuisance that children present (2005, 225). A casual web search reveals countless resorts, hotels, bed-and-breakfast establishments and restaurants that proudly advertise their 'adults only' environments.

Prior to revisions in the US Fair Housing Act in 1988, planned communities advertised their 'adults only' covenants, and the desire for such child-free living was clear as these developments became quite popular. Numerous developments went so far as to stipulate the length of visits allowed for grandchildren and other youth (in some cases restricting visits not to a number of weeks or days, but to a precise number of hours!), and to prohibit children and youth from playing on lawns and using facilities. Such restrictions were judged illegal age discrimination under the new rules, but this reprieve for children and their families was short-lived. The 1995 amendment to the Fair Housing Act (through the Housing for Older Persons Act – 'HOPA') permitted '55 and older' designations for communities in which at least 80 per cent of units were occupied by one or more persons aged 55 or older. The designation entitles communities to refuse to sell or rent to families with children, to limit visitation, and to deny access to facilities for visiting youth. Presumably, US law supports the position that 'older' adults' aversion to children is more understandable and acceptable than the discriminatory preferences of adults in their child-bearing years (see Allen, 1997 for details on HOPA).

If directed at any other group, the ill treatment of and disdain for children and youth that are exemplified here would not be long tolerated. Imagine the outcry and lawsuits that proclamations of 'Heterosexual-only housing development,' 'No unaccompanied atheists allowed,' or 'Whites only from noon to 4 pm' would provoke! But complaints about such discrimination against children are rarely heard. While many adults would not *themselves* prefer a 'kid-free' environment, that some do have such preference seems unremarkable and understood. The widespread tolerance for such discriminatory attitudes demonstrates the prevalence of the view of children as disruptive nuisance, an inferior 'other.'

Fear for children's safety

A second way that children are problems for adults stems not from annoyance with children's incomplete conversion into the 'religion of civility,' but from fear for naive and vulnerable children's safety in the dangerous modern world. Fear of children's victimization is tied to two related phenomena: first, a sentimental 'naive-child stereotype' (Van Ausdale and Feagin, 2001) that exaggerates children's innocence and incompetence; and secondly, the magnification of particular sinister, but very rare, events.

In their disturbing portrayal of preschool children's early understanding and use of race, Van Ausdale and Feagin (2001) argue that a prevalent 'naive-child stereotype' distorts adults' view of children's racists remarks and behaviours. 'She doesn't understand what she's saying' was the typical response from both parents and teachers to children's overtly racist remarks. The claim of children's naivety in such instances is a specific example of a more general position; that children of various ages are essentially innocents, ignorant of – and therefore also vulnerable to – unsavoury, hurtful or dangerous aspects of social life. (As I will elaborate later, such views tend *not* to be applied to children of colour, or to children whose parents are not middle class.)

The magnification of children's naivety, dependence and vulnerability is hardly new. The rapid decline of middle-class women's and children's productive labour that accompanied the upheavals of the industrial revolution provoked a sentimentalization and domestication of children that dramatically changed the nature of childhood (e.g., Best, 1990; Stacey, 1990; Corsaro, 2005). Children's 'need' for much nurturing and supervision was constructed and gained currency among the middle-class as these families' and communities' need for children's labour and independence declined. Two hundred years later, we are witnessing the further escalation of this historical trend, which might appropriately be termed the 'infantilization of middle-class childhood.'

With children defined as excessively naive and vulnerable, increasing fears about their safety logically follow, encouraged by the public posturing of reform-minded individuals and groups. Citing Zelizer (1985), Corsaro notes that children's safety campaigns in the 1920s and 1930s reduced both children's accidental deaths and their freedom to participate in social life (2005, 226). Best's (e.g., 1987, 1990) well-known explication of the social construction of the 'missing children' problem also demonstrates how sentimental exaggeration of children's vulnerability, coupled with exaggeration of the true risk of victimization, created high anxiety among parents and increased restrictions on children.

Throughout the 1980s until the present, media have fed the grisly details of a steady stream of high-profile stranger kidnappings to the American public, capturing their rapt attention and fostering perceptions that these rare events are actually commonplace – 'epidemic.' As Best notes, the 'atrocity tales' repeated by the media and by activists 'do not merely attract attention; they also shape the perception of the problem' (1987, 106) and 'shape the construction of...preventative measures' (1987, 113) that severely constrain children's freedom.

Likewise, a series of equally high-profile school shootings in the mid-1990s joined with stranger kidnaps to inspire irrational fear on the part of American parents that their children will fall victim to these heinous, but rare, events. School shootings at Paduka Kentucky, Jonesboro Arkansas, and of course 'Columbine' (Littleton Colorado) – among others – have inspired some of the most oppressive restrictions on the freedoms and rights of young Americans. Metal detectors greet students at entrances, and cameras and even armed guards are employed to create 'safe' schools. In the name of security, random searches of lockers and persons take place at schools around the country, sometimes executed by police and narcotic-detection dogs (Best, 2002; Rosier and Kinney, 2005; Waldron, 2005). 'Zero-tolerance' policies leave even sympathetic administrators unable to consider individual circumstances (Waldron, 2005), forcing suspensions and expulsions of thousands of students who are first-offenders of fighting or threatening violence, or who have repeated difficulties with truancy, use of profanity, and other nonviolent offences. Parental surveillance of children and adolescents has gone high-tech, with in-home drug tests, tracking devices on family cars and computers and family cell phone plans that keep children one-button accessible. In the name of safety, the activities of children and youth are constrained and monitored to an extent that was hardly imaginable only a generation or two ago.

The *reality* of the *rarity* of stranger kidnaps and school shootings seems largely irrelevant to popular discourse and imagination, and to preventative action taken by parents, schools and the larger society. Nonetheless, this rarity must be underscored here. The United States had a population of approximately 72.3 million individuals aged 17 and younger in 2000 (US Census Bureau, 2002). The US Department of Justice (Sedlak et al., 2002) cites an average figure of 115 'stereotypical' child kidnappings per year – that is, stranger kidnappings where the abductor is unknown to the child – and fewer than half of these result in the death of the child. The chance of stranger abduction for a US child in a given year is therefore about 1.5 per one million, and the chance a child would be killed as a result of the heinous crime is less than half that number. When comparisons are made between US Department of Justice estimates published in 1990 (Finkelhor et al.) and 2002 (Sedlak et al.), there is some evidence these extremely low rates are declining.

Violent deaths at school are even rarer than stranger abductions. Throughout the 1990s, as the hype and concern over school shootings grew, the number of deaths was actually on the decline (Donohue, Schiraldi and Ziedenberg, 1998; Best, 2002; Also see Newman et al., 2004, for analysis of changes in both rates over time and characteristics of shooters and shootings). There were 43 school-associated violent deaths in the United States during the 1997–1998 school year, the most deadly year in the late 1990s; there were 25 such deaths in 1996–1997, and 26 in 1998–1999 (these figures somewhat inflate the true incidence of 'school shootings,' including all homicides regardless of age of victims and perpetrators, as well as all suicides that occur at school). With approximately 54 million youths enrolled from kindergarten through to grade 12 in the year 2000 (US Census Bureau, 2002), the chance that an American school child will die a violent death at school is substantially less than one in a million. Nonetheless, Gallup reported that in 2005, three-quarters of respondents polled said a school shooting was likely to happen in their own communities.

Some increase in awareness of the rarity of stranger kidnappings and school shootings is apparent. For example, growing numbers of academic publications expose the sensationalized nature of reporting on these issues (Ayers, 1997/98; Donohue, Schiraldi and Zeidenberg, 1998; Glassner, 1999; Best, 2002). Mainstream media may also be tiring of their own portrayals: During their many hours of coverage of the recent recovery of two boys abducted in Missouri, CNN did a short 'Reality Check' (13 January 2007) that noted that kidnappings by strangers 'are actually very rare,' and cited the Justice Department estimate of 115 stranger kidnappings per year. Nonetheless, fears focused on the threat of sinister rare events like kidnappings and school shootings continue to create great anxiety, and to strongly influence parenting practice.

The hyped fears combine with both the perception that children are exces-sively naive and vulnerable, and with basic trends in family life (including smaller family size and growth in mothers' employment) to create real *prob-lems* for adults who are responsible for the care of children and youth. Dramatic declines in unsupervised neighbourhood play and in children's free time more generally, are well documented, as is the concomitant increase in children's involvement in adult organized and monitored activities (Adler and Adler, 1998; Hofferth and Sandberg, 2001; Dunn, Kinney and Hofferth, 2003; Lareau, 2003). With colleague David Kinney, I discuss elsewhere the issue of children's declin-ing freedom in the face of these developments (Rosier and Kinney, 2005). Here I want to emphasize the pressure these developments place upon *parents*, who devote increasing time and energy to managing and supervising their children's childhoods. 'Who's got time to be married?' one popular 'Marriage Movement' personality asked recently, 'if you have to be hyper-vigilant for kidnappers?' Doherty (2005) laments that 'many parents have little time for each other because they are full time activity leaders and chauffeurs for their children,' as he attempts to educate this large group of marriage advocates about the true rarity of stranger kidnappings.

Children's bad behaviour

While some children as seen primarily as innocent and naive, other children are viewed in a much less sympathetic, much more negative light. Corsaro notes 'the tendency to hold certain children personally responsible for the complex social and economic forces and problems that so dramatically affect their lives' (2005, 227). When adults see negative behaviours like teenage runaways, teen pregnancy, drug use, truancy and more serious juvenile crime as due primarily to the irresponsibility of youth themselves, they blame the victims of larger systemic failures like racism, sexism, poverty and extreme consumerism.

As the quote below illustrates, some social commentators have called attention to Americans' 'schizophrenic view of children,' which sees some children as vulnerable innocents while others are viewed as highly culpable villains:

> Our culture embraces a schizophrenic view of children: We romance childhood as a time of innocence and beauty, and we simultaneously construct an image of original sin and elemental evil lurking in those little bodies. Children are angels and devils – pure and wicked, clean and corrupt, lambs and devils. When children are left to themselves, however, our culture assumes the demon child has the upper hand... Young people today find themselves in a peculiarly precarious landscape – reified as consumers, demonized as a threat, they inhabit a cultural fault-line that is bumpy for all and fatal for some. (Ayers, 1997/98, 1)

Ayers' mention of the especially problematic nature of children 'left to themselves' is important. Above I noted the increase of adult-supervised activities, in part as strategy parents employ to protect children from lurking evils they perceive in our changing world. But this trend is not equally apparent for all children. Lareau (2003) documents a *'concerted cultivation'* approach to child-rearing – which emphasizes intense management of children's lives and activities – that is well-evidenced in middle-class families. Not so, however, for children whose parents and communities have fewer resources. Poor and working-class parents more often employ an approach that facilitates the *'accomplishment of natural growth.'* This style of child-rearing, which fits both the sensibilities and the material conditions of poor and working-class parents, allows children much more autonomy and control over their free time and leisure activities. Parents of poor and working-class children, who are also disproportionately non-white, seem to unsentimentally attribute to their children a high level of competence to manage their own time, schooling and general development. It is no coincidence that this type of parental ideology and practice is much more prevalent among those who have relatively few resources to devote to 'concerted cultivation' of their children.

It is arguably also no coincidence that those children and youth who are held responsible and at times vilified for their 'personal choices' and bad behaviour tend to be poor and working class. While Lareau notes that middle-class children develop and share with their parents a 'sense of entitlement,' learning quickly to expect and demand that interactions and institutions 'suit their preferences' (Lareau, 2003, 6), poor and working-class children more often resign themselves to the constraints and obstacles that they confront in schools and in the larger society. In the context of these constraints, those children who are neither well-served by nor well-prepared for schools that reflect middle-class styles and values are more likely to be truant, and much more likely to be suspended or expelled (Center on Juvenile and Criminal Justice, 2000). Those children whose daily environments provide them with little evidence that deferred gratification, hard work and perseverance pay off are more likely to drop out of school entirely, and to become pregnant and have children as teens. And those children whose parents' lives also reflect the frustration and constraints of social inequality are arguably also more likely to be neglected and abused, and more likely to run away from home.

And why not? Although examination of the many processes that privilege the outcomes of those with means over those without is beyond the scope of this chapter (but considered briefly in a later section), surely many of the advantages are systematic and entrenched in nature. Access to good schools, safe neighbourhoods, medical care and employment opportunity are largely determined by families' social class position. But systemic privilege is a hard-sell for America's middle-class (see, for example, Van Ausdale and Feagin, 2001), who maintain a 'presumption of moral superiority over the poor and the working class... [and employ] a moral vocabulary that blames individuals for their life circumstances and saves the harshest criticism for those deemed the "undeserving poor"' (Lareau, 2003, 257). In this view, even *children* are undeserving of dedicated assistance to overcome obstacles, when evidence of deservedness is found in *not* having the very problems that low-income children's circumstances provoke, the very problems that most demand assistance.

There are times and circumstances, however, when the bad behaviour of some children and youth appears to become so problematic and disturbing that concerted public action is deemed necessary. Unfortunately, public response is often punitive, blaming the victim, rather than helpful in nature. For example, the 'zero-tolerance' policies that will purportedly keep schools safe from 'random violence' wrought by 'school shooters' have contributed to growing suspension and expulsion rates that nearly doubled between 1974 and 1997, the vast majority of which are for non-violent offences. These administrative actions disproportionately eject low-income and minority students, whose ties to and benefits from school are most precarious. It is now widely known that suspension and expulsion rates of black students are nearly triple those of whites, and in some localities blacks are expelled at ten times the rate of whites (Center on Juvenile and Criminal Justice, 2000; Edelmen, 2005; Waldron, 2005).

Welfare reform enacted in the mid-1990s addressed the 'epidemic' problem of teen births – which had been declining for years – by severely restricting young mothers' ability to access funds and set up independent households, and by enforcing time limits that make completion of meaningful education or training beyond high school much more difficult. Hancock (2004) provides the following quotes from the *Los Angeles Times* and the *Washington Post*, demonstrating the punitive reproach apparent in public discourse prior to passage of the Personal Responsibility and Work Opportunities Act of 1996:

> Many…believe that cutting teenagers out of the program and capping family benefits are essential to reversing the high rate of out-of-wedlock births, which they regard as a cause of many of society's social ills. (Shogren, 1995, C52; as cited in Hancock, 2004, 78)

> To the [political] right, the goal is not punishing children, it is deterring teen-agers from having children. Ending the welfare mess may require more poverty for a generation or two, but that is the price of inducing responsible behavior and middle class values. (Kuttner, 1995, C7; as cited in Hancock, 2004, 81)

Consensus had taken shape that irresponsible teen mothers were not worthy of public support, beyond the 'tough love' sort intended to change 'values' and enforce 'morality.' The suffering of their young children (as well as the suffering of the children of older 'welfare queens') was a price worth paying for inducing the 'responsible behaviour' that would end the 'welfare mess'. And as Hancock (2004) and others (Gilens, 1997) demonstrate, public support for punitive 'tough love' welfare reform is tightly tied to whites' negative attitudes towards African-Americans in particular.

Perhaps the best example of the punitive public response to children's bad behaviour, however, is the trend towards prosecution of children as adults, in adult courts, with the potential for adult sentences to adult prisons. During the 1990s, nearly all US states passed legislation loosening prohibitions on adult prosecution of minors – Bishop (2000) reports that 44 states and the District of Columbia enacted such provisions between 1992 and 1997; in 2002, the Child Welfare League of America reported that 49 states had done so. Michigan made headlines in 1997 when it became one of only two states to abolish *any* legal age limit below which a child could not be prosecuted as an adult (since 1997, many other states have followed Michigan and Nebraska). That same year, a test case quickly materialized as the Oakland County Prosecutor's office moved to pros-ecute as an adult a child who was just 11 years old at the time of his offence. In a shooting that nearly all described as accidental, Nathaniel Abraham had fatally wounded 18-year-old Ronnie Greene outside a convenience store in the Detroit area. Abraham became one of the youngest people ever tried as an adult for mur-der in the United States, and on 16 November 1999, he was convicted of second-degree murder.

Thankfully, the judge in this case intervened at sentencing. Against the demands of the Prosecutor's office and many citizens, and despite his conviction in adult court, Abraham was given a juvenile sentence to remain in a detention centre until his twenty-first birthday. (Abraham completed his sentence and was released in January 2007.) Hundreds of young men (and some young women) currently serving time in adult US prisons have received less sympathetic treatment at sentencing. Consider this accounting from Florida:

> Florida leads the nation in incarcerating children between the ages of thirteen and seventeen in adult prisons. On 1 October 1999, a typical day, there were 465 children in Florida prisons. Of the 465 children, there were 3 fourteen-year-olds, 29 fifteen-year-olds, 108 sixteen-year-olds and 327 seventeen-year-olds. Occasionally, the Florida Department of Corrections (DOC) will admit a thirteen-year-old. As of 8 September 2000, there were 11 inmates in Florida prisons who were imprisoned for crimes that they committed when they were less than thirteen years old. One inmate committed his primary offence at the age of nine. (Annino, 2001, 471–472).

The growing number of minors incarcerated in adult prisons in the United States is viewed by many as a *solution* to yet another social problem that took shape in the United States in the 1990s – children without conscience, the 'super-predators.' Popularized in the mid-1990s, the 'super-predator' label for serious youthful offenders helped to shape public opinion and the 'get tough' solutions to the supposedly 'epidemic' problem of violent youth crime.

The social construction of the 'super-predators' problem mirrored the processes Best describes through which both the 'missing children' and 'school shootings' epidemics took shape. Best observes that contemporary Americans create new social problems through a claims-making process that follows a simple formula: 'Illustrate the problem with an awful example ... Give the problem a name ("school shootings") ... [and] Use statistics to suggest the problem's size and importance' (Best, 2002, 51; see also Glassner, 1999). This process is easily seen in the case of the 'super-predators.' Several dramatic and highly disturbing incidents involving young offenders' vicious attacks on younger children (e.g., a twelve-year-old Florida boy who killed a six-year-old girl using 'professional wrestling moves'; two Chicago youths who dropped an eight-year-old to his death out a fourteenth-story window) or on 'random' adults (most notably, the 'Central Park jogger') were repeatedly conjured by those proffering the 'super-predator' definition of the problem. And hyperbolic figures were repeated by politicians, social commentators, and respected scholars alike.

Most notable here was the simplistic equation of the size of the demographic group and crime rates: the more teenagers there are, the more crime there will be. Florida Representative Bill McCollum hawked his Juvenile Crime Control Act of 1997 (re-titled from the original 'Superpredator Incapacitation Act') by predicting growing chaos and mayhem as the size of the teen population grew: 'Today's super-predators are feral, pre-social beings with no sense of right and wrong,' and 'the really bad news' is that 'America will experience a 31 per cent increase in teenagers' (as quoted in Ayers, 1997/98, 1). A much-cited *USA Today* article entitled 'Violent Kids Can't Be Reformed' soberly cautioned: 'There are 40 million children in the United States under the age of 10, more than at any other time since the baby boom. People wonder whether there is anything that can be done to stop the potential super-predators among them before it's too late' (Estrich, 1996, A14). Finally, drawing on the work of criminologist James Q. Wilson, Princeton Professor and future head of the Bush White House Office of Faith-Based and Community Initiatives John Dilulio took the 40 million figure and extrapolated:

> By simple math, in a decade today's 4 to 7-year-olds will become 14 to 17-year-olds. By 2005, the number of males in this age group will have risen about 25 percent overall and 50 percent for blacks ... [we] can predict with confidence that the additional 500,000 boys who will be 14 to 17-years-old in the year 2000 will mean at least 30,000 more murderers, rapists, and muggers on the streets than we have today ... On the horizon, therefore, are tens of thousands of severely morally impoverished juvenile super-predators. They are perfectly capable of committing the most heinous acts of physical violence for the most trivial reasons ... (1995, A31; also see Bennett Dilulio and Walters, 1996)

Very scary indeed. But the predictions were simply wrong. The most recent figures from the Office of Juvenile Justice and Delinquency Prevention paint a very different picture of juvenile crime:

> In 2004, the juvenile arrest rate for Violent Crime Index offenses decreased for the tenth consecutive year, falling to half its 1994 peak and reaching its lowest level since at least 1980. The rate for each of the Violent Crime Index offenses – murder, forcible rape, robbery, and aggravated assault – has declined steadily since the mid-1990s. Between 1995 and 2004, the reduction in the number of violent crime arrests was greater for juveniles (31 per cent) than adults (14 per cent). Juvenile arrest rates for Property Crime Index offenses also declined in 2004, reaching their lowest level in at least three decades. (Snyder, 2006, 1)

While the coming wave of violent juvenile crime that was predicted and hyped by so many failed to materialize, their claims did produce intended results: the 'dismantl[ing of] the juvenile justice system by erasing distinctions between young and adult offenders' (Schiraldi and Kappelhoff, 1997). It is important to note that children and youth criminally processed as adults are denied the confidentiality afforded to minors, and their names and offences become part of public record. Even when their sentences do not involve prison, then, their criminal records are much more likely to hamper their future opportunities.

Like my earlier mentions of 'zero-tolerance' policies and 'welfare reform,' this more extensive discussion of 'get tough' changes in juvenile justice may seem somewhat inappropriate for a publication concerned with children, and children's problems. But these issues increasingly concern children under the age of 13. Although there are few (but some) children under age 14 in adult prisons, growing numbers of juveniles who committed their offences as children are eventually transferred to adult prisons. Likewise, although the majority of individuals suspended or expelled from schools are adolescents, rates for elementary children are growing as well. In 1974, about 3.7 per cent of all students were suspended; in 1997, it was 6.8 per cent (totalling over three million suspensions). National breakdowns by age or grade of student are not readily available; however, the Center on Juvenile and Criminal Justice (2000) reports that in one state, Maryland, the nearly 15,000 suspensions of *elementary* students constituted almost one-quarter of the 64,000 total students suspended in 1998. Finally, welfare reforms enacted in the mid-1990s reflected punitive attitudes towards teenage mothers and older welfare recipients, but these reforms were enacted with full knowledge that their negative impact would be felt not only by the 'irresponsible' welfare mothers, but also by their young children.

The punitive, victim-blaming attitudes that are evident towards certain children, and the policies these attitudes support, stand in sharp contrast to the protective stance society increasingly takes towards those children who are defined as essentially innocent and naive. Just as middle-class and white children are increasingly 'infantilized' and their dependency is often effectively extended well into their early twenties, the disdain many Americans feel for 'other' children – those who are not among the privileged middle-class – is evidenced in the public's support for increasingly harsh sanctions for the 'bad' behaviour of children and youth who are personally blamed and held responsible for the problems that their circumstances engender. The fact that a disproportionate share of the burdens imposed by 'get tough' changes in juvenile justice, 'zero-tolerance' policies, and welfare reform fall on the backs of low-income and minority youths is conveniently seen as just desserts for immoral and irresponsible children and/or their immoral and irresponsible parents.

A note on the demise of the 'super-predator' narrative

In his cynical pulling-no-punches style, Barry Glassner (2001) argues that the narrative of the depravity of youth and the 'coming super-predators' has lost favour in the shadow of 9/11, nearly disappearing from evidence in public discourse. Now that we must focus our fears on foreign threats, he argues, the aggressive villainy of American youths so popularly portrayed pre-9/11 is downplayed, as this same demographic group is ironically encouraged to risk their lives fighting external enemies that threaten middle-class Americans' way of life. Glassner's observations are powerful and painful – the callous manipulation nearly unthinkable – but it seems to me he is likely correct about the disappearance of the super-predator story, if not the cause of its demise. While it is of course difficult to demonstrate the absence of some phenomenon, Internet searches on 'super-predator' produce only pre-9/11 sources, and I can recollect no recent re-telling of the formulaic tale.

Be that as it may, I am pleased to acknowledge here a recent related development in US juvenile justice, which also suggests some softening of attitudes towards 'bad' children and youth. On 2 March 2005, the US Supreme Court abolished the death penalty for individuals who were under age 18 when their crime was committed. By a slim 5/4 margin, *Roper v Simmons* ruled that execution of juvenile offenders was excessive and cruel, and therefore unconstitutional. Seventy-three death row inmates in 12 states were granted reprieve by the ruling (Lane, 2005). With this ruling,[2] the United States joined all but a handful of other nations in forbidding juvenile executions; in the ten years prior to *Roper v Simmons*, the United States had executed 17 juvenile offenders, more than all other nations of the world combined (Juvenile Justice Center, 2004).

The problems of children

During the final two decades of the twentieth century, the United States experienced numerous 'moral panics' (Best, 1999; Filler, 1999) concerning children. Examination of these panics helps us to better understand the 'schizophrenic' view that Americans have of children and childhood. While some children are threatened innocents, others are threatening monsters. School shootings and stranger kidnappings (and such bizarre threats as Halloween sadism and satanic daycares), on the one hand, threaten naive good children, and much resources must be marshalled to protect them from these ever-looming dangers. On the other hand, unredeemably bad children themselves threaten the safety of good children and adults alike, and here again tremendous amounts of time, energy and money are devoted to their publication, prosecution and incarceration.

Widespread moral panics, then, drain society of both the energy and the will to confront the more mundane problems of children. While the details of each individual case are heart-wrenching and alarming, public obsession with these heinous but rare events does great injustice to the much larger number of children who suffer less sensational wrongs. More generally, the various ways outlined in this chapter that adults view children *as* social problems detract attention away from the very real social problems *of* children – such as child poverty, child abuse and maltreatment, lack of basic schooling or health care, and denial of children's rights as citizens – that are caused by complex social and economic forces that children have little ability to resist or control.

A recent authoritative and sophisticated analysis of child poverty in the United States and other 'rich' countries demonstrates that the United States 'leads the world' on this indicator of societal neglect and disregard for children. Using data from the Luxembourg Income Study, Rainwater and Smeeding (2003) present standardized poverty rates for children in fifteen of the world's wealthiest nations. These data from the mid-1990s reveals that nine of the fifteen countries had child poverty rates below 10 per cent (Sweden, Finland, Norway, Denmark, Belgium, Switzerland, Netherlands, France and Germany – listed from lowest child poverty rate to highest); five of the fifteen had child poverty rates above 10 but below 20 per cent (Spain, Australia, Canada, United Kingdom and Italy); and only one, the United States, had a child poverty rate above 20 per cent (20.3 per cent in 1997). The authors demonstrate that child poverty rates in the United States are dramatically higher for non-whites than for whites: while 'only' 12.4 per cent of white children are poor, 37.7 per cent of black children, 36.8 per cent of Hispanic children, and 32.5 per cent of Native American and Eskimo children are poor.

Rainwater and Smeeding also call attention to the dramatic increase in US child poverty rates in the final three decades of the twentieth century. By their estimates, child poverty rates rose from 13.1 per cent in 1969 to 22.9 per cent in the mid-1980s (corresponding with the dismantling of many 'War on Poverty' programs put in place in the 1960s), then dropped slightly but remained above 20 per cent through 1997. While the United States leads the world in child poverty among affluent countries, it is also true that the wealthiest children in the United States have much more disposable income than the wealthiest children in comparable nations (also see Corsaro 2005, 264–265). Child poverty rates, as well as the gap between the affluent and the poor, reflect priorities and resolve, not societal riches: 'the correlation between GDP per capita and poverty rates is effectively zero... there is simply no association between a country's wealth and the inequality of its income... distribution' (Rainwater and Smeeding, 2003, 26).

The dramatic inequality that these findings reveal is tightly tied to the most significant problems – beyond poverty – that US children suffer. Access to quality medical care, childcare and education is unequally distributed by income, as is access to safe and hospitable neighbourhoods. Poor children often live in communities with astronomical poverty and unemployment rates among adults; under-funded, dilapidated and failing schools; inadequate police and fire protection; few youth programs and facilities; and even an absence of grocery stores (such communities are sometimes referred to as 'food deserts'). In these blighted communities, children's risk of violent victimization is truly high and popular characterizations of violent events as 'random' effectively and conveniently avoid discussion of this unequal distribution of risk by social class and race (Best, 1999; Filler, 1999).

Earlier I detailed how popular rhetoric about youth and violence has tended to emphasize threats presented by amoral youthful predators; far less attention is called to typical child and adolescent victims of violence. In 1997, 2100 juveniles (i.e., individuals under age 18) were murdered, constituting 11 per cent of murder victims in the United States that year. Half of these juvenile victims were aged 15 through 17; one-third of juvenile murder victims were under age six. Nearly half (47 per cent) of juvenile murder victims that year were African-Americans, and about one-quarter resided in one of five major US cities: Los Angeles, Chicago, New York, Philadelphia and Detroit. Forty per cent of the victims were killed by family members, and the younger the victim the more likely their killer was a parent or other adult family member. Seventy per cent of the 700 murder victims in 1997 who were under age six were killed by family members, primarily parents, compared to only 10 per cent of those victims aged 15–17. All told, only about one in four (24 per cent) of juvenile murders were committed by other juveniles. (All above figures are drawn from Snyder and Sickmund, *Juvenile Offenders and Victims: 1999 National Report*.)

Much can be made of these facts, but here I want to underscore just three points. First, the 400–500 children under the age of six who are killed by their parents each year alone is more than four times the combined number of children who are killed in their schools or murdered by kidnappers. Secondly, the risk of death by homicide is much greater for male African-American teens that live in depressed inner-city neighbourhoods than it is for other juveniles. And thirdly, between 1980 and 1997, 77 per cent of all juvenile homicide victims were killed with a firearm. These facts suggest that helpful interventions should focus on family services, community revitalization and gun control – not policies aimed at incarcerating juveniles.

Other problems of children that receive little public attention include routine abuse and neglect that does not result in death, but does contribute to the high numbers of children who run away or are 'thrownaway' by their families. About 450,000 US juveniles run away annually and about one-third of these (133,000) are 'serious' cases where the child has no secure place to stay; about 130,000 juveniles are 'thrownaway,' and about half of these are 'serious' cases (Snyder and Sickmund, 1999). About four per cent of runaway/thrownaway children are under twelve years; nearly 70 per cent are aged 15 and older (Sedlak et al., 2002).

Great caution is necessary when reporting rates of child abuse and neglect. Increases in the number of cases that come to the attention of authorities are too often interpreted as increases in actual incidences. Given changes in laws for mandatory reporting, changes in the way reports are handled, and – most importantly – changes in social attitudes towards and definitions of abuse, these interpretations are not warranted (e.g., Strauss and Gelles, 1990). While it is ill-advised to speak confidently about recent change, then, in the rates of abuse and neglect of children, we can certainly continue to consider the total number of reported cases as conservative estimates of the true incidence of these offences against children at the hands of their parents and other adults. Data from the US Department of Health and Human Services suggest that *between ten and fifteen per cent of all US children and youth are victims of some type of abuse or neglect annually* (Corsaro, 2005, 245–246). Although most of these cases are not life-threatening, US children and youth suffer remarkably high rates of abuse and neglect, and they are much safer in their schools and in (most of) their communities than they are in their family homes.

In this section I have highlighted only a few of the problems of children that receive far too little recognition and attention in contemporary American society; more extensive discussion is beyond the scope of this chapter. Here I can simply reiterate that myopic focus on rare and sensational events, and on the criminal offences of a small number of children, does great injustice to large numbers of children that suffer less dramatic, but no less damaging, offences:

> Our society battles serious social difficulties that are never formally acknowledged as problems. At the same time, we dramatize other occurrences in ways that grossly overstate their extent or danger. As we decide how to spend limited resources – time, money, and personal freedom – it becomes necessary to explore how society constructs its concerns and fears. (Filler, 1999, 1098)

It is high time we begin to battle the real problems of children and youth with dedicated resources and diligent effort. To do otherwise continues a national shame that reduces our stature in the eyes of the world, and in the eyes of our own beleaguered children.

Concluding note on importing US fears and follies

This chapter has focused exclusively on children and problems in the United States. The extent to which the processes and problems outlined here are evident in other affluent countries surely varies widely, but is beyond my knowledge and scope. In *How Claims Spread* (2001), however, Best and his contributors suggest that the more similar other societies are to the United States in terms of both their individualist orientations and their federalist system of government, the more susceptible they are to the 'monster hypes' (Best, 2002) that create monumental social problems out of remarkably rare events. I recommend that volume, and also hope that readers find in the current chapter helpful direction for their own examinations of the social processes through which the problems of children and childhood are constructed and viewed in other societies.

Notes

1. This basic framework for considering the problematic nature of children and childhood is presented by Corsaro in *The Sociology of Childhood*, second edition, 2005, primarily pp. 225–228. This chapter elaborates, updates and extends the observations presented there.
2. Justice Scalia's dissent in this case strongly chastised the majority. Charging his colleagues with 'arbitrariness' and 'sophistry,' Scalia – joined by Justice Thomas and Chief Justice Rehnquist (Justice O'Connor penned a separate dissent) – opined that 'the Court's argument – that American laws should conform to the laws of the rest of the world – ought to be rejected out of hand' (Scalia, 2005). By only the slightest of margins, then, does the High Court concur with international opinion and law regarding the protected status of the most serious juvenile offenders.

References

Adler, P.A. and P. Adler (1998) *Peer Power: Preadolescent Culture and Identity.* New Brunswick NJ: Rutgers University Press.

Allen, M.T. (1997) 'Measuring the Effects of "Adults-Only" Age Restrictions on Condominium Prices', *Journal of Real Estate Research*, 14(3): 339–346.

Annino, P.G. (2001) 'Children in Florida Adult Prisons: A Call for a Moratorium', *Florida State Law Review*, 28: 471–490.

Ayers, W. (1997/98) 'The Criminalization of Youth', *Rethinking Schools, Online*, 12(2), Winter 1997/98. http://www.rethinkingschools.org/archive/12_02/kids.shtml.

Bennett, W.J., J.J. Dilulio and J.P. Walters (1996) *Body Count: Moral Poverty ... and How to Win America's War on Drugs and Crime.* New York: Simon and Schuster.

Best, J. (1987) 'Rhetoric and Claims Making: Constructing the Missing Children Problem', *Social Problems*, 34(2): 101–121.

Best, J. (1990) *Threatened Children: Rhetoric and Concern about Child-Victims.* Chicago: University of Chicago Press.

Best, J. (1999) *Random Violence: How We Talk about New Crimes and New Victims.* Berkeley CA: University of California Press.

Best, J. (2001) *How Claims Spread: Cross-National Diffusion of Social Problems.* New York: Aldine de Gruyter.

Best, J. (2002) 'Monster Hype: How a Few Isolated Tragedies – and Their Supposed Causes – Were Turned into a National "Epidemic"', *Education Next*, Summer, 51–55.

Bishop, D.M. (2000) 'Juvenile Offenders in the Adult Criminal Justice System', *Crime and Justice*, 27, 81–167.

Cahill, S. (1987) 'Children and Civility: Ceremonial Deviance and the Acquisition of Ritual Competence', *Social Psychology Quarterly*, 50(4): 312–321.

Center on Juvenile and Criminal Justice (2000) 'School House Hype: Two Years Later', Retrieved from Center on Juvenile and Criminal Justice, 15 January 2007. http://www.cjcj.org/pubs/shooting/shootings.html.

Child Welfare League of America. (2002) *Juvenile Offenders and the Death Penalty: Is Justice Served?* Washington DC: CWLA Press.

Corsaro, W.A. (2005) *The Sociology of Childhood.* 2nd edn. Thousand Oaks CA: Pine Forge Press.

DiIulio, J.J. (1995) 'The Coming of the Super-Predators', *The Weekly Standard*, 27 November 1995 (reprinted as 'Moral Poverty' in *The Chicago Tribune*, 15 December 1995: A31).

Doherty, W. (2005) 'Who's Got Time to Be Married If You Have to Be Hyper-Vigilant for Kidnappers?' Posting on the Smartmarriages.com website (accessed on 28 November 2005).

Donohue, E., V. Schiraldi and J. Zeidenberg (1998) 'School House Hype: School Shootings, and the Real Risks Kids Face in America', Retrieved from Center on Juvenile and Criminal Justice, http://www.cjcj.org/pubs/shooting/shootings.html (accessed in April 1999).

Dunn, J.S., D.A. Kinney and S.L. Hofferth (2003) 'Parental Ideologies and Children's after School Activities', *American Behavioral Scientist*, 46(10), 1359–1386.

Edelman, M.W. (2005) 'Increasing Criminalization of Children: How Did We Get Here?' *The Louisiana Weekly.* http://www.louisianaweekly.com (accessed on 28 November 2005).

Estrich, Susan. (1996) 'Violent Kids Can't be Reformed', *USA Today*, 8 August 1996: A14.

Filler, D.M. (1999) 'Random Violence and the Transformation of the Juvenile Justice Debate', Review of Joel Best, *Random Violence: How We Talk about New Crimes and New Victims. Virginia Law Review*, 86(5): 1095–1125.

Finkelhor, D., G. Hotaling and A. Sedlak (1990) *Missing, Abducted, Runaway and Thrownaway Children in America* (commonly known as 'NISMART-1'). U.S. Department of Justice, Office of Justice Programs, Office of Juvenile Justice and Delinquency Prevention.

Gilens, M. (1997) ' "Race Coding" and White Opposition to Welfare', *American Political Science Review*, 90, 593–604.

Glassner, B. (1999) *The Culture of Fear: Why Americans Are Afraid of the Wrong Things.* New York: Basic Books.

Glassner, B. (2001) 'The Fate of False Fears', *Chronicle of Higher Education.* 26 October 2001, B16–18.

Goffman, E. ([1955] 1982) *Interaction Ritual: Essays on Face-to-Face Behavior.* New York: Pantheon.

Goffman, E. (1963) *Stigma: Notes on the Management of Spoiled Identity.* Englewood Cliffs NJ: Prentice-Hall.

Hancock, A. (2004) *The Politics of Disgust: The Public Identity of the Welfare Queen.* New York: New York University Press.

Hofferth, S.L. and J.L. Sandberg (2001) 'How American Children Spend Their Time', *Journal of Marriage and the Family*, 63(2): 295–308.

Juvenile Justice Center (2004) 'Evolving Standards of Decency. Cruel and Unusual Punishment: The Juvenile Death Penalty', American Bar Association, January 2004. http://www.abanet.org/crimjust/juvjus/EvolvingStandards.pdf (accessed January 2007).

Kuttner, R. (1995) 'Don't Punish the Children', *Washington Post*, 30 April 1995: C7.

Lane, C. (2005) '54 – Supreme Court Abolishes Juvenile Executions', *Washington Post*, 2 March 2005: A1.

Lareau, A. (2003) *Unequal Childhoods: Class, Race, and Family Life*. Berkeley CA: University of California Press.

Leach, P. (1994) *Children First: What Our Society Must Do – and Is Not Doing – for Our Children Today*. New York: Alfred A. Knopf.

Newman, K.S., C. Fox, W. Roth, J. Mehta and D. Harding (2004) *Rampage: The Social Roots of School Shootings*. New York NY: Basic Books.

Rainwater, L. and T.M. Smeeding (2003) *Poor Kids in a Rich Country: America's Children in Comparative Perspective*. New York: Russell Sage.

Rosier, K.B. and D.A. Kinney (2005) 'Introduction to Volume 11: Historical and Contemporary Pressures on Children's Freedom', in D.A. Kinney and K.B. Rosier (eds) *Sociological Studies of Children and Youth*, vol. 11. Oxford UK: JAI/ Elsevier Science, 1–20.

Scalia, J. (2005) Dissenting, *Roper v Simmons* (036–33) 543 U.S. 551. http://www.law.cornell.edu/supct/html/036–33.ZD1.html (accessed on 29 August 2007).

Schiraldi, V. and M. Kappelhoff (1997) 'As Crime Drops, Experts Backpedal – Where Have the Superpredators Gone?' *JINN Magazine*, Pacific News Service, 3.09, 04/21/97–05/04/97. http://www.pacificnews.org/jinn/toc/3.09.html (accessed on February 2007).

Sedlak, A.J., D. Finkelhor, H. Hammer and D.J. Schultz (2002) *National Incidence Study of Missing, Abducted, Runaway and Thrownaway Children* (Commonly known as 'NISMART-2'), U.S. Department of Justice, Office of Justice Programs, Office of Juvenile Justice and Delinquency Prevention.

Shogren, E. (1995) 'Senate Welfare Plan Would Lessen Mandates for States', *Los Angeles Times* [Record Edition], 16 May 1995: C52.

Snyder, H.N. (2006) 'Juvenile Arrests 2004', *Juvenile Justice Bulletin*, December 2006. Office of Juvenile Justice and Delinquency Prevention.

Snyder, H.N. and M. Sickmund (1999) 'Juvenile Offenders and Victims: 1999 National Report', National Center for Juvenile Justice, Office of Juvenile Justice and Deliquency Prevention. http://www.ncjrs.gov/html/ojjdp/nationalreport99/toc.html (accessed in February 2007).

Stacey, J. (1990) 'The Making and Unmaking of Modern Families', chapter 1 in her *Brave New Families: Stories of Domestic Upheaval in Late Twentieth Century America*. New York: Basic Books.

Strauss, M.A. and R.J. Gelles (1990) 'Societal Change and Change in Family Violence', in M.A. Straus and R.J. Gelles (eds) *Physical Violence in American Families: Risk Factors and Adaptations to Violence in 8,145 Families*. New Brunswick NJ: Transaction Press, 113–131.

U.S. Census Bureau (2002) 'U.S. Summary: 2000. Census 2000 Profile', Tables DP-1 and DP-2 http://www.census.gov/prod/2002pubs/c2kprof00-us.pdf.

Van Ausdale, D. and J.R. Feagin (2001) *The First R: How Children Learn Race and Racism*. Lanham Maryland: Rowman and Littlefield Publishers.

Waldron, L.M. (2005) 'The Messy Nature of Discipline and Zero-Tolerance Policies', in D.A. Kinney and K.B. Rosier (eds) *Sociological Studies of Children and Youth*, vol. 11. Oxford UK: JAI/ Elsevier Science, 81–114.

Zelizer, V. ([1985] 1994) *Pricing the Priceless Child: The Changing Social Value of Children*. Princeton NJ: Princeton University Press.

18
Childhood: Leisure, Culture and Peers

Ivar Frønes

Childhood as free time

A child immersed in play or games is not only a child preoccupied with leisure activities, but the cultural image of childhood. The European working and agrarian classes were still at work when the bourgeoisie conceived of childhood as a period of play, peers and leisure. Childhood was also understood as a segregated strange world, a state of mind. The latter was vividly illustrated by Virginia Woolf's comments about Lewis Carroll and his vision in *Alice in Wonderland:* 'he could return to that world; he could re-create it, so that we too become children again' (Woolf, 1948, 83).

The childhood of peers and free time evolved parallel to the notion of childhood as a period of controlled socialization. In some cases the two ideas converged, as in Robert Baden-Powell's scouting movement. Free time, or leisure, is the primary arena of children's social and cultural autonomy, but there also appears to be a relationship between childhood leisure activities and later adult occupations (Hong et al., 1993). Some perspectives, in fact, interpret some activities, like hobbies, as a category between production and pure leisure (Gelber, 1999). This childhood of play, leisure and cultural socialization also evolved into a normative concept, the 'right to a childhood.'

Leisure, however, is unevenly distributed, both globally and by socio-economic status and gender. In developing countries today, about 16 per cent of all children are involved in what UNICEF defines as child labour. In sub-Saharan countries, 38 per cent are child labourers. Early marriages seek to ensure that women are under male control, illustrating that childhood is gendered as well as rooted in material standards and culture. The highest rate of child marriages is to be found in Niger, where 77 per cent of girls aged 20–24 were married at the age of 18. (UNICEF, 2001, 2006).

In developed countries, the modes of production of the industrial society and the increased affluence of the post-war era widened access to well-paid jobs for unskilled workers. This made earlier marriage possible and created a period of socialization where children were out of the work force, experienced fewer chores and burdens within the family than before, and relatively little pressure from an educational system most young people left after the compulsory period. Organized cultural and sport activities increasingly became a part of modern childhood – to some degree contrary to image of the free play and activities chosen by the children, evident today in the debates about the 'overscheduled' child (Elkind, 1981, 2007).

Current views place leisure both within the framework of a child's life in the present and within the child's life course development and the process of socialization. The functions assigned to leisure and cultural activities vary with children's development and historical period.

Cultural transfer, risk and cultural framing

Play and peers is understood as a fundamental mechanism of learning and development in human evolution. In modern societies, leisure activities and peer relations are understood as important in preparing children for a complex future (Frønes, 1995). Adolescence is described as a period of evolving autonomy, but also as a period of risk (Hall, 1904; Freud, 1937; Parsons, 1942). Adolescence as a period of increasing risk grew more salient in industrial society, as illustrated by the new teenage cultures (Coleman, 1961; Hebdige, 1979). The arena of risk was the free time after school. In these perspectives, organized activities contributed both to socialization and to keeping young people off street corners.

During the last several decades, the lifestyle of adolescence, with its risk-taking, has been inching down to younger age groups, as illustrated by new coinages such as 'tweens'. That more than one-third of boys in the United Kingdom in 2006 had vandalized property by age 14 or 15 (Beinart et al., 2002), and a similar proportion of those said they 'liked to see how much they could get away with', illustrates the prevalence of risky behaviours, as well as the potential for intergenerational conflict. That the majority of the young in general appeared to be well behaved and supervised underlines that the prevalence of risk is related to the life phase (Beinart et al., 2002).

Leisure activities are part of a system of domestic authority and ideological transfer, and an arena of autonomy and possible subversiveness. The freedom of leisure activities increases the possibility that new cultural activities and lifestyles will develop, understood by some as an innovative adaptation to the future, as illustrated by Margaret Mead's (1972) concept of pre-figurative socialization. In Mead's theory the pre-figurative functions were linked to young people's position as less rooted in the past under conditions of change, underlining the innovative and potentially subversive elements in children's culture and activities.

The future exists in the present as ideas and expectations. Traditions rule when the future is expected to be like the past. Under post-industrial conditions, with human capital at the centre of production, children are to prepare for uncertainty and increased demands for competence. This permeates leisure and cultural activities, influencing the amount of free time and, not least, the social framing of cultural and leisure activities. In this perspective, children's activities are formed by the pressure of the predicted future, not by the autonomy imagined by Mead and others. Within the framework of the post-industrial society, the dimension of integration/exclusion and the vocabularies of social and cultural capital gradually acquire dominance over the theories of the pre-figurative capacities of autonomous youthful activities, just as sociological interpretations of subcultures as cultural resistance gradually were replaced by models of lifestyles as symbolic expressions of social positions through consumption (Miles, 2000). At the same time, the post-industrial emphasis on self-realization and self-expression, and lifestyle as a constructed personal image of self-identity, position leisure as the arena of autonomy and construction of identity. The modern socialization often brings tensions between the dimension of competence and educational achievements and the youthful expressions of coolness and individualized identity.

Life course and leisure

In all industrial societies, the amount of leisure time has increased in the last decades, in the sense that less time is allocated to work outside the home or in the home. Books like *The Overworked American* (Schor, 1993) imply that work has impinged on leisure. However, studies of time use from a variety of countries, including the United States, indicate that the modern time squeeze is often more rooted in lifestyles outside of work. Among those of working age in the United States and Europe, hours at work have declined since 1960 (Aguiar and Hurst, 2006); Europeans work fewer hours than Americans. Men spend fewer hours at work than some decades ago, and women have acquired their extra leisure through less household work. The age for leaving the workforce has declined in all minority countries, with variations between countries often not reflected in the formal age for retirement. The effect has been to partly transform late middle age into a leisure age.

The increased productivity of the post-industrial societies brought, in general, increased free time, except for perhaps preadolescents and adolescents. Japanese junior-high students spend more time studying than college students, according to surveys on time use in 2001 (Statistics Bureau Japan, 2002). Chinese children often have little spare time after educational activities; more than 80 per cent were doing homework on weekends (Hongyan, 2003); 78 per cent of Chinese students chose studies as what worried them most, only beaten by students from South Korea (84 per cent) (Hongyan, 2007). The organized schedule also transforms the patterns of non-organized peer activities. 'I hear that kids these days make things called "play dates,"' a Japanese grandmother says. 'My boys didn't make dates – they ran around the neighbourhood and came home when the street lights went on,' she recalls, referring to little more three or four decades ago (Nagamura, 2005). The global educational competition, illustrated by the OECD's PISA studies (Programme for International Student Assessment – 32 countries took part in the first test in 2000) aiming to test and compare schoolchildren's performance across OECD countries, is likely to produce more parental and societal investment in educational leisure activities.

Time use, however, varies by country. Surveys in the United States indicate more time spent on homework (Juster, 2004), primarily among the youngest (Hofferth and Curtin, 2003). In the United Kingdom no increase is reported in the period from 1983 to 2005; from 1997 to 2005 there is a decrease. Young girls (12–13 year olds) seem to spend most time on homework (Trends, 2006). In Norway, children's time use has been analysed since the early 1970s, with no apparent increase in education or homework (Waage, 2002), even though the age of starting school has been lowered. Despite variations, in all post-industrial countries the need to qualify the youngest is underlined, as reflected in public investment in pre-schools and emphasis on educational parenting, especially among the middle classes. The 'hurried child' is rooted in the political economy of the educational post-industrial society, not just in busy and ambitious parents. Children spend in general less time outdoors than their parents did (Clements, 2004), and their independent mobility has declined (Hillman and Adams, 1992). Downtime and hanging out are increasingly domains of the lower classes and the groups living at the margins of society. Children of the upper classes that produced the childhood of play and leisure are gradually leaving Never Land.

The use of time

Time use studies largely focus on those aged 16 and older. Most data on children's time use refer to participation in activities, or being present in certain social contexts. Studies on time use in the United States show that children age 6–12 spend 5.5 to 6 hours of leisure each weekday, defined as time spent after sleep, school and personal needs (Hofferth and Curtin, 2003). The free time of children may be filled with both household chores and educational activities, and thus not be truly open to free choice. Children in post-industrial society generally spend little time on chores, while this is a dominant activity in developing countries.

Boys are in general over-represented in sports, girls in art, dance and drama, and increasingly in school-oriented activities. Australian studies of cultural activities (Australian Bureau of Statistics, 2006) indicate active participation in cultural expressions. Among 5-year-olds, 18 per cent had taken part in at least one singing, music, dancing or drama activity in the last year, increasing to 39 per cent by age 10. Most of these children were involved in lessons. From 2000 to 2003, the numbers participating in cultural activities decreased for boys and increased for girls. Children's activities are structured by the social and geographic context. Children in Melbourne travelled 3.9 hours per week by car (Ironmonger, 2007); children in the United Kingdom spent about 30 minutes per day in a car (UK National Statistics Time Use Survey, 2000).

In 2000, 10–13-year-olds in Finland spent almost one hour on sports and physical exercise a day, about two hours watching television, and 30–40 minutes at the computer, the latter increasing with the advent of Internet games and online chatting. Girls were more involved in domestic work and spent less time on sports. Total time on sports decreases with age when children reach their teens, even if it may increase for the most active (Statistics Finland, 2004). Participation in various organizations in the United States increased between 2000 and 2005 (US Department of Education, National Center for Educational Statistics, 2006). Eighth graders are the most active in this age range, but the percentage involved in organized activities shrinks during adolescence, which seems to be a general trend. Statistics on sports participation in the United States show varying trends between 1995 and 2005. Skateboarding and snowboarding show the strongest increase (NSGA, 2006), being less institutionalized than traditional sports, and more under the influence of the fads and fashions of youth culture. Time in school-based settings and highly structured activities has increased in the United States in the last decades (Hofferth and Sandberg, 2001). Boys are more likely than girls to participate in sport in the United States, as in other countries.

The concerns about safety, related to crime and traffic, as well as to parents' needs to supervise and support their children, move children from the outdoors to the indoors, a development also encouraged by spacious homes (Karsten 2005; Wridt 2004). Modern children stay home while communicating with others, and local friends meet in chat rooms as well as in their rooms. The Internet also provides for narrow, often international, interest groups and social networking sites like Facebook and MySpace, and participants in Internet games from all over the planet play in colourful landscapes in the 'World of Warcraft' and other games. Technology opens the door for new forms of social contact, as well as new risks, as illustrated by cyberstalkers and the growing protective strategies offered anxious parents (e.g., Cyber Angels).

Media act both as an activity and as a structuring of children's activities and social patterns. The decrease in time spent watching television and the increase in time spent on interactive media, such as chat rooms, Internet games and groups, challenges the notion of computers as a solitary endeavour (Buckingham, this volume).

The cultural framing of leisure

Leisure can be understood as time left when all work and chores are accomplished. Another perspective defines leisure as activities chosen for their own sake, not because they are profitable or educational, implying that the definition of the activity is created by the social or subjective framing. Mark Twain famously illustrated this when Tom Sawyer convinced his friend that whitewashing a fence was a chosen privilege, a persuasion later conceptualized by social scientists as 'reframing'. Young people reading to develop their future career versus those reading for fun illustrates the problem of definition and how social change may influence how activities are framed.

That certain cultural activities in childhood are seen as steps to acquiring social and cultural capital is not a new phenomenon, as illustrated by the English idle classes and their socialization into good manners and cultural codes. When one of Jane Austen's characters says she is mediocre at the piano, this is not primarily a statement about leisure interest. Even if class-related symbols and activities are abundant in modern societies, the differences among children seem to stem more from the amount of participation in organized leisure than from the types of activities, as illustrated by reports on social class and activities, which in general focus on frequency of participating. The globalization of sport and the media concentration on a few sporting activities have also promoted certain activities, as illustrated by the dominant position of football (soccer) for boys in most countries, and increasingly for girls. The increased participation in sport may be related to the fact that sport is understood as positive for children's development and to the local position of dominating sport activities. In a post-industrial framing, how sport and cultural activities contribute to children's cognitive and social development will be underlined (Perez and Gauvain, 2001).

In the childhood of the industrial society, leisure activities were understood less as a vehicle for educational development and more as a present phase of childhood. The function of activities as prevention was to keep children away from street corners and bad company. The post-industrial society reframes activities and directs them towards the future, as is evident in the term 'social education'. Risk is likewise reframed to focus on possible future success or failure. The degree to which the intense competition in educational systems permeates leisure activities is best illustrated by children in parts of Asia. Participating in educational activities such as music and sports (as well as academic subjects) influences the odds of acceptance to selective junior-high schools, high schools or universities. The cram schools in East Asia are not only part of children's education; they also transform their 'leisure' hours into long days of education and social education. On the micro level, such framing seems to be part of scholastic success to some ethnic groups, as when American families with Chinese background frame homework as family time, not as solitary 'time for homework' (Huntsinger, 1997, 1999).

The semiotics of cultural activities and the child as a subject

Traditional songs, dances and games are in general understood as anchoring children in their cultural traditions; cultural patterns, gender patterns and class patterns are conveyed as play and cultural activities. The cultural events and rituals of different ethnic groups reveal cultural roots through dance and songs, as illustrated by the fact that 35 per cent of Maoris surveyed in New Zealand had participated in a Maori activity in the last month (Statistics New Zealand, 2006). As Barthes (1973) illustrates in uncovering the hidden ideology of toys, children's leisure activities can be understood as reflecting dominating ideologies and through this, social reproduction. Rituals, toys and traditions are not only mirroring the past, but constructing it, in correspondence with interests and values of the present.

The increasing speed of change in industrial societies produced a new interest in the semiotics of youth subcultures, seen as indications of qualities of social change. Mannheim's (1952) theory of generations assigned children's culture and activities the function of transferring traditions, while the period of youth represented the active meeting of young subjects and dominating traditions, as in the theories of Freud and Erikson. Earlier biological and social maturation has increasingly assigned younger children a position as agents of change. Children's position as early adapters of new media is often held up as an illustration of their innovative capacities. In the Nordic countries, the vast majority of children have a mobile phone by age 10, and the age at which computers become a natural part of life is being lowered everywhere. Childhood as an intersection of the new and the old is vividly illustrated by digital storytelling: in the meeting of technology and the old art of storytelling, the child becomes the active constructor of the narrative. The past few years have introduced new leisure activities based on software that combines creative potential with low thresholds for technological competence. This opens the arena for a synthesis of children's creativity and parents' emphasis on educational framing, creating a new market for educational software. The first three years of life are increasingly exposed to this preparation for creativity, agency and scholastic success, as evident in the 'Baby Einstein' products and other educational products for the very youngest.

The over- or underscheduled child

The overscheduled child may, argue some researchers, limit the development of fundamental capacities, such as creativity or the capacity to cope with social complexity, and expose children to stress. Researchers worried about the overscheduled child and the vanishing open-ended play gained support from the American Academy of Pediatrics (AAP), who stressed that unstructured play fosters creativity and dexterity (Ginsburg, 2007). In the United Kingdom, the scripts of traditional play are available at governmental Internet sites, underscoring both the position that traditional play is assigned in socialization and the fear that play and games are endangered cultural artefacts.

Overscheduling may be a threat to creativity and development (Elkind, 2007). However, to others, underscheduling is the challenge, with a threat of future social exclusion. Only 25 per cent of elementary-school students reported doing three or more activities per week or spending more than four hours a week on their activities (Hofferth, in *USA Today* October 9, 2006); 40 per cent of all children are not active in any after-school activities (Mahoney, 2006a). Mahoney (2006b) declared overscheduling to be a myth, as did Hofferth (Cloud, 2007). Or, at the least, overscheduling is a class-based worry. Children of the upper classes are in general more scheduled, although this also varies by age and gender, illustrating that variations are in part institutionally embedded (Lareau, 2003).

The over- and underscheduling debate is partly rooted in a cultural framing where optimal leisure is seen as free personal time, as in play and art. Other discourses may frame this differently; the poles in a Chinese discourse on moral and social education are not primarily creativity versus tight scheduling, but social cohesion versus individualization and fragmentation, illustrating the common depiction of modernity as disintegration (Bakken, 2000). Different cultures and contexts may operate within different cultural and moral discourses.

Gender, age and phases

Activities convey cultural meaning, and one's choice of toys and activities is part of what constitutes social identity, age and gender. The social transitions of childhood imply changes in activities and symbols. Some activities are age graded; others are part of possibly lifelong patterns.

Leisure activities are still gendered, albeit much less so than in the past. In general, girls have gradually moved into activities and lifestyles that were once dominated by boys. The world of hobbies is often more gendered than sports; in general, one is more likely to find a female soccer player than a female owner of a miniature train. Girls move into gadget markets that fit with female social patterns: more women than men buy mobile phones, digital cameras and DVDs, while men and boys dominate electronic games.

The toys for preschoolers often present highly gendered fantasy universes, as evident in the advertisements on children's television. That Barbie got a home office more than two decades ago suggests that change may be subtle and often invisible from a distance. Research indicates that parents often encourage the gendered dimension of toys (Campenni, 1999), but also that parents' definitions of what constitutes appropriate toys for boys and girls are changing; the gender-neutral categories seem to be expanding (Wood, Desmarais and Gugula, 2002). Children are gender and age focused; activities, toys, and clothes thought of as too childish are dismissed. This search for mature activities contributes to puberty as a period of risk, creating a gap between contexts children may seek and their competencies. Changing gender patterns also alter risks. Gender differences in 'street-based' activities largely evaporated in some regions in the 1990s, contributing to the higher risk for girls (Sweeting and West, 2003).

Patterns of peer relations

In theories of socialization, peer activity is understood as a basic vehicle for developing social and cultural competencies, as well as a mechanism for transferring traditions, values and beliefs. In the hunting and gathering societies, as well as in village life, peer-oriented activities filled this function of cultural transfer by being a simulation of adult life. In some militarized societies, like Sparta and Aztec society, peer socialization was systematically utilized in military socialization (Frønes, 1995); the Sparta-inspired English boarding schools merged peer socialization and social control.

Educational institutions create a daily life filled with peers; the adults whom children meet are typically professionals whose focus is on children. Leisure activities are also a base for peer relations, when activities and companions are chosen. Studies from several countries indicate that 'hanging out' with peers is an important part of youth, and structured activities are often given priority because of the participation of peers, not because of the activity per se (see Corsaro, this volume). Again, social patterns of peer activities vary with demography, gender, class and life phase. Girls are often reported to have more dyadic relationships than boys. In Norway, however, studies show that teenage girls more often than boys are part of groups or networks (Øia, 1994), indicating changing social patterns.

Hanging out with peers, or being involved in activities with peers, increases with age and autonomy, but as suggested above, these idealized, unorganized activities are on the decline. While autonomous play may lose its position, peers do not. Among young people (age 15–24) in various European countries (Young Europeans, 2001), being with friends remains the favoured activity.

The size of homes has increased in most western countries, while fertility rates have declined, expanding a child's individual space. Having a room of one's own is in western culture part of the individualization of childhood. Children are increasingly moving inside for their leisure activities, a tendency strengthened by electronic media. Modern technology provides for new forms of peer contact, a new 'written talk' filled with signs and symbols is developed, and web cameras have opened up new socio-virtual patterns. Despite this increased reach, the time spent on solitary activities is increasing as growing affluence and fewer children increase privacy.

In Italy, the fertility rate is about 1.3, and children under age 15 constitute about 13 per cent of the Italian population, and even less in northern Italy. On the other side of the Mediterranean, Palestinian children under age 15 now make up 46 per cent of the population. Differences in living standards and the different demographic landscape make for different relationships between peers and between parents and children. When children constitute one-half of the population and homes are not as spacious, children will spend spare time outside with other children; affluence and small families bring them inside.

The 1980s and 1990s brought a gender educational revolution. Girls now outnumber boys at universities in most countries. In addition, girls are increasingly acquiring a culturally dominant position among young people. The development of strong peer groups among girls is a pivotal part of this development, both mirroring and driving the gender revolution (Frønes, 2001). Education and peers increasingly dominate life between age 20 and 30, a period that not long ago belonged to young families. The new breed of education-oriented girls profited from educational framing of leisure activities, while this development marginalized groups of working-class boys. The educational society and the reframing of leisure activities brought divergent consequences by class, gender, ethnicity and cultural context.

Time with parents

When women began entering the workforce in greater numbers, one worry was that time spent with children would be reduced. However, being home does not automatically mean being with the children. The bourgeois mother often had, as had the aristocrats, staff to deal with children. In some countries, the well off regard(ed) it as a plight of good parenthood to send their children to boarding school. Even among the non-elite, children were not at the centre of the housewife's priorities and activities in the era of the housewife, and they seldom intervened in children's days for educational purposes. But they were around; the children roaming the neighbourhood were dependant on the maternal figures that populated their environment.

Since the early 1980s, time spent with children has increased, paradoxically as the number of mothers in the workforce increased (Bianchi et al., 2006; George,

2007). At the same time, a substantial number of women work part-time in many countries, working hours and time spent on household activities have decreased and families are smaller. However, the main reason behind the increasing contact between parents and children, which seems to be in force everywhere in post-industrial countries, is simply that contact with children is given priority. Parents consider it important to stimulate their children. In particular, Asian parents seem to provide coaching of school work (Kagitcibasi, 1996); middle class parents everywhere seek to secure for their children an educational leisure.

An increasing number of commercial activities are directed towards the family, as when, for example, big amusements centres offer experiences for children and parents together. Amusement parks and holidays provide events that are increasingly acquiring positions as rituals of a good family, illustrating that leisure activities are constitutive of the family; the pictures of the family's leisure activities on the wall are important parts of its biography.

Leisure, cultural activities and risk: class, culture and social capital

Children's participation in leisure activities varies with parents' economic, cultural and social capital. American children who plan to go to college are more likely than other children to participate in after-school activities of all kinds, indicating that organized leisure is more a part of a lifestyle than simply narrow planning for educational success. Poor children are under-represented in organized activities and after-school activities, and spend more hours in sedentary activities, rooted both in lack of economic resources and in lack of cultural capital (Lareau, 2003). Children who watch television excessively do less homework and are less active in after-school activities and exercise (Child Trends, 2003). The causality in this relationship is less clear than the correlation, but the tension between television viewing and more active lifestyles is a recurring theme in discussions of children's use of time.

Risk reduction is a modern responsibility of parents; the parental minimizing of risks is at odds with the autonomy highlighted by the American paediatrics community. The culture of fear (as well as risk) is not distributed evenly around the globe. Japanese and Nordic children travel alone or with friends in city centres while American children are transported by their parents. In general, however, efforts to minimize risk converge with the emphasis on controlling children's environments and activities by scheduling their time. The socio-economic variations in this strategy increase the uneven distribution of risk.

The leisure activities of children are pivotal to the development of their social capital (Bourdieu, 1986; Coleman, 1988). Educational activities, social networks, social style and the bridges to wider society that local institutions provide, all of these function to expand social capital. While the perspective of risk focuses on keeping children away from harmful company, the perspective of social capital stresses the importance of the proper company on both the individual and institutional level. Social exclusion originates often with integration in subgroups that provide tight bonding and sub-cultural capital, but no bridging to the wider society and its institutions. Some leisure activities for children, like art, are providing both aesthetic competence and cultural capital in the more general sense; children with greater economic and cultural resources are over-represented both in these specific activities and in the amount of activities in general.

Risk varies with environment and resources, increases with the accumulation of sub-cultural capital, and decreases with general social and cultural capital. In the United Kingdom, 60 per cent of young people aged 11–14 in three relatively deprived areas had been injured within the prior month. Children truant from school, which is an indication of marginalization and often of specific sub-social attachment, were more likely to be injured. Few had spent time with other generations, and few participated in organized activities (Child Accident Prevention Trust, 2002). In highly deprived areas (Armstrong et al., 2005), about 50 per cent of secondary school children reported being involved in offending. Social deprivation correlates with high risk and low participation in activities that integrate young people into wider society. The perspective of risk underlines the importance of the qualities of the environment; the concept of toxic environment (Garbarino, 1995) illustrates the risk of some areas of socialization.

Children's leisure, socialization and social change

The activities of leisure are the arena where childhood and youth unfolds. The post-industrial conditions restructure the life course of childhood and youth, and reframe our understanding of leisure and cultural activities along an axis of integration versus exclusion, a basic dimension in the conceptualizations of all forms of capital.

Comparative analysis shows part of Asia as under a strong educational regime. The educational fever (Seth, 2002) is less strong in the United States and Europe; less of the leisure is spent in direct school-related activities, more in sport and other organized activities (Verma and Larson, 2003). The global variations illustrate the different cultural framing of leisure acitivites, but the numerous studies examining the correlations between activities and scholastic development illustrate the general post-industrial framing of leisure activities.

Cultural activities confirm cultural roots and operate as mechanisms of social distinction, and they are important to the transfer of traditions as well as for the evolving of possible pre-figurative patterns. In our traditional understanding of growing up, the tranquillity of childhood is succeeded by the *Sturm und Drang* of youth. The life course in an educated society produces a period of pre-youth, and transforms late childhood into 'tweens' and a social risk zone, while the educational framing defines the process of socialization as a time of continuous threat of exclusion. Sedentary activities such as watching television represent a controlled low-risk activity in the industrial framework, yet the educational society locates television in the risk zone, with its negative correlations with scholastic success.

The modern framing of leisure activities shows that the line between leisure and education is being blurred in the post-industrial childhood. The amount of leisure, and the categorization of leisure activities, does not emerge from the activities as such, but from the cultural framing. The culture of leisure and leisure activities is mirrored in deeper social structures, but it also provides a sphere of autonomy, positioning the leisure activities of young people as indications of social change and as an arena of social tension.

References

Aguiar, M. and E. Hurst (2006) *Measuring Trends in Leisure: The Allocation of Time over Five Decades*. Working Papers No 06–2 Federal Reserve Bank of Boston http://www.bos.frb.org/economic/wp/wp2006/wp0602.pdf.

Armstrong, D., J. Hine, S. Hacking, R. Armaos, R. Jones, N. Klessinger and A. France (2005) *Children, Risk and Crime; The On Track of Youth Lifestyles Surveys*. Home Office Research Study 278. http://www.homeoffice.gov.uk/rds/pdfs05/hors278.pdf.

Australian Bureau of Statistics (2006) *Participation in Cultural and Leisure Activities* http://www.googlesyndicatedsearch.com/u/AustralianBureauOfStatistics?q=children+cultural+activities&sa=Go&domains=abs.gov.au&sitesearch=abs.gov.au.

Bakken, B. (2000) *The Exemplary Society: Human Improvement, Social Control, and the Dangers of Modernity in China*. Oxford: Oxford University Press.

Barthes, R. (1972) *Mythologies*. London: Paladin.

Beinart, S., B. Anderson, S. Lee and D. Utting (2002). *Youth at Risk? A National Survey of Risk Factors, Protective Factors, and Problem Behaviour among Young People in England, Scotland and Wales*. (Report to the Joseph Rowntree Foundation). London: Communities That Care.

Bianchi, S., J.P. Robinson and M. Milkie (2006) *Changing Rhythms of American Family Life*. New York: Russell Sage.

Bourdieu, P. (1986) 'The Forms of Capital', in J.G. Richardson (ed.) *Handbook of Theory and Research for the Sociology of Education*. New York: Greenwood Press, pp. 241–258.

Campenni, C.E. (1999) 'Gender Stereotyping of Children's Toys: A Comparison of Parents and Non-Parents', *Sex Roles*, 40, 121–138.

Child Accident Prevention Trust (2002) *Taking Chances: The Lifestyles And Leisure Risk of Young People*. Project Summary http://www.capt.org.uk/pdfs/capt_risk_doc.pdf

Child Trends (2003) 'Watching Television', http://www.childtrendsdatabank.org/indicators/55WatchingTV.cfm.

Clements, R. (2004) 'An Investigation of the State of Outdoor Play', *Contemporary Issues in Early Childhood*, 5(1): 68–80.

Cloud, J. (2007) 'The Overscheduled Child Myth', *Times*. January 19.

Coleman, J. (1961) *The Adolescent Society*. New York: The Free Press.

Coleman, J. (1988) 'Social Capital in the Creation of Human Capital', *American Journal of Sociology*, 94, 95–120.

Cyber Angels: http://www.cyberangels.org/.

Elkind, D. (1981) *The Hurried Child*. Reading MS: Addison-Wesley.

Elkind, D. (2007) *The Power of Play; How Spontaneous, Imaginative Activities Lead to Happier, Healthier Children*. Cambridge: Da Capo Press.

Freud, A. (1937) *The Ego and the Mechanisms of Defence*. London: Hogarth Press,

Frønes, I. (1995) *Among Peers*. Oslo: Scandinavia University Press.

Frønes, I. (2001) 'Revolution without Rebels: Gender, Generation, and Social Change. An Essay on Gender, Socialization and Change', in A. Furlong and I. Guidikova (eds) *Transitions of Youth Citizenship in Europe: Culture, Subculture and Identity*. Strasbourg, France: Council of Europe Publishing, pp. 217–234.

Garbarino, J. (1995) *Raising Children in a Socially Toxic Environment*. San Francisco: Jossey-Bass Publishers.

Gelber, S. (1999) *Hobbies, Leisure and the Culture of Work in America*. New York: Columbia University Press.

George, D. (2007) 'Despite "Mommy Guilt," Time With Kids Increasing', Washington Post Staff Writer. Tuesday, 20 March 2007, page A01.

Ginsburg, K. (2007) 'The Importance of Play in Promoting Healthy Child Development and Maintaining Strong Parent–Child Bonds', *Pediatrics*, 119 Number 1 January.

Hall, S. (1922, first published 1904) *Adolescence: Its Psychology and Its Relations to Physiology, Anthropology, Sociology, Sex, Crime, Religion and Education*. New York: D. Appleton.

Hebdige, D. (1979) *Subculture: The Meaning of Style*. London: Methuen.

Hillman, M. and J.G. Adams (1992) 'Children's Freedom and Safety', Children's Environments, 9(2): 12–33.

Hofferth, S.L. and S. Curtin (2003) 'Leisure Activities in Middle Childhood', paper presented at The Positive Outcome Conference Washington DC. http://www.childtrends.org/Files/HofferthCurtinPaper.pdf

Hofferth, S.L. and J.F. Sandberg (2001) 'Changes in American Children's Time, 1981–1997', in S.L. Hofferth and T.J. Owens (eds) *Children at the Millennium: Where Have We Come From, Where Are We Going?* New York: JAI Press, pp. 1–7.

Hong, E., R.M. Milgram and S.C. Whiston (1993) 'Leisure Activities in Adolescents as a Predictor of Occupational Choice in Young Adults: A Longitudinal Study', *Journal of Career Development*, 19(3): 221–229.

Hongyan, S. (2003) 'Physical and Mental Health of Contemporary Chinese Children', *Journal of Family and Economic Issues*, 24(4): 355.

Hongyan, S. (2007) *China Daily*. 10 January 2007.

Huntsinger, C. (1997) 'Cultural Differences in Parents' Facilitation of Mathematics Learning: A Comparison of Euro–American and Chinese–American Families', Paper presented at the Annual Meeting of the American Educational Research Association (Chicago, IL, March 24–28).

Huntsinger, C. (1999) 'Homework' American Teacher, April 1999 http://www.aft.org/parents/k5homework.htm.

Ironmonger, P. (2007) 'Travel Behaviour of Women, Men and Children: What Changes and What Stays the Same?' 29th Annual Conference on Time Use Research 17–19 October 2007 Washington DC: USA.

Juster, T., H. Ono and F. Stafford (2004) *Changing Times of American Youth: 1981–2003*, Institute for Social Research, University of Michigan, Ann Arbor, Michigan http://www.umich.edu/news/Releases/2004/Nov04/teen_time_report.pdf.

Kagitcibasi, C. (1996) *Family and Human Development across Cultures: A View from the Other Side*. Mawah NJ: Lawrence Erlbaum.

Karsten, L. (2005) 'It All Used to be Better? Different Generations on Continuity and Change in Urban Children's Daily Use of Space', Children's Geographies, 3(3): 275–290.

Lareau, A. (2003) *Unequal Childhoods: Class, Race, and Family Life*. Berkeley CA: University of California Press.

Mahoney, J. (2006a) *Social Policy Report*, 12 August 2006; vol XX: no IV.

Mahoney, J. From Boston Globe. Interview http://www.timesargus.com/apps/pbcs.dll/article?AID=/20061001/NEWS/610010319/1016/FEATURES07.

Mannheim, K. (1952) 'The Problems of Generations', in his *Essays on the Sociology of Knowledge*. London: Routledge & Kegan Paul.

Mead, M. (1972) *Culture and Commitment: A Study of the Generation Gap*. London: Panther.

Miles, S. (2000) *Youth Llifestyles in a Changing World*. Buckingham: Open University Press.

Nagamura, K. (2005) 'At What Point Is a Child Being to Active?' *Japan Times* 4 October 2005.

NSGA (2006) http://www.nsga.org/public/pages/index.cfm?pageid=158

Øia, T. (1994) *Norske ungdomskulturer.* Lillehammer: Oplandske Bokforlag.

Parsons, T. (1942) 'Age and Sex in the Social Structure of the United States', *American Sociological Review*, 7(5): 604–616.

Perez, S. and M. Gauvain (2001) 'Children's After-School Activities as Opportunities To Develop Cognitive Skills', Paper presented at the Biennial Meeting of the Society for Research in Child Development. Minneapolis MN, 19–22 April.

PISA (The Programme for International Student Assessment) is a world-wide test of 15-year-old schoolchildren's scholastic performance. Coordinated by the OECD. The first PISA assessment was carried out in 2000.

Schor, J. (1993) *The Overworked American: The Unexpected Decline of Leisure.* New York: Basic Books.

Seth, M. (2002) *Education Fever: Society, Politics, and the Pursuit of Schooling in South Korea.* Honolulu: University of Hawaii Press.

Statistics Bureau Japan (2001) *Summary of Results of the 2001 Survey on Time Use and Leisure Activities.* Director General for Policy Planning & statistical Research and Training Institute Japan. http://www.stat.go.jp/english/data/shakai/index.htm.

Statistics Finland 2004; http://www.stat.fi/tk/el/kva_artikkelit_everydaylifesummary_en.html.

Statistics New Zealand (2006) http://www.stats.govt.nz/products-and-services/Articles/time-use-time-culture.htm.

Sweeting, H. and P. West (2003) 'Young People's Leisure and Risk-Taking Behaviours: Changes in Gender Patterning in the West of Scotland during the 1990s', *Journal of Youth Studies*, 6(4): 391–412.

Trends (2006) *Young People in the Uk Attitudes to and Experience of Leisure Activities 1983–2005.* http://www.sheu.org.uk/publications/exampleuk.pdf.

UK National Statistics Time Use Survey (2000) http://www.statistics.gov.uk/STATBASE/ssdataset.asp?vlnk=7054&More=Y.

UNICEF (2001) *Early Marriage : Child Spouse.* Innocenti Digest No. 7, March. Florence: UNICEF.

UNICEF (2006) *State of the World's Children 2006: Excluded and Invisible* http://www.unicef.org/sowc06/.

U.S. Department of Education, National Center for Educational Statistics (2006). *The Condition of Education 2006* (NCES 2006–071). Washington DC: US. http://nces.ed.gov/programs/coe/2006/pdf/34_2006.pdf.

Verma, S. and R. Larson (eds) (2003) *Examining Adolescent Leisure Time Across Cultures.* New Directions for Child and Adolescent Development, *No. 99.* San Francisco: Jossey-Bass.

Waage, F. (2002) Statistics Norway: *Barn og unges tidsbruk.* http://www.ssb.no/vis/samfunns-speilet/utg/200204/06/art-2002-10-08-01.html/.

Wood, E., S. Desmarais and S. Gugula(2002) 'The Impact of Parenting Experience on Gender Stereotyped Toy Play of Children', *Sex Roles: A Journal of Research*, 47(1–2): 39–49.

Woolf, V. (1948) *The Moment and Other Essays.* London: Hogarth Press, p. 83.

Wridt, P. (2004) 'An Historical Analysis of Young People's Use of Public Space, Parks and Playgrounds in New York City', *Children, Youth and Environments*, 14(1): 86–106.

Young Europeans (2001) Eurobarometer. http://ec.europa.eu/public_opinion/archives/ebs/ebs_151_summ_en.pdf.

Section V

Children's Practice – Children as Participants

19

From Child Labour to Working Children's Movements

Olga Nieuwenhuys

If we look at children's work from a world history perspective, children have always played an active role in the economy and have worked as soon as they were able to. At first playfully imitating the working kin in whose vicinity they spent most of their time, they gradually learned to lend a helping hand in and around the household, normally growing into full-fledged workers only in their teens. The industrial revolution made some of this work – for which I reserve the use of the term 'child labour' – problematic. Child labour was typically conceived as a fairly recent phenomenon limited to industrial societies in Western Europe and North America, distinct from the more mundane activities which children continued to undertake. It came to be closely related to the notion of exploitation and fuelled a growing public sensitivity to the wrongs it implied in respect to children. The prohibition of child labour became a major post staking out the project of modern childhood. But it also gave more mundane activities that did not qualify as child labour, such as helping out in and around the home, working on the land and in the household and going to school, a positive flavour that they often did not deserve.

With the globalization of the world economy from the 1980s, the Northern vision of childhood as a period in life devoted to play, socialization and school came under pressure. In the global confrontation between employers and organized labour that ensued, working children's movements that had sprung up in the developing world criticized the distinction that had been drawn during the industrial revolution between child labour and beneficial work. The movements rejected the idea that children, by their very nature, would be more vulnerable to some kinds of work than adults. Though admitting that children can be, and often are, exploited, they stressed that exploitation is not related to an innate vulnerability of the child but to conditions of work. Among these figure long working hours, lack of proper wages, insufficient ventilation, light, safety, medical services, holidays, training facilities and lack of freedom of association. From a childhood studies perspective, the critique should not only be taken seriously, but also intimates, as I shall highlight, a reassessment of child labour prohibition in the North, and this again has consequences for the conceptualization of childhood.

In this chapter I first argue that working children's movements are the logical outcome of a global economic order that has made attempts at regulating child labour through legal means obsolete. Second, I highlight why working children's movements do not want their work to be abolished. Finally, I discuss the claims put forward by working children's movements and tease out critical questions for further research on childhood in today's globalized world.

What is child labour?

Child labour is not necessarily the same as work condemned by custom and religion or on the ground of philosophical, ethical and political considerations. Rather than being a more or less accurate measure of what is good or bad for children, as commonly believed, child labour is a legal notion that emerged to regulate the interests of powerful groups in society during the industrial revolution. Three parties played a major role: employers, trade unions and the state. Broadly speaking, the stakes of these parties in child labour were as follows: employers were believed to be under constant pressure for ever-cheaper labour; trade unions needed to protect adult jobs against this pressure; and the state guaranteed the implementation of labour laws. These interests are still reflected in the tripartite nature of the International Labour Organisation (ILO). But in today's globalized world they no longer represent the interests at stake in regulating the work of children. Some employers, such as multinational corporations, have become vastly more powerful than many states, while trade unions have been superseded by a colourful array of charitable organizations or non-governmental organizations (NGOs). The changes imply first, that legal understandings of child labour have waned into vagueness; second, that child labour issues tend to arise as proxies for trade wars and, finally, that this makes the role children play in the economy more explicit than it has ever been before, paving the way for the rise of working children's movements.

I begin with waning legal understandings of child labour in the North. Historically, where trade unions were strong, as in factories, mining and transport by rail, child labour was described in great detail and effectively banned. Where unions were weak or non-existent – as in agriculture, shops and family undertakings, and in the household or domestic service – the work of children remained largely unregulated and became something different from 'labour'. The state had in addition the privilege of excluding from the definition of child labour work that fell under its direct control such as schoolwork or work in prisons and in the army. Also excluded was work done for churches, cultural institutions and political parties. Save for a few exceptions, child labour laws did not apply to children in the colonies. For the colonizers, colonies were purveyors of cheap raw materials both for industry and for the consumption of the working class. Workers in the colonies were overwhelmingly either peasants who had to pay taxes in colonial produce (cocoa, tea, cotton, indigo, etc.) or young men and women sent from the villages to plantations, factories and mines to earn money to pay for taxes, including heavily taxed necessities such as salt and cloth. Colonial authorities often refused to admit that either peasants or young migrants would be 'workers' and would need to organize. In the colonizers' imagination they would rather need their 'traditional' culture and way of life protected against what they saw as corrupting socialist ideas (Grier, 2006).

But after the first three decades of de-colonization after World War II, in which hardly any attention was paid to the issue of child labour in the world, globalization suddenly turned the spotlight on working children in the developing world. With globalization teeming, masses of extremely cheap and unorganized labour now became directly available to employers willing to outsource and invest in China, India, Brazil and the rest of the developing world. A heavy confrontation ensued between the 'old' working class in the North, keen on preserving jobs, and Northern investors keen on exploiting the cheap labour of the developing world. Child labour came increasingly to represent the stake of a confrontation between Northern labour and capital. But in so doing, it also changed meaning and turned into a nebulous notion. Compare for example the United States of America of the 1930s with India 50 years later. One of the first US federal laws on child labour was passed in 1938 under the Fair Labor Standards Act. The act defined child labour as the *employment* of children under the age of 16 and made exception for children between 14 and 16 years of age working under non-hazardous conditions that did not interfere with their schooling, health or well-being. The Indian Child Labour Act of 1986 did not define child labour as employment of children under a certain age in general, but only as children below 14 in a very limited number of *occupations*. It listed in addition 19 *sectors* where children's health could be at stake, such as the manufacture of carpets, cement and fireworks – where children's work was not to be regulated, but prohibited. All other work was left, by implication, unregulated, inspiring a heated debate on whether the Indian state had forsaken its children or had rather recognized at last working children's contribution to the economy (Ramanathan, 2000). Though the occupations and sectors earmarked for prohibition or regulation are claimed to be particularly damaging for children's health, there is no clear evidence that they would be so more for children than for adults nor that other sectors or occupations would be less harmful, notably in agriculture. Agriculture is the single largest employer of children in both India and the rest of the world but produces cheap raw materials critical for the level of corporate profits, which may account for its being systematically ignored when it comes to child labour policies. The earmarked sectors such as matches, fireworks, brass, glass blowing, carpets, embroidery and so on share in common that they are typically artisanal sectors that employ large numbers of people and provide cheap goods for the local consumer. Though in these sectors children undeniably work under severe conditions, their choice also serves the interests of corporations seeking to curtail competition from local business.

That legal understandings have become muddled transpires also from ILO legislation. The earliest ILO Convention on Minimum Age for Employment in 1919 defined child labour as industrial *employment* of children under 14, and excluded children in colonized or semi-colonized countries such as India and China where the Convention did not apply. Considering the nature of the Chinese and Indian economies of the time, this meant that vast numbers of children would have worked legally from the age of about three to four, even if this work was carried out in inhuman conditions and was, by today's standards, mere slavery. Eighty years later, the ILO recognized the problem with Convention 182 (1999) , stating that earlier child labour conventions did not cover *the worst forms of child labour,* comprising:

(a) all forms of slavery or practices similar to slavery, such as the sale and traf-ficking of children, debt bondage and serfdom, and forced or compulsory labour, including forced or compulsory recruitment of children for use in armed conflict;

(b) the use, procuring or offering of a child for prostitution, for the production of pornography or for pornographic performances;

(c) the use, procuring or offering of a child for illicit activities, in particular for the production and trafficking of drugs as defined in the relevant inter-national treaties;

(d) work which, by its nature or the circumstances in which it is carried out, is likely to harm the health, safety or morals of children.

ILO Convention 182 has officially been presented as a complement to earlier international law. But it can also be seen differently: if there are worst forms of child labour that need to be prioritized, then other forms become at least tem-porarily tolerated in the developing world, even if they remain prohibited in the North. The latter interpretation makes sense when looking, as I do next, at child labour issues as a proxy for trade war.

Concern with child labour in the developing world is now tied in with trade, be it in attempts to bar membership of the World Trade Organization (WTO) to countries who do not comply, to boycott products from developing countries or to start consumer actions. Here I give only a few examples. Child labour gained an international profile as developing countries were forced – under pressure of mounting debts to Western banks, incurred following the sharp rise in oil prices in the 1970s – to pursue an open door policy. Governments drastically cut down on public spending to invest in incentives to step up production for export and attract foreign investment. The cuts paved the road for making masses of children available for work in the promise that developing countries would benefit from the comparative advantage of exchanging labour-intensive goods with capital-in-tensive ones from the North. The strategy was in line with neo-liberal economic theory underpinning globalization. To protect their jobs, however, Northern exporters and trade unions started looking for ways to prevent cheap products from the developing world from entering Northern markets and threatening jobs. The 1990s saw mounting trade union pressure to introduce a 'social clause' as a condition for WTO membership. The social clause would exclude from member-ship countries that did not abide by minimum labour standards, including the prohibition of using slave, forced or child labour (Chan, 2003). The United States of America witnessed campaigns in favour of Senator Harkin's bill that anticipated the boycotting of products drenched, as the campaigners claimed, 'in the blood and sweat of children'. Though the bill was never passed, Bangladesh garment producers felt threatened and dismissed overnight the children working on their premises, with dramatic consequences for an alleged 50,000 children (Bachman, 2003, 2000; Nielsen, 2005). The boycott was never effectuated, because the WTO Singapore first ministerial meeting (1996) rejected the social clause and referred the issue of child labour to the ILO. As the ILO lacks the WTO system of sanctions and depends on voluntary cooperation, this was in fact a defeat. The trade unions were left with little else than to campaign for a new ILO Convention on child labour. As said, this may not be what ILO Convention 182 of 1999 actually does. Many signatory states in Africa, Latin America and Asia are deeply in debt and have higher priorities than a ban on child labour even in its worst forms. With boycotts out of the question, trade unions' strategies now aim at pressurizing corporations to adopt codes of conduct and run their business ethically, sensitizing the public, launching consumer actions in favour of child-labour-free products such as carpets, soccer balls and clothes, and supporting NGOs devoted to stopping the use of child labour.

NGO interventions place primary emphasis on children deemed at greatest risk, such as children in bondage, child soldiers or sexually exploited children. The typical package includes micro-credits to encourage parents to start a small business, non-formal education that can be combined with work, and training in children's rights advocacy. NGOs depend on Northern funding that merges corporate, government and church interests. They naturally target children in sectors of the urban economy and tend to ignore conditions in the supply chain, particularly in agriculture. They are, in addition, strictly monitored and kept on such a tight string that they can do little else than set examples and encourage working children to follow suit. Propping up media icons of the branded victims of 'the worst forms of child labour' to sensitize the public, NGOs have ushered working children on to the stage of national and international politics – with two consequences: suggesting, first, that child labour would be typically a problem of distant developing countries struggling with antiquated ideas of children's role in society; second, that working children actually want their work to be prohibited. I return to the first suggestion in the third section. The second suggestion is about what working children actually want, and is the topic of what follows.

Children's role in the moral economy

My argument here is that rather than wanting their work prohibited, working children feel that they should be offered, together with their families, reasonable alternatives that take their social and economic responsibilities into account. Both in the North and in the South children's roles are attuned to the performance of work that helps the family cope and contributes to creating long-term relations of solidarity and mutual support (for an elaboration see Nieuwenhuys, 2005). Even if we tend to believe that children in the South work because of abject poverty and those in the North because they wish to learn about the world, the reality is far more complex (Lavallette, 1994; Orellana, 2001; Mizen, 2005). The presence of a strong state in the North effectively controlling children's work does make a difference insofar as children have less choice in the jobs they do and must spend most of their time in school, where their work is unpaid and unacknowledged (Qvortrup, 2001). But both in the North and in the South, working outside school hours is for many children a way to help their families, gain respect and learn to work and be responsible (Leonard, 2004; Aitken, 2006). In spite of dramatic differences in wealth, these reasons are related to children being at the core of what anthropologists have termed the 'moral economy'. This economy is most visible where, in the absence of a strong state, the extended family is the sole source of support and long-term security. For the vast majority, schools do not lead to employment opportunities and incomes are at a depressingly low level; the majority of children start working at the earliest age, by the side of their parents. The legendary cheapness of products from the developing world flooding Northern markets is, as I highlight below, entrenched in entire families, including their often many children, working in close cooperation to enhance income and reduce expenditure.

Few children in the developing world enter in direct competition with adult workers, as Northern trade unions fear. Families work together, the children generally performing subsidiary tasks (De Suremain, 2000; Swaminathan, 1998; Chandrasekhar, 1997; Nieuwenhuys, 1994). Children's work is also often inseparable from a host of domestic chores such as caring for infants, collecting firewood or fetching water – crucial to make ends meet with the meagre proceeds of labour. Take for example the situation in Olinda, northwest Brazil, where children undertake a whole range of disparate odd jobs to help the family cope. Next to mandatory work in the home and in child care, even small children seek to earn a few coins by drawing water or running errands for a wealthier neighbour, while the older ones set out to sell flowers, sweets, newspapers and cigarettes, or work as shoe-shiners and tourist guides. Work is scarce and adults find it difficult to earn enough to feed the family. A man's wage will normally cover only a third of the necessary expenses. Children are lucky if they succeed in finding a more or less stable source of income that keeps them out of criminal circuits (Kenny, 2007).

The situation in Bhavnagar, a small town in northwest India near to Mumbai that specializes in dismantling and recycling material from shipwrecks and diamond cutting, is exemplary of how corporate interests weave into children's subsistence and domestic tasks. Swaminathan (1998) observed how children may be involved in a whole range of activities loosely connected with the expansion of corporate business: cleaning cement bags for reuse, sorting waste, helping out in shops and doing domestic work. It matters little whether the children have been to school; paid work is difficult to get and most have to engage in badly paid piece work or work that is paid in kind. Particularly girls and younger children will have to content themselves with domestic work, sorting waste and piece work at home. The older boys may think themselves lucky if they find work in diamond cutting (Swaminathan, 1998). A similar situation exists in match making, a sector that employs an estimated half a million children, most of them girls, working in inhumane conditions in a poverty-stricken dry region of southeast Tamil Nadu in South India, Sivakasi. The industry sprawls over the rural countryside where middlemen put out work to girls working at home on a piece rate. Only an estimated 100,000 children find employment in the small workshops that have sprung up around the city of Sivakasi. That match making is one of the sectors regulated by the Indian Child Labour Act may not be unrelated to the difficulties that foreign business finds in entering a market saturated by the cheap products of children clinging to the industry for their livelihoods (Chandrasekhar, 1997).

The volume of profits realized under such conditions can be gauged from my own study of children's work in fishing and coir making, two important export sectors in the south-western Indian state of Kerala. Children worked normally only as helpers of adults and received in compensation either only a reduction of the family's debt to the employer or some fish and pocket money. Children not only provided extremely cheap labour; they also contributed substantially to their upkeep, including schooling costs, so that adults could be paid daily wages barely sufficient for their personal maintenance. In the course of their daily routines, children undertook scores of activities such as child care, firewood collection, fishing, and gathering wild fruits and vegetables. In practice, this meant that the holder of capital invested in fishing and coir could realize profits of the order of 120 per cent (Nieuwenhuys, 1994). In other words, children's work is a highly profitable business precisely because it is embedded in the moral economy of the family and is done for a trifle out of love. When attempts at regulation deny children a proper wage, neglect to reduce their drudgery and are in addition highly selective, as is the case in today's developing world, it is difficult not to conclude that the real issue is about who reaps the profits. This is where the working children's movements come in.

Working children's movements

Far from seeing them as the victims of ignorant parents lacking a proper understanding of childhood, working children's movements see their members as active participants of their social world and want their right to work in dignity and to organize to fight exploitation recognized. They do not reject schooling, but believe that children also learn when at work. Schooling should be an option that is open to working children, which they can combine with work but which should not be compulsory or a tool to prevent them from working. Their position is far removed from the trade union model of child labour prohibition. The model would underestimate working children's ability to shoulder responsibilities towards their families and to contribute to the economy. They would view working children too exclusively as victims of poverty and ignorance and fail to recognize their agency in the making of their own societies. In their use of the term 'working children', the movements articulate that working to help their family and contribute to society does not render children less 'children' than their supposedly non-working peers in wealthier classes or countries (Hanson and Van Daele, 2003; Liebel, 2004).

Concerned activists in the developing world have triggered debates since the late 1970s on the political and economic role of children in society and helped draft labour laws that recognize that developing-world children normally work from a tender age. They have thrived on the multiplication of international meetings and declarations meant to unite working children behind a programme of action. A historical landmark was reached in 1996 in the south Indian town of Kundapur, where an international meeting of working children produced the *Kundapur Ten Points*. As country-wise consultations to draft ILO Convention 182 started in the course of 1996, activists had pressed for a consultation with working children. A number of NGOs with a record in child participation – among them CWC (India), ENDA (West Africa) and the Movement of Working Children and Adolescents from Christian Working Class Families (MANTHOC [Peru]) – sent delegates to Kundapur. About 30 working children, representing as many countries, discussed for two weeks their common concerns and drafted the following demands:

1. We want recognition of our problems, our initiatives, proposals and our process of organization.
2. We are against the boycott of products made by children.
3. We want respect and security for ourselves and the work we do.
4. We want an education system whose methodology and content are adapted to our reality.
5. We want professional training adapted to our reality and capabilities.
6. We want access to good health care for working children.
7. We want to be consulted in all decisions concerning us, at local, national or international level.
8. We want the root causes of our situation, primarily poverty, to be addressed and tackled.
9. We want more activities in rural areas and decentralization in decision-making, so that children will no longer be forced to migrate.
10. We are against exploitation at work but we are for work with dignity with hours adapted so that we have time for education and leisure.

Though demanding that adults respect their work and taking a firm stand against boycotts, working children do not want to compete with adults for jobs. They recognize adults' duties towards children and propose being their allies in a common struggle for the dignity of all workers. Their wish to organize separately is born out of the dreaded effects of anti-child-labour campaigning from which they are excluded, not from a feeling that their interests would be separate from those of adult workers. In points four ('we want an education system whose methodology and content are adapted to our reality') and five ('we want professional training adapted to our reality and capabilities') the children also criticize the type of low-cost, basic education programmes offered as an alternative to work. They feel that these programmes fail to build on their work experience and do not address their needs in terms of skills training (Bonnet, 2006).

What was the background of the delegates that drafted the Kundapur Ten Points? I will look at three organizations, one for each continent: Bhima Sangha (India); African Movement of Working Children and Youth (AMWCY) (West Africa); and MANTHOC (Peru). To start with Bhima Sangha, in the early 1980s trade union activists in south India discovered that many children attended the meetings they held for workers in the informal sector. Child labour being prohibited, none of the regulations applicable to adult workers were applicable in case the worker was a child: no minimum wage, no job protection, no security, and so on. Children were also by law barred from union membership. The situation was likely to worsen as the ILO was putting pressure on the Indian government to ratify its child labour Conventions. Realizing that most of the working children in Bangalore were migrants from rural areas, CWC activists started projects in surrounding villages to provide education and occupational training to working children. In 1989, they launched a newspaper for and by young workers, which eventually led to the founding of Bhima Sangha, a children's union that now has a membership of several thousand. The union organizes elections of children's village councils, runs a training centre for working children, entertains close links with a union for youths older than 18 and is also associated with working children's movements in other countries, notably in Asia.

The AMWCY formed out of groups of migrant children reaching the cities in the course of the 1980s in search of a livelihood as porters, shoe-shiners, rag-pickers and maids. A first meeting of street and working children was held in Grand Bassam (Ivory Coast) in 1985. Convinced of their ability to identify and sustain actions on their behalf, participants requested from a Dakar-based NGO ENDA the creation of a section for children and youth. A first movement went public on 1 May 1992, when a group of young maids in Dakar decided to participate in the celebrations of Workers' Day. Senegalese trade unions welcomed the initiative. During a meeting in 1994 in Bouaké (Ivory Coast), working children from a number of African countries founded the AMWCY and drafted a list of 12 rights that would inspire the Kundapur Ten Points.

MANTHOC (Peru) started in the 1970s, when the Peruvian state was under military dictatorship. Massive lay-offs swelled the ranks of children and youth working in Lima's streets. These children and youths faced outrageous working conditions. Charitable responses from the church and the voluntary sector at best rescued a few and at worst failed to equip them to survive independently when adults. Drugs trafficking worsened the situation, turning poor children into targets of police repression. Young militants of the left Catholic Young Christian Workers started organizing children with a view to preparing them for active union membership when adults. MANTHOC does not propose to eradicate child labour but to defend the rights of children as workers. It seeks to foster not just an individual, but also a collective social and political identity for these children as actors of social change.

The Kundapur delegates, then, came from movements emerging from the 1970s in the wake of the crisis sweeping across the developing world. By the time member states started, in 1998, consultations to draft ILO Convention 182, working children's movements had not only a reasonably well-developed agenda of action, but had networked internationally and could count on growing support both from developing country governments and the public. As said, the trade war that pitted the South against the North had crystallized around the child labour issue, propelling working children to the stage of world politics. There they could vent their critique that their situation had been ignored as long as the interests of the North had not been at stake. They could also propose new forms of global solidarity where adults unsuccessfully tried to apply old abolitionist formulas, intimating the depth of the changes that globalization has brought to bear on *children's* role in society as well as conceptions of childhood.

Conclusion

The difficulties that today's attempts at prohibiting child labour encounter imply that something has been missing in the Northern narrative of successful child labour abolition as a seminal ingredient of childhood in industrial societies. In spite of declarations of good intentions, the concerns of well-organized, relatively privileged adult workers in North America and Europe have formed the backbone of how child labour has informed the myth of childhood as divorced from political economy (Watson, 2004). With globalization turning working children in the developing world into icons of a new trade war the myth has exploded. As working children's movements rose to world attention with their claim that a ban on their products would rob them of their livelihood, they unveiled a truth glossed over by child labour legislation: that the world over, children work to support their families and need to be recognized and respected for their economic contribution.

The claim makes one ponder whether child labour was ever abolished in the North. Legislation remained limited to work where children could have competed against adults and endangered their job security. It created the illusion of childhood as a time of leisure, play and learning, underplaying mandatory work in the household, in the fields and at school. While children in the industrial North undoubtedly stood to gain, this conception of childhood naturalized the immense suffering of children that took place at the same time in colonized tropical countries. If we are to take the project of extending justice and equal opportunities to all children in the world seriously, a radical revision of childhood theory in the light of this omission may be a necessary step.

Three directions could be fruitfully pursued. The first pertains to problematizing the distinction between harmful and beneficial work. At issue is how the distinction naturalizes the exploitative practices that may take place when children perform their unpaid mandatory activities, including schoolwork or work outside school hours. In the North this type of work is treated as unproblematic and even a sign of the superiority of Northern childhood. In the South, it hides the crucial economic link between the exploitation of children's work and corporate profits. The second direction is about the reasons for the conspicuous absence of working children's movements in the North. I gauge that it is less on account of their not being exploited than of the state's power to enforce a regime of truth about the superiority of Northern childhood. The imagery of the coloured Asian child as the icon of today's child labour issue should leave no doubts that this regime rests on racist prejudice preventing working children from building solidarity on the basis of shared global interests and experiences. This brings me to the third direction. If working children organize in the developing world it is not only to fight day-to-day exploitation but perhaps even more to contest the construction of child labour as a phenomenon to be abolished for them but without them. The question is not merely about the fate of working children in the developing world. Globalization has also transformed the experience of childhood in the North in many different ways. Can childhood survive the challenge that globalization represents? How? The stage is set for a critical debate on the nature of both childhood and work from which working children can no longer be excluded.

References

Aitken, S., S.L. Estrada, J. Jennongs and L.M. Aguirre (2006) 'Producing Life and Labour: Global Processes and Working Children in Tijuana, Mexico', *Childhood*, 13(3): 365–388.

Bachman, S.L. (2000). 'A New Economics of Child Labor: Searching for Answers behind the Headlines', *Journal of International Affairs*, 53(2): 545–572.

Bachman, S.L. (2003) The (Limited) Case for Boycott Threats, Boycotts and Selective Purchasing, *Ethique Économique/Ethics and Economics,1, http:\\Ethique.economique.org*

Bonnet, M., K. Hanson, M.-F. Lange, O. Nieuwenhuys, G. Paillet and B. Schlemmer (2006) *Enfants Travailleurs: Repenser l' Enfance*. Lausanne: Page-deux.

Chan, A. and R.J.S. Ross (2003) 'Racing to the Bottom: International Trade without a Social Clause', *Third World Quarterly*, 24(6): 1011–1028.

Chandrasekhar, C.P. (1997) 'The Economic Consequences of the Abolition of Child Labor : An Indian Case Study', *Journal of Peasant Studies*, 24(3): 137–179.

De Suremain, C.-E. (2000) 'Coffee Beans and the Seeds of Labour: Child Labour in Guatemalan Plantations', in Schlemmer (ed.) *The Exploited Child*. London and New York: ZED, pp. 231–238.

Grier, B.C. (2006) *Invisible Hands: Child Labor and the State in Colonial Zimbabwe*, Portsmouth NH: Heinemann

Hanson, K. and A. Vandaele (2003) 'Working Children and International Labour Law: A Critical Analysis', *The International Journal of Children's Rights*. 11: 73–146.

Kenny, M.L. (2007) *Hidden Heads of Households: Child Labor in Urban Northeast Brazil*, Peterborough ON: Broadview Press.

Lavallette, M. (1994) *Child Employment in the Capitalist Labour Market*. Aldershot: Avebury.

Leonard, M. (2004) 'Children's Views on Children's Rights to Work: Reflections from Belfast', *Childhood*, 11(1): 45–62.

Liebel, M. (2004) *A Will of Their Own, Cross-Cultural Perspectives on Working Children*. London: ZED.

Mizen, P. (2005) 'A Little Light Work? Children's Images of their Labour', *Visual Studies*, 20(2): 124–139.

Nielsen, M.E. (2005) 'The Politics of Corporate Responsibility and Child Labour in the Bangladeshi Garment Industry', *International Affairs*, 81(3): 559–580.

Nieuwenhuys, O. (1994 and 2000) *Children's Lifeworlds, Gender, Labour and Welfare in the Developing World*. London: Routledge and New Delhi: Social Science Press.

Nieuwenhuys, O. (2005) 'The Wealth of Children: Reconsidering the Child Labour Debate', in Qvortrup, J. (ed.) *Studies in Modern Childhood*. London: Palgrave. pp. 167–183.

Orellana, M. (2001) 'The Work Kids Do: Mexican and Central American Immigrant Children's Contributions to Households and Schools in California', *Harvard Educational Review,* 71: 366–389.

Qvortrup, J. (2001) 'Children's Schoolwork: Useful and Necessary', *Brood & Rozen, Tijdschrift voor Geschiedenis van de Sociale Bewegingen,* 4: 145–162.

Ramanathan, U. (2000) 'The Public Policy Problem: Labour and the Law in India', in B. Schlemmer (ed.) *The Exploited Child.* London: ZED. pp. 146–159.

Swaminathan, M. (1998) 'Economic Growth and the Persistence of Child Labor: Evidence from an Indian City', *World Development,* 26(8): 1513–1528.

Watson, A.M.S. (2004) 'Seen but Not Heard: the Role of the Child in International Political Economy', *New Political Economy,* 9(1): 3–21.

20
Peer Culture
William A. Corsaro

Theoretical and conceptual issues

Much early work on peer culture focused on adolescents with the main concern being on outcomes (positive and negative) of experience with peers on individual development. New theoretical approaches to childhood studies see children and their peer cultures as worthy of documentation and study in their own right. From this new perspective peer culture is defined as a stable set of activities or routines, artefacts, values and concerns that children produce and share in interaction with peers (Corsaro and Eder, 1990; Corsaro, 2005).

From this definition it is clear that the concept of peer culture differs from that of peer group. Children are *members* of peer groups (i.e., groups of children of relatively the same age although the age range can vary), while children collectively *produce* their peer cultures. In fact, children produce and participate in a series of peer cultures that are affected by arrangements of children in various settings (neighbourhoods, schools, city streets, village compounds and so on) that result from age grading and other mechanisms of placing cohorts or groups of children together for extended periods of time.

To argue that children produce their own peer cultures does not mean that such cultures are separate from adult culture. Children's peer cultures are not a sort of tribal childhood (James, Jenks and Prout, 1998) making up some part of their lives separate from the adult world. Children are always participating in and are part of two cultures – children's and adults' – and these cultures are intricately interwoven in different ways across space and over time (Corsaro, 2005). This position is in line with Qvortrup's structural approach to childhood in which: childhood constitutes a particular structural form, childhood is exposed to the same societal forces as adulthood, and children are themselves co-constructors of childhood and society (1991). However, the production of peer culture is a matter neither of simple imitation nor of direct appropriation of the adult world. Children creatively appropriate information from adult culture to produce their own peer cultures. Such appropriation is creative in that it both extends or elaborates peer culture and simultaneously contributes to the reproduction and extension of the adult world.

This process of creative appropriation is seen as *interpretive reproduction* (Corsaro, 1992; 2005) in line with Giddens' notion of the duality of social structure in which he argues that 'structural properties of social systems are both medium and outcome of the practices they recursively organize' (1984, 25). It is in this sense that interpretive reproduction differs from other theories of social reproduction in that it sees social structure as both constraining and enabling. The process is interpretive because children do not simply individually internalize the external adult culture. Rather peer culture is at the core of reproduction and change. Children become a part of adult culture and contribute to its reproduction and extension through their collective negotiations and interactions with adults and their production of a series of peer cultures with other children (Corsaro, 2005).

Central themes in peer cultures

Given this is a handbook of child studies, this chapter will concentrate on empirical studies of children's peer cultures and not the rich literature on youth culture or subcultures. Although a wide range of features of children's peer cultures have been identified, two central themes consistently appear: Children make persistent attempts to *gain control* of their lives and to *share* that control with each other. In early childhood years (two to six years old), children have an overriding concern with social participation and develop strategies for challenging adult authority. In preadolescence (seven to twelve years old), the challenging of adult authority persists and is accompanied by increased desire for autonomy, but there is also often a gradual movement towards social differentiation within the peer culture.

Most of the empirical work on children's cultures has taken place in Western societies (primarily the United States, Canada and Europe). Studies in other cultures have focused on children's activities and primarily examined the types and frequencies of children's play and work in their households and communities. Recently, there have been more detailed ethnographic studies in a number of non-western societies which have gone beyond the documentation of children's activities to look closer at their daily lives and their interactions with peers.

Children's peer cultures in western societies

In this section I discuss generally what we know about sharing, participation and friendships as well as autonomy, control and differentiation in children's peer cultures in western societies. The review is by no means exhaustive; instead it focuses on what I see as key aspects in some detail in line with our earlier definition of peer culture. I concentrate primarily on younger children as other chapters in this volume (Evaldsson and Frønes) consider the activities of preadolescent children.

Sharing, participation and friendships

How early, given our definition, do children produce and participate in an initial peer culture? With the dramatic increase in dual-career and single-parent families in the United States and Europe, children as young as two years old are spending considerable time with peers in child care centres. Several studies in France, Italy, and Norway document how toddlers engage in routines that demonstrate shared emotional satisfaction and in some cases creatively use objects in areas of child care centres for other than their intended adult-designed purposes (Mussati and Panni, 1981; Corsaro and Molinari, 1990; Løkken, 2000a, 2000b).

One example, the 'little chairs routine', captures complex elements of toddler play (Corsaro and Molinari, 1990). This routine developed spontaneously among toddlers in an Italian preschool for two- and three-year-olds, and was extended and embellished over the course of the school year. It began as children played with the small chairs, first pushing them around the room like small cars and bumping them together. One day some children pushed the chairs to make a long line from one wall to a small platform sitting against the opposite wall. Once the line was finished, the children made sure that the chairs were together with no gaps and that the line was straight. Then the children walked across the room from chair to chair – sometimes swaying a bit and saying 'I'm falling! I'm falling!' but always keeping their balance – until they reached the platform and jumped down. The teachers noticed this play and told the children to be careful, but did not intervene. Over time the line of chairs was constructed in different ways, children sometimes hopped instead of walked, and always reminded each other that they must be careful.

In this example we see not only the creation and embellishment of a routine of peer culture among very young children, but also an implicit challenge of the teachers' authority. The chairs were to sit on and not walk on. However, the teachers were impressed with the children's invention and allowed it to occur as long as the children played carefully. Thus, the children felt a sense of control and took it upon themselves to monitor the correct and careful way to walk on the chairs.

Numerous studies document the complexity of young children's fantasy play in preschools and in homes in the United States and Europe. Children's fantasy play is emotion-laden and helps them deal with various concerns like being lost, facing a variety of dangers, and death (Corsaro, 1985, 2003; Löfdahl, 2005). Sawyer (1997), relying on work in metapragmatics, impressively identifies the poetic nature of American children's fantasy play. These poetic performances in children's fantasy play are part of shared peer culture in that they are created in an improvised fashion that Sawyer calls 'collaborative emergence' (Sawyer, 2002). By collaborative emergence Sawyer means that children's improvised play is unpredictable and contingent upon the ongoing turn-by-turn production of the fantasy play narrative. Thus, one child 'proposes a new development for the play, and other children respond by modifying or embellishing the proposal' (Sawyer, 2002, 340). Sawyer argues, however, that the researcher can interpret the particular episode of fantasy play by assuming that the play narrative ceases with the end of a particular play episode.

Johannesen (2004; also see Corsaro and Johannesen, 2007) in her study of children's fantasy play with Lego extends Sawyer's work by entering the practice of fantasy play in terms of the practice itself. She does this by considering the in-frame reality as voiced by the Lego play characters as a real world, and the voices as expressing real experiences. Given her work is longitudinal with the study of play with Lego by the same children over a long period of time, Johannesen demonstrates that the Lego characters remain intact even when they, as embodied in play artefacts, are stacked away from one day or week to the next. Over time the play-reality persists and becomes increasingly complex as the characters plan and experience recurring episodes of danger-rescue and other themes. These recurrent experiences materialize in the enduring relational identities, artefacts, and of the participants in the play. Thus we see many of the aspects of peer culture (play routines, values and concerns, and artefacts) in the shared production of fantasy play, over time (Corsaro and Johannesen, 2007).

In her work in 'doing reality with play,' based on observations of Finnish preschool children, Strandell (1997) makes a similar point, maintaining that play in the peer culture should not be seen only as a means of reaching adult competence. Rather she argues that play is a resource children use in their everyday life activities in the peer culture. Interestingly these and other studies of fantasy play demonstrate language and improvisational skills among the young children that some have argued surpass those of the majority of older children and adults.

Young children's dramatic role play differs from fantasy play in that children take on real roles that exist in society like mothers, police, construction workers and so on. Role play goes beyond mere reproduction of various real life scripts, as children appropriate and embellish adult models to fit their concerns and values. In role play children have a sense of status as power and authority over others, displayed in the children's action and language in role play in the home, neighbourhood and preschool (Garvey, 1977; Goodwin, 1990; Corsaro, 2003; Kalliala, 2006). Also, children tend to embellish role play themes to make them more interesting and dramatic in the peer culture. For example, in a role play scenario in an Italian preschool a girl created an ice cream store making ice cream from materials present in the outside yard (sand for vanilla, dirt for chocolate, leaves for pistachio). She then asked other kids if they wanted ice cream from her store, but she very specifically listed the only flavours available. Instead of first choosing one of these flavours the others always asked for one not on the list, such as lemon or in one case a very rare flavour *zuppa inglise* derived from the English dessert trifle. The girl who made the store was not upset with these orders, but instead enjoyed denying they were available saying '*Non c'é limone, non c'é zuppa inglise!*' with a great deal of relish. In this example, children go beyond enacting a role play theme to 'ply the frame' (Goffman, 1974) of the play and the whole role play becomes about 'playing with the play.'

Finally, in studies of role play across social class and racial groups in American preschools, Corsaro found interesting differences. Middle-class white children often mixed fantasy and reality in role play, while poor African-American children stayed very close to the reality of the real life models, often including challenging aspects of their lives and the lives of their families living in poverty (Corsaro, Molinari and Rosier, 2002).

It is in these routines and activities of the peer culture that children begin to talk about and form friendships. Shared play is verbally marked with the oft heard phrase 'We're friends, right?' Young children (three- to six-year-olds) often play regularly with a large number of other children in preschools (normally seven or eight children). However, gaining access to ongoing play is particularly difficult regardless of past shared experiences because play activities are fragile and children tend to protect their interactive space by resisting the entry of other children (Corsaro, 2003, 2005). Resistance of access attempts seems uncooperative or selfish to adults, but it is not that that children are resisting the idea of sharing. In fact, from the children's point of view they want to keep sharing what they are already sharing, and they know from past experience that entry of others often disrupts shared play. Over time in particular, preschool groups most children meet the challenge of resistance and develop a complex set of access strategies. These strategies are successful because they are composed of indirect techniques which communicate that the child attempting to gain entry has knowledge of the play theme and knows how to play without being disruptive (Corsaro, 2005).

Children's early friendships in preschools can become close with a good deal of shared understanding and intimacy (Corsaro, 2003; Dunn, 2004). They often become increasingly gender segregated in line with play preferences, but the degree of gender segregation is much less than in early elementary school and can vary across sub-cultural and cultural groups (Corsaro, 2003).

Autonomy, control, conflict and differentiation

Earlier I noted that a major theme of peer culture revolves around children gaining a sense of control over their lives. In fact, we know from numerous studies in the home and in schools that children and youth have a strong desire to achieve autonomy from the rules and authority of adult caretakers, and gain control of their lives (Adler and Adler, 1998; Corsaro, 2003, 2005). This issue of autonomy is apparent not only in children's active challenges of adult control, but also in a variety of play routines in which children confront confusions and fears from the adult world. These routines can be part of the peer culture in particular schools and also related to various festivals or rituals for children that are created by adults and celebrated in homes and communities.

Some researchers maintain that challenging and mocking adult authority may be a universal feature of peer cultures (Schwartzman, 1978; Corsaro, 2005). Such mocking of adults begins very early. In a study in a Finnish preschool when a group of three-year-olds were asked to show older children, who have just arrived back to the school from an outing, how nicely they can eat their snack, both the younger and older children instead begin calling out each others names and then the names of animals (Strandell, 1997). The teachers are not happy and tell the children to settle down. However, the mischief only escalates. When some children finish eating and run into the hall, a teacher calls them back saying, 'How about saying thank you!' One girl, Pia, stands by the dining room door and shouts, 'Thank you so much ladies!' All the other children now laugh and shout, 'Thanks ladies!' A teacher tries to control the situation by saying 'That's enough now' in a calm voice, only to have one of the children shout 'Enough!' to more laughter (Strandell, 1997, 459–460). The teachers are put in a difficult situation here because of the children's clever use of language. They do what they are told, but in a way that clearly puts them in control of the situation.

Corsaro (1985, 2003, 2005) has documented children's strategies for getting around adult conventional (as opposed to moral) rules in preschool in the United States and Italy. In line with Goffman's (1961) work on adults in total institutions, Corsaro refers to the children's strategies as *secondary adjustments* and the children's creation and sharing of these secondary adjustments as composing the *underlife* of preschools. For example, rules in most preschools limit or prohibit children from bringing personal items from home to school. The rule is conventional or organizational because teachers know that children often fight over such objects and these disputes can result in the items being damaged. But children get around the rule primarily by smuggling small objects to school which they hide in their pockets. Matchbox race cars, tiny dolls and small action figures are particular favourites. The smugglers almost never played with the toy alone, but show it to another child and then the two or sometimes more played with it surreptitiously, or so they thought. In fact, teachers usually saw what was going on, but ignored it as long as children did not fight over the toy.

The children were very careful in their play, returning smuggled objects to their pockets when a teacher passed and sharing a sly smile with their playmates. In fact, after a while 'getting around the rule' was just as important as playing with the forbidden object. Here we clearly see collective cultural production by the preschoolers. The children did not get the idea from parents, as it is extremely unlikely that a parent would advise, 'So the teacher says no bringing toys, well you can fool her by taking something small like your race car and hiding it in your pocket.' No, the kids come up with the idea themselves and then it can be passed on to other kids.

Corsaro identified many other types of secondary adjustments in preschools related to rules about indoor and outdoor play and especially the much dreaded 'clean up time' that occurs at different points (before snack, lunch, outside time and nap time) in a normal preschool day. Many kids did not see the logic of clean up time. Corsaro (1985) overheard one boy say to another, 'Clean up time is dumb, dumb, dumb. We could just leave our trucks here and play with them after snack time!'

The children Corsaro studied came up with many ways of avoiding or delaying their involvement in clean up including relocating as soon as the announcement is made; pretending not to hear the announcement; and using personal-problem delays (having some other pressing business that is more important). The last of these strategies is very inventive and involves things like feigning a personal injury or pretending to be dead as part of fantasy play, among others, including one boy's strategy of going around and giving all the other kids and teachers a 'big hug' during clean up (Corsaro, 2003).

Children also address shared fears, concerns and values in the types of fantasy and role play we discussed earlier. For example children in the pre-Civil War

South in the United States often engaged in auction role play which helped them deal with the very real fears of being separated from their plantation communities (Wiggins, 1985; Alston, 1992). Corsaro (2005) documented American and Italian children's approach-avoidance play in which a child is spontaneously forced into the role of a monster or wild animal who the other children then approach and avoid by running to a home base. This spontaneous play is related to a number of types of children's games (see Evaldsson, this volume).

Controlling fears and gaining a sense of autonomy can also be seen in children's participation in various rituals in western society. For example, children are fascinated with the tooth fairy, who brings them money for the painful experience of losing their baby teeth (Clark, 1995). Also figures like Santa Claus in many cultures and *La Befana* in Italy are primarily seen as benevolent, but will not bring toys or candy when children are bad. They also supposedly have magical powers and can see and remember children's bad behaviour and could bring lumps of coal instead of gifts (Clark, 1995; Corsaro, 2005). Clark (2005) in one of many interesting accounts of Halloween in the United States shows how this holiday for children and its various aspects from trick-or-treating, to the building of horrifying yard displays of tombs and skeletons, to even adults dressed as ghosts or vampires answering the door both give children a sense of control and instil real fears especially among younger children. Clark found that children love the idea of dressing up and being able to threaten adults with a trick for the reward of candy. On the other hand, many children were especially fearful of haunted houses and other frightening displays. As one child said, 'if you're really, really, really scared it's not fun' (Clark, 2005, 193).

Surprisingly, a good deal of work on children's peer relations and friendships documents the importance of discussion, debate and conflict (Rizzo, 1989; Corsaro, 1994, 2005). Corsaro found that Italian and African-American preschool children often develop friendship ties through debates and teasing. Neither these children nor their teachers were overly sensitive to conflict. On the contrary, disagreements, debates and teasing were valued in peer relations. In contrast, white middle-class American preschool children were highly sensitive to conflict and became upset when it occurred, often quickly going to teachers for aid in settling their disputes. On the other hand, the middle-class American children were much more likely to use the denial of friendship ('I won't be your friend' or 'You can't come to my birthday party') to try to control the behaviour of their peers (Corsaro, 1994). Corsaro discusses how these patterns are related to social relations and beliefs in the children's families and communities, reminding us again how peer and adult cultures are interrelated. These findings are similar to research on older preadolescent children (Fine, 1987; Rizzo, 1989; Goodwin, 1990, 1998; Poveda and Marcos, 2005; also see Evaldsson, this volume) that documents the role of conflict and peer relations among children of different social class, ethnic, and cultural groups.

As noted earlier the first sign of differentiation in young children's peer cultures is increasing gender separation, with children as young as age three preferring to play with children of the same sex. Differentiation by status in peer cultures is rare among preschool children and develops more in elementary school and reaches a peak in middle and high school (Adler and Adler, 1998; Eder and Nenga, 2003). Gender separation increases towards the end of the preschool period and in the early grades of elementary school (Berentzen, 1984; Davies, 1989; Thorne, 1993) leading Thorne to note that 'it is meaningful to speak of separate girls' and boys' worlds' (1986, 167).

However, as Thorne (1993) herself argued later, much of the work has a tendency to exaggerate gender differences and ignore similarities. Boys and girls do play and work together in educational settings, especially on group projects. Also features of composition, setting, culture and ethnicity are important. Goodwin (1990, 2003) found that African-American boys and girls often engaged in playful, cross-sex debates and teasing. Corsaro and Molinari (2005, also see Aydt and Corsaro, 2003) found that Italian children who stay together in the same group with the same teachers throughout elementary school display much less gender segregation than white middle-class American children. Evaldsson (1993, 2003, this volume) reports similar findings for Swedish elementary-school children.

These findings reflect new theories regarding gender identity which focus on children's collective practices in their peer cultures (Fine, 1987; Davies, 1989; Thorne, 1993). Following an interpretive and cultural perspective, Thorne (1993) and Goodwin (2003) advocate taking a non-gendered, contextual approach. They believe that when researchers enter the field expecting gender differences, they will limit their ability to see similarities among girls and boys. This approach also argues for comparative research in a wide variety of social and cultural contexts. This need for comparative research is important for understanding children's peer cultures more generally. We now turn to a discussion of what we know about children's peer cultures in non-western cultures.

Children's peer cultures in non-western societies

We know much less about the nature and complexity of children's peer cultures in non-western societies for a variety of reasons. First, most of the research focuses on children's psychological development rather than the nature of their childhoods and peer cultures. Secondly, children in non-western societies often live challenging lives due to poverty and political instability and often enter the adult world of work at an early age. Research on children in these circumstances is more applied and focuses on documenting the poor conditions of children's lives and developing programs and policies to provide them education and opportunities to have some degree of a childhood. Still some of these studies directly or indirectly document aspects of peer cultures among the children they study and for whom they advocate better lives. Thirdly, the dominance of the English language in the world (especially the western academic world) means that many studies and reports of children's lives in non-western cultures are not known beyond a particular society or group of societies which share the particular or a similar language. International conferences and journals have helped to better disseminate some of this work in English, but this process is still one way. We will know much more about children's cultures and childhood in general when more of us are literate in more languages and less dependent on English as the dominate language of the western academic world.

Sharing, participation and friendships

A rich set of data on children's activities in several non-western societies was collected as part of the six cultures studies (Whiting and Whiting, 1975). The main aim of this work was to document differences in individual child development across several cultures. With this focus on individual development the idea that children might have their own peer cultures was not considered. The original data were collected through observations of children aged three to ten years old between the years of 1954 and 1956 in Kenya, Mexico, Philippines, Okinawa, India and the United States. Edwards (2000) has recently done a re-analysis of the data which focuses specifically on play. Here we will examine her findings omitting information from the United States. Kenya was the country where children played the least as they were involved in work activities from a young age. However, girls who cared for younger siblings and boys who tended animals integrated play into their work. The boys made small ploughs out of sticks and they imitated agriculture work. Similar types of role play during work occurred in India with children using sticks and branches to fashion play materials. Role play was even more frequent in Mexico where children had more free time from work. Girls made houses and pretended to sew and to make tortillas while boys made roads and vehicles out of mud. In the Philippines children engaged in a wide variety of types of role play and fantasy play, including playing ghost and pretending to be horses. In Okinawa children younger then five were seldom given chores and they and older children participated in a rich variety of role and fantasy play (again often making needed props using available materials like mud, sand, pieces of tile and bamboo sticks).

We see in these materials that role play appeared to a large degree in all the cultures and it has also been documented in more recent studies in India (Roopnarine, et al. 1994) and the Sudan (Katz, 2004, this volume). Katz's longitudinal ethnography is especially fascinating in its detailed observations of Sudanese children's everyday life in Howa, a village in central eastern Arabic-speaking Sudan.

On a typical day in the village, children in mixed age, primarily same gender groups, spend time involved in a variety of types of work and play. Boys engaged in 'elaborate enactments in miniature of the behaviours and tasks associated with' *dukan* (store), *hawashaat* (tenancy), and *bildat* (subsistence fields) (Katz, 2004, 11). Central to tenancy play was a toy tractor one of the boys made from a variety of discarded objects with the help of an older brother. The boys made a plough for the tractor and cooperatively and painstakingly reproduced all the various elements of agricultural work from ploughing the fields, planting and watering the crops, to irrigating and weeding, and finally harvesting the crops and taking them to a pretend storehouse. They also reproduced the process of selling their harvest using artificial currency. Finally, they used their pretend profits to play store in which they bought a range of goods represented by objects like bits of metal and glass and battery tops (Katz, 2004, 12–13). Girls' role play was also elaborate. They made dolls from straw, gave a name to each doll who represented males and females of all ages, and played with the dolls in houses 'they established with dividers made of shoes, mortars, bricks and pieces of tins' (Katz, 2004, 17). The girls used these props to enact a wide range of domestic activities like cooking, eating, going to the well to fetch water, and visiting.

While Katz focuses on the elaborate nature of the role play and how it relates to processes of reproduction in this Sudan village, it is clear that the children in line with the notion of interpretive reproduction have also produced a rich peer culture. One in which they not only work and play, but also develop shared values and build close peer relations and friendships.

The nature of these friendships is quite different than the age-graded and extra kin friends of children in western societies. The need for a wider view of friendship that captures the mixed age groups of siblings, kin and neighbours that are typical of many non-western societies is evident. Gaskins in her research on Yucatan Mayan children's interactions in Mexico argues for a broader notion of friendship which is more reflective of family and kin networks and also more communal and collectivist. Gaskins argues that friendships 'can be re-conceptualized as a culturally specific form of providing children with close daily social interaction with other children rather than a unique, and presumed universal, social construct' (2006, 301). The peer cultures within which friendships emerge and are cultivated must also take cultural variation into account (also see Carvalho, 2004).

Autonomy, control, conflict and differentiation

The issue of autonomy and control from adult rules is less for children in many non-western societies because even though they have work obligations from a very early age, they also have a great deal of freedom from direct adult supervision (Nsamenang, 1992; Martini, 1994; Schildkrout, 2002). Martini in a study of a group of three to five year olds on the Marquesas Islands in Polynesia found that these young children 'organized activities, settled disputes, avoided danger, dealt with injuries, distributed goods and negotiated contact with passing others – without adult intervention' (1994, 74).

Studies of street children (children who work or both work and live on the streets) in urban areas of countries in Africa, Brazil and Turkey also display a great deal of autonomy from adults (Aptekar and Heinonen, 2003; Ennew and Swart-Kruger, 2003; Rizzini and Butler, 2003; Ataöv and Haider, 2006). Children live and work on the streets for many reasons. Almost all are poor, some are orphans, some are escaping maltreatment in the family or other settings and others are working to support themselves but also to contribute to the family. However, independence and freedom are important motivations for choosing street life (Rizzini and Butler, 2003). Yet, street children are often threatened by violence from police, other adults, and in some cases other street children. Still, street children report they often look out for one another and build strong group solidarity. (Rizzini and Butler, 2003; Ataöv and Haider, 2006)

Many children in non-western societies do spend much of their time under the direct supervision of adults in their families, schools and the work place. We know little about how children may challenge adult authority and how it is a product of peer cultures in non-western societies. However, Hadley (2003) found that Taiwanese kindergarten children used complex word play to both resist and accommodate the Confucian values that their teachers introduced to them. By manipulating and playing with adults' names and class names, the children collectively resisted the teachers' rules to act respectively towards adults. As Hadley notes, 'using word play to resist the value of being a good student could not be accomplished, however, without a parallel enactment of the very skills that characterize a good student. Understanding word structure, vocabulary and word placement were "good student" skills that facilitated the delivery of a disrespectful word play' (2003, 204).

Finally, regarding conflict, gender and status differentiation in peer cultures there are some patterns in the studies we have reviewed in this section. Gender differentiation begins at an early age and is often related to different types of work assigned to girls and boys. Girls and boys also show different patterns of play preferences even in the same general type of play (e.g., role play, Katz, 2004). Nonetheless many children do spend more time in age and gender mixed groups in non-western societies compared to at least most white middle-class children in western societies.

The issue of conflict is also important. None of the studies of non-western societies we reviewed reported intense personal conflicts among children or that adults were quick to enter into and settle such conflicts. In fact, the studies indicated that children are expected to be able to settle their own conflicts and disputes as part of learning to be members of their culture. For example, Martini in her study of young Marquesan children found that children are required to be compliant when dealing with adults, but peer relations are based on reciprocity. Martini discovered a complex hierarchy in the group with older children in the roles of noisy and quiet leaders, younger children in the role of initiate members, and the youngest toddlers as peripheral members of the group. Noisy leaders introduce activities, direct group play and keep players on track. Quiet leaders invent new play, monitor the bossiness of noisy leaders and care for the toddlers. Initiate members follow the leaders and support each other. The toddlers are interested observers. Their incompetence brings out the skills of the older children who gain status by helping and teaching dependent toddlers (Martini, 1994, 98).

Overall, Martini's research and other studies we have reviewed in this section remind us of the western bias that is evident in much research on children's peer cultures. In the mixed-age-and-gender groups of children in many non-western societies, attempts to control other children are most often pro-social rather than egoistic. That is, the goal is to maintain group cohesiveness rather than to attain individual desires (see Whiting and Edwards, 1988, 182). Martini contrasts this preference for pro-social versus egoistic control to peer interaction among white middle-class American children who learn to value goal-directness and individual achievement early in life.

The future of peer cultures

We see in this review that our knowledge of children's peer cultures has benefited greatly by more comparative studies both within and across cultural groups. It has also benefited from increasing cross-disciplinary work from anthropology, education, folklore, geography, history, psychology and sociology. The work of geographers has brought special insights to the role of space and place to understanding children's peer cultures (Rasmussen, 2004; Valentine, this volume). This work demonstrates that some types of play routines are very similar across western and non-western cultures. However, children from non-western societies and children who live in poverty in western societies often adapt their play routines more closely to the often harsh and challenging realities of their daily lives. These children are also more open to teasing and conflict as a part of peer relations than middle-class children in western societies.

As children's lives, especially in western societies, become more institutionalized and children are increasingly affected by media and new technologies, it is clear that future work on peer cultures must pay careful attention to these trends (Buckingham, this volume; Cook, this volume; Drotner, this volume). Finally, we must be open to new research methods that more directly involve the participation of children in the research process and in their social and political worlds including participatory action research (James, 1996; Kjørholt, 2003; Christensen, 2004; Ataöv and Haider, 2006; Christensen and James, 2008).

One thing is clear. Our understanding of children's peer cultures in the future depends on our appreciation of the diversity and complexity of their lives in the present.

References

Adler, P.A. and P. Adler. (1998) *Peer Power: Preadolescent Culture and Identity*. New Brunswick NJ: Rutgers University Press.

Alston, L. (1992) 'Children as Chattel', in E. West and P. Petrick (eds) *Small Worlds*. Lawrence KS: University of Kansas Press, pp. 208–231.

Aptekar, L. and P. Heinonen (2003) 'Methodological Implications of Contextual Diversity in Research on Street Children', *Children, Youth and Environments*, 13, retrieved 27 December 2006.

Ataöv, A. and J. Haider (2006) 'From Participation to Empowerment: Critical Reflections on a Participatory Action Research Project with Street Children in Turkey', *Children, Youth and Environments*, 16, retrieved 27 December 2006.

Aydt, H. and W.A. Corsaro (2003) 'Differences in Children's Construction of Gender Across Culture: An Interpretive Approach', *American Behavioral Scientist*, 46(10): 1306–1325.

Berentzen, S. (1984) *Children Constructing Their Social World*. Bergen, Norway: University of Bergen.

Carvalho, A.M. (2004) 'Brazilian Children at Play: Interactional Dynamics as a Locus for the Construction of Culture', Paper Presented at the International Seminar, 'The Culture Created by Children and Children's Participation', National Research and Development Centre for Welfare and Health, Helsinki, Finland.

Christensen, P. (2004) 'Children's Participation in Ethnographic Research: Issues of Power and Representation', *Children & Society*, 18(2): 165–176.

Christensen, P. and A. James (eds) (2008). *Research with Children: Perspectives and Practices.* 2nd edn. London: Falmer Press.

Clark, C.D. (1995) *Flights of Fancy, Leaps of Faith.* Chicago: University of Chicago Press.

Clark, C.D. (2005) 'Tricks of Festival: Children, Enculturation, and American Halloween', *Ethos,* 33(2): 180–205.

Corsaro, W.A. (1985) *Friendship and Peer Culture in the Early Years.* Norwood NJ: Ablex.

Corsaro, W.A. (1992) 'Interpretive Reproduction in Children's Peer Cultures', *Social Psychology Quarterly,* 55(2): 160–177.

Corsaro, W.A. (1994) 'Discussion, Debate, and Friendship: Peer Discourse in Nursery Schools in the US and Italy', *Sociology of Education,* 67(1): 1–26.

Corsaro, W.A. (2003) *'We're Friends, Right?': Inside Kids' Culture.* Washington DC: Joseph Henry Press.

Corsaro, W.A. (2005) *The Sociology of Childhood,* 2nd edn. Thousand Oaks CA: Pine Forge Press.

Corsaro, W.A. and D. Eder (1990) 'Children's Peer Cultures', *Annual Review of Sociology,* 16: 197–220.

Corsaro, W.A. and B.O. Johannesen (2007) 'The Creation of New Cultures in Peer Interaction', in J. Valsiner and A. Rosa (eds) *The Cambridge Handbook of Socio-Cultural Psychology.* Cambridge, England: Cambridge University Press, pp. 444–459.

Corsaro, W.A. and L. Molinari (1990) 'From *Seggiolini* to *Discussione*: The Generation and Extension of Peer Culture among Italian Preschool Children', *International Journal of Qualitative Studies in Education,* 3(3): 213–230.

Corsaro, W.A. and L. Molinari (2005) *I Compagni: Understanding Children's Transition From Preschool to Elementary School.* New York: Teachers College Press.

Corsaro, W.A., L. Molinari and K.B. Rosier (2002) 'Zena and Carlotta: Transition Narratives and Early Education in the United States and Italy', *Human Development,* 45(5): 323–348.

Davies, B. (1989) *Frogs and Snails and Feminist Tales: Preschool Children and Gender.* Boston: Allen & Unwin.

Dunn, J. (2004) *Children's Friendships: The Beginnings of Intimacy.* Oxford UK: Blackwell.

Eder, D. and S. Nenga (2003) 'Development and Socialization in Childhood', in J. Delamater (ed.) *Handbook of Social Psychology.* New York: Kluwer/Plenum, pp. 157–182.

Edwards, C.P. (2000) 'Children's Play in Cross-Cultural Perspective: A New Look at the *Six Cultures* Study', *Cross-Cultural Research,* 34(4): 318–338.

Ennew, J. and J. Swart-Kruger (2003) 'Introduction: Homes, Places and Spaces in the Construction of Street Children and Street Youth', *Children, Youth and Environments,* 13, retrieved 27 December 2006.

Evaldsson, A. (1993) *Play, Disputes and Social Order: Everyday Life in Two Swedish After-School Centers.* Linköping, Sweden: Linköping University.

Evaldsson, A. (2003) 'Throwing Like a Girl?: Situating Gender Differences in Physicality Across Game Contexts', *Childhood,* 10(4): 475–497.

Fine, G.A. (1987) *With the Boys: Little League Baseball and Preadolescent Culture.* Chicago: University of Chicago Press.

Garvey, C. (1977) *Play.* Cambridge MA: Harvard University Press.

Gaskins, S. (2006) 'The Cultural Organization of Yucatec Mayan Children's Social Interactions', in X, Chen, D. French and B. Schneider (eds) *Peer Relations in Cultural Context.* New York: Cambridge University Press, pp. 283–309.

Giddens, A. (1984) *The Constitution of Society.* Oxford UK: Polity Press.

Goffman, E. (1961) *Asylums.* Garden City NJ: Anchor.

Goffman, E. (1974) *Frame Analysis.* New York: Harper & Row.

Goodwin, M.H. (1990) *He-Said-She-Said: Talk as Social Organization Among Black Children.* Bloomington IN: Indiana University Press.

Goodwin, M.H. (1998) 'Games of Stance: Conflict and Footing in Hopscotch', in J. Holmes and C. Adger (eds) *Kids' Talk: Strategic Language Use in Later Childhood.* New York: Oxford University Press, pp. 23–46.

Goodwin, M.H. (2003) 'The Relevance of Ethnicity, Class, and Gender in Children's Play Negotiations', in J. Holmes and M. Meyerhoff (eds) *Handbook of Language and Gender.* New York: Blackwell, pp. 229–251.

Hadley, K.G. (2003) 'Children's Word Play: Resisting and Accommodating Confucian Values in a Taiwanese Kindergarten Classroom', *Sociology of Education,* 76(3): 193–208.

James, A. (1996) 'Learning to Be Friends', *Childhood,* 3(3): 313–330.

James, A., C. Jenks and A. Prout (1998) *Theorizing Childhood.* New York: Teachers College Press.

Johannesen, B.O. (2004) 'On Shared Experiences and Intentional Actions Emerging Within a Community of Lego-Playing Children', Paper Presented at the Third International Conference on the Dialogical Self. Warsaw Poland.

Kalliala, M. (2006) *Play Culture in a Changing World.* Berkshire, England: Open University Press.

Katz, C. (2004) *Growing Up Global: Economic Restructuring and Children's Everyday Lives.* Minneapolis MN: University of Minnesota Press.

Kjørholt, A.T. (2003) '"Imagined Communities": The Local Community as a Place for "Children's Culture" and Social Participation in Norway', in K.F. Olwig, and E. Gulløv (eds) *Children's Places: Cross-Cultural Perspectives,* London: Routledge, 2003, pp. 197–216.

Löfdahl, A. (2005) '"The Funeral": A Study of Children's Shared Meaning-Making and Its Developmental Significance', *Early Years,* 25(1): 5–16.

Løkken, G. (2000a) 'Tracing the Social "Style" of Toddlers Peers', *Scandinavian Journal of Educational Research,* 44(2): 163–176.

Løkken, G. (2000b) 'The Playful Quality of the Toddling "Style"', *International Journal of Qualitative Studies of Education,* 13(5): 531–542.

Martini, M. (1994) 'Peer Interactions in Polynesia: A View From the Marquesas', in J.L. Roopnarine, J.E. Johnson, and F.H. Hooper (eds) *Children's Play in Diverse Cultures.* Albany NY: State University of New York Press, pp. 73–103.

Mussati, T. and S. Panni (1981) 'Social Behavior and Interaction Among Day Care Center Toddlers', *Early Child Development and Care,* 7(1): 5–27.

Nsamenang, B. (1992) 'Early Childhood Care and Education in Cameroon', in M.E. Lamb, K.J. Sternberg, C. Hwang and A.G. Broberg (eds) *Child Care In Context: Cross-Cultural Perspectives.* Hillsdale NJ: Lawrence Erlbaum, pp. 419–439.

Poveda, D. and T. Marcos (2005) 'The Social Organization of a "Stone Fight": Gitano Children's Interpretive Reproduction of Ethnic Conflict', *Childhood,* 12(3): 327–349.

Qvortrup, J. (1991) *Childhood as a Social Phenomenon – An Introduction to a Series of National Reports.* Vienna, Austria: European Centre for Social Welfare Policy and Research.

Rasmussen, K. (2004) 'Places for Children – Children's Places', *Childhood,* 11(2): 155–173.

Rizzini, I. and U.M. Butler (2003) 'Life Trajectories of Children and Adolescents Living on the Streets of Rio de Janeiro', *Children, Youth and Environments,* 13, retrieved 27 December 2006.

Rizzo, T. (1989) *Friendship Development Among Children in School.* Norwood NJ: Ablex.

Roopnarine, J.L., Z. Hossain, P. Gill and H. Brophy (1994) 'Play in the East Indian Context', in J.L. Roopnarine, J.E. Johnson and F.H. Hooper (eds) *Children's Play in Diverse Cultures.* Albany NY: State University of New York Press, pp. 9–30.

Sawyer, R.K. (1997) *Pretend Play as Improvisation: Conversation in the Preschool Classroom.* Mahwah NJ: Lawrence Erlbaum.

Sawyer, R.K. (2002) 'Improvisation and Narrative', *Narrative Inquiry,* 12(2): 319–349.

Schildkrout, E. (2002) 'Age and Gender in Hausa Society: Socio-Economic Roles of Children in Urban Kano', *Childhood,* 9(3): 344–368.

Schwartzman, H. (1978) *Transformations: The Anthropology of Children's Play.* New York: Plenum.

Strandell, H. (1997) 'Doing Reality with Play: Play as Children's Resource in Organizing Everyday Life in Daycare Centres', *Childhood,* 4(4): 445–464.

Thorne, B. (1986) 'Girls and Boys Together…But Mostly Apart: Gender Arrangements in Elementary Schools', in W. Hartup and Z. Rubin (eds) *Relationships and Development*. Hillsdale NJ: Lawrence Erlbaum, pp. 167–184.

Thorne, B. (1993) *Gender Play: Girls and Boys in School*. New Brunswick NJ: Rutgers University Press.

Whiting, B.B. and C.P. Edwards (1988) *Children of Different Worlds: The Formation of Social Behavior*. Cambridge MA: Harvard University Press.

Whiting, B.B. and J.W. Whiting (1975) *Children of Six Cultures: A Psycho-Cultural Analysis*. Cambridge MA: Harvard University Press.

Wiggins, D. (1985) 'The Play of Slave Children in the Plantation Communities of the Old South, 1820–60', in N. Hiner and J. Hawes (eds) *Growing Up in America: Children in Historical Perspective*. Urbana IL: University of Illinois Press, pp. 173–192.

21
Play and Games

Ann-Carita Evaldsson

Introduction

In this chapter particular attention will be given to empirical studies on play and games as social action, with a focus on children's everyday play and game participation in situated activities across various settings. As will be demonstrated, studies of how children organize play activities *in situ* provide a special arena for rethinking a set of binarisms that consistently reappear in the literature, such as children's play as separate from the adult word, play and games as different activities, gender differentiation in play, and the distinctions between play and seriousness, play and work, and so on. Before that, in the first two sections, I will recapitulate how the study of play and games has evolved through several phases within different disciplines that have attributed to play and games an important role in (a) children's development of cognitive and social skills and (b) the production of a children's folklore, thereby providing a platform for further studies.

Developmentally oriented research on play and games

Theoretical and conceptual issues

Most traditional theoretical and empirical work on children's play has focused on the function of children's play activities for children's development of cognitive, language and social skills (Mead, 1934; Piaget, 1951; Vygotsky, 1966; see Garvey, 1977). Predominant in developmentally oriented research is to view children's development in regard to different types of play activities (i.e., symbolic play, make-believe or sociodramatic play and games with rules) associated with different cognitive stages and skills. In addition, symbolic play, make-believe or sociodramatic play versus games with rules have been clearly differentiated and thought to have distinct functions in relation to children's cognitive development.

Piaget, the most pre-eminent researcher on child development, is also responsible for the most widely used developmental model of children's play and games (1932, 1951). In Piaget's (1932) view games with rules prepare children for the final cognitive stage of formal thought while make-believe and sociodramatic play are associated with sensor-motor and preoperational stages. Although Piaget's main interest was not in children's folklore, but in moral and cognitive development, his study of upper-middle-class Swiss children's games provides one of the most detailed and careful observations of the game of marbles. Piaget's investigations of how children learn the rules for playing the game demonstrate that the ways children of different ages conceptualize rules can be associated with different stages of moral development, which Piaget outlined (ibid., 1932, 26–27). Also George Herbert Mead (1934) argued in his classic study of *Mind, Self and Society* that play and games have distinct functions in relation to children's development of social and cognitive skills. According to Mead, to take a perspective that is different from the one habitually or presently held is a cognitive skill learned in the context and course of games. When children engage in pretend play, as for example being teachers, parents and princesses, they are already 'taking roles', while it is only in rule-governed games that the participating child 'must have the attitude of all the others involved in the game' (54).

A number of scholars have commented on the description of play as mainly imitative and a preparatory activity that supports children in their cognitive development. For example, Sutton-Smith (1971, 341–342; 1972) argued in his critique of Piaget that Piaget reduced play to a function of cognition and by doing so disregarded the cognitive function of play transformations in early childhood. In contrast, Vygotsky (1966) put emphasis on the importance of play for cognitive development because 'it liberates the child from situational constraints' (11). In his view, preschool children's play enables them to discover the relationship between meanings, objects and actions, which supports the development of abstract thought. In addition Vygotsky (1966) argued that there is no such thing as play without rules. Moreover, so-called pure games with rules are essentially games within imaginary situations, in the sense that as soon as the game is regulated with certain rules, a number of actual possibilities for action are ruled out. Also Bateson (1971, 148–149), in his theory of play as transformations, suggested that it is in play that children learn that 'the choice of style or a role is related to the frame and context of behaviour'. The notion of play as transformations will be further developed in the last section.

Although developmentally oriented researchers differ in their view on the function of play and games, they assume that the play structures they have described are universal. Several scholars have demonstrated that Piaget's play sequences do not appear in the same way in their own studies (for a review of the critique see Schwartzman, 1978, 54–55). For example, Margaret Mead (1930) in her classic study *Growing Up in New Guinea* suggested that Manus children who grew up in a world of siblings or age-mates developed a naturalistic view of the world and did not engage in symbolic and imaginative play. Mead's early findings cast doubt on Piaget's theory of universal stages and highlighted the need for cultural explanations. More recently, the universalistic and evolutionary assumptions inherent in developmentally oriented research have been questioned and criticized for neglect of the sociocultural context by childhood researchers (James, Jenks, and Prout, 1998). Yet, childhood studies maintain an interest in the relationship

between play and individual development, but only as one aspect of the importance of play in children's lives. Play is seen as part of childhood and children's
meaning making, emotional sharing, and creativity in their everyday lives with
peers (Corsaro, 2005, this volume). Moreover, documentation of different types
of play (pretend and fantasy play, dramatic role play, play with toys and related
materials) and games with rules (and so on) is pursued as important in its own
right. This will be demonstrated in the last section.

Studies of play and games as children's folklore

Whereas developmentally oriented research has been claimed to not fully acknowledge the sociocultural context, the study of play and games across different times
and spaces has been a regular subject matter in folklore. Traditionally, studies of
folklore have had an interest in the origins, survival and history of games (Sutton-
Smith, Mechling, Johnson, and McMahon, 1995). For example Sutton-Smith
began his career by collecting children's games in New Zealand (1972) and then
studied changes in games over time and variations in games across cultures (game
preferences of New Zealand children, Maori children and American children). A
major work was undertaken by Opie and Opie (1959, 1969), who collected during
a period of around 30 years the speech play (riddles, rhymes, chants, nicknames
and satire) and games of over 5,000 English-speaking school children in England,
Scotland and Wales. The Opies' work on children's present-day games in the street
and playground was a response to a tendency at that time to study games 'as if
they were archaeological remains, rather than living organisms, which are constantly evolving, adapting to new situations and renewing themselves or being
replaced' (1969, vii). Like other researchers of children's folklore, Opie and Opie
(1969) imposed their own classifications, categorizing what children play on the
bases of selected features of the game (chasing games, hiding games, ball games,
marble games, hopscotch games, guessing games, jumping games, etc.) and developmental characteristics of the age group or sex of players (see also Sutton-Smith,
1972, 1979). Moreover, similar to the evolutionary assumptions in developmentally oriented research, a view of the child as primitive is also apparent in the
Opies' (1959) study:

> The folklorist and anthropologist can, without travelling a mile from his door
> examine a thriving unselfconsciousness culture (the word culture is used here
> deliberately) which is unnoticed by the sophisticated world, and quite as little
> affected by it, as is the culture of some dwindling aboriginal tribe living out its
> helpless existence in the hinterland of a native reserve...Like the savage, they
> are respecters, even venerators, of custom; and in their self-contained commu-
> nity their basic lore and language seems scarcely to alter from generation to
> generation. (22)

As shown, researchers on children's folklore strived to preserve childhood cus-
toms. Games were seen as the most vital form of play, which was related to a

tendency, at that time, to concentrate on descriptions of spectacular and ritual-ized events. The careful and detailed collections of children's present-day games advocated by the Opies were a reaction against the use of adults (i.e., teachers, university students, individual collectors, etc.) as informants (see Schwartzman, 1978, 92–97). Moreover, the emphasis given to children's culture as likely to remain intact for long time stands in contrast to the idea that children's play is based on imitation of adult activities (see for example Herron and Sutton-Smith, 1971; Levine, 1973).

More recently the notion of a separate culture of childhood – cut off from the family and the constraints of an adult world, transmitted in the cultural forms of play and games and, consequently, analysed in isolation – has been perceived as problematic by childhood researchers James, Jenks and Prout. As noted by them (1998, 85) the concept of children's culture 'slips in easily to describe what seems to be another world heard from, an otherness or difference characteristic of being a child, and in doing so takes up an enduring theme in literary and biographical accounts of the forgotten, tribal or marginal world of childhood'. In addition, they suggest that the concept of children's culture may 'be in part a product of the specificity of these research contexts' (87), thus referring to the fact that the spatial locations of studies are places dominated mainly by children, such as school playgrounds. As also noted by Schwartzman (1978, 92) the contextual character of play (i.e., how children play, with whom, the age and sex of players, how frequently a game is played and how it relates to the cultural context) was seldom taken into account in traditional research on children's folklore except for brief notes about the setting and region in which the game was collected. Nevertheless the systematic collection of what children play in different settings has generated a rich ethnographic material that has contributed to the under-standing of the place of play and games in children's worlds.

Play and games as situated activities and social orders

Theoretical background and conceptual issues

The study of play and games as situated activities implies a shift in focus from *what* children play – the preoccupation of traditional folklore studies – to *how* players actively contribute to the organization of play and games, generating qualitatively different versions and experiences through their everyday play and game participation (Goodwin, 1990, 1995, 2001; Evaldsson and Corsaro, 1998; Evaldsson, 2003, 2004, 2005). The notion of play and games as a situated activity emphasizes the interactive actions of separate participants in joint social projects (Goffman, 1961; Goodwin, 1990; see Evaldsson, 2003). Moreover, a situated activ-ity has 'transformation rules' or 'frames' that determine what experiences from the outside world are to be utilized as resources as well as what form they will be given in the activity (Goffman, 1961, 26–34).

As will be demonstrated, there are several reasons for studying play and games as situated activities and social orders (Corsaro, 2005, this volume; Kyratzis, 2004).

The most important is that participation in play is a central part of childhood and children's meaning making, emotional sharing, language use, and creativity in their everyday lives with peers. Second, an agentive view (see James, this volume) is taken of children's play and games, and the detailed documentation of how children organize different types of play (pretend and fantasy play, dramatic role play, play with toys and related materials) and games (play with rules such as games with marbles, jump rope, foursquare, hopscotch and so on) is explored to discover what children accomplish socially in play activities. Third, studies of play and games as situated activities across various settings are investigated as a central feature of how children accomplish social identities (age, gender, ethnicity, etc.) among peers, and, thus are important in the establishment and cultivation of different forms of peer cultures. Finally, studies of play and games as situated activities in children's everyday life focus on how children produce their own orders in play and how those orders are related to the adult world and society at large.

Play as transformations: cultural production, language use and authority in children's play

Schwartzman (1978) demonstrates that a study of children's play as transformations persuades researchers to rethink the pervasive division that western societies make between play and seriousness, play and work, fantasy and reality, and so on. The notion of play as transformation was first developed by Bateson (1971), who suggested that the passage to play and the creation of a reality predicated on play is keyed cognitively to a meta message 'this is play', which places a 'frame' around a space of immediate events, determining the type of 'sense' that will be accorded everything within the frame (see also Goffman, 1961, 1986). According to Schwartzman (1978) the notion of children's play as transformation points to the fact that 'children are continually constructing and reconstructing the contexts in which they exist in their efforts to make sense and sometimes nonsense, out of the worlds in which they find themselves' (1).

Several researchers have focused on how the social interaction in children's play is carried out and what kind of cultural and language competencies are inherent in particular play interchanges (Garvey, 1977; Goodwin, 1990; Goldman, 1998; Kyratzis, 2004; Corsaro, 2005, this volume). In an early study Garvey (1977) demonstrated that nursery school children (three to five-and-a-half years old) used different types of speech to accomplish the 'as if' framing of play and play roles in pretend play. The playing was set up in a variety of ways, for example, through *explicit mention of pretend transformations* ('I am a work lady at work,' 'Pretend you hated baby fish,' etc.) and *negation of pretend* ('I am not the dragon anymore'). It was found that the children used a considerable amount of speech to organize and negotiate the play frame, roles and plans, which suggested that for children of this age group 'the saying is the playing'. Also Goodwin (1993) and Whalan (1995) demonstrated that children in their play use language to maintain the specific definition of the situation as pretend play. Goodwin observed that 'pretend play differs from other domains of play in that children enact vocal and non-vocal scripts appropriate to their relative position in a pretend reality ... this is accomplished through skilful managing of staged identities, artful uses of a repertoire of voices, and careful attention to the framing of interaction' (160).

As reported by Kyratzis, Marx and Wade (2001) children use a variety of vocal and non-vocal resources to switch between different character voices in pretend play. Powerful adult roles in play such as mothers were portrayed as speaking with bald directives associated with high status (Aronsson and Thorell, 2002). Older children usually appropriated the Mom role to achieve authority in the peer group (see also Goodwin, 1993; Griswold, 2007). In a recent study Kyratzis (2007) demonstrated how American middle-class preschool children use directives and role-related speech acts to enact power and relationships within their own peer group in pretend play. Power was enacted in one friendship triad by a girl who assumed the lead role (head news reporter in news announcer play). Through the play, the same girl also took the lead role in dismissing other girls from the stage ('oops K., your doll's about to get snatched out of the leaves, you better pick it up quickly/ well, that's the end of our news for today'), thereby sanctioning and evaluating the behaviour of other members of the peer group.

Griswold (2007) found in a study of Russian preadolescent girls' pretend play that children in pretend play orient to multifunctional aspects of authority, including subordination, thereby providing an understanding of the co-construction of authority between the child displaying subordination and the child claiming authority. The girls ascribed power to a selected peer by assigning to her a position of familial authority, as Mother, even before the girl herself had a chance to claim a superior position. Simultaneously, they downgraded themselves to the less authoritative positions of children, seeking the girl's help as a mediator in disputes, and asking her to frame crucial elements of the play, such as ages and educational levels of the play characters or the boundaries of the play space. The girls' verbal actions (permission and information requests, directives, role negotiation and assistance appeals) were accompanied by bodily orientations to display their subordination and legitimate the power of one member of their group.

As will be further shown, several studies demonstrate that children display real-life power roles in role-play by appropriating language structures (voicing, directives, commands, requests, assessments) available in the adult culture, actively subverting them and recombining their features to construct 'meanings, moralities, and ideological responses of their own' (Goodwin and Kyratzis, 2007). Moreover, children appropriate language structures and social hierarchies to fit concerns and values within peer and sibling groups (Corsaro, this volume).

Rindstedt's (2001) ethnographic study of language use and play among Quichua children in an Andean community in Ecuador presents several examples of how children in a non-western society use language in play to display both powerful and subordinate adult roles that comment on the power structures in their community (see also Goldman, 1998; Reynolds, 2002; de

Example 1

1	Geovanni	Ya vas mamita. Dame almuerzo!	*Go now little mommy. Give me lunch!*
2	Miriam	Espera pues. Con-con éste. E<u>lace</u> e<u>lace</u> patrón. Ya traiga, traiga	*Wait then. With-with this one. T<u>a</u>ke t<u>a</u>ke patrón. Yeah bring bring*
3	Geovanni	Muchas gracias. Deme arroz con queso!	*Thank you very much. Give me rice with cheese!*
4	Miriam	Ya! ya! Comida<u>ca</u> no?	*Yeah! yeah! not the food?*
5	Geovanni	Po-	*Ch-*
6	Miriam	E<u>lace</u>!	*T<u>a</u>ke!*
7	Geovanni	Po- hace mucho tiempo.	*Ch- a ling time ago (sings)*
8	Miriam	E<u>lace</u>! E<u>lace</u>! E<u>lace</u>! E<u>lace</u>! E<u>lace</u>! E<u>lace</u>!	*T<u>a</u>ke! T<u>a</u>ke! T<u>a</u>ke! T<u>a</u>ke! T<u>a</u>ke! T<u>a</u>ke!*
9	Geovanni	Qué comida es? Si no- caldo de gallina me da. Qué da?	*What kind of food is it? If not- you give me chicken*
10	Miriam	Este- este- este- queso.	*This- this- this- cheese.*
11	Geovanni	No quiero queso. Quiero caldo de gallina.	*I don't want cheese. I want chicken soup.*

León, 2007). In Example 1, one older brother and his younger sister enact the roles of a landowner (patron) and a labourer (peón), who is commanded to serve him lunch.

During the entire sequence the older boy (the landowner/patron) uses various verbal resources such as directives, commands, requests to achieve authority while his younger sister (the labourer/peón) deploys information requests, asks for permission, appeals to him to eat, and 'readily does as told without showing any sign of disapproval' to display her subordination and obedience. The older children more often than the younger ones take the more powerful adult roles in play as mother, father, patron, and so on, privileged to speak with high status, thereby treating conventional authoritative language structures as means to establish social hierarchies in the sibling group. In their pretend play the Quichua children appropriate cultural background features of how speech is related to social hierarchies that exist between the indigenous people and the mestizos. Simultaneously they display their knowledge that mestizos eat better food such as 'cheese' and 'chicken soup', and do not eat the same kind of food as them. Interestingly enough, several studies show that young children in non-western societies actively manipulate and playfully exploit power roles and authoritative language registers (see also Goldman, 1998; Reynolds, 2002;

de León, 2007) in similar ways as have been described in the literature on children's pretend role play in the home, neighbourhood and preschool in western countries (Garvey, 1977; Corsaro, 1985; Goodwin, 1990; Elbers, 1996; Kyratzis et al., 2001). In addition de León (2007) demonstrates in her study of Zinacantec Mayan children that 'sibling-peer playful interactions resist order, and find powerful moments where hierarchies and roles are subverted or diluted through playful transformations of "pre-existing" structures'. Consequently she argues for a wider notion of sibling relations with mixed age, kin and neighbours in non-western societies that also takes children's peer cultures and agency into account.

All in all, the detailed analysis of children's play interactions based on longitudinal studies across various cultural settings dissolves dichotomies between western and non-western children and demonstrates that children's play is not separate from the adult word, but that children appropriate and creatively manipulate power and language structures available in the adult culture in play with siblings and peers. Moreover, the variations in play themes and the different ways children organize family and work play across settings point to play as an integral process of children's understanding of family and work, and show that play prepares children for future family and working lives. Thus, ethnographic studies of how children organize play activities across cultures demonstrate the fluidity between play and work, and the intertwining of children's play and the adult world.

Situating gender in play: critical remarks on a two-culture approach to gender and play

As James, Jenks and Prout (1998, 85) note in their critique of play as childhood cultures, children have been seen not only as possessing one culture that is different from the adult world but two, which are gendered. Most research in co-educational elementary school settings has provided strong evidence on gender differences in girls' and boys' games (Lever, 1978; Sutton-Smith, 1979; Thorne, 1993, 44–47; Adler and Adler, 1998; Maccoby, 1998). In analysing the differences between girls' and boys' games among white middle-class girls and boys in elementary school settings in the United States, researchers such as Lever (1978), Sutton-Smith (1979) and Maccoby (1998) demonstrate that girls' games involve partial body involvement and simple turn-taking, which emphasize cooperation and intimate relations, while boys engage in highly physical, competitive, complex games in large groups, taking up much playground space. In a study on popularity in elementary school Adler and Adler (1998, 183) note that 'the boys' culture embodies their expression of physicality' in its active involvement in extracurricular sport activities (American football), emphasizing physical ability, achievement, toughness, competitiveness and aggression. In contrast, a central aspect in girls' peer culture was 'conformity and compliance' (184). The girls organized games in which they practised established social roles, rules and relationships. Eder (1995) found similar patterns among adolescent boys' and girls' extracurricular activities in middle school, where boys in sports (American football) developed assertive behaviours while girls' activities (cheerleading) fostered a concern with appearance and popularity.

Recent research (Thorne 1993, 89–110) demonstrates that different gender orders in childhood cannot be attributed only to gender-segregated patterns in schools in contemporary society. As Thorne (1993) notes, studies on gender in childhood tend to exaggerate differences. 'A strategy of contrasts' is often built into the design of research that constructs and makes only gender differentiation visible. In separate studies, Evaldsson (2003, 2004), Goodwin (1995), Hughes (1988) and Hewitt (1997) have demonstrated that dichotomies such as 'girls are cooperative' versus 'boys are competitive' dissolve when interaction in particular game contexts is scrutinized in detail. These studies thus show that complexities in social interaction in games are lost as analysis proceeds through gender-linked contrasts.

Goodwin (1995) found that bilingual Spanish/English-speaking and African-American working-class girls playing hopscotch were involved in aggravated discourses and extended disputes about rules. Rather than being an eventless, typical girl game with simple rules (Lever, 1978), the girls treated the rules of hopscotch as resources to be probed and played with. In a longitudinal study of interactions in same-sex and cross-sex jump rope among fourth-grade middle-class children in an ethnically mixed elementary school in the United States, Goodwin (2001) demonstrated that girls' dominance in a jump rope game changed over time. Initially the girls set the agenda regarding how the game was to be played. As the boys gained more skill in the activity, they used the aggravated directive style of girls to control the girls' game participation. As boys gained proficiency in the girls' game, the boys became equal, and even more powerful, partners in calling plays and making decisions. The boys' and girls' use of directive forms in cross-sex jump rope was related to the players' acquired physical skills and achieved position in the particular game context, rather than being linked to unitary gendered behaviours.

In line with these findings, Evaldsson (2003, 2004) found that girls of ethnically mixed (Syrian, Kurdish and Chilean) and low-income backgrounds did not differ from boys with respect to use of physical moves such as slams or orientation toward competition in foursquare. The girls' use of throwing in same-sex and cross-sex foursquare shifted as the configuration of players changed. In the following example, two boys, Sherbel and William, play on the boys' team and two girls, Marion and Sarah, on the girls'. After several attempts to change the rules for throwing, Sherbel, one of the more physically skilled boys, finally takes off and slams the ball with great force in Marion's square. Although Sherbel ignores the rules for throwing (lines 15–16) Marion manages to catch the ball (line 19) and then slam it with force in William's square (line 20).

As shown, Marion's superior position with respect to her skills in slams entitles her to dictate the boys' game performance. By laughing at Willy's failure the girls both mock and challenge the image of boys as physical athletes, making the assumption very ambiguous. The different reactions on the part of the two boys also demonstrate that not all boys fit into the 'big man

Example 2			
15	Sherbel	((takes off)) uh: ((slams the ball in Marion's square))	
17	Sarah	det är inga låga (.) det är inga såna	*you are not allowed to (.) throw like that!*
18	Sherbel	vad är det då?	*what is it then?*
19	Marion	((catches the ball and bounces it with force in Willy's square))	
21	Sherbel	DU DU TA DE:N! ((runs after the ball))	*YOU YOU MUST TAKE I:T!*
22	Willy	((runs, fails to catch the ball,) lines up)	
23	Sarah	ha ha ha [ha]	
24	Marion	[ha ha [ha ha=	
25	Alice	[ha ha [ha ha	
26	Sherbel	[ha ha	
26	Marion	=ha:n gick ut	*=he: is out!*
27	Alice	härligt Marion!!	*great Marion!!*

bias', which assumes all boys to be physical and assertive (Thorne, 1993, 98). Whereas Thorne (1993) found that games such as 'boys against girls' strengthened gender boundaries and evoked stereotyped images, Evaldsson's study demonstrated that participants invoke, play with, pull apart and even resist traditional gender behaviours in the midst of cross-sex play. The ways in which the girls claimed entitlement to the game space, dictated the ground rules, mock-challenged and made fun of the boys and set the limits for their playful attempts differ from girls' game behaviour seen in other studies where boys dominate the playground in a physical way, thus disadvantaging girls (Thorne, 1993, 83; Sutton-Smith, 1995, 72).

Evaldsson's study (2003, 2004) demonstrated that cross-sex games such as 'boys against girls' were embedded in a framework constituted through humour, playfulness and laughter. For example boys, with expertise in the foursquare game, were eager to comply with the rules set up by the girls, but the same boys, who made a great effort to follow the agenda, playfully transgressed the game rules. The study demonstrates that the players operate with an imaginary overt situation similar to pretend play (Vygotsky, 1966), which in turn is in contrast to other findings that define games as mainly rule-governed in a more realistic framework (Piaget, 1932; Bateson, 1971). In this drama, the players invoke, play with, pull apart and even resist the meaning structure of the game. By importing actions from other genres (movies, real life) into the present game interaction, the participants alter the participation framework of the game into a make-believe realm. In so doing they manage to transcend the game format and play with the structure of separate gender teams. Thereby the participants give 'new' meanings to established gender roles, which maximize the fun of the cross-sex game and enhance cross-gender relationships.

All in all, the studies of children's games as situated activities by Goodwin (1990, 1995) and Evaldsson (2003, 2004) demonstrate that the relationship between the real and the unreal is so complex that a set of qualitative abstractions of boy versus girl games as regulated by particular rules has a quite limited value. Moreover, the notion that play and games have a set of essential and clearly differentiated characteristics is contradicted by the empirical subtleties in studies of how children actually play games *in situ*. Also the social organization of the school setting, boys' and girls' access to physical education and children's backgrounds (ethnicity, social class, age) are important (Goodwin, 1995, 2001; Corsaro and Molinari, 2005; Corsaro, this volume). For example, Evaldsson (2004) and Evaldsson and Corsaro (1998) found that more abstract contextual factors in the Swedish school setting – such as an ethos of gender equality and sameness, including sports and physical education available for girls and boys – encouraged girls and boys to rearrange physical behaviours and playfully challenge static and separate (gender, ethnic and class) positions in ongoing game activities on the playground.

The results indicate that detailed analysis of how gender is constituted in game interactions, with particular attention to girls and boys of low-income and minority backgrounds, in various settings is needed to overcome universalistic arguments about gender divisions in play. Moreover they point to the fact that the meaning of girls' (versus boys') behaviours is not intrinsically tied to the format of girl (versus boy) games, automatically giving rise to predictable and unitary gendered patterns of interactions.

The serious side of play: social inclusion and exclusion in children's play

The notion of play, from the romantized view of play as a free and not serious activity outside ordinary life, but at the same time absorbing players (Huizinga, 1938; Opie and Opie, 1959, 1969), to the antitethical view of play as rebellious, hierarchical and disorderly (Sutton-Smith, 1972), is contradicted by the findings of how children actually organize play and games *in situ*. As also Thorne (1993, 5–6) notes, an adult perception of play as not serious tends to misrepresent the full range of children's actions and feelings.

Researchers who examine children's play and games on their own terms show that play is a social process through which children produce their own orders and how those orders are related to society at large (see Danby & Baker, 1998; Evaldsson, 2005; Corsaro, 2005, this volume). Studies demonstrate that preschool and preadolescent children exploit the power of language in play to establish social hierarchies and maintain peer relations (Corsaro 1985, 2005, this volume; Goodwin, 1990, 1995, 2006; Sheldon, 1996; Danby and Baker, 1998; Evaldsson and Corsaro, 1998; Kyratzis et al, 2001; Aronsson and Thorell, 2002; Evaldsson,

2002, 2004, 2005; Cromdal, 2004; Griswold, 2007). Several of the speech activities explored illustrate that preschool children are being assertive, aggressive and even threatening as they protect their interactive space from intruders and organize ongoing joint activities. These features are important because they demonstrate that a bipolar distinction between play and seriousness dissolves in everyday peer group interactions. Moreover studies demonstrate that power, status and social exclusion are accomplished along with social inclusion and solidarity in play.

For example Sheldon (1996) showed that preschool girls participate in extended access disputes and verbally accomplish social exclusion in play. In keeping a third girl out of a play activity, the two girls who started the play ('Pretend you we-we wanted to get married, right?') used a range of verbal resources such as mitigators, indirectness, reframing, token agreements, dramatic imagery and so on that enabled them to confront others without being confrontational. Moreover the pretend frame enabled the two girls to delay the third girl's access to the play by saying 'You can be the baby brother, but you aint born yet.' Sheldon (1996, 58, 61) describes the techniques used by the girls as double-voice discourse, which has 'an overlay of mitigation and has the effect of softening rather than escalating discord'. Here, multifunctional aspects of play entry, including social exclusion, are analysed, providing an understanding of the collaboration between the child seeking access and the children protecting their ongoing play (see also Cromdal, 2001; Corsaro, 1979). Sheldon's (1996) work is interesting as it demonstrates white middle-class preschool girls' management of social exclusion and disagreements.

Danby and Baker (1998) provide another example of how Australian preschool boys use multiple verbal actions in gate-keeping their play. Danby and Baker (1998) demonstrate in their study how the boys learn lessons of masculinity in everyday play activities that radically differ from what the teachers intend the play to be: for example, that it is not masculine to cry and that bullying and 'being able to take it' is part of the masculine experience (166, see also Connolly, 1995; Evaldsson, 2005). Berentenzen's (1984) ethnographic study of Norwegian children's play in a preschool setting also demonstrated that the boys searched for possibilities for 'showing strength, courage and speed' (59). Moreover, similar to what Thorne (1993) found, Danby and Baker (1998) found that girls were more likely to call on the authority of the teacher. When there was trouble, the teachers usually interfered in the peer activities in order to resolve the conflict. This reflected the teachers' professional ambition to stop the disruptive nature of conflicts. When the boys called in the teacher, they were ridiculed more by their male peers than the girls were when they called in the teacher. As noted, 'a cry for help' or to 'call on the teachers' intervention' was a 'disastrous political move in terms of masculinity' (168, see also Evaldsson, 2002). The institutional framework is thus relevant to the repeated invocation and negotiation as well as the solidifying of particular behaviours such as 'crying' and 'calling on teachers' as non-acceptable behaviours for the boys in this preschool setting.

All in all, detailed studies based on long-term fieldwork in different preschool and school settings demonstrate that some girls and boys in play interactions position themselves as powerful and normal while others become deviant and powerless. Play interactions involve displaying alignments along with excluding other children from play. The pretend frame of play itself allows participants both to accomplish exclusion as well as solicit support, seek affiliation and strengthen alliances. These contrasting features, I would argue, do not indicate that boys' social organization is similar to girls' social concerns, but that boys and girls construct overlapping social identities in play interaction. In addition, studies demonstrate that as children play, they also reorganize their everyday emerging peer and sibling–peer culture (see Corsaro, this volume) for their own purposes: building social hierarchies, strengthening alliances, challenging stereotypical gender roles, having fun, through appropriation and resistance, in the midst of play episodes.

The future of play and games in children's everyday lives

This chapter has detailed some of the complexities and creativity in children's play and games across various settings. As demonstrated, the study of play and games *in situ* has been important for understanding children as active contributors to the complex process of cultural continuity and change within the group of peers and siblings, and in society at large. Moreover, it is through play interactions with peers and siblings, and across various settings, that social organization and identities, along with language competencies, are constituted. However, we still know little about what children accomplish socially in play and games outside of schools in their homes as well as how play is accomplished among working children in non-western cultures (Corsaro, this volume; de Leon, 2007). Moreover, future work on children's play and games needs to pay attention to popular culture, media and interactive technologies as integral parts of children's play and games as well as the allegiance to a broader youth culture (Aronsson and Sparrman, 2003; Buckingham, this volume; Drotner, this volume).

What this chapter emphasizes, then, is the need for more studies based on careful documentation and detailed analysis of children's play and game interactions across various settings, which will allow us to explore empirically the complex social process within which children actively reorganize their present peer and peer–sibling culture and future lives.

References

Adler, P.A. and P. Adler (1998) *Peer Power: Preadolescent Culture and Identity.* New Brunswick NJ: Rutgers University Press.

Aronsson K. and A. Sparrman (2003) 'Pog Game Practices, Learning and Ideology: Local Markets and Identity Work', in G. Walford (ed.) *Investigating Educational Policy through Ethnography.* Studies in Educational Ethnography Series, Vol. 8, 169–192.

Aronsson, K. and M. Thorell (2002) 'Voice and Collusion in Adult–Child Talk: Towards an Architecture of Intersubjectivity', in S. Blum-Kulka and C.E. Snow (eds) *Talking to*

Adults: The Contribution of Multiparty Discourse to Language Acquisition. Mahwah NJ: Erlbaum, pp. 277–293

Bateson, G. (1971) 'The Message This Is Play', in R. Heron and B. Sutton-Smith (eds) *Children's Play.* New York: Wiley, pp. 261–266.

Berentzen, S. (1984) *Children Constructing Their Social World.* Bergen, Norway: University of Bergen.

Connolly, P. (1995) 'Boys Will be Boys? Racism, Sexuality and the Construction of Masculine Identities among Infant Boys', in J. Holland, M. Blair and S. Sheldon (eds) *Debates and Issues in Feminist Research and Pedagogy.* Clevedon: Open University Press, pp. 169–195.

Corsaro, W.A. (1979) ' "We're Friends, Right?": Children's Use of Access Rituals in a Nursery School', *Language in Society,* 8(3): 315–336.

Corsaro, W.A. (1985) *Friendship and Peer Culture in the Early Years.* Norwood NJ: Ablex.

Corsaro, W.A. (2005) *The Sociology of Childhood.* 2nd edn. Thousand Oaks CA: Pine Forge Press.

Corsaro, W.A. and L. Molinari (2005) *I Compagni: Understanding Children's Transition From Preschool to Elementary School.* New York: Teachers College Press.

Cromdal, J. (2001) ' "Can I Be with"? Negotiating Play Entry in a Bilingual School', *Journal of Pragmatics,* 33: 517–545.

Cromdal, J. (2004) 'Building Bilingual Oppositions: Notes on Code-Switching in Children's Disputes,' *Language in Society,* 33(1): 33–58.

Danby, S. and C. Baker (1998) 'How to Become Masculine in the Block Area', *Childhood,* 5(2): 151–175.

De León, L. (2007) ' "*Mi chave*"?: *Chive', Chive', Chive'* ("Do You Want to Eat?": "I Will Eat, I Will Eat, I Will Eat"): Parallelism, Metalinguistic Play, and the Interactive Emergence of Zinacantec Mayan Sibling's Culture', *Research on Language and Social Interaction,* 40(4): 405–436.

Eder, D. (1995) *School Talk. Gender and Adolescent Culture.* New Jersey: Rutgers.

Elbers, E. (1996) 'Citizenship in the Making: Themes of Citizenship in Children's Pretend Play', *Childhood,* 3: 499–514.

Evaldsson, A.-C. (2002) 'Boys' Gossip Telling: Staging Identities and Indexing (Non-Acceptable) Masculine Behaviour', *Text,* 22(2): 1–27.

Evaldsson, A.-C. (2003) 'Throwing Like a Girl?: Situating Gender Differences in Physicality Across Game Contexts', *Childhood,* 10(4): 475–497.

Evaldsson, A.-C. (2004) 'Shifting Moral Stances: Morality and Gender in Same-Sex and Cross-Sex Game Interaction', *Research on Language and Social Interaction,* 37(3): 331–363.

Evaldsson, A.-C. (2005) 'Staging Insults and Mobilizing Categorizations in a Multiethnic Peer Group', *Discourse & Society,* 16(6): 763–786.

Evaldsson, A.-C. and W.A. Corsaro (1998) 'The Ethnographic Study of Play and Games in Children's Peer Culture. An Interpretative Approach', *Childhood,* 5(4): 377–402.

Garvey, C. (1977) *Play.* Cambridge MA: Harvard University Press.

Goldman, L.R. (1998) *Child's Play: Myth, Mimesis, and Make-Believe.* New York: Oxford University Press.

Goffman, E. (1961) *Encounters. Two Studies in the Sociology of Interaction.* Indianapolis: Bobs-Merill.

Goffman, E. (1986) *Frame Analysis.* New York: Harper & Row.

Goodwin, M.H. (1990) *He-Said-She-Said: Talk as Social Organization Among Black Children.* Bloomington IN: Indiana University Press.

Goodwin, M.H. (1993) 'Accomplishing Social Organization Multimodality in Girls' Play: Patterns of Competition and Cooperation in an African-American Working Class Girls Group', in S.T. Hollis, L. Pershing and M.J. Young (eds) *Feminist Theory and Folklore.* Urbana: University. Illinois Press, pp. 149–165.

Goodwin, M.H. (1995) 'Co-construction in Girls' Hopscotch', *Research on Language and Social Interaction,* 28(3): 261–281.

Goodwin, M.H. (2001) 'Organizing Participation in Cross-Sex Jump Rope: Situating Gender Differences within Longitudinal Studies of Activities', *Research on Language and Social Interaction*, 34(1): 75–106.

Goodwin, M.H. (2006) *The Hidden Life of Girls: Games of Stance, Status, and Exclusion*. Malden MA: Blackwell.

Goodwin, M.H. and A. Kyratzis (eds) (2007), Introduction: 'Children Socializing Children: Cultural Production and Authoritative Discourse in Peer Interactions', *Research on Language and Social Interaction*, 40(4): 279–290.

Griswold, O. (2007) 'Achieving Authority: Discursive Practices in Russian Pre-Adolescent Girls' Pretend Play', *Research on Language and Social Interaction*, 40(4): 291–320.

Hewitt, R. (1997) '"Box-Out" and "Taxing"', in S. Johnson and U.H. Meinhof (eds) *Language and Masculinity*. Oxford: Blackwell, pp. 27–46.

Hughes, L. (1988) 'But That's Not *Really* Mean: Competing in a Cooperative Mode', *Sex Roles*, 19(11–12): 669–687.

Huizinga, J. ([1938] 1955) *Homo Ludens*. A Study of the Play-Element in Culture. Boston: Beacon Press.

James, A., C. Jenks and A. Prout. (1998) *Theorizing Childhood*. New York: Teachers College Press.

Kyratzis, A. (2004) 'Talk and Interaction among Children and the Co-Construction of Peer Groups and Peer Culture', *Annual Review of Anthropology*, 33: 625–649.

Kyratzis, A. (2007) '"Now We Return Back to our Weather Report": Appropriating Authoritative Registers in Girls' Pretend Play', *Research on Language and Social Interaction*, 40(4): 321–352.

Kyratzis, A., T. Marx, and E.R. Wade (2001) 'Preschoolers' Communicative Competence: Register Shift in the Marking of Power in Different Contexts of Friendship Group Talk', *First Language*, 21: 387–431.

Lever, J.R. (1978) 'Sex Differences in the Complexity of Children's Play and Games', *American Sociological Review*, 43(4): 471–483.

Levine, R.A. (1973) *Culture, Behavior and Personality*. Chicago: Aldine.

Maccoby, E.E. (1998) *The Two Sexes: Growing Up Apart, Coming Together*. Cambridge MA: Harvard University Press.

Mead, G.H. (1934) *Mind, Self and Society*. Chicago: University of Chicago Press.

Mead, M. (1930) *Growing Up in New Guinea*. New York: Morrow, 1975 edn.

Opie, I and I. Opie (1959) *The Lore and Language of School Children*. Oxford: Oxford University Press, 1977 edn.

Opie, I and I. Opie (1969) *Children's Games in Streets and Playgrounds*. Oxford: Oxford University Press.

Piaget, J. (1932) *The Moral Judgment of the Child*. New York: Free press, 1965 edn.

Piaget, J. (1951) *Play, Dreams and Imitations in Childhood*. New York: W.W. Norton, 1962 edn.

Reynolds, J.F. (2002) *Maya Children's Practices of the Imagination: (Dis)Playing Childhood and Politics in Guatemala*, Los Angeles: (Ph.D.) Department of Anthropology, University of California.

Rindstedt, C. (2001) *Quichua Children and Language Shift in an Andean Community: School, Play and Sibling Caretaking*, Linköping: Unitryck: (Ph.D.) Linköping Studies in Arts and Science, 241, Linköping University.

Schwartzman, H. (1978) *Transformations: The Anthropology of Children's Play*. New York: Plenum.

Sheldon, A. (1996) 'You Can Be the Baby Brother, But You Aint Born Yet: Preschool Girls Negotiation for Power and Access in Pretend Play', *Research on Language and Social Interaction*, 29(1): 57–80.

Sutton-Smith, B. (1971) 'A Reply to Piaget: A Play Theory of Copy', in R. Herron and B. Sutton-Smith (eds) *Child's Play*. New York: Wiley, pp. 103–106.

Sutton-Smith, B. (1972) *The Folkgames of Children*. Austin: University of Texas Press.

Sutton-Smith, B. (1979) 'The Play of Girls', in C.B. Kopp and M. Kirkpatrick (eds) *Becoming Female*. New York: Plenum, pp. 229–257.

Sutton-Smith, B. (1995) 'Methods in Children's Folklore', in B. Sutton-Smith et al. (eds) *Children's Folklore: A Source Book*. New York and London: Garland, pp. 64–74.

Sutton-Smith, B., J. Mechling, T. Johnson, and F. McMahon, (eds) (1995) *Children's Folklore: A Source Book*. New York and London: Garland.

Thorne, B. (1993) *Gender Play: Girls and Boys in School*. New Brunswick NJ: Rutgers University Press.

Whalen, M. (1995) 'Working Towards Play: Complexity in Children's Fantasy Activities', *Language in Society*, 24(3): 315–348.

Vygotsky, L. (1966) 'Play and Its Role in the Development of the Child', *Soviet Psychology and Psychiatry*, 12(1): 6–18.

22
Children as Consumers

Daniel Thomas Cook

For the better part of a century, merchants, marketers and advertisers have recognized, attended to and engaged with children as consumers in some fashion.
Early twentieth-century dry goods and department stores in the United States,
Canadian and British cities assigned specific shelves or small sections of floor
space to display goods intended for children's possession or purchase. In the early
twenty-first century, the products, media, iconography and commercial spaces
designated for 'kids' hold a secure, significant place in the marketing plans of
many multi-billion dollar enterprises of global capitalism.

The change over this time extends beyond simple quantities or types of products made with children in mind. It is a change, rather, which involves cultural
understanding of childhood, the place and meaning of money and commerce
in social relations generally and the social valuation of children specifically. In
order for 'children,' generically, to be conceptualized and treated as a primary,
direct and significant market, merchants also found it necessary to acknowledge
their wants, desires and choices – even as these may have been mediated or otherwise directed by parents, specifically by mothers. Acknowledgement of children's
agentive involvement in the commercial world, moreover, entails a moral position and positioning by recognizing children as legitimate social participants –
as 'persons,' if you will (see James, this volume).

Children, in this sense, arise as subjects in and through consumer contexts, even
as they and their life-worlds continue to be subjected to a persistent onslaught of
commercial power in the form of promotions and packaged narratives. As 'consumers', children (or discursive constructions of children) capture the attention
of social structures, institutions and organizations to an extent and intensity that
often surpasses how they are regarded when framed as, say, citizens or workers. Specialized media, entire television networks, the design of retail spaces and
product packaging, publications, vacation destinations and leisure pursuits at
present have all been researched, tested, promoted and engineered for children's
(and, to a different extent, parents') edification. Children's consumption extends
beyond singular purchases and into meaningful engagement with the world and,
as such, needs to be understood not simply as individual acts but in reference to
an encompassing consumer culture of childhood.

Early recognition of the child consumer

'Before 1890', historian William Leach observes, 'most American children, wore, ate and played with what their parents made or prepared for them' (1993a, 85). By the early twentieth century, industries dealing in specially made and designed products for children, such as toys (Kline, 1993, 143–173; Leach, 1993a, 85–90, 328–330; Seiter, 1993; Cross, 1997), books, (Kline, 1993), magazines (Jacobson, 2004), clothing (Cook, 2004) and nursery ware (Forty, 1986, 67–72) began to proliferate in US cities. To be sure, these children's goods, including notably children's books (Kline, 1993, 79–99), were being manufactured outside the home and sold in stores prior to the twentieth century. In 1892, the Marshall Field's department store of Chicago published a 36-page Christmas catalogue listing playthings like cast iron horses, dolls and doll houses intended for children of the well-to-do 'carriage trade' (Cross, 1997, 11). The Sears mail-order catalogue included a section on children's clothing as early as 1896 (Huun and Kaiser, 2001).

It was during the first decades of the 1900s that key children's industries began to recognize themselves as industries by forming professional bodies, publishing trade journals and making appeals for and responses to government action. For the toy industry, *Toys and Novelties* started publication in 1903 and *Playthings* in 1909 (Cross, 1997). The first trade journal devoted exclusively to children's clothing, *The Infants' Department*, began in 1917. In 1924 the *Horn Book* was founded to promote books for children, although as early as 1874, *Publishers Weekly* listed children's books. Creating markets for children's goods was becoming an increasingly collective, organized and purposeful endeavour.

These developments notwithstanding, the 'child market' until the 1920s and 1930s appears to have been fairly circumscribed in terms of sales. In urban department stores there were few separate children's clothing departments (Cook, 2004). The 'toy department' usually consisted of a few shelves, perhaps an aisle or two, within a large emporium of other goods (Cross, 1997; Leach, 1993b). The icon of Santa Claus was only beginning to solidify the connection between children, shopping and Christmas (Leach, 1993a). Taken individually – a few toys, some candy purchased at a local drugstore candy counter, a game obtained from a mail-order catalogue – these things would not amount to anything notable beyond their specific instances of purchase, something unremarkable in themselves.

The cultural foundations of the child consumer can be found in significant part in an ideology of domesticity arising from the well-to-do classes of the eighteenth and nineteenth centuries which legitimized the home as a 'woman's place' and sentimentalized children – upper- and middle-class children initially – as innocent, vulnerable beings in need of nurturance and protection (Gillis, 1996; Douglas, 1977; Hall and Davidoff, 1987; Heininger, 1984). Sentimental domesticity, as a set of beliefs, situated the home as something of a haven from the 'external' world of work, commerce and pecuniary interests – a moral opposition which would seem to be unfavourable for the rise of the child consumer. Indeed, sociologist Viviana Zelizer (1985) offers evidence that the sentimentalization of childhood spread beyond the upper classes. From the 1880s through 1930s, she argues, the social value of children underwent a transformation whereby their worth increasingly came to be assessed in emotional rather than economic terms, as illustrated in debates about child labour, black market babies and child insurance. Zelizer understands the change as one in the cultural conception of childhood whereby children had become sacralized by virtue of their moral incompatibility with, and distance from, commercial, monetary interests.

The growing cultural presence and visibility of the child consumer over this same time, however, tells a different if complementary tale about the intermixing – rather than the separation – of pecuniary considerations and the social-emotional value of children. Advertisers in the early 1900s were unsure of the extent of children's purchasing power or influence on parents' spending. Nonetheless, they targeted children as an audience and market for their promotions and used images of children as product endorsers (Jacobson, 2004). Historian Gary Cross argues that many advertisements of and for children encoded an emerging sensibility regarding childhood that was not found either in traditional religious views of child depravity or in the proscriptions of developmentalist childrearing advice which stressed rational nurturing. 'Wondrous innocence' (Cross, 2004a, 2004b), found in the child's look of wonder, expressed the joys of having and consuming goods which were experienced as much by the gifting adults as the receiving child.

Promotional expressions of innocent wonder in the 1920s represent the beginnings of a deep and progressive blending of the values of the consumer culture with constructions of childhood. It was not due to the size of the market, to children's purchasing power, nor, for that matter, to their ability to cajole their parents into great purchases that provided the original and enduring impetus for the children's market. The great change in the commercialization of childhood, one from which modern societies have not retreated, involves the cultural recognition of, and institutional support for, children who are seen to have something of a social right and wherewithal to be desirous of goods and to act upon those desires. Beyond advertising images and promotions, the infrastructure of retail enterprises transformed and adjusted to welcome and accommodate the child consumer to create what Leach (1993b) calls a 'child-world' of goods.

Key departments in department stores – children's clothing departments in particular – began to organize and structure selling space around the child's, rather than mother's, presumed perspective. In the 1930s, departments for children's clothing began to be fitted with child-apportioned fixtures and child-height mirrors. In the younger children's shops and areas, nursery-story characters adorned the walls and 'child' music was piped in, all to offer a sense of propriety and cultural ownership for the children – that is a sense that the place was 'theirs.' These spaces also effectively linked differently aged children into an ascending hierarchy of social prestige, nuanced by commercial goods, based on presumed age-gender differences (Cook, 2003). Anecdotes from retailers appeared regularly on the pages of retail trade publications, like *The Infants' Department, Printers' Ink* and *The Dry Goods Merchandiser*, throughout the 1920s and 1930s, testifying to the increasing influence children appeared to be wielding with their parents on the sales floor regarding the purchase of their attire and other goods (see Cook, 2004).

The shift in orientation from parent to child – and the accompanying celebration of the child's desires as natural, good and primary – dovetailed with other trends in American, middle-class culture. Childrearing advice in books and parent magazines over these decades increasingly urged mothers to take the child's point of view (Wolfenstein, 1955). The rise of radio and programming for children helped make the child into a targeted audience to tune into programs produced with her or his interests in mind (Cross, 1997, 100–129). Moreover, children's films, the rise of Disney during this time (Sammond, 2005), along with the solidification of age-grading in schools (Chudacoff, 1989) together formed a significant part of the cultural context where children could be addressed as a distinct entity with values, viewpoints and desires of their own.

Orienting commercial spaces, merchandise, stock and department design in deference to the presumed perspective of the child (it is presumed because no systematic research on children's consumer views was undertaken during these decades) made for a shift beyond simply naming the child as a 'consumer.' It institutionalized 'the child' and, importantly, childhood in commercial terms and in business agendas and priorities to the extent that some began to build their enterprises in conversation with children's desires, choices and viewpoints, rather than ignoring or marginalizing them. This shift, which began in earnest in the 1920s, did not remove mothers or parents from the consumer equation; it repositioned them increasingly as reactive and responsive vis-à-vis the overtures originating from the marketplace (Seiter, 1993).

From 'knowing' to researching children

The commercial impetus to 'know' the child as a consumer followed logically and practically from the commercial impetus to 'sell' the child. Initially, an understanding about children (and mothers) as consumers was garnered through retailers' anecdotal observations of selling floor interactions between mothers and children, some of which circulated nationally in the form of features and stories in trade magazines (see Cook, 2000, 2004, chapter 4). Some market observers apparently would extrapolate from the experiences of their own children to offer generalizations about the 'child consumer' (e.g., Howell, 1930, 118). In many ways, these stories invoked models or constructs of 'the child' which served as a vital currency of business knowledge at a time well before any direct market research on children existed (see Cook, 2000, 2004, chapter 4).

Knowledge about children's consumer inclinations began to acquire a systematicity and organization when scholars and observers sought to apply insights from the emerging field of developmental child psychology to the children's market behaviour. The most prominent practitioner in this area in the 1930s was E. Evelyn Grumbine, assistant publisher and advertising director of *Child Life* magazine. Grumbine had written a number of articles summarizing and extending academic research on topics such as children's colour preferences.

The research, according to Grumbine, was conducted to assist the merchandiser in 'artistically satisfying' the child by designing advertisements, books and illustrations which are 'pleasing.' (Grumbine, 1938a, 39–40). In 1938, she published *Reaching Juvenile Markets* wherein she matched the known traits and tendencies of children at various developmental stages with the characteristics of goods, toys or games appropriate for that age. For instance, children in GROUP II (age 4–6) exhibit 'imagination with a broader scope' and their attention can be captured with products utilizing fairy tales and fantastical characters (1938b, 34–35).

Matching developmental stages with appropriate products, now standard practice for both business and consumers, did not constitute a simple case of the market exploitation of children. Indeed, for Grumbine and others, the effort to determine the child's orientation and skill level at a particular age stage enabled children's autonomy by encouraging children's 'choice' and 'participation' in the marketplace (Grumbine, 1938b, ix). Grumbine and others at this time did not ask children directly about their product preferences, but she did conduct interviews about their satisfactions with premiums (see Jacobson, 2004, 203–205), demonstrating further the growing effort to coordinate children's desires and views with commercial interests. By the 1950s, the 'youth market,' which included 'children' into their twenties, had become a cultural phenomenon with the ascent of the 'teenager' (Palladino, 1996) in public culture. In this context, marketers like Eugene Gilbert (1957) baldly encouraged appealing to the child and youth market without apology.

In the 1960s, market researchers found it analytically useful and ethically workable to forego notions from developmental psychology and interview young children directly about their knowledge of goods and icons, their preferences and desires. Marketing professors like William Wells (1965; see Cook, 2000) and James McNeal (1964, 1969) brought children into the research process in order to assess their knowledge of and preferences for products and brands. Instead of simply being imputed, intuited or assumed, the child's view and understanding was elicited from children themselves. The significance of this research lays not so much in the accuracy of the detailed findings as in its acknowledgement that children can and should be treated as knowing, able consumers and, as Sammond (2005) argues, seen as 'normal' children.

Television and the problem of children's cognitive abilities

During this same time, specialized 'children's' television came into its own in terms of content and, perhaps more significantly, in terms of its social and temporal place in children's and families' lives. In the 1960s, three television networks devoted programming specifically geared for preschool and elementary school-aged children's consumption during Saturday mornings at a time when there were no more than five channels in total available to households (Hendershot, 1998). With programming comes advertising. Young, school-aged children provided a clear target audience for many promotions. This concentrated advertising and programming eventually sparked resistance from consumer watchdog groups, most notably Action for Children's Television (ACT).

ACT objected that children's programs had become 'thirty-minute commercials' for products such as Hot Wheels toy cars. They argued that insidious and unchecked commercialism was overriding the potential educational value of television for children. Opponents of children's television and commercialism based much of their argument on emerging research about the relationship between children's developmental age and their ability to process commercial information. Instead of seeking details about children's product recall and preferences, social researchers began to investigate the extent to which young children are able to understand the persuasive intent and content of ads, their ability to judge the truth of promotional claims, and capacity to determine the value of goods (Martin, 1997; John, 1999).

The concerns here centre on the child's facility, as an individuated social-psychological entity, to comprehend commercial messages in ways necessary to make knowledgeable choices, where it is thought that a clear distinction between 'commercial speech' and other forms of communication can be made. In this emerging sensibility – one which recalls debates over children's cinema in the 1930s (Sammond, 2005) – the market arises as a threat to children and their childhoods mainly by virtue of the manner through which children encounter their values and messages, and not as a categorically corrosive force.

In 1974, the advertising industry, under pressure from ACT and other groups, set up the Children's Advertising Review Unit (CARU) of the US government's Better Business Bureau as a way for the industry to regulate itself and avoid government intervention. ACT continued to push for governmental regulation of American television programming for, and advertising to, children throughout the 1970s and 1980s. Their efforts culminated in the Children's Television Act of 1990, a watered-down version of earlier legislative initiatives, which placed limits on the amount of commercial time that could be aired during children's shows. The legislation also required 'separators' between program and commercial (e.g., 'We'll be right back after these commercial announcements.') to help children distinguish between program content and advertising.

Ultimately, the Children's Television Act was argued and decided on the free market principle of choice in the marketplace. ACT and others were only partially successful in invoking the model of the child actor/consumer as vulnerable to commercial manipulation. President G.H.W. Bush did not sign the Act (which could become law without his signature), stating that: 'The legislation limits the amount of advertising that broadcasters may air during children's programming…. The First Amendment [to the US Constitution], however, does not contemplate that government will dictate the quality or quantity of what Americans should hear – rather, it leaves this to be decided by free media responding to the free choices of individual consumers' (http://www.presidency.ucsb.edu/ws/index.php?pid=18939).

These statements position 'the child' not as a special audience in need of regulation or protection, but as an 'American' who deserves to be afforded all the 'rights' of the First Amendment. Chief among these rights is the right to choose, to act as a full person in a democratic capitalist society. The regulations that did make it into the 1990 legislation were essentially impotent on arrival as a new arrangement between media, properties and goods was already in the making in the 1980s with the meteoric rise of character licensing and co-branding.

Commodity and media synergies through character licensing

Character licensing, as Tom Englehardt (1986) points out, has existed in some form at least since the early twentieth century, and has been present in children's television since the 1950s with the likes of Buffalo Bob in *Howdy Doody*. A turning point in the relationship between children, products and media, he argues, occurred during the 1980s with the advent of what he has dubbed 'the Shortcake Strategy.' Strawberry Shortcake is a feminine character developed by an offshoot of the American Card Company in 1980 as both a doll and an intellectual property to be licensed. The licensed property found widespread success on greeting cards, clothing accessories and eventually as a cartoon.

Strawberry Shortcake reinforced earlier lessons learned by corporate onlookers that characters can exist outside of specific narrative genres and thus can be transferred to other, purportedly non-related products. School lunchboxes, for instance, have been a popular medium to display television show and cartoon characters since the 1950s.[1] Strawberry Shortcake, and subsequent licensing efforts in the 1980s, demonstrated something fundamental and new about the interaction between the children's market and media: characters could be conceived from the outset as transferable and mobile, and thereby could be amenable to making multiple partnerships among industries and across brands. It became feasible and economically viable to plan and develop entire lines of interconnected products woven together by a character's back-story (Englehardt, 1986).

In response to the deregulatory environment of the Reagan–Bush administrations (1981–1993) and the legal compromises that the Children's Television Act of 1990 represents (Kline, 1993; Kunkel and Roberts, 1991), media interests had found a formula that combined the synergistic qualities of co-branding and marketing partnerships with the benefits of owning and maintaining the back-stories and narratives of characters. The result has been children's television shows that are conceived and developed in tandem with an entire array of merchandising arrangements. Many shows now are essentially 30-minute commercials for their own brands, brand extensions and media networks – the very format against which Action for Children's television had campaigned. The distinctions between advertising and program – as well as between program and food, toys and clothing – have been disintegrating and blurring for several decades.

Examples of product extensions and corporate partnerships abound, from the early 1990s success of the Power Rangers, to the Power Puff Girls later in the decade to the continuing dominance of Barney, Blues Clues, Dora the Explorer,

Teletubbies and SpongeBob SquarePants characters in the early twenty-first century, each targeting a specific age-gender market niche. Many of these partnerships are now familiar. Disney toys, which usually represent characters from their films, are found as premiums in McDonald's Happy Meals. Famously, the 1990 film *Teenage Mutant Ninja Turtles*, a huge global success, featured Pizza Hut as part of the story line of the pizza-loving characters. In 2002, the licensed Veggie Tales cartoon characters followed suit (Burgess, 2002). Many children's shows are owned and developed by the media interests that produce and televise them, like the Cartoon Network, Nickelodeon and the Disney Channel in the United States of America.

Characters and cartoons often serve as the vehicles for the nurturing of cross-national and global markets and audiences. The characters of Sesame Street, for instance, which often have been lauded as 'educational' programming on American public television, are now shown and tailored to the local linguistic 'idiom' and cultural 'tone' towards media and education in over a dozen countries (Hendershot, 1998, 179–186), complete with growing lines of licensed products and brand extensions. Adjusting characters and narratives to local, cultural tastes accounts largely for the phenomenal success of the Pokemon franchise, a Japanese product, since the late 1990s in the United States (Allison, 2006). The marketing of Pokemon in the United States, according to Allison (2006, 237–249), had to contend with the tension between the general avoidance of conflict that is characteristic of the original Japanese story line, and the corporate belief that American children in particular preferred 'loud' characters who were easily identifiable as 'good' or 'evil' to create dramatic action and winners and losers. Nintendo capitalized on the Pokemon cartoon, trading card and film craze in 1999 by offering Pokemon fruit roll-ups with five of the collectible cards from combination game and cartoon series (Thompson, 1999, 10).

Cartoons and shows in general exist not simply for the sake of telling stories or imparting 'lessons,' but to deliver an audience to advertisers and a market to retailers. They serve foremost as promotional vehicles for the brand and for brand extensions across product categories, such as food, clothing, school supplies, bedding and toys. In this new world of child marketing, the characters and shows do not only sell products, they *are* the commodities. Intertextuality – the extension of media characters and narratives beyond a single genre or medium (Spigel, 1992) – is the purpose of producing the characters and narratives, from the sellers' perspective. Intertextuality ensures that consumption is always multiple. Watching the SpongeBob SquarePants show, for instance, *is* in itself a form of brand exposure, but having the Kraft Corporation's SpongeBob Macaroni and Cheese meal for lunch is exposure to a brand of another order. When a child eats the Kraft Corporation's macaroni with the character on the box, she also simultaneously ingests SpongeBob *and* Nickelodeon Network (its corporate owner) as a kind of semiotic fare which accompanies the carbohydrates, protein, fat and sodium. The 'consumption' here is multiply articulated along gustatory, semiotic and cultural dimensions and, significantly, oriented to the child's views, preoccupations and desires.

New childhoods arising?

Since the 1980s, there have been growing concerns expressed that something fundamental about childhood has changed, or is in the process of changing. Some social critics and observers contend that childhood is disappearing or eroding – that some basic, elemental beliefs, practices and understandings about how children move through the early life course, and what that movement means for children as well as adults, no longer pertain. It is a view that has risen to the level of public discourse and common sense since the 1990s and to some degree is shared by marketers as well as by parents, psychologists and medical doctors. A common thread uniting these views – though few would concur about the exact causal relationships and consequences of this change – is a sense that the intense and prolific commercial-media environment in which children are embedded has altered how children interact with and come to know the world.

In the 1980s, a number of authors put forward the thesis that childhood is disappearing mainly under the tutelage of modern life due to the increasingly ubiquitous environment of electronic media, particularly the growing centrality of television (Elkind, 1981; Postman, 1982; Suransky, 1982; Meyrowitz, 1985; see Buckingham, 2000, 21–40 and in this volume for discussion and critique). Neil Postman's argument in *The Disappearance of Childhood* (1982) is perhaps the most famous and most celebrated of this view. He contended that the rise of electronic media, particularly television, has made knowledge available to children that previously was out of their purview, or which was to be revealed to them in a measured way as they grew older. For Postman, the visual nature of televisual media is characterized by an immediacy of, and a 'total disclosure' of information, implicating children of virtually all ages because it does not require literacy and education to grasp and to take in. Consequently, the lines traditionally distinguishing adulthood from childhood are disappearing as adults are no longer able to control the 'symbolic environment of childhood' and thus cannot set the 'conditions by which a child was to become an adult' (ibid., 45).

Postman and others made their assertions at a time before the rise of the World Wide Web and associated communication technologies came into widespread use and before the computer was conceptualized and used as a communication device on par with the telephone. As several cohorts of children have grown into and come of age in a world of virtually instant access to images, news, information and other people, the dynamic outlined by the 'disappearance' theorists has itself transformed in a variety of ways. For one, many children quickly become adept at using computers and other devices, often exceeding their parents' abilities to the extent that many children educate their elders in technology matters. As well, with email, instant messaging, text messaging, blogs and the like, children interact through and participate in global networks well outside the immediate surveillance of their parents. Moreover, the possession, use and consumption of many communication technologies are themselves a sign of 'youth' and are used by some as a form of social distinction from adults. Thus, electronic media in these ways reverses or otherwise disrupts basic power-knowledge relationships which have traditionally pertained between children and adults (Buckingham, 2000, this volume; Livingstone, 2002; Seiter, 2005; Marsh, 2005)

If childhood is transforming in a fundamental way, it is not simply due to a technological determinism, as Buckingham (2000) argues. The 'disappearance of childhood' authors did not recognize the tight relationship between media and consumption and, as well, did not account for the increasing specification of children's consumer markets which have offered an ever-expanding array of goods and entertainment designed and promoted for children of specific ages and age grades. Marketers recognize the change in childhood citing the phenomenon of KGOY (Kids Getting Older Younger) as a noticeable form of 'age compression' whereby goods previously desired by children of a certain age are now shunned as immature or 'babyish' (Sutherland and Thompson, 2001, 40–42). For instance, the traditional 'toy' market in the United States now has difficulty selling to children older than 10 years old. Mattel's famous Barbie doll used to be part of 14-year-old girl's play repertoire. Now, the company only seems to be able to sell to girls eight years old and younger, or to nostalgic adults (Payne, 2002; Shen, 2002).

Marketers and advertisers were also quick to note children's attraction to and use of technology in the 1990s. Some of them argue that contemporary children are media savvy and thus consumer savvy. Children's comfort with media and technology and their ability to learn about the world, including products, through the internet makes them increasingly difficult to persuade through standard advertising messages and means. A few marketers contend that children have, in recent years, developed a keen scepticism about marketing and advertising claims (as gathered through their own research on and with children). The new 'savvy' child consumer, marketers maintain, constitutes someone who is, except in a few cases, not a passive subject to be 'exploited,' but an extremely knowledgeable person to be engaged.

In this new ideology of children's consumption, emergent in the 1990s and in full force in the early twenty-first century, marketers implore that goods 'empower' children by the very fact that children can and do make choices and see the products as their own (Schor, 2004, 177–181; Cook, 2007). Because children are being given an increasing array of choices, some argue, they are better equipped to choose in an informed manner and thus can be sold to with little concern about 'exploitation' (Del Vecchio, 1998; Sutherland and Thompson, 2001; Johnson, 2005). A knowledgeable, engaged child is antithetical to manipulation, in this view. Marketers present the function of market research – especially the kind of research where children are questioned or observed directly about their preferences and knowledge – as ultimately befitting children by consulting children's views and offering things children, not adults, want (Schor, 2004, 99–118).

The key issue in the loss or disappearance of childhood resides in the changing power relationship between adults and children and more specifically between parents, particularly mothers, and their children. Children's new found 'power' in this sense arises from consumer power in terms of the money they spend, of what is spent on or for them and of the increasing array and kinds of goods designed with their views, social worlds, peer cultures (see Corsaro, this volume) and preferences in mind. Children's 'desires' – whether presumed, imputed or 'discovered' through research – hold a firm central place in marketing efforts, including the role played by parents.

The changing political economy of the household and the economic status of mothers have provided the fertile soil where children's wants could not only be acknowledged but engaged and incorporated into family practice. Mothers have entered the paid workforce in greater numbers than in previous decades and, by the late 1990s, a second (i.e., woman's) source of income was seen as a necessity by many (Schor, 1998). A steady, high rate of divorce and remarriage made blended families a common experience for many children. In addition, two prolonged periods of relative economic prosperity in the 1980s and 1990s, punctuated by only a brief downturn, made conditions favourable for children to become recognized as an economic influence and force by marketers and economists.

Together, these sets of factors also helped chip away at lingering moral hesitations about the extent to which children could be addressed and targeted as direct consumers beyond the traditional Christmas season and gift-giving occasions such as birthdays. Many observers point to women's absence from the home to work in the labour force as a source of guilt for mothers who often 'compensate' by acquiescing to children's requests for things more than they might have otherwise. Mothers' relative absence has also made for a market of convenience foods which can be easily prepared by them or by the children or fathers. Dining out or ordering food for take-out or home delivery has increased dramatically for similar reasons. Marketers began to realize that children consequently were gaining a stronger voice in family purchasing decisions, not only in the area of their own food, toys and clothes as might be expected, but also in having a say in the choice of such big ticket items as the family car, vacation destination, large appliances and even the location of the new home (McNeal, 1992, 1999; Guber and Berry, 1993; Sutherland and Thompson, 2001).

The change in childhood, it appears, is less about its disappearance and more centred on an adjustment in the relationship between parents and children vis-à-vis consumption and media activities. Moreover, the relationship does not consist simply of dichotomous terms in simple opposition: for example adults vs children; parent vs child. Rather, the world and practices of economic actors like marketers, advertisers, merchandisers and market researchers must be included as a third term in the relations which continue to re-form the dynamic boundaries of childhood (Coffey, Siegel and Livingston, 2006).

Conclusion

Children, in practical terms, no longer enter life independent of the world of commerce and subsequently 'become' consumers through a process of socialization. Rather, they unfold as persons in and, in significant ways, through a consumer society. Children can't escape consumption, in part, because their parents and virtually everyone around them are avid consumers as today's adults have come of age in their own historically specific versions of consumer culture. They can't escape consumption because their toys, stories, clothing, media, and food and games (Moore, 2006) are awash in commercial meaning, brands and icons; their schools in the United States promote consumerism through Channel One, fast food cafeterias and corporate sponsorships (Molnar, 1996; Stole and Livesay, 2006).

Consumption does not include everyone equally. Children from low-income families find themselves on the outside looking in. Single and low-income mothers sometimes find that their most difficult-to-handle concern is their inability to outfit their children with the 'gear' and goods of their peers, thus marking their kids as 'different' and sub-par (Pugh, 2004; Power, 2005; Thorne, 2005). Those who live in difficult economic circumstances may find themselves desiring a good not because of its use value or even potential to offer pleasure, but because possession itself may serve as a sign of 'belonging' to a peer group and perhaps in a larger sense to 'society' (Chin, 2001). In the global division of labour and wealth, many children remain in circumstances where they have little choice but to labour to create goods that others consume.

Consumer capitalism, in its modern form, has never existed without some-how incorporating children and childhood into its mix. As it continues it glo-bal march, it is clear that childhood is centrally positioned in this process. Media entertainment, global brands and fast food restaurants are among the key vehicles for the intermixing of childhoods and consumption in various coun-tries, cultures and contexts (Yan, 1997; Langer, 2004; Peterson, 2005). It remains an open question as to the extent to which the forces of capital will shape child-hoods or perhaps homogenize them into the figure of a 'global child.' What is clear is that these questions need to be posed. It is also clear that the issue of children's place in consumer culture must be engaged in ways that recognize the hand of corporate power in the hyper-commercialization of childhoods while also acknowledging children's stake in commercial life as something other than exploitation.

Note

1. See Smithsonian Institution documents online at: http://www.smithsonianeducation.org/idealabs/ap/artifacts/lunchbox.htm, accessed 20 May 2008.

References

Allison, A. (2006) *Millennial Monsters: Japanese Toys and the Global Imagination*. Durham NC: Duke University Press.

Buckingham, D. (2000) *After the Death of Childhood*. Cambridge: Polity Press.

Burgess, A. (2002) 'VeggieTales Nibbles Its Way to Mass Market with an Upcoming Feature Film', *KidScreen*, 1 May, 19.

Bush, G.H.W. (1990) 'Statement on Public Television Act of 1990', http://www.presidency.ucsb.edu/ws/index.php?pid=18939 (accessed on 20 May 2008).

Chin, E. (2001) *Purchasing Power*. Minneapolis: University of Minnesota Press.

Chudacoff, H.P. (1989) *How Old Are You? Age Consciousness in American Culture*. Princeton NJ: Princeton University Press.

Coffey T., D. Siegel and G. Livingston (2006) *Marketing to the New Super Consumer: Mom & Kid*. Ithaca NY: Paramount Marketing Publishers.

Cook, D.T. (2000) 'The Other "Child Study": Figuring Children as Consumers in Market Research 1910's–1990's', *The Sociological Quarterly*, 41(3): 487–507.

Cook, D.T. (2003) 'Spatial Biographies of Children's Consumption', *Journal of Consumer Culture*, 3(2): 147–169.

Cook, D.T. (2004) *The Commodification of Childhood*. Durham NC: Duke University Press.

Cook, D.T. (2007) 'The Disempowering Empowerment of Children's Consumer "Choice": Cultural Discourses of the Child Consumer in North America', *Society and Business Review*, 2(1): 37–52.

Cross, G. (1997) *Kids' Stuff*. Cambridge: Harvard University Press.

Cross, G. (2004a) *The Cute and the Cool: Wondrous Innocence and American Children's Culture*. Oxford UK: Oxford University Press.

Cross, G. (2004b) 'Wondrous Innocence', *Journal of Consumer Culture*, 4(2): 183–201.

Del Vecchio, G. (1998) *Creating Ever-Cool: A Marketer's Guide to a Kids' Heart*. Gretna LA: Pelican Publishers.

Douglas, A. (1977) *The Feminization of American Culture*. New York: Avon.

Elkind, D. (1981) *The Hurried Child*. Reading MA: Addison-Wellesley.

Englehardt, T. (1986) 'The Shortcake Strategy', in T. Gitlin (ed.) *Watching Television*. New York: Pantheon, pp. 68–110.

Forty, A. (1986) *Objects of Desire*. London: Thames and Hudson.

Gilbert, E. (1957) *Advertising and Marketing to Young People*. Pleasantville NY: Printer's Ink Books.

Gillis, J. (1995) *A World of Their Own Making*. New York: Basic Books.

Grumbine, E.E. (1938a) 'Pictures and Colors Children Like', *Printer's Ink Monthly*, March, pp. 39–40.

Grumbine, E.E. (1938b) *Reaching Juvenile Markets: How to Advertise, Sell, and Merchandise through Boys and Girls*. New York: McGraw-Hill.

Guber, S. and J. Berry (1993) *Marketing To and Through Kids*. New York: McGraw-Hill.

Hall, C. and L. Davidoff (1987) *Family Fortunes*. Chicago: University of Chicago Press.

Heininger, M.L.S. (1984) 'Children, Childhood, and Change in America, 1820–1920', in Heininger (ed.) *A Century of Childhood, 1820–1920*. Rochester NY: Margaret Woodbury Strong Museum, pp. 1–33.

Hendershot, H. (1998) *Saturday Morning Censors*. Durham NC: Duke University Press

Howell, W.F. (1930) 'With Designs Upon the Next Generation', *Printer's Ink Monthly*, October, 118.

Huun, K. and S.B. Kaiser. (2001) 'The Emergence of Modern Infantwear, 1896–1962: Traditional White Dresses Succumb to Fashion's Gender Obsession', *Clothing and Textiles Research Journal*, 19(3): 103–119.

Jacobson, L. (2004) *Raising Consumers*. New York: Columbia University Press.

John, D.R. (1999) 'Consumer Socialization of Children: A Retrospective Look at Twenty-five Years of Research', *Journal of Consumer Research*, 26(3): 183–213.

Johnson, S. (2005) *Everything Bad is Good for You*. New York: Riverhead Books.

Kline, S. (1993) *Out of the Garden: Toys and Children's Culture in the Age of TV Marketing*. London: Verso.

Kunkel, D. and D. Roberts 'Young Minds and Marketplace Values: Issues in Children's Television Advertising', *Journal of Social Issues*, 47(1): 57–72.

Langer, B. (2004) 'The Business of Branded Enchantment: Ambivalence and Disjuncture in the Global Children's Culture Industry', *Journal of Consumer Culture*, 4(2): 251–276.

Leach, W. (1993a) *Land of Desire: Merchants, Power and the Rise of a New American Culture*. New York: Pantheon.

Leach, W. (1993b) 'Child-World in the Promised Land', in J. Gilbert (ed.) *The Mythmaking Frame of Mind*. Belmont CA: Wadsworth.

Livingstone, S. (2002) *Young People and New Media*. London: Sage.

Marsh, J. (ed.) (2005) *Popular Culture, New Media and Digital Literacy in Early Childhood*. London: Routledge Falmer.

Martin, M.C. (1997) 'Children's Understanding of Intent in Advertising: A Meta-Analysis', *Journal of Public Policy and Marketing*, 16(2): 205–216.

McNeal, J.U. (1964) *Children as Consumers*. Austin TX: Bureau of Business Research, University of Texas.

McNeal, J.U. (1969) 'The Child as Consumer' *Journal of Retailing*, 45: 15–22.

McNeal, J.U. (1992) *Kids as Customers*. New York: Lexington Books.

McNeal, J.U. (1999) *The Kids' Market: Myths and Realities*. Ithaca NY: Paramount Market Publishing.

Meyrowitz, J. (1985) *No Sense of Place: The Impact of Electronic Media on Social Behavior*. New York and Oxford: Oxford University Press.

Molnar, A. (1996) *Giving Kids the Business: The Commercialization of America's Schools*. Boulder CO: Westview Press.

Moore, E. (2006) 'Its Child's Play: Advergaming and the On-line Marketing of Food to Children', Kaiser Family Foundation Report. Publication #7536. http://www.kff.org/entmedia/upload/7536.pdf (accessed on 20 May 2008).

Palladino, G. (1996) *Teenagers*. New York: Basic Books.

Payne, E. (2002) 'Tweens: The Latest Sale Bait: Too Young to Woo?: The Preteen Kids of the Youngest Baby Boomers Drive Billions of Dollars in Consumer Spending. But as Objects of Marketers' Desire, Will Tweens Lose Their Childhood?' *The Ottawa Citizen*, April 28, D3.

Peterson, M.A. (2005) 'The *Jinn* and the Computer: Consumption and Identity in Arabic Children's Magazines', *Childhood*, 12(2) May: 177–200.

Postman, N. (1982) *The Disappearance of Childhood*. New York: Laurel.

Power, E. (2005) 'The Unfreedom of Being Other: Canadian Lone Mothers' Experiences of Poverty and "Life on the Cheque"', *Sociology*, 39(4): 643–660.

Pugh, A. (2004) 'Windfall Child Rearing: Low-income Care and Consumption', *Journal of Consumer Culture*, 4(2): 229–249.

Sammond, N. (2005) *Babes in Toyland*. Durham NC: Duke University Press.

Schor, J. (1998) *The Overspent American: Why We Want What We Don't Need*. New York: Basic Books.

Schor, J. (2004) *Born to Buy: The Commercialized Child and the New Consumer Culture*. New York: Scribner's.

Seiter, E. (1993) *Sold Separately: Parents and Children in Consumer Culture*. New York: Basic Books.

Seiter, E. (2005) *The Internet Playground*. New York: Peter Lang.

Shen, F. (2002) '"Toys? But I'm 10 Now!" As the Barbie Set Gets Younger and Younger, The Industry Retools', *Washington Post*, 17 February, H01.

Smithsonian Institute 'Lunchboxes, 1950's–1980's', SI neg. #89–5015, www.smithsonianeducation.org/idealabs/ap/artifacts/lunchbox.htm. (accessed on 20 May 2008).

Spigel, L. (1992) *Make Room for TV*. Chicago: University of Chicago Press.

Stole, I.L. and R. Livesay (2006) 'Consumer Activism, Commercialism, and Curriculum Choices: Advertising in Schools in the 1930's', *Journal of American Culture*, 30(1): 68–80.

Suransky, V. (1982) *Erosion of Childhood*. Chicago: University of Chicago Press.

Sutherland, A. and B. Thompson (2001) *Kidfluence*. Toronto: McGraw Hill.

Thompson, S. (1999) 'Dole Pumps Fun into Fruit in $20M Effort', *Brandweek*, 29 March, 40, 13: 14.

Thorne, B. (2005) 'Unpacking School Lunchtime', in C.R. Cooper, C. Garcia Coll, T. Bartko, H. Davis and C. Chapman (eds) *Rethinking Diversity and Contexts as Resources for Children's Development*. Hillsdale NJ: Lawrence Erlbaum Publishers, pp. 63–87.

Wells, W. (1965) 'Communicating with Children', *Journal of Advertising Research*, 5(1): 1–12.

Wolfenstein, M. (1955) 'Fun Morality: An Analysis of Recent American Child-Training Literature', in M. Mead and M. Wolfenstein (eds) *Childhood in Contemporary Cultures*. Chicago: University of Chicago Press, pp. 168–178.

Yan, Y. (1997) 'McDonald's in Beijing: Localization of Americana', in J. Watson (ed.) *Golden Arches East*. Stanford CA: Stanford University Press, pp. 39–76.

Zelizer, V. (1985) *Pricing the Priceless Child*. Princeton NJ: Princeton University Press.

23
Children and Television

David Buckingham

Both in academic research and in popular debates about television, children are frequently identified as a special audience with distinctive characteristics and needs. Although watching television is a routine everyday activity for people of all age groups, it is often children who are singled out for particular attention and concern. Their behaviour is closely measured and monitored; they are experimented upon, surveyed and canvassed for their views; and the 'problem' of their relationship with television is frequently a focus of concern among parents, pundits and politicians.

On one level, this might be seen simply as a response to the relative importance of television in children's lives. It is frequently pointed out that children today spend more time watching television than they do in school, or indeed on any other activity apart from sleeping. While newer digital media are proving increasingly popular among teenagers, statistics show that television remains the dominant medium in children's lives, even in countries with high levels of access to computer technology (Livingstone and Bovill, 2001; Roberts and Foehr, 2003; Ofcom, 2006). Yet in fact, it is elderly people who are the heaviest viewers – although there has been little discussion, either of their needs in relation to television or of any potential effects it might exert upon them.

This identification of children as a 'special' audience for television is thus not simply a matter of viewing figures. On the contrary, it invokes all sorts of moral and ideological assumptions about what we believe children – and, by extension, adults – to be. As histories of childhood have shown, the definition and separation of children as a distinct social category is itself a relatively recent development, which has taken on a particular form in Western industrialized societies (Ariès, 1973; Hendrick, 1997). This process has been accompanied by a veritable explosion of discourses, both *about* childhood and directed *at* children themselves. The emergence of developmental psychology, and its popularization in advice literature for parents, for example, has been one of the means by which norms of 'suitable' or 'natural' behaviour for children have been enforced. Likewise, the production of children's literature and children's toys – and eventually of children's television – has invoked all sorts of assumptions about what it means to be a child.

347

As these examples imply, this construction of 'the child' is both a negative and a positive enterprise: it involves attempts to restrict children's access to knowledge about aspects of adult life (most obviously sex and violence), and yet it also entails a kind of pedagogy – an attempt to 'do them good' as well as protect them from harm. The constitution of children as a television audience, and as objects of research and debate in this field, has been marked by a complex balance between these positive and negative motivations. In the early days of television, for example, one of the primary advertising appeals made by the equipment manufacturers was on the grounds of the medium's educational potential for the young (Melody, 1973); and while some have argued that this pedagogical motivation has increasingly been sacrificed to commercialism, it remains a central tenet of public service provision for children. Likewise, early debates about the role of television in the family, both in the United Kingdom and in the United States, were characterized by genuine ambivalence about its potential, as either an attack on family life or as a means of securing domestic harmony (Spigel, 1992; Oswell, 2002).

This definition of the child audience is an ongoing process, which is subject to a considerable amount of social and historical variation. Policies on the regulation of children's programming, for example, often reflect much more fundamental assumptions about the nature of childhood, which vary from one national context to another (Hendershot, 1998; Keys and Buckingham, 1999; Lisosky, 2001). Likewise, the struggle between parents and children over what is appropriate for children to watch and to know is part of a continuing struggle over the rights and responsibilities of children. Indeed, the definition of what is 'childish' or 'adult' is also a central preoccupation among children themselves, not least in their discussions of television (Buckingham, 1994; Davies, Buckingham and Kelley, 1999).

A history of concern

It is important to locate the concern about children and television historically, in the context both of evolving definitions of childhood and of recurrent responses to new cultural forms and communications technologies. Fears about the negative impact of the media on young people have a very long history (Starker, 1989). Over 2000 years ago, the Greek philosopher Plato proposed to ban dramatic poets from his ideal Republic, for fear that their stories about the immoral antics of the gods would influence impressionable young minds. In more recent times, popular literature, music hall, the cinema and children's comics have all provoked 'moral panics' which have typically led to greater censorship designed to protect children in particular from their allegedly harmful effects. In this respect, more recent controversies such as the 'video nasties' scare of the 1980s or the debates about screen violence that followed the killing of James Bulger in Britain in 1993 can be seen as heirs to a much longer tradition (Barker, 1984; Buckingham, 1996). And of course these concerns are now being echoed yet again in contemporary discussions of children's uses of the internet and computer games.

Yet, such concerns about the harmful influence of television on children cannot be dismissed as simply irrational scare mongering. Indeed, different versions of such concerns would seem to recur among many social groups, and right across the political spectrum. The most vocal groups, and perhaps the most influential, are those of the so-called moral majority. The concern here, often motivated by traditional religious beliefs, is essentially with the moral and behavioural impact of television, most obviously in terms of sex, violence and 'bad' language. Yet there are also concerns which might be seen as more 'liberal', for example to do with the impact of television viewing on children's academic achievement, their imagination and their capacity for social interaction. Popular books like Marie Winn's symptomatically titled *The Plug-In Drug* (1985) typically urge parents to encourage more 'healthy' viewing behaviour and to wean their children away from their 'addiction' to television. Meanwhile, on the political Left, it is possible to identify parallel concerns with the negative influence of television – for example, on the grounds that it encourages consumerism, militarism, sexism, racism, and just about any other objectionable ideology one might care to name (e.g., Goldsen, 1977).

Of course, it is important to distinguish between these different areas of concern, and the motivations which underlie them. Yet they share a fundamental belief in the enormous power of television, and in the inherent vulnerability of children. Television has, it would seem, an irresistible ability to brainwash and narcotize children, drawing them away from other, more worthwhile activities and influences. From this perspective, children are at once innocent and potentially monstrous: the veneer of civilization is only skin-deep, and can easily be penetrated by the essentially irrational appeals of the visual media (Barker, 1984). Such arguments often partake of the fantasy of a 'golden age' before television, in which adults were able to 'keep secrets' from children, and in which innocence and harmony reigned. By virtue of the ways in which it gives children access to the hidden, and sometimes negative, aspects of adult life, television is frequently accused of having caused the 'disappearance of childhood' itself (Postman, 1983; and for further discussion, see Buckingham, 2000a).

These arguments reflect a form of displacement that often characterizes popular debates about the media. Genuine, often deep-seated anxieties about what are perceived as undesirable moral or social changes lead to a search for a single causal explanation. Blaming television may thus serve to deflect attention away from other possible causes – causes which may well be 'closer to home' or simply much too complicated to understand (Connell, 1985). The symbolic values that are attached to the notion of childhood, and the negative associations of an 'unnatural' technology such as television, make this a particularly potent combination for social commentators of all persuasions. Yet they also make it extremely difficult to arrive at a more balanced and less sensationalist estimation of the role of television in children's lives.

Psychological research: From 'effects' to 'active audiences'

Research is itself an inextricable part of this process. The production of 'scientific' knowledge about children inevitably helps to define what it means to be a child, and thus invokes the kinds of assumptions I have been discussing (Luke, 1990). The discipline of psychology – which, until fairly recently, enjoyed an effective monopoly of the study of children – has been particularly implicated in this process (Burman, 1994).

Broadly speaking, the fundamental aim of most psychological research in this field has been to establish evidence of the negative effects of television. By comparison, research on positive effects has been a very marginal concern. As new media forms and technologies have been introduced, the same basic questions have tended to recur (Reeves and Wartella, 1985). Thus, the questions researchers began asking about television in the 1960s were very similar to those which had been investigated (and indeed, largely superseded) in relation to film 30 years previously – and which are now recurring yet again in research on computer games and the internet.

This is most obviously the case with research about the effects of television violence on children – an area which has been exhaustively reviewed elsewhere (a useful critical account can be found in Freedman, 2002). The problems with this research are partly methodological – for example, to do with the limited validity of laboratory experiments as a guide to real-life behaviour, or with the frequent confusion in survey research between correlation and causality. They are also theoretical, reflecting fundamental confusions about the definition of 'violence' and the ways in which it is deemed to influence people's behaviour (Barker and Petley, 2001). Above all, however, the key issue is a political one: it is to do with how media research has been used by politicians to deflect attention away from other potential causes of violence that seem to be much more difficult for them to address – for example, by means of gun control. Here, as in many other areas, the focus on children enables campaigners to command assent in a way that would be much harder to achieve were they to propose restrictions on adults (see Jenkins, 1992).

Similar arguments might be made in relation to other key preoccupations of media effects research, such as the effects of advertising or gender stereotyping (for a review, see Buckingham, 1998). Yet in fact, research in these areas has gradually moved away from the cruder form of behaviourism (the so-called magic bullet theory) which continues to characterize research on children's responses to television violence. While the influence is still seen to flow in one direction, the emphasis now is on the range of 'intervening variables' which mediate between the stimulus and the response. In the process, many effects researchers have tended to adopt rather more cautious estimates of the influence of the medium.

For example, research on the place of television in cultivating 'sex roles' has increasingly drawn attention to the influence of the broader social context – for example, of family communication patterns, and of relationships within the peer group. Durkin (1985), for example, agrees that television tends to provide stereotyped representations of male and female roles, but he rejects the view that these are somehow 'burned' into the viewer's unconscious, or that they necessarily have a cumulative effect. He argues that research in this field needs to take much greater account of the developmental changes in children's understanding and use of the medium as they mature, and of how they actively make sense of what they watch.

In this respect, effects research has gradually given way to paradigms that conceive of children as 'active viewers'. The notion of 'activity' here is partly a rhetorical one, and it is often used in rather imprecise ways. Yet what unites this work is a view of children, not as passive recipients of television messages, but as active interpreters and processors of meaning. The meaning of television, from this perspective, is not delivered *to* the audience, but constructed *by* it.

This emphasis is apparent in some research within the 'uses and gratifications' tradition. Rosengren and Windahl (1989), for example, paint a complex picture of the heterogeneous uses of television among Swedish adolescents, and its interaction with other media such as popular music. In the process, they challenge many generalized assertions about media effects, not least in relation to violence: they argue that the socializing influence of television will depend upon its relationship with other influences, and upon the diverse and variable meanings which its users attach to it. Thus, for example, television viewing will have a different significance depending upon the child's orientation towards the school, the family and the peer group. As they indicate, the influence of variables such as age, gender and social class means that different children can effectively occupy different 'media worlds' – an argument which clearly undermines any easy generalizations about 'children' as a homogeneous social group.

This notion of 'active viewing' is particularly evident in psychological studies that adopt broadly 'constructivist' or cognitive approaches (for reviews, see Gunter and McAleer, 1997; van Evra, 2004). Rather than simply responding to stimuli, viewers are seen here as consciously processing, interpreting and evaluating information. In making sense of what they watch, viewers use 'schemas' or 'scripts', sets of plans and expectations which they have built up from their previous experience both of television and of the world in general. In studying children's understanding of television, cognitive psychologists have tended to concentrate on the 'micro' rather than the 'macro' – for example, aspects of mental processing such as attention and comprehension, the understanding of narrative or the ability to distinguish between fantasy and reality. Thus, there is some extremely detailed research about the ways in which particular elements of television 'language' (such as camera angles or editing) may 'stand in' for internal mental processes or 'model' cognitive skills which children do not possess (Salomon, 1979). Much of this work has attempted to map the ways in which children's understanding of television changes along with their general intellectual development.

This research provides many insights into the kinds of mental processing that are involved in understanding television, but it suffers from some limitations that are characteristic of mainstream psychology in general. 'Cognition' has largely been considered in isolation, not only from 'affect' or emotion, but also from the social and interpersonal aspects of the viewing experience. The focus on the individual's internal mental processes has made it difficult to assess the role of social and cultural factors in the formation of consciousness and understanding. While some psychological researchers do acknowledge these factors in theory, much of the research itself appears to adopt a notion of 'the child' that is abstracted from any social or historical context. Ultimately, the relationship between children and television is conceived as a matter of the isolated individual's encounter with the screen. The central questions are about what television does to the child's mind – or, more recently, about what the child's mind does with television. In the process, television itself, and the social processes through which its meaning is established and defined, have tended to be neglected.

A cultural studies perspective

By contrast, these latter issues have been a particular focus of concern for Cultural Studies researchers. In principle, the Cultural Studies approach moves beyond many of the limitations both of effects research and of 'active audience' theories. It disputes normative models of child development, focusing attention instead on the changing social, historical and cultural construction of childhood. It seeks to understand children's uses of media in their own terms and from their own perspectives, rather than comparing them with those of adults; and it seeks to explore the *social* experiences of children, not least as these are constructed through the operation of other dimensions of social power, such as social class, gender and ethnicity – as well as focusing on intergenerational differences and relationships. In these respects, Cultural Studies approaches to children and media have much in common with recent work within the sociology of childhood represented elsewhere in this volume.

Cultural Studies is a multifaceted, interdisciplinary endeavour that is typically conceptualized in terms of the interaction between *institutions, texts* and *audiences* (e.g., Johnson, 1985/1986). In accounting for the role of television in children's lives, it suggests that it is not enough to look at children in isolation. On the contrary, we also need to take account of the economic and institutional context of television production, and the nature of television 'texts' themselves. In this way, it becomes possible to understand the relationships between children's agency as users or consumers of television and the broader structural contexts in which they are located. The following brief review seeks to identify a range of relevant studies in each of these three areas.

Production

Accounts of television production for children written from within the industry have perhaps inevitably tended towards public relations; but critical academic studies are relatively few and far between. Early studies of children's television such as those by Melody (1973) and Turow (1981) adopted a broad 'political economy' approach, focusing on questions of ownership, marketing and regulation. Aside from the work of Buckingham et al. (1999) and Hendershot (2004a), there has been very little analysis of producers' assumptions and expectations about the child audience; and while there has been some historical and international comparative research on the evolution of regulatory policy on children's television (e.g., Hendershot, 1998; Keys and Buckingham, 1999; Lisosky, 2001), this too has remained under-researched.

Perhaps the most interesting work in this field in recent years has related to broader concerns about the commercialization of children's culture (see Cook, this volume). This issue has generated a growing body of popular commentary (e.g., Linn, 2004; Schor, 2004); and while much of this has been driven by a view of children as especially vulnerable to influence and exploitation, it has also shed light on the increasingly sophisticated and often 'invisible' practices of children's marketers. While advocates of a traditional 'political economy' approach tend to regard the market as inherently inimical to children's best interests (e.g., Kline, 1993), others have adopted a more sanguine approach, arguing that critiques of consumer culture are often driven by implicitly elitist conceptions of taste and cultural value (Seiter, 1993). Our own research on the political economy of children's television (Buckingham et al., 1999) and of 'edutainment' media (Buckingham and Scanlon, 2005) also suggests that success in the marketplace is far from secure or guaranteed, and that producers often face considerable challenges in identifying children's wants and needs in the first place. This kind of research serves as a caution against overstated assumptions about the 'power' of the media; yet it also draws attention to the growing significance of commercial forces in the production and circulation of children's culture.

Texts

Of course, children's use of television is far from confined to material that is specifically designed for them; yet the analysis of children's television does provide interesting insights into some of the broader tensions that surround dominant definitions of childhood. For example, research on children's television has focused on well-established concerns such as gender representation (Seiter, 1993; Griffiths, 2002), as well as more novel issues such as its implicit models of adult citizenship (Northam, 2005), how it handles the relationship between 'information' and 'entertainment' (Buckingham, 1995), and how it addresses the child viewer (Davies, 1995). There have also been fruitful discussions of specific genres of children's programming such as costume drama (Davies, 2002), news (Buckingham, 2000b; Banet-Weiser, 2004), action-adventure shows (Jenkins, 1999) and preschool programming (Buckingham, 2002; Oswell, 2002). As in research on children's literature, the analysis suggests that the position of the medium as a 'parent' or 'teacher' and the process of attempting to 'draw in' the child are fraught with difficulties and uncertainties (cf. Rose, 1984).

Some of the most interesting work in this area has focused on the widely denigrated area of children's cartoons. As against the continuing use of quantitative content analysis (e.g., Kline, 1995), there have been several studies that have applied semiotics (Hodge and Tripp, 1986; Myers, 1995), psychoanalysis (Urwin, 1995) and postmodernist theory (Kinder, 1991) in qualitative analyses of this apparently simple genre. This work raises interesting hypotheses about the ways in which cartoons offer the potential for 'subversive' readings, and enable viewers to explore and manage anxiety, thereby perhaps bringing about more protean forms of subjectivity (Hendershot, 2004b; Nixon, 2002; Wells, 2002). Disney has proved a particularly fertile ground for textual studies, generating competing analyses informed by a range of theoretical perspectives including feminism (Bell, 1995), post-structuralism (McQuillan and Byrne, 1999) and more conventional forms of ideological critique (Giroux, 2001).

Audiences

It is in the area of audience research that Cultural Studies researchers have made the most significant contribution to this field. As I have implied, the primary aim of audience research in Cultural Studies is to understand the social processes through which the meanings and pleasures of media are constructed, defined and circulated. While this research is not necessarily qualitative, most of the work that has been undertaken relies either on focus-group or individual interviews or on 'ethnographic' observation.

In their ground breaking study, Hodge and Tripp (1986) applied a social semiotic perspective, both to the analysis of children's programming, and to audience talk. Although they regard children as 'active' producers of meaning, they are also concerned with the ideological and formal constraints exerted by the text. In the process, they explore how children's talk about television depends upon the context in which it occurs, and how it enacts social relationships with others (including researchers themselves). This approach has been pursued in my own work, which places a central emphasis on how children define and construct their social identities through talk about television and other media (Buckingham, 1993a, b; 1996; 2000b; Buckingham and Bragg, 2004). Rather than applying a narrowly semiotic approach, this research uses arguments drawn from discourse analysis to challenge the positivist use of audience data within mainstream research: instead of regarding what children say at face value, as some kind of self-evident reflection of what they 'really' think or believe, it argues that talk should itself be seen as a form of social action or performance (cf. Potter and Wetherell, 1987). Children's judgements about genre and representation, and their reconstructions of television narrative, for example, are studied as inherently social processes; and the development of knowledge about television ('television literacy') and of a 'critical' perspective are seen in terms of their social motivations and purposes. (For other examples of audience studies using a similar approach, see McKinley, 1997; Robinson, 1997; and Tobin, 2000.)

In parallel with this work, some researchers have adopted a more 'ethnographic' approach to studying children's uses of media, based primarily on observation. Thus, there have been studies of the use of television and other media, both within the home (e.g., Palmer, 1986; Lindlof, 1987; Richards, 1993) and in the context of the peer group (Wood, 1993); as well as research on the use of media in schools and informal educational settings, mainly in the context of media education programmes (e.g., Buckingham and Sefton-Green, 1994; Buckingham et al., 1995;

Marsh, 1999; Burn, 2000; de Block and Buckingham, 2007). However, the term 'ethnographic' is perhaps best reserved for studies that have entailed long-term immersion in a particular community; and work of this kind is comparatively rare in media research more broadly. Marie Gillespie's (1995) study of the use of television among a South Asian community in London is a rare exception, which combines an analysis of the role of television within the family and the peer group with an account of children's responses to specific genres such as news and soap opera. Television is used here partly as a heuristic means of gaining insight into the broader culture of this community, although (as with the work discussed above), there is a self-reflexive emphasis on the role of the researcher, and on the power-relationships between researchers and their child subjects, which is typically absent from mainstream psychological research; (similar observational studies using different methods can be found in Marsh (2004) and Seiter (1999)).

While this is a developing body of research, there are several broader issues within it that remain to be resolved. Like sociologists of childhood, Cultural Studies researchers are broadly inclined to regard children as 'active' participants in the process of making meaning – as competent social actors, rather than as passive and incompetent victims. This kind of argument offers an important challenge to many of the assumptions that typically circulate in public debate – particularly in arguments about media violence. Yet there is a risk of adopting a rather simplistic 'child-centred' approach, which seeks to celebrate the sophistication of the 'media-wise' child, and to prove (endlessly) that children are not as gullible or as passive as they are often made out to be. There is often an implicit assumption here that if children are 'active', then they are somehow not going to be influenced by what they watch (and of course similar assumptions are made about adults in this respect). Yet this does not necessarily follow: indeed, one could argue that in some instances to be 'active' is to be more open to influence – and 'activity' should not in any case be equated with agency, or with social power. Furthermore, this kind of celebration of children's sophistication as users of television can lead us to neglect the fact that there are areas they need to know more about – which is inevitably a key concern both for educators and for media regulators.

This reflects a broader tension here between structure and agency that is characteristic of the human sciences in general (see Buckingham and Sefton-Green, 2004). The temptation to celebrate children's agency – and, in doing so, to speak 'on behalf of the child' – can lead researchers to neglect the broader economic, social and political forces that both constrain and produce particular forms of audience behaviour or meaning-making. The intellectual, cultural and indeed material resources that children use in making meaning are not equally available to all. The actions of media producers and the structures and forms of media texts clearly delimit and to some extent determine the possible meanings that can be made. From the perspective of 'structuration theory' (Giddens, 1984), we would argue that structure works through agency, and agency works through structure: in order to create meanings and pleasures, the media depend upon the active agency of audiences; and yet (to paraphrase another well-known commentator,

Karl Marx!) audiences can only make meanings in conditions that are not of their own choosing.

This is why, in my view, it remains crucially important for researchers to combine the different areas of investigation identified here. Yet while there have been significant contributions in each of these areas, there have been comparatively few attempts in media research to bring them together, or to theorize the relationships between them. Janet Wasko's studies of Disney (Wasko, 2000; Wasko et al., 2001) do address the economic, textual and audience dimensions of the phenomenon, and look across a range of media; while Stephen Kline et al. (2003) provide a similarly multidimensional analysis of video games, albeit one that is significantly more effective in its analysis of the industry than in accounting for other aspects. Yet, while both studies cover the relevant bases, neither offers a convincing theoretical reconciliation of the different perspectives. However, Joseph Tobin's edited volume on the Pokemon phenomenon manages to combine these elements more effectively (Tobin, 2004a): the contributions by Tobin (2004b) and by the present author (Buckingham and Sefton-Green, 2004) seek to move beyond polarized accounts of the operation of 'media power', combining each of the three aspects identified above. As we suggest, this is not simply a matter of balancing the equation, and thereby finding a happy medium between the 'power of the text' and the 'power of the audience'. Nor is it something that can be achieved in the abstract. Ultimately, the relationship between children and television can only be fully understood in the context of a wider analysis of the ways in which both are constructed and defined.

References

Ariès, P. (1973) *Centuries of Childhood*. Harmondsworth: Penguin.
Banet-Weiner, S. (2004) ' "We Pledge Allegiance to Kids": Nickelodeon and Citizenship', in H. Hendershot (ed.) *Nickelodeon Nation: The History, Politics and Economics of America's Only TV Channel for Kids*. New York: New York University Press, pp. 337–385.
Barker, M. (ed.) (1984) *The Video Nasties*. London: Pluto.
Barker, M. and J. Petley (eds) (2001) *Ill Effects: The Media/Violence Debate* 2nd edn. London: Routledge.
Bell, E., L. Haas and L. Sells (1995) *From Mouse to Mermaid: The Politics of Film, Gender, and Culture*. Bloomington IN: Indiana University Press.
de Block, L. and D. Buckingham (2007) *Global Children, Global Media: Migration, Media and Childhood*. Basingstoke UK: Palgrave Macmillan.
Buckingham, D. (1993a) *Children Talking Television: The Making of Television Literacy*. London: Falmer.
Buckingham, D. (ed.) (1993b) *Reading Audiences: Young People and the Media*. Manchester: Manchester University Press.
Buckingham, D. (1994) 'Television and the Definition of Childhood', in B. Mayall (ed.) *Children's Childhoods Observed and Experienced*. London: Falmer.
Buckingham, D. (1995) 'On the Impossibility of Children's Television', in C. Bazalgette and D. Buckingham (eds) *In Front of the Children*. London: British Film Institute.
Buckingham, D. (1996) *Moving Images: Understanding Children's Emotional Responses to Television*. Manchester: Manchester University Press.
Buckingham, D. (1998) 'Children and Television: A Critical Overview of the Research', in R. Dickinson, O. Linne and R. Harindranath (eds) *Approaches to Audiences*. London: Edward Arnold.

Buckingham, D. (2000a) *After the Death of Childhood: Growing Up in the Age of Electronic Media*. Cambridge: Polity.

Buckingham, D. (2000b) *The Making of Citizens: Young People, News and Politics*. London: University College London Press.

Buckingham, D. (2002) 'Teletubbies and the Educational Imperative', in D. Buckingham (ed.) *Small Screens: Television for Children*. Leicester: Leicester University Press, pp. 38–60.

Buckingham, D. and S. Bragg (2004) *Young People, Sex and the Media: The Facts of Life?* Basingstoke UK: Palgrave Macmillan.

Buckingham, D. and M. Scanlon (2005) 'Selling Learning: Towards a Political Economy of Edutainment Media', *Media, Culture and Society*, 27(1): 41–58.

Buckingham, D. and J. Sefton-Green (1994) *Cultural Studies Goes to School: Reading and Teaching Popular Culture*. London: Taylor and Francis.

Buckingham, D. and J. Sefton-Green (2004) 'Gotta Catch 'Em All: Structure, Agency and Pedagogy in Children's Media Culture', in Tobin, J. (ed.) *Pikachu's Global Adventure: The Rise and Fall of Pokemon*. Durham NC: Duke University Press, pp. 12–33.

Buckingham, D., J. Grahame and J. Sefton-Green (1995) *Making Media: Practical Production in Media Education*. London: English & Media Centre.

Buckingham, D., H. Davies, K. Jones and P. Kelley (1999) *Children's Television in Britain: History, Discourse and Policy*. London: British Film Institute.

Burman, E. (1994) *Deconstructing Developmental Psychology*. London: Routledge.

Burn, A. (2000) 'Repackaging the Slasher Movie: Digital Unwriting of Film in the Classroom', *English in Australia*. pp. 24–34: 127–128.

Connell, I. (1985) 'Fabulous Powers: Blaming the Media', in L. Masterman (ed.) *Television Mythologies*. London: Comedia/MK Media Press.

Davies, H., D. Buckingham and P. Kelley (1999) 'Kids' Time: Television, Childhood and the Regulation of Time', *Journal of Educational Media*, 24(1): 25–42.

Davies, M.M. (1995) 'Babes 'n' the Hood: Pre-school Television and Its Audiences in the United States and Britain', in C. Bazalgette and D. Buckingham (eds) *In Front of the Children*. London: British Film Institute.

Davies, M.M. (2002) 'Classics with Clout: Costume Drama in British and American Children's Television', in D. Buckingham (ed.) *Small Screens: Television for Children*. Leicester: Leicester University Press, pp. 120–140.

Durkin, K. (1985) *Television, Sex Roles and Children*. Milton Keynes: Open University Press.

Freedman, J. (2002) *Media Violence and Its Effect on Aggression: Assessing the Scientific Evidence*. Toronto: Toronto University Press.

Giddens, A. (1984) *The Constitution of Society*. Cambridge: Polity.

Gillespie, M. (1995) *Television, Ethnicity and Cultural Change*. London: Routledge.

Giroux, H. (2001) *The Mouse That Roared: Disney and the End of Innocence*. New York: Rowman and Littlefield.

Goldsen, R. (1977) *The Show and Tell Machine*. New York: Dial Books.

Griffiths, M. (2002) 'Pink Worlds and Blue Worlds: A Portrait of Infinite Polarity', in Buckingham, D. (ed.) *Small Screens: Television for Children*. London: Leicester University Press, pp. 159–184.

Gunter, B. and J. McAleer (1997) *Children and Television* 2nd edn. London: Routledge.

Hendershot, H. (1998) *Saturday Morning Censors: Television Regulation Before the V-Chip*. Durham NC: Duke University Press.

Hendershot, H. (ed.) (2004a) *Nickelodeon Nation: The History, Politics and Economics of America's Only TV Channel for Kids*. New York: New York University Press.

Hendershot, H. (ed.) (2004b) 'Nickelodeon's Nautical Nonsense: The Intergenerational Appeal of *Spongebob Squarepants*', in H. Hendershot (ed.) *Nickelodeon Nation: The History, Politics and Economics of America's Only TV Channel for Kids*. New York: New York University Press.

Hendrick, H. (1997) *Children, Childhood and English Society. 1880–1990*. Cambridge: Cambridge University Press.

Hodge, B. and D. Tripp (1986) *Children and Television: A Semiotic Approach.* Cambridge: Polity.

Jenkins, H. (1999) 'Her Suffering Aristocratic Majesty: The Sentimental Value of *Lassie*', in M. Kinder (ed.) *Kids' Media Culture.* Durham NC: Duke University Press.

Jenkins, P. (1992) *Intimate Enemies: Moral Panics in Contemporary Great Britain.* New York: Aldine de Gruyter.

Johnson, R. (1985/6) 'What Is Cultural Studies Anyway?' *Social Text,* 16: 38–80.

Keys, W. and D. Buckingham (eds) (1999) *International Perspectives on Children's Media Policy* special issue of *Media International Australia/Culture and Policy* 93.

Kinder, M. (1991) *Playing with Power.* Berkeley: University of California Press.

Kline, S. (1993) *Out of the Garden: Toys and Children's Culture in the Age of TV Marketing.* London: Verso.

Kline, S. (1995) 'The Empire of Play: Emergent Genres of Product-Based Animations', in C. Bazalgette and D. Buckingham (eds) *In Front of the Children.* London: British Film Institute.

Kline, S., N. Dyer-Witheford and G. de Peuter (2003) *Digital Play: The Interaction of Technology, Culture and Marketing.* Montreal: McGill-Queens University Press.

Lindlof, T. (ed.) (1987) *Natural Audiences.* Newbury Park CA: Sage.

Linn, S. (2004) *Consuming Kids: The Hostile Takeover of Childhood.* New York: New Press.

Lisosky, J. (2001) 'For *All* Kids' Sakes: Comparing Children's Television Policy-Making in Australia, Canada and the United States', *Media, Culture and Society,* 23(6): 821–845.

Livingstone, S. and M. Bovill (eds) (2001) *Children and Their Changing Media Environment.* Mahwah NJ: Erlbaum.

Luke, C. (1990) *Constructing the Child Viewer.* New York: Praeger.

Marsh, J. (1999) 'Batman and Batwoman Go to School: Popular Culture in the Literacy Curriculum', *International Journal of Early Years Education,* 7(2): 117–131.

Marsh, J. (ed.) (2004) *Popular Culture, Media and Digital Literacies in Early Childhood.* London: Routledge Falmer.

McKinley, E.G. (1997) *Beverly Hills 90210: Television, Gender and Identity.* Philadelphia PN: University of Pennsylvania Press.

McQuillan, M. and E. Byrne (1999) *Deconstructing Disney.* London: Pluto.

Melody, W. (1973) *Children's Television: The Economics of Exploitation.* New Haven CT: Yale University Press.

Myers, G. (1995) '"The Power Is Yours": Agency and Plot in *Captain Planet*', in C. Bazalgette and D. Buckingham (eds) *In Front of the Children.* London: British Film Institute.

Nixon, H. (2002) '*South Park*: Not in Front of the Children', in D. Buckingham (ed.) *Small Screens: Television for Children.* Leicester: Leicester University Press, pp. 96–119.

Northam, J. (2005) 'Rehearsals in Citizenship: BBC Stop-Motion Animation Programmes for Young Children', *Journal of Cultural Research,* 9(3): 245–263.

Ofcom (2006) *The Communications Market 2006.* London: Ofcom.

Oswell, D. (2002) *Television, Childhood and the Home: A History of the Making of the Child Television Audience in Britain.* Oxford: Oxford University Press.

Palmer, P. (1986) *The Lively Audience.* Sydney: Allen and Unwin.

Postman, N. (1983) *The Disappearance of Childhood.* London: W.H. Allen.

Potter, J. and M. Wetherell (1987) *Discourse and Social Psychology.* London: Sage.

Reeves, B. and E. Wartella (1985) 'Historical Trends in Research on Children and the Media, 1900–1960', *Journal of Communication,* 35(2): 118–133.

Richards, C. (1993) 'Taking Sides? What Young Girls Do with Television', in D. Buckingham (ed.) *Reading Audiences: Young People and the Media.* Manchester: Manchester University Press.

Roberts, D.F. and U. Foehr (2003) *Kids and the Media in America.* New York: Cambridge University Press.

Robinson, M. (1997) *Children Reading Print and Television.* London: Falmer.

Rose, J. (1984) *The Case of Peter Pan: Or the Impossibility of Children's Fiction*. London: Macmillan.

Rosengren, K.E. and S. Windahl (1989) *Media Matter: TV Use in Childhood and Adolescence*. Norwood, NJ: Ablex.

Salomon, G. (1979) *Interaction of Media, Cognition and Learning*. San Francisco CA: Jossey-Bass.

Schor, J. (2004) *Born to Buy: The Commercialized Child and the New Consumer Culture*. New York: Scribner.

Seiter, E. (1993) *Sold Separately: Parents and Children in Consumer Culture*. New Brunswick NJ: Rutgers University Press.

Seiter, E. (1999) *Television and New Media Audiences*. Cambridge: Cambridge University Press.

Spigel, L. (1992) *Make Room for TV: Television and the Family Ideal in Postwar America*. Chicago: University of Chicago Press.

Starker, S. (1989) *Evil Influences: Crusades against the Mass Media*. New Brunswick NJ: Transaction.

Tobin, J. (2000) *'Good Guys Don't Wear Hats'; Children's Talk About Television*. New York: Teachers College Press.

Tobin, J. (ed.) (2004a) *Pikachu's Global Adventure: The Rise and Fall of Pokemon*. Durham NC: Duke University Press.

Tobin, J. (2004b) 'Conclusion: The Rise and Fall of the Pokemon Empire', in Tobin, J. (ed.) *Pikachu's Global Adventure: The Rise and Fall of Pokemon*. Durham NC: Duke University Press, pp. 257–292.

Turow, J. (1981) *Entertainment, Education and the Hard Sell*. New York: Praeger.

Urwin, C. (1995) 'Turtle Power: Illusion and Imagination in Children's Play', in C. Bazalgette and D. Buckingham (eds) *In Front of the Children*. London: British Film Institute.

Van Evra, J. (2004) *Television and Child Development*. Mahwah NJ: Erlbaum.

Wasko, J. (2000) *Understanding Disney*. Cambridge: Polity.

Wasko, J., M. Phillips and E. Meehan (eds) (2001) *Dazzled by Disney?* London: Leicester University Press.

Wells, P. (2002) '"Tell Me About Your Id, When You Was a Kid, Yah?" Animation and Children's Television Culture', in D. Buckingham (ed.) *Small Screens: Television for Children*. Leicester: Leicester University Press.

Winn, M. (1985) *The Plug-In Drug*. Harmondsworth: Penguin.

Wood, J. (1993) 'Repeatable Pleasures: Notes on Young People's Use of Video', in D. Buckingham (ed.) *Reading Audiences: Young People and the Media*. Manchester: Manchester University Press.

24
Children and Digital Media: Online, On Site, On the Go

Kirsten Drotner

Charting the relations between children and digital media immediately invites a bottom-up perspective on media, a perspective that focuses on the multiple ways in which children take up and appropriate digital media, be they audiences of media produced by adult professionals or content creators themselves. But one need not venture far in that direction to realize that this perspective is intimately bound up with a top-down perspective on these relations, a perspective that focuses on the ways in which adults debate and intervene in children's media uses. This dual perspective is important to keep in mind simply because it serves as a useful reminder that children's media uses are a set of contextualized sociocultural practices that must be analysed and understood in relation to a grander canvas of modern childhood and adulthood.

Modern, westernized childhood is ambiguously defined in three capacities, namely in relation to time, to space and to the social relations that children are part of. Children grow *up*; that is, childhood is regarded as a phase of development, and often a vulnerable phase, too. Childhood is equally seen as giving shape to, and being shaped by, particular spaces such as the nursery and kindergarten, the school and the sports club; and all of these sites are, ideally, positioned outside the spheres of paid employment. Fundamentally, childhood is defined in relation to its social networks and relations – parents, siblings and peers, for example. As is evident, such a definition of childhood positions children within regimes of power, transgression and accommodation in temporal, spatial and sociocultural terms. For example, children outpacing or lagging behind designated ages and stages are labelled as brainy and laggards, respectively. And children evading approved leisure activities have often met with adult disapproval. In their everyday interactions, children must handle such labelling, even if they are unaware of its existence. When it is remembered that such discourses and practices are acted out in tandem with the development of modern media, it is easily recognized that media may become objects both of adult debate and children's engagements.

Today, children's media cultures are or can be digitized – from books and music to television and the internet. This is because it is now technically possible to digitize what media are made of, namely signs such as text, images, numbers and sound. Digitization facilitates an interlacing of traditional mass media such as books, newspapers, radio and television, with information and communication technologies (ICTs) such as the telephone, the personal computer and the internet. In practice, the notion of digital media often implies technologies that are 'born' digital such as the computer and the internet, computer (or video) games and mobile media. This is also the focus of the present chapter. But the possibilities of having these media interact fairly seamlessly with, for example, print media and television should be remembered when studying children and digital media, because they facilitate attentiveness to the ways in which certain modes of address and expression or particular uses carry over from one medium to another. For example, children may download a jingle from a popular television series via the internet as a ring tone for their mobile phone. So, the relations between children and digital media cannot be studied meaningfully in isolation from children's wider media cultures.

So, children's relations to digital media are played out and must be analysed against a grander sociocultural canvas where changing perceptions of childhood take centre stage. Moreover, these relations must be understood as part of a wider media culture that encompasses print and audio-visual media such as books and magazines, radio and television. But, adult discourses on these relations rarely display such contextual awareness. On the contrary, they largely underestimate the complexities found in children's media engagements in favour of simple statements. Since these discourses serve as perhaps the most decisive parameters of children's digital practices, they merit closer inspection.

Discourses of concern

Public discourses on children's digital media practices are mostly created by adults, and so by their very nature these discourses serve to articulate issues of generational power, often in a very tacit manner. Whenever a new medium has entered the social scene since the advent of the first books and magazines, its entrance has spurred often heated public debates. Across boundaries of time and place, these debates display some central characteristics irrespective of the actual medium in question, namely that the new medium operates as a catalyst for debates in which adults are subjects and children are objects; the debates are often very normative; and they may be mapped on to two basic oppositions, namely discourses of concern and discourses of celebration (see also Buckingham, this volume).

Because of their intense and emotional character, the discourses of concern have been termed media panics (Drotner, 1999; Critcher, 2008) in emulation of the term moral panics which the Canadian media scholar Marshall McLuhan coined in 1964 in his famous book *Understanding Media*, and which British sociologist Stanley Cohen established as a sociological concept to denote processes of public labelling and handling of perceived deviance (Cohen, 1972). Not all public debates on children's media uses attain the emotional heights and temporal coherence to be defined as media panics, and it may be claimed that the complexities of the current media culture and its permeation of children's everyday lives in many parts of the world operate so as to deflate the debates. So, rather than demarcated peaks of panic we see recurrent ripples of concern. In terms of digital media, public discourses of concern focus on two related areas of tension, one of which is to do with perceived dangers and transgressions, while the other one focuses on identity performance and display. The internet has been at the core of these concerns because it dramatically widens young users' access to unsolicited information, and because of its domestic and often private patterns of use. The internet pushes boundaries between public and private issues and between children's personal and peer uses, to a degree which radio and television do not.

Sex, violence and bodily harm are central issues for debate and deliberation. It is well known that the military and the pornographic industries are the primary movers of internet technology developments, and children are singled out as a risk group of this development in two capacities. They are victims of sexual assault through paedophile content production, and they are objects of encountering harmful or illegal content when surfing on the net. Detection of transnational networks of paedophile internet users makes headlines in the press, and child protection agencies have expanded, and partly reoriented, their activities to cover virtual actions of sexual abuse. Public organizations and private corporations – from UNICEF to content providers – demonstrate citizenship and corporate responsibility by adopting internet codes of conduct ('netiquette') that prioritize advice on the sexual protection of young users. Evidently, the definition of childhood as being bounded by particular sites and settings is challenged by children's possible access to, and engagements with, virtual worlds.

Particularly, computer games have given rise to renewed debates on the media's perceived ill-effects on the young (for a historical account, see Barker and Petley, 1997). Spurred by tragic incidents such as the school shootings in 1999 at Columbine High School in the United States of America, in 2002 in Erfurt, Germany, and in 2007 in Jokela in Finland, first-person shooter games such as *Doom* and *Grand Theft Auto* and their sequels are singled out as causes of untamed aggression and violent behaviour that may lead to innocent deaths. In the United States of America, a former military psychologist, David Grossman, terms these games 'murder simulators', a term that encapsulates a widely claimed connection between virtual and real violence (Grossman and Gaetaeno, 1999).

More recently, health issues have added to an already steady stream of issues through which children's relations to digital media are socially negotiated. The very acute rise in obesity in many parts of the world coincides with the rapid take-up of personal computers and internet communication, and quick, if contested, correlations are made between the two trends. Children's use of digital media is seen as an alternative, even a threat, to physical activity, irrespective of the fact that the earliest and most rapid take-up of computing and internet use is in high-income families where obesity rates are low (d'Haenens, 2001). At the other end of the spectrum, so to speak, teenage anorexia and self-harm is linked to children's wider access, not only to visual content, but, more importantly, to support and exchange of information on social network sites.

Mobile devices have added to many of these concerns, not least because so-called MMS (multimedia message services) allow for easy (if not inexpensive) exchange of still and live images. Since most children over the age of ten in most westernized societies use mobile communication as an integral part of their social practices, few are immune to acts of cyber-bullying and other forms of personal harassment through the exchange of virtual hate material which they may encounter virtually everywhere and at all times. Shutting off one's mobile or disregarding received messages is like cutting off a social life-line, and young internet and mobile users rarely consider that a real option.

Still, digital media have not only spurred discourses of transgression in terms of sex, violence and the body. Also, children's personal identities are seen as being under threat. In particular, the onset and early adoption of computer games and internet communication gave rise to debates over the possible ways in which users would design online identities very different from their offline selves. The title of Sherry Turkle's book *Life on the Screen* (Turkle, 1995) neatly sums up a position that has attained wide, public resonance, namely that digital engagements are an alternative to, some would say a poor substitute for, social life beyond the computer, the mobile phone or the games console. Such deliberations posit a dichotomy between virtual and real aspects of life, a dichotomy that easily slides into an opposition between fake and original, false and true. Such normative divides are well known from debates over children and television (Buckingham, this volume; Davies, 1997), and they are sharpened when mapped on to widely held assumptions of modern childhood as a vulnerable phase of development. From such assumptions, it is obviously worse for children to enter into acts of identity experimentation through gaming or extensive cyber-communication, since their personal identities are only in the making in the first place.

Discourses of concern over children's uses of digital media are highly gendered even if this difference is rarely explicitly addressed. Public anxiety over aggressive behaviour caused by gaming primarily pertains to boys and young men. Conversely, issues of visual sexual abuse and bodily harm are mostly defined as a girls' problem, although in the case of cyber-paedophilia age takes pride of place. These differences are partly a result of gendered media practices – avid gaming is mostly a male affair, while mobile forms of communication top girls' usage of digital media. Still, the dis-cursive gendering also maps on to a long tradition in which male aggression is more widely accepted than female aggression ('boys will be boys'), while girls and women are primary objects of bodily grooming and visual performance. So, the discourses of concern over children's relation to digital media may display new objects on the social scene, but their causes and explanations remain well rehearsed.

Discourses of celebration

Children's widespread, but uneven, take-up of digital media since the mid-1990s has offered a cause not only for concern, but also for celebration. Indicative of the adult attempts to locate the assets of innovation have been the ways in which children's relation to digital media has been labelled in terms of either generation or technology. Young users have been termed a net generation (Tapscott, 1998), a digital generation (Papert, 1996), cyberkids (Holloway and Valentine, 2003) and the thumb tribes (Rheingold, 2002). Behind such general catch phrases lie optimistic claims of social transformation and development for children, largely brought about single-handedly by the young users themselves. Some of these claims take a personal focus, locating the aims of transformation with children who eagerly assume a new voice of their own, while others point to more structural discussions concerning children's future competence formation.

Not surprisingly, commercial content producers and distributors are among the most fervent proponents of optimism on children's account. Much has been made of the ways in which the personal computer is a so-called lean-forward medium, favouring content creation and active engagement, a concept that only makes sense when contrasted to so-called lean-back media such as radio, television and newspapers where usage is arguably a passive process of consumption. Such rhetorical claims assume an equation between medium and audience that does not hold up to closer scrutiny – any reader knows that meaningful interpretation of a text requires active engagement, just as few parents are unaware of the ways in which very young television audiences will demonstrate their active involvement by talking to or physically emulating characters on the screen.

The personal computer does widen and sophisticate users' opportunities for manipulating text, image and sound, just as mobile devices facilitate virtual forms of synchronous communication between individuals. Beyond commercial circles, adults interpret these options along neo-liberal lines as new ways in which children may make their personal voice heard, and as ways in which they may evade adult supervision and form virtual peer friendships, thanks to mobile message systems and participatory social networking sites such as the video-sharing website YouTube, the photo-sharing website Flickr or online game communities (Huffaker, 2004; boyd, 2007). Others assess such online and portable practices within more welfarist frameworks as important new ways in which children may exercise democratic participation and citizenship (Loader, 2007; Hamelink, 2008). The ambivalent adult discourses on children's online and portable communication practices invoke the UN Convention on the Rights of the Child and they speak to particular tensions of the Convention, as is evident, for example, in article 13 that states:

> The child shall have the right to freedom of expression; this right shall include freedom to seek, receive and impart information and ideas of all kinds, regardless of frontiers, either orally, in writing or in print, in the form of art, or through any other media of the child's choice (Convention, 1989).

Public discourses on children's rights of (virtual) forms of articulation and reception latch on to wider debates on individual freedom of expression vs democratic participation and deliberation, debates that take on a particular tone because they invoke tacit assumptions about power relations defined by age rather than the more explicitly acknowledged oppositions of social class, ethnicity and gender (see also Freeman, this volume).

So far, we have examined discourses of optimism that address children's social position either as media-savvy and discerning consumers in their own right or as future citizens training for their full entry into democratic participation. In addition to these more general positions, children's relations to digital media are debated with a view to a more specific social framework, namely that of school. In the history of childhood, formal education plays a pivotal role in two capacities. It trains children selectively in particular skills and competences, so that they will take up different future roles in paid or unpaid employment; and for some years it offers a joint space of generational interaction and engagement. Formal education, then, acts as a catalyst for both social division and generational unity.

Particularly since the 1980s, ICTs have acted as catalysts for heated educational debates and policymaking on competence formation. While these debates play out different sociocultural scenarios of the future, they speak to very real current tensions between proponents of established forms of literacy (reading, writing and numeracy) and proponents of new forms of literacy. The latter are often among the most optimistic advocates of the perceived social transformations brought about by offering 'one laptop per child', as MIT professors Nicholas Negroponte and Seymour Papert favour, or by paving the way for 'the information superhighway', a term that is attributed to Al Gore, former vice-president of the United States of America. These debates have had considerable, if conflictual, policy impact (Drotner, 2007). For example, Singapore is currently reforming its school system to allow for more differentiated and creative work processes stimulated by virtual forms of collaboration and participation, while in the United States of America and most of Europe, the pendulum is swinging in the opposite direction: here policymakers put increasing emphasis on national tests and on evidence-based learning through well-defined steps in order to counter what are perceived as too permissive frameworks of education.

Addressing childhood while speaking of media

As may be expected, public discourses on children's relations to digital media are partly framed by the enablers and constraints of the particular technologies under scrutiny. For example, overt and systematic regulation of output is clearly much more difficult to enact for digital technologies such as the hyper-complex internet than for broadcast media such as traditional radio and television. Broadcasters may be legally bound to restrict certain types of content to certain times of the day (known in Britain as the nine o'clock watershed), a regulatory option that is clearly not feasible when it comes to the internet with its enormous storage capacity and its immediate trans-border exchange of information.

Regulation of digital media output that underage users may access and appropriate is largely enacted as self-regulation and this may take different forms. Within the home and often dependent on age, parents may directly ban certain computer games or limit access to certain internet sites, perhaps through the use of filters. Many exercise little regulation of content, often because they are simply ignorant of the possible uses to which the internet or the computer may be put. Instead, much parental regulation takes the form of limitations on time or money. When this situation is coupled with the fact that policymakers 'stop their regulatory scrutiny at the front door', the result is often a domestic power struggle whose unintended results are to undermine 'the trust-based negotiations within the family that are central to attempts to democratize the family' (Livingstone and Bober, 2006, 110).

Self-regulation or co-regulation is also found on a more structural level, as when content providers follow labelling of computer games such as those offered, for example, by the ESRB (Entertainment Software Labeling Board) in the United States of America or by PEGI (Pan European Game Information), whose labelling system operates in over 30 countries. Although the research literature is still somewhat sparse, qualitative studies indicate that most practices of self-regulation and transgression are carried out by children themselves, either in the form of self-monitoring or as peer-guidance (Facer et al., 2003; Livingstone and Bober, 2004).

While technological enablers and constraints do impact on the forms that regulation and transgression of digital media may take, these technological traits are played out against changing perceptions of childhood and a refashioning of children's sociocultural practices, both of which serve to orchestrate children's digital appropriations. For example, the increased role played by self- or co-regulation from the 1980s on coincides with more widespread assumptions that children are capable, social actors in their own right, not vulnerable individuals or potential victims in need of adult protection. The tacit co-production of optimistic discourses on childhood and on digital media does not go unchallenged, as we have seen. More importantly, there are considerable variations when it comes to the ways in which discourses transmute into everyday practices.

The results from a pan-European study on children's take-up and appropriation of print, audiovisual and digital media demonstrate that media practices and sociocultural practices are intimately intertwined; and these complex constellations map on to different perceptions of what it takes to be a vulnerable or a competent child. In the Northern countries of Europe there is widespread adult encouragement of forming strong peer cultures in childhood, just as it is deemed safe for children over the age of eight or nine to bike to the local sports club or music school. Southern Europe displays more family-oriented child cultures with less adult acceptance of children's autonomous exploration of public space. In between are countries such as Britain, Germany and Switzerland where children's peer culture is closer to the pattern found in Northern Europe while restrictions made on children's physical independence are similar to those found in Southern Europe (Suoninen, 2001).

The proliferation and integration of games consoles and mobile phones, of portable music players and personal computers with internet access into many children's lives – from bedrooms and schools to cybercafés and shopping malls – serve to question and possibly rework established boundaries of power. In discursive terms, adults assume the loudest voice, as we have seen; irrespective of their stance in particular debates on children and digital media. And while these debates address profound issues of independence and social inequality, of future competence formation and physical mobility, they do so through rhetorical gestures that position children as others – be they exotic, menacing or vulnerable others. In media scholar Crispin Thurlow's words, 'that adults get away with misrepresenting young people on such a scale says a great deal about the relations of power that structure youth' (Thurlow, 2006).

Still, there are more similarities in the discourses than those pertaining to power. Both optimists and pessimists take a normative stance in their descriptions and evaluations, and such a perspective foregrounds certain aspects, often emotionally charged ones, while downplaying others. Sex, violence and bodily harm get bigger headlines and more energetic action from special interest groups than do more structural issues such as the commercial ramifications within which so many of children's digital media appropriations take place today. Some of the biggest, and most spectacular, mergers and acquisitions since the 1990s involve media and ICT corporations. And yet these transformations are belittled in public debates on gaming, social networking sites and mobile texting. The much-touted celebratory claims for democratic participation on file-sharing sites such as Flickr and Facebook rarely mention that the search engine corporation Google bought YouTube for USD 1.65 billion in 2006 and that the social networking website MySpace, linking user-generated, personal profiles, photos and music, is owned by News Corporation, the world's third-largest media conglomerate.

Debates on children and digital media enter and address a complex and constantly transmuting set of relations. The way in which these challenges are handled is through rhetorical processes of selection and simplification. Concerned adults will tend to focus on the negative aspects or potential hazards of children's digital engagements, unlike proponents of celebratory assertions, who will single out the empowering, playful and innovative elements of the youthful engagements. Such rhetorical choices may be inevitable parts of being heard and seen in public debate, and because of the multiplicity of digital uses, such choices are perhaps made easier than before. But, by the same token, this makes public discourses harder to use as bases for assessment and action in scholarly, industry and policy terms – contextualized insights into children's digital media practices need to substantiate the adult knowledge base.

Defining digital media and children

What, then, characterizes these digital media practices? Most importantly, media are particular technologies that facilitate the storage and modification, articulation and exchange, of signs, be they text, images, numbers or sound. Signs are tools of meaning-making, and so media may be defined as meaning-making technologies. They are material tools, and mostly commercial tools (books, television sets, mobile phones), and as such media are like many other tools such as cars, toothbrushes and saucepans. But, unlike such object-like tools, media are also immaterial tools of signification, of meaning-making. This dual definition of media as both material and immaterial tools (Carey, 1989) places them at a particular cultural vantage point. Unlike interpersonal forms of meaning-making, such as dinner conversation, the forms of meaning-making taking shape through media may be preserved and handed down through time, and they may cross boundaries of place. Media are also selective cultural resources, in that they mostly require a bit of money, some free time and sometimes also some formal knowledge of the semiotic codes (reading, writing, numeracy) as prerequisites of use. In short, media are means through which we may express ourselves and reflect upon the world, and they are means through which we may connect to other people, times and places beyond our immediate spheres of interaction.

In terms of the material aspects of media, then, children's relations to media may be defined as means through which they can connect to and encounter other realities and as means of engaging with other people beyond their physical reach. In terms of the material aspects of media, these encounters and relations may be regulated through organizational or personal rules of access and use, such as broadband availability at school and parental time limitations on gaming; through structural or economic shortcomings such as lack of books, computers or money; or through insufficient skills to break the codes of expression, understanding and use, such as illiteracy, ignorance of internet distribution networks or sparse insights into the handling of texts and images.

Digitization has been taken up in a big way only since the 1990s, and so children's digital media cultures are a relatively new phenomenon. But they latch on to existing media cultures which serve to modify the introduction of mobile media, computer games and the internet, just as these digital media serve to relocate existing media cultures in terms of adult discourses, regulations and children's uses. Crucially, media that are digital from their inception, such as the personal computer, the games console and mobile devices, are all commercial products whose survival is largely dependent upon their success on globalized markets. Unlike some radio and television channels that belong to a public-service and often a national domain, children's access to most digital media depends on their (or their parents') economic acumen and priorities. Since economic divides and sociocultural patterns of production and use change at a much slower pace than do technologies, the transformations brought about by digital media in children's lives should not be overstated. Still, four characteristics of digital media serve as catalysts for qualitative changes in relation to children's everyday practices, namely:

Semiotic codes – digital media invite more-seamless forms of multimodal (co-) production and interactivity;

Time – digital media allow immediate exchange of mediatized forms of communication and, for mobile media, ad hoc coordination;

Place – digital media widen options of mediatized communication virtually everywhere;

Social relations – digital media intensify meaning-making practices as forms of action, participation, collaboration and reflexivity.

As for the multimodality of codes, it should be noted that this is not particular to digital media. Even the earliest books for children display a mixture of text and images, so the novelty of digital media is rather the ease with which different sign systems may be brought on to the same platform and manipulated there. Moreover, this manipulation of signs is also well known from other media – writing letters or modifying photo negatives through special forms of development. Again, it is the relative ease with which such manipulations may be carried out that is particular to digital media – most children with access to a computer attempt to download music and many edit and remix images and text (Gilje, 2008; Perkel, 2008) – and this immediacy is unknown to analogue media apart from the telephone. Some young users also (co-)produce new mixtures of visuals, graphics and sound, and these processes involve often complex handling of a range of semiotic codes and conventions. Several studies demonstrate that it takes a good deal of training to shape the complexity of semiotic resources in ways that are relevant not only to the young producers but also to the ones to whom the results are addressed (Tyner, 1998; Jewitt and Kress, 2003). Very few children exert any form of digital literacy or multimodal literacy without systematic training.

That media help orchestrate children's time is well known from studies of television, for example, especially prior to the introduction of the VCR; and this still holds true for young children and special programmes such as Disney animated cartoons in some countries (Lemish, 1987; Drotner, 2004). Exchanging communication across time through media is also known to many children of earlier generations who have treasured letters to distant pen pals, who have coordinated arrangements on the family landline phone, and who may have written to the so-called agony columns of teenage magazines in search of advice on looks, friendship or fashion. But mobile phones, internet messaging and social networking internet sites allow synchronous, continuous and easy exchanges between peers. Moreover, these forms of communication serve to integrate what we may term distant intimacies as mundane, and increasingly mobile, elements of children's everyday lives. Not least the mobile phone has catalysed ad hoc coordination among teenagers and between parents and children, and this virtual life-line is used by many parents to legitimize their purchase and upkeep of their children's mobiles (Drotner, 2005; Ito et al., 2005; Ling and Haddon, 2008).

Children and young people have been among the earliest and most avid consumers of mobile phones. Indeed, the mediatized physical mobility of children is one of the most distinctive and, perhaps, far-reaching innovations brought about by digital media. Even if transistor radios of the 1960s, Discmans of the 1980s and Game Boys of the early 1990s meant that particularly music listening and later gaming became part of children's increased physical mobility, the advent in the 1990s of mobile phones, MP3 players and mobile multimedia platforms implied an enormous widening of juvenile media engagements in terms of entertainment, information and communication, and did so nearly everywhere and at all times.

In more general terms, the internet serves to widen users' options of communication and action across space, and these options become increasingly globalized (Holloway and Valentine, 2003). Since the 1980s, satellites in the sky, cables under the sea and corporate mergers and acquisitions have brought about an intensified media globalization and commodification, so that today children, irrespective of their actual options of engaging with globalized media, know about their existence and relate to perceived assumptions about mediatized forms of otherness (Feilitzen and Carlsson, 2002; de Block and Buckingham, 2007). Globalized media, then, are both a symptom of and a solution to the demands made on children in late-modern societies to exert temporal coordination, spatial flexibility and personal identity performance. As such, they have attained a central importance, not accorded to media among former generations of children. This importance should be kept in mind by policymakers who address and attempt to minimize the so-called digital divides found in children's lives today. These divides are often tackled as problems of access, while their most drastic implications are possibly to do with inequalities of use – of children having very pronounced differences in terms of learning and knowing how to handle the complexities of media in ways that are relevant to their current lives and future situation (Warschauer, 2004). Digital divides demonstrate an intimate connection to familiar fault-lines in terms of class, gender, ethnicity, age and region (Fox, 2005; Peter and Valkenburg, 2006).

Digital practices and personal identity performance are precisely some of the contested aspects of children's digital media uses, as we shall see below. In general, the social relations which media are intertwined with are key to current debates on, and adult interventions into, children's media uses, and for obvious reasons. For, on a day-to-day basis, social relations are more visible than the dimensions of time and space, and so these relations assume an overarching role in the public eye. Much has been made of the interactive options of digital media, not least the internet. But media that are analogue from the outset also entail options of social interaction, such as phone-in radio programmes where selected audiences may enter into a dialogue with the programme host, or debate programmes on TV where the studio public may cast their vote or may offer their opinion. Digital media serve to widen these interactive options and to make the processes of selection less transparent, as is evident from virtual communities where users do not immediately detect the web-host's possible gatekeeping.

Because of the ease with which signs may be manipulated and modified, digital media offer more, and more advanced, possibilities of semiotic production, such as is evident when users make their own profiles on Facebook or MySpace. Moreover, because of their flexible and often mobile nature of joint meaning-making, digital media intensify modes of virtual co-production and collaboration, as when peers edit images and circulate them via their mobile or do homework together on the internet. In particular, the so-called second-generation services on the internet, called web 2.0 – such as social networking sites, free user-generated encyclopaedias (Wikipedia or wikis) and internet diaries (weblogs or blogs) – offer more and easier ways of social participation and networking, of shaping and sharing content. The rapid take-up of these services by the younger generation in many parts of the world has meant an enormous expansion of informal communication, participation and play. Even if the research literature is still limited and inconclusive, several studies indicate that these virtual social sites offer children new ways both of expressing intimacies and of reflecting upon the reactions brought about by their articulations (Brake, 2008). Some of the most advanced digital experiences are brought about through gaming, since these processes both assume and advance virtual action – to be a gamer one has to *do* something in a very concrete sense, such as manipulating objects or figures, and thereby one helps create and sustain universes of practice (Gee, 2005). These universes offer spaces of articulation, collaborative experimentation and playful action, to which are sometimes added options for reflection if the gamer joins one of the many game communities.

Back to the future?

As we have noted, such practices are open to often intense and dichotomous debates. As we have also seen, the mundane, the social and the commercial aspects of these practices are routinely downplayed in favour of the extraordinary, the personal and the transformative aspects (in both a negative and positive sense). Future developments in children's mediatized forms of meaning-making are very likely to recapitulate some of these debates. In the meantime, children go on exploring, engaging with – and disbanding – these objects and processes. Since the current trend is for digital media to be embedded within or enhance physical objects, these uses and their implications may be more difficult to detect and follow in future. For example, media are no longer simply tie-ins to toys, or vice versa, as has long been the case. Toys are becoming digitized and offer ways of meaning-making and use that go well beyond a cuddly Mickey Mouse figure or a super-shaped Barbie doll. Conversely, digital gaming is fast moving away from the screen and into the playground or the street (Goldstein et al., 2004). These developments undoubtedly offer young users new options for interaction and participation, just as they offer lucrative new means of corporate development. In addition, these developments challenge researchers of children and researchers of digital media to engage with one another's research traditions in ways not yet explored. Technology developers, content producers and avid young users will lead the way. It is to be hoped that level-headed researchers will follow closely on their heels.

References

Barker, M. and J. Petley (eds) (1997) *Ill Effects: The Media/Violence Debate*. Routledge: London.

de Block, L. and D. Buckingham (eds) (2007) *Global Children, Global Media: Migration, Media and Childhood*. Basingstoke: Palgrave.

boyd, d. (2007) 'Why Youth ♥ Social Network Sites: Contemporary American Teenage Social Life', in D. Buckingham (ed.) *Youth, Identity and Digital Media*: Cambridge MA: MIT Press. The McArthur Foundation series on Digital Media and Learning. Retrieved December 2007 from http//:www.mitpressjournals.org/toc/dmal/-/6.

Brake, D. (2007) 'Examining My Life or just "About Me?" In the Shallows of the Digital Self', Paper presented at the International Communication Conference, San Francisco: May.

Carey, J.W. (1989) *Communication as Culture: Essays on Media and Society*. Boston: Unwin Hyman.

Cohen, S. (1972) *Folk Devils and Moral Panic*. London: McGibbon & Kee.

Convention on the Rights of the Child (1989) United Nations Office of the High Commissioner for Human Rights: New York. Retrieved August 2007 from http://www.unhchr.ch/html/menu3/b/k2crc.htm

Critcher, C. (2008) 'Making Waves: Historical Aspects of Public Debates About Children and Mass Media', in K. Drotner and S. Livingstone (eds) *The International Handbook of Children, Media and Culture*. London: Sage, pp. 91–104.

Davies, M.M. (1997) *Fake, Fact & Fantasy: Children's interpretation of television reality*. Mahwah NJ: Lawrence Erlbaum.

d'Haenens, L. (2001) 'Old and New Media: Access and Ownership in the Home', in S.Livingstone and M. Bovill (eds) *Children and their Changing Media Environment: A European Comparative Study*. New York: Lawrence Erlbaum, pp. 53–84.

Drotner, K. (1999) 'Dangerous Media? Panic Discourses and Dilemmas of Modernity', *PaedagogicaHistorica*, 35(3): 593–619.

Drotner, K. (2004) 'Disney Dilemmas: Audience Negotiations of Media Globalization', *Nordicom Review*, 25 (1–2). Special issue, ed. U.Carlsson, 16th Nordic Conference on Media and Communication Research. Retrieved August 2007 from http://www.nordicom.gu.se/common/publ_pdf/157_137-148.pdf.

Drotner, K. (2005) 'Media on the Move: Personalised Media and the Transformation of Publicness', in S. Livingstone (ed.) *Audiences and Publics: When Cultural Engagement Matters for the Public Sphere*. Bristol: Intellect Books, pp. 187–211.

Drotner, K. (2007) 'Leisure is Hard Work: Digital Practices and Future Competences', in D. Buckingham (ed.) *Youth, Identity and Digital Media*. Cambridge MA: MIT Press. The McArthur Foundation series on Digital Media and Learning. Retrieved December 2007 from http//:www.mitpressjournals.org/toc/dmal/-/6.

Facer, K., J. Furlong, R. Furlong and R. Sutherland (2003) *ScreenPlay: Children and Computing in the Home*. London: RoutledgeFalmer.

Feilitzen, C.V. and U. Carlsson (eds) (2002) *Children, Young People and Media Globalization*. Gothenburg: Nordicom.

Fox, S. (2005) *Digital Divisions: The Pew Internet and American Life Project*. Retrieved August 2007 from http//www.pewinternet.org.

Gee, J.P. (2005) *Why Video Games are Good for Your Soul: Pleasure and Learning*. Melbourne: Common Ground.

Gilje, Ø. (2008) 'Googling Movies: Digital Media Production and the "Culture of Appropriation"', in K. Drotner, H. Siggaard-Jensen and K.C. Schrøder (eds) *Informal Learning and Digital Media: Constructions, Contexts, Critique*, Cambridge: Cambridge Scholars Press, pp. 29–48.

Goldstein, J., D. Buckingham and G. Brougère (eds) (2004) *Toys, Games and Media*. Mahwah NJ: Lawrence Erlbaum.

Groosman, D. and G. Degaetano (1999) *Stop Teaching Our Kids to Kill: A Call to Action against TV, Movie and Video Game Violence*. New York: Crown Publishers.

Hamelink, C.J. (2008) 'Children's Communication Rights: Beyond Intentions', in K. Drotner and S. Livingstone (eds) *The International Handbook of Children, Media and Culture*. London: Sage, pp. 502–513.

Holloway, S.L. and G. Valentine (2003) *Cyberkids: Children in the Information Age*. London: RoutledgeFalmer.

Huffaker, D. (2004), 'Spinning Yarns Around a Digital Fire: Storytelling and Dialogue Among Youth on the Internet', *First Monday* 9(1). Retrieved August 2007 from http://www.firstmonday.org/issues/issue9_1/huffaker/index.html. Rpt. in*Information Technology in Childhood Education Annual 2004*, pp. 63–75.

Ito, M., D. Okabe and M. Matsuda (2005) *Personal, Portable, Pedestrian: Mobile Phones in Japanese Life*. Cambridge MA: MIT Press.

Jewitt, C. and G. Kress (eds) (2003) *Multimodal Literacy*. New York: Peter Lang.

Lemish, D. (1987) 'Viewers in Diapers: The Early Development of Television Viewing', in T. R. Lindlof (ed.) *Natural Audiences: Qualitative Research of Media Uses and Effects*. Norwood NJ: Ablex.

Ling, R. and L. Haddon (2008) 'Children, Youth and the Mobile Phone', in K. Drotner and S. Livingstone (eds) *The International Handbook of Children, Media and Culture*. London: Sage, pp. 137–151.

Livingstone, S. and M. Bober (2004) *UK Children Go Online: Surveying the experiences of young people and their parents. Second project report*. London School of Economics. Retrieved August 2007 from: personal.lse.ac.uk/bober/UKCGOsurveyreport.pdf.

Livingstone, S. and M. Bober (2006) 'Regulating the Internet at Home: Contrasting the Perspectives of Children and Parents', in D. Buckingham and R. Willett (eds) *Digital Generations: Children, Young People and New Media*. Mahwah NJ: Lawrence Erlbaum.

Loader, B.D. (ed.) 2007, *Young Citizens in the Digital Age: Political Engagement, Young People and New Media*. London: Routledge.

McLuhan, M. (1964) *Understanding Media: The Extensions of Man*. New York: McGraw Hill.

Papert, S. (1996) *The Connected Family: Bridging the Digital Generation Gap*. Atlanta GA: Longstreet Press.

Perkel, D. (2008) 'Copy and Paste Literacy? Literacy Practices in the Production of a MySpace Profile', in K. Drotner, H. Siggaard-Jensen and K.C. Schrøder (eds) *Informal Learning and Digital Media*. Cambridge: Cambridge Scholars Press, pp. 203–224.

Peter, J. and P.M. Valkenburg (2006) 'Adolescents' Internet Use: Testing the "Disappearing Digital Divide" versus the "Emerging Differentiation" Approach', *Poetics*, 34(4–5): 293–305.

Rheingold, H. (2002) *Smart Mobs: The New Social Revolution*. Cambridge MA: Perseus Publishing.

Suoninen, A. (2001) 'The Role of Media in Peer Group Relations', in S. Livingstone and M.Bovill (eds) *Children and their Changing Media Environment: A European Comparative Study*. New York: Lawrence Erlbaum, pp. 201–219.

Tapscott, D. (1998) *Growing Up Digital: The Rise of the Net Generation*. New York: McGraw-Hill.

Thurlow, C. (2006) 'From Statistical Panic to Moral Panic: The Metadiscursive Construction and Popular Exaggeration of New Media Language in the Print Media', *Journal of Computer-Mediated Communication*, 113(1). Retrieved August 2007 from http://jcmc.indiana.edu/vol11/issue3/thurlow.html.

Turkle, S. (1995) *Life on the Screen*. London: Phoenix.

Tyner, K. (1998) *Literacy in a Digital World*. Mahwah NJ: Lawrence Erlbaum.

Warschauer, M. (2004) *Technology and Social Inclusion: Rethinking the Digital Divide*. Cambridge MA: MIT Press.

Section VI

Children's Rights and Place in the World

25

Children's Rights as Human Rights: Reading the UNCRC

Michael Freeman

In *The Alchemy of Race and Rights* Patricia Williams writes:

> For the historically disempowered, the conferring of rights is symbolic of all the denied aspects of their humanity: rights imply a respect that places one in the referential range of self and others, that elevates one's status from human body to social being. (Williams, 1991, 163)

She is not writing about children – they do not feature in her argument – but about African Americans and women. But what she says is all too pertinent in other contexts too: to children, to the learning disabled, the mentally ill and older people. There are trenchant critiques (within Critical Legal Scholarship, for example) of this emphasis on the importance of rights – these can be traced back to Bentham (1987) for whom rights were 'nonsense upon stilts' and Sumner (1987, 111–112), and to Marx's famous essay 'On the Jewish Question' (1992); but, as Robert Williams (1987) noted in an essay advocating 'taking rights aggressively', this may reflect blindness to the privileged position from which they make their arguments.

It is true that rights may be a disciplinary – or at least a potentially disciplinary – practice (Foucault, 1977; Brown, 1995). The early children's rights movement – this spoke in the language of rights but was concerned exclusively with welfare (Platt, 1979) – can be seen as a vehicle for enlarging state power over both children and their caregivers (Donzelot, 1979; Grossberg, 1985). But it does not have to operate in this way. We must not overlook the importance of rights where rights are the currency in use. Rights may atomize: communitarians recoil at the horror of this (Etzioni, 1993). But, as Patricia Williams notes: 'For me, stranger–stranger relations are better than stranger–hattel' (1991, 148).

This language is most apposite to children who, for much of history, have been little more than property. The sacrificial son is at the root of two of the world's great religions (Delaney, 1998). It is in classic epics like the *Aeneid* of Virgil (1956), in Shakespeare's plays (*Hamlet, The Winter's Tale*) (Belsey, 1999), in Dickens' *Dombey and Son,* and much else (Miller, 2003). Custody disputes were often – and sometimes still are – fought as unseemly squabbles over possessions (Mason, 1994). A leading English judge had to caution not long ago against treating children like 'packages'.[1] In England, the *Gillick* decision[2] in the mid-1980s is often seen as a watershed. It acknowledged that 'parental right yields to the child's right to make his own decisions when he reaches sufficient understanding and intelligence to be capable of making up his own mind on the matter requiring decision'.[3] But the decision shocked and also offended: a national campaign to 'protect the family from interference from officialdom' (*The Times*, 28 May 1985) was established. Popular sentiment supported parental rights, and *Gillick* had undermined them.[4] It is not surprising that there has been a retreat from *Gillick* (Freeman, 2005).

Litigation is still brought – in England but of course also elsewhere – where children appear to be little more than objects in a battle between others. A good recent illustration is the *Williamson* case.[5] Parents alleged that their human rights were infringed by legislation which removed from schools the liberty to inflict corporal punishment on children.[6] The parents were Christians who wanted to ensure that their children were educated in conformity with their religious convictions (but see Greven, 1990). Throughout, the dispute was conceived as one between the State – its right to ban corporal chastisement in schools – and parents (as well as their teachers). The children were not represented: their views were not known or sought. It is, of course, possible that, indoctrinated as they were, they would have agreed with their parents, as the Amish children in the US Supreme court case of *Wisconsin v. Yoder*[7] apparently had. But that is not the issue: more significant is the potential impact upon children as a class. The courts found against the parents (and teachers). But had they not done so, children would once again have been exposed to being beaten at school to uphold the human rights of adults. It is of significance that the State did not argue in this case that corporal punishment necessarily involved an infringement of any of the rights of children.[8] Of course, it does, as a cursory glance at Article 19 of the United Nations Convention on the Rights of the Child would reveal.[9] In an impressive judgement, Baroness Hale proclaimed:

> This is, and always has been, a case about children, their rights and the rights of their parents and teachers. Yet there has been no one here...to speak on behalf of the children. The battle has been fought on ground selected by the adults.[10]

Her judgement, she said, was 'for the sake of the children'.[11] She noted that instead of focusing, as the courts were expected to do, on 'whether the beliefs of the parents and teachers qualified for protection',[12] it should have examined, at least additionally, the rights of children. The result would have been the same, but the arguments and the reasoning would have looked very different.

That you don't have to be a fundamentalist Christian to view children as rightless is superbly illustrated by an article published in *The Guardian* newspaper in the summer of 2006 (Bindel, 2006). That it was written by the founder of 'Justice for Women' is all the more telling: that it was published in a leading liberal newspaper says much about how children are still perceived. If the article had focused on women or Muslims, there would have been an outcry. Julie Bindel's argument is that school holidays should be cut (in half) because the presence of children in her space – streets, parks, museums, public transport, restaurants – offends her. A little of her diatribe will illustrate its venom:

> I live in an area where kids (*sic*) are routinely taken to proper restaurants for lunch, but I was here before it became Nappy Valley.... There seems to be no escape this summer. Ken Livingstone [the mayor of London] has made it easier for the little monsters to follow me around London by giving school children free bus travel.... There they are, in the museums when you least expect them.

Imagine *The Guardian* publishing an article which objected to black people in restaurants or gay people in museums!

Reading Bindel, I am reminded of what the American court said in the *Dred Scott* case – that slaves 'were so far inferior, that they had no rights which the white man was bound to respect'.[13] And this is understood by Hannah Arendt. In *The Origins of Totalitarianism* (1986), and commenting upon the Holocaust, she observed that before the Nazis started exterminating the Jews they deprived them of all legal status. 'The point is', she notes, 'that a condition of complete rightlessness was created before the right to live was challenged' (Arendt, 1986, 296). The most fundamental of rights is the right to possess rights. Arendt adds:

> Slavery's fundamental offence against human rights was not that it took liberty away...but that it excluded a certain category of people even from the possibility of fighting for freedom. (Arendt, 1986, 297)

Those who would deny children human rights – rights such as the participatory freedoms in the UN Convention, for example freedom of expression, thought, conscience and religion, association and peaceful assembly[14] – sometimes argue, as Onora O'Neill famously did, that 'a child's main remedy is to grow up' (O'Neill, 1988, 453). In other words, unlike slaves or women for example, there is a finite limit on rightlessness. But is this really a satisfactory objection to giving children rights now? We impose responsibilities on children, including criminal responsibility:[15] in some systems this is at a very young age (in England for example at 10).[16] Those who are uncomfortable at according rights to children rarely protest this incongruence. We expect children to obey laws before they are enfranchised. But try running the argument that the age for voting in elections should be set at the same age as that for criminal responsibility.[17] Even suggestions that the age of voting should be lowered to 16 – it is 18 in most democratic countries – are repelled.[18] Voting rights for prisoners seem to command more support.[19]

If we accept the case for human rights[20] – of course, not everyone does – we must ask why some of those who support human rights do not do so when it comes to children. There is an argument that there is no point or value in talking about children's rights. There are those who believe it is misguided to think that rights can achieve something positive for children. This is the view of the prominent Kantian thinker, Onora O'Neill. In an influential article, first published in 1988, she argues that 'taking rights as fundamental in ethical deliberation about children has neither theoretical nor political advantages' (O'Neill, 1988, 447). In her view, if we care about children's lives, we should rather identify what obligations parents, teachers and indeed the wider community have towards children. 'We can perhaps go *further* to secure the ethical basis of children's positive rights if we do *not* try to base them on claims about fundamental rights' (O'Neill, 1988, 446), she argues. She adds: 'in the specific case of children, taking rights as fundamental has political costs rather than advantages' (O'Neill, 1988, 447). But 'a construction made from the agent's perspective may deliver more, though it promises less, since it does not aim at an "all or nothing" construction of ethical requirements' (O'Neill, 1988, 457).

Does it deliver more? Consider the *Williamson* case.[21] How would we identify the parental obligation in this case? From the perspective of the child? It is unlikely that O'Neill intends this. From that of the parents or perhaps even through the lens of Christianity (and, if so, which Christianity – the one as interpreted by the fundamentalist parents and schools?) If, as I suspect, it would be the parents' perspective that would count, the obligation would presumably be to raise children in an environment which encourages physical chastisement. And one, it may be added, in which the package of participatory rights in the UN Convention (Articles 12, 13, 14 and 15)[22] would count for very little. An emphasis on obligation places parents and other adult authorities centre stage – it marginalizes children. As so often in the past, where there was no concern for, or interest in, children's rights, children appear to be little more than objects of concern. O'Neill's model, on reflection, is the conventional deficit one.

And this underlies much other contemporary philosophical writing about children. Thus, to Harry Brighouse, there is 'something very strange about thinking of children as bearers of rights' (Brighouse, 2002, 31). In his view, 'the further an agent departs from the liberal model of the competent rational person, the less appropriate it seems to be to attribute rights' (Brighouse, 2002, 31). It hardly needs saying, but it was once thought inappropriate to attribute rights to women, who were certainly thought to fall short of the 'liberal model'. Brighouse does not have difficulty with seeing children as bearers of welfare rights, but he has problems with agency rights, at least as far as young children are concerned. It is, of course, easier to justify welfare rights, and there are likely to be some limitations on agency rights. But welfare rights work better in a rights culture where agency, for example the right to participate in decisions about oneself, is acknowledged. Children are better protected (from abuse, neglect, etc.) where their rights are also recognized.[23] Brighouse is particularly critical of three agency rights, all of which are recognized in the UN Convention: to freedom of expression (Article 13),[24] to freedom of religion (Article 14),[25] and to enjoyment of one's own culture (Article 30).[26] But why should children not have these rights? Why – to take one of his examples – should it be thought that the child's right to cultural identity 'jeopardizes the family as an institution' (Brighouse, 2002, 29)? Is a small child not entitled to adopt a vegetarian lifestyle or express an opinion on schooling (perhaps opting for or out of a faith school)?

The conventional deficit model is also exemplified in the concern of some critics of children's rights that children will make mistakes. Thus, Carol Brennan's main reason for refusing to acknowledge that children have autonomy is that 'often children do not choose well or wisely' (Brennan, 2002, 59). She accepts that adults can also fail to make the right decisions. It is, of course, fundamental to believing in rights that we accept that there is a right to do what we consider to be wrong, to make mistakes, to let others do things which we would not do (Dworkin, 1977). We have to balance, what Joel Feinberg has called, the child's 'right to an open future' (Feinberg, 1980) with an acceptance that we learn how to act autonomously by being allowed to do so. To train children to become autonomous requires, among other things, that we treat them in some respects as if they already were. Should we respect the person, the dignity of the child now or see her as a person whose *future* dignity is the important consideration? This dilemma can be seen starkly in cases where children refuse medical treatment. In an English case, not so long ago, an intelligent 15-year-old girl, who clearly met the test for competence in *Gillick*[27] refused to consent to a heart transplant.[28] She insisted she would rather die with her own heart than live with someone else's. Nor is this case unique. In all of them, the courts have come to the decision that nearly everyone would make – for most of us are paternalists when it comes to children. And so they have held that a competent child can consent to treatment,[29] but cannot refuse it.[30] Those who think the courts right to take decisions away from young persons are unashamedly paternalistic. It is important, as Brazier and Bridge acknowledge, that decision-makers should satisfy themselves that a choice is 'maximally autonomous' (Brazier and Bridge, 1996, 109). But what does this involve? I have argued that it requires us to understand the young person's decision, to see how it fits their value system and coheres with their goals (Freeman, 2005). There are cases where an adolescent is able to make a competent, maximally autonomous choice, even one to refuse life-saving treatment. Respecting such a choice is difficult, but we would respect it if the young person was 18. Arbitrary discrimination on the basis solely of age is not justifiable.

But are we not putting too much faith in the power of rights and rights discourse, particularly when it comes to children? One to pose this question is Michael King (1994; see also 2004). Why, he asks, has it become important – for advocates of children's rights that is – to move from seeing rights as 'dignified statements' and 'manifesto rights' into 'rules designed to regulate relationships' (King, 1994, 385). So, why was it that those who called for and drafted the UN Convention think it was important that this document was accepted as 'law'? This is an important question, though it is not one that needs to be asked exclusively with reference to children. And there are answers. Law is one of the most significant symbols of legitimacy (Ball and Friedman, 1965). When enacted, it is an accomplished fact, one which it is difficult to resist (Hyman and Sheatsley, 1964). And it can change attitudes as well as behaviour (Berger, 1952). For King, however, law is one version of reality, and whether it is experienced as 'real' hinges upon whether it can 'deliver the goods' (King, 1994, 393), that is, improve the welfare and enhance the interests of children (King, 1997).

Getting a worldwide convention to recognize the rights of children was not easy. The gestation process was lengthy. There was a 'Declaration' as early as 1924 (Marshall, 1999) and a second one in 1959. But it was only in 1979, 10 years later, that the process to construct what became the UN Convention on the Rights of The Child, began. There were five issues upon which a consensus was difficult to achieve (Johnson, 1992). Freedom of thought, conscience and religion – now in Article 14 – was a major stumbling block. The representative of Bangladesh commented that this ran counter to the major religious systems of the world, in particular to Islam (and see Sait, 2000). From the Islamic perspective, to give children freedom of religion was unacceptable since it did not recognize the Koranic practice of forbidding the child the possibility of changing his or her religion.

On adoption there was also Islamic opposition. This is not surprising as adoption is not a recognized institution of Islamic law. But opposition was also voiced by Venezuela, which was concerned about the abuses involved in inter-country adoption.

A third area of contention was the issue of the rights of the unborn child. The Declaration of 1959 had recognized the claim of the unborn child to protection: 'the child needs special safeguards and care, including appropriate legal protection, before as well as after birth.'[31] Debates around the 1989 Convention centred on how 'child' was to be defined. Discussion divided between those who argued that childhood should begin 'at the moment of conception' and those who argued that any attempt to establish 'a beginning point should be abandoned' and that wording accordingly be adopted which was compatible with the wide variety of domestic legislation on the subject.[32] The latter viewpoint prevailed, and the article adopted does not provide for the inclusion of the unborn in the Convention.

The fourth contentious issue was traditional practices. The delegations of Canada, the United States and the United Kingdom wanted express reference to be made to female circumcision. But, as an African NGO pointed out, there were other traditional practices harmful to children, such as son preference. The resulting article does not specify any specific practice, though it is clear that female circumcision, in particular female genital mutilation, is the main target of it.[33]

The fifth issue upon which opinion divided was on whether the Convention should specifically recognize that children had duties to respect parents, and, in case of need, to give them assistance. The origins of this – at least the duty to respect – are biblical (it is the fifth commandment). The Senegalese delegation to the Convention Second Reading urged the acceptance of 'this cultural value of Africa and Asia'.[34] This was opposed by Australia and the United States, which pointed out that the obligation of a child towards his or her parents was unenforceable by the State, and therefore outside the purport of an international convention. The International Labour Organization, which agreed, also pointed out that requiring a child to render assistance in case of need was tantamount to a call for child labour, and unacceptable for this reason.[35] The result is Article 29(c), which states that 'States Parties agree that the education of the child shall be directed to the development of respect for the child's parents, his or her own cultural identity...' The concern of Senegal was thus met. It took ten years to get a convention. But it was ratified by more countries and more swiftly than any previous comparable international treaty. Only Somalia – mainly because it does not have a government – and the United States – perhaps because it does – have failed to ratify it (Todres et al., 2006). The Convention, and, one may add, the World Summit which followed it, were greeted with such euphoria that it is all too easy to assume that the Convention itself represents the final word on children's rights. However, in a world in which the child's voice was genuinely heard, the Convention itself might have looked quite different. It is generally accepted that Article 12 is the linchpin of the Convention: it requires states to:

> assure to the child who is capable of forming his or her own views the right to express those views freely, on all matters affecting the child, the views of the child being given due consideration in accordance with the age and maturity of the child.

Yet, of course, on the major 'matter' of the contents of the Convention itself, there is no evidence that children or children's groups as such, participated in drafting or had any real influence in preliminary discussions.

The Convention has been described as 'an important and easily understood advocacy tool – one that promotes children's welfare as an issue of justice rather than one of charity' (Veerman, 1992, 184). But it is more than this. It is a convention in which the child is constructed, for the first time, as a 'principal' (Pais, 1992, 76), a subject in their own right, rather than a concern or an object of intervention. There are general rights (the right to life,[36] prohibition against torture,[37] freedom of expression,[38] thought[39] and religion,[40] and the right to information and privacy[41]); rights requiring protective measures (including measures to protect children from economic and sexual exploitation,[42] to prevent drug abuse[43] and other forms of abuse and neglect[44]); rights concerning the civil status of children (including the right to acquire nationality,[45] the right to preserve one's identity,[46] the right to remain with parents unless the best interests of the child dictate otherwise,[47] and the right to be reunited with family[48]); rights concerning development and welfare (including the child's right to a reasonable standard of living,[49] the right to health and basic services,[50] the right to social security,[51] the right to education,[52] and the right to leisure[53] and play); rights concerning children in special circumstances or 'in especially difficult circumstances' (these extend to such children as handicapped children,[54] refugee children[55] and orphaned children,[56] and include special regulations on adoption,[57] cultural concerns of minority and indigenous children,[58] and rehabilitative care for children suffering from deprivation,[59] as well as a prohibition on the recruitment of soldiers under 15 years,[60] which has now been extended by an optional Protocol to 18[61]). The Convention also contains a monitoring mechanism, with State Parties required to submit reports every five years and an international committee of experts to monitor compliance.[62]

If children's rights are human rights, they should have the characteristics of human rights. Thus, they should be universal (Lukes, 1993; Van Boven, 2002; Mahoney, 2007), to be held by children simply because they are children. Race, sex, sexual orientation, religion, social position, nationality, fortune, etc., are in these terms irrelevant (Besson, 2005); hence the important non-discrimination principle in Article 2 of the Convention (Hitch, 1989). At their basis, as John Rawls puts it, is a 'common good conception of justice' (Rawls, 1993). In his view, human rights cannot be rejected 'as peculiarly liberal or special to our Western tradition'. He sees them as 'politically neutral' (Rawls, 1993, 12). There is no doubt that children's rights could be undermined by cultural relativism (Freeman, 1995).

But of course different societies have different understandings of childhood.[63] There are different views on such questions as parent–child relationships (the issues of respect and support have already been discussed), on child labour (Weston, 2007), on the age of marriage (it is noticeable that the African Charter on the Rights and Welfare of The Child of 1990 refers to this,[64] although the UN Convention does not). And views differ also on such basics as education, punishment and medical treatment. As Ncube, a leading thinker on children in Zimbabwe, recognizes, 'the normative universality achieved in the definition and formulation of children's rights has to contend with diverse and varied cultural and traditional conceptions of childhood, its role, its rights and obligations' (Ncube, 1998a, 5). And he describes some aspects of the traditional African conception of childhood that are very different from the model found in the developed world. Thus, he notes, 'in the African cultural context childhood is not perceived and conceptualized in terms of age but in terms of intergenerational obligations of support and reciprocity. In this sense an African "child" is often always a "child" in relation to his or her parents who expect and are traditionally entitled to all forms of support in times of need and in old age' (Ncube, 1998b, 18).

It is standard, when culture is discussed in the context of human/children's rights, to confine discussion to cultural practices in Africa, Asia or other parts of the developing world. So the emphasis tends to be on female genital mutilation, child marriage (particularly forced marriage), and issues like child soldiers. It is as if the norm were the practices of the developed world, though there are cultural practices in this part of the world too which may be considered to be against the human rights of children.

A valuable way of looking at the debate is suggested by Philip Alston, who urges the analogy drawn from European Human Rights Jurisprudence of a 'margin of appreciation' (Alston, 1994, 20). This allows for some flexibility, some discretion, but would not allow culture to be accorded 'the status of a metanorm which trumps rights' (Alston, 1994, 20). Looked at in this way, certain practices will fall outside the pale of acceptability: slavery and practices similar to slavery, such as imprisonment within brothels and forcing children into prostitution. Nor can there be space for the so-called cultural defence (Renteln, 2004), for female infanticide or for female genital mutilation.

To recognize that children's rights are human rights is also to recognize that children are humans, that they are not animals or pieces of property. But this does not mean that we have to overlook the fact that they are also children and, as such, vulnerable.[65] This is one of the reasons why the UN Convention on the Rights of the Child adopts, as one of its two most important principles (the other is in Article 12, already quoted in part), the normative standard that 'in all actions concerning children, whether undertaken by public or private social welfare institutions, courts of law, administrative authorities or legislative bodies, the best interests of the child shall be a primary consideration'.[66] This provision puzzles some. As Robert Mnookin pointed out in 1975, 'deciding what is best for a child poses a question no less ultimate than the purpose and value of life itself' (Mnookin, 1975, 260). And yet the standard has come to be seen as 'neutral' (Mnookin, 1975, 235). However, it is vague and indeterminate. One of the dangers of this is that in upholding the standard, other principles and policies can exert an influence from behind a smokescreen. It can cloak prejudices, for example anti-gay sentiments (Reece, 1996, 295–296). It can also be merely a reflection of 'dominant meanings' (Théry, 1989, 81). Different cultures will also and inevitably operate with different concepts of what is in a child's best interests. An example, recently litigated in the courts in England, occurred when a Christian parent confronted a Muslim one over whether their son should be circumcised.[67]

But there is a more important concern for those who wish to proclaim children's rights. There is, it will be pointed out, some incongruity in emphasizing best interests – a concept rooted in paternalism – when the goal is to propagate children's rights. Article 3(1) of the Convention talks of best interests, not best rights. Indeed, it neither creates any rights, nor for that matter does it impose any duties.

The relationship between interests and rights must, therefore, be teased out. Suppose it is not considered – the question does, of course, arise by whom – that actualizing a particular right in the Convention is in a child's best interests. Does the emphasis on best interests trump other considerations? Does it afford space to values other than those sanctioned in the Convention? Are there circumstances where a consideration other than the best interests of the child should prevail? For example, can cultural or religious norms override a child's best interests? Take the headscarf controversy, which has arisen in a number of European countries recently (Brems, 2006a). Or take the issue of immigration control: here decisions are often taken with considerations other than the child's best interests to the fore (Sawyer, 2006).

There are answers to this within the Convention itself. The 'best interests' principle must be seen both as informed by and constrained by the rights provided for by the Convention. As John Tobin has argued:

> a proposed outcome for a child cannot be said to be in his or her best interests where it conflicts with the provisions of the Convention. (Tobin, 2006, 287)

He looks at this in relation to a child's health rights and notes that this requires a consideration of the other guiding principles under the Convention such as protection against violence, the right to an adequate standard of living, the right to education, the right to play and leisure and protection against all forms of exploitation. All of these 'inform any assessment of the best interests of a child' (Tobin, 2006, 287). It is significant that the United Nations Committee on the Rights of The Child maintains that the obligation to consider children's best interests requires a child-impact assessment and evaluation with respect to all legislation and other forms of policy development to determine the impact of any proposed law or policy or budgetary allocation on children's rights.

The 'best interests' principle can also be seen to supplement any catalogue of children's rights, such as those in the UN Convention. Stephen Parker is surely right to appreciate that it offers guidance where there is a lacuna in the Convention (Parker, 1994). For example, the Convention does not specifically focus on street children (Ennew, 2000). Of course, in so far as they are children, it is possible to read nearly every article in the Convention as applicable to them. But they have specific problems: for example, they may need greater employment protection than other children. Issues relating to reunification with their families may have different implications for them.

The 'best interests' principle may be used to reinterpret rights or construct new ones. No catalogue of rights for children should ever be seen as definitive. The 'best interests' principle may also be valuable where rights conflict. Philip Alston sees it as 'a mediating principle which can assist in resolving conflicts between different rights' (Alston, 1994, 16).

One of the rights in the Convention, and unquestionably a central human right, is participation (Roche, 1999; Thomas, 2007). Indeed, at the root of the cluster of participation rights in the Convention is the normative value of autonomy, the idea that persons have a set of capacities that enables them to make independent decisions regarding appropriate life choices. Kant expressed this by asserting that persons are equal and autonomous in the kingdom of ends (Kant, 1987). To believe in autonomy is to believe that everyone's autonomy is as morally significant as anyone else's. To respect a child's autonomy is to treat that child as a person, and as a rights-holder. We now have the evidence to enable us to do this to a much greater extent than we thought possible until relatively recently. Priscilla Alderson's work – for example that on children's consent to surgery and more recent publications – offers clear evidence of this (Alderson, 1993; Alderson, Hawthorne and Killen, 2005).

At the same time, as I have argued, the Convention emphasizes that the best interests of children should guide decision-makers. Is there a conflict here? And, if so, can it be resolved? There is, of course, a let-out in Article 12: the 'views of the child' are to be given 'due weight in accordance with the age and maturity of the child'. The Convention gives no indication as to how to judge maturity, or indeed what is meant by maturity. It is, however, clear that this is judged by adults, and not by the child himself or herself. Thus, English law permits a child space to make decisions if *Gillick*-competent, but it is clear that whether a child is *Gillick*-competent and thus able to participate is a decision made by adults, teachers, doctors, administrators, etc. But what if a child's views conflict with what adults think is in his or her best interests? What is the point, it may be asked, of giving the child the opportunity to be heard, if at the end of the day we do not listen or we override his/her views in the name of upholding what we consider to be his/her best interests?

When can we impose limits on rights in the name of 'best interests'? One answer is posited by John Eekelaar, who situates children's rights within dynamic self-determinism (Eekelaar, 1994). The goal of this, he explains, is 'to bring a child to the threshold of adulthood with the maximum opportunities to form and pursue life-goals which reflect as closely as possible an autonomous choice' (Eekelaar, 1994, 53). It is dynamic because it appreciates that the optimal course for a child cannot always be mapped out at the time of decision, and may need to be revised as the child grows up. It involves self-determinism because the child is 'given scope to influence the outcomes'. Note 'influence', not 'determine'. Virginia Morrow explains that autonomy requires 'not the straightforward delegation of decision-making to children, but rather enabling children to make decisions in controlled conditions, the overall intention being to enhance their capacities for mature well-founded choices' (Morrow, 1999, 166). And Jane Fortin is of the opinion that there are 'respectable jurisprudential arguments for maintaining that a commitment to the concept of children's rights does not prevent interventions to stop children making dangerous short-term choices, thereby protecting their potential for long-term autonomy' (Fortin, 2004, 259).

The burden lies on those who wish to deny rights to children. An argument from age alone will not do. Arguments based on competence (or its absence) are often suspect, and we should remember Katherine Hunt Federle's comment that children, unlike women for example, have been 'unable to redefine themselves as competent beings', so that 'powerful elites decide which, if any, of the claims made by children they will recognize' (Federle, 1994, 344). Arguments drawn from best interests tend to be weak, as rights can be shown to be grounded in best interests. There is a distinction between 'having' rights and being allowed to exercise them. But there are also dangers in dichotomizing in this way. Nevertheless, it may explain and justify those very few decisions where autonomy is denied to children. In *The Rights and Wrongs of Children* I explained this in terms of 'liberal paternalism' (Freeman, 1983, 54–60). I might not use this expression today, but the idea remains, I believe, convincing.

It would legitimate interventions in children's lives to protect them against actions which are generally held to be irrational. There may not be universal standards of 'irrationality', any more than there are universal standards of best interests, or, for example, of what constitutes abuse. There must therefore be sensitivity to culture, including religious belief. It is also important to recognize the potential dangers of curbing autonomous action. For this reason, what is to be regarded as 'irrational' must be strictly confined. The subjective values of the would-be protector – judge, doctor, teacher, even parent – cannot be allowed to intrude. What is 'irrational' must be defined in terms of a neutral theory capable of accommodating pluralistic visions of the 'good'. We need to understand the experiences and the values of the child we wish to protect. We must engage with them. The space should be created for a child advocate to assist the child. Merely imposing a decision, for example medical treatment, achieves nothing in the long term. On the contrary, it may alienate both the child in question and others in a comparable situation. We must look at decisions we take in relation to children not just in terms of the impact they may have on the child in question, but with an understanding of what they say about our concept of childhood. 'Liberal paternalism' is a two-edged sword: its goal is rational independence, and those who exercise constraints must thus do so in such a way as to enable children to develop their full capabilities.

It is best to see the United Nations Convention on the Rights of The Child as a beginning rather than the final word on children's rights. The Convention's scope is too narrow – there is, for example, too little attention to the girl child and to gay children (Freeman, 2000) or to indigenous children (Libesman, 2007) or to citizenship rights (Lister, 2007). Its enforcement procedures are too weak. States Parties are allowed to enter reservations and thus to opt out of important obligations (Bissett-Johnson, 1994). Many countries have considered rhetoric and symbolism to be sufficient. King explains that 'once political and economic rights have been reconstructed as legal communications, it is possible and indeed appropriate, for governments to respond by further legal communications, declaring that their policies are "lawful" within the terms of the convention' (King, 1994, 398). Sad to say this has happened. But unlike King I do not think this is inevitable. Nor does it stop others, children's organizations and NGOs in particular, from establishing that this is not so, and campaigning for change. The Convention is a convenient benchmark. Judged against it, the world continues to fail children.

Notes

1. Dame Elizabeth Butler-Sloss, then the President of the Family Division in *Re B* [1992] 2 F.L.R. 1, 5. She is best known for chairing the Cleveland Inquiry into Sexual Abuse, on which see Freeman, 1989.
2. *Gillick v. West Norfolk and Wisbech Area Health Authority* [1986] A.C. 112.
3. Ibid., p. 186.
4. See *The Times*, 28 May 1985. Concerns pre-*Gillick* were voiced by some on the 'Right': see, for example, Mount, 1982.
5. *R (Williamson) v. Secretary of State for Education and Employment* [2005] 2 F.L.R. p. 374.
6. The United Kingdom was, of course, most dilatory in effecting this abolition which it achieved in stages, first abolishing it in state schools in 1986, and subsequently in private schools in 1998. See the discussion in Freeman, 2007b, pp. 193–198.
7. 406 US 205 (1972). And see Dwyer, 1998.
8. It could hardly do so since it obstinately adheres to the view that corporal punishment by parents is permissible so long as it does not leave a mark. See Children Act 2004 section 58. Also see Freeman, 2007b.
9. This states that 'States Parties shall take all appropriate legislative, administrative, social and educational measures to protect the child from all forms of physical or mental violence, injury or abuse, neglect or negligent treatment, maltreatment or exploitation, including sexual abuse, while in the care of parent(s), legal guardian(s) or any other person who has care of the child'. Also see Bitensky, 2006.

10. *R (Williamson) v. Secretary of State for Education and Employment* [2005] 2 F.L.R. p. 395.
11. Ibid., p. 395.
12. Ibid., p. 396.
13. In 1857, this deprived free blacks of citizenship and prohibited Congress from even conferring to territorial legislatives the power to deprive citizens of slave property.
14. See Articles 13, 14, and 15 (and see Brems, 2006b; Thorgeirsdóttir, 2006).
15. This is discussed in Fortin, 2003, p. 550ff.
16. Children between 10 and 14 formerly had the protection of a doctrine (the *doli incapax* doctrine) which presumed them incapable of committing crime unless they could be shown to understand the difference between serious wrong and mere naughtiness or mischief. This was abolished in the aftermath of the trial of two 11-year-olds for the murder of James Bulger. This case is discussed by Asquith, 1996; Freeman, 1997; Hay, 1995 and King, 1995.
17. One to do so is Archard, 2004, pp. 98–105.
18. A few countries – Brazil is one – permit 16-year-olds to vote in elections.
19. These are discussed in a 'Special Issue' of *Journal of Applied Philosophy*: see (2005) vol. 22(3): 211–273.
20. Mahoney (2007), who does, curiously totally ignores children's rights.
21. Above, n.5.
22. See Articles 12, 13, 14 and 15 of the UN Convention.
23. Of course, this depends upon what one interprets to be the cause(s) of child abuse. It is clearly the case if, as I do, you adopt a cultural interpretation.
24. Article 13.
25. Article 14.
26. Article 30.
27. Above, n.2.
28. Re M [1999] 2 F.L.R. 1097.
29. In the *Gillick* decision, n.2 above.
30. See *Re R* [1991] 4 All E.R. 177; *Re W* [1992] 4 All E.R. 627.
31. Preamble.
32. UNDoc. E/CN.4/L 1542, para. 29 (1980).
33. And see UN Doc. E/CN.4/1986/42.
34. Some Western nations supported Senegal, notably the Federal Republic of Germany and Ireland.
35. UNICEF made the point that if this proposal were adopted it would be the first time that duties other than those of States would be enumerated in a UN international human rights instrument. On child labour and children's rights issues see Weston, 2007.
36. Article 6(1).
37. Article 37(a). Capital punishment is not permitted – one of the main reasons why the United States failed to ratify. But it has now accepted such punishment is unconstitutional.
38. Article 13.
39. Article 14.
40. Article 14.
41. Articles 16 and 17.
42. Articles 32, 34, 35, 36.
43. Article 33.
44. Article 19.
45. Article 7.
46. Article 8. The right includes that to preserve nationality, name and family relations.
47. Article 9(1).
48. Article 9(3), including a right to maintain personal relations and direct contact with both parents on a regular basis. On relationship rights further see Dwyer, 2006.

49. Article 27(1).
50. Article 24.
51. Article 26, and see Scheinin, 1995.
52. Article 28. See Article 29 on the broad aims of education.
53. Article 31.
54. Article 23.
55. Article 22.
56. Article 20.
57. Article 21.
58. Article 30.
59. Article 39.
60. Article 38(2).
61. On this and further developments see Mendez, 2007.
62. Articles 43 and 44.
63. See Ariès, 1960 and 1962 (for history – though now heavily criticized), and Jenks, 1996.
64. Article 21(2) and see Chirwa, 2002.
65. See Murphy, 1999: the protection of children is the 'core value' in family law.
66. Article 3, and see Freeman, 2007(a).
67. *Re J* [1999] 2 F.L.R. 678, affirmed by the Court of Appeal in [2000] 1 F.L.R. 571.

References

Alderson, P. (1993) *Children's Consent to Surgery.* Buckingham: Open University Press.
Alderson, P., J. Hawthorne and M. Killen (2005) 'The Participation Rights of Premature Babies', *International Journal of Children's Rights*, 13(1–2): 31–50.
Alston, P. (1994) 'The Best Interests Principle: Towards a Reconciliation of Culture and Human Rights', *International Journal of Law and the Family*, 8(1): 1–25.
Archard, D. (2004) *Children: Rights and Childhood.* 2nd edn., London: Routledge.
Arendt, H. (1986) *The Origins of Totalitarianism.* London: André Deutsch.
Ariès, P. (1960) *L'Enfant et la Familiale Sous L'Ancien Régime.* Paris: Librairie Plon.
Ariès, P. (1962) *Centuries of Childhood.* London: Jonathan Cape.
Asquith, S. (1996) 'When Children Kill Children 3', *Childhood*, 3(1): 99–116.
Ball, H.V. and L.M. Friedman (1965) 'The Use of Criminal Sanctions in the Enforcement of Economic Legislation: A Sociological View', 17 *Stanford Law Review.* 197.
Belsey, C. (1999) *Shakespeare and the Loss of Eden.* New Brunswick NJ: Rutgers University Press.
Bentham, J. (1987) 'Anarchical Fallacies', in J. Waldron (ed.) *Nonsense Upon Stilts.* London: Methusen.
Berger, M. (1952) *Equality By Statute.* New York: Columbia University Press.
Besson, S. (2005) 'The Principle of Non-discrimination in the Convention on the Rights of the Child', *International Journal of Children's Rights*, 13(4): 433–461.
Bindel, J. (2006) 'Six Weeks of Suffering', *The Guardian*, 18 August, p. 35.
Bissett-Johnson, A. (1994) 'What Did States Really Agree To? Qualifications of Signatories to the United Nations Convention on the Rights of the Child', *International Journal of Children's Rights*, 2(4): 399–411.
Bitensky, S.H. (2006) *Corporal Punishment of Children – a Human Rights Violation.* Ardsley NY: Transnational Publication.
Brazier, M. and C. Bridge (1996) 'Coercion or Caring: Analysing Adolescent Autonomy', *Legal Studies*, 16(1): 84–109.
Brems, E. (2006a) 'Above Children's Heads: The Headscarf Controversy in European Schools from the Perspective of Children's Rights', *International Journal of Children's Rights*, 14(2): 119–136.

Brems, E. (2006b) *Article 14 – the Right to Freedom of Thought, Conscience and Religion*. Leiden: Martinus Nijhoff.

Brennan, C. (2002) 'Children's Choices or Children's Interests: Which Do Their Rights Protect?' in D. Archard and C. Macleod (eds) *The Moral and Political Status of Children*. Oxford: Oxford University Press, pp. 53–69.

Brighouse, H. (2002) 'What Rights (If any) Do Children Have?' in D. Archard and C. Macleod (eds) *The Moral and Political Status of Children*. Oxford: Oxford University Press, pp. 31–52.

Brown, W. (1995) *States of Injury*. Princeton NJ: Princeton University Press.

Chirwa, D.M. (2002) 'The Merits and Demerits of the African Charter on the Rights and Welfare of The Child', *International Journal of Children's Rights*, 10(2): 157–177.

Delaney, C. (1998) *Abraham on Trial*. Princeton NJ: Princeton University Press.

Donzelot, J. (1979) *The Policing of Families*. New York: Patheon Books.

Dworkin, R. (1977) *Taking Rights Seriously*. London: Duckworth.

Dwyer, J.G. (1998) *Religious Schools v. Children's Rights*. Ithaca NY: Cornell University Press.

Dwyer, J.G. (2006) *The Relationship Rights of Children*. New York: Cambridge University Press.

Eekelaar, J. (1994) 'The Interests of the Child and the Child's Wishes: The Role of Dynamic Self-Determinism', *International Journal of Law and the Family*, 8(1): 42–63.

Ennew, J. (2000) 'Why the Convention Is Not about Street Children', in D. Fottrell (ed.) *Revisiting Children's Rights*. The Hague: Kluwer Law International, pp. 169–182.

Etzioni, A. (1993) *The Spirit of Community*. New York: Simon and Schuster.

Federle, K.H. (1994) 'Rights Flow Downhill', *International Journal of Children's Rights*, 2(4): 343–368.

Feinberg, J. (1980) 'The Child's Right to an Open Future', in W. Aiken and H. LaFollette (eds) *Whose Child?* Totowa NJ: Rowan and Littlefield.

Fortin, J. (2003) *Children's Rights and the Developing Law*. London: Lexis Nexis.

Fortin, J. (2004) 'Children's Rights: Are the Courts Taking Them More Seriously?' *King's College Law Journal*, 15: 253–273.

Foucault, M. (1977) *Discipline and Punish*. London: Allen Lane.

Freeman, M. (1983) *The Rights and Wrongs of Children*. London: Frances Pinter.

Freeman, M. (1989) 'Cleveland, Butler-Sloss and Beyond – How Are We To React to the Sexual Abuse of Children?' *Current Legal Problems*. 42: 85–134.

Freeman, M. (1995) 'The Morality of Cultural Pluralism', *International Journal of Children's Rights*, 3(1): 1–17.

Freeman, M. (1997) 'The James Bulger Tragedy: Childish Innocence and the Construction of Guilt', in M. Freeman (ed.) *The Moral Status of Children*. The Hague: Martinus Nijhoff, pp. 235–253.

Freeman, M. (2000) 'The Future of Children's Rights', *Children and Society*, 14(4): 277–293.

Freeman, M. (2005) 'Rethinking "Gillick"', *International Journal of Children's Rights*, 13(1–2): 201–217.

Freeman, M. (2007a) *Article 3: The Best Interests of The Child*. Leiden: Martinus Nijhoff.

Freeman, M. (2007b) *Understanding Family Law*. London: Sweet and Maxwell.

Greven, P. (1990) *Spare the Child*. New York: Random House.

Grossberg, M. (1985) *Governing the Hearth: Law and Family in Nineteenth Century America*. Chapel Hill NC: North Carolina Press.

Harris-Short, S. (2003) 'International Human Rights Law: Imperialist, Inept and Ineffective? Children's Rights and the UN Convention on the Rights of The Child', *Human Rights Quarterly*, 25(1): 130–181.

Hay, C. (1995) 'Mobilization through Interpretation: James Bulger, Juvenile Crime and the Construction of a Moral Panic', *Social and Legal Studies*, 4(2): 197–224.

Hitch, L.M. (1989) 'Non-discrimination and the Rights of the Child: Article 2', *New York Law School Journal of Human Rights*, 7(1): 47–63.

Hyman, H.H. and P.B. Sheatsley (1964) 'Altitudes towards Desegregation', *Scientific American*, 211(1): 16.

Jenks, C. (1996) *Childhood*. London: Routledge.

Johnson, D. (1992) 'Cultural and Regional Pluralism in the Drafting of the UN Convention on the Rights of the Child', in M. Freeman and P. Veerman (eds) *The Ideologies of Children's Rights*. Dordrecht: Martinus Nijhoff, pp. 95–114.

Kant, I. (1987, originally 1790) *Critique of Judgment*. Indianapolis: Hackett.

Keating, H. (2007) 'The "Responsibility" of Children in the Criminal Law', *Child and Family Law Quarterly*, 19(2): 183–203.

King, M. (1994) 'Children's Rights as Communication; Reflections on Antipoetic Theory and the United Nations Convention', *Modern Law Review*, 57(3): 385–401.

King, M. (1995) 'The James Bulger Murder Trial: Moral Dilemmas and Social Solutions', *International Journal of Children's Rights*, 3(2): 167–187.

King, M. (1997) *A Better World for Children?* London: Routledge.

King, M. (2004) 'The Child, Childhood and Children's Rights within Sociology', *King's College Law Journal*, 15: 273–300.

Libesman, T. (2007) 'Can International Law Imagine the World of Indigenous Children?' *International Journal of Children's Rights*, 15(2): 283–309.

Lister, R. (2007) 'Why Citizenship: Where, When and How Children?' *Theoretical Inquiries in Law*, 8(2): 693–718.

Lukes, S. (1993) 'Five Fables about Human Rights', in S. Shute and S. Hurley (eds) *On Human Rights*. New York: Basic Books, pp. 19–40.

Mahoney, J. (2007) *The Challenge of Human Rights – Origin, Development and Significance* Oxford: Blackwell.

Marshall, D. (1999) 'The Construction of Children as an Object of International Relations: The Declaration of Children's Rights and the Child Welfare Committee of the League of Nations 1900–1924', *International Journal of Children's Rights*, 7(2): 103–148.

Marx, K. (1992) 'On the Jewish Question', L. Colletti (ed.) in *Early Writings*. Harmondsworth: Penguin.

Mason, M.A. (1994) *From Father's Property to Children's Rights*. New York: Columbia University Press.

Mendez, P.K. (2007) 'Moving from Words to Action in the Modern Era of Application: A New Approach to Realising Children's Rights in Armed Conflicts', *International Journal of Children's Rights*, 15(2): 219–249.

Miller, D.L. (2003) *Dreams of the Burning Child*. Ithaca NY: Cornell University Press.

Mnookin, R. (1975) 'Child – Custody Adjudication: Judicial Functions in the Face of Indeterminacy', *Law and Contemporary Problems*, 39(3): 226–294.

Morrow, V. (1999) 'We Are People Too: Children's and Young People's Perspectives on Children's Rights and Decision Making in England', *International Journal of Children's Rights*, 7(2): 149–170.

Mount, F. (1982) *The Subversive Family*. London: Jonathan Cape.

Murphy, J.C. (1999) 'Rules, Responsibility and Commitment to Children: The New Language of Morality in Family Law', 60 *University of Pittsburgh Law Review* 1128.

Ncube, W. (1998a) 'Prospects and Challenges in Eastern and Southern Africa: The Interplay between International Human Rights Norms and Domestic Law, Tradition and Culture', in W. Ncube (ed.) *Law, Culture, Tradition and Children's Rights in Eastern and Southern Africa*. Aldershot: Dartmouth.

Ncube, W. (1998b) 'The African Cultural Fingerprint? The Changing Concept of Childhood', in W. Ncube (ed.) *Law, Culture, Tradition and Children's Rights in Eastern and Southern Africa*. Aldershot: Dartmouth.

O'Neill, O. (1988) 'Children's Rights and Children's Lives', *Ethics*, 98(3): 445–463.

Pais, M.S. (1992) 'The United Nations Convention on the Rights of the Child', *Bulletin of Human Rights*, 91/2: 75–82.

Parker, S. (1994) 'The Best Interests of the Child; Principles and Problems', *International Journal of Law and the Family*, 8(1): 26–41.

Platt, A. (1979) *The Child Savers*. Chicago: University of Chicago Press.

Rawls, J. (1993) 'The Law of Peoples', in S. Shute and S. Hurley (eds) *On Human Rights*, New York: Basic Books, pp. 41–82.

Reece, H. (1996) 'The Paramountcy Principle: Consensus or Construct?' 46 *Current Legal Problems*, 267.

Renteln, A.D. (2004) *The Cultural Defense*. New York: Oxford University Press.

Roche, J. (1999) 'Children: Rights, Participation and Citizenship', *Childhood*, 6(4): 475–493.

Sait, M.S. (2000) 'Islamic Perspectives on the Rights of The Child', in D. Fottrell (ed.) *Revisiting Children's Rights*. The Hague: Kluwer Law International.

Sawyer, C. (2006) 'Not Every Child Matters: The UK's Expulsion of British Citizens', *International Journal of Children's Rights*, 14(2): 157–185.

Scheinin, M. (1995) 'The Right to Social Security', in A. Eide, C. Krause and A. Rosas (eds) *Economic, Social and Cultural Rights: A Textbook*. Dordrecht: Nijhoff.

Sumner, L. (1987) *The Moral Foundation of Rights*. Oxford: Clarendon Press.

Thomas, N. (2007) 'Towards a Theory of Children's Participation', *International Journal of Children's Rights*, 15(2): 199–218.

Thorgeirsdóttir, H. (2006) *Article 13 – the Right To Freedom of Expression*. Leiden: Martinus Nijhoff.

Tobin, J. (2006) 'Beyond the Supermarket Shelf: Using a Rights-Based Approach to Address Children's Health Needs', *International Journal of Children's Rights*, 14(3): 275–306.

Todres, J., M. Wojcik and C. Revaz (2006) *The UN Convention on the Rights of the Child*. Ardsley NY: Transnational Publications.

Van Boven, T. (2002) 'Children's Rights Are Human Rights: Current Issues and Developments', in J. Williams (ed.) *Developmental and Autonomy Rights of Children*. Antwerp: Intersentia, pp. 11–19.

Veerman, P. (1992) *The Rights of the Child and the Changing Image of Childhood*. Dordrecht: Martinus Nijhoff.

Virgil (1956) *The Aeneid*, transl. W.F. Jackson Knight, Harmondworth: Penguin.

Weston, B.H. (2007) *Child Labour and Human Rights*. Boulder CO: Lynne Rienner Publishers.

Williams, P. (1991) *The Alchemy of Race and Rights*. Cambridge MA: Harvard University Press.

Williams, R. (1987) 'Taking Rights Aggressively: The Perils and Promise of Critical Legal Theory for Peoples of Color', 5 *Law and Inequality*, 103–134.

26
Interests in and Responsibility for Children and Their Life-Worlds

Doris Bühler-Niederberger and Heinz Sünker

It is a commonplace that children are the future of society. This basic assumption can be incorporated into different approaches: investment in children as human capital, disciplining of children to guarantee social order, educating children as citizens. In bourgeois societies these mostly take place at the same time. As a result religious, voluntary and state organizations have a long history of intervening in children's lives. This has led to a systematization of interest in, and responsibility for, children. Paradoxically, though, such systematization has resulted in concerns which often fail to incorporate specific, real living children and the needs they might have articulated if there had been anybody listening to their voices.

Saving poor children as social ordering – lessons from history

The work of the pedagogic innovators of the seventeenth and eighteenth centuries in France, the Christian Brothers, illustrated well that an interest in poor children was also a decisive striving for an orderly, efficient society.[1] Of course this was not the first attempt to deal with poor children, who were often orphaned, vagrant and begging. Institutions of enclosure were developed during the seventeenth century in France, England and other European countries – so-called workhouses or *Zucht-Häuser* which combined apprenticeship and strict religious exercises to prepare the children for a decent way of life. But these institutions reached only a few children and probably had a minor effect on the amount of begging and vagrancy. Meanwhile the efforts of schooling by the Christian Brothers included a large proportion of poor children.[2] The Christian Brothers invented a technology of schooling with a strict schedule of lessons and subjects. The order of teaching was meticulous: the movements and speech of the pupils were directed by signals, as in military exercises. This allowed permanent and comprehensive monitoring and registering of minor deviancies. Foucault (1975) refers repeatedly to the inventions of the Christian Brothers to illustrate the techniques of discipline in the classical age, constructing what he calls the disciplinary individual.[3] But their inventions reached far beyond teaching technology. Pupils were surveyed in the streets by other pupils entrusted with such control.

Above all, parents were enrolled in the endeavour that education now had to be. Teachers and parents had to establish an alliance with regular conferences in which parents were admonished not to listen to any complaints from their children, and a special advice book for parents was written and sold or given to them. Parents were taken to be too tender-hearted, and Jean-Baptiste de La Salle, one of the prominent leaders of this reform movement, complained that parents were in love with their children in a foolish way.[4] If parents remained reluctant the charity commissions of the parish were informed to cut the provision of alms in such cases. All together, this was a comprehensive occupation of the child and the end of the old childhood with its 'légèreté', 'libertinage' and 'vagabondage', about which de La Salle complained in his writings.

Factories and manufactures would be filled with hard-working and faithful apprentices, and vice and idleness, which were poisoning the whole society, would be eradicated only if the children of the common people were educated in the new way.[5] Such were the arguments to gain the support and patronage of the authorities made by the advocates of the reform movement. This is the vision of a society which is orderly because it is composed of useful individuals. To reinforce the dedication to poor children, the Christ Child was adduced. The Child Jesus had to be worshiped in the figure of the poor child in his rags. This is an old rhetoric of charity, but appeared now in a new context, completely different from the one of alms. It was a social utilitarian approach relying on disciplined individuals and developing techniques to produce such individuals. In this new approach the child became a crucial figure, he who among the other poor deserved attention and support, as this was profitable and justifiable since the child was not to be made responsible for his poverty.

At the end of the eighteenth, and in the nineteenth, century we find an accumulation of interventions on the part of social reform movements and public authorities, all targeting poor children. The instruments became more subtle and more pervasive than before; they included a radical redefinition of the roles of husbands and wives, new experts, home visits, urban planning and architecture, large-scale scientific studies and police control. One cluster of measures can be characterized as the 'policing of families' (Donzelot, 1979). Such policing was designed to mould family life around proper child socialization. In the new families women had to be the central figure, as devoted mothers, albeit under the aegis of paediatricians and controlled by visiting baby-nurses. Families should live in newly built residential areas with symmetrical architecture and aesthetic greens, with allotment gardens, kindergartens and welfare agents. Different from the overcrowded downtown areas where life happened on the street, in backyards, courts and pubs, the new architecture clearly separated private and public life and in this way especially disciplined men; a transformation of men into fathers and allotment gardeners was to start (Joseph, Fritsch and Battegay, 1977). And if this re-education of men was not sufficiently successful an additional instrument was found towards the end of nineteenth century: a guardian for the child appointed by the courts. This was an important step in the change of generational order, from patriarchal order towards socialization order, in which education should be for the collective good and not for a family's particular business. In this whole rebuilding of the family, children had the double function of hostage and missionary. As hostage their progress as well as their misbehaviour offered the possibility of checking parents' virtues. As missionary they could teach at home the lessons of domesticity and disciplined way of life that they themselves were taught in school. At least in France the policing of families was a scientific project and from 1830 surveys described and explained the life conditions of working-class families (Joseph, Fritsch and Battegay, 1977, 271–282). The second cluster of measures concerned the way to deal with children still hanging around in the streets. In England, France and the United States the name given to poor children lingering in the streets and sometimes trying to make some money there was 'Arab boys'. A declining tolerance towards them resulted in police chases. Several historical analyses of court records, police protocols and penalty orders of the late eighteenth and the nineteenth century in French towns[6] show that the 'crimes' of these children were often banal and their prosecution ridiculous; in many cases they were just gambling in the streets. But the prosecution was a question of principle: the child that was a dawdler was no better than a thief. Such practice was not limited to France – in several other European countries and the United States a real barracking of children occurred, which worsened at the end of the nineteenth and the beginning of the twentieth century. Smoking in the streets or just being outside after sunset was also sufficient reason for legitimate detainment, as the newly rising theory of the 'criminal career' declared that little misdeeds had severe consequences if not radically combated (Maynes, 1985; Mahood, 1995; Coninck-Smith, 1997; Hendrick, 1997; Bühler-Niederberger, 2005a). The same logic of the theory of the criminal career and a growing moral panic can be found in the Crime and Disorder Act of 1998 and the Youth Justice and Criminal Evidence Act of 1999 in the United Kingdom (Goldson and Muncie, 2006; Muncie 2002). By the way, the punchline of this story is that the coercive interventions did not really succeed in removing children from the street. It was traffic and therefore the twentieth century which 'solved' this problem, and a new place was invented and offered to children: the playground (Zelizer, 1985).

Social policy in the twentieth century – absence of the child and social inequality

An outline of twentieth-century childhood policies in Germany is interesting, as there were many political changes – Empire, Weimar Republic, Nazi time, partitioning of Germany into the German Democratic Republic and German Federal Republic and the reunited Germany after 1989. All these breaks urged reevaluations of social policies, but the redefinitions which followed mostly confirmed the essential elements of an approach in which children were far more an object of concern than persons with individual needs and interests.

From the beginning of the twentieth century until now the interventions, laws, subsidies, and so on which concerned the child aimed, above all, at shaping families. The favoured pattern was the family with a male breadwinner, only minor-wage working by any other family members, and with two or more children. Such families were taken to be the guarantor of children's moral development and also of the growth of population, or at least of what was taken to be a balanced demographic development. In short, they were considered as producers of human capital and important pillars of social order. The Preussische Landrecht of 1794 already explicitly defined this type of family and the civil law of 1896 codified it. It allowed women's wage work only in exceptional cases, and the child-saving law of 1903 reduced drastically children's possibilities to work, even for any kind of business in the child's family. The Weimar Republic paid family allowances to civil servants and an extra 'women's allowance' if wives stopped working. Later on such family allowances were repealed and Germany fell behind in this kind of family support in comparison with France and Belgium. In addition, public and private welfare did not hesitate to interfere in families that did not correspond to these expectations in the form of 'friendly visitors' to poor families through to more harsh interventions such as detaining people in workhouses. At the beginning of the twentieth century the German *Länder* (states) passed a veritable flood of laws concerning compulsory education (*Fürsorgeerziehung*). The President of the German Association of Private and Public Welfare formulated the following guidelines to govern welfare and legal measurements: 'The frequently made objection that interference in parental educational rights means a disturbing restriction of personal freedom is not of sufficient importance to abstain from such intervention. The limits of personal freedom are determined by the prevailing social order and nobody may interpret this term in a way that may allow him to do whatever he wants.'[7] A 1922 youth-welfare law guaranteed all children the right to an education, but its focus on social order could not have been expressed more clearly, as it stated: 'Every German child has a right to be educated for physical, mental and social prowess... In cases in which the rights of the child to education cannot be realized within the family, then public youth assistance ensues' (Peukert, 1986, 22). The practices of the Nazi system even exceeded the Weimar Republic as far as social disciplining of the youth was concerned (Steinacker, 2007), and welfare policy was perverted by racial dogma and followed a clearly populationist goal (Sünker and Otto, 1997). But the difference was not the interest in children's utility – this interest is universal; the difference was the brutal radicalization of this interest and the way to argue blatantly.

After Fascism and the Second World War a system of tax allowances and child benefits was developed in the German Federal Republic to support families, once again with the clear intention to mould them. The argument was still unambiguous. A splitting system, introduced in 1958, meant considerable tax reduction for families with one breadwinner, but none if husband and wife earned about the same amount of money. When it was introduced it was explicitly legitimated by the 'intention behind family policies of not furthering mothers' inclinations towards wage work and... with the special appreciation of women as mothers and housewives' (Langer-El Sayed, 1980, 102). Additionally, this regulation of family support was more advantageous for higher- than lower-income families, a differentiation which was intentional and overt. The then-minister for the family said: 'The fulfilment of cultural duties should not be made impossible for our middle classes just when they are passing cultural values to their children' (Langer-El Sayed, 1980, 100). In contrast he spoke of 'stray children' who did not grow up in these 'inwardly healthy families', but in problematic family circumstances, as those found in one-child, lone-parent or fractured families, and those with wage-earning mothers (Langer-El Sayed, 1980). The regulations of family support were constantly revised, the amount of support was considerably augmented, and additional *Erziehungsgeld* and *Elterngeld* were introduced (monthly amounts paid during the first two or three years if one parent reduces or stops work). The topic of family support was very prominent in electoral campaigns towards the end of the twentieth century. Social democrats in particular latched onto it and gained moral, and probably also political, credit by accusing the then-governing Christian and Free Democrats with a rhetoric of the poor and needy child and the threat such children might pose later for the whole of society (Bühler-Niederberger, 2003). The preferential treatment of breadwinner families and higher-income families was never changed. There remained a clear (at least monetary) preference for the family pattern which promises to produce human capital. In contradiction to the guideline that the state should protect private life and not interfere with it – which the German state had already declared in 1896 and repeated ever since – a whole range of laws, financial regulations, institutional arrangements and discourses established and conserved this family pattern during the whole twentieth century.

Efforts to establish a long and protected childhood for every German child resulted in many other protective laws. Since the first half of the twentieth century public commitment towards childhood has also involved laws and institutions protecting children from influences that might compete with the ideal or ideology of childhood. These include violent and sexual content of films, literature and theatre; the consumption of alcohol and cigarettes; adult sexual contact with children; the protection of young people in employment; the protection of young people in public life; and so on. All these laws have been frequently revised to avoid new 'dangers' and to afford new protections for young people. The Act Concerning the Protection of Young People in Public was revised again in 2003. The Protection of Young Persons at Work Act of 1976 (revised in 2000) and the Children's Work Protection Decree of 1998 forbade child labour up to the age of 15 – or rather until the completion of full-time compulsory education (mostly ending at 17). Furthermore, young people under 18, the age of majority, are not subject to criminal law. Under the age of 14 there is no criminal responsibility at all, due to the general assumption that these children cannot be guilty in the sense of the law. Between 14 and 18 years they are subject to the Penal Law Relating to Young Offenders. The difference between criminal law and criminal law for juveniles concerns the punishment imposed. While adults can be punished with imprisonment or fines, the criminal law for juveniles is first oriented towards education and help; actions should aim at re-socialization. A new Child and Youth Services Act was passed in 1990 and was an attempt to regulate the interventions of social workers and foster carers over and above pure social disciplining, with the overall goal of education and individual development. In 1992 Germany ratified the UN Convention on the Rights of the Child. This required some legal changes, especially a new law according equal rights to children whether born in or out of wedlock. Some private organizations occasionally complain of a disregard for children's rights, but this mainly concerns the immigration rights of non-adult refugees, who are treated like adults as regards the restriction of entrance into Germany.

Taken together the attempts to establish childhood as a protected phase of socialization do guarantee this in most cases, but there are considerable inequalities concerning gender and social class associated with childhoods in Germany – this finding was also established by the PISA 2000 and PISA 2003 international comparative studies of school achievement and cognitive competence of 15-year-old students in OECD countries. The effect of social background variables on competence was found to be especially high in Germany.[8] To state it clearly: such inequalities are not only by-products, but are principles of construction of normal childhood, deliberately maintained for the sake of social order and its reproduction. While other European countries may have been more flexible in the adaptation of their gender and family policies to the new exigencies of private and economic life or more sensitive about social inequality, it probably remains true for most of them that children are mainly seen as objects of concern and not as persons with a voice, or at least that societies are ambiguous on this point (Prout, 2003, 1; cf. Qvortrup et al., 1994). Susan Pedersen summarizes saliently her analysis about the history of welfare states: 'Children, like Marx's peasants, could not represent themselves and had to be represented, and their well-being was shamelessly linked to efforts to increase the population, stabilize the labour force, restore paternal authority, or emancipate wives' (1993, 425–426). Accordingly, the problems of children may be defined beyond empirical reality and needs – even those that are vociferously articulated. Mirja Satka (2003) shows how child welfare in Finland ignored palpable reality at least in two moments of its history, once when, at the turn of the twentieth century, Continental discussions and fears concerning industrialization and urbanization were adopted and followed by a series of reform efforts in Finnish child welfare, even though Finland was still a predominantly agrarian society and the actual numbers of deprived children was small. Another moment occurred after the Second World War when many children had to manage on their own while their mothers – often war widows – were at work, as leading scientists were absolutely convinced that day-care for small children would cause social problems and society relied on science in its decision about children's programmes.

The interest in children – its heritage and traps

Six characteristics of the organized interest in children may be mentioned:

1. The absence of children from the definition of problems and solutions and sometimes even the absence of any realistic attempt to analyse their problems;

2. A moral argument relying on the 'power of innocence' (Bühler-Niederberger, 2005b) to gain support for reforms and eventual costs, sacralizing the needy child;

3. An additional moral argument insisting on the danger the child may be for society; these two moral arguments do not intersect at all, which means that the image of the child in such movements is extreme – evil or sacred and sometimes both in the same discourse. As the danger of the child is used to justify interventions there is no difference admitted between endangered and dangerous children (see Rosier in this volume), between children as victims and children as wrongdoers; both are treated with the same instruments (while in the United Kingdom there is meanwhile a tendency to punish children like adults and to send them to jail);

4. An attempt to create an orderly society in which useful individuals are taken to be the royal road to social order. In such a social utilitarian view children constitute human capital. This vision of social order implies a refusal of common people's way of living and especially their patterns of private life; as a consequence it does not reduce social inequalities but creates additional ones;

5. An approach which claims to be based on expert knowledge and has a visible technology and which therefore cannot easily be questioned or challenged by trivial reproaches such as complaints by parents or children, or children running away;

6. A certain unwillingness of authorities to spend too much money on such endeavours.

The above-mentioned characteristics of child welfare and social interventions for the sake of the child are no mere problems of the past. If we look at recent programmes we may easily recognize that these problems still inhere in such actions in spite of good intentions – and sometimes they are even openly approved and chosen as guidelines to action.

Such is true for instance of Truancy Watch, an action launched in England in 1993 as a reaction to the murder of James Bulger. Shops display 'truant-free zone' stickers and staff are trained to challenge suspects and fill in confidential forms for education welfare officers. Buses carry posters asking 'Are you sure your child is in school?' (Jenks, 1998). The theory of a criminal career exposes practically every child who is in the wrong place at the wrong time to suspicion. Children have to be watched carefully. This is especially the case for boys of lower classes, as the inevitable consequence of a minor misdeed might be that the child becomes a real criminal. Sure Start[9] is an English government program with the declared aim to increase educational and care provision for preschool children for the best possible development of the children and to support parents both as parents and in aspirations towards employment. Sure Start concentrates its effort in disadvantaged areas. However, one of the effects is also a massive increase in the monitoring of poor children. The UK Children Act 2004,[10] which aims at the improvement of children's life, merges education and welfare services and provides the basis for a central electronic database on which all encounters between children and those professionals should be recorded. All in all these programs and legislation represent a serious concern for endangered children, but also anxiety about dangerous children; they provide a mixture of care, monitoring, and outright stigmatizing. In the Respect Agenda and Respect Action Plan of 2006 such measures of family and child welfare are integrated into a larger plan of a new and more efficient ordering of society and above all into a clearly social utilitarian vision of society (Schütter, 2006).

Alternatives and perspectives

Interests in children

Against the background of parental interests in children and ruling powers instrumentalizing them in a specific manner, there have always been different ideas about how children should be dealt with and trajectories of these in history. This is not to deny that there were compassion and honest motives to help, too, but *who* was to be helped and in *what way* – these were often neither matter to be decided by the recipients of such help nor in the common interest.[11]

The challenge embedded in conceptualizing a politics of childhood is to find a normative frame of reference which allows arguments in favour of defending or developing children's rights in contemporary societies. The status of children needs to be addressed in societies in the interest of both children's and society's capacities of development. One salient approach for this is found in the Enlightenment in Kant's concept of mediating childhood with the future state of the art of mankind: 'Children ought to be educated, not for the present, but for a possibly improved condition of man in the future; that is, in a manner which is adapted to the idea of humanity and the whole destiny of man' (Kant, 1968, 704).[12]

Following the Kantian line Schleiermacher considered education to always be based in the intergenerational relationship and concluded that 'the younger generation should be delivered to the great communities of life in which it has to act autonomously'. Schleiermacher particularly used the tense relationship that could be observed between community life and free self-activity to derive his perspective for applying the tasks of 'conserving' and 'changing' to deal with the following generation (Schleiermacher, [1826] 1983, 94).

A second approach to answering the question of interest in children is linked to the previous problem: it points to the difficulties of establishing a singular scientific foundation for our topic of how we should understand the lives of children and how we should act on that. Understanding childhood in the historical context of charting societies brings to the fore the significance of the intellectual, theoretical, political and empirical stance taken in any historical inquiry towards the relationship between children, childhood, society and individuals. How society deals with children, and how interests are constituted and acted upon, influence the way in which histories of childhood are written. This is evident in the contrast between the work of Ariès and deMause. Both of these controversial approaches to the history of childhood consider processes of excluding and integrating children in social contexts, and the consequences of different modes of societalization, in terms of the consequences for the specificities of children's lives, but they reach different conclusions. Whilst Ariès maps a decline in the way society deals with children from a golden age, deMause argues that there has been improvement over time. The heart of the argument and empirical controversy is that Ariès' argument (1978), which is based on a theory of social control in which the education of everyday life and the disciplining of children are interwoven, is confronted with deMause's ideas (1975) of an optimistic approach based on evolution theory that assumes that the situation of children will improve as social contexts develop further towards civilization. The outcomes of this controversy have been that the historical societal formation of the life of children and ideas about childhood have been worked out more clearly.

Thereby, insights into the relationship between theories of childhood, images of childhood and the real lives of children can be contrasted empirically with those ideas in which the child is reduced to the state and estate of a natural being alone.

Interest in democracy

Overcoming 'naturalism' in childhood studies and the empirical analyses of children's different lives (based on class, gender, race/ethnicity, culture, abilities) necessarily involves engaging with concepts of democracy, self-determination, advocacy, the relationship of dependency and autonomy in different life stages, and adult–child relationships. This means social theory, social policy and childhood studies have to be integrated.

Overcoming 'naturalism' therefore means, too, generalizing the interest in children and responsibilities for children's lives in a way that allows, first, the 'child' to be conceptualized in the interest of adults and children. Second, this approach defends children against the colonizing grasp of adults maintaining that they know the best interests of the child.

As the starting point, the common interest should be an interest in democracy and a decent life for everyone.[13] This interest should be embraced and owned by all generations because the quality of the future of individuals and of societies is at stake. This includes especially a need to look for indications of changes in social life conditions and life opportunities, in the forms of appropriating social reality, and thereby revealing children's spaces of experience and their subjectivity potential in contemporary societies. These ideas entail the task of finding answers to the question of how children can be supported in the democratic processes and decision-making mechanisms of our societies. One possible answer has been found by Bowles and Gintis – against the background of their social theory and analysis of real existing capitalist societies[14] – since they interrelate democratic capacities, processes of education and institutional conditions: 'Because the growth and effectiveness of democratic institutions depend on the strength of democratic capacities, a commitment to democracy entails the advocacy of institutions that promote rather than impede the development of a democratic culture. Further, because learning, or more broadly, human development, is a central and lifelong activity of people, there is no coherent reason for exempting the structures that regulate learning – whether they be schools, families, neigh-bourhoods, or workplaces – from the criteria of democratic accountability and liberty' (1987, 204).

This orientation moves towards and partially achieves the transcendence of adult or parental behaviour against children which is – as we have shown – guided by interest in social control, maintaining generational capital, and so on. Within the framework of this analysis of generational relations, it is a matter of an eman-cipatory and liberating perspective which Benjamin – reminiscent to some extent of Schleiermacher and Kant – proposed: 'Is education not above all the necessary ordering of the relations between generations and thus, if one wishes to speak of governance, the governance of the generational relationship rather than of chil-dren?' (Benjamin, 1991, 147).

Children's rights and politics of childhood

At the centre of this alternative perspective is a conception of a politics of child-hood based on the discourse on children's rights. The starting point for this is the distinction between concepts of politics for children and politics with chil-dren. This distinction is based on different, contested theoretical and political positions. The background of this controversy is multifaceted. In very traditional terms it concerns an image of childhood in which childhood is defined as a defi-cient transitional stage in the process of becoming adult, and which, through the deployment of traditional concepts such as 'care' and 'protection', refuses any far-reaching discussion of children's rights. The measure of all things in relation to 'rights' is a particular model of adulthood, characterized by autonomy and performative competence (cf. Qvortrup et al., 1994). In political terms this discus-sion was and is tied to conceptions of childhood as 'family childhood' which can be extended to positioning children as the property of their parents (cf. Mason, 1994).

In opposition to that, there is a position defending a concept of politics with children that recognizes the anchoring of children in multiple forms of family life, as well as the fragility of the status of children in family and society – pre-cisely as a result of social changes and their consequences for the lives of chil-dren – and which bases the rights of children on human and civil rights in the modern welfare state. This constitutes the relevance of the UN Convention on the Rights of the Child (see Freeman in this volume).

Attempts to structure and determine the content of the Convention through the 'three Ps' (protection, provision, participation) indicate the need to give the Convention some substance, especially by giving it a more precise political foun-dation, and to demand implementation.

(a) Protection: This clearly is first based on a traditional approach to childhood (a child is an especially vulnerable individual), without either addressing or resolving the issue of the possible coercion built into protection and care.

Child protection deals with classical problems such as violence against children, child neglect, street children, and so on. The task remains until today (cf. Brinkmann and Honig, 1984) one of developing new concepts of protection which go beyond models which are either paternalistically or patriarchally oriented, and thus geared to tutelage or social control. The question remains: what/when is help help, and not regulation of the self/individual?

(b) Provision: Here too we seem at first glance to have a rather traditional approach, although (at least beyond the 'Third/Fourth World' problematic and that of 'basic needs') in relation to western societies it can be, at least, an approach taken up by the welfare state and in social policy, as well as in private and public education, and hence in the framework of educational and child/youth welfare policy. Today it is facing more and more the challenges of poverty/poor children, poverty and education, and social exclusion.

(c) Participation: This category is linked on the one hand with positions concerned with the theory and practice of democracy on different social/political levels which hope for a strengthening of democratic relations oriented towards the society as a whole and its developmental potential. But it is also concerned with positions which can only imagine an improvement in children's living conditions and their perspectives through their own active participation and which also aim to resolve the question of the relationship between dependency and autonomy in a way showing that this isn't only a question for children. It is dealing – in the core – with the problem of giving children a voice and studying their social competences (Hutchby and Moran-Ellis, 1998).

The paternalism of the classical ideology of family, protection and immaturity conflicts with important formulations in many articles of the UN Convention where it concerns the participation of children in matters which affect them: this means that it can be said that there is now some official recognition that children should be involved in decisions concerning their well-being and living conditions. Although such an assessment doesn't overlook the fact that the Convention does not put forward any sort of children's rights radicalism, at the same time the positions it brings to the fore have potential for theoretical questions concerning childhood – centred on 'child subjectivity' – and policies concerning childhood – with the priority on 'participation' rather than on 'representation'. The question of realizing participation operates at a number of levels and in diverse constellations and formulations, which move between the problem of freedom of expression and participation in decisions dealing with life conditions.

It can be said that the UN Convention's challenge for the issue of interest in and responsibility for children has to be seen in the new relationships that need to be brought about between protection, provision and participation. Against the old favouring of protection alone it not only favours participation but brings this into the problem of formulating a perspective on children and their lives.

Notes

1. We refer here especially to Julia (1998) and Maynes (1985); with respect to German developments cf. Dreßen (1982) and Wild (1985).
2. According to Maynes (1985) between a quarter and half of the boys in French towns attended these schools and they were also to be found in Italy, Belgium and Germany.
3. Dekker (2001) argues against the interpretation of Foucault and in favour of pedagogy.
4. J.-B. de La Salle, *Conduite des écoles chrétiennes divisée en deux parties*. Avignon 1720, S, 681; quot. from Julia (1998, p. 92).
5. Such was the argumentation of Charles Demia in 1666 while applying for the support of the authorities for the Christian Schools (Julia, 1998, p. 15).
6. Farge (1992) as well as the analyses of Michelle Perrot and of Jean and Claire Delmas quoted in Ariès (1994).
7. Peukert, 1986, p. 128; with respect to the situation in the United States of America cf. Pelton (1989).
8. PISA 2003, *Ergebnisse des zweiten internationalen Vergleichs*, edited by PISA-Konsortium Deutschland. http://pisa.ipn.uni-kiel.de/Ergebnisse_PISA_2003.pdf; cf. Sünker (2007, chapter 1).
9. http://www.surestart.gov.uk/aboutsurestart/.
10. http://www.dfes.gov.uk/publications/childrenactreport/.
11. See for example with respect to contemporary debates Law (2006).
12. From an educational point of view this is the classic problem in dealing with the relationship between 'new people' and 'old structures' or education and social change.
13. This, of course, includes a criticism of approaches aiming at 'children at risk' as children as dangerous class members, processes of 'therapeutization', and so on. (cf. Sünker, 1991). Quite opposite to this, this approach is based on the demand of 'education for all', democratic education and educating for democracy (cf. Sünker, 2007).
14. Essential here is the recognition 'that no capitalist society today may reasonably be called democratic in the straightforward sense of securing personal liberty and rendering the exercise of power socially accountable' (Bowles and Gintis, 1987, p. 3).

References

Ariès, Ph. (1978) *Geschichte der Kindheit*. München: DTV.

Ariès, Ph. (1994) 'Das Kind und die Stadt – von der Stadt zur Anti-Stadt', *Freibeuter, Vierteljahreszeitschrift für Kultur und Politik*, 60: 75–94.

Benjamin, W. (1991) 'Einbahnstrasse', in W. Benjamin: *Gesammelte Schriften IV, 1*. Frankfurt/M.: Suhrkamp, pp. 83–148.

Bowles, S. and H. Gintis (1987) *Democracy & Capitalism. Property, Community, and the Contradictions of Modern Social Thought*. New York: Basic Books.

Brinkmann, W. and M.-S. Honig (1984) *Kinderschutz als sozialpolitische Praxis: Hilfe, Schutz und Kontrolle*. München: Kösel.

Bühler-Niederberger, D. (2003) 'The Needy Child and the Naturalization of Politics: Political Debate in Germany', in Ch. Hallett and A. Prout (eds) *Hearing the Voices of Children. Social Policy for a New Century*. London, New York: RoutledgeFalmer, pp. 89–105.

Bühler-Niederberger, D. (2005a) *Kindheit und die Ordnung der Verhältnisse*. München: Juventa.

Bühler-Niederberger, D. (ed.) (2005b) *Macht der Unschuld – das Kind als Chiffre*. Opladen: VS-Verlag.

Coninck-Smith, N. de (1997) 'The Struggle for the Child's Time – at All Times. School and Children's Work in Town and Country in Denmark from 1900 to the 1960s', in N. De

Coninck-Smith et al. (eds) *Industrious Children: work and Childhood in the Nordic Countries 1850–1990*. Odense: University Press, pp. 129–159.

Dekker, J. (2001) *The Will to Change the Child: Re-education Homes for Children at Risk in Nineteenth Century Western Europe*. Frankfurt am Main: Peter Lang.

Donzelot, J. (1979) *The Policing of Families*. London: Hutchinson.

Dreßen, W. (1982) *Die pädagogische Maschine. Zur Geschichte des industrialisierten Bewusstseins in Preußen/Deutschland*. Frankfurt/M. et al.: Ullstein.

Farge, A. (1992) *Vivre dans la rue à Paris*. Paris: Gallimard.

Foucault, M. (1975) *Surveiller et punir. La naissance de la prison*. Paris: Gallimard.

Goldson, B. and J. Muncie (eds) (2006) *Youth Crime and Justice*. London: Sage.

Hendrick, H. (1997) *Children, Childhood and English Society 1880–1990*. Cambridge: Cambridge University Press.

Hutchby, I. and J. Moran-Ellis (eds) (1998) *Children and Social Competence. Arenas of Action*. London: Falmer.

Jenks, Ch. (1998) 'Childhood and Social Space – Examples from the UK', in D.K. Behera (ed.) *Children and Childhood in Our Contemporary Societies*. New Delhi: Kamla-Raj Enterprises, pp. 91–109.

Joseph, I., Ph. Fritsch and A. Battegay (1977) 'Disciplines à domicile. L'édification de la famille', *Recherches*, 28.

Julia, D. (1998) 'L'enfance entre absolutisme et Lumières', in E. Becchi and J. Dominique (eds) *Histoire de l'enfance en Occident*. Paris: Seuil, pp. 7–111.

Kant, I. (1968) 'Über Pädagogik', in I. Kant: *Werke in 10 Bänden*. Bd. 10.2.: Schriften zur Anthropologie, Geschichtsphilosophie, Politik und Pädagogik, (ed.) W. Weischedel. Wissenschaftliche Buchgesellschaft (WBG): Darmstadt, pp. 693–761.

Langer-El Sayed, I. (1980) *Familienpolitik: Tendenzen, Chancen, Notwendigkeiten*. Frankfurt: Campus.

Law, S. (2006) *The War for Children's Minds*. London/New York: Routledge.

Mahood, L. (1995) *Policing Gender, Class and Family*. London: UCL Press.

Mason, M.A. (1994) *From Father's Property to Children's Rights*. New York: Columbia University Press.

deMause, L. (ed.) (1975) *The History of Childhood*. New York: Harper.

Maynes, M.J. (1985) *Schooling in Western Europe*. Albany: State University of New York Press.

Muncie, J. (2002) 'Children's Rights and Youth Justice', in B. Franklin (ed.) *The New Handbook of Children's Rights*. London: Routledge.

Pedersen, S. (1993) *Family, Dependence, and the Origins of the Welfare State: Britain and France, 1914–1945*. Cambridge: Cambridge University Press.

Pelton, L.H. (1989) *For Reason's of Poverty. A Critical Analysis of the Public Child Welfare System in the United States*. New York: Praeger.

Peukert, D.J.K. (1986) *Grenzen der Sozialdisziplinierung: Aufstieg und Krise der deutschen Jugendfürsorge von 1878 bis 1932*. Köln: Bund Verlag.

Prout, A. (2003) 'Introduction', in Ch. Hallett and A. Prout (eds) *Hearing the Voices of Children. Social Policy for a New Century*. London, New York: RoutledgeFalmer, pp. 1–8.

Qvortrup, J., M. Bardy, G.B. Sgritta and H. Wintersberger (eds) (1994) *Childhood Matters. Social Theory, Practice and Politics*. Aldershot: Avebury.

Satka, M. (2003) 'Finnish Conception of Children and the History of Child Welfare', in Ch. Hallett and A. Prout (eds) *Hearing the Voices of Children. Social Policy for a New Century*. London, New York: RoutledgeFalmer, pp. 73–88.

Schleiermacher, F. (1983) *Pädagogische Schriften I. Die Vorlesungen aus dem Jahre 1826*. Frankfurt/M.: Ullstein.

Schütter, S. (2006) 'Die Regulierung von Kindheit im Sozialstaat', *neue praxis*, 36(5): 467–482.

Steinacker, S. (2007) *Der Staat als Erzieher: Jugendpolitik und Jugendfürsorge im Rheinland vom Kaiserreich bis zum Ende des Nazismus*. Stuttgart: Ibidem-Verlag.

Sünker, H. (1991) 'Childhood, Subjectivity, and Prevention', in G. Albrecht and H.-U. Otto (eds) *Social Prevention and the Social Sciences.* Berlin/New York: de Gruyter, pp. 143–156.

Sünker, H. (2007) *Politics, Bildung and Social Justice. Perspectives for a Democratic Society.* Rotterdam: Sense.

Sünker, H. and H.-U. Otto (eds) (1997) *Education and Fascism. Political Identity and Social Education in Nazi Germany.* London/Washington: Falmer.

Wild, R. (1985) *Die Vernunft der Väter. Zur Psychographie von Bürgerlichkeit und Aufklärung in Deutschland.* Stuttgart: Metzler.

Zelizer, V. (1985) *Pricing the Priceless Child. The Changing Social Value of Children.* New York: Basic Books.

27

Transnational Mobilities and Childhoods

Adrian Bailey

Introduction

While discourses on the spatiality of children and childhoods (broadly defined) continue to inform both structural and constructionist scholarship in childhood studies (Holloway and Valentine, 2000a, b; McKendrick, 2001), this chapter argues that discourses of mobility have a profound but understated influence upon the relationship between childhood and cultural reproduction. Just as research on spatiality suggests childhood is mutually constitutive of social organization (including the spheres of education, family and the market [Hengst, 1997]) and spatial organization (including local–global relations [Ruddick, 2003; Katz, 2004]), I contend that socio-spatial discourses of mobility implicate the re-negotiation of childhood in the cultural reproduction of society. The chapter explores how this occurs as mobility becomes scaled and placed in transnational ways.

I start from the position that research on the international migration of children generally limits itself to black-box treatments of childhood (but see Bhabha, 2004; van Blerk and Ansell, 2006; and Waters, 2002 as important exceptions). Studies assume, a priori, naturalized classifications of migration (international, national, regional, local and so on) and differences between types (including forced and voluntary), and struggle to identify links and commonalities, despite considerable empirical evidence to the contrary (Richmond, 1994). The use of such neoclassical typologies limits the view of children and childhood. At one extreme, and as represented by human capital accounts of voluntary migration, typologies accept the prevailing (global North) view that children fall outside the world of work and, because they assume voluntary migration is labour-market driven, render children invisible. Likewise, there is a conservatism associated with conceptualizing how the migration of children may recast local–global relations which stems from the conflation between mobility and the sphere of production. Authors including Doreen Mattingly (2001) and Rhacel Parreñas (2005) show how care chains specifically, and the social reproduction of society more generally, inextricably link childhood, production, social reproduction and globalization.

To contribute to more open theorizations of childhood and mobility, I draw inspiration from post-structural accounts that explore how discourses of mobility (and more broadly migrancy and nomadism) are in tension with norms and expectations of sedentarism (Braidotti, 1994; Brah, 1998; Lawson, 2000). Reading childhood through the mobility-sedentarist optic sensitizes our account to the instances when mobility can put children 'out of place', and to the possibilities for regaining visibility. It also connects these re-negotiations to the intersections and re-scaling of regimes of production and social reproduction (Marston, 2000). Crucially, the rupturing of sedentarist society undermines the sustainability of territorialization as supposedly fixed referents of identity, nation and state drift apart, and is accompanied by moral panics that revolve around questions of mobility. Across the global North, increased immigration and asylum applications, combined with securitization and tightening access to social citizenship, have created moral panics which, as in the case of the Cuban boy Elian Gonzalez, hold world attention and spark debates on family, home and rights. Children can also be displaced and excluded when, as in the example of Roma youth in the United Kingdom, they are ascribed nomadic sensibilities of ethnicity that stand in opposition to dominant sedentarist ideals, and when they transgress the sedentarist norms of a classroom-based education system (Vanderbeck, 2005).

The increased intensity and complexity of international migration has only sharpened moral panics around mobility and children. Almost one-fifth of children in the United States live in immigrant families (Leiter et al., 2006, 11). The number of children moving either with or without family members and seeking asylum is at near-record level. Structural poverty in the global South and the demand for child prostitutes and sex tourism underlie the significant growth in the movement of children for purposes of exploitation. UNICEF (2007) estimates as many as 1.2 million children worldwide are affected each year by trafficking. More children are being affected by international adoption. The emergence of discrete and highly connected labour markets for skilled workers has increased the number of parents and children moving for temporary sojourns overseas (Conradson and Latham, 2005). By far the largest category of international migrants is so-called economic migrants. Individuals and complex family networks respond to the worsening conditions of economic, environmental, and political security in many countries of the global South; the appetite of metropolitan economies for low wage disposable workers; reduced social support in destinations; anti-immigrant sentiment; and the availability of instant and near instant communications through increasingly flexible migration strategies (Castles and Davidson, 2000; Pribilsky, 2001).

Such contemporary migration – be it forced, voluntary, and so on – is complementary to a transnationalization of society that brings into daily local and virtual contact those from the global South, many of whom have very diverse expectations of mobility and belong to states that explicitly promote mobility and cultural exchange, with those in the global North, many of whom have more defensive expectations of mobility and belong to societies where nativism fuels anti-immigrant panics (Hannerz, 1996; Smith, 2001; Jackson et al., 2003). Norms around mobility and sedentarism collide. Such collisions emphasize the need to write open accounts of childhood and mobility, and prompt two specific questions pursued here: first, how do discourses of mobility work to 'displace' and re-negotiate childhoods as part and parcel of the reproduction of society and, secondly, how can a more visible and constitutive view of childhood inform accounts of the post-colonial geographies of transnationalism (Bailey, 2001)? After describing what I understand by the transnationalization of society, I review research that describes variations in the experiences of mobile children and childhoods. The conclusion discusses the relevance of further work on multilocal and relational family networks, and what multiple belongings to these social fields might mean for childhood.

The transnationalization of society

There is a growing consensus that diverse childhoods are emerging hand in hand with the transnationalization of society (Olwig, 1999; 2003; Waters, 2002). A re-awakening of interest in the connections and cultures of overseas migrant communities reveals groupings of immigrants who participate on a regular basis in non-local fields of relationships, practices and norms (Cohen, 1997; Smith, 2001). These social networks tie together local places separated by long distances (multilocality), encourage the pursuit of daily life in two or more places at once (simultaneity), and support the construction of overlapping and shifting identity positions (multiplicity). Transnational and diaspora scholarship not only describes corporeal movement and physical communities but, increasingly, constituent social fields that, in simplest terms connect actors, through direct and indirect relations across borders (Levitt and Glick Schiller, 2004). In respect to global systems of production (for example, remittances sent home by overseas migrants are currently estimated to be worth in excess of $230 billion), social reproduction (for example, global care chains), and cultural reproduction (for example, the growth of internet-based movements), such transnationalism is having a profound and interrelated affect upon daily lives, social networks and fields, communities, and nations (Jackson et al., 2003).

As transnationalization connotes how experiences of multilocality, simultaneity and multiplicity emerge through social fields that extend from, and transcend, national institutions – in short, how mobile people, networks and practices transform social institutions – post-structural readings of mobility-sedentarist norms help us access changing meanings of childhood. First, the experience, organization and management of international migration under transnationalization are distinctive (Smith and Bailey, 2004). Minimizing – or at least, being as flexible as possible in the face of – risk and insecurity, provides a backdrop to how many in the global South approach transnational (im)mobility. Insecurity arises in both origins and destinations, and as a consequence of, for example, global economic restructuring, the retrenchment of welfare provisions, regime change, ecological disasters and nativist sentiment. For states, insecurity of the distant other – heightened by moral panics around terrorism – has affected how immigrants, asylum seekers and children enter and become residents. There are significant contrasts in the opportunities available to 'elite' transnational migrants and their family members compared to opportunities available to the vast majority of transmigrants (Castles and Davidson, 2000). As Olwig argues 'families constitute a central sociocultural framework of life where specific notions of livelihood emerge which lead family members to engage in a wide range of migratory movements' (2003, 788).

Tied to the diversification of migration strategies, the rise of what have been termed 'transnational families' comprises one of the most overt features of transnationalization. A vibrant body of literature accents the ways in which simultaneity and multiplicity transform, and are being transformed by, the transnational family (for example, Orellana et al., 2001; Parreñas, 2001; Al-Ali, 2002). Bryceson and Vuorela define transnational families as: 'families that have some or most of their time separated from each other, yet hold together and create something that can be seen as a feeling of collective welfare and unity, namely "familyhood", even across national borders' (2002, 3). The barriers, costs and experiences of entry and settlement encourage many families to 'split' and organize themselves in geographically flexible ways. Parreñas (2001) argues that separation is often extended by a set of structural factors that include the difficulty of accessing family reunification in many countries, the reluctance of overseas parents to bring their children into a low wage and often difficult living environment offshore, the lower costs of reproduction in most origin areas, and discourses of nativism and anti-immigration sentiment. Indeed, split family organization is not new, and may become culturally sanctioned and normalized in different geographic places at different moments (Zlotnik, 1995). What transnationalization does, however, is to bring these geographically and culturally variable constructions of proximity/sedentarism and dispersion/mobility into sharp, and daily, focus.

Within families, research suggests that roles and ideologies associated with mothering and fathering are affected by a relationality where, for example, efforts to create family space and network ties are complicated and often undermined by the lack of proximity and face-to-face interaction (Asis et al., 2004). Hondagneu-Sotelo and Evila (1997) examine how US-socialized women balance the role expectation of mothers who are in constant proximity to, and who hold responsibility for, their children with the reality of daily lives that extend beyond social reproduction tasks. In taking on mothering responsibilities for these US housewives, Mexican-socialized nannies in turn had to re-negotiate their own constructions of motherhood and childhood. While many of these women arranged and subcontracted care for their children in Mexico, they firmly distinguished this transnational version of motherhood from estrangement, abandonment, adoption and disowning. Accounts of transnational fatherhood (for example, Pribilsky, 2001) also expose the stress that some men feel from being unable to follow (locally) defined pathways towards manhood on account of their absence from children.

The opportunities for, and constraints upon transnational families are heavily linked to discourses around, and policies towards immigration, citizenship and human rights. Just as transnationalization is associated with a new web of relations between mobility, families, and childhoods, it is also associated with a new web of relations between mobility, states and childhoods. In many cases, individual states respond to increased global mobility and a media-fuelled apparent loss of control over their borders through entrance and residence restrictions, and more discursive tactics that increase individualization and ideologies of active citizenship. Crucially, these discourses can turn on socio-spatial norms about child–parent proximity – that is culturally specific constructions of children within family space. In her review of recent UK government practice, Heaven Crawley argues that children seeking asylum (or children with parents seeking asylum) are more likely to be constructed as migrants than as (resident) children: 'children who are separated from their parents or primary carers and who claim asylum in the United Kingdom struggle to negotiate an asylum system designed for adults and a child protection system focused on children who live in their own community within their own families' (2006, 13). More broadly, supra-national (for example, the UN Convention of the Rights of the Child) and national (for example, the United Kingdom's *Every Child Matters* framework and subsequent Children Act, 2004) initiatives aimed at protecting the rights of children still trump the child's place of birth as the key location for the provision of protection. As Leiter's review of recent changes in immigration legislation in the United States concludes: 'children's dependence upon adults, particularly the ways in which parents must act as proxies for their children in relations with the state, calls into question the extent to which children have direct, independent relationships with the state' (Leiter et al., 2006, 13).

As transnationalization reworks mobility, family and governance, it brings the local and the global, and multiple locals together in non-hierarchical ways that support the formation and circulation of multiple and overlapping identities and cultural constructions (Castells, 1996). That is, as expectations of daily, quotidian life are no longer confined to transactions in fixed bounded spaces and spheres like nation-states, physically located communities, and family spaces, new opportunities for identity formations arise in hybridized third spaces (Anderson, 1985; Appadurai, 1996). Most broadly, whereas cultural diffusion has often been studied as a process mediated by contiguity and connectivity to key networks of influence, the possibilities afforded by instantaneous, decentralized, and mass information and communications technologies have given groups – including children – the potential to be aware of and shape cultural practices in new ways (examples include web sites like MySpace and Runescape).

However, the extent to which multiplicity is genuinely open is contested (Mitchell, 1997). Empirical work points to (family) role entrenchment (Asis et al., 2004), and the re-inscription of gendered, raced, and classed access to rights of entry and social support in immigration policy (Kofman and England, 1997). Quota-led work visas reinforce the dependence upon male target workers and further naturalize female care roles. In the Canadian context, Walton-Roberts notes that the 'highly gendered dependency provides a context for the transmission and reinforcement of patriarchal assumptions about female behaviour across both Indian and Canadian space' (2004, 364). The entrenchment of gendered subject positions also arises when women move first to take up particular work (including domestic service, sex trade, [Hondagneu-Sotelo and Avila, 1997]) with women expected to expand (but not give up) caring to encompass paid employment. Extremist and fundamentalist views have also been cited as the basis for group affinities among disaffected migrant youth. Referring to those involved in the World Trade Centre bombings of 2001 Bryceson says: 'These young men constructed purposeful associational networks that largely displaced long-distance familial ties. Their networks were based on the rejection of the values of their home areas and their host countries' (2002, 265).

To summarize, the transnationalization of society raises a number of questions for our understanding of children and childhood. Strategies of international migration – their cultural endorsement, coordination and meaning – are strongly mediated by transnational families. The spaces of these familial social fields become sites of containment and transgression for children. However, transnational families exhibit considerable diversity in prevailing norms around parent–child proximity which can spark tensions around mobility-sedentarism. For example, tensions can arise between parents in such families and local sentiment around attitudes towards parenting, and between parents seeking to live transnational lives and maintain multilocal obligations and their children who seek to conform to playground norms of local families. One cannot essentialize migration in ways that divorce spatial practices (including the separation of split families) from constituent social practices (including the reshaping of idealized childhoods). This in turn raises questions about accounts of migration that stress simple cause and effect epistemologies, and explanations that stress either economic or political factors alone (both of which render children invisible). Under transnationalism, the link between mobility and childhood is constitutive rather than causal, and cuts across the spheres of production, social reproduction and consumption. Indeed, transnationalization, and its seeming technological and cultural permissiveness, apparently offers children unparalleled access to new sites of identity formation and multiplicity. Of course, the children of immigrant families have long been caught up in the re-negotiation of rules over, for example, consumption (bringing to the fore discrepancies between traditional and modern), and are recognized as playing constitutive roles in mobile households (Ewen, 1976). However, a series of empirical questions remain about, for example, the extent to which childhoods are footloose; the extent to which age grading reflects the daily realities of production, social reproduction, and consumption; how family context affects identity and multiplicity. The next section tackles these questions.

Writing transnational childhoods

Existing empirical work on children and childhoods under transnationalism focuses on experiences and conditions at destinations (i.e., following migration), and experiences and conditions at geographical origins (among those left behind, sent back, or resettling). To date, most work describes destinations located in the minority, global North, and origins located in the majority, global South. Turning first to destinations, the discussion below highlights three overlapping themes: the organization of families and their caring responsibilities; the well-being of children (defined broadly to include economic standing of households with children, access to education, health, community participation, and so on); the operation of influence, authority and power.

The care responsibilities for children who have moved internationally encompass a diverse suite of local arrangements. As Erel notes, because 'the process of migration often does not take place at the same time for the whole family' (2002, 130) a wide (and changing) network of individuals and resources is called upon to assist in the range of roles traditionally associated with mother figures. Aunts, siblings, partners, grandparents (particularly grandmothers), foster parents and hired carers are among those involved. Conversely, concern about the security and quality of these arrangements is a major reason for the non-migration of children (and sending children home [Erel, 2002, 134]). In situations where children (some of whom may be orphans) are forced to leave their homes – including civil unrest, war, famine, HIV-AIDS – adoption, fostering, and the use of extended care networks has implications beyond social reproduction to work and education (van Blerk and Ansell, 2006). In general, there is a paucity of child-centred, biographical analyses that follow the experiences of children over space and time (cf. Marcus, 1995).

By contrast, more attention has been given to how the well-being of children varies across ethnicity (Landale and Lichter, 1997; Zhou, 1997; House of Commons; 2004), religion (Barat, 2002), and the time and sequencing of arrival in destination (Portes and Zhou, 1993; Smith and Bailey, 2004). Acknowledging how the dynamic context of migration unfolds across the life course of family members and social networks, research emphasizes how tensions between parents and children impact the well-being of children. Local context – including the opportunities for interaction between children and access to secular norms – plays a mediating role in these negotiations, and mitigates sweeping generalization. For example, the children of second generation Moroccans living in multiethnic areas of the Netherlands generally derived positive cultural capital from their parents' tolerant and culturally relativist attitude towards daily life, and its challenges (Bryceson, 2002, 57). The same kind of empathy was less in evidence in the relations between the parents and children of Bosnian refugees living in the United Kingdom and the Netherlands over the issue of language (Al-Ali, 2002). While parents felt their children should learn Bosnian to participate in and be closer to this ethnic community, children felt they should acquire and master the language of the school playground. Such clashes may also be gendered. Noting how social roles and positions are differentiated in traditional Sahelian Muslim family space, Timera describes how the relatively greater access that girls had to education in France compared to compatriots in the Sahel promoted a kind of feminist consciousness 'at odds with familial and community norms'; by contrast, the relatively reduced access boys had to public space in France compared to that experienced by their fathers in the Sahel led to boys being 'rebels against public order', and to criticisms from beyond the community about the parenting capacity of Sahelian immigrants (Timera, 2002, 150–151). Barat saw similar antipathy among Gujarati youth in London but noted 'youth rebellion and individualist paths are tempered by the external forces of racism, especially the climate of intimidation, harassment and violence that the young face and cause them to develop a community-based defensive posture' (Barat, 2002, 210).

Research suggests that influence, authority and the circulation of power between children who have moved internationally and their transnational social fields revolves around the negotiation of otherness. For some authors, transnational childhoods and consumption activities can remove childhood from the particularist spaces of family networks and locales, and evidence a deeper structural underpinning to group identity. For example, Hengst's survey of transmigrant children in Germany and England pointed to the importance of play activities for bringing migrant and native children into daily contact, although contact was mediated by class with 'children from the lower classes typically have more contact with the children of immigrants than do those from the upper middle class' (1997, 55). In arguing for a kind of 'Children's International' identity, Hengst noted that children connected with each other through the consumption of globally circulating cultures: 'all children are fascinated by globally distributed games and by leisure and sports fashions ... the media and consumer industries for their part do everything to create children's culture as independent of adults. A basis for the establishment of global solidarity has arisen' (1997, 58) (see Hengst in this volume). Participation in online consumption activities stressed connections between children, and differences between children and their own parents.

Markers of otherness like language may simultaneously be foregrounded by immigrant youth in their efforts to claim an alternative identity from their parents (by quickly adopting the native language), and backgrounded in their negotiation for influence with other young persons. The dynamic place of language in the social field suggests that migration acts through the re-negotiation of childhood to undermine (global North) family forms that derive authority from sedentarism/parent–child proximity. More broadly, migration disrupts the long-standing isomorphism between family, identity and nation (Stephens, 1997; Erel, 2002, 139).

While patterns of social reproduction involving transnational children in destination areas across the global North were often at odds with locally prevailing norms, the practice of communal caregiving is well established in many origin areas. While preferring care to be delivered by a close relative, particularly their own mothers, migrant mothers reached out to godmothers, female kin, the child's father, and paid caregivers (Hondagneu-Sotelo and Avila, 1997). Parreñas (2001) reported that Filipino mothers paid for the care of their children with remittance income. Elsewhere, Mattingly (2001) noted a similar global care chain with those unable to afford the costs of migration 'left behind' and at the bottom of the production system, and providing care for the families of migrants.

Many studies discuss the experiences of children 'left behind' in 'either/or' terms, that is by developing a debate between those who argue that parents' (and particularly mothers') migration is detrimental to the development of the child, and those who feel the effects upon the child are both positive and negative (Zlotnick, 1995). Findley (1997, 127) linked family separation to parents' perceptions of control problems and caring for young children, and to a rise in child abuse. Parreñas (2001) investigates how feelings of loneliness, vulnerability and insecurity lead to a set of resentments among the 'left behind' children of Filipino mothers. Here, children's well-being was diminished by the disconnection between their own expectations of childhood, based on traditional gender norms and ideologies, and their daily experience of commodified love at a distance, and extended separation from their mothers. Aitken et al. (2006) likewise caution against making blanket generalizations about the impact of broader processes of globalization upon well-being without considering local social norms pertaining to production and reproduction expectations.

The relevance of understanding local context for appreciating well-being is amplified by research by Jason Pribilsky (2001). He focused on a pronounced rise of 'new' disorders among the children of Ecuadorians working overseas. Villagers described a state of extreme sadness, explosive anger, malicious acts of violence and an uncooperative attitude towards daily activities (labelled collectively as *nervios*) and connected this to the absence of fathers or parents. For Pribilsky *nervios* is a strategy that some Ecuadorian children use to make sense of their world and to bring voice to transformations they may not fully understand (2001, 268). Indeed, he argues that it may be the mismatched placement of childhood roles and responsibilities that is the greatest source of trauma for children of transnational families.

Globalized consumption practices offer new connections to and between children, and in so doing transform the authority structure within families. Exploring the images in children's cartoons in Egypt, a state with a growing transmigrant population, Peterson notes: 'through such media, Egyptian children may enter into an imagined community…of other children like themselves playing and consuming, both elsewhere in the Middle East and in the wider worlds of America, Europe, and Japan' (2005, 179). What is communicated is a 'style of imagination' that constructs 'a particular ideology of regional identity that is simultaneously Arab and Islamic, but also part of a larger global community of consumption…much of the power of these regional images derives from their juxtaposition with…the world of consumer goods and…a transnational world of commodities' (189–190). Parents appear complicit in the development of their children's hybrid identities in this newly imagined community, supplying pocket money and the like. What is less clear is the extent to which consumption norms influence behaviour across the transnational field, change constructs of childhood and/or persist.

Indeed, while access to 'global' commodities and resources may be a reality for an increasing number of children, the circumstances of split families puts the abstractions of commodification in a new light. Distant (absent) parents seek to compensate for a lack of expected proximity with their children by 'commodifying love' – in providing remittances and material goods from the global

North parents act as agents of westernization and the diffusion of global norms (Parreñas, 2001). While children disagree that such gifts are adequate substitutes for 'love', and frame the transnational child–parent relationship as a 'money or family' problematic, 'the intergenerational conflicts engendered by emotional tensions in transnational households are aggravated by the traditional ideological systems of the patriarchal nuclear family' (ibid., 10).

In a similar vein, and exposing the public discourse about the changing meanings of parent–child (often, father–child) bonds in transnational families, Pribilsky cautions against the over-celebratory nature of some transnational discourse: 'while transmigration may de-territorialize social relations, it cannot dissolve the realities of borders and the costs they exact for those who cross them and their families…Ideas about "proper" childhood and "modern" parenting styles that circulate through the global economy are not neatly grafted onto the local situation, but rather the fit is incomplete…Global structures of childhood provide a common set of formats and channels for the forms of childhood in Ecuador, but it is the local mediation of these forms by family and by community that dictate the experience' (2001, 269). Similarly, Bey (2003) argues that Western norms of idealized childhoods as placed in proximity to their parents and revolving around formal education may not translate everywhere equally. This pattern both changes the relationship children have for these institutions (particularly the family and the state) but also trivializes and obscures the still-present hierarchies of control in space. Furthermore, transnationalization means that contingencies extend beyond the local to include memory, with ideas about affinity and influence referencing sets of accumulated offshore experiences (constructed pasts). Olwig's interviews with one family who had returned to Dominica in 1978 found that 'a few younger family members had rebelled…against the emphasis upon education and moral respectability, emphasized by the family, and rejected the pressure for individual achievement and the value judgements that this involved. Some of them, instead, developed an interest in black, "diaspora" culture and participated in black cultural events' (2003, 807).

Conclusions

This chapter has aimed to contribute to the development of an open view of the links between childhood, mobility, and the cultural reproduction of society. Adopting a post-structural lens, I have argued that discourses of mobility are scaled and placed in particular ways that are constitutive of transnational society, and experiences of simultaneity, multilocality and multiplicity have highlighted the importance of relational family (social) networks. The development of, and embedding of transnational family forms have implications both for structural views of childhood (with some pointing to the emergence of universal childhoods in technologically enabled transnational space) and for (western) constructions of sedentary isomorphism between identity, family, and nation.

The account emphasized mobility as opposed to migration per se, and urged attention to flows that extend beyond demographic movement of individuals to encompass materials, cultures and power. It is important to recognize that spaces of belonging are not defined by 'privileged' acts of mobility operating in isolation, but by the multilocality and simultaneity begotten by the possibilities and experiences of mobility. In this way we might begin to address what Holloway and Valentine (2000a), Ross (2005) and others have referred to as the 'imaginative' aspects of spaces of childhood.

There is also a methodological implication here. The relativizing family suggests that research cannot afford to adopt an origin or destination perspective, but most narrate both, preferably simultaneously. While strength of current accounts is their sensitivity to contingency, such contingencies are almost always local ones, with geographic origins and destinations treated as separate entities. Without following children through their constitutive networks, the active ways in which re-negotiated childhoods change such networks and relations are lost. Re-imagined childhoods, and with these new patterns of relationality and multiplicity are being overlooked. Both continuity (of commitment to family members multiply located) and discontinuity (identity, experiences of discrimination, status) flow through transnational networks, and necessarily change the relationships of individuals and institutions to each other. This implies going beyond multi-sited ethnography because such a design falls short of following childhoods by focusing on individual children, rather than social networks (Marcus, 1995).

My second objective focused on how re-negotiated transnational childhoods gave form to the free-floating hybridities of post-colonial interactions between the global South and North. In particular, the rescaling of belonging through frontiering and relativizing family networks brought to the fore traditional entrenchments around gendering and racialization, and a new set of engagements between members of generations. Further research can usefully explore what Vanderbeck (2007) has referred to as the process of 'generationing' by linking mobility discourses to age-graded expectations for children, adults, and the elderly, and the normalized intergenerational relations between them (see also Pain, 2006; see also Alanen in this volume). Indeed, a similar point is emphasized by Bryceson and Vuerola who note that individuals within the same transnational family may imagine this family differently – mediated, for example, by their sense of belonging within the family (2002, 15).

Acknowledgements

I enjoyed – and this paper has benefits from – immensely valuable conversations with a number of colleagues, including Kirsty Finn, Larch Maxey, and Robert Vanderbeck; the normal disclaimers apply.

References

Aitken, S., S.L. Estrada, J. Jennings and L.M. Aguirre (2006) 'Reproducing Life and Labor: Global Processes and Working Children in Tijuana, Mexico', *Childhood*, 13(3): 365–387.

Al-Ali, N. (2002) 'Loss of Status and New Opportunities? Gender Relation and Transnational Ties among Bosnian Refugees', in D. Bryceson and U. Vuorela (eds) *The Transnational Family*. Oxford: Berg, pp. 83–102.

Anderson, B. (1985) *Imagined Communities*. London: Verso.

Appadurai, A. (1996) *Modernity at Large: Cultural Dimensions of Globalization*. Minneapolis MN: University of Minnesota Press.

Asis, M., S. Huang and Y. Brenda (2004) 'When the Light of the Home Is Abroad: Unskilled Female Migration and the Filipino Family', *Singapore Journal of Tropical Geography*, 25(2): 198–215.

Bailey, A.J. (2001) 'Turning Transnational: Notes on the Theorisation of International Migration', *International Journal of Population Geography*, 7(6): 413–428.

Barot, R. (2002) 'Religion, Migration and Wealth Creation in the Swaminarayan Movement', in D. Bryceson and U. Vuorela (eds) *The Transnational Family*. Oxford: Berg, pp. 197–216.

Bey, M. (2003) 'The Mexican Child: From Work with the Family to Paid Employment', *Childhood*, 10(3): 287–299.

Bhabha, J. (2004) 'Seeking Asylum Alone: Treatment of Separated Trafficked Children in Need of Protection', *International Migration*, 42(1), 141–148.

Braidotti, R. (1994) *Nomadic Subjects: Embodiment and Sexual Difference in Contemporary Feminist Theory*. New York: Columbia University Press.

Brah, A. (1998) *Cartographies of Diaspora: Contesting Identities*. London: Routledge.

Bryceson, D. (2002) 'Epilogue', in D. Bryceson and U. Vuorela (eds) *The Transnational Family*. Oxford: Berg, pp. 265–267.

Bryceson, D. and U. Vuorela (eds) (2002) *The Transnational Family*. Oxford: Berg.

Castles, S. and A. Davidson (2000) *Citizenship and Migration: Globalization and the Politics of Belonging*. New York: Routledge.

Castells, Manuel (1996) *The Information Age. The Rise of the Network Society* (vol. 1). Oxford: Basil Blackwell.

Cohen, R. (1997) *Global Diasporas*. Seattle WA: University of Washington Press.

Conradson, D. and A. Latham (2005) 'Friendship, Networks, and Transnationality in a World City: Antipodean Transmigrants in London', *Journal of Ethnic and Migration Studies*, 31(2): 287–305.

Crawley, H. (2006) *Child First, Migrant Second: Ensuring That Every Child Matters*. Immigration Law Practitioners' Association Policy Paper. London: ILPA.

Erel, U. (2002) 'Reconceptualizing Motherhood: Experiences of Migrant Women from Turkey Living in Germany', in D. Bryceson and U. Vuorela (eds) *The Transnational Family*. Oxford: Berg, pp. 127–146.

Ewen, S. (1976) *Captains of Consciousness*. New York: McGraw-Hill.

Findley, S. (1997) 'Migration and Family Interactions in Africa', in A. Adepoju (ed.) *Population and Development in Africa*. London: Zed Books, pp. 109–138.

Hannerz, U. (1996) *Transnational Connections*. London: Routledge.

Hengst, H. (1997) 'Negotiating "Us" and "Them": Children's Constructions of Collective Identity', *Childhood*, 4(1): 43–62.

Holloway, S. and G. Valentine (eds) (2000a) *Children's Geographies: Playing, Living, Learning*. London: Routledge.

Holloway, S. and G. Valentine (2000b) 'Spatiality and the New Social Studies of Childhood', *Sociology*, 34(4): 763–783.

Hondagneu-Sotelo, P. and E. Avila (1997) '"I'm Here but I'm There" – the Meanings of Latina Transnational Motherhood', *Gender and Society*, 11(5): 548–571.

House of Commons (2004) *Child Poverty in the UK: Second Report of Session 2003–4, Work and Pensions Committee*. Available from: www.publications.parliament.uk/pa/cm200304/cmselect/cmworpen/85/85.pdf.

Jackson, P., P. Crang and C. Dwyer (2003) *Transnational Spaces*. London: Routledge.

Katz, C. (2004) *Growing up Global*. Minneapolis MN: University of Minnesota Press.

Kofman, E. and K. England (1997) 'Citizenship and International Migration: Taking Account of Gender, Sexuality, and Race', *Environment and Planning A* 29(2): 191–194.

Landale, N. and D. Lichter (1997) 'Geography and the Etiology of Poverty among Latino Children', *Social Science Quarterly*, 78(4): 874–894.

Lawson, V. (2000) 'Arguments Within the Geographies of Movement: The Theoretical Potential of Migrants' Stories', *Progress in Human Geography*, 24(2): 173–189.

Leiter, V., J. McDonald and H. Jacobsen (2006) 'Challenges to Children's Independent Citizenship: Immigration, Family and the State', *Childhood*, 13(1): 11–27.

Levitt, P. and N.G. Schiller (2004) 'Transnational Perspectives on Migration: Conceptualizing Simultaneity', *International Migration Review*, 38(3): 1002–1039.

McKendrick, J. (2001) 'Coming of Age: Rethinking the Role of Children in Population Studies', *International Journal of Population Geography*, 7(6): 461–472.

Marcus, G. (1995) 'Ethnography in/of the World System: The Emergence of Multi-sited Ethnography', *Annual Review of Ethnography*, 24: 95–117.

Marston, S.A. (2000) 'The Social Construction of Scale', *Progress in Human Geography*, 24(2): 219–242.

Mattingly, D. (2001) 'The Home and the World: Domestic Service and International Networks of Caring Labor', *Annals of the Association of American Geographers*, 91(2): 370–386.

Mitchell, K. (1997) 'Different Diasporas and the Hype of Hybridity', *Environment and Planning D: Society and Space*, 15(5): 533–553.

Olwig, K. (1999) 'Narratives of the Children Left Behind: Home and Identity in Globalised Caribbean Families', *Journal of Ethnic and Migration Studies*, 25(2): 267–284.

Olwig, K. (2003) '"Transnational" Socio-cultural Systems and Ethnographic Research: Views from an Extended Field Site', *International Migration Review*, 37(3): 787–811.

Orellana, M., B. Thorne, A. Chee and W.S. Lam (2001) 'Transnational Childhoods: The Participation of Children in Processes of Family Migration', *Social Problems*, 48(4): 572–591.

Pain, R. (2006) 'Paranoid Parenting: Rematerializing Risk and Fear for Children', *Social and Cultural Geography*, 7(2): 221–243.

Parreñas, R.S. (2001) 'Mothering from a Distance: Emotions, Gender, and Inter-generational Relations in Filipino Transnational Families', *Feminist Studies*, 27(2), 361–390.

Parreñas, R.S. (2005) *Children of Global Migration*. Stanford CA: Stanford University Press.

Peterson, M.A. (2005) 'The Jinn and the Computer: Consumption and Identity in Arab Children's Magazines', *Childhood*, 12(2): 177–200.

Portes, A. and M. Zhou (1993) 'The New Second Generation: Segmented Assimilation and Its Variants', *Annals of the American Academy of Political Science*, 530: 74–96.

Pribilsky, J. (2001) 'Nervios and "Modern Childhood": Migration and Shifting Contexts of Child Life in the Ecuadorian Andes', *Childhood*, 8(2): 251–273.

Richmond, A. (1994) *Global Apartheid*. Oxford: Oxford University Press.

Ross, N. (2005) 'Children's Space', *International Research in Geographical and Environmental Education*, 14(4): 336–341.

Ruddick, S. (2003) 'The Politics of Aging: Globalization and the Restructuring of Youth and Childhood', *Antipode*, 35(2): 334–362.

Smith, D. and A. Bailey (2004) 'Linking Transnational Migrants and Transnationalism', *Population, Space and Place*, 10(5): 357–360.

Smith, M. (2001) *Transnational Urbanism*. Oxford: Blackwell.

Stephens, S. (1997) 'Editorial Introduction: Children and Nationalism', *Childhood*, 4(1): 5–17.

Timera, M. (2002) 'Righteous or Rebellious? Social Trajectory of Sahelian Youth in France', in D. Bryceson and U. Vuorela (eds) *The Transnational Family*. Oxford: Berg, pp. 147–154.

UNICEF (2007) *State of the World's Children 2006*. Accessed at: http://www.unicef.org/sowc06/profiles/trafficking.php.

Van Blerk, L. and N. Ansell (2006) 'Children's Experiences of Migration: Moving in the Wake of AIDS in Southern Africa', *Environment and Planning D: Society and Space*, 24(3): 449–471.

Vanderbeck, R. (2005) 'Anti-Nomadism, Institutions, and the Geographies of Childhood', *Environment and Planning D Society and Space*, 23(1): 71–94.

Vanderbeck, R. (2007) 'Intergenerational Geographies: Age Relations, Segregation, and Re-Engagements', *Geography Compass*, 1(2): 200–221.

Walton-Roberts, M. (2004) 'Transnational Migration Theory in Population Geography: Gendered Practises in Networks Linking Canada and India', *Population, Space and Place*, 10(5): 361–373.

Waters, J. (2002) '"Flexible Families?": Astronaut Households and the Experiences of Lone Mothers in Vancouver, B.C.', *Social and Cultural Geography*, 3(1): 117–134.

Zhou, M. (1997) 'Growing up American: The Challenge Confronting Immigrant Children and the Children of Immigrants', *Annual Review of Sociology*, 23: 63–95.

Zlotnik, H. (1995) 'Migration and the Family: The Female Perspective', *Asian and Pacific Migration Journal*, 4(2): 253–271.

28
Closing the Gap Between Rights and the Realities of Children's Lives

Natalie Hevener Kaufman and Irene Rizzini

Introduction

With the almost universal ratification of the Convention on the Rights of the Child (CRC), the international community has acknowledged that children and youth are entitled to basic rights regardless of the country of their origin, nationality, or even that of their residence, whether permanent or temporary. In this chapter we will explicate some of the most important content of international law that affects children and youth, discuss the usefulness as well as the limitations of this set of legal norms, and suggest some steps that we believe are important if legal rights are going to serve to help address the profound problems that face children and youth in their everyday lives (see also Freeman in this volume).

The underlying assumption of most law on human rights is the dignity of the individual. Individuals are posited to have rights because they are human, aside from their membership in any particular national group. When we speak of inalienable rights, we are acknowledging an understanding that rights are not coterminous with nationality. One indication that this belief is fundamental is that when governments historically have deprived whole groups of people of their rights, they first deny their humanity and next deny them citizenship in the state.[1]

Thus, one of the hurdles for the group we call children was the presumption in many cultures that children are less than fully human; children can be denied fundamental rights until they reach an age of maturity, at which time they are considered fully human. The rejection of the notion that children lack human rights developed throughout the twentieth century, most notably since the Declaration of the Rights of the Child in 1924. The 1989 CRC sets aside any lingering idea that children are not entitled to human rights.[2]

The Convention covers the largest scope of any single human rights treaty, and states take on extensive obligations for the survival, development, protection, and participation of children. The language includes all children and is in the form of binding obligations. 'States shall respect and ensure the rights set forth in the present Convention to each child within their jurisdiction without discrimination of any kind, irrespective of the child's or his or her parent's or legal guardian's race, colour, sex, language, religion, political or other opinion, national, ethnic or social origin, property, disability, birth or other status' (Article 2, paragraph 1). It is of interest that there was controversy about defining the age of the child, and the list of bases for non-discrimination does not include age. The Convention does allow discrimination based on age since certain rights are linked to the child's developmental capacity, such capacity being determined by adults.

There are a number of regional rights documents that reinforce the international claim that children have legal rights. The European Convention on Human Rights and Fundamental Freedoms (1950) uses 'everyone' in Article 5 (liberty, and security of person) and Article 8 (respect for privacy, family life, home and correspondence), so one might assume that children are included. The European Social Charter (1961), most specifically in Article 7 (protection of children and young people at work), Article 10 (right to vocational education), and Article 17 (social and economic protection for mothers and children), specifically includes children as those having rights.

In the American Convention on Human Rights (1969) Article 16 is devoted entirely to the 'Rights of children'; it protects children's status as minors, and states their right to be with their parents and their right to free education. Under Article 19 the child is entitled to protection by the family, society and the state. The child's education rights are elaborated in Article 13 of a protocol to this convention focusing on economic, social and cultural rights (1988).

Africa is the only region that has a separate regional agreement on children's rights, the African Charter on the Rights and Welfare of the Child (1990) (ACRWC). This document covers the same rights domains as the CRC and has specific articles devoted to regional concerns, such as Article 26 on protection against apartheid and discrimination and Article 30 on children of imprisoned mothers. The charter also sets up a regional committee to monitor the rights of the child as set forth in the treaty.

The role of international law in establishing human rights

One of the purposes of international law is to lay out the common ground of understanding between two or more states and formulate that understanding into an agreement. Over time such agreements have come to be treated as creating binding obligations. Readers who are only familiar with international law through instances like the dramatic treaty-breaking of Hitler's forces or the Iranian government's approval of the taking of the United States embassy mistakenly associate international law with pie-in-the-sky idealism or paper promises cast into a void. But the fact remains that the representatives of sovereign states take international law seriously. They are very reluctant to enter into internationally binding agreements; they meticulously and painstakingly peruse each word and comma, struggling to limit the nature and extent of the serious obligations they are accepting on paper, which they know all too well they cannot cast aside without painful consequences. That some state leaders do in fact act contrary to the obligations they have voluntarily accepted in no way changes the seriousness of their obligation or the relative ease with which the rest of the world can then identify that the state has indeed committed a violation of law.

The fact that human rights treaties have been drafted and ratified in substantial numbers and with substantive content in an age when sovereignty and nationalism are thriving is itself a phenomenon worth investigating. Not only do the treaties define serious substantive obligations, but most lay out, as well, a system of monitoring and implementation and some form of dispute resolution. We are surprised by this international legal development because human rights were until the second half of the twentieth century, for the most part, a subject of purely national consideration. Human rights issues in fact appeared to the drafters of the United Nations Charter, towards the close of the first half of the century, to be perfect examples of the need for Article 2 paragraph 7, which retained to the member states the right to cite national law in order to limit the international organization's jurisdiction.

The Charter and Judgment at Nuremberg and the Universal Declaration of Human Rights signalled a fundamental change in the conceptualization of the legal status of the individual, but the seriousness with which states have enlarged and expanded the domain of human rights has signalled as well a fundamental change in the conceptualization of the state, for to take internationally defined human rights seriously is to acknowledge that the idea of the state as the sole arbiter of those rights is an anachronism.

What this means is that a new set of global norms has been emerging, the very existence of which challenges our thinking about national/international dichotomies. If a state cannot claim exclusive jurisdiction over its own citizens within its own borders, to what extent is the concept of sovereignty useful? If we consider the large number of human rights treaties, the extensive ratification of these treaties with relatively few limiting attachments or conditions, it is impossible to deny that the formal apparatus of the state system has embraced a set of fairly consistent obligations which represents a new level of consensus on moral and ethical norms. Along with these treaties, we find an even larger number of declarations from international conferences, United Nations resolutions, regional international organization resolutions, unilateral supportive statements by official representatives of governments, and individual state constitutional and statutory action which testify to the global governmental acknowledgement of the obligatory nature of international human rights norms.

Even when representatives of states publicly agree to statements of norms which they may not intend to implement fully or speedily, they are giving added force to the legitimation of the norms they adopt. And although the International Court of Justice stands symbolically as the ultimate arbiter of international law, it is in the national courts, national legislatures, national administrations, and national public-policy debates that the impact of these norms will be most strongly felt. Often government officials, members of legislatures, and national representatives at international organizations embrace the language of human rights standards with a view to applying them to foreign strangers only to discover that they are being asked to apply those same standards at home.

Using international law to address problems in children's everyday lives

Even at the level of the national state, law cannot transform society overnight. It can, however, set forth an expectation of governmental as well as non-governmental behaviour, and these expectations can in turn legitimize policies and programmes which contribute to changing attitudes and actions. Normally, some attitudes have changed in order to bring about a change in law and the law can then provide a basis for moving forward that particular set of values. In any participatory political system some important groups, and under normal circumstances some important coalition of elites, have created the climate and preconditions for the emergence of sufficient consensus to move to change stated values and expectations. The same can be said for global efforts to improve the lives of children. International legal norms can become powerful tools in advocacy by national, as well as international, organizations on behalf of children.

Respect for the dignity of the child

To exemplify the globalization of human rights norms for children, we can look first at the concept of the dignity of the person, which is essential to the very definition of what it means to have rights, and finds a central place in the CRC. One example of a norm that was newly developed in the second half of the twentieth century is that of the right of the child to protection from abuse. Here is an issue which is still controversial within states, basically in tension with the right of the family to privacy and in line with longstanding attitudes that the child is the property of the parents. As Van Bueren (1995, 87) has pointed out, the lack of reservations to the CRC articles on abuse and neglect is a positive sign that states are willing to entertain the idea that children have the right to live in families without being subject to emotional or physical abuse (Article 19 paragraph 1).

One good example of what it would mean to respect the dignity of the child is the even more controversial emergent norm prohibiting corporal punishment as degrading and humiliating. The Riyadh Guidelines aimed at the prevention of juvenile delinquency, for example, recommend the 'Avoidance of harsh disciplinary measures, particularly corporal punishment' (section IV paragraph 21 (h)). An example of this changing norm is the effort in Scandinavia to prohibit parental corporal punishment. The European Commission on Human Rights upheld a Swedish law prohibiting parental corporal punishment, when it was challenged by Swedish parents, on the grounds of the vulnerability of children. In 2004, the Council of Europe adopted a ban on corporal punishment (Council of Europe, 2004). The decision means that states that have ratified the European Convention are not required to abolish parental corporal punishment, but that if they choose to do so, they are not violating the rights of parents. One may hope that as research on the damage of corporal punishment and its conflict with the dignity of the child is more widely promulgated, a potential limitation on parental abuse may gain international status.

Although the CRC does not specifically prohibit parental corporal punishment, it is increasingly difficult to reconcile such practice with the Convention's emphasis on the dignity of the child (see though Freeman in this volume on Article 19). The convention does provide a basis for eliminating corporal punishment in schools in one of the articles on education. Article 28 paragraph 2 requires states to 'ensure that school discipline is administered in a manner consistent with the child's human dignity'. For children in the juvenile justice system – an especially vulnerable population – the United Nations Standard Minimum Rules for the Administration of Juvenile Justice (The Beijing Rules) (1985) clearly states that 'juveniles shall not be subject to corporal punishment' (Article 17.3).

International cooperation to improve the lives of children

As the world has grown smaller through communications and technological advances, awareness has increased of problems and progress. Globalization has made it easier to bring about cooperative ventures to collectively address the challenges that face children and youth (Kaufman and Rizzini, 2002). There are many treaties aimed at closing gaps between and among national systems in both law and implementation that are exploited by violators of children's rights. One example is traffic in children.

Governments for over a century have joined together to address the international dimensions of slavery. Although there have for decades been agreements outlawing traffic in women, and later children, the CRC contains the most universally ratified and broadly defined treaty provision outlawing this crime. States have accepted an obligation to 'take all appropriate national, bilateral and multilateral measures to prevent the abduction of, the sale of or traffic in children for any purpose or in any form' (Article 35). Clearly in matters of this kind it is essential to maximize the number of cooperating states, since national laws are ineffective for preventing and punishing criminals if violators are free to move without penalty across state borders. The African Children's Charter also prohibits traffic in children (Article 29) and prohibits, as well, the use of children in begging. Most recently, this issue has been addressed in the Optional Protocol to the CRC on the Sale of Children, Child Prostitution and Child Pornography that entered into force on 18 January 2002.

Unfortunately, individuals also take children across state borders when they are unhappy with custody arrangements. Again, multilateral agreements are necessary to provide for prevention of this, as well as effective and safe return of children. States are obligated under the CRC to help prevent the illegal removal of children from the state and to enter into agreements, including already existing ones, aimed at ending such activity (Article 11). The Convention on the Civil Aspects of International Child Abduction (1980) states as its purpose ensuring 'that rights of custody and of access under the law of one Contracting State are effectively respected in the other Contracting States' (Article 1).

Several regional treaties were specifically drafted for the purpose of promoting international cooperation for the return of children illegally taken across national borders. The European Convention on Recognition and Enforcement of Decisions Concerning Custody of Children and on Restoration of Custody of Children (1980) lays out legal and technical arrangements aimed at uniformly and systematically applying one another's custody agreements within Europe. And the Inter-American Convention on the International Return of Children (1989) makes similar arrangements for the Americas.

Obstacles to bringing legal rights to bear on the everyday lives of children

Even though international and national law has been used effectively to improve children's lives, it is clear from the *State of the World's Children*, as reported each year by the United Nations Children's Fund (UNICEF), that many children are living lives that appear to be untouched by the obligations that their governments assumed in ratifying the CRC and other related treaties. Some of the forces preventing full implementation of the law are themselves of a legal nature; others, the most important ones, are in fact the result of the social, economic and political context in which the law is expected to operate. We will discuss both types of obstacles below.

First, human rights treaties, including the CRC, have also been challenged on the grounds that they often reflect western law and values and neglect the rich legal and cultural traditions of non-western societies (see Bühler-Niederberger & Sünker and Freeman, both in this volume). Although there is some merit in this accusation, it is important to note that multilateral human rights treaties were drafted by representatives of all the governments of the world and large numbers of non-governmental organizations. The normal drafting process also allows for numerous opportunities for input from those not in attendance at the drafting conferences. Following adoption of the treaty there is, of course, a national process of ratification, which is in the minds of each delegation during the drafting process. Finally, most countries have a process in national legislation that they use to incorporate the treaty provisions into their domestic constitutional system. Thus, a careful analysis of the drafting process of most human rights treaties reveals a very thoughtful and necessarily slow deliberation about each word and phrase, primarily because the drafters aim for universality with respect for flexibility within maximally perceived allowable limits.

'Tradition' alone should not be a basis for setting aside widely accepted human rights norms. Often those who are the primary victims of human rights abuses have been, by these same 'traditions', without voice or power. To use a painful example from the southern states of the United States, many slave owners claimed that slavery was an important southern 'tradition'; the application of 'outside' legal and moral standards was necessary to challenge the 'tradition' on behalf of the slaves, who were allowed no voice. Infant betrothal, infanticide, rape and other ritualized mistreatment of children should not be removed from the application of international standards on the grounds that they are 'traditional'. One positive dimension of globalization is the ease of promulgation of human rights standards. A crucial source of opposition to arguments that 'tradition' should take precedence over human rights standards is the active support for human rights norms by indigenous groups of formerly powerless citizens who are challenging the traditional system.

The global recognition of human rights is one of the most significant dimensions of an emerging system of globally shared values. The extension of human rights regimes to encompass the least powerful citizens – ethnic, racial and religious minorities, women and children – means that even the most vulnerable are now entitled to equal protection of the law. The creation of a High Commissioner for Human Rights is a more recent development that highlights the importance nations are attaching to the monitoring and implementation in this one area of global values consensus.

However, there are still many challenges to be faced until those laws are truly enforced. In the sphere of children's rights, for example, the gap between theories that talk about the 'defence and guarantee of children's rights' and their implementation is enormous. The most basic rights of children are violated on a daily basis throughout the world. Equally problematic is the premise of equality enshrined in the idea of rights; all children have equal rights and rights should be the same for all, but massive discrimination, hostility and injustice against certain groups continue to exist today and in some places seem to be getting worse. The gap between the privileged and the under-privileged is not diminishing. See, for example, the case of countries with progressive child rights laws that have not been widely implemented. Brazil, for example, passed its Statute of the Child and Adolescent in 1990 and it has been making very slow progress in improving actual children's lives.[3]

Second, some have argued (Kaufman and Lindquist, 1995) that since the validity of international law partially depends on overt or tacit consent to the obligations set forth in the law, a process of law-making or ratification which excludes significant groups may not be globally valid. For example, children and youth or those who genuinely claim to speak on their behalf are rarely included in the formal governmental delegations that draft international law and may be absent, as well, from the governmental-level ratification process. An important exception to the normal process, however, was the very active involvement of non-governmental organizations in the drafting of the children's convention, including several child advocacy groups. Hopefully this example and the involvement of these groups, as well, in the monitoring process augur well for future international law codification. In addition to the participation of particular organizations, since children are not monolithic groups, it is especially important to seek diverse input into the interpretation and implementation of human rights treaties if they are to achieve the level of consent that would give them maximum validity.

It is difficult to imagine a definition of democracy that does not rest on fundamental civil and political rights. The CRC guarantees rights to freedom of speech (Article 12; ACRWC Article 7) and to assembly and association (Article 15; ACRWC Article 11). Also, children have the right to privacy and the right to be protected by law from any interference with their privacy (Articles 16, 40; ACRWC Article

10). Basic legal protections are spelled out for children in the legal system, among them the presumption of innocence, the right to be informed of charges, to not be forced to testify against oneself, to legal assistance, to an interpreter, and to a hearing by an independent and impartial authority (Article 40; ACRWC Article 40).

The Beijing Rules also provide extensive protections, including 'presumption of innocence, the right to be notified of the charges, the right to remain silent, the right to counsel ... the right to confront and cross-examine witnesses and the right to appeal to a higher authority shall be guaranteed at all stages of proceedings' (Article 7 paragraph 1).

Yet the most crucial link between human rights and democracy is the prevention of unjust exercises of authority by participation in the life of one's society.

The nature of civic life has been changing in the late twentieth and early twenty-first centuries. With increased democratization more people than ever before are eligible to participate in the public life of their countries. Also, as barriers to participation such as gender, minority group membership, property ownership, and age, among others, are eliminated, formerly disenfranchised groups have access not only to voting and holding public office, but also to more active participation throughout public life, in their communities and in national policy debates.

Some have argued that the strength of a democracy is best measured by how well it treats its weakest members. Children's awareness of democratic processes and their participation in them are required on the basis of the dignity of the child and the experience of childhood as a stage in itself. But it is, of course, also necessary for the growth of a healthy democratic future for the society. Therefore, we are not surprised that human rights instruments place a heavy emphasis on the participation of the child in decision-making, not only in public life, but also in private life.

The idea of children's participation has been gaining a broader international acceptance. Several authors have been highlighting the importance of cultural constructs of the notion of childhood in historically situated ways (Flekkøy and Kaufman, 1997; Reddy, 1997; Morrow, 1999; Weis and Fine, 2000; Limber and Kaufman, 2002; James, 2004; Smith, 2005). In order to increase opportunities for truly meaningful participation in culturally responsive ways, it is important to know more about how particular cultures and societies and the children who live in them understand and exercise these rights of participation (Rizzini and Thapliyal, 2006).

The CRC lays down strong bases for the child's participation in public life. First, children have the right to the knowledge about the system and information for decision-making that are the prerequisites for meaningful participation. In defining the right to education, the CRC emphasizes the development of the child's personality, respect for human rights, and the preparation of the child for 'responsible life in a free society' (Article 29). Similar language appears in the ACRWC in Article 11 and in the Additional Protocol to the American Convention on Human Rights in the area of Economic, Social and Cultural Rights (1988) in Article 13.

As important, research indicates that children need experience of participation in decisions affecting them if they are to feel efficacious as participants during their childhood and also as adults (Limber and Kaufman, 2002; Melton, 2006). In fact, in some ways children's rights documents present a model for participation that might be instructional for enhancing adult participation. The CRC encourages attention to the child's environment in promoting the child's developing capacities for participation.

A good example of this approach is found in the United Nations Standard Minimum Rules for the Administration of Juvenile Justice (the Beijing Rules). In setting forth the 'Fundamental perspectives,' Article 1.2 calls upon states to 'endeavour to develop conditions that will ensure for the juvenile a meaningful life in the community, which during that period in life when she or he is most susceptible to deviant behaviour, will foster a process of personal development and education that is as free from crime and delinquency as possible'. Finally, Article 1.3 asks that states focus on positive measures that mobilize family, community groups and schools to promote the young person's well-being.

Creating an environment conducive to the child's well-being would require increasing opportunities and incentives for child participation. For example, the environmental approach to participation is found more clearly elaborated in the UNESCO Recommendation on Education (1974), which devotes an entire section (V) to civic education. There is a call for civic education which appeals to children's 'creative imagination' in helping them to learn about their rights and how to actively exercise their rights and freedoms (paragraph 12). Furthermore, the recommendation promotes 'active civic training' aimed at helping young people to learn about how public institutions operate and how to solve problems, and to 'increasingly link education and action to solve problems at the local, national, and international levels' (paragraph 13).

The Riyadh Guidelines (1990) recommend a similar approach, emphasizing the importance of developing active rather than passive roles for children. One of the Fundamental Principles in the Guidelines is that 'young people should have an active role and partnership within society and should not be considered as mere objects of socialization or control' (1.3).

Third, economic conditions frequently are responsible for the failure of governments to move more rapidly and more effectively to implement their legal obligations to improve children's lives. There are at least two levels to the economic obstacles. One is the lack of government funds; the other is the lack of economic power of the children themselves. Both result in serious deprivations to children and youth.

One good example of the way in which economic conditions militate against the implementation of the state's legal obligations towards children is in the area of child labour. The CRC reveals the drafters' serious concern about child labour and exploitation. There is proactive language that states recognize the child's right to 'rest and leisure', to time for play and recreation (Article 31 paragraph 1). There is also prohibition on the economic exploitation of the child and affirmation of a prohibition on children performing work which is hazardous to the child's health, would interfere with the child's education, or be harmful to the child's 'physical, mental, spiritual, moral or social development' (Article 32 paragraph 1). Provision is made for a minimum age for employment, regulation of hours and working conditions, and enforcement sanctions for child labour matters (Article 32 paragraph 2).

The regional treaties also address issues of child labour and exploitation. The ACRWC covers the same ground as the CRC (Article 15). The drafters of the European Social Charter devoted an article to 'the right of children and young persons to protection' which covers among other concerns a minimum age for work, with special attention to the potential hazards to the young person in setting the age, the need to ensure that work does not interfere with education, the number of working hours, and the right to fair wages and fair benefits (Article 9).

The International Labour Organisation has also overseen the development of a number of treaties on child labour, including the Convention Concerning Minimum Age for Admission to Employment 1973, the Medical Examination of Young Persons (Industry) Convention 1946, and a treaty that supplements the slave trade convention and bans practices in which children are bonded for labour when they reach maturity.

Treaty provisions may also reflect an understanding of the impact of the economics of the family environment on the child. The CRC obligates states in Article 27 to assist families in providing a standard of living adequate for the physical, mental, spiritual, moral and social development of the child, thus linking economic conditions to child development. As with so many economic rights, the treaty's provision is primarily important in indicating that the family is the appropriate conduit for economic aid to the child, and also that an inadequate standard of living is directly connected to so many dimensions of the child's development. Given the widespread poverty in the world, we may conclude that most governments have failed to take their obligations seriously either to redistribute wealth within their countries or to contribute to international efforts to financially aid those countries whose children are most in need. There is also an awareness of the potentially negative impact on children's lives of instability and unpredictability of family economic situations. The Riyadh Guidelines, in discussing Socialization Processes (section IV), draw attention to the need for special attention to 'children of families affected by problems brought about by rapid and uneven economic, social and cultural change' (Article 15).

Fourth, social conditions also account for shortcomings in implementing the rights of children and youth. For example, although governments for over a century have joined together to address the international slave trade, including the traffic in children, there continue to be gross violations of these laws. There have for decades been agreements outlawing traffic in women, and later children, and the CRC contains the most universally ratified and broadly defined treaty provision outlawing this crime. States have accepted an obligation to 'take all appropriate national, bilateral and multilateral measures to prevent the abduction of, sale of, or traffic in children for any purpose or in any form' (Article 35). Clearly in matters of this kind it is essential to maximize the number of cooperating states since national laws are ineffective for preventing and punishing criminals if violators are free to move without penalty across state borders. As mentioned, the African Children's Charter also prohibits traffic in children (Article 29) and prohibits, as well, the use of children in begging. There is as well the relatively recent Optional Protocol focused on traffic in children. Yet, we are far from eliminating this practice, and in fact, there has been a dramatic increase in moving young girls across borders for sex work. Here, as in other areas, poverty and powerlessness combine to create social conditions which limit governments' attention to the weakest members of their society.

Conclusions

The CRC is the leading global legal agreement that international and domestic groups rely upon as the basis for their claims that children are the holders of fundamental human rights – rights to which they are entitled independent of their nationality. This treaty and many regional and special topic agreements establish a broad and deep understanding of what is necessary for children to grow up in families and communities that respect their dignity, foster their well-being and honour their contributions. If we now have a shared global understanding of the importance of taking children's rights seriously, why are we still failing to make these rights a reality in their everyday lives?

What we have argued here is that the international law and the national law aimed at increasing its impact can achieve success only if all those involved in the lives of children acknowledge the crucial role of social, economic and political forces in constraining the usefulness of legal efforts. Children and youth are not equal participants in the governmental and non-governmental decision-making processes. They do not hold substantial economic assets and have little influence in private and public economic planning. They have little if any role to play in the administrative and judicial deliberations that result in interpretations and judgments about the meaning and implementation of the law. As we have learned from the history of non-represented groups, those in power are often able to ignore the interests of those who are absent from the table. For all these reasons, increased attention needs to be paid to how to address the context in which the laws are expected to operate and to openly acknowledge the limited capacity of children and youth to make their own case and to gain access to the financial and other resources necessary to bring the goals represented by the law into fruition.

This work will take planning, organization, policy formation and implementation, as well as measuring and monitoring the success of policies through constant evaluation of children's well-being. Many organizations, national and international, public and private, are engaged in various stages of this work. One leading one is the Committee on the Rights of the Child. The Committee reviews the required reports from member states and receives, as well, shadow reports from national child advocacy groups, which usually raise issues of weaknesses in the government's programmes. These reports enable the Committee to raise significant questions with governmental representatives and put them in a position to make useful and well designed recommendations for improved compliance with the state's obligations under the Convention.

Though there is still much to be done, there are several initiatives that have been established that identify and begin to address the mains challenges. The annual publication *State of the World's Children* (UNICEF) presents significant data on the strengths and deficiencies of the situation for children in particular countries and regions on specific topics of central concern. Non-governmental organizations like Childwatch International Research Network and Save the Children focus on research and services that increase our ability to see what programmes are actually working and why. They also help develop standardized interpretations of the provisions of the CRC and have developed guidelines to enable governments to more easily produce competent and useful national reports to the Committee. One important example of a variety of efforts that are being made to monitor children's well-being and changes in their well-being over time is the work of a study group on Measuring and Monitoring Children's Well-Being Beyond Survival. Their initial findings are reported in *Measuring and Monitoring Children's Well-Being* (Ben-Arieh et al., 2001) and their work continues to promote the use and refinement of such indicators as a part of the policy planning and implementation process, nationally and internationally.

All that we have observed does not mean that there are not significant and even powerful groups attempting to introduce into these deliberations some attention to childhood and children's lives. Similarly children and child advocates are themselves part of the process of globalization and may make critical and powerful use of international legal arrangements designed to promote the rights and interests of children and youth. Probably most of us, at least some of the time, feel like children in the sense of wonder and helplessness that the world is changing in ways that seriously affect us but offer us minimal opportunities for participation. These are times in which thinking globally and acting locally invites personal strategizing for ourselves and with 'our' children. The international legal arrangements that have been forged by representatives of governmental and non-governmental organizations offer a child-centred philosophy, practical steps for action, legitimacy for our undertakings, and reason to hope that we may even succeed.

Notes

1. For example, Jews in Germany under the Third Reich and African slaves in the United States prior to 1860.
2. The Convention was preceded by the non-binding United Nations Declaration on the Rights of the Child, 1959.
3. Brazil is a southern tier country with a very high percentage of low-income people. It is one of the ten largest economies in the world and at the same time considered one of the four most unequal countries.

References

Ben-Arieh, A., N. Kaufman, A. Andrews, R. Goerge, B. Lee and L. Aber (2001) *Measuring and Monitoring Children's Well-Being*. Dordrecht: Kluwer Academic Press.

Council of Europe. Parliamentary Assembly. *European-Wide Ban on Corporal Punishment of Children*. Document 10199. 4 June 2004.

Flekkoy, M.G. and N.H. Kaufman (1997). *The Participation Rights of the Child: Rights and Responsibilities in Family and Society*. London: Jessica Kingsley Publishers.

James, A. (2004) 'Understanding Childhood from an Interdisciplinary Perspective: Problems and Potentials', in P.R. Pufall and R.P. Unsworth (eds) *Rethinking Childhood*. New Brunswick: Rutgers University Press.

Kaufman, N.H. and I. Rizzini (eds) (2002) *Globalization and children*. New York: Kluwer Academic/Plenum Publishers.

Kaufman, N.H. and S. Lindquist (1995) 'Critiquing Gender-Neutral Treaty Language: The Convention on the Elimination of All Forms of Discrimination Against Women', in A. Wolper and J. Peters (eds) *Women and Human Rights: An Agenda for Change*. London: Routledge.

Limber, S. and N.H. Kaufman (2002) 'Civic Participation by Children and Youth', in N. Kaufman and I. Rizzini (eds) *Globalization and Children's Lives*. New York: Kluwer Academic/Plenum.

Melton, G.B. (2006) *Background for a General Comment on the Right to Participate: Article 12 and Related Provisions of the Convention on the Rights of the Child* [Report to the U.N. Committee on the Rights of the Child]. Clemson, SC: Clemson University, Institute on Family and Neighborhood Life.

Morrow, V. (1999) '"We Are People Too"; Children and Young People's Perspectives on Children's Rights and Decision-Making in England', *The International Journal of Children's Rights*, 7(2): 149–170.

Reddy, N. (1997) *Have We Asked the Children: Different Approaches to the Question of Child Work?* Paper Presented at the Urban Childhood Conference, Trondheim, Norway.

Rizzini, I. and N. Thapliyal (2006) Perceptions and experiences of participation of children and adolescents in Rio de Janeiro, Brazil. Colorado: University of Colorado (in print).

Smith, A. (2005) *Research Forum on Children's Views of Citizenship: Cross-Cultural Perspectives. an Introduction and Overview of Results*. Dunedin: University of Otago, New Zealand. Oslo: Symposium on Children and Young People's Views on Citizenship and Nation Building at conference *Childhoods 2005* Oslo, Norway, 29 June–3 July .

Van Bueren, G. (1995) *The International Law on the Rights of the Child*. Dordrecht, Netherlands: Martinuis Nijhoff.

Weis, L. and M. Fine (2000) *Construction Sites: Excavating Race, Class and Gender among Urban Youth*. New York: Teachers College, Columbia University.

Name Index

Subject Index

The editors are grateful to Mr. Christian Haag for his conscientious preparation of the index.

447